DIVINE FREEDOM AND THE DOCTRINE OF THE IMMANENT TRINITY

'The first edition of this book in 2002 was a now-classic account of the freedom of God as understood in the doctrine of the immanent Trinity. The second edition is not just a reprint but a thorough revision with a reconfigured preface, a new chapter on Divine Freedom, and many revisions and updates to material on Jenson, Moltmann, Pannenberg, Jüngel and Schleiermacher. In clarity, power and effectiveness, it takes its place at the heart of contemporary discussion of the doctrine of God. I thoroughly recommend this new edition.'

Iain R. Torrance,
President Emeritus of Princeton Theological Seminary, USA

'The reissue of this weighty tome in revised and expanded form is welcome news indeed. It had already established itself as one of the two or three most important English-language treatises on the doctrine of the Trinity in recent theology. In its new form it includes rich and detailed discussions of theologians like Moltmann, Pannenberg and Jenson, not to mention McCormack and his followers, that are sure to generate interest. Molnar is one of the most distinguished interpreters of the Trinity in our time. His powerful book is indispensable for anyone interested in these questions.'

George Hunsinger,
Princeton Theological Seminary, USA

'The first edition of Paul Molnar's *Divine Freedom and the Doctrine of the Immanent Trinity* was one of the most significant books to appear in trinitarian theology in a generation. In this new edition, Professor Molnar has enhanced the case made in that study, demonstrating with even greater depth, clarity and nuance why it is that the doctrine of the essential Trinity must hold material primacy if Christian theology is to confess the God of the gospel well. This is an even more powerful book than its predecessor, enriched by further engagement with contemporary debates on freedom, election and history. The central argument concerning God's antecedent plenitude in himself remains of crucial importance for theology today. More than ever: Take, read!'

Ivor J. Davidson,
University of Aberdeen, UK

'Paul Molnar in his *Divine Freedom and the Doctrine of the Immanent Trinity* illumines in refreshingly clear prose the errors in method in many contemporary theologies by his resolute insistence that God is the only fit witness to Who He is. Molnar adroitly opens for the reader the understanding that theology to be truly theological must start from and be normed by what is unfolded in the doctrine of the Immanent Trinity, that is, an account of the eternal life of the Father-Son-Holy Spirit. Therein theology is poised to hear the divine direction for our creaturely lives, attitudes and actions. Molnar, critical of theologies which proceed from a centre in ourselves and our own experiences, is yet careful and judicious in his description of these various contemporary Roman Catholic and Protestant theologies. This book is a bright beacon bringing clarity to current theological discussion.'

David Demson,
Wycliffe College, Toronto School of Theology, Canada

'In the face of several challenges, Paul Molnar offers us a robust defence of the doctrine of the immanent Trinity. With his characteristically clear and robust style, he outlines the intellectual and existential reasons for maintaining the classical position. This new expanded edition should be widely studied and cited.'

David Fergusson,
University of Edinburgh, UK

DIVINE FREEDOM AND THE DOCTRINE OF THE IMMANENT TRINITY

In Dialogue with Karl Barth and Contemporary Theology

Second Edition

Paul D. Molnar

Bloomsbury T&T Clark
An imprint of Bloomsbury Publishing Plc

B L O O M S B U R Y
LONDON · OXFORD · NEW YORK · NEW DELHI · SYDNEY

Bloomsbury T&T Clark
An imprint of Bloomsbury Publishing Plc
Imprint previously known as T&T Clark

50 Bedford Square   1385 Broadway
London   New York
WC1B 3DP   NY 10018
UK   USA

www.bloomsbury.com

**BLOOMSBURY, T&T CLARK and the Diana logo are trademarks of
Bloomsbury Publishing Plc**

First published 2017

© Paul D. Molnar, 2017

Paul Molnar has asserted his right under the Copyright, Designs
and Patents Act, 1988, to be identified as Author of this work.

British Library Cataloguing-in-Publication Data
A catalogue record for this book is available from the British Library.

ISBN: PB: 978-0-5676-5679-7
ePDF: 978-0-5676-5680-3
ePub: 978-0-5676-5741-1

Library of Congress Cataloging-in-Publication Data
A catalog record for this book is available from
the Library of Congress.

Typeset by Newgen Knowledge Works (P) Ltd., Chennai, India
Printed and bound in Great Britain

CONTENTS

PREFACE

In the preface to the first edition of this book I stated that 'all Christian theologians realize that the purpose of a doctrine of the immanent Trinity is to recognize, uphold and respect God's freedom'.[1] By this I meant to assert the importance of what Karl Barth described as the 'antecedent' existence of the Father, Son and Holy Spirit such that the inner life of God as Father, Son and Holy Spirit is the free life of God and is so in such a way that God did not and does not need to relate with us in any way in order to be or to become who God eternally is. When I stated that all Christian theologians realized the importance of acknowledging this freedom of God, I meant that even those who simply paid or might pay lip service to the truth affirmed in this doctrine at least understood that Christians must be able to recognize and distinguish God from the world in order to speak coherently about God's *relationship* with us and about our *relationship* with God from within history. This was a crucial issue when the first edition of this book was published since some theologians argued that it was downright impossible to say anything at all about the immanent Trinity while others claimed that the doctrine referred to nothing more than God's involvement with us in history. While some maintained that to speak of the immanent Trinity was nothing more than speaking of our experience of God in the economy, others asserted that the economic Trinity must in some way have a retroactive effect on the immanent Trinity such that there is a mutually conditioning relationship between the immanent and economic Trinity. Still others claimed that the point of the doctrine of the Trinity was not to provide objective or literal information about God but only to protect our experience of God in the economy of salvation. Today, there are some who claim that it is pure speculation to assert that the God who meets us in the economy could have been God without us. Yet, as I will continue to claim in this second edition, it is just that thinking that undermines the proper function of the doctrine of the immanent Trinity. It does so because such a perspective always

---

1 Paul D. Molnar, *Divine Freedom and the Doctrine of the Immanent Trinity: In Dialogue with Karl Barth and Contemporary Theology* (London: T & T Clark/Continuum, 2002), ix.

leads those who embrace it to argue that in some sense God's creative function has absorbed his essence.

By analyzing and comparing the views of a number of prominent theologians on these issues I attempted to explain why a properly understood and properly functioning doctrine of the immanent Trinity was crucial for theologians then as it was in the early church. My main thesis was that without such a doctrine, anything said about God merely became little more than an attempt to discuss our religious experiences using theological categories. It was my claim that, in the end, such an approach to theology turned out to be little more than mythology or the projection of human conceptuality onto what is imagined to be the divine being. My goal in the book was to engage in what Thomas F. Torrance has called 'scientific theology' or theology that allows the reality of what is being reflected on to determine the truth of what is said.[2]

In this sense I followed Karl Barth's view that God's eternal being and act as Father, Son and Holy Spirit 'is the basis of His whole will and action even *ad extra*, as the living act which He directs to us'.[3] Put another way, I held that 'the antecedent eternal Trinity was, in his [Barth's] eyes, the necessary and sufficient condition of God's trinitarian self-revelation ... As such, the antecedent Trinity was in fact not "abstract" but the *ens concretissimum*. It was not "speculative" but the essential guarantee of revelation's freedom, veracity and reliability'.[4] This is why Barth could say:

2 For Torrance, 'precise, scientific knowledge was held to result from inquiry strictly in accordance with the nature (κατὰ φύσιν) of the reality being investigated, that is, knowledge of it reached under the constraint of what it actually and essentially is in itself, and not according to arbitrary convention', *The Trinitarian Faith: The Evangelical Theology of the Ancient Catholic Church* (hereafter: *The Trinitarian Faith*) (Edinburgh: T & T Clark, 1988), 51. See also Paul D. Molnar, *Thomas F. Torrance: Theologian of the Trinity* (hereafter: *Torrance: Theologian of the Trinity*) (Farnham: Ashgate, 2009), chapter one and passim.

3 Karl Barth, *Church Dogmatics*, 4 vols in 13 pts (hereafter: *CD*). Vol. IV, pt 2: *The Doctrine of Reconciliation*, trans. G. W. Bromiley, ed. G. W. Bromiley and T. F. Torrance (Edinburgh: T & T Clark, 1958), 345.

4 George Hunsinger, *Reading Barth with Charity: A Hermeneutical Proposal* (hereafter: *Reading Barth with Charity*) (Grand Rapids, MI: Baker Academic, 2015), 36.

God is love in Himself. Being loved by Him we can, as it were, look into His 'heart'. The fact that He loves us means that we can know Him as He is. This is all true. But if this picture-language of 'the heart of God' is to have any validity, it can refer only to the being of God as Father, Son and Holy Spirit ... We cannot say anything higher or better of the 'inwardness of God' than that God is Father, Son and Holy Spirit, and therefore that He is love in Himself without and before loving us, and without being forced to love us. And we can say this only in the light of the 'outwardness' of God to us, the occurrence of His revelation.[5]

Here Barth clearly explains that our only access to the immanent Trinity (God's inwardness) is through the economic Trinity (God's outwardness) and that it is the revelation of God the Father through his Son and in the Spirit that enables and guarantees our knowledge of God in himself. Thus, there are not two trinities, the economic (God's actions for us within history) and the immanent (God's eternal existence as Father, Son and Spirit – the One who loves in freedom), but only one Trinity who lives in freedom and acts for us in the freedom of his love. Nonetheless, one can never suggest, imply or openly advocate the idea that who God is as triune is contingent on his relations with us in history. In the words of T. F. Torrance: 'We cannot think of the ontological [immanent] Trinity as if it were constituted by or dependent on the economic Trinity, but must rather think of the economic Trinity as the freely predetermined manifestation in the history of salvation of the eternal Trinity which God himself was before the foundation of the world, and eternally is.'[6] In the sovereign freedom of his love God did of course decide to create us and to relate with us. However these relations are 'external relations' in that God did not and does not need creation or incarnation in order to exist as the one who loves. The God with whom we are related is none other than the eternal Father, Son and Holy Spirit; thus, as Barth put it, this is not merely 'picture language' with no content – this is the revealed name of God as disclosed in the history of Jesus Christ and through the power of the Holy Spirit and understood within faith.

---

5 *CD* I/2, 377.

6 Thomas F. Torrance, *The Christian Doctrine of God, One Being Three Persons* (hereafter: *The Christian Doctrine of God* (Edinburgh: T & T Clark, 1996), 108–9.

My statement about the purpose of the doctrine of the immanent Trinity and the assertions concerning the freedom of God's love were as important then as they are today. If anything, these descriptions of God's freedom, which were made against the background of the many attempts to understand the Trinity in ways that seemed to undermine that freedom, are even more important to recognize today. It is now assumed that the doctrine of the immanent Trinity is indeed important and that it has something crucial to say since it is for certain generally recognized by Christian theologians as the 'ground and grammar of theology'. T. F. Torrance thus affirms that 'it is finally in our understanding of the trinitarian relations in God himself that we have the ground and grammar of a realist theology'.[7] However exactly what that is remains the subject of continued debate since so-called social or relational trinitarians continue to base their understanding of the Trinity in generally understood religious experience instead of in revelation, as they should. Even sophisticated theologians who claim to be basing their thinking on revelation actually allow history and experience rather than God himself as disclosed to us in history and experience to shape what is said about God and our relations with God. In this second edition I significantly expand the discussion in the first chapter to make my position clear. I argue that, while we cannot say anything about the triune God without an experience of God in faith, since it is by grace and revelation and thus through the Holy Spirit that this God is known with what Barth termed 'apodictic certainty',[8] we immediately and necessarily realize that it is God himself and never our experience that is the basis for our understanding God. That is why Barth and Torrance repeatedly assert that it is only through God that God is known. Hence, I agree with Barth that because it is by God that God is known, therefore, a proper theological starting point for understanding God can 'neither be an axiom of reason nor a datum of experience. In

---

7 Thomas F. Torrance, *The Ground and Grammar of Theology* (Charlottesville: University Press of Virginia, 1980), xi and 158–9, where Torrance explains that he thinks of the doctrine of the Trinity 'as the ultimate ground of theological knowledge of God, the basic grammar of theology, for it is there that we find our knowledge of God reposing upon the final Reality of God himself, grounded in the ultimate relations intrinsic to God's own Being, which govern and control all true knowledge of him from beginning to end'.

8 Cf. *CD* II/1, 162.

the measure that a doctrine of God draws on these sources, it betrays the fact that its subject is not really God but a hypostatised reflection of man'.[9]

As I argued in the first edition, a doctrine of the immanent Trinity is an attempt to say something about who God actually is based on the revelation of God in history. This assertion also has become a particularly thorny issue today even among Barth scholars, as we shall see, because those who think it is appropriate to 'correct' Barth by logically reversing the doctrines of election and the Trinity have in reality undermined the proper function of a doctrine of the immanent Trinity. Hence, this is not just a problem in relation to more radical views of the Trinity that explicitly argue against the doctrine of the immanent Trinity or merely pay lip service to the doctrine. It is a much more subtle problem today because those Barth scholars who seek to advance their so-called revisionist thesis (revisionist because they are attempting to revise Barth's actual stated position to meet the demands of their thesis that election logically should precede Trinity), do so precisely by marginalizing God's eternal freedom as the one who loves. We will consider this issue at various points along the way in this second edition. Unfortunately, as we shall see, even those so-called revisionists who realize that logically reversing these doctrines is something Barth himself would reject, end up caught in the problematic thinking that gave rise to that original proposal in the first place.

Therefore it is still extremely important to realize that without theoretical and practical awareness of the freedom of God recognized in and through a properly formulated doctrine of the immanent Trinity, all theological statements about the significance of created existence become ambiguous and constitute merely human attempts to give meaning to creation, using theological categories. At issue in a proper understanding of a doctrine of the immanent Trinity is the fact that, although we obviously have no alternative but to understand God in the categories available to us in our human experience, it is not anything

---

9 *CD* II/2, 3. This is why Barth claimed that the Gospel must be respected such that 'Jesus Christ is the first and the last word of Christian faith' (*CD* II/1, 162). All theological certainty is grounded in Jesus Christ himself as the one who has reconciled us to God and mediates true knowledge of God to us through his Holy Spirit. Apodictically certain knowledge of God is lost, however, 'when from an object of faith the Gospel becomes the object of our own experience of faith' (*CD* II/1, 141).

within our experience or inherent in those categories that prescribes who God is in se and ad extra. This is an extremely important point and, as we shall see, much of the controversy that continues to exist regarding the doctrine of the Trinity concerns just this issue. The paramount problem here concerns the fact that since we know the triune God by grace and through faith, we cannot, as it were, read back our concepts and experiences into God. A properly conceived doctrine of the immanent Trinity, while not designed to prevent this, will indeed do so to the extent that God's freedom as the one who loves is recognized and upheld through such a doctrine. The crucial point here of course is that God is love in himself and without us and does not need us in order to create, to reconcile and to redeem.

This was essentially the issue in the controversy between Athanasius and Arius. God is who he is, independent of creation, and while he has indeed chosen not to remain isolated in himself, but to create us out of his free love and to enable us to know and love him by overcoming the enmity created by human sin, the fact remains that he can be known with certainty only through his own self-disclosure. As Athanasius put it: 'It is more pious and more accurate to signify God from the Son and call him Father, than to name him from his works and call him Unoriginate.'[10] This is one of the most pressing problems facing contemporary trinitarian theology: how do we speak accurately of God as Father, Son and Spirit, and about God's relationality and temporality without projecting our limited human relations of fathers, of sons and of the human spirit and created temporality into the divine life, thus compromising not only God's sovereignty, but our genuine contingent freedom which is grounded in God's freedom for us in the incarnation and at Pentecost? Or to put it another way, how may we know God in accordance with his nature rather than creating God in our own image?

In face of this critical question, this second edition will be an effort once again to articulate a contemporary doctrine of the immanent Trinity.[11] First, a contemporary doctrine should eschew irrelevant

---

10 Athanasius, *Contra Ar.* 1.34, in *A Select Library of Nicene and Post-Nicene Fathers of the Christian Church Second Series*, trans. and ed. Philip Schaff and Henry Wace (Edinburgh: T & T Clark, 1987), 326. Cf. also Torrance, *The Trinitarian Faith*, 6 and 49.

11 In *Faith, Freedom and the Spirit: The Economic Trinity in Barth, Torrance and Contemporary Theology* (hereafter: *Faith, Freedom and the Spirit*) (Downers Grove, IL: InterVarsity Press, 2015), I explore what it means

speculation about God's inner nature, abstracted from God's own self-revelation, in the awareness that this is and has been damaging to theology and practice within the Church. We will therefore avoid both separating and confusing the immanent and economic Trinity and adhere to the economic Trinity for our information about the immanent Trinity. Second, a contemporary doctrine of the immanent Trinity also will be aware of the fact that numerous theologians today continue to either directly polemicize against such a doctrine or simply pay lip service to it because they know its importance in recognizing and upholding God's freedom and distinction from creation such that God never ceases to live his own eternal life even in his closest relations with us in history as our creator, reconciler and redeemer. Neither of these alternatives, as we shall see, does justice to the function and theological importance of a doctrine of the immanent Trinity; its function is to direct us to the fact that God is uniquely who he is without needing us and that out of his own love and wisdom he willed to have communion (fellowship) with us in his grace and mercy.

We have already noted that for Karl Barth we can have accurate knowledge of this God as Father, Son and Spirit only in and through God's own revelation of himself in history in his Word and Spirit; but this must be recognized as the free love of God's grace, which enables us, who are sinners and prone to create the God we want, to know God as he truly is for us. Recognizing the problem created by the fact that people often create the God they want instead of relying on God himself to know who he is and who we are, Barth wrote that 'the content of the doctrine of the Trinity ... is not that God in His relation to man is Creator, Mediator and Redeemer, but that God in Himself is eternally God the Father, Son and Holy Spirit ... [God acting as Emmanuel] cannot be dissolved into His work and activity'.[12] In order to show why this remark by Barth is and remains so important for a proper understanding of the Trinity today, a new chapter (Chapter 4) is being added to this second edition. The purpose is to consider the divine freedom once again especially as this relates to a proper understanding of Barth's concepts of primary and secondary objectivity, the proper place of the *Logos asarkos* and why it is problematic to assume that God's determination to be God for us means that God thereby gives himself his

to think about God in faith by focusing on the role of the Holy Spirit in knowledge of and experience of God in the economy.

12 *CD* I/2, 878–9. Cf. also *CD* I/2, 35–7; and *CD* II/1, 309, 313.

triune being. I will also discuss various misunderstandings that arose in connection with the first edition as I attempt to point the way forward. Some readers claimed that I was arguing for a God who lives in isolation and is far removed from us here in history. However that is exactly the opposite of what I argued and what I am now arguing. My position was and remains that the God who meets us in the economy and enables us to know him and thus to relate with him is and remains God and therefore never becomes dependent on us; consequently I firmly argue against any idea of a dependent deity – not because I am proposing a separation of the economic from the immanent Trinity, but because I am refusing to collapse the latter into the former.

As this idea of a dependent deity has become so central to the thinking of several well-known theologians such as Wolfhart Pannenberg, Robert Jenson and Jürgen Moltmann, I have expanded my discussion of some of their thinking in this second edition; this is especially true with regard to Pannenberg. It is in opposition to such thinking, with its indebtedness to Hegel, that I then argued and will still argue that trinitarian doctrine or trinitarian thinking or relationality as we experience it cannot displace God as the foundation of true knowledge since God's action in revelation is not a dogma, view or principle but the actual Word of God working ad extra as creator, reconciler and redeemer. This is also why I then argued and will still argue that any separation of the Spirit from the Word indicates that those who do so have in reality confused the Holy Spirit with the human spirit. To have the Holy Spirit means to be united to the incarnate Word and thus to the Father. In light of this, the doctrine of the immanent Trinity therefore depends on this Word which cannot be reduced to anything within history. It can help clarify who God is in revelation and is itself the central Christian doctrine as already mentioned, but it is not itself the controlling center of dogmatics. Since God is and remains this center, I will continue to argue that grace, faith and revelation, which include creation in a genuine communion with God from creation to consummation, always remain grounded *exclusively* in God and never jointly in God and creation. God lives, discloses himself anew and has to be discovered anew because theology has no sovereignty in relation to God. Thus, as Barth noted,

> wherever there is knowledge of Jesus Christ, it takes place in the power of His witness, in the mystery and miracle, the outpouring and receiving, of the gift of the Holy Spirit ... He is the *doctor veritatis*: He is the finger of God ... which causes the reason of man ... to receive

the truth ... Wherever there is Christian *gnosis* it is His work. That is why it has no other sources or norms. That is why it can be had without any demonstrations of its origin.[13]

Unfortunately, however, the way many leading contemporary theologians continue to employ trinitarian categories actually leads from agnosticism to monism and dualism and thus compromises divine and human freedom just because they either have simply paid lip service to God's freedom or have completely rejected the idea that we can or should know the immanent Trinity. Most modern theologians adopt Karl Rahner's axiom that 'the immanent Trinity is strictly identical with the economic Trinity and vice versa'[14] in some form, even if only to move beyond it, to speak about God's involvement with the world. Certainly there is a perfectly noncontroversial way to understand this axiom, that is, it may simply mean that the God with whom we are involved in Christ and the Spirit is none other than the eternal Father, Son and Holy Spirit. However, as in the first edition, a question to be explored in this book will be whether or not this axiom, as it stands and as it actually functions for many modern theologians, can truly respect God's freedom as a doctrine of the immanent Trinity must. Does the vice versa obscure God's freedom, so that any attempt to reconcile God's freedom with this axiom, as it stands, inevitably underplays God's actual pretemporal, supratemporal and posttemporal freedom as Barth explicated these concepts? Does it not encourage theologians to introduce some type of logical necessity into the inner life of the Trinity such that God's inner freedom is conceptualized more in terms of our experiences of love and freedom than in terms of God's actual freedom for us in sending his Son to become incarnate so that we might have life in his name (Jn. 3:16)?

Some confusion and reversal of the creature/creator relationship inevitably follows the failure to consistently distinguish without

---

13 *CD* IV/2, 126. See also Karl Barth, *Evangelical Theology: An Introduction* (hereafter: *Evangelical Theology*), trans. Grover Foley (Grand Rapids, MI: Eerdmans, 1963), 6: 'The separation and distinction of this one true God from all the others can only be continually his own deed.'

14 Karl Rahner, 'Theology and Anthropology,' *Theological Investigations* (23 vols) (hereafter: *TI*), Vol. 9, trans. by Graham Harrison (New York: Herder and Herder, 1972), 28–45, 32. See also *TI* 9, 130. Cf. Karl Rahner, *The Trinity* (hereafter: *Trinity*), trans. Joseph Donceel (New York: Herder and Herder, 1970), 22ff.

separating the immanent and economic Trinity while at the same time recognizing that there is indeed only one triune God such that, as T. F. Torrance liked to say, there is no God 'behind the back of Jesus Christ'.[15] Of course everything depends on how this remark is understood. If it is taken to mean that Jesus's human history is in any sense constitutive of who he is as the eternal Son of the Father, then all is lost – such a view in fact illegitimately reads history back into eternity in exactly the wrong way and, as we shall see, that makes it impossible to recognize grace in distinction from nature and revelation in distinction from our experience of ourselves. With this in mind, I will argue that several indications that such a reversal remains all too prevalent today are: (1) the trend toward making God, in some sense, dependent on and indistinguishable from history; (2) the lack of precision in Christology which leads to the idea that Jesus, in his humanity *as such*, is the revealer; (3) the failure to distinguish the Holy Spirit from the human spirit; and (4) the trend to begin theology with experiences of self-transcendence, thus allowing experience rather than the object of faith to determine the truth of theology. Exploring these indicators by seeing what a number of prominent contemporary theologians have to say in these areas, I hope, will lead toward a contemporary doctrine of the immanent Trinity which clarifies divine and human freedom and avoids agnosticism, monism and dualism. Such a doctrine will be able to affirm what Barth calls God's 'antecedent' existence in such a way that the irreversibility of the creator/creature relation will be seen and maintained, as will the irreversible relationship between grace and nature and revelation and reason. Without recognizing the sovereignty of grace and of the creator in relation to creatures, it will be impossible to maintain that God's love for us in Christ and his Spirit is the firm basis on which sin, suffering, evil and death are overcome in Jesus Christ for our benefit. None of this should be taken to imply that God in Christ undercuts our freedom and independence or that grace displaces nature instead of perfecting it or that revelation destroys reason instead of enabling it to live in and from the truth in its identity with Jesus, who is the way, the truth and the life. It is because Jesus is God himself acting for us even now as the risen, ascended and advent Lord that we have access to the eternal God as the Holy Spirit actualizes the reconciliation of our minds and hearts to God the Father as this has already happened in Jesus vicariously for our benefit.

15 See, for example, Torrance, *The Christian Doctrine of God*, 17, 24, 199. See Torrance, *The Trinitarian Faith*, 23, for how he applies that thinking.

ACKNOWLEDGMENTS

Once again I would like to thank the Very Reverend Professor Iain R. Torrance for his consistent support, encouragement and friendship. At his invitation, I presented what is now Chapter 2 as a lecture to a graduate seminar at the University of Aberdeen in March 1999. Iain and his wife Morag went to great lengths to make that a wonderfully memorable event. Our many conversations over the years have greatly enhanced my knowledge of trinitarian theology. Professor David Fergusson also went out of his way to make my visit to Aberdeen a success and offered valuable advice as well. I also remain grateful to Professor Trevor Hart for his invitation to deliver the same lecture at the University of St. Andrews and for his hospitality during my visit there. Everyone at both universities made me feel very welcome and helped me think through important issues related to Barth's Christology. In addition, I remain grateful to the Very Reverend Professor Thomas F. Torrance for reading and commenting on material contained in a number of chapters and for his encouragement to proceed with the first edition of this work. Over the years since the publication of that first edition I have come to appreciate even more the monumental contributions T. F. Torrance has made to contemporary reflections on the doctrine of the Trinity. Further, his thinking, as especially expressed in his major works on the Trinity, has been extremely helpful to me and his influence will be seen throughout the book. I am also grateful to St. John's University for consistently supporting my work and specifically for providing me with a number of research reductions so that I might be able to finish this second edition of *Divine Freedom*.

As with the first edition, this book also has developed over many years, and there are dialogue partners, friends and colleagues who have contributed to my thinking; special thanks are due to Professors George Hunsinger, David Demson, John Webster, Ivor Davidson, Myk Habets, Christopher Holmes, D. Stephen Long and Nick Healy. John Webster was a good friend to me in the years since the first edition was published and, like many others, I am grateful to have experienced his keen theological insight and spectacular sense of humor. I would also like to thank George Hunsinger and Walt Lowe for invitations to speak at two meetings of the Karl Barth Society of North America and especially for featuring the first edition of this book at another meeting of the Barth

Society in Toronto in November 2002. In November 1994 I presented an abbreviated version of what is now Chapter 6 and in November 1999 I presented a version of what is now Chapter 3. In addition, I am grateful to the many members of the Karl Barth Society of North America whose intense scholarship makes that one of the most important and rewarding scholarly meetings I attend. Special thanks are also due to Anna Turton of Bloomsbury T & T Clark for her support, encouragement, patience and for her many good ideas. Working with her makes the job of writing much easier. I would also like to thank Miriam Cantwell for her helpful assistance along the way as well as Malarvizhi for her very able copy-editing. In addition, I would like to thank my graduate assistant Connor Shea for proof-reading the entire manuscript during the spring semester of 2016. Finally, I would like to extend a sincere thank you to John J. McCormick who generously gave his time and expertise in reading and re-reading several versions of this manuscript over the years and offering valuable editorial suggestions at each stage. Still, it goes without saying that the sole responsibility for any errors resides with the author.

Also, I am grateful to the following for permission to reprint previously published material: T&T Clark for Karl Barth, *Church Dogmatics*, 4 vols in 13 pts., 1958–81; Paul D. Molnar, 'Robert W. Jenson's Systematic Theology Volume I: The Triune God', *Scottish Journal of Theology* 52 (1999), 117–31; Paul D. Molnar, 'Toward a Contemporary Doctrine of the Immanent Trinity: Karl Barth and the Present Discussion', *Scottish Journal of Theology* 49 (1996), 311–57; Paul D. Molnar, 'God's Self-Communication in Christ: A Comparison of Thomas F. Torrance and Karl Rahner', in *Scottish Journal of Theology* 50 (1997), 288–320; Paul D. Molnar, 'The Function of the Immanent Trinity in the Theology of Karl Barth: Implications for Today', *Scottish Journal of Theology* 42 (1989), 367–99; *The Thomist* for Paul D. Molnar, 'Is God Essentially Different From His Creatures? Rahner's Explanation from Revelation', 51 (1987), 575–631; *Theological Studies* for Paul D. Molnar, 'The Function of the Trinity in Moltmann's Ecological Doctrine of Creation', 51 (1990), 673–97; Blackwell Publishers for Paul D. Molnar, 'Some Dogmatic Implications of Barth's Understanding of Ebionite and Docetic Christology', *International Journal of Systematic Theology* 2 (2000), 151–74; Crossroad Publishing for Karl Rahner, *Foundations of Christian Faith: An Introduction to the Idea of Christianity*, trans. William V. Dych. A translation of *Grundkurs des Glaubens: Einführung in den Begriff des Christentums* © Verlag

Herder Freiburg im Breisgau 1976; Fortress Press and SCM Press for Jürgen Moltmann, *The Trinity and the Kingdom*, originally published by Harper & Row and by SCM Press, 1981; Darton, Longman & Todd for Karl Rahner, *Theological Investigations, Vol. IV: More Recent Writings*, trans. Kevin Smith. A translation of *Schriften zur Theologie, IV*, published by Verlagsanstalt. Benziger & Co. A.G., Einsiedeln. Translation © Darton, Longman & Todd, 1966 and 1974. InterVarsity Press for Paul D. Molnar, *Faith, Freedom and the Spirit: The Economic Trinity in Barth, Torrance and Contemporary Theology*, chapter three, 129–86. Copyright © 2015 by Paul D. Molnar. Used by permission of InterVarsity Press, P. O. Box 1400, Downers Grove, IL 60515 USA www.Ivpress.com.

ABBREVIATIONS

CD	Karl Barth, *Church Dogmatics*
KD	Karl Barth, *Kirchliche Dogmatik*
FCF	Karl Rahner, S.J., *Foundations of Christian Faith: An Introduction to the Idea of Christianity*
GMD	Gordon D. Kaufman, *God – Mystery – Diversity: Christian Theology in a Pluralistic World*
HW	Karl Rahner, S.J., *Hearers of the Word*
IFM	Gordon D. Kaufman, *In Face of Mystery: A Constructive Theology*
SJT	*Scottish Journal of Theology*
ST	Gordon D. Kaufman, *Systematic Theology: A Historicist Perspective*
STI	Robert W. Jenson, *Systematic Theology Volume 1: The Triune God*
SW	Karl Rahner, S.J., *Sprit in the World*
TI	Karl Rahner, S.J., *Theological Investigations*
TNA	Gordon D. Kaufman, *Theology for a Nuclear Age*
TS	*Theological Studies*

Chapter 1

THE PURPOSE OF A DOCTRINE OF THE IMMANENT TRINITY AND ITS NEGLECT TODAY

In this chapter I will explore two important questions which will lead to a more precise understanding of how a doctrine of the immanent Trinity ought to function today. The first concerns the role of experience in theology; the second deals with issues raised by feminist theologians about the *locus* of trinitarian theology. Should the experience of a person, male or female, be the starting point for understanding the triune God? With such a starting point, how can one avoid allowing experience to also become the norm for such understanding? The issue here is not whether we are capable of viewing and conceiving 'the divine'. Of course we can do this since we have the capacity to view and conceive images. The issue, rather, is whether or not there is some capacity in us (in our viewing and conceiving as such) to know the one true God of Christian faith, namely, the eternal Father, Son and Holy Spirit. The answer to this question for Karl Barth and, as he asserted, 'for the whole Early Church and theology' was an unequivocal 'No', because theology, as faith seeking understanding, must 'keep to the fact that God is known only by God'.[1] Hence we cannot know God by the 'inner power' of our views and concepts, by virtue 'of their own capacity' or 'in virtue of a potentiality of our cognition which has perhaps to be actualized by revelation'.[2] Certainly, we are active as knowers when it comes to knowing the triune God – our capacities for viewing and conceiving are not eliminated when it comes to knowing God. Thus 'we are definitely active as the receivers of images and creators of counter-images'.[3] However, this ability of ours to receive and create images and counter-images, Barth insists, does not owe 'its truth to any capacity of

---

1 *CD* II/1, 182.
2 *CD* II/1, 182.
3 *CD* II/1, 182.

our own to be truly recipients and creators in relation to God' because 'we ourselves have no capacity for fellowship with God'.[4]

In this assertion one might wonder whether or not Barth has made it impossible for us to truly know the God of Christian faith. The answer is 'No' for one simple reason. Barth unambiguously and consistently ascribes the possibility and actuality of human knowledge of the tri-une God not to us but to the miracle of God's grace in ordaining and creating 'fellowship between Himself and us'. This, Barth insists, 'does not happen in the actualising of our capacity, but in the miracle of His good-pleasure'.[5] When true knowledge occurs, it does so therefore in the power of the Holy Spirit; it is thus not something accomplished by our own power or wisdom, but 'in a freedom which is given' in Christ himself so that while it is our own 'free decision', it is enabled by the power of the risen Lord through the Holy Spirit. In this regard Barth can say of one who responds to the Word of God enacted in Christ that

> in the work of the Holy Spirit this man ceases to be a man who is closed and blind and deaf and uncomprehending in relation to this disclosure effected for him too. He becomes a man who is open, seeing, hearing, comprehending. Its disclosure to all and consequently to him too, becomes his own opening up to it. In the work of the Holy Spirit it comes about that the man who with the same organs could once say No thereto, again with the same organs, in so far as they can be used for this purpose, may and can and must say Yes. In the work of the Holy Spirit that which was truth for all, and hence for him too, even without his acceptance, becomes truth which is affirmed by him.[6]

Here, as elsewhere in his theology, Barth is simply applying to the knowledge of God the doctrine of our justification by faith and by grace. Hence he insists that even though our views and concepts cannot of themselves 'apprehend God', this does not inhibit God from empowering such knowledge.[7] There is no power 'inherent in these works of ours', says Barth. 'But there is a power of the divine indwelling in both the broad and the narrow which our works cannot withstand for all

---

4 *CD* II/1, 182.

5 *CD* II/1, 182.

6 *CD* IV/4, 27–8.

7 *CD* II/1, 212.

their impotence.'[8] This is the case because God enables us, in spite of our inability, to participate in his own truth by grace and through revelation. Barth thus maintains that 'in all his impotence he becomes a place where his honour dwells – not his own, but God's. As a sinner he is justified.'[9]

This means that Barth believes we have a certainty of knowledge that many contemporary theologians suspect is impossible because they suppose that knowledge of God is metaphorical and symbolic in the sense that our metaphors are based on those experiences which matter most to us, but do not and cannot actually describe the nature of God since God is transcendent. Contrary to such thinking, however, Barth pointedly and rightly insists that in this situation 'we are dealing with a cognition which does not have merely relative certainty, but the absolute, simple and indisputable certainty of God Himself.'[10] How can someone who himself admits to being an 'unprofitable servant' even in this work make such a remarkably definite statement concerning the knowledge of the transcendent God? The answer once again is simple, but with profound implications: 'It [knowledge of God] cannot be established in this certainty otherwise than by God Himself; but otherwise than by God Himself it cannot be attacked and annulled.'[11] Thus, 'although the knowledge of God certainly does not come about without our work, it also does not come about through our work, or as the fruit of our work' because 'God can be known only by God' so that 'in faith itself, we know God in utter dependence, in pure discipleship and gratitude.'[12]

It is for this positive reason that Barth continually insists that we cannot rely on our own capacities since, as sinners who need fellowship with God to know God in truth, all we can do on our own is create idolatrous pictures of God by projecting images of ourselves and of our world onto the 'divine'. Here theologians must admit, Barth rightly claims, that 'in faith itself we are forced to say that our knowledge of God begins in all seriousness with the knowledge of the hiddenness of God'.[13] This means that 'we know, view and conceive God, not as a work

---

8 *CD* II/1, 212.
9 *CD* II/1, 213.
10 *CD* II/1, 180.
11 *CD* II/1, 180.
12 *CD* II/1, 183.
13 *CD* II/1, 183.

of our nature, not as a performance on the basis of our own capacity, but only as a miraculous work of the divine good-pleasure, so that, knowing God, we necessarily know His hiddenness'.[14] It is crucial, however, to realize that at this point God's hiddenness is a 'property of God' and not a last statement of the limits of human epistemology. It is simply a statement that in knowing God by God 'we do not comprehend how we come to know Him, that we do not ascribe to our cognition as such the capacity for this knowledge, but that we can only trace it back to God'.[15] In this sense, because it is God's revelation and our faith in that revelation that drive our human knowledge of God, we must respect the fact that our capacity for knowing God always comes from God alone through revelation. Any other view in this matter would have to mean that revelation was 'at our own disposal', and that would suggest we were no longer utterly dependent on God for fellowship and for such knowledge.

Having said all of this, it should now be easy to see why Barth stated with great clarity that his 'starting-point in [the] first part of the doctrine of God was neither an axiom of reason nor a datum of experience. In the measure that a doctrine of God draws on these sources, it betrays the fact that its subject is not really God but a hypostatised reflection of man'.[16] He was simply applying what he understood to be true about God on the basis of God's own revelation in and through the cross and resurrection of Jesus Christ and the fellowship established by God in and through those events and in the revelation of that truth through the power of his Holy Spirit.

It is in this context that I ask the question concerning human experience, which includes all of our various self-determinations: shouldn't all our experiences, including our viewing and conceiving, important as they are, be continually assessed by the extent to which their relation to the truth shapes them? I will follow the view held by Karl Barth and clearly articulated by Thomas F. Torrance that theology must allow the unique nature of its object to determine what can and cannot be said about the triune God. While both of these theologians rely on the thought of Athanasius, Torrance has made this reliance especially explicit. It should also be noted that these two contemporary theologians are not alone in asserting that it is only by God that the

---

14 *CD* II/1, 184.

15 *CD* II/1, 184.

16 *CD* II/2, 3.

Christian God is known. Walter Kasper himself makes that exact same assertion: 'God, therefore, can be known only through God; he can be known only when he himself allows himself to be known.'[17] Indeed, he also acknowledges that 'the starting point for a systematic understanding of the trinity of divine persons can only be revelation'; that is, we must start 'with the revelation of the Father through the Son in the Holy Spirit.'[18] However, these assertions, as we shall see later on in our exploration of Rahner's theology, do not carry the same weight and meaning as they do in Barth's thinking precisely because Kasper and Rahner also ascribe the possibility of knowing the God of Christian revelation to us in our supposed *obediential potency* for revelation. It is just at this point, as we shall see, with respect to the doctrine of justification as it applies to the knowledge of God, that Barth's evangelical theology and Roman Catholic theology remain at loggerheads.

The Role of Experience

Among contemporary American theologians, perhaps the most notorious examples of those who at least indirectly have helped shape trinitarian theology in exactly the wrong way are Gordon Kaufman and Sallie McFague.[19] Their thinking makes it impossible to speak of the immanent Trinity and thus reduces speech about God to our human attempt to give meaning to our existence using theological categories. Their thinking in turn has strongly influenced the trinitarian theology of Catherine LaCugna and the feminist theology of Elizabeth Johnson. I will illustrate how this influence affects the theology of LaCugna and Johnson as the chapter proceeds with a view toward seeing how experience displaces God's free actions ad extra when the doctrine of the immanent Trinity is ignored or compromised.

Both Gordon Kaufman and Sallie McFague are correct to call attention to the important issue of idolatry and to the fact that in the

17 Walter Kasper, *The God of Jesus Christ*, trans. Matthew J. O'Connell (New York: Crossroad, 1986), 113.

18 Kasper, *The God of Jesus Christ*, 299–300.

19 For a thorough analysis and critique of their thinking, see Paul D. Molnar, 'Myth and Reality: Analysis and Critique of Gordon Kaufman and Sallie McFague on God, Christ, and Salvation', *Cultural Encounters: A Journal for the Theology of Culture*, summer 2005, vol. 1, no. 2 (Summer 2005): 23–48.

past the Church has misunderstood the faith when it was thought that Christianity could or should be imposed on others, as happened during the Inquisition and the Crusades. Along with many others, I share their concerns about the fact that Christians have often misused Christian symbols. They are also correct in believing that the imagination is part of the theological enterprise. However I disagree with them on two extremely important issues: (1) they think that because theology merely represents our human attempt to give meaning to existence using theological symbols, it should be 'judged in terms of the adequacy with which it is fulfilling the objectives we humans set for it'[20] and (2) thus when they speak of theology as 'imaginative construction' they mean that its truth is not governed by a unique object (the triune God) which exists independently of the mind, but that *we* are the ones who actually create truth by the way we think and act.[21]

20 See Gordon D. Kaufman, *Theology for a Nuclear Age* (hereafter: *TNA*) (Philadelphia: Westminster Press, 1985), 19. See also Gordon D. Kaufman, *God – Mystery – Diversity: Christian Theology in a Pluralistic World* (hereafter: *GMD*) (Minneapolis, MN: Fortress Press, 1996), 42.

21 Thus, in rejecting a traditional approach to theology as an understanding of truth existing in its own right, Kaufman can say that according to that traditional view 'theological truth is not something we humans discover (or create) in our work; it is, rather, something already present and available in tradition – especially the Bible – awaiting our appropriation ... What the truth is, is already determined; we simply believe and seek to understand' (*TNA*, 17). In one sense, of course, the truth in its identity with God is not simply there awaiting our appropriation – our appropriation of the truth, as argued earlier, is enabled here and now by the active movement of God toward us and is not in the least dependent on us. Therefore even biblical truth cannot simply be identified with tradition as Kaufman seems to think the traditional view does. Beyond this, however, Kaufman honestly does believe that we create truth through conversation such that 'truth is ... a process of becoming, a reality that emerges (quite unexpectedly) in the course of conversation ... This truth will harden and die away, moreover, if the participants in the conversation attempt to reify it into legalistic definitions and formulas ... no single voice can lay claim to it, for each understands that only in the ongoing conversation as a whole is it *brought into being* ... truth is never final or complete or unchanging' (*GMD*, 199–200; emphasis mine). Sallie McFague argues that metaphorical theology offers us 'new possibilities in place of others. In this sense *we create the reality in which we live*; we do not copy it or to put it more pointedly, there are no copies, only creations' (*Models of God: Theology for an Ecological, Nuclear Age*

They believe that to speak of a really existing God who is the creator and who before that was the eternal Father, Son and Holy Spirit, represents what they call a false form of reifying symbols, or as Kaufman puts it: 'It is "treating our thoughts as things." We reify the symbols "creator" and "lord" and "father" when we take them to mean that God *really is* a creator/lord/father (The literal meaning of the word "reify" is simply "to make into a thing.").'[22] They therefore believe that any contemporary talk about an immanent Trinity represents irrelevant speculation.

Gordon Kaufman

For Kaufman, theology is *essentially* imaginative construction, that is, the human imagination uses the image/concept of God as the 'ultimate point of reference', to organize its experiences in the world and to enable humans to come to terms with those things that threaten the survival of civilization, such as a potential nuclear holocaust. Any theology that would begin with revelation would be considered 'authoritarian'. Kaufman thus sees two alternatives: (1) we can admit that theology is essentially imaginative construction or (2) we can accept the fact that our terms refer to reality.[23] He insists that if, mistakenly, we were to choose the second alternative, we would be guilty of reifying our images, that is, we would have failed to realize that our concepts are simply imaginative constructs governed by the way we think humanity ought to function in community in a movement toward peace. Such a failure would lead us to think that God is an objective reality existing independently of our conceptions. Since he can only conceive of God as a symbol we invest with meaning and use to create a better world, Kaufman thinks the symbol God is a myth.[24] Because of this, he is

(hereafter: *Models*) (Philadelphia: Fortress Press, 1987), 26; emphasis mine). Hence, for her the only way to reach 'reality' is 'by creating versions of it' (*Models*, 26).

22 Gordon D. Kaufman, *In Face of Mystery: A Constructive Theology* (hereafter: *IFM*) (Cambridge, MA: Harvard University Press, 1993), 330.

23 Kaufman, *IFM*, 49. Re: Theology as essentially imaginative construction, cf. also Kaufman, *TNA*, 26ff.

24 Kaufman, *IFM*, 332, that is, 'this symbol is actually but one feature of a larger mythic map of reality'.

unable to acknowledge or describe the Christian God at all since, as Barth put it, the triune God

> reveals Himself as the One who, even though He did not love us and were not revealed to us, even though we did not exist at all, still loves in and for Himself as surely as He is and is God; who loves us by reason and in consequence of the fact that He is the One who loves in His freedom in and for Himself, and is God as such.[25]

Hence Barth also rightly insisted that 'we cannot say anything higher or better of the "inwardness of God" than that God is Father, Son, and Holy Spirit'.[26] But we can say this because God has enabled us to know him as he truly is.

Thus, genuine knowledge of God is in no sense achieved by reifying our concepts, but only by allowing God himself, who is the truth, to empower us to participate in the truth of God's own self-knowledge and love. In any case, it is just because Kaufman thinks of God as a symbol and as part of a mythic map of reality that, although he rightly opposes dualism (any separation of God from the world), he himself is led into the most extreme form of it. For while he insists that 'if genuine revelation is affirmed, the character of God's relating himself to his world must express the inmost essence of his being and will', he also insists that 'to the internal *structure* of this innermost essence we have no access in history or revelation; and anything said about it is pure speculation'.[27] Ultimately this truly rigid dualism leads Kaufman to the position that 'God will no longer be pictured or conceived as a personal being in the heavens above who "before the foundation of the world" ... devised a detailed divine plan ... we will no longer ... be able to imagine ourselves as in direct personal interaction with this divine being'.[28]

Catherine LaCugna

It is just this dualistic thinking that structures what Catherine LaCugna thinks about the Trinity. For instance, she approves Kaufman's refusal to

25 *CD* IV/2, 755.

26 *CD* I/2, 377.

27 Gordon D. Kaufman, *Systematic Theology: A Historicist Perspective* (hereafter: *ST*) (New York: Charles Scribner's Sons, 1968), 102 n.9.

28 Kaufman, *IFM*, 332.

make a distinction between the immanent and economic Trinity because she believes, with him, that theology should not accept the fact that the immanent Trinity 'is equivalent to "God as he is in himself" or "God's essence"'.[29] She believes that 'the economy itself does not *necessarily* imply real distinctions "in" God that are of a different ontological order than the distinctions in the economy. There *may be* such distinctions, and it *may be* a legitimate enterprise for a purely speculative theology to posit such intradivine distinctions, but there is no transeconomic perspective from which to establish their existence.'[30] What she quite rightly wishes to avoid is thinking that ignores the economy. However, she assumes, incorrectly, that if a theologian argues on the basis of the intradivine distinctions, then the economy must be left behind, with the result that the Trinity then would have no bearing on our life or faith. Thus, she supports Schoonenberg's view that on the basis of revelation we cannot know whether or not God would have been a Trinity apart from salvation.[31] Unquestionably we all agree that *we* cannot leave the economy behind without disrupting the important connection between the Trinity and the life of faith. Yet it is precisely on the basis of revelation that we do indeed know that God would still be the eternal Father, Son and Spirit without the world, even though he freely created the world and has acted to save the world in his Word and Spirit.[32] While we are in no position

29 Catherine Mowry LaCugna, *God for Us: The Trinity and Christian Life* (hereafter: *God for Us*) (San Francisco: HarperSanFrancisco, 1991), 226–7.

30 LaCugna, *God for Us*, 227.

31 See LaCugna, 227 and 218. LaCugna summarizes her understanding of Schoonenberg's point this way: 'the question of whether God would be trinitarian apart from salvation history is purely speculative and cannot be answered on the basis of revelation' (227). One of the key problems with this sort of thinking is that it leads Schoonenberg to argue that God *becomes* triune by deciding to relate with us and then by relating with us in history. Hence Schoonenberg remarks that 'it is not impossible that God becomes Trinity through communicating himself in a total way to, and being present in, the man Jesus as Word, and through being in the Church as Spirit', Piet Schoonenberg, S.J., *The Christ: A Study of the God-Man Relationship In the Whole of Creation and in Jesus Christ* (New York: Herder & Herder, 1971), 85. From this he concludes that 'on a Trinity in God from eternity and by necessity we as creatures cannot make any statements, either in the affirmative or in the negative', *The Christ*, 86. For a discussion of this point, see Molnar, *Faith, Freedom and the Spirit*, 210–11.

32 On this point in current discussion, see esp., Molnar, *Faith, Freedom and the Spirit*, chapter three. See also George Hunsinger, *Reading Barth with*

to say anything about God in himself (the immanent Trinity) except on the basis of what is revealed by the economic Trinity, it is imperative, as Thomas F. Torrance never tires of reminding us, that we recognize that all of our theological knowledge is grounded in the fact that God is toward us what he is eternally in himself. While LaCugna makes statements that sound similar to this, as when she cites Roger Haight's view that 'God must in some way be such that God corresponds to the way God communicates God's personal self to human beings',[33] her inability to admit that the immanent Trinity does indeed refer to God's life independent of his relations with us in the economy leads her to reduce the immanent to the economic Trinity, against her own stated desire not to do so.[34]

LaCugna's entire trinitarian theology is built on a foundation of sand precisely because she refuses to acknowledge the importance of the immanent Trinity as the presupposition, meaning and goal of any trinitarian theology.[35] Unless our knowledge of God for us is anchored in a firm knowledge of who God eternally is as Father, Son and Holy Spirit, it has no objective validity. One not only does not have to leave the economy to know this God with certainty. In light of the fact that God himself has come to us in time, space and history and in light of the fact God enables such knowledge in his Word and Spirit, it is clear that God enables such knowledge within the economy so that any thought that knowing God on our part must require an escape from the economy represents a failure to respect the importance of the incarnation. The ultimate guarantee of that knowledge is, as T. F. Torrance rightly contends, the fact that Christ himself rose from the dead and is himself the guarantee of that validity.[36] As we shall see later in more detail, it is just this thinking that leads LaCugna to reduce God's existence to his existence in the economy: 'The doctrine of the Trinity is not ultimately a teaching about "God" but a teaching about *God's life with us and our life with each other*.'[37] Indeed she believes that 'to speak about God in

---

Charity, who maintains that for Barth 'God would be the antecedent Trinity whether the world had been created or not', 36. This is a point that Barth constantly reiterated (106) and it is in harmony with the tradition regarding God's freedom in se.

33 LaCugna, *God for Us*, 228.

34 See, for example, LaCugna, *God for Us*, 211–21.

35 This is a point which has been made forcefully and helpfully with respect to Barth's theology by George Hunsinger in *Reading Barth with Charity*.

36 See Molnar, *Faith, Freedom and the Spirit*, 127.

37 LaCugna, *God for Us*, 228.

immanent trinitarian terms is nothing more than to speak about God's life with us in the economy ...'.[38] It is important to note here, however, that we cannot speak intelligibly about God's life with us unless the God of whom we speak is distinguishable from us and from our life with each other. This is the very thing that LaCugna is unable to do precisely because of her refusal to allow the doctrine of the immanent Trinity a genuine function in her thinking about God for us.

To be fair, it is quite obvious that she believes that some talk of an immanent Trinity is legitimate because she does claim that 'God's presence to us does not exhaust without remainder the absolute mystery of God'.[39] She even acknowledges that 'the distinction between the economic and immanent Trinity is a way of holding on to the truth that God is personal, that God is free, that God cannot be reduced to human history or human perception'.[40] Nonetheless, for her, there can be no equating the immanent Trinity with God's life apart from us. So any talk of the immanent Trinity for LaCugna can be nothing more than an analysis of the economy. She is of course ambiguous about this. On the one hand she speaks as if it were extremely important to distinguish God in se from God for us in order to avoid the appearance of projection. On the other hand, she insists that any grounding of the economy in an immanent Trinity represents a separation of God from us. Thus she believes that '*theologia* is not the Trinity *in se* but, much more modestly and simply, the mystery of God ... *an "immanent" trinitarian theology of God is nothing more than a theology of the economy of salvation*'.[41] This leads to the idea that divine *perichoresis* should be understood as the 'divine dance' that signifies not 'intradivine communion' but

> divine life as all creatures partake and literally exist in it ... Everything comes from God, and everything returns to God, through Christ in the Spirit. This *exitus* and *reditus* is the choreography of the divine dance which takes place from all eternity and is manifest at every moment in creation. There are not two sets of communion – one among the divine persons, the other among human persons ... The one *perichoresis*, the one mystery of communion includes God and humanity as beloved partners in the dance.[42]

38 LaCugna, *God for Us*, 229.
39 LaCugna, *God for Us*, 228.
40 LaCugna, *God for Us*, 304.
41 LaCugna, *God for Us*, 223–4.
42 LaCugna, *God for Us*, 274. It is important to realize that *perichoresis* did indeed come to refer to the inner relations of mutual participation and

By way of summary LaCugna points out that 'the exodus of all persons from God and the return of all to God is the divine dance in which God and we are eternal partners'.[43] Having said that, however, LaCugna clearly reveals her own inability to distinguish God from creatures precisely because her thinking has already incorporated them under the umbrella of her relational feminist ontology at the outset. Her polemic against the doctrine of the immanent Trinity will not allow her to admit with Barth that God 'would be no less and no different even if they [creatures] all did not exist or existed differently'; that even in relating with us, 'God is who He is in independence of [us] even in this relatedness'; and that God 'does not mingle and blend Himself with [us] … Even in His relationship and connexion with them [creatures], He remains who He is … He would be who He is even without this connexion'.[44] These important statements by Barth are made because he allows his thinking to be shaped by who God eternally is within his immanent divine life precisely as the God who relates with us not by necessity but by grace and in the freedom of his love. They are thus quite different from LaCugna's rather confused statements: 'The life of God is not something that belongs to God alone. *Trinitarian life is also our life*'[45] and 'To be God is to be the Creator of the world'.[46] Barth rightly insists that God's life is and remains uniquely his, even as he draws us into relationship with himself through his grace. Barth's

containing of the trinitarian persons. On that basis, and by the grace of God's movement toward us in his Word and Spirit, we may, through faith, participate in God's own knowledge and love through union with Christ in the Spirit. However, simply to assert that God and we are eternal partners in 'the divine dance' makes it conceptually impossible to distinguish God's eternal perichoretic relations from God's relations with us as just described. Perhaps the culprit here is the image of the divine dance which T. F. Torrance noted rests on a confusion of the terms 'χωρέω' with 'χορεύω'. The former term refers to the mutual containing of one another in which the persons of the Trinity eternally exist, while the latter term means to dance as in the Greek word χορός or chorus. See Thomas F. Torrance, *The Christian Doctrine of God*, 170n. 8.

43 LaCugna, *God for Us*, 304.

44 *CD* II/1, 311–12.

45 LaCugna, *God for Us*, 228.

46 LaCugna, *God for Us*, 355.

thinking unequivocally and rightly eschews any reduction of God's eternal being into his creative function, as happens in LaCugna's thinking.

No wonder Colin Gunton believes that LaCugna's position seems more like that of John Scotus Erigena, one of the founders of modern pantheism, than the Cappadocians, to whom she frequently appeals.[47] And that is the problem. LaCugna's thinking ultimately leads her into both the pantheism and dualism which she quite obviously attempts to avoid by paying lip service to God's freedom; but lip service is not enough for her to avoid making God dependent on us and allowing an abstract concept of relationality to determine her view of God and Christ. More will be said about this later. Here I simply wish to establish the fact that LaCugna's thinking about the Trinity at the outset is not really dictated by God, Christ or the Holy Spirit just because she allows her theology to be shaped by the historicist, Kantian[48] and pantheistic views of Gordon Kaufman. It may be noted here that Kaufman's understanding of God, as dictated by the evolutionary process, is in fact pantheistic because he cannot distinguish God from the evolutionary process itself:

> The symbol 'God' suggests a reality, an ultimate tendency or power, which is working itself out in an evolutionary process ... God – this whole grand cosmic evolutionary movement – is giving birth, after many millennia, to finite freedom ... God is here understood as that ecological reality behind and in and working through all of life and history ...[49]

Sallie McFague

Sallie McFague reconceives God from generally accessible human experience, explicitly claiming that we must 'image God according to what we find most desirable in ourselves and what we find constitutive of

---

47 See Colin E. Gunton, *Scottish Journal of Theology* (hereafter: *SJT*), vol. 47, no. 1, 1994, 137. See also Colin E. Gunton, *The Promise of Trinitarian Theology Second Edition* (Edinburgh: T & T Clark, 1997), xvii–xix.

48 Kaufman believes the idea of God is a regulative idea that we use to order our existence. Cf. Gordon D. Kaufman, *An Essay on Theological Method* (hereafter: *Method*) (Atlanta, GA: Scholars Press, 1990), 24.

49 *TNA*, 43–5.

our world'.[50] She also asserts that she does 'not know whether God (the inner being of God) can be described by the models of mother, lover and friend'.[51] Through these significant experiences she employs her model of God as mother and describes a God who is dependent on and *intrinsically* related to the world;[52] a God who needs the world since the world is God's body;[53] and thinks the doctrine of the Trinity simply gave dogmatic status to relationality.[54] By describing only our experiences of relationality, however, her panentheistic view which inevitably devolves into pantheism destroys the free basis which our human relations have in God who becomes 'our friend and co-worker,' one who needs many saviors[55] instead of our Lord, Savior, Helper and Friend as the Incarnate Word. Following Schleiermacher, Tillich and process theologians, McFague thinks of the Trinity 'as a summation of ... ontology or of the Christian experience of God'[56] so that her models can replace the Father, Son and Spirit;[57] thus, she focuses

> on God's activity in relationship to the world and our talk about that activity. It makes no claims about the so-called immanent or intrinsic trinity, for I see no way that assumptions concerning the inner nature of God are possible. My interest centers on the economic trinity, on the experience of God's activity in relation to the world.[58]

This thinking is of a piece with her belief that while she cannot *know* the reality of God, she can still speculate about God's reality by creating new mythologies rather than replicating past traditional mythologies such as these were embodied in the doctrine of creation. Hence she writes: 'I do not *know* who God is, but I find some models better than others for constructing an image of God commensurate with my trust in a God as on the side of life.'[59] Thus, she believes that

50 McFague, *Models*, 134.
51 McFague, *Models*, 192.
52 McFague, *Models*, 72 and 78, 167.
53 McFague, *Models*, 112–13, 131, 133–5.
54 McFague, *Models*, 166.
55 McFague, *Models*, 135, 150.
56 McFague, *Models*, 223 n.2.
57 McFague, *Models*, 181.
58 McFague, *Models*, 224.
59 McFague, *Models*, 192 n.37. McFague thus specifically rejects the idea that we actually can know anything about the immanent Trinity, 224. It is worth

through remythologizing the doctrines of God and human beings in light of the picture of reality from contemporary science – through the use of the organic model as a way of reconceiving the relation of God and the world – the appropriate human stance vis-à-vis God and our planet will emerge. Remythologizing ... is a form of embodied thought combining image and concept that calls forth both a feeling and a thinking response ... If one uses the model of the universe as God's body ... one would, or at least might, act differently toward it than if one used the model of creation as a work of art (one possible model from the Genesis story).[60]

Yet the problem with this thinking is that if she cannot know the immanent Trinity, that is, the reality of God, but can only speculate in a mythological way about God by projecting possibilities from our experiences of motherhood, love and friendship, then any claim she might make to actually know God is simply vacuous. All that is really known are our experiences and our supposed knowledge of God is nothing more than projection. Indeed this projection leads directly to the pantheism, modalism and dualism that mark her reflections.

Her particular modalist idea that we only have to do with an economic Trinity, however, results from the same methodological agnosticism that marks Catherine LaCugna's work and which cannot describe God who really *is* Father, Son and Spirit in eternity and in time. So while Christian prayer, following Jesus's own instruction, has always been related to the coming of the kingdom, McFague sees prayers as a conjuring of images which will enable *us* to think of the world as special so that we will preserve it as God's body,[61] that is, as a reality that 'is not something alien to or other than God but is from the "womb" of God, formed through "gestation".'[62] It is apparent that the very idea of the world as God's body is a panentheistic attempt (which clearly collapses

---

noting that McFague actually describes herself as having been an 'erstwhile Barthian' in her book *The Body of God: An Ecological Theology* (hereafter: *The Body of God*) (Minneapolis, MN: Fortress Press, 1993), who had to overcome her resistance to 'nature spirituality' (208), and holds the same view espoused in *Models*: 'The transcendence of God frees us to model God in terms of what is most significant to us' (193).

60 McFague, *The Body of God*, 81.

61 See McFague, *Models*, 187.

62 McFague, *Models*, 110. T. F. Torrance in particular avoids these kinds of analogies because he insists that analogies must be governed by God's

back into pantheism) to bypass the uniqueness of the incarnation as an event in the life of Jesus and to visualize the God/world relation as one in which 'God will therefore need the world, want the world, not simply as a dependent inferior (flesh subordinated to spirit) but as offspring, beloved, and companion'.[63] Apotheosis thus issues in self-justification just because for her Jesus is *'paradigmatic of God the lover but is not unique. This means that Jesus is not ontologically different from other paradigmatic figures* ... He is special to us as our foundational figure: he is our historical choice as the premier paradigm of God's love'.[64] McFague's mythological view of the incarnation suggests that:

> The world as God's body, then, may be seen as a way to remythologize the inclusive, suffering love of the cross of Jesus of Nazareth ... God is at risk in human hands: Just as once upon a time in a bygone mythology, human beings killed their God in the body of a man, so now we once again have that power, but, in a mythology more appropriate to our time, we would kill our God in the body of the world.[65]

self-revelation and cannot simply be read back into God from our experiences of faith. We thus refer to God as Father and Son, he says, in an *imageless* way, 'that is in a diaphanous or "see through" way, to the Father and the Son without the intrusion of creaturely forms or sensual images into God. Thus we may not think of God as having gender nor think of the Father as begetting the Son or of the Son as begotten after the analogy of generation or giving birth with which we are familiar among creaturely beings', *The Christian Doctrine of God*, 158.

63 McFague, *Models*, 112–13.

64 McFague, *Models*, 136, emphasis mine. McFague thinks Jesus is a 'paradigmatic' manifestation 'of God as lover', but considering this love 'in an ecological evolutionary context does not allow the work of one individual to be effective for all space and time' (143). Consequently, sin is redefined as failure to realize our interdependence with the world as God's body (136) and salvation is redefined as 'the ongoing healing of the divided body of our world which we, with God, work at together' (143). It is not something that is accomplished by Jesus doing anything for us – it is rather the work of many saviors attempting to reunify 'the shattered, divided world' and it must be 'done and done again, by many minds, hearts, hands, and feet' (150). For further discussion of these ideas, see Paul D. Molnar, *Incarnation and Resurrection: Toward a Contemporary Understanding* (hereafter: *Incarnation and Resurrection*) (Grand Rapids, MI: Eerdmans, 2007), 214–32.

65 McFague, *Models*, 72–3.

The point here is that McFague is deeply influenced by the thinking of Gordon Kaufman, and for that very reason she is led to reject what has always been the only sure foundation for Christian knowledge of God, that is, the existence and activity of the eternal (immanent) Trinity. For her, using her model of God as lover based on our experiences of love, Jesus is one significant example of God's love for us among others and he is this since Christians chose to make him their foundation. Precisely because of her agnosticism with respect to the immanent Trinity, she ascribes true knowledge of God and of Christ to us instead of recognizing that true knowledge of God can only come from God. The triune God does not become who he is based on our choices but can only be known in truth when and if our choices correspond with his choice of us in Christ through the Holy Spirit. Indeed, as Colin Gunton has observed, any compromise of divine freedom means that human freedom is also endangered: 'God's personal otherness from the world is needed if there is to be a true establishing of the world in its own right.'[66]

Feminist Concerns/Elizabeth Johnson

In her book *She Who Is: The Mystery of God in Feminist Theological Discourse*, Elizabeth A. Johnson patterns her entire discussion of God methodologically and in terms of content after the theologies of Gordon Kaufman and Sallie McFague. Thus, she argues that the symbol God functions as our 'ultimate point of reference'. Hence, if we speak of God as an arbitrary tyrant or as a war-God we will have an aggressive and intolerant community, while if we speak of a loving and forgiving God we will have a community of forgiveness and caring. God is described as a 'matrix' within which human life is lived and understood. Indeed her basic argument is that 'the symbol God functions'[67] and that we must make it function today so as not to exclude women. The suggestion clearly is that it is we who invest this symbol with meaning and it is we who thus must change the symbol in order to obtain the desired social results. This is in harmony with Kaufman's view that theology must be

66 Gunton, *The Promise of Trinitarian Theology second edn*, xix.

67 Elizabeth A. Johnson, *She Who Is: The Mystery of God in Feminist Theological Discourse* (hereafter: *She Who Is*) (New York: Crossroad, 1992), 4. See also Elizabeth A. Johnson, *Quest for the Living God: Mapping Frontiers in the Theology of God* (hereafter: *Quest*) (New York/London: Continuum, 2008), 98.

judged by the objectives we humans set for it. It is just this assumption that makes it impossible to argue consistently that the triune God alone is the judge of the truth of our human knowledge of God.

Consequently, instead of allowing her thought to be shaped by the fact that the truth of our symbols for God must be grounded in God acting for us in history and thus in revelation, Johnson argues that women have been excluded 'from the realm of public symbol formation and decision making' and have thus been subordinated to 'the imagination and needs of a world designed chiefly by men'.[68] While Johnson admits that God is officially seen as spirit and beyond male or female sexuality, nevertheless she argues that the church's daily language in worship, preaching and teaching conveys the message that 'God is male, or at least more like a man than a woman, or at least more fittingly addressed as male than as female'. Since the symbol God functions and it has thus functioned to subordinate women, the task of contemporary theology is to make it function so as to enhance women's dignity as equally created in God's image. What is needed, according to Johnson, is a 'creative "naming toward God," as Mary Daly so carefully calls it, from the matrix of their own experience'.[69] As active subjects in their own right, women wish to name God out of their emerging identity. Language for God in female images is thus necessary to overcome any subordination of women and any false domination by men.

There can be no doubt that women frequently have been mistreated and still are mistreated today by men and other women. Further, women are quite justified in reacting against their exclusion from certain positions in the church and to some of the rather odd arguments used to explain their exclusion.[70] Here I want to make it perfectly clear

---

68 Johnson, *She Who Is*, 4. *Quest*, 99.

69 Johnson, *She Who Is*, 5. Kevin J. Vanhoozer, *Remythologizing Theology: Divine Action, Passion, and Authorship* (Cambridge: Cambridge University Press, 2010), 120–1, thinks that Johnson's is 'ultimately an experiential theology' since 'it is difficult to escape the impression that human experience … serves as the interpretative framework for the being of God rather than vice versa'. Vanhoozer rightly intends to argue that the meaning of our experiences of love and relationality should be interpreted in light of the 'ontological implications' of the biblical images and metaphors. Thus, he opposes Johnson's attempt to substitute 'new images/metaphors for biblical ones' (120).

70 For a very helpful discussion of some of those issues and arguments, see George Hunsinger, *The Eucharist and Ecumenism: Let us Keep the Feast*

that I fully support the feminist desire and drive for equality for women in dignity, rights and opportunity because, as Roland Frye has argued, following Elizabeth Achtemeier, '"the Christian gospel is a gospel of freedom and service, in Christ, for male and female alike".'[71] This desire and drive for equality, however, cannot mean that theology should now exchange the revelation of God for the experience of women (or anyone else's experience as argued earlier) and thus collapse theology into anthropology. Such a move inevitably leads Johnson to think that we can never 'literally' know who God is. This approach surely will not enhance the stature of women and will ultimately obscure rather than illuminate the truth, which alone can set all of us free in this matter. Since Jesus is the way, the truth and the life, any theological understanding of this issue must begin and end its thinking with him. To the extent that the fight for women's equality in the church is grounded in the freedom that comes from Christ alone freeing us to live as those who really are one in him, it will be seen that we do not need to change the symbols for who God is.

Indeed, it is crucial to realize that changing the language for the God of Christian faith is not, as Roland Frye correctly notes, a true solution to the problems women face; it is instead what he calls a 'distractor' since 'it identifies an answer that may look right but is not'.[72] Changing the language for God at the end of the day ends up changing the faith itself because it leads to a different God than the God revealed in Jesus Christ. In the words of Elizabeth Achtemeier: 'The church cannot and it must not accede to feminist demands that language about God be changed to feminine, for then the church will have lost that God in whom it truly lives and moves and has its being.'[73] Therefore, our God-talk cannot and should not be arbitrarily constructed based on any social or religious agenda. Moreover, it certainly cannot be grounded in anyone's experience since in reality it is and must remain grounded in revelation in its identity with Jesus Christ himself and is known through the present action of his Holy Spirit.

(Cambridge: Cambridge University Press, 2008), 231–44. Hunsinger wonders whether or not 'the refusal of the sacramental churches to admit women into holy orders rests very largely on a theologically misguided theory of imagistic or iconic "representation"', 231.

71 Frye, 'Language for God', *SJT* (1988), 441.
72 Frye, 'Language for God', *SJT* (1988), 443.
73 Achtemeier cited in Frye, 441–2.

Critical Issues

Because Elizabeth Johnson's main concern is to overcome women's subordination, she sees theology more as an imaginative way to achieve that goal politically, socially and religiously, than as an attempt to understand who God really is and what he has actually done and is doing in history. While she does believe that 'we would lose a great deal if we ceased speaking altogether of the immanent triune God',[74] her starting point for reflecting on the Trinity is the experience of 'holy mystery'. Hence, 'this language [for the Trinity] is not a literal description of the inner being of God who is in any event beyond human understanding. It is a pointer to holy mystery'.[75] Since 'holy mystery' can go by many names other than the eternal Father, Son and Holy Spirit and since, as we shall note later, Johnson effectively equates God's incomprehensibility with the fact that we cannot literally know who God is when we speak of the immanent Trinity, she leaves herself in an essentially agnostic position when it does come to knowing God's inner being. For this reason there are several serious errors and inconsistencies evident in Johnson's thinking which need to be explained and overcome.

Naming God from the Matrix of Women's Experience

As already noted, Johnson argues that while the Christian God in reality is neither male nor female[76] and so should not be understood as sexually defined, one of her main arguments is that throughout church history God, as Father and Son, has been understood to be male and was so named by men in order to subordinate women.[77] This is simply wrong

74　Johnson, *She Who Is*, 200.

75　Johnson, *She Who Is*, 200.

76　Johnson, *She Who Is*, 4–5, 54–5.

77　Johnson, *She Who Is*, 5, 21, 44 and 48ff. Johnson literally cannot think of the Persons of the Trinity as uniquely personal without mistakenly introducing gender into God via Christology. Hence, instead of thinking of Jesus in his uniqueness as recognized at Chalcedon, she claims that 'if Jesus as a man is the revelation of God ... then this points to maleness as an essential characteristic of divine being itself', Elizabeth A. Johnson, 'Redeeming the Name of Christ', in *Freeing Theology: The Essentials of Theology in Feminist Perspective*, ed. Catherine Mowry LaCugna (HarperSanFrancisco: Harper Collins, 1993), 115–37, 119. She believes that this view 'is intensified by the

and, as Roland Frye has shown, follows the errant assumptions of Mary Daly's slogan 'Since God is male, the male is God'[78] with the implication that God must be emasculated for women to achieve equality. Neither in scripture nor in the history of dogma has God, as Father and Son, been understood to be male – not even subliminally. Unfortunately, Johnson believes the conflicts that break out over naming God 'He' or 'She' 'indicate that, however subliminally, maleness *is* intended when we say God'.[79] And the reason she says this is extremely revealing. It is because she thinks that when people call on God as Father they are naming God 'in the image of powerful men'[80] when in reality Christians who confess the Nicene Creed are naming God the Father based on the revelation of his Son, Jesus Christ. Such speaking of God is not in the

almost exclusive use of the father-son metaphors to interpret Jesus' relationship with God' (119) and follows Rosemary Radford Reuther's view that: ' "The unwarranted idea develops that there is a necessary ontological connection between the maleness of Jesus' historical person and the maleness of *Logos* as male offspring and disclosure of a male God' " (119). All of this reasoning is extremely problematic because it literally will not allow God acting *as* man in Jesus Christ to be uniquely who he is in eternity and in history as the revealer of God's own identity. Instead, Jesus the man is visualized in connection with a supposedly male *Logos* in a way that subordinates women to men and Jesus's maleness is erroneously thought to introduce gender into the eternal relations of the Father and Son. It is crucial to realize that the terms 'Father' and 'Son' are not simply metaphors *projected* by Christians interpreting Jesus's relation with God. Such a view would have to mean that revelation comes *from* us in our imaginative theological constructions (Kaufman) instead of from God alone *to* us. In reality these metaphors are used analogically to speak of the God who came into history from outside and enabled a knowledge of the Trinity in its internal relations – a knowledge which would have been closed to us without our inclusion in the eternal Father–Son relation by the Spirit.

78 Cited in Roland Frye, 'Language for God and Feminist Language: Problems and Principles' *SJT*, vol. 41, no. 4 (1988): 441–69, 443. See also Roland Frye, 'Language for God and Feminist Language: Problems and Principles', *Speaking the Christian God: The Holy Trinity and the Challenge of Feminism*, ed. Alvin F. Kimel, Jr. (Grand Rapids, MI: Eerdmans, 1992), 17–43, 19. See Mary Daly, *Beyond God the Father: Toward a Philosophy of Women's Liberation* (Boston: Beacon Press, 1985), 19.

79 Johnson, *Quest*, 98.

80 Johnson, *Quest*, 98.

image of any man, but takes place on the basis of who God eternally is in relation to his Son and in relation to the Holy Spirit as revealed in the history of Jesus Christ and the outpouring of his Holy Spirit. This Father exercised his power by sending his Son to suffer and die for our sakes. That is hardly the image of 'powerful men' used by men to subordinate women. In any case, the reason why Johnson thinks this way is because her basic theology is grounded in the experience of women. She is, as she says, naming God from the matrix of women's experience. Thus, while she continues to use the traditional name for God sparingly she ultimately changes its meaning by associating it 'with metaphors and values arising from women's experience'.[81] This, however, might be considered merely an interim strategy, she says, until some new word arises

> for the as yet unnameable understanding of holy mystery that includes the reality of women as well as all creation. On the way to that day, language of God/She is aimed at generating new content for references to deity in the hopes that this discourse will help to heal imaginations and liberate people for new forms of community.[82]

The truth, however, is that in scripture and in doctrine, God was understood from a center in God rather than from a center in human experience, whether male or female. That is the significance of Athanasius's statement mentioned earlier that 'it is more pious and more accurate to signify God from the Son and call Him Father, than to name Him from His works only and call Him Unoriginate'.[83] Here the Father–Son relation has priority over the creator–creature relation in an irreversible way so that God's nature is neither defined nor measured by our own human nature. True knowledge of God in this context could take place *only* through Christ who was and is one in being with the Father. The deity of Christ therefore was central to a proper view of the Trinity. As Thomas F. Torrance remarks: 'The Deity of Christ is the supreme truth of the Gospel, the key to the bewildering enigma of Jesus …'[84] Athanasius thus made it clear that

81 Johnson, *She Who Is*, 43.

82 Johnson, *She Who Is*, 43.

83 Athanasius, *C. Ar.* I, 34, in *A Select Library of Nicene and Post-Nicene Fathers of the Christian Church*, trans. and ed. Philip Schaff and Henry Wace, *Volume IV, St. Athanasius: Select Works and Letters* (Grand Rapids, MI: Eerdmans, 1987), 326. See also Torrance, *The Trinitarian Faith*, 49.

84 Torrance, *The Christian Doctrine of God*, 46. While Douglas Farrow, *Ascension and Ecclesia: On the Significance of the Doctrine of the Ascension for*

those who would call God the Unoriginate were those who named him only from his works because they did not know the Son who is the very same being as God the Father.[85] Our knowledge of God as creator then is taken from knowledge of God as Father and as Son because all things were created through the Son. As Hilary of Poitiers makes clear:

> You hear the name *Son*; believe that He is the Son. You hear the name *Father*; fix it in your mind that He is the Father. Why surround these names with doubt and illwill and hostility? The things of God are provided with names which give a true indication of the realities; why force an arbitrary meaning upon their obvious sense? Father and Son are spoken of; doubt not that the words mean what they say.[86]

What all of this means is that we cannot have precise theological knowledge of God as the almighty creator 'in terms of abstract possibilities and vague generalities – from what we imagine God is not, or from examining what God has brought into being in complete difference from himself'.[87] It was the Gnostic Basileides from Alexandria who, relying on Plato's notion that 'God is beyond all being' taught that 'we cannot say anything about what God is, but can only say something about what he is not'.[88] But Gregory of Nazianzen (*Or.* 28.9) held in opposition to this thinking that 'if we cannot say anything positive about what God is, we really cannot say anything accurate about what he is not'.[89] As Thomas F. Torrance rightly explains, Nicene theologians refused to speak of God in empty negative conceptions because if we

Ecclesiology and Christian Cosmology (hereafter: *Ascension and Ecclesia*) (Grand Rapids, MI: Eerdmans, 1999), 13, argues that theologians today are more prone to stumble over Christ's humanity than his divinity, I hope to show throughout this book that it is mainly the failure of modern theologians to begin and end their thinking with the man Jesus who was and is the eternally begotten Son of the Father that causes much of the trouble that now exists in connection with our understanding of the immanent and economic Trinity.

85 Torrance, *The Trinitarian Faith*, 76.

86 St. Hilary of Poitiers, *On the Trinity*, Book III, 22 (hereafter: Hilary, *Trinity*), in *A Select Library of Nicene and Post-Nicene Fathers of the Christian Church Second Series, Vol. IX*, trans. Philip Schaff and Henry Wace (Grand Rapids, MI: Eerdmans, 1997), 68.

87 Torrance, *The Trinitarian Faith*, 78.

88 Torrance, *The Trinitarian Faith*, 50.

89 Torrance, *The Trinitarian Faith*, 50.

do not think of the Father in his relation to the Son but only as creator in relation to creatures then we will think of the Son himself as one of the works of the Father. This will mean that we are then speaking of God 'in a way that is not personally grounded in God himself, but in an impersonal way far removed from what he is in himself'.[90] Further, if we try to reach knowledge of God from some point outside of God, then there is no point within God 'by reference to which we can test or control our conceptions of him' and so we 'are inevitably flung back upon ourselves'.[91] In this case our God-talk will be arbitrary and grounded in human experience rather than God himself. This is just what Athanasius accused the Arians of doing. Hilary was also unhappy with such a procedure arguing that 'the action of God must not be canvassed by human faculties; the Creator must not be judged by those who are the work of his hands'.[92] Throughout this book it will be noted that whenever and wherever the deity of the man Jesus is undermined or ignored, then and there God is defined *by* human experience rather than *by* revelation and thus *through* human experience.

Divine Incomprehensibility

It is extremely important that this point be made clear because when Johnson calls God 'holy mystery', an expression taken from Karl Rahner, she is referring ultimately to a God who remains unknown, as noted previously, and attempts to ground this thinking in a view of divine incomprehensibility that accords with the basic agnosticism of Sallie McFague and Gordon Kaufman. It is God's incomprehensibility, she believes, that makes it legitimate to speak of God as a 'matrix surrounding and sustaining life'.[93] And yet, as we shall see in more detail later, this is essentially a vague pantheistic description of God employed by theologians who refuse to think from a center in God and who explicitly and implicitly deny or exclude the deity of Christ. Johnson believes, with Anne Carr, that because of God's incomprehensibility we need more images of God, and the more we have, the better God's incomprehensibility will be preserved.[94]

90 Torrance, *The Trinitarian Faith*, 50.

91 Torrance, *The Trinitarian Faith*, 51.

92 Hilary, *Trinity*, Book III, 26, at 70.

93 Johnson, *She Who Is*, 45.

94 See Anne E. Carr, *Transforming Grace: Christian Tradition and Women's Experience* (San Francisco, CA: Harper & Row, 1988), 141: 'the father symbol …

While it is certainly true that the triune God is and remains incomprehensible and that no human concept can grasp the divine being, this cannot mean that we may now know God by stepping outside the Father–Son relation in and through which God has actually revealed himself by including us within his own internal relations by grace. Here Johnson follows Gordon Kaufman and argues that we know both God and the world through 'imaginative constructs'.[95] Undoubtedly God can be known through our imagination; but this cannot mean that our imagination is what makes God known. Yet this latter view is precisely the view of Kaufman and McFague who both fall into pantheism and both explicitly deny the deity of Christ in order to affirm their imaginative views of God, Christ and salvation.[96]

At this point Johnson follows Tillich's view that symbols point beyond themselves to something else in which they participate. Symbols open depths of our own being and grow from a 'collective unconscious'. They live and die based on their ability 'to bear the presence of the divine in changing cultural situations'.[97] Today, she says, we have reached the crossroads of dying and rising religious symbols and can see that the 'patriarchal idol is cracking' while female symbols for the divine are emerging. Thus she suggests that the historical reality of women should function as a symbol for the mystery of God; they are to be seen as channels for speaking about God. Johnson resists addressing this situation by adding feminine qualities to God or by finding a feminine dimension in God. Such approaches, she says, might only reinforce the

must be relativized by the use of many other images for God'. Hence, 'The use of many images more clearly affirms the fully transcendent and incomprehensible reality of God ...' 143. Like Elizabeth Johnson, Carr sees the experience of women as a source for theology (145) and mistakenly believes that when Christians refer to God as Father they believe God is male, 136ff.

95 Johnson, *She Who Is*, 45 and 283 n.12.

96 See, for example, Kaufman, *IFM*, 320: 'we were created by cosmic evolutionary and historical processes on which we depend absolutely for our being'. Regarding Christ, Kaufman argues against the idea that Jesus is unique as the 'only begotten son of God' stating that such thinking represents false reification *IFM*, 390–3. As noted earlier, Sallie McFague maintains both that God needs the world as 'offspring, beloved, and companion' (pantheism) and denies Jesus's uniqueness by asserting that 'Jesus is not ontologically different from other paradigmatic figures either in our tradition or in other religious traditions'.

97 Johnson, *She Who Is*, 46.

patriarchalism that she wishes to overcome. Instead she will speak of God using female, male and cosmic reality as divine symbols! Her basic point is that if women are created in God's image then 'God can be spoken in female metaphors in as full and as limited a way as God is imaged in male ones'.[98]

Experience as a Source and Norm for Theology

The major problem with this reasoning, however, is the simple methodological fact that it uses human experience, in particular the experience of women, as its source for theology. Once this is done, unfortunately, such experience also becomes the norm for theology as well, whether inadvertently or by design. From revelation, however, we know that the only proper norm for theology is God himself, since God can be known only through God. As Hilary of Poitiers declared, if we are to understand God we must take our 'stand upon the sure ground ... of God ... [we] must not measure the Divine nature by the limitations of [our] own, but gauge God's assertions concerning Himself by the scale of His own glorious self-revelation ... He Whom we can only know through His own utterances is the fitting witness concerning Himself.'[99] Of course Karl Barth and Thomas F. Torrance have fundamentally taken over this patristic insight.[100] It is an indispensable insight for fruitful theological investigation because it begins with the acknowledgment that theology can only take place as faith seeking understanding, that is, the object of faith, God himself, promises to lead those who accept his Word to a true knowledge of himself and his purposes for creation. Thus if our knowledge of God is not grounded in the very being and action of God himself – and consequently in his Word and Spirit, then it is in fact nothing more than our own religious or irreligious speculation grounded in our self-experience. Thinking thus, from a center in God rather than from a center in ourselves yields a very different method and very different conclusions in

98 Johnson, *She Who Is*, 54.

99 Hilary, *Trinity*, Book I, 18, 19, at 45.

100 See *CD* II/1, 179 where Barth stresses that 'God is known only by God' and that 'our viewing and conceiving is adopted and determined to participation in the truth of God by God Himself in grace'. Torrance considers this a 'biblically grounded principle' and cites Irenaeus who, relying on Matt. 11:27 and Lk. 10:22, explicated this in the second century: 'The Lord has taught us that no one can know God unless God himself is the Teacher, that is to say, without God, God is not to be known', *The Christian Doctrine of God*, 13.

this matter. This is where contemporary trinitarian theology has something to contribute. As Karl Rahner rightly indicated, trinitarian theology detached from an experience of Christ and the Spirit, can easily lead to 'wild and empty conceptual acrobatics'.[101] Yet, it would be disastrous for anyone to assume that experience of the self should be the condition for the possibility of experiencing and knowing God or that such experience should be seen as a source or ground for theology. Any such assumption means that, methodologically, one has begun to think theologically from a center in oneself rather than from a center in God; this unfortunately is the legacy of Rahner's transcendental method.[102]

We cannot rehearse the entirety of Rahner's transcendental method here. However, we can point out several key ingredients that are picked up and used by Elizabeth Johnson and which lead to her basic view of theology.[103] *First*, she argues that among possible historical mediations of encounter with God, 'the experience of oneself has a unique importance'.[104] *Second*, she believes that Rahner's theological investigation of

---

101 Rahner, *Trinity*, 48.

102 See Chapter 5 for a discussion of how Rahner's method affects his trinitarian theology. See also Chapter 6 for an exploration of how the theology of Ted Peters is shaped by this method. It is exactly because Ted Peters thinks about the Trinity on the basis of an experience of the beyond and intimate that he finally compromises God's freedom *in se* and *ad extra*. See also Molnar, *Incarnation and Resurrection*, chapters two and four for how this approach plays out in Rahner's Christology.

103 Francis Martin, *The Feminist Question: Feminist Theology in the Light of Christian Tradition* (Grand Rapids, MI: Eerdmans, 1994), notes that Rahner would most likely not acknowledge Johnson's conclusions drawn from his chapter 'Experience of Self and Experience of God' in his *Theological Investigations*, Vol. 13. Still, Martin believes that Rahner 'must take some responsibility for them. Rahner's transcendentalist foundationalism easily elides from a description of an unthematic experience and its correlate … to a quite thematic experience that also finds its correlate in God and his plan of salvation … his identification of the necessary background of all thought with being, and then this being with God, neglects a fundamental biblical teaching, namely that God, as creator, is not to be identified with the constructs or demands of the structure of the thinking subject' 181. Walter Kasper criticizes Rahner on this point as well, arguing that 'the Thou of God … is in danger of being lost in Rahner's thematizing of the subjectivity of man in his theology of the Trinity' (*The God of Jesus Christ*, 302).

104 Johnson, *She Who Is*, 65.

the unity between the self and the symbol God sheds light on the way forward regarding women's experience today. Since we are 'spirit in the world', an experience of radical questioning and the possibility of free and responsible action before a constantly receding horizon shows that humans 'are dynamically oriented toward fathomless mystery as the very condition for the possibility of acting in characteristic human ways'.[105] Thus she contends that, in their most personal actions, human beings display 'an openness toward infinite mystery' as the basis of their existence and so they are 'dynamically structured toward God'.[106] *Third*, she believes that the experience of God is primordially mediated 'through the changing history of oneself'. God cannot be experienced directly but 'as the ultimate depth and radical essence of every personal experience such as love, fidelity, loneliness, and death'. In fact, our own mystery arises in these 'prethematic' experiences and so we thus 'experience and are grasped by the holy mystery of God as the very context of our own self-presence. In fact the silent, nonverbal encounter with infinite mystery constitutes the enabling condition of any experience of self at all'.[107] *Fourth*, since the connection between one's self-experience and the experience of 'holy mystery' is intrinsic in this way, it follows that if one experience changes, so does the other. Any personal development will mean development in the experience of God, while any diminishment of personal identity represents a loss of experience of God. These can be seen accordingly as 'two aspects of one and the same history of experience ... Each mutually conditions the other'.[108] *Fifth*, when a person thus has new experiences of freedom or accepts oneself, this evokes a change in the experience of God. Also when one rejects an idol, sees some truth about God or transcends particulars to reach 'toward unfathomable mystery', these experiences of God belong to one's self-experience. Following Rahner then, Johnson sums up: ' "The personal history of the experience of the self is in its total extent the history of the ultimate experience of God also" '.[109]

While Johnson notes that Rahner's individualism has been criticized by Metz and others, it is clear that she takes his basic method as foundational: self-experience illuminates who God is, and indeed the two

105 Johnson, *She Who Is*, 65.
106 Johnson, *She Who Is*, 65.
107 Johnson, *She Who Is*, 65.
108 Johnson, *She Who Is*, 65–6.
109 Johnson, *She Who Is*, 66.

are mutually conditioning factors. Furthermore, she accepts Rahner's basic conception of God as the 'holy mystery' or the silent term of the experience of transcendence which everyone experiences in the experiences of love, freedom, loneliness and death.[110] So she contends that it is in this 'deeply personal-and-religious dimension that women are caught up in new experiences, which when articulated move toward new speaking about God'. As women have new experiences of liberation from male domination, she believes that God is being experienced in new ways.

> Through women's encounter with the holy mystery of their own selves as blessed comes commensurate language about holy mystery in female metaphor and symbol, gracefully, powerfully, necessarily ... speaking about God and self-interpretation cannot be separated. To give but one example, conversion experienced not as giving up oneself but as tapping into the power of oneself simultaneously releases understanding of divine power not as dominating power-over but as the passionate ability to empower oneself and others ... in the ontological naming and affirming of ourselves we are engaged in a dynamic reaching out to the mystery of God ...[111]

Clearly, Johnson has not only redefined who God is, but has done so from a center in herself, and so unfortunately calls into question the

---

110 We will explore the problem with this assumption by Rahner in detail in Chapter 5. Cherith Fee Nordling, *Knowing God by Name: A Conversation between Elizabeth A. Johnson and Karl Barth* (New York: Peter Lang, 2010), offers a compelling analysis of how Rahner's thinking affects Johnson's position in relation to the theology of Karl Barth.

111 Johnson, *She Who Is*, 66-7. In this thinking Johnson is explicitly following the reasoning of Mary Daly. It is worth mentioning here that Karl Barth links conversion to sanctification and argues that 'God is the active Subject not only in reconciliation generally but also in the conversion of man to Himself' (*CD* IV/2, 500). What this means is that God who 'is indeed holy in and for Himself' acts in history to establish fellowship between us and himself; God in his majesty 'sanctifies the unholy by His action with and towards [us]' thus giving us a 'derivative and limited, but supremely real, share in His own holiness' (*CD* IV/2, 500). It should be noted that conversion in this context has to do with our relations with God himself and is neither founded in nor derived

ultimate authority and freedom of God, of scripture and finally of Christ himself. In her thinking, conversion no longer means accepting God as he exists self-sufficiently and as one who loves us in freedom and by grace and thus as the one who makes us holy by enabling communion between himself and us. Rather, conversion means self-reliance and self-acceptance. In classical theology, she believes, sin was understood as pride because it was described from the perspective of the ruling male. However today, she contends, sin cannot be seen as pride because for those whose sense of self has been devalued or those who have been excluded from 'self-definition' by a dominant group, pride is not a pitfall. For these persons any suggestion of turning from self-love or losing oneself functions ideologically to 'rob them of power' and to keep them subordinate.[112] Thus we are told that women's basic temptation is not to pride but to the lack of it! This is why God must be named in female categories today – this is the female call to conversion or to empowerment, according to Johnson. We are told that: 'In and through women's conversion experience and its many articulations new language about God is arising, one that takes female reality in all its concreteness as a legitimate finite starting point for speaking about the mystery of God.'[113]

One extremely important point, however, is completely overlooked in this analysis. That is, whether we like it or not, whether we are male or female, whether we have a good sense of self or a poor one, God remains who he is and sin remains the failure to accept God as immeasurably superior to ourselves; sin remains the failure to acknowledge that it is by grace that we are saved, and so we cannot in any sense equate self-experience or self-acceptance with experience of God or acceptance of God. By what right can anyone change the definition of sin or of salvation from the revelation of both in Jesus Christ as attested in scripture, unless they strip the terms of their theological meaning and invest them

from our own self-experience. Our holiness exists in our relationship with God established and maintained in Christ. Hence, Barth insists that 'we cannot be too strict or consistent in looking away from ourselves. It is a matter of knowing ourselves but of knowing ourselves in Christ … in this Other who is not identical with me, and with whom I am not, and do not become identical, but in whose humanity God Himself becomes and is, and always will be another, a concrete antithesis' (*CD* IV/2, 283). Christ is the one in whom we are converted to God and in him we can live as part of the new creation.

112 Johnson, *She Who Is*, 64.
113 Johnson, *She Who Is*, 75.

solely with a sociological or psychological meaning? Astonishingly, those today who would insist that the traditional understanding of sin as pride does not apply to women because they have been excluded from power and need to take that power back, have in fact shown by their own analysis that the original sin remains pride. For, while it is important to assist people whose sense of self has been devalued, and while it is important to recognize that women should not be dominated or subjected to patriarchal ideology (or any other kind), any appeal to pride in order to solve these difficulties will only make matters worse. Relying on pride to overcome false domination by others will lead one to conclude that it was exactly through one's own self-reliance that a person must overcome such false domination in the first place. Almost without noticing it then, theological language comes to be used simply to empower women and others who have been falsely dominated, so that they can and must free *themselves* from this enslavement.

But it matters how one is set free. If I can free myself, then I am indeed self-reliant and even God cannot contradict my aims, goals and methods for achieving self-reliance. That is to say God is a symbol that I create and recreate in order to achieve a desired social, political and religious end. On the other hand, if God frees me from false domination, then it is an act of grace which claims me for God's service in such a way that I know that God is other than myself as my Creator, Savior and Lord – one who can be and is my helper and friend, but not on my terms. I then know that God is not some vague and indescribable mystery that can be experienced in experiencing love, freedom and death. Yes, these are experiences which raise questions about existence and ultimately questions about the existence and nature of God. However, in order to answer these questions, it is necessary to think from a center in God rather than from a center in myself. That is precisely the problem of sin. Without the grace of God revealed and active in Jesus Christ and his Holy Spirit, it is impossible to think from a center in God; it is also impossible to grasp the true meaning of sin. Sin means the attempt to commandeer God to the service of my agenda rather than allowing God the freedom to create a new heart in me according his own purposes and goals.

Agnosticism: Docetic and Pantheistic Implications

Before drawing this chapter to a conclusion, it is important to note that it is precisely Johnson's agnosticism, which is part and parcel of her method, that allows her to change the content of the trinitarian doctrine. This she does by advocating the kind of Docetic Christology that

Karl Barth correctly rejected and that will be discussed in detail in the next chapter. It also allows her to change the meaning and content of the resurrection and Christology itself. Hence she contends that: 'Jesus in all his physical and spiritual historicity is raised into glory by the power of the Spirit. What this ringing affirmation precisely means is inconceivable.'[114] Indeed, in a manner not unlike that of Robert Jenson, and also closely allied to that of Gordon Kaufman, she argues that

> the biblical symbol Christ … cannot be restricted to the historical person of Jesus … but signifies all those who by drinking of the Spirit participate in the community of disciples. Christ is a pneumatological reality, a creation of the Spirit who is not limited by whether one is Jew or Greek … male or female … the body of the risen Christ becomes the body of the community.[115]

114 Johnson, *She Who Is*, 163. In 'Redeeming the Name of Christ' Johnson says that 'the cross … is the parable that enacts Sophia-God's participation in the suffering of the world' and concludes that the 'the victory of love, both human and divine, that spins new life out of this disaster [the cross] is expressed in belief in the risen Christ. The resurrection itself cannot be imagined' (125). An agnostic picture of the resurrection is presented here because for Johnson the resurrection does not refer to an event in the life of Jesus on the basis of which he continues to act humanly and divinely for us. Instead it is a symbolic expression of belief in the power of love over death. This sort of vague assertion differs radically from the very definite remark of Barth: 'The resurrection of Jesus Christ from the dead, with which His first *parousia* begins to be completed in the second, has in fact happened. It has happened in the same sense as His crucifixion and His death, in the human sphere and human time, as an actual event within the world with an objective content' (*CD* IV/1, 333). For more on the resurrection in Barth, see R. Dale Dawson, *The Resurrection in Karl Barth* (Aldershot: Ashgate, 2007) and John Drury, *The Resurrected God: Karl Barth's Trinitarian Theology of Easter* (Minneapolis, MN: Fortress, 2014).

115 Johnson, *She Who Is*, 162. Jenson's understanding of the church as Christ's risen body will be discussed in Chapter 3. Again, for Johnson, 'Christ' is a symbol and following the thinking of Sandra Schneiders, she claims that 'the Christ is composed of all the baptized. That means that Christ, in contrast to Jesus, is not male, or more exactly not exclusively male. Christ is quite accurately portrayed as black, old, Gentile, female, Asian or Polish. Christ is inclusively all

This confusion of Christ and the Church allows Johnson to argue in a way clearly indebted to the thought of Sallie McFague, that Jesus is named Christ in 'a paradigmatic way' but that 'multiple redemptive role models' are available to us![116] Her ultimate aim of course is to argue that Jesus's maleness must be reinterpreted in light of the 'whole Christ' so that '*Christa* and *Christus* alike, the wisdom community' contribute to the Christian story by constituting Christ in his entirety.[117]

Johnson actually believes that she escapes a Docetic interpretation of Jesus. However, the fact is, it is her unwillingness to accept the truth that the man Jesus from Nazareth *IS* the Christ simply because he is, and not because we think he is an important redemptive role model, that leads her directly into Docetism. She substitutes *Sophia* for the eternal Word to argue once more that:

> God is not male ... feminist theological speech about Jesus the Wisdom of God shifts the focus of reflection off maleness and onto the whole theological significance of what transpires in the Christ event. Jesus ... is confessed as Sophia incarnate, revelatory of the liberating graciousness of God imaged as female; women ... can freely represent Christ, being themselves, in the Spirit, other Christs.[118]

the baptized,' 'Redeeming the Name of Christ', 129. This confusion of Christ and Christians of course undermines Jesus's exclusive uniqueness as the Christ of God and his inclusive ability to enable the baptized to become holy in fellowship with him by grace and through faith as the risen Lord acts now in the power of his Holy Spirit. See also n. 118 below.

116 Johnson, *She Who Is*, 162.

117 Johnson, *She Who Is*, 163.

118 Johnson, *She Who Is*, 166–7. Importantly, Barth thinks that Christians are those who live by faith in Jesus Christ himself so that a Christian can live 'in conformity with the One in whom he believes, that he can and will be man only in the likeness of Jesus Christ as the One who died and rose again for him' (*CD* IV/1, 769). However, Barth adds to this the fact that this must not lead to the 'fantastic notion that I am a kind of second Christ. That would lead me out of faith and its knowledge, in which He [Christ] has for me the form of another, in which He is object, and there would be no solid ground under my feet. And the notion could only be an illusion. I am not the Lord who became a servant ... the Son who in obedience to the Father allowed Himself to be judged as my Judge and the Judge of all [humanity]. The glory of God has not been revealed in me as in His resurrection' (*CD* IV/1, 769).

Clearly, Johnson believes that on the one hand God is imaged as male, in spite of her stated recognition that this is not the case. Indeed, as already noted earlier, she really believes that in identifying Jesus as male and as logos 'a certain leakage of Jesus' human maleness into the divine nature' takes place so that 'maleness appears to be of the essence of the God made known in Christ'.[119] On the other hand, she believes that by focusing attention on the Christ event, understood from her feminist analysis of wisdom, instead of on the man Jesus, she can image God as female. However, the point of this chapter has been to argue that a proper doctrine of the Trinity begins and ends its reflections with Jesus Christ himself who *alone* can enable us to think from a center in God and not from a center within our male or female experience. This does not discount our experience but simply acknowledges that the norm for theological truth is and always remains God *alone*. In experiencing God in faith, we know that it is God and not our experience that dictates truth when it comes to knowing God the Father, Son and Holy Spirit.

It is worth noting here that those theologians, Johnson included, who use the feminine gender of Wisdom in Hebrew and Greek 'to suggest something akin to a divine feminine apotheosis or hypostasis' have ignored the fact that such passages 'should be read as examples of Hebrew personification'.[120] Gender should not be confused with sex; thus the mere fact that a word is feminine or masculine in gender does not necessarily imply reference to an actual male or female being. Those who elevate Sophia to a divine feminine are in fact 'in line with the Gnostic heresy, as when Ptolomaeus declared that the "celestial mother Sophia" bestowed the Logos upon Jesus at his baptism'.[121] Such thinking

---

119 Johnson, *She Who Is*, 152.

120 See Roland Frye, *Language for God and Feminist Language*, in Kimel (ed.), *Speaking the Christian God*, 34.

121 Frye, 'Language for God', *Speaking the Christian God*, 35. See also G. L. Prestige, *God in Patristic Thought* (London: SPCK, 1952), 130. Frye identifies Elisabeth Schüssler Fiorenza as one theologian who repeatedly refers to the Hebrew's ' "gracious Sophia-God" and the "Sophia-God of Jesus" ' ('Language for God', *Speaking the Christian God*, 35). Frye concludes that: 'Whether by feminist apotheosis or by an inherent divine nature, *Sophia-Hōkmāh* is thus presented as a divine feminine being or hypostasis.' As Schüssler Fiorenza puts it: 'Divine Sophia is Israel's God in the language and *Gestalt* of the Goddess' ('Language for God', *Speaking the Christian God*, 35). This, in Frye's judgment, places her thinking with that of other feminists who adopt this approach 'in line with Gnostic heresy' ('Language for God', *Speaking the Christian God*, 35).

also opens the door to polytheism. In addition, those who believe that Sophia is in some sense divine, basically repeat an Arian argument 'for the subordination of Son to Father by interpreting Jesus Christ as the incarnation not of God but of God's Wisdom'.[122]

Furthermore, in feminist interpretation, simile and metaphor are often confused so that the occasional biblical comparisons of God's love to that of a mother 'are given the same force as if they were names or identifications'.[123] It is a fact that where God is called Father in scripture, metaphor and naming are used and these are grounded in God's revelation to us, that is, in his naming himself to us. Wherever God is compared to a mother, simile is used. What difference does this make? According to Roland Frye, simile 'states resemblance, while metaphor boldly transfers the representation'.[124] Similes are more restricted than metaphors. Metaphors can be 'stretched' so that even though Jesus is never said to have literally herded sheep, Jn. 10:11 takes the metaphor from the twenty-third Psalm and presents Jesus as the good shepherd. Thus, while the Lord is spoken of in scripture as a shepherd (metaphor) (Psalm 23), in Isaiah 42:13 it is said that 'the Lord goes forth like a mighty man …' (simile) and again the Lord says 'now I will cry out like a woman in travail, I will gasp and pant' (simile).[125] God is not here identified as mother any more than God is identified as warrior. These similes are used in a very restricted sense and do not make the same claim to identify God as the metaphoric language of 'good shepherd' and 'Lamb of God' or the language that speaks of God as Father and Son does.[126] The upshot of all this is that it is important to recognize the scriptural use of language in order to avoid the kind of polytheism and Gnosticism that follows when it is thought that we can name God *from* our experiences, whether they be male or female. God is not named Mother in the Bible because God has revealed himself as the Father of Jesus Christ – not as a male, but as a unique Father of a unique Son, who is eternally begotten before all worlds. Here it is important to remember, with Barth, that: 'If we call what is said about Father and Son figurative, it should be remembered that this can apply only to our human speech as such but not to its object'.[127] The object in question is the

---

122 Frye, 'Language for God', *Speaking the Christian God*, 36.

123 Frye, 'Language for God', *Speaking the Christian God*, 34.

124 Frye, 'Language for God', *Speaking the Christian God*, 37.

125 Frye, 'Language for God', *Speaking the Christian God*, 39.

126 Frye, 'Language for God', *Speaking the Christian God*, 39.

127 *CD* I/1, 432; *CD* I/1, 392–3.

eternal Father, Son and Holy Spirit who, in Barth's thinking, is who he is in an utterly unique sense which transcends all human experience of fatherhood and sonship. Hence, as noted earlier, for Barth there really is nothing higher or better that can be said of the immanent Trinity than that God is the eternal Father, Son and Holy Spirit. Revelation therefore is not the projection of human experience into God, but the action of God naming himself to us and including us in a genuine relationship with himself by faith and grace. Therefore, as Elizabeth Achtemeier notes, while 'Israel was surrounded by peoples who worshiped female deities',[128] the Israelites themselves worshiped one God who, unlike the religions of Israel's neighbors, could not be identified with creation: 'It is precisely the introduction of female language for God that opens the door to such identification of God with the world.'[129]

Finally, it is just because Johnson has failed to respect God's actual freedom for us in the history of the man Jesus of Nazareth and has instead substituted her abstract notion of liberation for Christ's atoning liberation that she reaches what can only be described as the Gnostic conclusion that women can represent Christ because they are in fact other Christs.[130] The truth of the gospel hinges on the fact that there

128 Elizabeth Achtemeier, 'Exchanging God for "No Gods"', in Kimel (ed.), *Speaking the Christian God*, 7.

129 Achtemeier, 'Exchanging God for "No Gods"', 8–9.

130 Elaine Pagels, in her University Lecture in Religion at Arizona State University titled *The Gnostic Jesus and Early Christian Politics*, 28 January 1982, asserts that according to the Gnostic Gospel of Thomas, Jesus says '"when you come to know yourselves" (and discover the divine within you) then "you will recognize that it is *you* who are the sons of the living Father" – just like Jesus! … The Gospel of Philip makes the same point … you are to "become not a Christian, but a Christ."' From this she concludes that the Gospel of Thomas really intends to say that '"you, the reader, are the twin brother of Christ;" when you recognize the divine within you, then you come to see, as Thomas does, that you and Jesus are, so to speak, identical twins' (6). Of course, if we are identical twins with Jesus we no longer need to rely on him but may instead rely on ourselves in typically Gnostic fashion. As Pagels herself puts it: 'One who seeks to "become not a Christian, but a Christ" no longer looks to Jesus, as orthodox believers do, as the source of all truth' (7). Indeed Pagels argues that it was the Gnostics and not the orthodox Christians who named God mother and father precisely because their norm was not Jesus himself but their own self-consciousness. While Pagels approves of this misguided theology, Roland

never was and never will be another Christ than the one incarnate Son of God whose name was Jesus of Nazareth. This Christ represents himself in the power of the Holy Spirit. It is no wonder that Johnson's work, like that of LaCugna, is marked by a distinct tendency toward pantheism: Sophia is seen as becoming incarnate because 'Her essence … might well be called connectedness, for … she is a breath, an emanation … The power of relation built into wisdom metaphors comes to unique fruition in the doctrine of Jesus-Sophia, Sophia incarnate. Sophia is present in and with her envoy Jesus …'[131] Here it is obvious that the incarnation is no longer seen as a free act of grace, but is conceptualized as a necessary relation dictated by the essence of wisdom with its connectedness and which emanates in and through Jesus, who is no longer the unique mediator actively reconciling us to the Father and enabling our true knowledge of God here and now, but is reduced to an envoy representing God's love that can be categorized in any one of a number of freely chosen metaphors.[132]

Frye makes plain why such Gnostic thought is antithetical to the Gospel: *SJT* (1988) 454ff. It is worth noting that Ludwig Feuerbach wrote that Christ is 'the consciousness of the species. We are all supposed to be one in Christ. Christ is the consciousness of our unity. Therefore, whoever loves man for the sake of man, whoever rises to the love of the species … is a Christian; he is Christ himself,' Ludwig Feuerbach, *The Essence of Christianity*, trans. George Eliot, intro. by Karl Barth, foreword by H. Richard Niebuhr (New York: Harper Torchbooks, 1957), xviii. See Barth's view of this notion above, n. 118.

131 Johnson, *She Who Is*, 168–9. Even though Johnson quite rightly intends to uphold the idea that there is an 'asymmetrical reciprocity' between God and the world so that it is theologically legitimate to focus 'solely on God', the very way she conceptualizes the relation of God and history within her panentheistic perspective (which inevitably collapses into pantheism) becomes ambiguous because she immediately speaks of God 'who is never not related to the world' (*She Who Is*, 236). Such a view literally cannot envision the fact that God eternally existed and the world did not eternally coexist with God but was created out of nothing at a particular point in time.

132 For Johnson, Jesus can be viewed as a 'filter through whom God is made known' (*Quest*, 217), or employing a 'pneumatological inflection', one could say that we never have 'one straight-as-an-arrow name' for God because God's name 'cannot be fixed in a single form of speech nor in a fixed name' (*Quest*, 221). This thinking is diametrically opposed to the traditional Christian view that there is salvation in no other name than that of Jesus himself (Ac.

Johnson even argues that 'Jesus' death was an act of violence brought about by threatened human men, as sin'.[133] The clear implication is that only men are implicated in Jesus's death. Are we to suppose that women are exempt from the sin that led to Jesus's death on the cross? The answer seems to be that we are, since Johnson claims that women disciples 'are the moving point of continuity between the ministry, death, burial, and resurrection of Jesus'.[134] What is so astonishing about this analysis is that: (1) it divides humanity by separating men from women and (2) it implicitly makes the Docetic claim that women are free of sin while men are the sinners. Tragically, this thinking misses the point of the atonement, which is that what was not assumed was not saved. All humanity is implicated in Christ's death – his rejection manifests the depth of human sin. Since he died for all (women as well as men), all are saved by him alone. Johnson's failure to acknowledge Jesus as the One Mediator clearly leads to a confused view of the atonement so that she can argue that the suffering of Jesus 'is neither passive, useless, nor divinely ordained, but is linked to the ways of Sophia forging justice and peace in an antagonistic world ... the cross is part of the larger mystery of pain-to-life, of that struggle for the new creation evocative of the rhythm of pregnancy, delivery, and birth so familiar to women of all times'.[135] This interpretation of the atonement misses its essential nature which includes Jesus's active and passive obedience as the one who, from the divine side, reconciles us to God from within our sinful situation and passively accepts the suffering and death caused by sin as the Judge judged in our place so that God's opposition to sin would not fall on us. As T. F. Torrance insisted, if Jesus is just a man dying on the cross, then Christianity is immoral because we have an image of a God who will only love us on condition of being placated by Jesus's sacrifice on the cross. However if you put God on the cross, Torrance

4:12) and that we are in fact baptized not into any name other than that of the Father, Son and Holy Spirit. Johnson's view that 'no expression for God can be taken literally' (*Quest*, 18) follows from the agnosticism that will not allow her to recognize that we can and must have an objectively true knowledge of God based on revelation if there is to be true knowledge of the triune God at all. See, for example, *Quest*, 19–21 and *She Who Is*, 116–18.

133 Johnson, *She Who Is*, 158.
134 Johnson, *She Who Is*, 159.
135 Johnson, *She Who Is*, 159.

holds, the whole picture changes because we then have the picture of God unconditionally loving us in the experience of God-forsakenness that Jesus willingly accepted in sacrifice for us.[136] Everything depends on who Jesus was and is so that if he is only paradigmatic of God's love, then he cannot be the unique savior of the world acting both from the divine and human side for us and for our salvation.

These christological errors are ultimately traceable to Johnson's own agnosticism, which roots the doctrine of the Trinity in experience. For her, analogy means that, based on the Christian experience of faith which 'is the generating matrix for language about God as triune' one can say 'the Trinity is a legitimate but secondary concept that synthesizes the concrete experience of salvation in a "short formula".'[137] Because the Trinity is not controlled from a center in God but from a center within the Christian experience of salvation, Johnson concludes that analogy points to the 'holy mystery'. Indeed this

> language is not a literal description of the inner being of God ... It is a pointer to holy mystery ... At rock bottom it is the language of hope. No one has ever seen God, but thanks to the experience unleashed through Jesus in the Spirit we hope ... that it is the livingness of *God*

---

136   For Torrance's view of active and passive obedience and the atonement, see Molnar, *Torrance: Theologian of the Trinity*, 229–34 and 146–51 and 12 for his view that unless Christ is God acting for us *as* man, Christianity is immoral.

137   Johnson, *She Who Is*, 198. According to Johnson: '... analogy ... means that while it [human naming of God] starts from the relationship of paternity experienced at its best in this world, its inner dynamism negates the creaturely mode to assert that God is more unlike than like even the best human father' (*She Who Is*, 173). Of course the analogy of faith starts from Jesus Christ who encounters us and who alone can liberate us to speak of God in truth. Thus true knowledge of God not only begins and ends with Christ himself as attested in the New Testament but it never claims knowledge of God's fatherhood by negating our human experience of fatherhood. God is revealed as Father in an *utterly unique* way and is as such the key to understanding human fatherhood. It is never the other way around. This is why, as we shall see in Chapter 6, Barth rightly insists that: 'It is not true that in some hidden depth of His essence God is something other than Father and Son. It is not true that these names are just freely chosen and in the last analysis meaningless symbols whose original and proper non-symbolical content lies in that creaturely reality. On the contrary, it is in God that the father-son relation, like all creaturely relations, has its original and proper reality' (*CD* I/1, 432–3).

who is with us in the suffering of history, and so we affirm that God's relation to the world is grounded in God's own being capable of such relation.[138]

Clearly, it is the experience of hope that provides the impetus for what Johnson has to say about the Trinity and what she says is that we do not know God in his inner essence as Father, Son and Holy Spirit.[139] Rather, God is holy mystery, which can go by many other names such as Mother and not just by one name as Father, Son and Holy Spirit. Hence,

> the symbol of the Trinity is not a blueprint of the inner workings of the godhead, not an offering of esoteric information about God. In no sense is it a literal description of God's being *in se*. As the outcome of theological reflection on the Christian experience of relationship to God, it is a symbol that indirectly points to God's relationality … Our speech about God as three and persons is a human construction that means to say that God is *like* a Trinity, *like* a threefoldness of relation.[140]

138 Johnson, *She Who Is*, 200–1.

139 Johnson consistently insists that we have no 'literal' knowledge of who God is: 'Even when used almost exclusively, the paternal symbol never signifies theologically that God is a father in a literal or ontological sense' (*She Who Is*, 173). For Johnson, 'God is not literally a father or a king or a lord but something ever so much greater', that is, 'incomprehensible source, sustaining power, and goal of the world, holy Wisdom, indwelling Spirit, the ground of being, the beyond in our midst, the absolute future, being itself, mother, matrix, lover, friend, infinite love, the holy mystery that surrounds and supports the world' (*Quest*, 99). These additional references, unfortunately, are not at all governed by who God is both in eternity and in history as the eternal Father, Son and Holy Spirit confessed in the Nicene Creed since Johnson's thinking is governed by the perspective embraced by Sallie McFague as discussed earlier and by Roger Haight who believes that the point of the doctrine is to 'assert and protect' the experience of salvation from which the doctrine derives; hence, 'the doctrine is not intended to provide information about the internal life of God, but is about how God relates to human beings' (Roger Haight, *Jesus: Symbol of God* [Maryknoll, NY: Orbis, 1999], 485). Compare to Johnson: 'Anyone who talks of Trinity talks of God as Love in an idiom particular to the Christian story. Conversely, the symbol of the Trinity safeguards this Christian experience of God' (*Quest*, 222).

140 Johnson, *She Who Is*, 204–5.

This abstract understanding of God is not at all grounded in the economic trinitarian self-revelation but is instead explicitly grounded in experience, so that in the end it is the creature who defines the creator based on experiences of suffering within history or any one of a number of other experiences of relationality between us and the 'divine' however that is named. This is especially problematic in connection with Johnson's rhetoric regarding the Spirit because, as Stanley Grenz put it: 'Johnson's declared starting point is not the divine self-disclosure in Jesus Christ but the experience of the Spirit as "God's livingness subtly and powerfully abroad in the world"'.[141] But this 'starting point' entails the separation of the Holy Spirit from the incarnate Word. It does this just because anyone who claims to have the Spirit and thinks of the Spirit without reference to Jesus Christ has, in reality, detached the Spirit from the Word. Once that happens, the Spirit will always be located directly in universally accessible experiences that are not necessarily tied to the revelation of God in Jesus himself. This is why Grenz describes her view of the experience of the Spirit as 'seemingly universal' when he refers to Johnson's statement: 'Wherever we encounter the world and ourselves as held by, open to, gifted by, mourning the absence of, or yearning for something ineffably more than immediately appears, whether that "more" be mediated by beauty and joy or in contrast to powers that crush, there the experience of the Spirit transpires.'[142] This universalist thinking is clearly in keeping with Johnson's understanding of transcendental experience. That is why she can say that 'at the end of the day the pneumatological inflection cannot be fixed in a single form of speech nor in a fixed name. Its specific task is to express the inexhaustible fullness of the mystery of the living God, a fullness for which *no one expression is ever totally adequate*.'[143] Detaching the Spirit from the Word seems to be required by the agnosticism that refuses to allow the name of Jesus Christ to be the starting point leading to an understanding of the eternal Trinity itself.[144]

141 Stanley Grenz, *Rediscovering the Triune God: The Trinity in Contemporary Theology* (Minneapolis, MN: Fortress, 2004), 172.

142 Johnson, *She Who Is*, 124–5.

143 Johnson, *Quest*, 221, emphasis mine.

144 For Barth, of course, the only fact which justifies the Christian religion in the form of forgiveness is the free judgment of God as the one who forgives so that 'this freedom and inscrutability is identical with the revealed name of Jesus Christ' (*CD* I/2, 355).

Ultimately, what makes this move, and the difficulties that follow from it possible and even necessary, is Johnson's failure to distinguish the immanent and economic Trinity – more accurately what makes this move possible and necessary is her failure to acknowledge the immanent Trinity, which is known only from the economic self-revelation of God in his Word and Spirit, as the norm for truth when discussing the Trinity. Instead, she substitutes the experience of salvation, which is supposedly unleashed by Jesus; an experience which clearly can be had without any reference to his name. It is clear, however, that Jesus, who is the Word incarnate, cannot really be the active subject in relation to us in Johnson's thinking. Rather, he is seen as one messenger or one model among others that we use to try to achieve equality and liberation. Ultimately, her agnosticism, like LaCugna's, leads to the dualist conclusion that Jesus is an envoy or a Spirit endowed human being and not the very presence of God within history in his unique history and subsequently in and through the community of faith in the power of his Holy Spirit. It leads to the dualist conclusion that God is *like* a Trinity rather than the God who is one and three (as Father, Son and Holy Spirit) from all eternity.[145] Finally, it leads to the dualist conclusion that

145 While Stanley Grenz seems to be quite open to Johnson's attempt to redescribe Jesus as *Sophia* and curiously thinks that Johnson should be numbered among those contemporary theologians who want to return to the doctrine of the immanent Trinity, he also realizes that saying that God is *like* a Trinity is problematic (*Rediscovering the Triune God*, 181). It is no accident that, at the Eleventh Council of Toledo (675), it was explicitly stated that 'it cannot correctly be said that there is a Trinity in one God but that *the one God is a Trinity*' (John F. Clarkson, S.J. et. al. trans. and ed., *The Church Teaches: Documents of the Church in English Translation* (hereafter: *The Church Teaches*), (London: Herder, 1955), 147, emphasis mine). Strangely, in his defense of Elizabeth Johnson against my critique, Veli-Matti Kärkkäinen, *The Trinity: Global Perspectives* (Louisville, KY: Westminster John Knox Press, 2007), completely ignores the connection that I made between Rahner's method (which even he acknowledges begins with experience [191] and to that extent allows experience rather than revelation in its identity with Jesus Christ to dictate theological truth) and then also misses the connection that I made between her approach and that of Kaufman and McFague. He also missed the significance of Johnson's mistaken view that 'God is *like* a Trinity'. This leads him to confuse her rather overt agnosticism with a properly conceived apophaticism so that he erroneously believes that she is upholding a proper doctrine of the immanent Trinity. This is naïve at best. He thinks my

holy mystery, which can be known in everyone's transcendental experience without actually relying on Jesus himself as the risen, ascended and coming Lord, but which for that reason, cannot be equated with the immanent Trinity (which ultimately remains unknown and unknowable), is the true God and that any literal view of God as Father must therefore be an idol.

In fact, however, the point of this chapter has been to show that wherever and whenever trinitarian theology takes its bearings from a center in human experience and not from a center in God (through Christ himself) it necessarily leads to agnosticism, dualism and finally to pantheism. It cannot lead to true knowledge of the triune God, which can only come to us from God through his Word and Spirit. Naturally enough Johnson's concept of analogy is meant to suggest that calling God mother is not only appropriate but desirable. Yet the unfortunate result of her failure to appreciate that only God can name God leads to the pantheist idea that, as mother and child have a relation of 'interdependence', so God's relation with creation is one of interdependence.[146]

charge that she has exchanged the experience of women for the revelation of God is wrong because it 'assumes that traditional theology does not have any "agenda" but rather is interest-free, and that the experience of salvation as a human category in principle would be antagonistic to the revelation of God' (212). He thinks that such a view is 'dualistic' and undercuts the possibility of a 'contextual approach'. Once again Kärkkäinen completely missed the point of my analysis. His own thinking is rather confused. On the one hand, he admits that her starting point is 'women's experience' (212). On the other hand, he thinks she is only taking women's experience seriously and that it is pneumatology and Christology that drive her thought. However, as I just demonstrated, her 'pneumatology' operates by separating the Spirit from the Word such that Christology is marginalized and Jesus is merely seen as an envoy while the risen Lord is somehow blended into the community. Indeed, her equation of 'holy mystery' with the Trinity allows her to think of the Trinity without being bound to think of the Father through the Son in faith, that is, without actually relying on the Holy Spirit as the enabling condition of our knowledge of God. The fact that she thinks the doctrine of the Trinity is a 'symbol that indirectly points to God's relationality' proves that in her thinking it is relationality and not the unique eternal relations of the trinitarian persons that dictates her understanding. That indeed is what leads her to say we have no 'literal' knowledge of God and that 'God is *like* a Trinity'. Both of those statements miss the point of the doctrine as classically understood and as Torrance and Barth understand it.

146 Johnson, *She Who Is*, 178–9.

Hence, 'the mother image points to an intrinsic relatedness between God and the world, a loving relationality that belongs to the very essence of being a mother and never ends'.[147] Here relationality has become God while the eternal Father, Son and Holy Spirit has been relegated to the domain of freely chosen metaphor. It goes without saying that whenever God's relations with the world are thought to belong to his essence, then his creative function has absorbed his essence in a typically Cartesian fashion. Pantheism always implies that God cannot exist without the world. Johnson's position clearly bears that out.

It is time that contemporary theologians face this problem squarely. Theology needs to begin and end its task with Jesus Christ as the revelation of God in history. Any other starting point will mean a self-chosen one and thus one that stands in conflict with God's freedom for us exercised in Christ. This is where trinitarian theology is important. A theology of the Trinity recognizes who God is who meets us in Christ and then thinks about various contemporary issues and problems in light of the relation between creator and creatures reconciled by God in Christ. In this first chapter then we have seen how very important it is for theology to think from a center in God provided by God himself in the incarnation and outpouring of the Holy Spirit. No theology can provide that center for itself. This can only be received from God himself as grace. Thinking that takes place within faith will always find that center in Jesus Christ himself, the Son of God. This chapter has shown that contemporary theologians who think about God as a symbol or as a freely chosen metaphor that we use to create a better world have simply missed the essential point about a contemporary doctrine of the immanent Trinity. The point is, that unless God is acknowledged at the outset as the one who alone creates, reconciles and redeems us, then we are left alone with ourselves and any attempt to find freedom and truth are doomed to the agnostic conclusion that we never truly know God; we only image God in ways that seem appropriate to ourselves. In the next chapter we shall see how this problem arises and takes shape in Christology. I will continue to suggest that the proper solution to this problem is a return to Jesus Christ himself as the starting point and norm for theology.

---

147 Johnson, *She Who Is*, 185.

Chapter 2

CHRISTOLOGY AND THE TRINITY: SOME DOGMATIC IMPLICATIONS OF BARTH'S REJECTION OF EBIONITE AND DOCETIC CHRISTOLOGY

One of the most vexatious aspects of contemporary Christology is the fact that so many theologians do not begin where Karl Barth began and in so doing miss the importance of distinguishing the immanent and economic Trinity. Hence they end by trying to build a Christology on a historically or idealistically reconstructed Jesus whose uniqueness is more a creation of the community than a reality whose genuine recognition rests on a simple acknowledgment of his lordship. Barth's starting point for thinking about the person and work of Jesus Christ was, as is well known, the simple fact of Jesus Christ himself who was the Son of God by virtue of his unique relation to the Father. This may sound like a simple or even simplistic point. It is in fact loaded, because by this statement Barth was not only trying to say that thinking must be determined by the unique object being considered, but he was also asserting that accurate thinking about revelation (and thus about Jesus Christ) could begin neither with our ideas nor with our experiences.[1] At bottom, revelation was not the disclosure of something hidden within history, but the disclosure of God himself who had entered history from outside. Beginning with ideas would lead to what he labeled Docetic Christology, while beginning with experience would lead to what he called Ebionite Christology. In both instances, confession of Jesus's deity would be no more and no less than a confession of the power of human ideas or the power of human experience. Such starting points therefore would necessarily deny the content of Christian confession at the outset. They would deny the fact that Jesus is the Son of God, independently of what we may think and independently of our experiences, beliefs or feelings. Ultimately, what was at stake for

1 *CD* I/2, 20.

Barth was the difference between genuine Christian insight and a kind of Feuerbachian reversal of divine and human predicates. In the last chapter we saw that this predicament is still a lively issue because much contemporary Christology and trinitarian theology begins from experience and not from Jesus Christ himself. It should be noted that Barth's starting point does not simply reject or annul human experience and self-determination in some christomonistic sense. It merely means that the unique object that determines our thinking is and always remains God, the Father of Jesus Christ, who meets us in and through our experiences in the power of the Holy Spirit, without becoming identical with them or dependent on them; this God claims our obedience.[2]

Some of the dogmatic implications of Barth's rejection of Ebionite and Docetic Christology and for his concern to distinguish the immanent and economic Trinity then are: (1) Christology must begin with Jesus Christ himself as attested in the New Testament. Any other starting point will necessarily distort who Jesus was and is, precisely because God has indeed exercised his freedom to be for us in Christ and not in some other way. (2) Failure to recognize Jesus's true deity means failure to recognize God as he really is for us. Thus, recognition of Jesus's true deity means acknowledging his antecedent existence as the eternally begotten Son of the Father, and so it has trinitarian implications and suggests an important distinction between the immanent and economic Trinity. (3) Jesus's humanity as such does not reveal because he is veiled in his revelation and thus he causes offense. Revelation thus means the unveiling of what is by nature veiled and it is identical with the power of the resurrection. This means that it must be understood as an *exception* and as a *miracle*. (4) Recognition of Jesus's deity is an analytic and not a synthetic statement. Therefore, Jesus's uniqueness is in no way dependent on the community's recognition of him to be true and valid. Since this is so, there can be no confusion of Christ and Christians and no suggestion of adoptionism or subordinationism in Christology or in trinitarian reflection. Any such suggestion once more implies the reversal of divine and human being and action and thus the collapse of theology into anthropology.

Situating the Question

To focus the issues here, consider for example, where Jürgen Moltmann begins his Christology in *The Way of Jesus Christ*. He begins his

2 See *CD* I/1, 198ff.

'pneumatological christology'[3] with the community's experience of discipleship and argues against the traditional christologies, on the *basis* of 'christopraxis' or what he calls a 'doxological' Christology which he says is the 'source from which christology springs'.[4] A doxological Christology is grounded 'on the experience of men and women who follow the path of Jesus Christ'.[5] Moltmann's self-stated goal is to overcome traditional metaphysical and more modern anthropological errors. His Christology therefore marks a transition from the metaphysical to the historical and finally to the post-modern type 'which places human history ecologically in the framework of nature'.[6] In other words, he intends to criticize Karl Rahner's Christology as a form of what he calls 'Jesuology', which he connects with the Christology of Schleiermacher, and rightly questions. His main criticism concerns the fact that Rahner attempted to reverse 'incarnation christology into a christology of self-transcendence' in accordance 'with the new interpretation of metaphysical christology by way of anthropological categories which we find in Kant and Schleiermacher'. Thus Rahner mistakenly sets Christology 'in the framework of anthropology' with the result that he 'ends up with Jesus, the perfect image of God, because he equates "the idea of Christ" with fulfilled human existence'.[7] Moltmann cleverly notes that for Rahner 'If it were not for the "idea of Christ" in the general make-up of human existence, no one would be in a position to recognize Jesus as "the Christ", and to believe in him'.[8] Moltmann rightly links this thinking with Rahner's theory of 'anonymous' or 'seeking christology' so that a person 'who arrives at his essential nature and its true fulfilment is a "Christian" whether he knows it or not, for "he also accepts this revelation whenever he really accepts *himself completely*, for it already speaks *in him*"'.[9] Moltmann

3 Jürgen Moltmann, *The Way of Jesus Christ: Christology in Messianic Dimensions* (hereafter: *The Way*), trans. Margaret Kohl (San Francisco: HarperSanFrancisco, 1990), 73ff. For analysis and critique see Paul D. Molnar, 'Moltmann's Post-Modern Messianic Christology: A Review Discussion', in *The Thomist*, vol. 56, no. 4 (October, 1992): 669–93.

4 Moltmann, *The Way*, 41, xiv.

5 Moltmann, *The Way*, xiv.

6 Moltmann, *The Way*, xvi.

7 Moltmann, *The Way*, 62.

8 Moltmann, *The Way*, 62.

9 Moltmann, *The Way*, 62. See the discussion of Rahner's idea that self-acceptance is the same as accepting Christ, in the following and in Chapters 5, 6 and 7.

also intends to criticize Karl Barth's Christology as a metaphysical one that he mistakenly thinks 'de-historicizes' the events of Christ's life, especially his resurrection,[10] while locating his own Christology in a 'cosmological perspective' that 'integrates human history in the natural conditions in which it is embedded'.[11] Some very odd conclusions follow from this. I will mention just two of them.

First, Moltmann argues that 'Jesus *is* the Lord because God *has raised* him from the dead. His *existence* as the Lord is to be found in God's eschatological *act* in him, which we call raising from the dead'.[12] This thinking is, of course, echoed in the reasoning of very many prominent contemporary theologians among whom are Wolfhart Pannenberg and Robert Jenson. The most unfortunate part of this thinking concerns the fact that it does not begin with the simple fact that Jesus is the Lord simply because he *is*. Thus it negates his antecedent existence as the preexistent Word which is so critically important for a proper trinitarian understanding of divine–human relations. It is interesting to note, as we will see shortly in more detail, that Barth's rejection of Ebionite and Docetic Christology led him to argue that: 'The resurrection can give nothing new to Him who is the eternal Word of the Father; but it makes visible what is proper to Him, His glory'.[13] In connection with his trinitarian theology Barth insisted that

> ... we have to accept the simple presupposition on which the New Testament statement rests, namely, that Jesus Christ is the Son because He is (not because He makes this impression on us, not because He does what we think is to be expected of a God, but because He is).

10 Moltmann, *The Way*, 231.

11 Moltmann, *The Way*, xvi.

12 Moltmann, *The Way*, 40.

13 *CD* I/2, 111. This, of course, is a point that Moltmann criticizes in Barth (Moltmann, *The Way*, 231). However, his criticism is thoroughly misplaced because Barth does not 'de-historicize' the resurrection by speaking of it as an act of God, since that very act of God was an act of raising the man Jesus from the dead so that the risen Lord himself was, in a second history (the Easter history), the inauguration of his second coming. Thus, one could never say, with Moltmann, that for Barth, 'What really happened in human history is only Christ's death' (Moltmann, *The Way*, 231). That is exactly the kind of thinking Barth rejected. For a discussion of Barth's view of Christ's resurrection, see Molnar, *Incarnation and Resurrection*, esp. Chapters 1 and 4.

With this presupposition all thinking about Jesus, which means at once all thinking about God, must begin and end.[14]

It is also interesting to note the importance of the hiddenness of revelation. Jesus's being as the Word incarnate meant that, as the Word, he was completely hidden[15] to those who met the man Jesus and to us, and indeed he was an offense to those who encountered him, as he is to us. For Barth, nothing could be more hidden than revelation and we must be offended at it precisely because it is something completely new and contrary to what would normally be acceptable to our thinking and experience.[16] As we shall see, it is this offending element in revelation that theologians such as Karl Rahner have obviated with their attempts to find an a priori way of approaching the study of Christology.

Second, Moltmann's own understanding of Jesus's preexistence and resurrection is flawed. He argues that in their mutual experience, the child Jesus and Abba 'discover themselves mutually through one another. In his relationship to Jesus, God becomes "Abba"; and in his relationship to his Abba God Jesus becomes "the child" … this mutual relationship is constitutive for both persons and precedes the history they share.'[17] From this it follows that 'Jesus' personhood does not exist in isolation, per se; nor is it determined and fixed from eternity. It acquires its form in living relationships and reciprocities …'[18] Hence,

> The divine power of healing does not come from his side alone … The healings are stories about faith just as much as they are stories about Jesus. They are stories about the reciprocal relationships between Jesus and the faith of men and women. *Jesus is dependent on*

---

14 *CD* I/1, 415.

15 Cf. *CD* I/2, 41–4.

16 Cf. *CD* I/2, 61. See also *CD* IV/2, 406 where Barth says that sin, in the form of sloth, leads to the 'rejection of the man Jesus' in favor of belief in simply a 'higher or supreme being' since this 'higher' being tolerates and confirms us as we are. However, the presence and action of God in Jesus basically illuminates and radically questions us, along with our belief in a higher being, and at this we are 'disturbed and therefore offended by the deity of God in the concrete phenomenon of the existence of this man'. Rejection of this man thus means rejection of God himself.

17 Moltmann, *The Way*, 143.

18 Moltmann, *The Way*, 136.

this faith, just as the sick are dependent on the power that emanates from Jesus.[19]

In connection with the resurrection, although Moltmann does quite rightly wish to assert the importance of Jesus's bodily resurrection,[20] he nonetheless reached the strangely Docetic conclusion that 'Resurrection means not a *factum* but a *fieri* – not what was once done, but what is in the making: the transition from death to life'.[21] This, because

> the early Christian faith in the resurrection was not based solely on Christ's appearances. It was just as strongly motivated ... by the experience of God's Spirit ... Believing in Christ's resurrection therefore does not mean affirming a fact. It means being possessed by the life-giving Spirit . . .[22]

Even though Moltmann later insists that 'Christ's "appearances" were bodily appearances',[23] what is actually described by resurrection language here is not really a factual event in the life of Jesus that is independent of the disciples' faith and our faith such that the risen Lord was the sole enabling condition of the disciples' faith and through the power of his Spirit the sole enabling condition of ours. Here Moltmann's focus is on something grounded in 'visionary phenomena'[24] which have as their foundation the 'inner experience'[25] of those who had them. Thus the controlling factor here for Moltmann is not Jesus, risen bodily from the dead, but the fact that 'The "seeing" of the risen Christ became faith'.[26] Moreover, it is just this Ebionite explanation of the resurrection at this point and Moltmann's apparent Docetic conclusions that are at odds with Barth's emphasis on the importance of Jesus's bodily resurrection as the factor that gives meaning to faith without becoming dependent on faith.[27] Far from de-historicizing the events

---

19 Moltmann, *The Way*, 111–12, emphasis mine.
20 Moltmann, *The Way*, 241 and 256–7.
21 Moltmann, *The Way*, 241.
22 Moltmann, *The Way*, 218.
23 Moltmann, *The Way*, 257.
24 Moltmann, *The Way*, 217–18.
25 Moltmann, *The Way*, 216.
26 Moltmann, *The Way*, 218.
27 See esp. *CD* III/2, 448ff. and IV/2, 143 and IV/1, 351. In an important discussion of the resurrection helpfully comparing, in typological fashion,

of Christ's life, as Moltmann believed, Barth decisively maintained the historicity of the resurrection as an event in Jesus's life that could be as little proven from history as the event of revelation could. As we will see later, it is Moltmann's panentheism, which starts from experience and reconstructs theology in process terms, that cannot allow for an 'an immanent Trinity in which God is simply by himself, without the love which communicates salvation'.[28] Thus, Moltmann must 'surrender the traditional distinction between the immanent and the economic Trinity', and affirm

> Rahner's thesis that 'the economic Trinity *is* the immanent Trinity, and vice versa' ... The thesis about the fundamental *identity* of the immanent and the economic Trinity of course remains open to misunderstanding as long as we cling to the distinction at all ... The

differing ways of thinking about it, George Hunsinger compares the views of Schleiermacher, Bultmann and Tillich with Pannenberg and Wright and also with Moltmann, Frei and Barth. See 'The daybreak of the new creation: Christ's resurrection in recent theology' *SJT*, vol. 57, no. 2: 163–81. In connection with Moltmann's presentation, Hunsinger expresses the following critical comment: 'It seems fair to say that in Moltmann's theology it remained uncertain whether the risen Christ was really the center or merely the prototype of the new creation' (175).

28 Jürgen Moltmann, *The Trinity and the Kingdom, The Doctrine of God* (hereafter: *Trinity and Kingdom*), trans. Margaret Kohl (New York: Harper & Row, 1981), 151. Moltmann literally cannot make a distinction between God's eternal love and God's free act of love ad extra. So he insists that: 'The distinction between the immanent and economic Trinity would be necessary if, in the concept of God, there were really only the alternative between liberty and necessity' (*Trinity and Kingdom*, 151). He then claims that 'if God *is* love, then his liberty cannot consist of loving or of not loving' (*Trinity and Kingdom*, 151). The implication in this remark is that since God is love he cannot but love us. Indeed that is where his panentheistic thinking leads him when he says: 'it is impossible to conceive of a God who is not a creative God' and 'God cannot find bliss in eternal self-love if selflessness is part of love's very nature' (*Trinity and Kingdom*, 106). While Moltmann claims that God is not compelled by some inner or outer necessity (*Trinity and Kingdom*, 151), his thinking is shaped by his desire to unite *freedom* and *necessity* in God. This confusion seems to compel him to conclude that since God is love God cannot just as well exist without us. For more on this, see Chapter 8.

economic Trinity not only reveals the immanent Trinity; it also has a retroactive effect on it.[29]

This thinking opens the door to the mutually conditioned relationship Moltmann sees between Jesus and those he heals. As we shall see, Moltmann uncritically enlists the principle of mutual conditioning and eliminates any need to conceptualize a God truly independent of creatures.[30] Any real notion of Lordship applying to God's love revealed in Christ is simply reinterpreted by the experience of suffering, drawing God into the vicissitudes of creation itself.[31]

Karl Barth was able to avoid these and other difficulties simply because his starting point for Christology was Jesus Christ himself: 'The explanation of their [Palestinian Jews of Jesus' time] statement that Jesus is Lord is to be sought only in the fact that for them He was the Lord, and was so in the same factual and self-evident and indisputable way as Yahweh was of old Israel's God.'[32] What led Barth to this conclusion? It was his consideration of 'God the Son' in § II of *CD* I/1 where he wrote: 'The one God reveals Himself according to Scripture as the Reconciler ... As such He is the Son of God who has come to us or the Word of God that has been spoken to us, because He is so antecedently in Himself as the Son or Word of God the Father.'[33] It is in this part of his trinitarian theology that Barth first discusses Ebionite and Docetic Christology as ways of thinking that are excluded by the simple fact of revelation, namely, by the fact that Jesus Christ is truly God and truly human at the same time.[34]

In *CD* I, 1, Barth begins by noting that 'What God reveals in Jesus and how He reveals it, namely, in Jesus, must not be separated from

---

29 Moltmann, *Trinity and Kingdom*, 160.

30 Moltmann, *Trinity and Kingdom*, 4, 32ff. 38ff. and Jürgen Moltmann, *God in Creation: A New Theology of Creation and the Spirit of God* (hereafter: *Creation*), trans. Margaret Kohl (New York: Harper and Row, 1985), 13ff., 86–9, 101ff. and 204ff. See also Chapter 8.

31 For Barth, God was deeply affected by creatures but not *because* of any mutually conditioning relationship between himself and another. See, for example, *CD* II/1, 307ff., 312, 496, and esp. 510–11.

32 *CD* I/1, 405.

33 *CD* I/1, 399.

34 Of course, without using the designations Ebionite and Docetic Christology similar thinking already appears in Karl Barth, *The Göttingen Dogmatics: Instruction in the Christian Religion*, vol. 1, ed. Hannelotte Reiffen,

one another according to the New Testament'.[35] Without denying Jesus's distinction from the Father, Barth then considers 'the unity of the Son with the Father attested [in the Bible] … and therefore the deity of Jesus Christ … as definitive, authentic and essential'.[36] For this reason and unlike Bultmann in his book *Jesus*, Barth insists that we cannot understand the Jesus of the New Testament one-sidedly by focusing only on his sayings and excluding his miraculous actions. Both must be seen together as is evidenced in Mk. 2:1–12 in the story of the paralytic. If the two are seen together, then Jesus will be acknowledged in his essential and authentic deity as the eternally begotten Son of the Father. Thus, for Barth,

> The New Testament statement about the unity of the Son with the Father, i.e., the deity of Christ, cannot possibly be understood in terms of the presupposition that the original view and declaration of the New Testament witnesses was that a human being was either exalted as such to deity or appeared among us as the personification and symbol of a divine being.[37]

This statement is a direct rejection of the manner in which M. Dibelius formulated the problem of New Testament Christology, that is, 'as the way in which "knowledge of the historical figure of Jesus was so quickly transformed into faith in a heavenly Son of God"'.[38] Barth rejects this thinking because in presupposing 'that knowledge of a historical figure came first and a transforming of this into faith in the heavenly Son of God came second', so that we must then ask 'in terms of the history of thought how this came about', can only lead to a blind alley; it can only lead to modern historical versions of what he calls Ebionite and Docetic Christology.[39]

It may be noted that John Macquarrie in his book, *Jesus Christ in Modern Thought*, echoes the very perspective that Barth here rejects when he claims to find, following J. D. G. Dunn, 'a unifying idea amid the diversity of the New Testament, an idea which he [Dunn] expresses

---

trans. Geoffrey W. Bromiley (hereafter: *The Göttingen Dogmatics*) (Grand Rapids, MI: Eerdmans, 1991), 115–18.

35 *CD* I/1, 399.
36 *CD* I/1, 400.
37 *CD* I/1, 402.
38 *CD* I/1, 402.
39 *CD* I/1, 402.

as the conviction that the historical figure, Jesus the Jew, becomes an "exalted being".[40] Interestingly, it is just this thinking that leads Macquarrie to argue that the term 'Christ' should not be restricted to the man Jesus of Nazareth, but should instead describe the Christ-event, that is, 'Jesus and the community as together embraced in the Christ-event'. Thus, for Macquarrie 'there is no sharp dividing line between

40 John Macquarrie, *Jesus Christ in Modern Thought* (hereafter: *Jesus Christ*) (Philadelphia: Trinity Press International, 1990), 12. On this basis Macquarrie is critical of Barth for discussing Christ's two natures in the Chalcedonian sense arguing that: 'The determination of His divine essence is *to* His human, and the determination of His human essence *from* His divine' (*CD* IV/2, 70). Of course Barth was attempting to explain that God assumes human nature into union with his divine being as the Son without ceasing to be God and without changing the human nature he assumed into something other than his true humanity exalted into fellowship with God. So Barth spoke of a mutual participation of the divine and human natures in Christ noting that 'the relationship between the two is not reversible' so that while 'He became man' that did not mean that 'as the Son of Man ... He became God' (*CD* IV/2, 71). Barth asks: 'How could He just become that which He already was from all eternity as the Son of God, and which He did not cease to be even as the Son of Man?' (*CD* IV/2, 71–2). The point Barth was making was that Jesus was from the very first who he was as God who became man for us and for our salvation, and that his humanity had its reality in the fact that he was God acting *as* man. His human essence was truly human only because of the unique union of natures in the assumption of that human nature by the Son who was and is the Subject of the incarnation. However, because Macquarrie thinks that this entails moving into 'a realm of unreal distinctions' (*Jesus Christ*, 12), he claims that Barth's position here undermines 'the full humanity of Christ' and pushes 'us in a monophysite direction' (*Jesus Christ*, 14). In reality, of course, Barth did not move in a monophysite direction but deliberately avoided it precisely by describing the relationship between the divine and human natures without undermining Jesus's divinity or his humanity exactly because he thought of his humanity as it truly was in and through his being as the Son of God incarnate. Macquarrie takes this position just because he begins 'with the simple assertion that Jesus Christ was a man, a human being' (*Jesus Christ*, 360) and asks the very question Barth insists is disallowed by the fact that Jesus exists as the incarnate Word: ' "How does a man become God?" ' (*Jesus Christ*, 360). That very question illustrates his Ebionite starting point that posits an adoptionist Christology that Barth rightly claims is excluded by a Chalcedonian Christology which recognizes the mystery of Jesus Christ as both divine and human. For a fuller

Jesus and the community'.[41] The Christ-event refers to 'something larger than the career of Jesus of Nazareth. In that larger reality there were joined inseparably the career of Jesus and its impact on the believing community'.[42] This is of a piece with his belief that there are 'two sources for the knowledge of Jesus Christ – the testimony of the past and the experience of the present'.[43]

All of this thinking steadfastly refuses to begin from Jesus Christ who was the Son of God, and the result is a form of Ebionite Christology that sees the relation between Jesus and the community as one that is mutually conditioned.[44] Indeed, it leads exactly to the notion that it is an idea rather than Jesus himself that unifies the New Testament. Strangely, while Macquarrie mistakenly criticizes Barth for being unhistorical in his Christology, it is this very thinking that fails to respect the fact that it is precisely Jesus the man from Nazareth who is the Christ and so is itself quite unhistorical and thus Docetic in the end.

Moreover, this thinking leads Macquarrie to argue that the resurrection 'is one element in that potentiality for being that was given to the human race as created in the image and likeness of God'.[45] Instead of seeing that the resurrection is the miraculous power of divine action itself which unveils the true meaning of Jesus as the incarnate Word, Macquarrie believes that: 'Those whose lives had been deeply influenced by Jesus spoke of a "resurrection,"'[46] and that to assert that Jesus is risen does not 'mean an actual rising from the dead' in a historical sense. Rather the historical event is 'the rise of the Christian church ... considered as part of the Christ-event and not only something in the career of Jesus'.[47] What then is the historical fact that empowers the church to be the body of Christ? According to Macquarrie: 'There is a solid historical fact here, namely, that the birth of the church depended on the belief of the disciples that Jesus had been resurrected.' Thus only 'a belief in the resurrection provides anything like a sufficient reason for the rise

discussion of Macquarrie's thinking, see Molnar, *Incarnation and Resurrection*, 163–71.

41 Macquarrie, *Jesus Christ*, 21.
42 Macquarrie, *Jesus Christ*, 20.
43 Macquarrie, *Jesus Christ*, 6.
44 Macquarrie, *Jesus Christ*, 22–3.
45 Macquarrie, *Jesus Christ*, 66.
46 Macquarrie, *Jesus Christ*, 5.
47 Macquarrie, *Jesus Christ*, 406.

of Christianity after the death of Jesus'.[48] But does Macquarrie believe that Jesus rose bodily from the dead or not? According to Macquarrie 'what is resurrected is not the dead body that has been laid in the grave' because he believes that this would lead to the idea that resurrection was only the resuscitation of a corpse. Hence, Macquarrie suggests that 'perhaps resurrection is transcendence to a new level in the being of the human person, a level which eludes our understanding so long as we are seeing it only from below'. Since he follows a trend also evident in the thought of Karl Rahner to explain reality through the concept of self-transcendence, he insists that we are not restricted 'to these visionary experiences recorded in the New Testament'.[49]

Here it is clear that it is not and cannot be Jesus himself risen bodily from the dead who gives meaning to the faith of the Church. He has instead been absorbed into the faith of the Church under the idea of the Christ-event. This just misses the main point that Barth correctly insisted on, that is, that the power of the resurrection is identical with the power of the Word and Spirit evident in Jesus's life from Christmas to Good Friday to Easter and beyond; a power over which we have no conceptual, existential or ontological control.

Ebionite Christology

What then is Barth rejecting and affirming here with his opinion about M. Dibelius, whose views, as we have just seen are alive and well in the theology of John Macquarrie? He rejects any suggestion that Christ's deity can be 'taken individualistically as the apotheosis of a man' whose effect on others led to 'the impression and idea that He was a God'.[50] Barth is here repudiating all forms of adoptionism and all notions that a hero figure (Jesus included) could be 'idealised upwards as God ... This is Ebionite Christology, or Christology historically reconstructed along the lines of Ebionitism'.[51] There are then at least two problems that Barth identifies here for us.

First, reading the New Testament or the dogmatic tradition with the assumption that we first know Jesus as a historical figure and then,

48 Macquarrie, *Jesus Christ*, 406.
49 Macquarrie, *Jesus Christ*, 408–9.
50 *CD* I/1, 402.
51 *CD* I/1, 403.

supposedly like the disciples, we believe in him as Son of God suggests that his deity is grounded in and results from the experience (the
response) of the community of faith.[52] In *CD* I/2, more light is shed on
this when Barth says: 'As Docetism starts from a human conception to
which it logically returns in due course, so does Ebionitism start from
a human experience and impression of the heroic personality of Jesus
of Nazareth. On the basis of this impression and experience, divinity is
ascribed to this man.'[53] Barth never ceased to emphasize this fact in all
his dogmatic reflections. Hence, in the doctrine of reconciliation when
Barth considered the important topic of human vocation he insisted
that 'we must maintain at all costs that the living Jesus Christ is the
subject acting in it [vocation] here and now in the allotted time of the
lives of specific men … [instead of speaking] more or less abstractly of
the structure of the experience of the man who is called. To be realistic at this point, we must speak quite concretely and unequivocally
of Jesus Christ Himself.'[54] Interestingly, Barth goes on to note that the
Holy Spirit must not be seen as in any sense independent of Christ but
as 'His Spirit, as the power of His presence, work and Word' if we are to
speak properly of vocation. Barth's thinking always was shaped by the
fact that Jesus, who rose from the dead and is coming again, is present
now between Easter and his final revelation in the power of his resurrection, and thus in the power of the Holy Spirit. Consequently, Barth
insisted that: 'If we are to speak with true relevance and clarity in this
matter, we have not only to mention Jesus Christ but to name Him as
the One whose sovereign action alone gives to the subjective experience
the power and profundity which otherwise it could not have.'[55]

In fact, it is not too much to say that all Barth's thinking about
Christology and trinitarian theology is unmistakably structured by his
positive and negative assertions developed in relation to the categories

---

52 Thomas F. Torrance makes a similar point in *Preaching Christ Today: The
Gospel and Scientific Thinking* (Grand Rapids, MI: Eerdmans, 1994), 8ff.
Torrance explains why he rejects Ebionite and Docetic Christology in *The
Trinitarian Faith*, 111–16. Each in its own way separated Jesus's divinity and
humanity and thus distorted the New Testament emphasis on 'the undivided
wholeness of his divine-human reality as God become man' (*The Trinitarian
Faith*, 114).

53 *CD* I/2, 20.

54 *CD* IV/3.2, 502.

55 *CD* IV/3.2, 503.

Ebionite and Docetic Christology both in *CD* I/1 and I/2. As we shall see, the resurrection plays a decisive role in Barth's understanding of revelation and reconciliation. His view of the resurrection stands in stark contrast to the views of Moltmann, Pannenberg, Jenson and others. While Barth insists that the resurrection discloses who Jesus was and is as the Son of God,[56] these theologians and others argue, in different ways, that the resurrection constitutes his being as the eternal Son to some extent. Barth's view also sharply contrasts with Rahner's since Rahner is unable to distinguish consistently between the resurrection as an event in the life of Jesus and the disciples' experience as well as our experience of the risen Lord himself. In the end Rahner places more emphasis on our transcendental experience of hope than on the risen Lord himself.[57] That, of course, is why Rahner could argue for an 'anonymous experience' of the resurrection while Barth as well as Torrance insisted that an experience of Christ's resurrection was necessarily tied to Jesus himself as the object and active subject enabling that experience through his Holy Spirit.[58]

Second, such Ebionite thinking is individualistic and adoptionistic and thus further suggests that Jesus was not the eternally begotten Son of the Father but had to become this by virtue of his ministry, the effect he had on others or by God's adopting him as his Son either at his birth, transfiguration or at his resurrection.[59] This is certainly a major problem in contemporary Christology. Thus, while Barth is extremely

---

56 See, for example, *CD* IV/3.1, 44 where Barth writes: 'When we say that Jesus Christ lives, we repeat the basic, decisive, controlling and determinative statement of the biblical witness, namely, that He, very Son of God and Son of Man, the Mediator between God and man, the One who lives the life of grace … the Fulfiller of the divine act of reconciliation, that He, this One, has risen from the dead, and in so doing shown Himself to be who He is. He lives as and because He is risen, having thus shown that He lives this life. If there is any Christian and theological axiom, it is that Jesus Christ is risen, that He is truly risen. But this is an axiom which no one can invent. It can only be repeated on the basis of the fact that in the enlightening power of the Holy Spirit it has been previously declared to us as the central statement of the biblical witness.'

57 For a discussion of Rahner on these issues, see Chapter 7, 358–63 and 373 and Molnar, *Incarnation and Resurrection*, chapter two, 60–4 and chapter four.

58 See again Chapter 7, 359 and Molnar, *Incarnation and Resurrection*, chapters one and four.

59 *CD* I/1, 402–3.

clear that we must be precise in emphasizing Christ's centrality and uniqueness in accordance with the precision of Chalcedon, Wolfhart Pannenberg is notably vague and positively ambiguous when he says that Jesus's eternal sonship

> precedes his historical existence on earth and must be regarded as the creative basis of his human existence. If the human history of Jesus is the revelation of his eternal sonship, we must be able to perceive the latter in the reality of the human life. The deity is not an addition to this reality. It is the reflection that the human relation of Jesus to God the Father casts on his existence, even as it also illumines the eternal being of God.[60]

Thus for Pannenberg, 'Apart from Jesus' resurrection, it would not be true that from the very beginning of his earthly way God was one with this man. That is true from all eternity *because* of Jesus' resurrection'.[61] Indeed, for Pannenberg, 'Jesus resurrection is not only constitutive for our perception of his divinity, but it is ontologically constitutive for that divinity'.[62] It is not surprising that Barth's own reaction to Pannenberg's *Jesus – God and Man* was one of horror.[63] Pannenberg continues to insist that 'Only the Easter event determines what the meaning was

60 Wolfhart Pannenberg, *Systematic Theology Volume 2* (hereafter: *Systematic Theology 2*), trans. Geoffrey W. Bromiley (Grand Rapids, MI: Eerdmans, 1994), 325. Chapter 10 concerns the deity of Christ.

61 Wolfhart Pannenberg, *Jesus – God and Man* (Second Edition), trans. Lewis L. Wilkins and Duane A. Priebe (Philadelphia: Westminster Press, 1977), 321.

62 Pannenberg, *Jesus – God and Man*, 224. Such thinking apparently is no problem for Kam Ming Wong, *Wolfhart Pannenberg on Human Destiny* (Aldershot: Ashgate, 2008), 10 and 163–4. Wong criticizes Paul Fiddes for supposing that Pannenberg's emphasis on the priority of the future was merely epistemological and not ontological, insisting that Pannenberg meant to say that 'without the resurrection Jesus would not be the Son of God ... Jesus' resurrection ... is ontologically constitutive for that divinity' (10).

63 *Karl Barth Letters 1961–1968*, ed. Jürgen Fangmeier and Hinrich Stoevesandt, trans. and ed. Geoffrey W. Bromiley,(Grand Rapids, MI: Eerdmans, 1981), 178. Barth wrote to Pannenberg: 'My first reaction on reading your book was one of horror when ... I found you rejecting M. Kähler in a way which led me to suspect that, like others, you ... intended to pursue a path from below to above ... Is not this to build a house on the sand – the shifting sand of historical

of the pre-Easter history of Jesus and who he was in his relation to God'.[64] By contrast of course Barth held that in the resurrection 'the man Jesus appeared to them ... in the mode of God ... He had always been present among them in His deity, though hitherto this deity had been veiled'.[65]

And Pannenberg is not alone. According to Robert Jenson ' "the Son" in trinitarian use [does not] first denote a simply divine entity. Primally, it denotes the claim Jesus makes for himself in addressing God as Father ... this Son is an eternally divine Son only in and by this relation'.[66] Obviously if Jesus is only the eternal Son in and by this relation, then his antecedent existence, which alone gives meaning to his historical existence is compromised. Barth very clearly countered this kind of thinking when he wrote that:

'Begotten of the Father before all time' means that He did not come into being in time as such ... That the Son of God becomes man and that He is known by other men in His humanity as the Son of God are events, even if absolutely distinctive events, in time ... *But their distinction does not itself derive or come from time* ... because the power of God's immanence is here the power of His transcendence,

probabilities ... *In its positive content is your christology – after the practice of so many modern fathers – anything other than the outstanding example and symbol of a presupposed general anthropology, cosmology, and ontology?*' emphasis mine. For additional discussion of Pannenberg's Christology, see Molnar, *Incarnation and Resurrection*, 261–310. There I argue that Pannenberg's opposition to the Chalcedonian view of Jesus as truly divine and truly human results from his own inability to hold together, as he should have, the incarnation and the resurrection instead of seeing the incarnation as the result of his Christology from below, which will not explicitly acknowledge Jesus's divinity as the basis for his human history throughout his earthly life. Pannenberg believed that a Christology which holds that the preexistent Word became flesh had to mean that 'Jesus could not be conceived as a real, individual man' (*Jesus – God and Man*, 290, 301). This is why he was compelled to seek the validation of Jesus's uniqueness in history and anthropology and thus outside of Jesus himself as the incarnate Word.

64   Pannenberg, *Systematic Theology 2*, 345.

65   *CD* III/2, 448, cf. also 451.

66   Robert W. Jenson, *Systematic Theology Volume I: The Triune God* (hereafter: *ST I*) (New York: Oxford University Press, 1997), 77. Jenson here explicitly relies on the thinking of Pannenberg.

their subject must be understood as being before all time, as the eternal Subject, eternal as God Himself, Himself eternal as God.[67]

Docetic Christology

Here it is important to note that in Barth's thinking Ebionitism does not stand on its own but is closely related to what he labels Docetism: 'There was and is a counterpart and extension of Docetism in the shape of an equally arbitrary Christology of Ebionitism'.[68] From another point of view then, one could take the New Testament statement of Jesus's deity in a collective sense suggesting that 'In Him ... we have the personifica-tion of a familiar idea or general truth, e.g., the truth of the communion of deity and humanity, or the truth of the creation of the world by God's word and wisdom'.[69] Importantly, this view pays little attention to the historical Jesus, who is more or less dispensable. 'He was believed in as theophany or myth, as the embodiment of a general truth ... As and to the degree that the symbol of this idea was seen and venerated in Jesus of Nazareth, He was called Kyrios'.[70] In other words 'what was in view was the idea, not the Rabbi of Nazareth, who might be known or not known as such with no great gain or loss either way, whom there was at any rate a desire to know only for the sake of the idea. This is Docetic Christology, or Christology historically reconstructed along the lines of Docetism'.[71] It will be recalled that John Macquarrie, for instance, begins his thinking about Jesus with the community's experience of transcend-ence and ends by displacing Jesus, God and man with the idea of an exalted being.

What both of these views have in common is that 'strictly speaking the New Testament statement about Christ's deity is a form of expres-sion that is meant very loosely and is to be interpreted accordingly'.[72] More importantly, what both these views have in common is their refusal to begin thinking about the 'problem of Christology',[73] or about Jesus Christ, from Jesus himself as we meet him in the New Testament

---

67 *CD* I/1, 426–7, emphasis mine.
68 *CD* I/2, 19.
69 *CD* I/1, 403.
70 *CD* I/1, 403.
71 *CD* I/1, 403.
72 *CD* I/1, 403.
73 See *CD* I/2, 122ff.

witness. The Jesus we meet in the New Testament witness is one who really is true God and true man and whose mystery cannot be resolved by thinking of him as one or the other or as some *tertium quid*. 'As the true humanity of Christ is ultimately dispensable for Docetism, so is the true divinity of Jesus for Ebionitism – in fact, in the last resort it is a nuisance'.[74] Of course, for Barth, one could hardly say that Docetic thinking had recognized true divinity, since the divinity alleged by that viewpoint is dictated by an idea of divinity conjured by people apart from and in contradiction of the particular God revealed in Jesus Christ.

In *CD* 1, 2 Barth argues that, however important the incarnation may be – and it is important, 'we ought not to say that the incarnation is the proper content of the New Testament' since all religions and myths can produce the idea of an incarnation. What is central to the New Testament and only to the New Testament is the fact that 'the Son of God is called Jesus of Nazareth, and Jesus of Nazareth the Son of God'.[75] The name of Jesus of Nazareth signifies the reality of revelation, that is, that God has entered history in the person of his Son in order to save humanity from sin, suffering, evil and death. For Barth, knowledge of the triune God meant knowledge of a force that was disturbing to and 'even destructive of, the advance of religion, its life and richness and peace' and that it was bound to be so because

> Olympus and Valhalla decrease in population when the message of the God who is the one and only God is really known and believed … No sentence is more dangerous or revolutionary than that God is One and there is no other like Him … Let this sentence be uttered in such a way that it is heard and grasped, and at once 450 prophets of Baal are always in fear of their lives … Beside God there are only His creatures or false gods, and beside faith in Him there are religions only as religions of superstition, error and finally irreligion.[76]

But the most important point to be noted here is that 'to gain a real understanding of Christ's God-manhood, does not rest upon our choice or goodwill, for the decision concerning whether it is reached or not depends not upon us, but upon the object whose reality is here to be seen and understood'. For Barth the discovery that Jesus is God's Son

---

74 *CD* I/2, 20–1.
75 *CD* I/2, 14.
76 *CD* II/1, 444.

and that God's Son is Jesus 'is not to be conceived of as though those who thus thought and spoke had first a definite conception of God or of a Son or Word of God, of a Christ, and then found this conception confirmed and fulfilled in Jesus. That would be an arbitrary Christology, docetic in its estimate and in its conclusions on the basis of which there can be no serious recognition of the divinity of Christ'.[77] As we shall see, Rahner begins his questing Christology just this way and thus falls foul of this Docetic Christology. As we have seen in Chapter 1, Elizabeth Johnson interpreted Christology from the matrix of women's experience and both substituted Sophia for the Word incarnate and saw Jesus as an envoy and model of God's love alongside others. Barth's decisive thinking is also in marked contrast, say, to the popular view espoused by Sallie McFague when she writes:

> Jesus' response as beloved to God as lover was so open and thorough that his life and death were revelatory of God's great love for the world. His illumination of that love as inclusive of the last and the least, as embracing and valuing the outcast, is *paradigmatic of God the lover but is not unique. This means that Jesus is not ontologically different from other paradigmatic figures* either in our tradition or in other religious traditions who manifest in word and deed the love of God for the world. He is special to us as our foundational figure: he is our historical choice as the premier paradigm of God's love.[78]

While McFague's thinking is intended to reject Christ's uniqueness, Barth's thinking also diverges sharply from Wolfhart Pannenberg's more sophisticated attempt to ground his understanding of Jesus as God's Son in the experience of anticipation.[79] Of course it must be emphasized that Pannenberg, Moltmann and Rahner all were trying to explain and maintain Christ's uniqueness in a way that would make sense to modern people. Thus they differ in that important way from such theologians as Sallie McFague and Gordon Kaufman, whose wider Christology, as we shall see, is an almost classic case of Docetic Christology which, like McFague's, does not intend to acknowledge Jesus's uniqueness.

From what has been said so far, it appears that the key problem with much modern Christology is its inability to admit, with Barth, that

---

77   *CD* I/2, 15–16.

78   McFague, *Models*, 136, emphasis mine.

79   Cf. Paul D. Molnar, 'Some Problems with Pannenberg's Solution to Barth's "Faith Subjectivism"' *SJT*, vol. 48, no. 3 (1995): 315–39.

'among the realities of this cosmos there is not one in which God would be free for man. In this cosmos God is hidden and man blind'.[80] This is exactly why revelation meets us as a mystery and a miracle, that is, 'an exception from the rule of the cosmos of realities that otherwise encounter man'.[81] It contradicts what the phenomena seem to be saying.[82] Thus God's hiddenness itself can only be known from revelation. Several crucial points that are instructive for us today follow from this thinking and set Barth apart from much contemporary Christology.

First, God can and indeed did cross the boundary between himself and us in the incarnation; his nature does not prevent him from being 'God within the sphere indicated by this nature of ours'. While we are limited to and by our nature, as a flame must shoot upward and is bound to its nature as a sign of its creatureliness: 'It corresponds with the greatness of God ... not to be tied down and limited by His own nature.'[83] The fact that deity became human without ceasing to be divine is thus a miracle.

Second, God is free for us in such a way that God the Son or Word becomes man – not God the Father or the Holy Spirit. Yet 'God in His entire divinity became man'. For those who accuse Barth of modalism it should be noted that he says here: 'It is not the one nature of God as such with whose operation we have to do here. It is the one nature of God in the mode of existence of the Son, which became Man.'[84] While we cannot understand *how* this can be so, it is a fact that Jesus Christ is the incarnate Word. There is no absolute necessity here, and so Barth approves the fact that Thomas Aquinas grants that the Father or the Spirit could have become incarnate. This is a thought that would be abhorrent to Karl Rahner, who repeatedly rejects this very idea.[85] While Rahner's positive intention is to avoid an abstract consideration of the Word as one of a nonnumerical three, it is also clear that there is a certain logical necessity to the way Rahner conceives the Word, in accordance with his theology of symbolic expression. This leads him

80 *CD* I/2, 30.

81 *CD* I/2, 28.

82 *CD* I/1, 166.

83 *CD* I/2, 31.

84 *CD* I/2, 33.

85 See, for example, Rahner, *Trinity*, 11 and Karl Rahner, S.J., *Foundations of Christian Faith: An Introduction To The Idea of Christianity* (hereafter: *FCF*), trans. William V. Dych (New York: A Crossroad Book, Seabury, 1978), 214.

to compromise God's freedom in various ways, as we shall see more explicitly later. While Barth here acknowledges God's freedom, he nonetheless argues that we must accept the factual necessity (as distinguished from any logical necessity) attested by scripture that Jesus is the incarnate Word.

Third, while God assumes a form 'known to us' and so can be known 'by analogy with other forms known to us',[86] it is still true that God's entry into history is a veiling of the eternal Word, that is, a kenosis that will lead to an unveiling, even in the veiling. However, here is the key difference between Barth's thinking and that of many contemporaries, what is known here can be known only by grace and not at all by nature – 'not on the ground of an *analogia entis* already visible to us beforehand'.[87] This means that we can neither seek nor will we find any possibility of knowing God's revelation by exploring human experiences of self-transcendence, even if we argue that such experiences are graced at the outset. For Barth, grace as grace exposes us as those who continually bypass Jesus Christ and thus are in conflict with grace by nature since the fall.[88] Revelation shows us the 'factual resistance of man to the divine act of lordship, a resistance in which he who makes this statement will be aware that he participates, and shares in its guilt'. For Barth, God's revelation is genuinely hidden and offensive. This can be seen in his analysis of God's time and our time: 'God in Himself is not offending. Time in itself is also not offending. God in time is offending because the order of rank mentioned is thereby set up, because we are

86 *CD* I/2, 35.

87 *CD* I/2, 37.

88 Thus Barth writes: 'To believe means to believe in Jesus Christ. But this means to keep wholly and utterly to the fact that our temporal existence receives and has and again receives its truth, not from itself, but exclusively from its relationship to what Jesus Christ is and does as our Advocate and Mediator in God Himself ... in faith we abandon ... our standing upon ourselves (including our moral and religious, even Christian standing) ... for the real standing in which we no longer stand on ourselves (on our moral and religious, or even our Christian state) ... but ... on the ground of the truth of God ... We have to believe: not to believe in ourselves, but in Jesus Christ' *CD* II/1, 159. The certainty of faith thus comes only from Jesus Christ, risen, ascended, coming again and continually mediating between us and his Father. Thus, any question about the certainty of our knowledge of and participation in God can only be answered correctly if it 'does not start from the believing man but from Jesus Christ as the object and foundation of faith' (*CD* II/1, 156).

thereby gripped by God ... in the delusion that we possessed time.'[89] The problem is that we want to destroy or render innocuous or conceal this fulfilled time, the time of Jesus Christ, which can only be known from itself. In connection with our knowledge of God, Barth insists that our life in the Holy Spirit is a life of faith, that is,

> the temporal form of [our] eternal being in Jesus Christ and therefore in truth ... Our truth is not the being which we find in ourselves ... [this] will always be the being in enmity against God ... Our truth is our being in the Son of God, in whom we are not enemies but friends of God, in whom we do not hate grace but cling to grace alone, in whom therefore God is knowable to us.[90]

Seen in this light, Barth argues that the crucifixion can be viewed as a very primitive form of self-preservation and self-defense that includes Israel and the nations. Barth insists that it was not just the Jews who were offended by Jesus but also the Gentiles. In fact he notes that the very man who thought he was the exception here, Peter, had to submit to being told that he would deny Jesus. This, because offense is inevitable at the servant form of revelation, that is, at 'God in time'. This is a hiddenness contrary to nature. It is because we seek ourselves and resist God that we take offense at revelation. We thus contradict and resist it. The cross represents our attempt to get clear of the offense of revelation and to make God's time the same as ours – to level up the order of rank.[91] We think we can set aside the offense in revelation but in fact we cannot. That is why the fact that revelation nevertheless takes place is a miracle and an offense. That God has time for us, that 'there is a divine time in the midst of our time' is a miracle. It cannot be explained 'otherwise than by the special direct new act of God'.[92] A miracle is 'the special new direct act of God in time and in history. In the form in which it acquires temporal historical actuality, biblically attested revelation is always a miracle, and therefore the witness to it, whether direct or indirect in its course, is a narrative of miracles that happened. Miracle is

---

89 *CD* I/2, 61.

90 *CD* II/1, 158–9.

91 See above, n. 16 for how Barth explains sloth as the form in which we are offended by the fact that God meets us in Jesus and not as an unobtrusive 'supreme being' who simply approves of us as we are.

92 *CD* I/2, 64.

thus an attribute of revelation.'[93] So the most important point to make here is that there is no loss of majesty on God's part when he condescends to become man and to suffer and die on our behalf. There is a veiling of his majesty but not an abandonment of or a lessening of his divinity. 'He who the third day rose from the dead was no less true God in the manger than on the cross.'[94]

Fourth, the Word became flesh means that he assumed our sinful alienated flesh and thus became everything that we are and also experienced death; but he could not sin because God cannot be untrue to himself. While we cannot explain *how* this mystery can be so, it remains the case that Jesus's humanity is both a barrier (a veil) and also 'a door that opens'.[95] It is a problem for us but a solution as well because while Jesus died as man, he also rose from the dead. This thinking explains why Barth insisted that Jesus, in his humanity as such was not the revealer. His humanity 'receives its character as revelation and its power to reveal solely from the Word and therefore certainly cannot in itself ... be the object of faith and worship'.[96] There is therefore no divinization of his human nature.[97]

Contemporary Examples of Ebionite Christology

Let us explore further examples of what Ebionite Christology might look like today in order to set in relief the positive and negative insights to be gained from Barth's position. Regarding the problem of Christology, Paul F. Knitter believes that John Hick 'works out a solution that allows Christians to continue to adhere to Christ as *their* unique savior without having to insist that he is necessarily unique or *normative* for others'.[98] Belief in Christ's divinity is thus considered mythical. Hence, it

---

93 *CD* I/2, 63–4.

94 *CD* I/2, 38.

95 *CD* I/2, 41.

96 *CD* I/2, 138. We will discuss the important christological question of whether or not Jesus's humanity as such reveals in more detail later.

97 *CD* IV/2, 72.

98 Paul F. Knitter, *No Other Name? A Critical Survey of Christian Attitudes Toward the World Religions* (hereafter: *No Other Name?*) (Maryknoll, NY: Orbis, 1985), 149, emphasis mine. For more analysis and critique of Paul F. Knitter see Paul D. Molnar, 'Some Dogmatic Consequences of Paul F. Knitter's Unitarian

must be reinterpreted to get to the reality of Jesus. Hick believes it is understandable that early Christians spoke of the Father–Son relation and of Jesus's consubstantiality with the Father. However, this view is no longer possible today, he thinks, because it leads to all the 'uncomfortable "onlys" in Christian self-consciousness: Christ is the "only Savior" or the "only final norm" for all other religions.'[99] Thus, Hick concludes: 'The real point and value of the incarnational doctrine is not indicative but expressive, not to assert a metaphysical fact but to express a valuation and evoke an attitude.'[100] For Hick: 'Christians can declare that God is *truly* to be encountered in Jesus, but not *only* in Jesus ... Such a Christology lays the foundation not only for the possibility but the necessity of interreligious dialogue.'[101]

This is an almost classic contemporary expression of what Barth categorized as Ebionite Christology simply because both Knitter and Hick refuse to begin their thinking about Jesus Christ from the fact that Jesus himself is the unique incarnate Son of the Father. Thus, they refuse to acknowledge that he alone must be the proper object of thought in Christology. Instead, Paul Knitter and John Hick change the very nature of truth by arguing that Christians can accept Christ as unique and normative for themselves but not for others. What kind of

---

Theocentrism' in *The Thomist*, vol. 55, no. 3, (July 1991): 449–95 and *Incarnation and Resurrection*, 171–90.

99 Knitter, *No Other Name?*, 150.

100 Knitter, *No Other Name?*, 151. Also see John Hick, *The Metaphor of God Incarnate: Christology in a Pluralistic Age* (Louisville, KY: Westminster/ John Knox Press, 1993). Incarnation is a metaphor that describes in Jesus 'the ideal of human life lived in openness and response to God ... In so far as Jesus lived a life of self-giving love ... he "incarnated" a love that is a finite reflection of the infinite divine love' (105). This idea continues to express Hick's basic Ebionite view which is closely allied to his Docetic Christology which sees Jesus as one instance of divine love among others at work in the world. For Hick, no metaphysical claim can be made here because Jesus's being as God is nothing more than the expression of a personal value judgment, or a 'historical judgment' (110) on the part of people who saw in him a special human openness to God. Thus, for Hick, anyone could be an incarnation of God: 'To the extent that a man or a woman is to God what one's own hand is to oneself, to that extent God is "incarnate" in that human life' (106). For further discussion of John Hick's thinking, see Molnar, *Incarnation and Resurrection*, 243–60.

101 Knitter, *No Other Name?*, 152.

truth is it that is not objectively the same for every one? Paul Knitter explains that:

> Truth will no longer be identified by its ability to exclude or absorb others. *Rather, what is true will reveal itself mainly by its ability to relate to other expressions of truth and to grow through these relationships –* truth defined not by exclusion but by relation ... The new model reflects what our pluralistic world is discovering: no truth can stand alone; no truth can be totally unchangeable. Truth, by its very nature, needs other truth ... Truth, without 'other' truth, cannot be unique; it cannot exist ... the model of truth-through-relationship allows each religion to be unique ...[102]

This relativistic understanding of Christ and of truth follows from the fact that both theologians are uncomfortable in interreligious dialogue when it comes to acknowledging Christ's uniqueness precisely because they assume that the New Testament meant to affirm Christ's deity only in a mythological sense. That is to say Christians were only expressing the fact that they valued Jesus and they were trying to engender similar reactions in others. Thus Hick argues that the point of the incarnation was to express a valuation and evoke an attitude and definitely not to describe a metaphysical fact.[103] It is precisely the Ebionite assumption at work here that leads to Paul Knitter's nonnormative Christology, the hallmark of which, is to assert that Jesus is one savior among others.[104]

---

102 Knitter, *No Other Name?*, 219, some emphases mine.

103 Hick, *The Metaphor of God Incarnate*, 104ff.

104 See Knitter, *No Other Name?* 171ff. For Knitter, 'Jesus *is* unique, but with a uniqueness defined by its ability to relate to – that is, to include and be included by – other unique religious figures. Such an understanding of Jesus views him not as exclusive or even as normative but as *theocentric*, as a universally relevant manifestation (sacrament, incarnation) of divine revelation and salvation ... such a nonnormative, theocentric christology does not contradict the New Testament' (172). For Knitter, neither Christ's incarnation nor his resurrection are to be seen as 'one and only'. That is why other saviors are possible and necessary for him as well. It goes without saying that both his initial assumption and his further explanation of Jesus's supposed uniqueness are completely at variance with the New Testament witness which identifies Jesus himself as the 'way, and the truth, and the life' and thus as the only way to the Father (Jn. 14:6). See also Hick, *The Metaphor of God Incarnate*, 89–98

This particular Ebionite thinking has definite implications for how the resurrection itself is interpreted. Knitter argues that 'belief in the resurrection originated from a deeply personal faith experience, which can be described as a "revelation" or "conversion" experience'. Hence the appearance accounts and the empty tomb are seen 'as attempts to express and give more tangible form to these conversion experiences' and the New Testament account of the resurrection is seen 'as a richly mythic account ... of experiences that could never be photographed'. This leads Knitter to assert that the reality behind the Easter stories need not be limited to an experience of Jesus just because the particular conversion experience on the part of the disciples is not much different from the conversion or faith experiences of countless others after the deaths of their archetypal religious leaders. Consequently, in Paul Knitter's opinion, this fact shows that 'the resurrection of Jesus, in all its authentic mystery and power, does not necessarily imply "one and only"'.[105]

But has Knitter thought about Jesus's resurrection as attested in the New Testament at all with this analysis? Is Jesus's personal resurrection from the dead the factor determining what Knitter has to say about this matter? I am afraid the answer has to be that Paul Knitter has substituted the conversion or faith experiences of the disciples for the event which the gospels and Paul claim took place in the life of Jesus as the basis of their faith. Thus, for Knitter resurrection language is not only mythological but it describes an experience that is universally accessible without faith in the risen Jesus. It is this Ebionite thinking that leads him to believe first that what happened to Jesus could have happened to others and second, that who he is as the risen savior derives its significance from the impression he made on the disciples rather than from who he was and what he did in his own life history. Moreover, Knitter assumes that the origin from which resurrection

where he explicitly argues for 'Plural Incarnations'. Hick is not alone in this as Roger Haight, with his 'Spirit christology', claims 'it is not necessary to think that God as Spirit can be incarnated only once in history' (*Jesus: Symbol of God*, 456). John Macquarrie explains that he never 'understood why theologians have maintained that there could be only one incarnation' (*Jesus Christ*, 170); he believed that the idea of many savior figures makes sense as long as 'incarnation is not supposed to be an isolated event in Jesus Christ alone' (*Jesus Christ*, 421).

105 Knitter, *No Other Name?*, 198–200.

language sprang was a deeply personal faith experience or a conversion experience.[106]

This is in conflict with the New Testament understanding of the matter because in the Synoptics and in John and Paul the assumption is that the origin of their descriptions was the man Jesus himself who had risen from the dead and in his glorified existence really encountered the disciples during the Easter history as the Lord of history. As Barth put it: 'The Easter story, Christ truly, corporeally risen, and as such appearing to His disciples, talking with them, acting in their midst – this is, of course, the recollection upon which all New Testament recollections hang.'[107] 'What happened here according to the witness of the New Testament cannot, by its nature, cease to be, any more than it cannot yet exist. This witness has in view a being immune from dissolution and above the need of coming into being. And yet this being is the object of recollection.'[108] Indeed Barth astutely insists, in the doctrine of reconciliation, that attempts to explain Jesus's appearances with the notion of visions subjectively or even objectively interpreted (as, for instance, John Macquarrie and Moltmann do):

> Smacks … of an apologetic to explain away the mystery and miracle attested in the texts … The texts do not speak primarily of the formation of the Easter faith as such but of its foundation by Jesus Christ Himself, who met and talked with His disciples after His death as One who is alive (not outside the world but within it), who by this act of life convinced them incontrovertibly of the fact that He is alive and therefore of the fact that His death was the redemptive happening willed by God … its objectivity, not taking place in their faith but in

---

106 It should be noted that for John Hick, *The Metaphor of God Incarnate*, the resurrection refers 'to the transitional event or events in virtue of which the Jesus movement survived the death of its founder … Precisely what this transitional event was we cannot now discern with confidence' (23). This conclusion would have come as quite a surprise to Paul who argued that without Christ's resurrection, his preaching and their faith would be without substance (1 Cor. 15:14–15). In any case, Hick prefers to speak of 'an experience essentially similar to Paul … of a supernatural light' (24) instead of an actual event in the life of the historical Jesus which gave meaning to Paul's faith.

107 *CD* I/2, 114.

108 *CD* I/2, 115.

conflict with their lack of faith, overcoming and removing their lack of faith and creating their faith . . .'[109]

Contemporary Examples of Docetic Christology

What about contemporary examples of Docetic Christology? Remembering that Ebionite and Docetic Christology are closely connected and seem to run into each other, I will briefly discuss two examples. Gordon D. Kaufman is an almost classic example of Docetic Christology while Karl Rahner, though far more serious and orthodox than Kaufman, has what could be considered a Christology that more noticeably combines both the Ebionite and Docetic tendencies.

Gordon Kaufman

Gordon Kaufman explicitly maintains that, when speaking of Christ and salvation, the New Testament texts 'do not in fact refer exclusively to the man Jesus of Nazareth'. The term 'Christ' is sometimes applied to Jesus but other times applied to the community and its transformation. Thus, when Paul says that 'In Christ God was reconciling the world to himself' (2 Cor. 5:19) he cannot have meant that God's relationship to the world had changed in the man Jesus. For Kaufman this is unintelligible! Instead the term 'Christ' points us to the 'complex of events and new relationships that grew up in and around this man'. Therefore it is wrong to suggest that God was incarnate in this man since the New Testament meant to say that God was incarnate in the larger community, that is, in its spirit of love, freedom, mutual caring and forgiveness. 'It is in this new order of interpersonal relationships that the incarnation of God is to be found.'[110]

It is not surprising then that Kaufman thinks that Muslims and Jews were right in criticizing Christians for compromising God's absoluteness (oneness) with their erroneous belief in the deity of the man Jesus.[111] Kaufman therefore argues for what he terms this wider

---

109   *CD* IV/1, 340–1.

110   Kaufman, *IFM*, 382–3. For a fuller discussion of Kaufman's Christology, see Molnar, *Incarnation and Resurrection*, 191–213.

111   Kaufman, *IFM*, 392. See also *GMD*, 11 and 40. See also 119: 'From early on Jews and Muslims realized that Christians were falling into idolatrous attitudes toward Christ (and the church), and they criticized these in the name

Christology. He believes it will have the advantage of avoiding Christian chauvinism and the oppression and weirdness associated with the archaic traditional belief in the incarnation. For Kaufman then 'the humaneness of God – the tendency toward the human and the humane (toward "Christ") in the ultimate nature of things – has existed from the very beginning'. So the term 'Christ' refers to 'this new order of human relationships' and this provides a perspective to discover 'the direction in which the evolutionary-historical process … has been moving from its beginning'.[112]

Christians reconceived the ideals of justice, love and peace 'in the light of the vision of the human and the humane which had become visible in Christ'. For Kaufman, 'Any reification of Christ … into a kind of absolute standard to which all human ideas and values and conduct must conform is clearly a confusion and mistake which should be forth-rightly rejected today.' Any belief that Jesus is the 'only begotten son of God' is to be rejected as false reification.[113]

The obvious problem with this thinking is both its Ebionite and Docetic perspectives. On the one hand Kaufman really believes that Christian recognition of Christ's deity represents the objectification of Christian self-consciousness and the projection of certain attitudes such as triumphalism onto what he calls the story of the man Jesus who simply suffered for others. Such an Ebionite stance prevents him from acknowledging that Jesus Christ himself is utterly unique in such a way that his uniqueness is in no way grounded in the community's response to him. On the other hand, Kaufman is clearly re-defining who Jesus really was as reported in the New Testament in order to make him conform to his own process idea of divinity which sees God as a 'ser-endipitous creativity' at work in the world. Thus Jesus is seen by him as one manifestation of divine love among others and indeed the term 'Christ' itself is not dictated by who Jesus was and is, but by a wider Christology that is defined by the community's ideas of God and the process of humaneness that it thinks it has found in Jesus. However, like all Docetic Christology it is not bound to Jesus, the man from Nazareth. It can equally make these assertions from the perspective of many other

of the One High God. But to this day most Christians have failed to acknowledge this quite proper theological critique of the ways in which they employed their central religious symbols'.

112 Kaufman, *IFM*, 387–8.
113 Kaufman, *IFM*, 390–1.

religions and even from the perspective of humanism itself as Kaufman himself insists. Unfortunately, Kaufman's perspective leads him to conclude that 'the resurrection was preeminently an event in the *history of meaning*'[114] rather than an event in the life of Jesus. Of course, the meaning is identical with the transformations evident within the community of faith.

Karl Rahner

In *Foundations of Christian Faith* Rahner begins his Christology by calling attention to the fact that there is an 'anonymous Christianity'. By this he means that anyone can be a 'justified person who lives in the grace of Christ' even if that person has no specific, historical contact with 'the explicit preaching of Christianity'. Such a person 'possesses God's supernatural self-communication in grace not only as an offer, not only as an existential of his existence; he has also accepted this offer and so he has really accepted what is essential in what Christianity wants to mediate to him: his salvation in that grace which objectively is the grace of Jesus Christ'.[115]

It is extremely significant that Rahner began his theology in *Foundations* insisting that we cannot start our thinking with Jesus Christ. Although Rahner notes that the Second Vatican Council said that theologians should be introduced to the mystery of Christ right at the beginning of their study, he wishes to avoid a

> *too narrowly Christological approach* ... [because] a too narrow concentration of the foundational course on Jesus Christ as the key and the solution to all existential problems and as the total foundation of faith would be too simple a conception ... Today Jesus Christ is himself a problem ... Why and in what sense may one risk his life in faith in this concrete Jesus of Nazareth ...? This is what has to be justified. Hence we cannot begin with Jesus Christ as the absolute and final datum, but we must begin further back than that.[116]

So where does Rahner choose to begin? He begins with 'a knowledge of God which is not mediated completely by an encounter with Jesus

---

114 *ST*, 433.
115 *FCF*, 176.
116 *FCF*, 13.

Christ.[117] He begins with our transcendental experience which he claims mediates an 'unthematic and anonymous … knowledge of God'.[118] He thus claims that knowledge of God is always present unthematically to anyone reflecting on themselves so that all talk about God 'always only points to this transcendental experience as such, an experience in which he whom we call "God" encounters man in silence … as the absolute and the incomprehensible, as the term of his transcendence'.[119] This term of 'transcendence' Rahner eventually calls a holy mystery because he believes that whenever this experience of transcendence is an experience of love, its term is the God of Christian revelation.[120]

It is worth noting that Rahner does not insist, as Barth does, that true knowledge of God begins only at the place where God has freely made himself known, that is, where God has become 'God for us'. For Barth, as we have already seen, any attempt to begin theology by bypassing Jesus Christ, true God and true man, means that we have failed to acknowledge revelation in its uniqueness. It means the failure to recognize grace as grace. It is amazing that Rahner, who is so famous for having re-oriented Catholic theology toward the importance of the doctrine of the Trinity, has himself methodologically ignored the most significant point of that doctrine completely. Instead of allowing his thought about God and Christ to be governed by the Father of Jesus Christ known in faith through the Holy Spirit, Rahner begins with transcendental experience. This Ebionite starting point leads to his conclusions about Christ and grace which are disastrous just because they manifest all the difficulties associated with Ebionite and Docetic Christology.

In connection with his view of the incarnation, Rahner understands God first as 'that nameless mystery which is the vehicle of all understanding' and 'the incomprehensible mystery – which is … the

---

117 *FCF*, 13.

118 *FCF*, 21.

119 *FCF*, 21.

120 For more on this see Paul D. Molnar, 'Is God Essentially Different From His Creatures? Rahner's Explanation From Revelation,' in *The Thomist*, vol. 51, no. 4 (October, 1987): 575–631 and Chapter 5. We have already seen how Elizabeth Johnson exploits the expression 'holy mystery' in Chapter 1. For a discussion of Rahner's understanding of unthematic or prethematic knowledge of God and how it relates to the thinking of Barth and Torrance who explicitly reject what they call nonobjective or nonconceptual knowledge of God, see Molnar, *Faith, Freedom and the Spirit*, Chapter 1.

condition of possibility of grasping and comprehending anything, the all-encompassing incomprehensibility of the Whole, no matter how it is named.'[121] By contrast, Barth argued that the content of revelation cannot be separated from the form: 'The form here is essential to the content, that is, God is unknown as our Father, as the Creator, to the degree that He is not made known by Jesus.'[122] Clearly, Rahner's abstract understanding of God as the term of our transcendental dynamisms yields a concept of God that is at variance with the very heart of what is or should be understood in light of the trinitarian self-revelation of God the Father. Although Barth is today frequently criticized for over-stressing the *analogia entis* as a problem, the fact is that it is the *analogia entis* or the attempt to find God apart from Christ that really is the problem here.

Beginning with our unthematic experience, Rahner is led to con-clude, in his treatment of the incarnation, that self-acceptance is the same as accepting Christ. Answering his own question about what it means to say that God became man Rahner says: 'Man ... is ... an inde-finability come to consciousness of itself' and indeed one can only say what man is by describing what he is concerned with 'and what is con-cerned with him', that is, 'the boundless, the nameless'.[123] Since we are a mystery in this way, Rahner concludes that 'Our whole existence is the acceptance or rejection of the mystery which we are'.[124] What could be a more logical conclusion once one assumes that our confession of Christ is grounded in our transcendental experience? In fact in his Christology in *Foundations* Rahner insists that transcendental theology 'must develop in a general ontology and anthropology an a priori doc-trine of the God-Man, and in this way try to construct the conditions which make possible a genuine capacity to hear the historical message of Jesus Christ'.[125] In his mind this then is joined with the historical testimony regarding Jesus's life, death and resurrection. Rahner insists that such an a priori doctrine could not in fact be developed prior to the actual appearance of the God-man or prior to an encounter with him.

But given the facts that Rahner believes in an anonymous Christianity, that he rejects a too narrowly christological starting point, and he begins Christology in Ebionite fashion with transcendental experience,

121 Karl Rahner, 'On the Theology of the Incarnation', *TI* 4, 106.
122 *CD* I/1, 390.
123 *TI* 4, 107–8.
124 *TI* 4, 108.
125 *FCF*, 176–7.

how can Rahner possibly avoid reducing theology to anthropology? I believe he cannot. For in the end, Rahner argues that 'the transcendence which we are and which we accomplish brings our existence and God's existence together: and both as mystery'.[126] In this respect, Rahner believes that in light of this understanding of our indefinable human nature we can better understand the incarnation. When God assumes this human nature then it 'simply arrived at the point to which it always strives by virtue of its essence'.[127] Human nature must disappear Rahner says into the incomprehensible. This happens, strictly speaking, 'when the nature which surrenders itself to the mystery of the fullness belongs so little to itself that it becomes the nature of God himself. The incarnation of God is therefore the unique, *supreme*, case of the total actualization of human reality, which consists of the fact that man *is* in so far as he gives up himself'.[128] It is difficult to avoid the conclusion that on the one hand Rahner is suggesting that the incarnation is the result of the human achievement of ultimate self-transcendence.[129] On the other hand it is hard to avoid the conclusion that Jesus is only the highest instance of this anthropological achievement.[130] The former insight is almost classically Ebionite while the latter insight is almost classically

126 *TI* 4, 108.

127 *TI* 4, 109.

128 *TI* 4, 109–10.

129 After explaining how Rahner's theology of the symbol influences his view of the incarnation, one Rahner commentator actually writes: 'In the light of Rahner's evolutionary view of Christology, this process wherein the Word becomes flesh is identical with the process wherein flesh becomes the Word of God' William V. Dych, S.J., *Karl Rahner* (Collegeville, MN: The Liturgical Press, 1992), 79.

130 This is why Colin Gunton criticizes Rahner's Christology as a form of *degree* Christology. See Colin E. Gunton, *Yesterday and Today: A Study of Continuities in Christology* (Grand Rapids, MI: Eerdmans, 1983), 15ff. See also Molnar, *Incarnation and Resurrection*, 68ff. Though John Hick, *The Metaphor of God Incarnate*, differs from Rahner by explicitly rejecting Chalcedonian Christology, his is also a degree Christology: 'We are not speaking of something that is in principle unique, but of an interaction of the divine and the human which occurs in many different ways and degrees in all human openness to God's presence' (109). John Macquarrie explicitly adopts a degree Christology (*Jesus Christ*, 361) while Roger Haight employs his Spirit Christology to embrace a degree Christology as well (*Jesus: Symbol of God*, 463–4). See also Molnar, *Incarnation and Resurrection*, 164ff. and 238f.

Docetic because the former suggests the apotheosis of a man while the latter suggests that it is Rahner's idea of God as the mysterious nameless incomprehensible Whole that determines his thought about Jesus.

Therefore, the problem with Rahner's thinking is enormous. He believes that the incarnation must be the end and 'not the starting point of all Christological reflection' since that starting point 'lies in an encounter with the historical Jesus';[131] yet he argues that God's revelation or self-communication 'in the depths of the spiritual person is an a priori determination coming from grace and is in itself unreflexive ... it is not something known objectively, but something within the realm of consciousness'. This is what Rahner calls transcendental revelation, that is, 'God's gift of himself, the gratuitously elevated determination of man'.[132] It is mediated categorically because we exist in history; but it is not identical with this categorical knowledge. This 'non-objective and unreflexive self-revelation in grace must always be present as mediated in objective and reflexive knowledge'.[133]

Given these presuppositions, Rahner is literally unable to conceptualize the two things that were most important to Barth – the two things that in my opinion acknowledge grace as grace and the incarnation as a free miraculous and utterly unexpected act of God for us.

1. *His thinking does not reflect the fact that revelation is an exception and a miracle and thus the occurrence of something utterly new in history.* This failure leads to a very odd interpretation of the resurrection

---

131 *FCF*, 177. While Rahner wants to hold together his 'ascending Christology' (Christology from below) with a 'descending Christology' (Christology from above), it is significant that, at this point in his reflections he writes that: 'If Jesus as the Christ has ever actually encountered someone, the *idea* of a God-Man ... and hence a descending Christology, also has its own significance and power' (*FCF*, 177, emphasis mine). Is it enough to speak of the idea of a God-Man arising from an encounter with Jesus? Must we not speak of Jesus himself as uniquely divine and human from the outset and thus as one for whom there is no analogy in our experiences on the basis of which he can be recognized and discussed in his factual uniqueness as the incarnate Word? And if that is so, as I believe it is, then Rahner's 'searching Christology' is shown to be little more than a search for the 'idea' of a savior and to that extent merely a reflection of our own anthropological a priori perspective.

132 *FCF*, 172.

133 *FCF*, 173.

as 'an inevitable part of the interpretation of my existence imposed on my freedom ... The message of Jesus' resurrection says in addition that his definitive identity, the identity of his bodily history, has victoriously and irreversibly reached perfection in God'.[134] Thus Rahner actually believed that 'the knowledge of man's resurrection given with his transcendentally necessary hope is a statement of philosophical anthropology even before any real revelation in the Word'.[135] Such a statement clearly reflects the fact that for Rahner it is our transcendental experience of hope that is the determining factor in his thinking and not the man Jesus who rose from the dead and enabled the disciples' faith.[136] It could hardly be otherwise because, as one Rahner commentator puts it: 'Faith sees meaning and significance in the data which history provides, and sees it in an act of recognition of that for which it had been searching'.[137] Thus, for Rahner, without a transcendental experience of hope, it would be impossible for us to share in the disciples' experience of the risen Jesus. Objective and subjective elements are here mutually dependent.

Indeed one of Rahner's own disciples, Dermot Lane, attempts to deal with the resurrection by following Rahner and concludes that we cannot be overly objective or overly subjective in our interpretation of the resurrection. So, attempting to avoid what he views as a kind of fundamentalism on the one hand and Bultmann's reduction of the Easter event to the rise of faith on the other, Lane formulates the view, based on an interpersonal model of a 'person-to-person transforming experience' that 'The issue here cannot be reduced to either "faith creates resurrection" or "resurrection creates faith". Rather, these are *intrinsically* related dimensions of the *same transforming experience*'.[138] And Lane

134 Karl Rahner and Karl–Heinz Weger, *Our Christian Faith: Answers for the Future*, trans. Francis McDonagh (hereafter: *Our Christian Faith*) (New York: Crossroad, 1981), 111.

135 *TI* 17, 18.

136 For more on this see Chapter 7 for how Thomas F. Torrance and Karl Rahner interpret the resurrection differently because of their contrasting understanding of God's self-communication in Christ. See also Molnar, *Incarnation and Resurrection*, Chapters 2 and 4.

137 William V. Dych, S.J., *Karl Rahner*, 56.

138 See Dermot A. Lane, *The Reality of Jesus* (hereafter: *The Reality*) (New York, Paulist Press, 1975), 60–1, emphasis mine. Compare this to

really believes that this obvious confusion of "cause" (resurrection) and "effect" (the apostles' experiences of the risen Lord) adequately presents the resurrection as the actual foundation of the church and the sacraments. This finally leads to his belief that what happened in Christ's death and resurrection was already anticipated in our experiences of the world. Thus, the resurrection is seen as reasonable:

> Is it not reasonable to ask whether there is any point within the history of mankind in which these deeply-rooted aspirations and hopes of mankind have been fulfilled and realised? ... Within such an horizon the resurrection appears not as some exception or isolated incident but rather as the *realisation and crystallisation of man's deepest aspirations* ... nor is it a violation of the laws of nature ... the resurrection is, in the case of Jesus, the full realisation and actual fulfilment of those *seeds of indestructibility* which exist within the heart of every individual.[139]

Rahner: 'There is such a thing as Easter faith. Those possessing it are beyond all reckoning. It is present first in the disciples of Jesus, and the witness *which they bear to their Easter experience* and their Easter faith is to acknowledge him who was crucified ... It may be that we of today cannot draw any clear distinction within the Easter event as understood here between Easter itself (precisely the fact of the risen Christ) and the Easter experience of the disciples ... In the case of Jesus' disciples their Easter faith and their Easter experience (their belief and the grounds for that belief) are already blended into each other indissolubly', *TI* 7, 164, emphasis mine.

139 Lane, *The Reality*, 64, emphasis mine. Closely allied with this thinking is Rahner's view that understanding the resurrection means that one yearns for one's own resurrection because 'on any true anthropology, he can only understand himself as a man who hopes for that which is described in terms of resurrection' (*TI* 11, 213). From this Rahner concludes that this means such a person 'has also achieved an *a priori* perspective such that ... it does justify him in believing in such a thing as the Resurrection of Jesus, i.e. in accepting the Easter experience of the disciples' (*TI* 11, 213). The question that must be asked here is: Can any anthropological a priori perspective justify belief in Jesus's resurrection without undermining the fact that the only justification for such belief is the risen Lord himself empowering people to recognize him and acknowledge him – first the disciples and after his ascension, others who never directly met him, through the power of his Holy Spirit? For a discussion of this as it relates to Rahner's theology see Molnar, *Incarnation and Resurrection*, 61ff.

It is obvious from this reasoning that the seeds of indestructibility within the heart of every person are the basis of and foundation for both the reality of and meaning of Jesus's own resurrection. The horizon, constructed on this foundation, leads to a denial of the miraculous element in the resurrection of Jesus; it blurs the distinction between his activity and our experiences and aspirations; and finally it makes Jesus's resurrection a particular instance of the general experience of hope found within everyone.

2. *Rahner's thinking does not allow for the fact that revelation, which is identical with Jesus Christ, actually causes offense.* It is not something for which we have any a priori capacity whatsoever just because it is and remains identical with the risen Christ. And when revelation is accepted for what it really is, then we actually know that we lack this capacity. However, Rahner insists upon this capacity just because of his belief that we have an obediential potency and a supernatural existential, which structure his notion of transcendental revelation. This very belief is the motor that runs his transcendental method. Thus these categories compel him to reflect first upon human experience, which he assumes is an experience of God and of Christ, and only then upon the meaning of revelation. Rahner's conclusions are more than a little problematic.

First, he concludes that revelation is at least in some sense identical with our transcendental dynamisms. Hence, Rahner conceives the universal offer of grace as 'always and everywhere and primarily to the transcendentality of man as such' which is accepted and justifying 'when this transcendentality of man is accepted and sustained by man's freedom'. Indeed, Rahner believes that 'the universality of the factuality of grace from the outset [is] ... an existential of man's transcendentality as such'.[140] These beliefs undergird his anonymous Christianity, but given what we have shown earlier, it also confuses the universal Lordship of the man Jesus with our own transcendental experience and thus allows Rahner to direct us to accept ourselves instead of directing us away from ourselves toward Christ. This was exactly the conclusion that Barth sought to avoid and actually did avoid by defining and rejecting both Ebionite and Docetic Christology; such thinking in the end is both Pelagian and compromises Christ's uniqueness.

140 *TI* 18, 182.

Second, Rahner concludes that Christology and anthropology are mutually conditioning because he will not begin his Christology with 'the Church's official Christology as such', that is, with the Church's acknowledgment of Jesus as the eternal Word of God. As Rahner puts it:

> We are not starting out from the Christological formulations of the New Testament in Paul and John ... we are not assuming the impossibility of going behind such a 'late' New Testament Christology to ask about a more original and somewhat more simple experience of faith with the historical Jesus, in his message, his death, and his achieved finality that we describe as his resurrection.[141]

He really believes his starting point in transcendental experience, with what he calls a 'questing Christology', will lead to what the Church teaches regarding Jesus. Since for Rahner 'all theology is ... eternally an anthropology'[142] he believes that 'Christology is the end and beginning of anthropology'[143] and that 'anthropology and Christology mutually determine each other within Christian dogmatics if they are both correctly understood'.[144] By contrast, Barth argued that 'there is a way from Christology to anthropology, but there is no way from anthropology to Christology'.[145] Indeed, Barth consistently insisted that there was an order of priority or rank that remained even in the incarnation because he started and ended his reflections with the man Jesus who was the Word incarnate. Thus, the relationship between grace and nature remained an irreversible one that was not conditioned by human belief or unbelief. Further, Barth believed that the incarnation was best understood by saying that the Logos assumed flesh while Rahner believed that the Logos 'empties himself' because God expresses himself. This validates Rahner's belief that the humanity as such is God's self-utterance; but Barth believed that 'one cannot subsequently speak christologically, if Christology has not already been presupposed at the outset, and in its stead other presuppositions have claimed one's attention'.[146] Barth's entire attack on natural theology was his attempt to say that we have real knowledge of God and real communion with God

141   *TI* 18, 145.
142   *TI* 4, 116.
143   *TI* 4, 117.
144   *TI* 9, 28.
145   *CD* I/1, 131.
146   *CD* I/2, 123.

only in Christ because in him God was ready for us and in him we are no longer at enmity with God as we are when we try to live apart from Christ.[147]

147 *CD* II/1, 149ff. Thus, while Rahner is in search of an a priori anthropology on the basis of which he can make sense of Jesus Christ, Barth unequivocally and consistently insists that: 'If we look past Jesus Christ, if we speak of anyone else but Him, if our praise of man is not at once praise of Jesus Christ, the romance and illusions begin again' and it again becomes impossible to speak of 'the man who is ready for God in life and in truth'. For Barth no one in himself or herself 'as such' is ready for God. As sinners we have no aptitude for God. That is what was and is revealed by Jesus Christ who, as the eternal Son of God, participated in our enmity against God in becoming flesh for our sakes and in that way he experienced God's judgment in our place and enabled and as eternal high-priest enables our human knowledge of God through participating in the Son's knowledge of the Father (*CD* II/1, 151–2). Perhaps it would be helpful here to consider R. Kendall Soulen's critique of Barth for having a 'blind spot' with regard to natural theology. Soulen thinks that the Nicene Creed authorizes 'three patterns of naming to identify' the three persons of the Trinity: (1) 'A pattern characterized by the oblique reference to the Tetragrammaton'; (2) 'A pattern characterized by the vocabulary of Father, Son, and Holy Spirit'; and (3) 'A pattern characterized by the open-ended multiplicity of names'. He thinks of these three patterns as 'theological, christological and pneumatological' claiming that in the Nicene Creed 'the three patterns are clearly distinct, intimately related, and equally important' (*The Divine Name(s) and the Holy Trinity: Distinguishing the Voices Volume One* [Louisville, KY: Westminster John Knox Press, 2011], 120). From Barth's perspective, this portrayal of patterns for naming the triune God is inherently problematic, however, from within the perspective of the Nicene Creed since, for the Creed, theology is shaped precisely by who God is in Jesus Christ his only begotten Son who is (against Arianism) true God from true God, begotten and not made. This means that to think about God the Father, one must as Athanasius insisted, think about the Father through the Son. As T. F. Torrance rightly argues, for Athanasius knowledge of the Holy Spirit is controlled by knowledge of the Son since all three persons of the Trinity are *homoousios*. Therefore, to suggest that it might be appropriate, on pneumatological grounds, to name God as Soulen does, using an open-ended 'multiplicity' of names leads directly to the idea that such names do not have to be controlled by who God *is* in his incarnate Word. Then one could claim to be speaking pneumatologically and theologically without allowing one's thinking to be shaped by who God is in Jesus Christ, that is, one could claim that one is speaking of the God of the Nicene

Third, Rahner concludes that one can be a Christian without specifically hearing about Christ or knowing him; but for Barth one cannot believe in the God of Christian faith without knowing about him through the articles of the creed which specifically refer to the Father, the Son and the Holy Spirit. As Barth put it:

> What gives faith its seriousness and power is not that man makes a decision, nor even the way in which he makes it … On the contrary, faith lives by its *object*. It lives by the call to which it responds … The seriousness and the power of faith are the seriousness and power of the *truth*, which is identical with God Himself, and which the believer has heard and received in the form of definite truths, in the form of articles of faith … In believing, man obeys by his decision the decision of God.[148]

faith while referring to God as 'nameless'. Such a view in reality undercuts the point of the Nicene Creed which identifies God as Father, Son and Holy Spirit. In reality we are baptized in the name of the Father, Son and Holy Spirit and not in the name of the 'nameless'. Relying on these patterns of naming, Soulen makes the following strange assertion: 'On the Reformation side, the vaunted imperative of naming God exclusively from "revelation" continuously obscures the fact that it has pleased God to make "revelation" unintelligible apart from the church's reliance on intellectual resources that belong to the wider culture' (122). Based on this assertion Barth's opposition to natural theology is deemed to be a 'blind spot'. Unfortunately, however, Soulen has missed the most important aspect of Barth's thinking, which is that, in light of the doctrine of justification by faith, we are utterly reliant on God alone and God always to make himself intelligible to us by grace and through faith. For Barth, this meant above all that the church does not rely on intellectual resources from the wider culture for the intelligibility of 'revelation', but only on the actual revelation of God in his Word and Spirit as God speaks his Word to us through the scriptural witness and through theological thinking that is obedient to that specific revelation using categories and intellectual resources of the wider culture in specific circumstances. So the church is free to use a variety of intellectual resources in thinking about revelation. However, those resources are never what make revelation intelligible; only God can do that. Barth's theological epistemology is built precisely on that point since he insists that it is nothing in our knowing that enables us to know God because true knowledge of God comes about not through our knowing but by God enabling that knowing in faith and through our obedience to the Word heard and believed.

148 Karl Barth, *Credo*, trans. Robert McAfee Brown (New York: Charles Scribner's Sons, 1962), 2.

For Barth a person

> might suppose himself appointed and able to set divinity in motion
> in his life, or possibly to create it ... Such presumptuous faith might
> befit a pious Hindu ... but it should not represent itself as Christian
> faith [which] occurs in the *encounter* of the believer with him in
> whom he believes. It consists in communion, not in identification
> with him.[149]

Fourth, Rahner believes that self-acceptance in our transcendental
experience is the same as acceptance of God and Christ. Thus:

> Anyone therefore, no matter how remote from any revelation
> formulated in words, who accepts his existence, that is, his humanity
> ... in quiet patience, or better, in faith, hope and love – no matter
> what he calls them, and accepts it *as* the mystery which hides itself in
> the mystery of eternal love and bears life in the womb of death: such
> a one says yes to something which really is such as his boundless
> confidence hopes it to be, because God has in fact filled it with the
> infinite, that is, with himself, since the Word was made flesh. He says
> yes to Christ, even when he does not know that he does ... Anyone
> who accepts his own humanity in full ... has accepted the son of
> Man ...[150]

Here the container concept of space determines Rahner's view in
accordance with his theology of the symbol and thus tends to compromise God's freedom with the inference that human nature can be
filled with divine grace and that the humanity of Jesus is filled with
the Logos in its self-emptying or self-expression, as a symbol is full

---

149 Barth, *Evangelical Theology*, 99. For a full discussion of how the object
of faith shapes Barth's thinking about the truth of theology and how this relates
in detail to Rahner's perspective, see Molnar, *Faith, Freedom and the Spirit*,
Chapter 1. It should be very clear from what has been said here, however, that
Rahner's theory of anonymous Christianity subverts Barth's understanding of
faith as tied explicitly to Jesus himself always and everywhere. It is not too much
to say that the idea of anonymous Christians both leads toward and follows
from the idea that a too narrow focus on Jesus Christ as, in Rahner's words, 'the
total foundation of faith would be too simple a conception' *FCF*, 13 and above.

150 *TI* 4, 119. Joseph Cardinal Ratzinger, *Principles of Catholic Theology:
Building Stones for a Fundamental Theology*, trans. Sister Mary Frances

of the thing symbolized.[151] For Rahner, Jesus is the supreme symbolic presence of God in history, and because of the nature of symbolic reality, 'the finite itself has been given an infinite depth and is no longer a contrast to the infinite, but that which the infinite himself has become'.[152] This is the basis of Rahner's assertion that Jesus, in his humanity as such, is the revealer and it stands in stark contrast with Barth's consistent emphasis on the fact that our lives are hidden with Christ in God – really hidden.[153]

Thus, Barth argues that God separates himself from us in uniting himself to us in Christ and that Jesus's humanity actually conceals his uniqueness as the Son of God and that this must be miraculously revealed or unveiled by God himself if we are truly to know it at any given time. Barth thus rejected the idea that Jesus in his humanity as such reveals because he does not believe that God's majesty is diminished in the incarnation and he believes that created reality is not infinitely extended by virtue of the incarnation because Christ remains distinct from the rest of history as one who is utterly unique. Barth argues that we participate in the person and work of Jesus Christ only through the power of the Holy Spirit and only in faith and by grace.[154]

McCarthy, S.N.D. (San Francisco: Ignatius Press, 1987), astutely argues that this very thinking compromises the newness of Christianity by resolving the particular into the universal and by reducing 'Christian liberation into pseudoliberation … Self-acceptance – just being human – is all that is required [to be a Christian]' (167). Ratzinger properly rejects this kind of thinking as a type of rationalism that fails to come to grips with the particularity of Christianity that calls for conversion and not self-acceptance. As noted above, Moltmann rightly criticized this aspect of Rahner's thinking as well. In its own way such thinking reduces theology to anthropology. For more on this issue see Chapters 5, 6 and 7.

151 *TI* 4, 239, 251. See Chapters 5 and 6 for more on this point. For a discussion of the difficulties bequeathed to theologians with the 'container concept' of space, see Molnar, *Torrance: Theologian of the Trinity*, 124–35. See also, Molnar, *Incarnation and Resurrection*, 90–6.

152 *TI* 4, 117.

153 Barth writes: 'In Christian doctrine, and therefore in the doctrine of the knowledge and knowability of God, we have always to take in blind seriousness the basic Pauline perception of Colossians 3:3 which is that of all Scripture – that our life is our life hid with Christ in God' (*CD* II/1, 149).

154 Thus, 'the Holy Spirit is the temporal presence of the Jesus Christ who intercedes for us eternally in full truth … life in the Holy Spirit is the life of

Conclusion

Karl Barth is still criticized today for overdoing his attack on an *analogia entis*, which he supposedly invented to some degree in order to attack it. Yet, what Barth was trying to avoid in his rejection of the *analogia entis* was *any* attempt to understand God which bypassed Jesus Christ as the *only* possible starting point. This procedure denies and subverts God's grace and thus manifests the fact that fallen humanity is indeed in conflict with grace and revelation. This is the real problem that affects much modern Christology, and I believe that Barth's original development of what he labeled Ebionite and Docetic Christology helps us to see a bit more clearly through this problem today by focusing on Jesus himself and on no one and nothing else in order to understand that God really is 'for us'. Since it is God himself who is 'for us' we must make a deliberate and sharp distinction between the immanent and economic Trinity,[155] a distinction that Rahner and many who follow

faith. Faith does not consist in an inward and immanent transformation of man, although there can be no faith without such a transformation ... as the work of the Holy Spirit it is man's new birth from God, on the basis of which man can already live here by what he is there [in Christ's eternal representing us before his Father] in Jesus Christ and therefore in truth' (*CD* II/1, 158). Barth was always clear that the proper answer as to our human ability to know and love God can only be given in faith, but such an answer, he insisted, 'does not start from the believing man but from Jesus Christ as the object and foundation of faith' (*CD* II/1, 156).

155 As George Hunsinger helpfully indicates, Karl Barth continued to make this 'sharp distinction' in *CD* IV/2 (*Reading Barth with Charity*, 124) when he spoke of the fact that divine and human essence can only be properly understood 'in a sharp distinction and even antithesis'. He argued for that same deliberate and sharp distinction between the immanent and economic Trinity earlier as well in order to maintain the free basis that our relations with God have in God himself saying, in opposition to Bultmann, that 'it is not just good sense but absolutely essential that along with the older theology we make a deliberate and sharp distinction between the Trinity of God as we may know it in the Word of God revealed, written and proclaimed, and God's immanent Trinity, i.e., between "God in Himself" and "God for us"' (*CD* I/1, 172). This statement was not made in order to suggest that God remains aloof from us. Rather, it was made to assert that the God who acts for us in the history of Jesus Christ and in the outpouring of his Holy Spirit is truly God whose actions are free actions of love and must not be seen as necessary for his eternal being or as conditioning

him do not make. The consequences of this were discussed throughout this chapter. In the next chapter we will see exactly how a number
of prominent contemporary theologians wrestle with the implications
of Christ's pretemporal existence as this relates to the doctrine of the
immanent Trinity. It will be my contention that any outright rejection
of a *Logos asarkos* would compromise God's freedom with the implication that the economy, rather than God himself, defines his eternal
being. One of those theologians, Robert Jenson, accepts Rahner's axiom
of identity and goes beyond what Rahner would have maintained in
order to understand the person and work of Christ. As a result of that,
his failure to properly distinguish the immanent and economic Trinity
leads him to compromise God's freedom and to misunderstand some
key aspects of Christology in ways similar to Rahner. However, he is
not alone. With many others, Bruce McCormack blurs the distinction
between the immanent and the economic Trinity by failing to appreciate the function of the *Logos asarkos* in Barth's theology. It will be
instructive to see exactly how failure to appreciate the proper relation
between the immanent and economic Trinity affects many aspects of
theology, including how to understand Christ's humanity, his resurrection, his relation with the church and the proper relation between time
and eternity.[156]

his eternal being. This could never be seen as a pretext for separating the
immanent and economic Trinity as some readers have mistakenly supposed.

156 Additional discussion of those who do not appreciate the proper
function of the *Logos asarkos* in Barth's theology will be provided in the next
chapter and can be seen as well in Molnar, *Faith, Freedom and the Spirit*.

Chapter 3

CHRISTOLOGY, RESURRECTION, ELECTION AND THE TRINITY: THE PLACE OF THE *LOGOS ASARKOS* IN CONTEMPORARY THEOLOGY

We begin this chapter noting that because the relevance of the *Logos asarkos* is so important to a proper understanding of the relation of the immanent and economic Trinity it would be helpful to begin by considering an influential contemporary proposal that will open the door to a wider analysis and critique of the theology of Robert Jenson with the help of distinctions made by Karl Barth. That proposal was made by Bruce McCormack. It has been some 15 years since McCormack first made his suggestion that Barth should have logically reversed the doctrines of election and the Trinity because he believed that such a reversal would make his theology more consistent. Much ink has been spilled discussing the role of the *Logos asarkos* in Barth's theology and in trinitarian theology in general. Some have argued that the idea of a *Logos asarkos* is sheer idolatry.[1] Others see a limited role for the *Logos asarkos*, while others think that for Barth it was merely a 'placeholder' for the humanity that would be assumed in the incarnation.[2] An extensive literature developed around this issue.[3] I will not reiterate the many ideas that were developed in the course of these publications. They are

---

1 See Benjamin Myers, 'Election, Trinity, and the History of Jesus: Reading Barth with Rowan Williams', in *Trinitarian Theology After Barth*, ed. Myk Habets and Phillip Tolliday (Eugene, OR: Pickwick Publications, 2011), 121–37, at 130–3. From this Myers erroneously concludes that Jesus is 'the one who (so to speak) makes God God' (Myers, 133). See also Molnar, *Faith, Freedom and the Spirit*, 138–49 and Chapter 4.

2 Darren O. Sumner, *Karl Barth and the Incarnation: Christology and the Humility of God* (hereafter: *Karl Barth and the Incarnation*) (London: Bloomsbury T & T Clark, 2014), 81–4 uses this concept to argue against the idea of a *Logos asarkos* and for the idea that this is simply a placeholder for Jesus of Nazareth.

3 See, for example, *Trinity and Election in Contemporary Theology* ed. Michael T. Dempsey (Grand Rapids, MI: Eerdmans, 2011); Kevin W. Hector,

available for anyone to study. What I would like to do here is simply show that whenever the *Logos asarkos* is disregarded, marginalized or even banished from consideration, such a move can be seen as an indicator of some sort of confusion of the immanent and economic Trinity, with disastrous results. It must be noted here, however, that while Barth did strongly criticize the *Logos asarkos* because, as George Hunsinger has pointed out, it 'had no role to play in our coming to know God'; any attempt to establish such a role in the end would amount to the pursuit of some sort of natural theology, which Barth rejected. In reality, we are granted to 'share in God's own self-knowledge as Father, Son and Holy Spirit' only through the Word who was made flesh and not through the *Logos asarkos*. Hence, 'the only form of the divine Word to which we had access was the incarnate Word, Jesus Christ'.[4] Nonetheless, Hunsinger rightly insisted that for Barth there still was a role for the *Logos asarkos* because he continued to affirm the *extra Calvinisticum* and thus he believed that in the incarnation 'the Word was totally but

'God's Triunity and Self-Determination: A Conversation with Karl Barth, Bruce McCormack, and Paul Molnar', *IJST*, vol. 7, no. 3 (2005): 246–61; George Hunsinger, 'Election and the Trinity: Twenty-Five Theses on the Theology of Karl Barth', *Modern Theology*, vol. 24, no. 2 (April 2008): 179–83; George Hunsinger, *Reading Barth with Charity: A Hermeneutical Proposal* (Grand Rapids, MI: Baker Academic, 2015); Bruce L. McCormack, 'Election and the Trinity: Theses in Response to George Hunsinger', *SJT*, vol. 63, no. 2 (2010): 203–24; McCormack, 'Seek God Where He May be Found: A Response to Edwin Chr. Van Driel', *SJT*, vol. 60, no. 1 (2007): 62–79; Paul D. Molnar, "Can the Electing God Be God without Us?" *Neue Zeitschrift für Systematische Theologie*, vol. 49 (2007): 199–222; Molnar, 'Can Jesus' Divinity Be Recognized as "Definitive, Authentic and Essential" if It Is Grounded in Election?', *Neue Zeitschrift für Systematische Theologie*, vol. 52 (2010): 40–81; Molnar, 'Orthodox and Modern: Just How Modern Was Barth's Later Theology?', *Theology Today*, vol. 67, no. 1 (2010): 51–6; Molnar, 'Was Barth a Pro-Nicene Theologian? Reflections on *Nicaea and Its Legacy*', *SJT*, vol. 64, no. 3 (2011): 347–59; Molnar, 'The Perils of Embracing a "Historicized Christology"', *Modern Theology*, vol. 30, no. 4 (October 2014): 454–80; Molnar, "The Trinity, Election and God's Ontological Freedom: A Response to Kevin W. Hector," *IJST*, vol. 8, no. 3 (2006): 294–306; Molnar, *Faith, Freedom and the Spirit: The Economic Trinity in Barth, Torrance and Contemporary Theology* (Downers Grove, IL: InterVarsity Press, 2015); D. Stephen Long, *Saving Karl Barth: Hans Urs Von Balthasar's Preoccupation* (Minneapolis, MN: Fortress Press, 2014).

4 Hunsinger, *Reading Barth with Charity*, 158.

not exhaustively present'. In other words, 'there was more to the eternal God's self-relationship than just this world-relationship'.[5]

This is the point I tried to establish and argue for in the first edition of this book. It is this that I still wish to present here because I think my original argument is more pertinent than ever: marginalizing or rejecting the reality of the *Logos asarkos* inevitably leads to a reduction of the immanent to the economic Trinity and thus to a perspective that makes God's eternal being and action dependent on history. In a real sense everything here depends on the recognition that while God is known in his entirety according to his good-pleasure (*Wohlgefallen*) as he meets us in Jesus Christ, still 'God's being and nature are not exhausted in the encroachment in which He is God among us and for us, nor His truth in the truth of his grace and mercy'.[6] And, of course, marginalizing or simply paying lip service to the reality of the *Logos asarkos* makes it impossible to see the forceful and effective actions of God for us within history because such views inevitably do maintain in some way, wittingly or unwittingly, that God's being is indeed 'exhausted' in his relationship with us. So this issue is extremely important because it also unavoidably leads to some notion of a dependent deity; and any idea of a dependent deity makes it impossible to distinguish divine from human action and thus makes it impossible to see divine action in history as the basis of human freedom.[7] Since a new chapter considering divine freedom once again in light of the many developments in Christology and in the doctrine of the Trinity in the years after this issue first arose will

5 Hunsinger, *Reading Barth with Charity*, 158.

6 *CD* II/1, 75.

7 The idea of a dependent deity can take a number of forms. See, for example, Ted Peters, *GOD as Trinity: Relationality and Temporality in Divine Life* (hereafter: *Trinity*) (Louisville, KY: Westminster/John Knox Press, 1993), who maintains that Wolfhart Pannenberg 'believes that the reciprocity in the relationship of the divine persons makes room for the *constitutive* significance of the central events of salvation history for the Godhead of God' with the result that he believes that not only is 'the sending of the Son with his crucifixion and resurrection . . . to be understood as *constitutive* of the divine life, but also the work of the Spirit who dynamically realizes the kingdom of God in the world'. Hence, 'Without this kingdom, God could not be God' (135, emphasis mine). In Peters' estimation, for Pannenberg, 'the divinity of the eternal God is in the process of being determined and defined in the historical events of Jesus' destiny. The eternal nature of God is at least in part dependent upon temporal events' (137). It is my contention that whenever the relationship between God and history is

follow this chapter, I will address some of that recent literature there. In this chapter, as is already clear, I am adding one key participant to this discussion, George Hunsinger. He has presented an invaluable set of reflections on the significance of the *Logos asarkos* in Barth's theology and in theology generally. His reflections will help us see very clearly that Bruce McCormack and those who follow his thinking on this issue are in conflict with what Hunsinger calls the 'textual Barth'. Hunsinger calls these Barth scholars 'revisionists' because they mistakenly think that the textual Barth needs to be revised so that his thinking will conform to the logic they have imposed on Barth's thinking. However in reality their thinking is at variance not only with the 'textual Barth' but also with the classical doctrine of the Trinity and with Christology as well. This is what I hope to show in this chapter.

Bruce McCormack

When Bruce McCormack first considered the conception of the *Logos asarkos* in relation to Barth's theological ontology and election, he acknowledged that Barth did not wish to 'deny the propriety of the distinction between the *Logos asarkos* and the *Logos ensarkos* altogether'.[8]

conceptualized as one that is mutually conditioned, then the freedom of grace has been obliterated and the distinction between God and creation becomes blurred. I will discuss this a bit more in the next chapter and again in connection with the theology of Ted Peters in a later chapter. For now it is important to recognize that the problem here concerns the fact that 'Pannenberg abandoned the idea of God's absolute perfection and unqualified self-sufficiency' so that 'the perfection of God's essence was somehow subsequent, contingent, and teleological rather than (as for Barth) antecedent, necessary, and primordial' (George Hunsinger, 'Karl Barth's Doctrine of the Trinity, and Some Protestant Doctrines After Barth' *The Oxford Handbook of the Trinity*, ed. Gilles Emery, O.P. and Matthew Levering (Oxford: Oxford University Press, 2011), 294–313, at 311. That is why Pannenberg mistakenly thought of the immanent Trinity as 'a function of the economic Trinity' (311), and adopted what Hunsinger rightly recognizes as the 'startling claim' that '"with the creation of a world God's deity and even his existence become dependent on the fulfillment of their determination in his present lordship"' (311).

8 Bruce McCormack, 'Grace and being: The role of God's gracious election in Karl Barth's theological ontology', in *The Cambridge Companion to Karl Barth*, ed. John Webster (Cambridge: Cambridge University Press, 2000), 96.

McCormack here correctly indicated that for Barth, Jesus's human nature did not exist until a particular time in history: 'It was not eternal; the Logos did not bring it with him, so to speak, in entering history. Hence there could be no denying the reality of a *Logos asarkos* prior to the incarnation (and, Barth would add, in agreement with his Reformed forebears, after the incarnation as well).'[9] Again, this is an accurate and important statement of Barth's view. However, here McCormack cites Barth's statement opposing speculation about the being and action of a *Logos asarkos* and thus 'about a God who could be known and whose divine essence could be defined on some other basis than in and from the perception of his presence and action as the incarnate Word'[10] to argue that this assertion by Barth was not simply meant to express an epistemological concern to exclude any sort of natural theology. Rather, 'what was really at stake … was divine ontology.'[11] Accordingly, Barth

9 McCormack, 'Grace and being', 96.

10 *CD* IV/1, 181.

11 McCormack, 'Grace and being', 96. It is here that a subtle difference between the views of McCormack on the one side and Hunsinger and me on the other side can be seen. We all agree that God cannot be known on any other basis than through his incarnate Word, but we disagree that 'divine ontology' is 'at stake' because it is just this assumption that leads McCormack to a problematic view of divine self-determination. In reality it is the triune God who, in election, eternally determines himself to be for us in Jesus Christ. However, for McCormack, self-determination means that in electing us, God constitutes his own triunity (i.e. the ontological implication). In a real sense then, by extending this view into 'ontology' McCormack is led to embrace a kind of dependent deity that is not terribly dissimilar to the deity envisioned by Pannenberg. What George Hunsinger has shown definitively is that this is certainly not Karl Barth's view of the matter. Nor is it a view that upholds the traditional doctrine of the Trinity. See Hunsinger, *Reading Barth with Charity*, 'For Barth something can be "determined" (or modified) only if it has already been "constituted"' (49). For Hunsinger's criticism of Pannenberg, see notes 7 and 68. The point to be noted here is this: McCormack fails to distinguish God's internal actions from God's external actions and so he mistakenly thinks God's act of graciously establishing his covenant with us is the ground of his triunity. However, it is God's eternal triune being and act that is the ground of God's eternal determination to be God for us. That is the central difficulty here. One therefore does not have to say that God's essence precedes his act of being as Father, Son and Spirit because the immanent Trinity is eternally who God is in his act of being Father, Son and Spirit. However, one must still distinguish

was not just saying that there was no rift between what God is in himself and what God does as reconciler, so that we could say that God's essence 'precedes act as the ground of the latter'. In McCormack's view, Barth was 'suggesting that the activity of God the Reconciler is in some sense (yet to be specified) *constitutive* of the divine essence'.[12] The ontological implications of this simply are that since Barth thought of Jesus Christ and not the Logos as the subject of election, this had to mean that: 'The eternal act of establishing a covenant of grace is an act of Self-determination by means of which God determines to be God, from everlasting to everlasting, in a covenantal relationship with human beings and to be God in no other way'.[13] McCormack went on to say that 'if the eternal being of God is constituted by His eternal act of turning towards the human race – if that is what God is "essentially" – then God's essence is not hidden to human perception. It is knowable because it is *constituted* by the act of turning towards us. God in himself *is* God "for us"'.[14] The questions that I raised briefly in the first edition of this book concerned whether or not this thinking was (1) a faithful explication of Barth's views and (2) whether or not this thinking led McCormack to blur the distinction between the immanent and economic Trinity that he himself said was important to maintain.[15]

In any case, McCormack grapples with the implications of Barth's doctrine of election, namely, that God's decision to establish a covenant

this eternal act and being from God's actions ad extra as creator, reconciler and redeemer, and that is what McCormack here fails to do.

12 McCormack, 'Grace and being', 96–7.

13 McCormack, 'Grace and being', 98.

14 McCormack, 'Grace and being', 99. When compared to Barth's statement noted earlier that 'God's being and nature are not exhausted in the encroachment in which He is God among us and for us' (*CD* II/1, 75), this view is an almost classic case of reducing the eternal Trinity to God for us.

15 Thus, 'the distinction between the immanent and the economic Trinity has also been shown to be a necessary one (it is the distinction between eternity and time which may not be eradicated)', McCormack, 'Grace and being' , 107. As indicated in the previous note, it is not clear to me that there can be any distinction between the immanent and economic Trinity once one claims that 'God in himself *is* God "for us"' as McCormack does, since for him this means that God's eternal triunity is *constituted* by his turning toward us while for Barth God's triunity is who God is and would be who God was and is and even if he never turned toward us in electing us in Jesus Christ.

of grace also meant a self-determination on God's part to be God for us in Jesus Christ. This raises the question of whether or not the incarnation should be construed as being '*constitutive*' of God's eternal being. McCormack carefully and rightly distinguishes Barth's position from Hegel's insisting that for Barth, in opposition to Hegel, the incarnation is God's free act; that Barth sharply distinguished the creator/creature relation; that Barth insisted that God preexisted creation; and that God's eternal actions could not be collapsed into history. Hence, 'The immanent Trinity is complete, for Barth, before anything that has been made was made (including time itself).'[16] Still, McCormack wishes to argue that both the incarnation and outpouring of the Holy Spirit are in some sense 'constitutive' of God's eternal being, by way of anticipation. Will such an interpretation of Barth respect God's freedom, which indeed is the basis for human freedom and for human self-determination?

Here McCormack asks about the logical relation of God's election to his triunity, arguing that this is not a 'chronological relation'. Thus, 'Election is an *eternal* decision and as such resists our attempts to temporalize it; i.e., to think of it in such a way that a "before" and an "after" are introduced into the being of God in pretemporal eternity. If election is an eternal decision, then it has never not taken place.'[17] It is at this point in the first edition that I asked the following question: But if God's election has always taken place, how then can it be construed as a decision; does it not then become a necessity (a logical necessity at that), that is, the very opposite of what Barth intended with his doctrine of the immanent Trinity? This question was meant to underscore the fact that in God's pretemporal eternity, which for Barth was not timeless, but consisted of God's unique time that was not limited by the opposition of past, present and future as ours is, there really could be a 'before' and an 'after' because God's eternal decision involved a decision of the eternal triune God.[18] His eternal triunity was not constituted by

---

16 McCormack, 'Grace and being', 100.

17 McCormack, 'Grace and being', 101.

18 I explain this thinking in *Faith, Freedom and the Spirit*, 140, 198ff. George Hunsinger speaks of such a before and after as well because for Barth there 'are "temporal" distinctions in God's eternity but no "separations"' (*Reading Barth with Charity*, 48). Indeed, because 'Eternity is the simultaneity of beginning, middle, and end' (*CD* II/1, 608 and *Reading Barth with Charity*, 49), Barth can hold that 'Jesus Christ is present at the beginning of all things because he is made to participate in the dynamics of the divine eternity' (*Reading Barth with Charity*, 49). Thus, for Barth '"God's 'before' and 'after' … are not separated

his eternal decision to be our God in the covenant of grace. This is why Barth continually stressed that God did not need fellowship with us and that God has his own unique temporality as the one who alone is eternal in such a way that he did not need time. So Barth can speak of eternity surrounding our time and of God's lordship over time as the one who could create and control time. He also insisted that 'this does not mean that it was necessary for it [eternity] to create time and therefore to give it reality. It does not mean that God would be any less eternal if time did not exist outside Himself.'[19] This is why Barth repeatedly spoke of the fact that God did not need us or fellowship with us because he could have done without us since 'He is who He is before it [our existence] and without it.'[20] Of course, he then adds that for the very same reason God 'can have it [our existence] as a reality in His sight without owing it to us or to Himself'.[21] Barth describes this pre-time of God as 'the pure time of the Father and the Son in the fellowship of the Holy Spirit' – a clear reference to the immanent Trinity – and indicates that God did not in fact choose to be without us, but decided to be in relation with us in and through Christ in his pretemporal eternity. Such thinking confirms Barth's own insistence that 'Jesus Christ's identity as

from one another"' (49, referring to *CD* II/1, 623). Following Thomas Aquinas, Karl Barth makes an interesting distinction between *potentia absoluta* (God's power to do 'that which He can choose to do, but does not have to') and *potentia ordinata* ('the power which God does actually use and exercise in a definite *ordinatio*'). Barth concludes: 'Interpreted in this way, the distinction is simply a description of the freedom of the divine omnipotence' so that in answer to the question of whether or not God could do what he has not done, Thomas answered that question with a 'yes'. Barth concludes that: 'The question is certainly to be answered in the affirmative. God would not have power, nor would His power be in His hands nor would it be the power of a Lord, real power over everything, if it amounted only to His omnicausality' (*CD* II/1, 539). Of course Barth goes on to explain that this question was not always answered correctly as Thomas had done and is always incorrectly answered when we attempt to ascribe a capacity to God which is different from that revealed in his work or which contradicts it. 'His real capacity is not one which contradicts and therefore compromises the capacity in which He actually manifests Himself' (*CD* II/1, 541).

19 *CD* II/1, 619.
20 *CD* II/1, 621.
21 *CD* II/1, 621–2.

God's Son "of course did not rest on election".[22] Language which was subsequently developed with the help of George Hunsinger clarified this question further. One could say that God's eternal triunity is necessary in the sense that God could not not be Father, Son and Holy Spirit and still be God while election is eternally contingent in the sense that God could have been triune without electing us. However, in light of further developments, it has become very clear that McCormack did indeed introduce a logical necessity into the divine being with his logical reversal of the doctrines of election and the Trinity precisely by claiming, in opposition to the 'textual Barth', that Barth needed to retract some of his earlier views, even though Barth never did so.

One of those views was Barth's denial that 'God is triune *for the sake of* his revelation'.[23] Having thus claimed that Barth should not have made this first statement, McCormack then insists that when Barth wrote that 'In Himself and as such [God – the second "person" of the Godhead] is not revealed to us. In Himself and as such He is not *Deus pro nobis*, either ontologically or epistemologically' McCormack asks: 'What context could there possibly be which would justify speaking in this way?'[24] He thinks it is unfortunate that Barth referred to the second person of the Trinity as such as a necessary and important concept needed to understand the freedom of God's grace in dealing with us in connection with the doctrine of the Trinity. McCormack's conclusion is that in making such a statement, either Barth did not fully realize the implications of his own doctrine of election for the doctrine of the Trinity or that he did not draw the conclusions 'for reasons known only to himself'. In any case, it was McCormack's stated task from here to 'correct' this supposed inconsistency in Barth's thought.[25] What George Hunsinger has shown with respect to McCormack's claims, however, is that Barth was not at all inconsistent in making these assertions and that the supposed inconsistency only follows from the fact that Barth's thinking stands opposed to logic embedded in McCormack's fundamentally erroneous claim that God's election of us is the ground of God's triunity. It is not. Indeed that is the position which I have presented from the beginning and which both George Hunsinger and I continue to espouse.[26] Here,

22 See Hunsinger, *Reading Barth with Charity*, 13, referring to *CD* II/2, 114.
23 McCormack, 'Grace and being', 101.
24 McCormack, 'Grace and being', 102 referring to *CD* IV/1, 52.
25 McCormack, 'Grace and being', 102.
26 See Hunsinger, 'Twenty-Five Theses', in *Modern Theology* as well as *Reading Barth with Charity*. See also Molnar, *Faith, Freedom and the Spirit*.

then, is the difficulty at this point: these were statements that Barth made in order to stress that God's actions for us are free actions of grace that are not necessitated by his nature. That is why Barth not only did not retract them but held firm to them throughout his work. Since McCormack logically claims that 'God in himself *is* God "for us"', God can no longer exist as *Logos asarkos* within the immanent Trinity since the *Logos asarkos* in McCormack's thinking has been reduced to the *Logos incarnandus*. While McCormack claimed that he did not intend to do away with the *Logos asarkos* altogether, his subsequent arguments very clearly did exactly that, so that he now maintains not only that God has to give himself his being in his act of electing us[27] but that '*There is a triune being of God – only in the covenant of grace*'.[28] It hardly needs to be stated that if God *only* has his triunity in the covenant of grace, then God's eternal existence as Father, Son and Holy Spirit has in fact been conceptualized in such a way that it is 'exhausted in the encroachment in which He is God among us and for us'.[29]

How then does McCormack 'correct' Barth's theology? He argues that we must understand God's triunity

> logically as a function of divine election ... the eternal act of Self-differentiation in which God is God 'a second time in a very different way' ... and a third time as well, is *given in* the eternal act in which God elects himself for the human race. The *decision* for the covenant of grace is the ground of God's triunity and, therefore of the eternal generation of the Son and of the eternal procession of the Holy Spirit from the Father and Son ... the works of God *ad intra* (the trinitarian processions) find their ground in the *first* of the works of God *ad extra* (viz. election). And that also means that eternal generation and eternal procession are willed by God; they are not natural to him if 'natural' is taken to mean a determination of being fixed in advance of all actions and relations.[30]

McCormack therefore argues that this thinking is compatible with Barth's view of the doctrine of the Trinity and that the doctrine might

---

27 See *Faith, Freedom and the Spirit*, 194.

28 McCormack, 'Election and the Trinity', 128, emphasis mine. See also, *Faith, Freedom and the Spirit*, 194.

29 See *CD* II/1, 75 and above.

30 McCormack, 'Grace and being', 103; emphasis in original.

have been 'subordinated in the order of treatment to the doctrine of election'.[31]

Here I stand firmly with my original statement in the first edition that this thinking once again highlights the importance of a proper doctrine of the immanent Trinity. For Barth, God exists eternally as the Father, Son and Holy Spirit and would so exist even if there had been no creation, reconciliation or redemption.[32] Thus, the order between election and triunity cannot be logically reversed without in fact making creation, reconciliation and redemption necessary to God.[33] It is precisely this critical error that is embodied in McCormack's proposal. Barth insisted that the Trinity exists eternally in its own right and thus even the electing God is not subject to any necessities, especially a necessity that would suggest that the ground of his triunity is the covenant of grace. It is exactly the other way around. The covenant of grace is a covenant of *grace* because it expresses God's free decision to create, to reconcile and to redeem the world. That free decision takes place in pretemporal eternity in what Barth called the 'pure time of the Father and the Son in the fellowship of the Holy Spirit'.[34] This pretemporal eternity is

31 McCormack, 'Grace and being', 103.

32 Here it is important to realize that for Barth: 'The necessary and sufficient condition for the possibility of all God's ways and works toward the world is always located in God's antecedent being as the eternal Trinity' Hunsinger, *Reading Barth with Charity*, 8. That is why Hunsinger rightly insists that the 'actualistic ontology' advocated by the 'Barth revisionists' abandons Barth's 'signature doctrine of antecedence' (*Reading Barth with Charity*, 8). They mistakenly replace this doctrine with a doctrine of 'subsequence' so that for them 'What God is eternally in himself is subsequent to what he determines himself to be relative to the world' (*Reading Barth with Charity*, 8). This is why Hunsinger can and does argue consistently and correctly that for Barth, God 'could become the Trinity in the economy because he was already the Trinity to all eternity' and that 'He did not need to constitute himself as the Trinity, nor did he need to "historicize" his eternal being' (*Reading Barth with Charity*, 165). All of this is true because 'In Barth a doctrine of divine antecedence took precedence over all elements of subsequence' (*Reading Barth with Charity*, 165).

33 Even those who rightly criticize McCormack's thesis that election and Trinity should be logically reversed do not always entirely escape the thinking that led McCormack to his thesis in the first place or the problematic thinking that follows. In the next chapter we will see that Kevin Hector does not entirely escape some of the problematic aspects of McCormack's own position.

34 *CD* II/1, 623.

the eternity in which God 'could have done without [us], because He is who He is before [us] and without [us]' but nonetheless 'He did in fact choose not to be without us'.[35] This decision certainly was not the basis of God's triunity, but rather the expression of the fact that God is truly free (and did not need us to be the one who loves in freedom) and so God is *also* truly free to be for us in a way that is not at all dependent on us either. None of this is subject to a principle of love, and God's being is not the result of his will; were that the case the door would be opened wide to the Arianism which Athanasius firmly rejected.[36] Rather, his will to elect expresses his freedom to be God in a new way as God for us. It expresses the fact that, as we shall see in more detail later, God is Lord of his inner life as well as of his actions ad extra. However, none of this is required by his essence, and his essence most certainly is not contingent on his works ad extra. Indeed, as we shall also see later, God's will cannot be played off against his nature here because his free will expresses his nature as the one who loves in freedom. We will explore the limited way in which the *Logos asarkos* was advocated by Barth when we consider Robert Jenson's outright rejection of the concept; as already noted, Barth was certainly leery of the concept if it suggested any attempt to think of God by going behind the God revealed in Christ, but he insisted on its necessity in connection with the doctrine of the Trinity and Christology and was certainly right to do so.

---

35 *CD* II/1, 621–2.

36 See discussion of this point in the next chapter, 164ff. George Hunsinger rightly notes that the ' "strong" (revisionist) reading' of the way Barth conceives God's nature and will rides 'roughshod' over subtle distinctions that Barth makes when speaking of this, for instance, in *CD* I/1, 435 and concludes that 'Revisionism would insist that for Barth, God's nature is merely a function of his will, that the form taken by his nature is discretionary, that God might or might not have been trinitarian, and that his trinitarian nature is the result of a pretemporal decision, namely, that of election' (*Reading Barth with Charity*, 105). For Barth the begetting of the Son is indeed a work of God's will in which God freely wills himself. However, it is not an act of God's will 'in the way that the freedom to will this or that is expressed in the concept of will'. God is free in this regard with respect to creation but he does not have this freedom with respect to his being the triune God (*Reading Barth with Charity*, 104–5). Hunsinger rightly believes that any idea that the form of God's nature is discretionary is a tacit form of modalism (*Reading Barth with Charity*, 37–8).

Here is where a 'deliberate and sharp' distinction between the immanent and economic Trinity is essential.[37] While McCormack admits that
such a distinction is necessary, it plays no conceptual role at this point
in his argument. Consequently, it is just because McCormack failed to
make such a distinction at this important point, that he is misled into
believing that God became the triune God only in virtue of his self-
determination to be our God. The reason Barth never changed his view
on this matter is because he consistently recognized and maintained
God's freedom; that is, the freedom of God's love without which the
doctrine of the Trinity becomes nothing more than a description of
our relations among ourselves, which we then dubiously attribute to
the God of our own invention.[38] Paramount here, as we shall see later
in more detail, is Barth's insistence that we cannot explain the *how* of
the mystery of God's triunity, election and incarnation – we can only
accept these divine actions as facts grounded in God's primal decision
to be God for us. However, election is a decision of the living God and
thus while it is irreversible, once made, it still was freely made and continues to be freely affirmed by God in his faithfulness to the covenant,
and therefore we cannot simply equate the immanent and economic
Trinity in the manner suggested by McCormack, without actually making God dependent on the world in precisely the Hegelian way that he
recognizes is so mistaken in this regard. This important example should
serve as a warning that we cannot just dispense with a *Logos asarkos*, or
merely pay lip service to it as McCormack apparently finally did, first by
reducing the *Logos asarkos* to the *Logos incarnandus* and then by arguing that 'there is no "eternal Son" if by that is meant a mode of being in
God which is not identical with Jesus Christ'.[39] For Barth, as we shall see
in more detail shortly, the *Logos asarkos* is a necessary concept in the

37 This language is not meant to affirm any separation of the immanent
and economic Trinity. It is meant simply to affirm the fact that what God
does in relation to us is always an act of grace – it is not necessary for God to
create, reconcile and redeem us – that he does so is an act of his free love. See
Hunsinger, *Reading Barth with Charity*, where he notes that it is completely
proper to argue for a 'sharp distinction' between the immanent and economic
Trinity (124).

38 Hunsinger correctly notes that the later Barth of *CD* IV appealed to his
own explication of the doctrine in *CD* I/1 and did not change the position he
originally espoused in *CD* I/1, *Reading Barth with Charity*, 104–5.

39 Bruce L. McCormack, 'Karl Barth's Historicized Christology: *Just How
"Chalcedonian" Is It?*, *Orthodox and Modern: Studies in the Theology of Karl*

doctrine of the Trinity and Christology that recognizes and maintains God's freedom, that is the freedom of God's love. One might ask at this point whether Barth is not more concerned with God's freedom here than God himself might be. The simple answer to such a question is that he plainly recognizes that a compromise of God's freedom here means dissolution of human freedom and ultimately the collapse of theology into anthropology.[40] Before proceeding to our consideration of Robert Jenson's thinking about the *Logos asarkos*, it is worth discussing very

Barth (hereafter: *Orthodox and Modern*) (Grand Rapids, MI: Baker Academic, 2008), 201–33, 219. Even more pointedly McCormack claims that 'Any talk of the eternal Son in abstraction from the humanity to be assumed is an exercise in mythologizing; *there is no such eternal Son – and there never was*' (Bruce L. McCormack, *Engaging the Doctrine of God: Contemporary Protestant Perspectives*, ed. Bruce L. McCormack (hereafter: *Engaging the Doctrine of God*) (Grand Rapids, MI: Baker Academic, 2008), 'The Actuality of God: *Karl Barth in Conversation with Open Theism*', 185–242, 218, emphasis mine). Peter Goodwin Heltzel and Christian T. Collins Winn, 'Karl Barth, Reconciliation and the Triune God', in *Cambridge Companion to the Trinity*, ed. Peter C. Phan (Cambridge: Cambridge University Press, 2011), 190 read McCormack to be saying that 'there is no eternal Logos *in abstraction* (no *logos asarkos*), but only the Logos manifest eternally in the incarnation of Jesus Christ (i.e. *logos ensarkos*)'. In a much more nuanced and accurate way George Hunsinger argues that 'the relationship of the Logos *ensarkos* to the Logos *asarkos* is not one of dialectical identity … They do not form a single self-identical reality that can be looked at in two different ways … as if the two were dialectically one and the same without remainder', *Reading Barth with Charity*, 57. Indeed, Hunsinger rightly maintains that the *Logos asarkos* does not 'simply disappear into the Logos *ensarkos*, as if the former were merely a preliminary stage on the way to the latter. The Logos *asarkos* is not exhausted in its secondary form as the Logos *incarnandus/incarnatus/ensarkos* … The Logos *asarkos* in itself and as such is not preliminary but antecedent, not transitory but eternal, not provisional but perpetual and enduring' (*Reading Barth with Charity*, 57). As mentioned earlier, this is exactly the position for which Barth argued.

40 As will be noted in the next chapter, Robert B. Price (*Letters of the Divine Word: The Perfections of God in Karl Barth's Church Dogmatics*, ed. John Webster, Ian A. McFarland and Ivor Davidson, T & T Clark Studies in Systematic Theology [New York: T & T Clark, 2011]), captures the issue that I have been discussing here nicely when he notes that McCormack's proposal emphasizes the divine love at the expense of the divine freedom, 11.

briefly Douglas Farrow's attempt to maintain Christ's uniqueness while simultaneously arguing against any idea of a *Logos asarkos*.

Douglas Farrow

In his important book *Ascension and Ecclesia*, which we will discuss in more detail in Chapter 9, Douglas Farrow praises Barth for his apparent thoroughgoing rejection of a *Logos asarkos* without paying sufficient attention to the fact that this concept performed a significant but limited role in Barth's theology. Farrow indicates that Irenaeus similarly rejected such a concept and links Barth to Irenaeus in a positive way.[41] Farrow himself believes that such a concept brings 'us dangerously near to the gnostic conviction that Jesus himself is somehow incidental to the Word. Flirtation with that idea was and is common enough, of course, preserving even among orthodox theologians traces of the gnostic bias against the redemption of the material world.'[42] Indeed Irenaeus too, when he referred to Jesus as 'God of God; Son of the Father; Jesus Christ; King for ever and ever' and so thought of him as the one 'who sailed along with Noah, and who guided Abraham; who was bound along with Isaac', causes Farrow to ask 'whether so much has been claimed for Jesus that his humanity must be crushed after all under the weight of these claims'.[43] Moreover, Farrow argues that Karl Barth, in spite of his supposed thoroughgoing rejection of a *Logos asarkos*, has a difficulty similar to that of Irenaeus: 'Is not *our* reality somehow threatened if we take such statements about Jesus too seriously?'[44] This leads Farrow to conclude that Barth 'has spoken the name of Jesus so loudly that other names cannot even be heard; that once again humanity is being swallowed up, if not by God directly then by "the humanity of God." '[45]

The simple answer to these reflections is that for Barth one can never stress God's freedom too strongly as long as it is properly understood as his freedom disclosed and active in the history of Jesus Christ and the outpouring of the Holy Spirit. This is the case because it is precisely God's freedom for us in Christ that establishes and maintains human

---

41 See Farrow, *Ascension and Ecclesia*, 53ff. and 243.

42 Farrow, *Ascension and Ecclesia*, 54.

43 Farrow, *Ascension and Ecclesia*, 83.

44 Farrow, *Ascension and Ecclesia*, 83.

45 Farrow, *Ascension and Ecclesia*, 243.

freedom itself.[46] The mystery of Jesus Christ indeed consists in the fact that he was both the eternal God and a contingent human being at the same time – one did not in fact overwhelm the other; but by the grace of God, Jesus lived as a man of his time and was at the same time Lord of history. This is indeed the heart of the Christian faith, but Farrow appears to be in search of 'Jesus-history' which is defined as 'the sanctification of our humanity through the life and passion and heavenly intercession of Jesus',[47] and so emphasizes his humanity that no decisive function is allotted to Jesus as God incarnate, even though he also admits that 'if Jesus really is God giving himself to us, then we must be prepared to speak of his pre-existence *as* God'.[48] Still, it seems that Jesus's human preexistence is such that in Farrow's thinking this appears to replace the eternal Word who was with God and was God according to Jn. 1:1. That is why for Karl Barth the *Logos asarkos* was a necessary and important trinitarian insight that recognizes and helps us to maintain God's freedom. As we have been seeing, it allows him to recognize that the Trinity exists in its own right and that our trinitarian thinking can never substitute historical relations for the relations of the Father, Son and Spirit that are decisive for the events that take place within the economy.

Farrow concludes that there were two types of preexistence attested in the New Testament, that is, Jesus's preexistence as a man and as God. Like Barth, he stresses the importance of the immanent Trinity, but unlike Barth he refuses to acknowledge that there ever was a *Logos asarkos*. Referring to John's Gospel, Farrow contends '*That* he [Jesus] goes [ascends] makes him the way [to the Father]'.[49] But wasn't Jesus the way, the truth and the life precisely because, as Son he was eternally *homoousion* with the Father from the beginning? Doesn't the entire gospel hinge on this fact – a fact which, as we have been seeing, becomes unrecognizable whenever Jesus's preexistence as God is obscured? Does Farrow's belief in Jesus's human preexistence take due cognizance of the need to distinguish the immanent and economic Trinity and of election as a free act of grace as Barth did? As we shall see later in Chapters 6 and 8, Barth accepted the fact that God once existed in isolation from us, in the sense that the God who meets us as Lord in freedom does

---

46 See, for example, *CD* IV/3.1, 378ff.
47 Farrow, *Ascension and Ecclesia*, 6.
48 Farrow, *Ascension and Ecclesia*, 281.
49 Farrow, *Ascension and Ecclesia*, 36.

not just have his existence in that relation to us but first in himself and on that basis in relation to us; this is the God who elected us in Jesus Christ as the beginning of his ways and works and executed that election in his life, death, resurrection, ascension and session at the Father's right hand. Thus, the doctrine of the immanent Trinity clearly recognizes God's freedom to exist as the eternal Father, Son and Spirit without need of creation. That is precisely why election is God's covenant of grace – it is freely exercised on our behalf. Further, Barth argued that one's vocation, like one's justification and sanctification,

> prior to its actualisation in his own history it has its basis as we must say first and supremely, in his election in Jesus Christ 'before the foundation of the world' (Eph. 1:4). It has as the seed and root of its historical reality, truth and certainty the absolutely prevenient 'history' which as the *opus Trinitatis internum ad extra* is in God Himself the eternal beginning of all His ways and works, namely, the election of grace of the God who loves in freedom and is free in love, in which the Son, thereto ordained by the Father and obedient to the Father, has elected Himself for sinful man and sinful man for Himself. In light of this, the one true God is the true God of man in ... His pre-temporal, supra-temporal and post-temporal eternity ... Not in and of himself, but in Jesus Christ as the eternal beginning of all God's ways and works, no man is rejected, but all are elected in Him to their justification, their sanctification and also their vocation. This is the prior history which precedes and underlies the event of vocation in their own history, which is purely and totally divine, but which in intention is already divine-human.[50]

Does Farrow's own understanding of 'Jesus-history' not become his theological criterion, with the result that the living Lord is kept from acting decisively in this context? Indeed, noticeably missing throughout Farrow's book is any notion of Christ's active Lordship, namely, of his ability, as the Word incarnate, to interact with us now through the power of the Holy Spirit.

One wonders whether Farrow's search for a 'eucharistic world-view'[51] indicates that in the end he is not as reliant on the living Lord as he intends. Wasn't Barth right to observe that *all* world-views

---

50 *CD* IV/3.2, 483f. See also *CD* III/4, 595–646.

51 Farrow, *Ascension and Ecclesia*, 73, 88.

represent human attempts to avoid the Lordship of Jesus Christ?[52] Indeed, far from advancing some sort of Christomonism, Barth very clearly argued that because God in Jesus Christ has become our brother 'man has become the brother of God in Jesus Christ, and as such cannot adopt an attitude of hostility, neutrality or passivity in relation to the name and cause of God'.[53] For Barth we are set free for our active life and our vocation in Jesus Christ, but he insists that our active life in freedom is a participation in the life of the man Jesus by being disciples and allowing ourselves 'to be claimed by Him for an active life under his leadership'.[54] Still, for Barth, 'Man neither is nor can be a second Jesus Christ … His freedom, activity and achievements will always be very different from the freedom, activity and achievements of God.'[55] Our relation with Christ then takes place in an unlikely miracle in which we participate in his freedom while remaining active ourselves: 'It is the miracle of miracles that man may be genuinely active as a subject in this sense where God acts and speaks … Yet it is true because in Jesus Christ it is revealed and commanded that it should continually become real.'[56] While Farrow thinks that Barth is open to the criticism of falling into a type of Christomonism,[57] the reality is that for Barth there can be no Christomonism because our union with Christ 'does not mean the dissolution or disappearance of the one in the other, nor does it mean identification. It does not mean a conjunction of the two in which one or the other, and perhaps both, lose their specific character, role and function in relation to the other, the reciprocal relation being thus reversible.'[58] Instead our union with Christ preserves the independence, activity and uniqueness of each.

By contrast, is it not Farrow's very understanding of 'Jesus-history' that tends toward the Docetism he thinks he finds in Barth with the idea that Jesus humanly preexisted his birth, life, death, resurrection and ascension? How can Jesus truly share our humanity if his is a humanity that preexisted his birth on earth, even if this is only understood

52 *CD* IV/3.1, 254ff.
53 *CD* III/4, 482.
54 *CD* III/4, 482.
55 *CD* III/4, 482.
56 *CD* III/4, 483.
57 See Farrow, *Ascension and Ecclesia*, 243.
58 *CD* IV/3.2, 540.

retroactively?[59] It is one thing to say that Jesus's humanity existed one way in God's primal decision to be God for us in Jesus Christ. Such a view is delicately and clearly explained by George Hunsinger when he analyzes important biblical texts such as Jn. 17:24 which speaks of Jesus being loved by the Father 'before the foundation of the world', 1 Pet. 1:20 which speaks of Jesus as ' "foreknown" by God as the one who could die like a spotless lamb', and finally Rev. 13:8 which refers to Jesus 'as the Lamb "slain before the foundation of the world" '.[60] Hunsinger rightly notes that Barth did not invent this difficult idea. He also explains that it was never meant to suggest that Barth believed in an eternal incarnation[61] and that Barth definitely did not wish to reject entirely any notion of a *Logos asarkos*. Hence, Hunsinger argues that:

> To say that Jesus Christ was present 'in the beginning' does not make him into a constitutive member of the Trinity (as the Logos *ensarkos*), for his humanity obviously has a beginning. It is therefore not the Logos *ensarkos* as such who is eternally begotten of the Father but rather (as in all traditional ecumenical theology) the Logos *asarkos*. Nor is the Logos begotten merely for the sake of becoming *ensarkos*, as if God had no subsistence in and for himself.[62]

The point here is that 'Jesus Christ enjoys a unique place by grace in both time and eternity, and therefore at the beginning of all things. He is made to exist at the beginning as the One he will be in time. He is present in the eternal foreknowledge and counsel of God.'[63] But it is quite another thing to say, as Farrow does, that there is a 'pre-existence of a *man*, a pre-existence which is disclosed to us and interpreted for us chiefly through the ascension.'[64] Here it seems that Farrow's complete rejection of any notion of a *Logos asarkos* leads him to project Jesus's eternal existence after the resurrection and ascension into pretemporal

---

59 See Farrow, *Ascension and Ecclesia*, 297.

60 Hunsinger, *Reading Barth with Charity*, 41ff.

61 Thus, Hunsinger maintains that 'Barth should not be mistaken as teaching a pretemporal incarnation' since the incarnation is only proleptically present to God in his eternal foreknowledge prior to the actual event of incarnation, *Reading Barth with Charity*, 66.

62 Hunsinger, *Reading Barth with Charity*, 42.

63 Hunsinger, *Reading Barth with Charity*, 49.

64 Farrow, *Ascension and Ecclesia*, 283.

eternity with the result that he is unable to distinguish the immanent and economic Trinity at that point. This leads him to suggest that the historical events of Jesus's life somehow contribute to his unique existence in precisely the Hegelian manner that we have seen is so problematic in contemporary theology.

Robert W. Jenson

Robert Jenson's *Systematic Theology Volume I: The Triune God* intends to show that contemporary theology must find its meaning in the triune God or else it will in fact contradict the gospel. Many theologians find Jenson's approach to the doctrine of the Trinity just the answer that is needed by contemporary theology in its attempts to avoid modalism, dualism and pantheism. Jenson's positive contribution rests on his insistence that reflection about God cannot take place except on the ground of the gospel, and that such reflection ought to be faithful to the God of the gospel rather than to anyone's particular tradition, whether Roman Catholic, Lutheran or Reformed. While tradition certainly is important to Jenson, he is very clear that the norm for theological truth must always be the triune God himself who is present to us as event, or as he puts it toward the end of the book, as a fugue![65]

Jenson strongly emphasizes the importance of Jesus's resurrection; the necessity of the church and the sacraments as the sphere in which we experience our inclusion in God's own self-knowledge and love; and the importance of not understanding God, with Greek metaphysics, as timeless and impassible or in a modalist or subordinationist way. Jenson seeks to plot the narrative of Jesus's life, death and resurrection in contrast to the Greek and medieval thought forms in which this story was told so that the reader can see that the concerns of the gospel were in conflict with the concerns of Aristotle and Plato. Without doubt, Jenson makes every effort to start and end his reflections with the gospel in such a way that Israel and the church are bound together in their dependence on the very same God who raised Jesus from the dead. This important point shows that, while Jesus the Son is at the center of his thinking, Jenson feels free to allow the living Christ, the risen Lord, to continue to exercise his mediatorial function in the world today. Unlike many contemporary theologies of the

---

65 Jenson, *STI*, 236.

Trinity, Jenson's presentation sets out to make room for Christ's active mediation of himself to us today and does so with a renewed emphasis on the Holy Spirit that deliberately does not separate the Holy Spirit from Jesus himself or from the Father.

Despite his positive intentions, however, Jenson's trinitarian theology as articulated in *Systematic Theology Volume 1* and *The Triune Identity* raises serious questions that center on four important interrelated areas: (1) the proper relation of the immanent and economic Trinity; though, as far as I am aware, while Jenson deliberately adopted Rahner's axiom and gave it an eschatological twist in his previous book, *The Triune Identity*, this question does not even arise in *Systematic Theology Volume I*; (2) the person and work of Jesus Christ, the Son of God; (3) the proper significance of Jesus's resurrection from the dead, including how we ought to understand Jesus's glorified body; and finally (4) Jenson's understanding of the relation between time and eternity.

The Proper Relationship between the Immanent and Economic Trinity

As I have stated throughout this book, a properly conceived doctrine of the immanent Trinity aims to recognize, uphold and respect God's freedom – not just God's freedom in se (though it certainly includes that), but God's freedom to act for us in history in a way that is recognizable as an act of free grace. As Jenson himself once maintained, 'it must be that God "in himself" could have been the same God he is, and so triune, had there been no creation, or saving of fallen creation'.[66] At the same time Jenson accepted, with Rahner, the identity of the immanent and economic Trinity, writing that 'the two most important contemporary trinitarian theorists, Karl Rahner and Eberhard Jüngel, agree on the rule for [the contemporary task of trinitarian theology]: the "economic" Trinity *is* the "immanent" Trinity, and vice versa'.[67] Now, as we have begun to see already, the problem with Rahner's axiom as it

---

66 Robert W. Jenson, *God According to the Gospel: The Triune Identity* (hereafter: *The Triune Identity*) (Philadelphia: Fortress Press, 1982), 139. Today Jenson no longer thinks this is a valid question. After rethinking his position on the *Logos asarkos*, Jenson now believes this is not even a 'real question'. He claims that this question is 'nonsense' because we cannot say anything about God's triunity apart from creation. See Robert W. Jenson, 'Once more the *Logos asarkos*' *IJST*, vol. 13, no. 2 (April 2011): 130–3, 130.

67 Jenson, *The Triune Identity*, 139.

stands is that it tends to blur the distinction between God and history, especially in terms of Christology as Rahner explicates matters from within his philosophy and theology of the symbol.[68] Thus, for example, as we have already seen, Rahner contends that Jesus, in his humanity *as such* reveals God.[69] In a similar way Jenson, citing Rahner's assertion that: 'What Jesus as man is and does, *is* the existence [*Dasein*] of the *Logos*, that reveals the *Logos* himself', argues that 'Jesus' human action and presence is without mitigation God's action and presence, with whatever that must do to and for creatures'.[70] Here we must insist, however, that while it is true that God did not merely come in the man Jesus but *as* man, it is still necessary to make the Chalcedonian distinction at this point or else the revealing power that comes from the Word and is not transferred to Jesus's humanity will be merged with history and

68 George Hunsinger rightly notes that Rahner's axiom or rule 'is systematically ambiguous' and 'has led to a great deal of confusion' ('Karl Barth and Some Protestant Doctrines', 309). While he believes it can be given a 'Barthian interpretation' as Jüngel did in part but Moltmann and Pannenberg failed to do, he notes that for Barth the relation of the two forms of the Trinity (eternal and temporal or immanent and economic) is one of 'correspondence' which allows us to understand the one Holy Trinity in 'two forms' as a 'unity-in-distinction' and not one of ' "dialectical identity" – as if when looked at in one way the Trinity was eternal but in another way it was historical, or as if eternity and history were merely two sides of a single process' ('Karl Barth and Some Protestant Doctrines', 310). Such thinking would indeed obliterate the necessary and important distinction without separation of the immanent and economic Trinity. As will be noted in the next chapter, while Bruce McCormack wholeheartedly accepts Rahner's axiom and thinks that Moltmann and Pannenberg do not disturb the distinction between the immanent and economic Trinity, Hunsinger rightly notes that McCormack's position is one of 'dialectical identity' and so it does indeed stand in conflict with Barth's view. This relates decisively to McCormack's misconception of the *Logos asarkos* since he seems to think of the *Logos asarkos* and *Logos ensarkos* as 'a single self-identical reality that can be looked at in two different ways ... as if the two were dialectically one and the same without remainder' (*Reading Barth with Charity*, 57). Against such thinking Hunsinger rightly insists that 'the Logos *asarkos* in itself and as such is not preliminary but antecedent, not transitory but eternal, not provisional but perpetual and enduring' (*Reading Barth with Charity*, 57).

69 See above, 85–6. For more on this see Chapter 6, esp. 325–30.

70 Jenson, *STI*, 144.

then become dependent on it.[71] Jenson's thinking leads to such puzzling statements as: 'the events in Jerusalem and on Golgotha are themselves inner-triune events' and 'the Spirit who will raise the Son finds his own identity only in the *totus Christus*, in the Son who is identified with us'.[72] Such suggestions seem to blur the distinction between events in God and events in history and further suggest that the Spirit does not eternally have his identity but must find it through events within history.

The Person and Work of Jesus Christ, the Son of God

In answering the question of whether or not Jesus in his humanity as such is revelation, Karl Barth, noting that it is one of the hardest problems of Christology,[73] rejected this idea because he insisted, correctly in my view, that revelation involved both a veiling and an unveiling. He was relying here on the Chalcedonian formulation of the two natures as unmixed (and therefore not identical), distinguished but also not separated.[74] Thus, Barth insisted on a 'deliberate and sharp [*scharf*]

71 Thomas F. Torrance, *Theology in Reconciliation* (London: Geoffrey Chapman, 1975), 151ff. and 201ff. follows Athanasius and Cyril of Alexandria and presents a positive understanding of Christ's vicarious humanity that neither falls into Apollinarian substitution of divinity for his humanity nor into Nestorian separation. Thus, 'since the Son of God did not just come into man but came *as man*, yet without ceasing to be God, the same subject in the Incarnation occupies two roles that are not just two roles or modes but real natures', 155. See also Torrance, *The Christian Doctrine of God*, 40–1. For a comparison of how T. F. Torrance's trinitarian theology helps us see the problems in the historicist thinking of Jenson and McCormack, see Paul D. Molnar 'The Perils of Embracing a "Historicized Christology"', *Modern Theology*, vol. 30, no. 4 (2014): 454–80 and *Faith, Freedom and the Spirit*, chapter 5.

72 *STI*, 191.

73 *CD* I/1, 323. More will be said about this in Chapter 6.

74 *CD* IV/2, 63ff. For more on the Chalcedonian character of Barth's Christology, see George Hunsinger, *Disruptive Grace: Studies in the Theology of Karl Barth* (Grand Rapids, MI: Eerdmans, 2000), chapter six. This idea of the Chalcedonian pattern has been questioned by Paul Nimmo, 'Karl Barth and the *concursus Dei* – A Chalcedonianism Too Far?', *IJST*, vol. 9, no. 1 (2007), 58–72. However, George Hunsinger rightly notes in response that in *CD* IV/3.1, 40 Barth deliberately uses terms taken directly from the Chalcedonian formulation to speak of the living Christ acting divinely and humanly for us without transforming the one into the other, without mixing the one with the

distinction' between the immanent and economic Trinity[75] in order to avoid ascribing to history or humanity as such, what can only become real within and for history and humanity by the grace of God active in Christ and the Spirit. Barth argued that 'the Godhead is not so immanent in Christ's humanity that it does not also remain transcendent to it, that its immanence ceases to be an event in the Old Testament sense, always a new thing, something that God actually brings into being in specific circumstances'.[76]

As already mentioned, Barth also maintained the importance of the *Logos asarkos* within the strict doctrine of the Trinity and within Christology. He believed that this abstraction[77] was necessary because

other and without separating or dividing the one from the other. He also notes that the same 'relational terms' appear in *CD* IV/2, 499–511 in connection with 'justification' and 'sanctification' and again in *CD* III/2, *Reading Barth with Charity*, 123. Shao Kai Tseng, *Karl Barth's Infralapsarian Theology: Origins and Development 1920–1953* (Downers Grove, IL: InterVarsity Press, 2016), rightly notes that Bruce McCormack and Paul Jones have also argued against Hunsinger's idea of the Chalcedonian pattern on the basis of their own 'historicized' view of Christology and concludes that Barth's theology does indeed retain a 'basically Chalcedonian' pattern, 123, 215. Against Paul Nimmo's version of actualism Tseng rightly argues that Barth retained aspects of classical 'substantialism' within his actualistic perspective. See also Molnar, 'The Perils of Embracing a "Historicized Christology"', *Modern Theology*, vol. 30, no. 4 (2014): 454–80 and *Faith, Freedom and the Spirit*, chapter 5 for a discussion of how the historicized Christology of McCormack and Jenson leads them to problematic views of the relationship between the immanent and economic Trinity.

75 See *CD* I/1, 172. See Hunsinger, *Reading Barth with Charity*, 124, n. 10 where he connects this important point with Barth's later use of the same term [*scharf*] (sharp) in *CD* IV/2, 61 to distinguish the relationship between creator and creature and also between the immanent and economic Trinity.

76 *CD* I/1, 323.

77 John Webster 'Trinity and Creation', *IJST*, vol. 12, no. 1 (January 2010): 4–19, 18, has criticized Barth for referring to the second person of the Trinity as an 'abstraction'. However, by abstraction Barth simply may mean that, given the reality of the incarnation, we must abstract from that in order to posit a *Logos asarkos* from the perspective of history in which God has acted for us. He is not denying the reality of the second person of the Trinity as such. Rather he is saying that any attempt to conceptualize this second person as such must not be

God acting for us must be seen against the background of God in himself who could have existed in isolation from us but freely chose not to. He rejected a *Logos asarkos* in his doctrine of creation if it implied a 'formless Christ' or 'a Christ-principle' rather than Jesus who was with God as the Word before the world existed; he rejected it in connection with reconciliation if it meant a retreat to an idea of God behind the God revealed in Christ; but he still insisted it had a proper role to play in the doctrine of the Trinity and in Christology, describing it as 'indispensable for dogmatic enquiry and presentation'.[78] In stark contrast, Jenson rejects such a concept, because history (creation) is allowed to determine God's eternal existence in his thinking; it is noteworthy that in his book *The Triune Identity*, Jenson was indeed trying to reconcile God's freedom to be God without us with Rahner's axiom as it stands (with the vice versa).[79] Barth refused to discredit this 'antecedently in

formed in abstraction from what is revealed in Jesus Christ. For a discussion of this point, see Molnar, *Faith, Freedom and the Spirit*, 139 and Chapter 4.

78 *CD* III/1, 54. Cf. *CD* IV/1, 52. Cf. also *CD* I/2, 168ff. and *CD* III/2, 65f., 147f. and *The Göttingen Dogmatics*, 160 where Barth wrote: 'The Son is both *logos ensarkos* and *logos asarkos*. Do we not have to say this afresh and for the first time truly the moment we speak about the union of God and man in revelation lest we forget that we stand here before the miracle of God? Can we ever have said it enough?' Darren Sumner thinks that my appeal to this statement by Barth is anachronistic (Sumner, *Karl Barth and the Incarnation*, 75). However, the point I was making was that the Logos could and did exist in distinct forms without ceasing to be the *Logos asarkos*. This point is made well by George Hunsinger as noted earlier when he argues correctly that for Barth the Logos exists in distinct forms as *asarkos* and *ensarkos* such that the 'Logos *asarkos*' does not simply disappear and is not 'exhausted' in 'its secondary form as the Logos *incarnandus/incarnatus/ensarkos*' (*Reading Barth with Charity*, 57). Cf. also, *CD* I/2, 136 where Barth writes: 'The Word is what He is even before and apart from His being flesh.'

79 Cf. *The Triune Identity*, 138–41. Jenson believes that any concept of a *Logos asarkos* prevents the procession of the Son from being the same as Jesus's mission. Indeed it does; precisely in order to prevent God's eternal freedom from being confused with his freedom for us. This is not to suggest a separation of Jesus's humanity and divinity but to say that, unless his mission is seen against the background of his being in se before the world was, then his deity will be equated with or seen as the outcome of history. Jenson, following Wolfhart Pannenberg, sees it this way. Thus, 'the Trinity is simply the Father and the man Jesus and their Spirit as the Spirit of the believing community', 141. This is a most curious

footnote 79 (*cont.*)

statement because, as George Hunsinger has observed, it has monophysite overtones (George Hunsinger, 'Robert Jenson's Systematic Theology: a review essay' *SJT*, vol. 55, no. 2: 161-200, 168) as when Jenson also says that: 'According to our Christological conclusions [in *STI*, 134-8], the identity of the eternal Son is the human person Jesus' (Robert W. Jenson, *Systematic Theology Volume 2, The Works of God* [New York: Oxford University Press, 1999]), 99. What happened to the eternal Trinity which preexisted, exists now and is also future? This Trinity is banished into a future: 'This "economic" Trinity is eschatologically God "himself," an "immanent" Trinity' (*The Triune Identity*, 141). Hence, Jenson substitutes Jesus's resurrection for God's *ousia* (168) and argues that: 'The divine *ousia* is no longer our first concern. It is the work, the creative event done as Jesus' life, death, resurrection' (113); here historical events displace God's eternal being and action. This is the major problem that follows Rahner's axiom of identity with its vice versa. Part of the difficulty here is that Jenson's thought drifts in the direction of a type of panentheism that allows events in history to determine God's eternal being, as Hunsinger notes (Hunsinger, *SJT* [2002], 176ff.). However, here also, the key issue concerns the fact that 'for Jenson, the Son enjoys no antecedent reality prior to his coming to be in history' so that 'the eternal trinity enjoys no antecedent reality, strictly speaking, prior to the creation of the world' (Hunsinger, *SJT* [2002], 171-2). Hunsinger maintains that Jenson solves this problem by investing the 'triune life' in the Father alone. Thus, his thought has both Arian and subordinationist tendencies. In Hunsinger's words: 'It is Jenson's teleological self-constitution of the trinity, along with his historical constitution of the Son's deity, that puts him on a collision course not just with the intentions of Arius [because for Arius God was primordially determinate and not primordially indeterminate as suggested by Jenson], but precisely with those of Nicaea [because for Nicaea and Constantinople God was primordially determinate as the eternal Father, Son and Holy Spirit]' (Hunsinger, *SJT* [2002], 173). Hunsinger is not alone in criticizing Jenson on this point. Simon Gathercole: 'Pre-existence, and the Freedom of the Son in Creation and Redemption: An Exposition in Dialogue with Robert Jenson, *IJST*, vol. 7, no. 1 (January 2005): 38-51, referring to Phil. 2:6-11, thinks that Jenson's position is incoherent because, in his attempt to speak about Jesus's preexistence, he will not speak of 'the transition from pre-existent Sonship to incarnate Sonship' and thus of the incarnation not as 'something which *happens to* the Son, but which comes about by the very action of the Son himself' so that his emptying himself refers to 'an action whereby the Son freely determines his being in the incarnation' (46). This 'pre-existent Jesus' has 'a personal act of *choice*' and does not simply find himself in the world 'independently of any will on his part' (47). In light of this, Gathercole rightly argues that 'Jenson's Christology fails in that

himself' as 'untheological metaphysical speculation'. Christ's deity has to do with 'the distinction between the Son of God in Himself and for me. On the distinction between the "in Himself" and "for me" depends the acknowledgment of the freedom and unindebtedness of God's grace, i.e., the very thing that really makes it grace'.[80]

What happens in *Systematic Theology Volume I* is instructive. What Jenson seeks to interpret 'is a birth of the *Logos* as God that enables and therefore must be somehow antecedent to his birth as man'. On the one hand we are told that: 'There must be in God's eternity – with Barth, in his eternal decision – a way in which the one Jesus Christ as God precedes himself as man, in the very triune life which he lives eternally as the God-man.' On the other hand he argues that: 'What in eternity precedes the Son's birth to Mary is not an unincarnate *state* of the Son, but a pattern of movement within the event of the incarnation, the movement to incarnation, as itself a pattern of God's triune life.'[81] While Jenson notes that he inadequately made this distinction in his earlier work, he nevertheless believes that his rejection of a *Logos asarkos* preceding the incarnation was correct. Now the problem with

it cannot accommodate a real, personal "before and after" in the incarnation. As a result, his Christology fails to provide the "before and after", which the Son's free act entails' (47). The problem here then is expressed in Jenson's misguided remark that in reading John's prologue 'we may not, if we follow the Gospel it introduces, conceive the pre-existence of the Son as the existence of a divine entity that has simply not yet become the created personality of the Gospels' (Jenson, *STI*, 139). For Jenson, Christ's preexistence is his preexistence in the history of Israel since for him we can 'see how the Son indeed precedes his human birth without being simply unincarnate: the Son appears as a narrative pattern of Israel's created human story before he can appear as an individual Israelite within that story' (Jenson, *STI*, 141). What precedes Christ's birth to Mary, for Jenson, 'is the narrative pattern of *being going to be* born of Mary' and this cannot be 'an unincarnate *state* of the Son' (Jenson, *STI*, 141). This leads Jenson to two further problematic assertions: (1) 'Jesus is the second hypostasis of the Trinity' (in reality the second hypostasis of the Trinity is the eternal Son who became incarnate for us) and (2) he continues 'to regard *Logos asarkos*, used for something "before" the incarnation on any sort of line, as a *Vorstellung* [an idea] in futile search of a *Begriff* [concept]' (Jenson, '*Once more the* Logos asarkos', *IJST*, 133).

80 *CD* I/1, 420. Cf. also *CD* I/1, 416ff.
81 *STI*, 141.

this reasoning is that it leads directly to the idea that history constitutes God's eternal being, that is, to the idea of a dependent deity.[82] And that in fact compromises the freedom that Jenson intends to maintain as when he writes that: 'The "hypostases" are Jesus and the transcendent Will he called "Father" and the Spirit of their future for us ... What happens between Jesus and his Father and our future *happens in God* – that is the point.'[83]

But what happened to Christ's sonship here? It appears to be equated with the human Jesus in his relation to the Father. To that extent one

82 Importantly, as George Hunsinger notes, Jenson's 'denial of the Son's full ontological antecedence, is precisely what gives Jenson's Christology its "adoptionist" and "Arian" features' (Hunsinger, *SJT* [2002], 187). There are two fatal moves evident in Jenson's idea of the Trinity: 'He denies that God is a person, and he denies that God is simple' (Hunsinger, *SJT*, 187). These ideas together 'lead inexorably toward subordinationism and tritheism' and when these ideas are combined with 'the metaphysics of panentheistic historicism ... they also lead ... toward monism. Subordinationism, tritheism, and monism – these are the steep price of God's total Hegelian immersion' (Hunsinger, *SJT*, 188). Divine simplicity means that we must uphold the traditional concepts of 'divine immutability, impassibility and timelessness' (Hunsinger, *SJT*, 189). It is these ideas that Jenson's Hegelian thinking inexorably opposes. Hunsinger convincingly explains Jenson's tritheistic tendencies (Hunsinger, *SJT*, 194ff.) explaining that for Jenson there are 'three divine subjects in one coherent story' since 'God ... is constituted by the outcome of narrated events' (Hunsinger, *SJT*, 194). Interestingly, Francesca Aran Murphy thinks that Jenson is also open to the charge of modalism because his approach ends in 'an Hegelian absorption of the three hypostases into a single process or grammar' in spite of appearances to the contrary (Francesca Aran Murphy, *God is Not a Story: Realism Revisited*, [Oxford: Oxford University Press, 2007]), 278. She astutely notes that the 'axis' for our identifying the trinitarian God in Jenson's thought 'is not the divine-human *uniqueness* of Jesus, but the instrumental process of *identification*' (268). This occurs, she thinks, because: 'The unitary process into which descriptive Trinitarianism ingests the three-personed God is human storytelling' (268). Consequently, she thinks 'a unitary Fate presides over the fortunes of Jenson's Father, Son, and Holy Spirit' since she believes 'an apparent "hyper-Trinitarianism" is effectively a modalism' (262).

83 Jenson, *The Triune Identity*, 106. Scott R. Swain, *The God of the Gospel: Robert Jenson's Trinitarian Theology* (hereafter: *The God of the Gospel*) (Downers Grove, IL: InterVarsity Press, 2013), also notices this difficulty in

may either say that the human Jesus exists eternally, that is, before the Word became incarnate (in which case his human existence is compromised), or one may say that the human Jesus became the Son of God in his actions in history (in which case he did not in fact preexist as the eternally begotten Son of the Father). However, one cannot say that Jesus as such is one of the trinitarian hypostases without blurring the distinction between God in se and God acting for us ad extra. What happens in Jenson's thinking, in my opinion, is that Jesus is actually stripped of his eternal uniqueness as Son. Here I agree with George Hunsinger that 'Jenson's understanding of Christ's person is so close to that rejected by the Council of Nicaea that it may fairly be called, if not "Arian", then certainly at least "neo-Arian".'[84] And this is captured in the statement that:

> What the event of God happens to is, first, the triune persons. The fundamental statement of God's being is therefore: God is what happens between Jesus and his Father in their Spirit ... [also] God is what happens to Jesus and the world. That an event happens to something does not entail that this something must be metaphysically or temporally prior to it.[85]

Jenson's thought when he points out two seemingly irreconcilable statements that undergird Jenson's thinking: (1) 'Jenson asserts that God determines who and what he will be by determining to be the God of his people' and (2) 'he also affirms in certain places that God could or would have been the same God that he is *apart from* his people', 155. According to Swain: 'These statements are difficult, if not impossible, to reconcile', 155. I would lean in the direction of saying they are impossible to reconcile because God is who he is as the one who loves in freedom, precisely as the eternal triune God and God would be that God even if he never had decided to create, reconcile and redeem the world. Jenson's God is essentially a dependent deity and that very idea undercuts God's sovereignty and makes it impossible to see his actions ad extra as acts of free grace.

84 Hunsinger, *SJT* (2002), 171.

85 *STI*, 221. Even here, however, Jenson attempts to maintain God's freedom by saying that: 'It might not have been so. God might have been the God he is without this world to happen to. However, again, we can know only the counterfactual; how God would have described his own being had he been without the world, we cannot even inquire' (*STI*, 221). This same idea appears in *STI*, 65 as well. That once again is the problem because according to Barth it is precisely on the basis of revelation that we do know that God is not a

Here once again Jesus's antecedent existence as the eternally begotten Son of the Father is simply denied in order to advance a Hegelian notion of God's involvement with history. Part of the difficulty here is the fact that Jenson believes that ' "the Son" in trinitarian use' does not 'first denote a simply divine entity. Primally, it denotes the claim Jesus makes for himself in addressing God as Father; as we will see, this Son is an eternally divine Son only in and by this relation'.[86]

Additionally, there is a problem in the way Jenson understands Barth's notion of divine *decision*. By choosing to unite himself with us in the man Jesus, God not only chooses that he *will be* the man Jesus, but since 'God *is* his act of choice ... he *is* the man Jesus'.[87] In other words, the way Jenson conceptualizes the divine choice, it appears that God is not really free to decide to become incarnate and then carry out that primal decision in history; rather the incarnation happens in eternity as the ground of its happening in time, 'in eternity as the act of decision that God is'. Here God's choice is equated with God's nature, and this seems to me to compromise God's freedom. The corrective here is the fact that Barth held that God's unity with us is something new as an act of will which 'has its basis neither in the essence of God nor in that of man, and which God does not owe either to Himself or to any other being ... That is what we can call ... God's free election of grace ...'[88] More will be said about this shortly.

'counterfactual' but the eternal Father, Son and Holy Spirit who would have been exactly who he was and is as the one who loves in freedom without us but nevertheless freely chose not to be without us. By dismissing the *Logos asarkos* Jenson is unable to recognize and maintain the freedom of the eternal Trinity. In other words there is no clear doctrine of the immanent Trinity functioning in Jenson's thought as it did indeed function in Barth's thought.

86 *STI*, 77. Here Jenson appeals to the thinking of Wolfhart Pannenberg.

87 *STI*, 140.

88 *CD* IV/1, 66. Earlier we noted that God is not the result of an act of his will and discussed the distinctions that Barth carefully made between God willing his own being and the fact that God is not free to will to be God or not since he cannot not be who he is as the eternal Trinity. Here it should be noted that Barth's thinking about God's nature and will as mentioned earlier represents what George Hunsinger has called a 'subtle modification' of Athanasius's insight that the begetting of the Son is a work of will because in God, nature and will are the same (*CD* I/1, 435). However, since God's eternal being is not a 'counterfactual' as Jenson seems to think, one cannot think of his eternal nature as the result of his decision or will to relate with us. So the begetting of the Son is

The Proper Significance of Jesus's Resurrection from the Dead: How to Understand Jesus's Glorified Body

This difficulty evident in Jenson's view of Jesus's eternal sonship becomes especially evident when we are told that Christ's sonship is neither determined by his birth nor by his preexistence but by his Resurrection: 'He is Son in that he is resurrected.'[89] Or 'In that Christ's Sonship comes "from" his Resurrection, it comes from God's future into which he is raised.'[90] Or again 'Jesus would not be the Word without the Resurrection.'[91] And '*fully* reliable love can *only* be the resurrected life of one who has died for the beloved ones'.[92] Finally, we are told not only that 'the way in which the triune God is eternal, is by the events of Jesus' death and resurrection' but that his 'individuality is constitutive of the true God's infinity'.[93] All these descriptions unfortunately allow events that take place in creation (in

not an act of will in the sense that God might or might not have been the eternal Trinity. A freedom not to will himself, Barth says, would be 'an abrogation of his freedom' (*CD*, I/1, 435). All of this, Hunsinger says, 'gives the lie to the idea that [Barth] regarded the triune God's being merely as "decision"' as Robert Jenson claims in his 'Karl Barth on the Being of God', *Thomas Aquinas and Karl Barth*, ed. Bruce L. McCormack and Thomas Joseph White, O.P. (Grand Rapids, MI: Eerdmans, 2013, 48-9) (Hunsinger, *Reading Barth with Charity*, 105–6). Strangely, Jenson here argues that God 'needs nothing to be and to be what he is, not even possession of his own essence, not even an antecedent "himself" with which to begin' Jenson, 'Karl Barth on the Being of God', 49. This denial of God's antecedent triunity is consistent with Jenson's firm rejection of the *Logos asarkos*. However, it is also completely antithetical to Barth's insistence that all God is and does in history is grounded in his antecedent existence as the eternal Father, Son and Holy Spirit. Scott R. Swain, *The God of the Gospel*, rightly maintains that there is a serious problem with Jenson's idea that 'God is perfect in that the contingent fact of his freely *willed* existence determines the *nature* of his existence' (156). Swain argues that the problem with this view is that 'if God's manner of being God is determined by his decision to be our God, then God's decision to be our God cannot be a decision to give God, for there is no antecedently existent God to be given' (156). Jenson's thinking, Swain rightly argues, undermines the reality of the 'economy of grace' (156).

89 *STI*, 142.
90 *STI*, 143.
91 *STI*, 171.
92 *STI*, 199.
93 *STI*, 219.

history) to determine or define God's supposedly preexistent being and nature. This is precisely the confusion of the immanent and economic Trinity that Barth was able to avoid by distinguishing God in se from God *for us*. Even Jenson's own insight expressed in *The Triune Identity* that God could be the triune God without creation or incarnation is here called into question by the fact that Jesus could not have been the Word without the Resurrection. Here history and Jesus's sonship are reversed. Is this not just because the function of the *Logos asarkos* is rejected in his doctrine of the Trinity and in his Christology? It certainly appears that this rejection compromises God's genuine preexistence by making it dependent on a historical event or a series of historical events. Could this situation be otherwise, given Jenson's assertion that: 'Since the Lord's self-identity is constituted in dramatic coherence, it is established not from the beginning but from the end, not at birth but at death, not in *persistence* but in *anticipation*?'[94] Furthermore, and against Jenson's best intentions, does this thinking not compromise the historicity of the resurrection itself because it ascribes to history a power that it cannot actually have, that is, the power to constitute God's eternal being and nature?

Compromising the fact that Jesus is the Son of God simply because he is (and not because of the resurrection), this thinking opens the door to the idea that salvation is conditioned. Thus, Jenson believes that 'the very existence of the Gospels as a corpus depends on the community constituted by the faith that so judges',[95] whereas the existence of 'the Gospels' depends on the work of the Holy Spirit rather than the community. Also, we are told that 'the occurrence of the gospel depends on the chain of witnesses who have brought the news from the first witnesses to those who now hear'.[96] Is it not the case that while we are dependent on these witnesses, the occurrence of the gospel is not? And finally, this thinking leads to the idea that once we have heard the gospel our question should become: 'what *shall* we now say and enact that the gospel may be spoken?'[97] Should the question instead not be whether and to what extent our actions and speech acknowledge God's freedom for us and thus allow him to speak to us through our dogmatic work?

---

94 *STI*, 66. By contrast, as seen earlier, Barth writes: 'He who the third day rose from the dead was no less true God in the manger than on the cross' *CD* I/2, 38.

95 *STI*, 174.

96 *STI*, 14.

97 *STI*, 16.

In his book *The Triune Identity*, Jenson suggested that: 'If we bend the old language a little, instead of replacing it, we may say that the resurrection is this God's [the Christian God's] *ousia*.'[98] But as we have just seen, this thinking simply eliminates a genuinely existing immanent Trinity. God's *ousia* is his triunity, his eternal being and act as the one who loves in freedom; it is the fact that God eternally exists and acts as Father, Son and Holy Spirit. The problem here concerns making the resurrection the center of theology without making this important distinction between the immanent and economic Trinity.[99] This affects what is said about the resurrection and the risen Lord himself.

Jenson very astutely rejects the idea that the resurrection could be construed as a vision or in any other reductionist way that would divest from the New Testament narrative its true meaning which is that Jesus is risen bodily from the dead.[100] With or without the empty tomb, he believes that 'Somehow there now exists a body that is the living Jesus' human body'.[101] Jenson embarks on a very interesting analysis of the

---

98 Jenson, *The Triune Identity*, 168.

99 Among contemporary theologians Ivor J. Davidson gets this just right, 'Salvation's Destiny: Heirs of God' in *God of Salvation: Soteriology in Theological Perspective*, ed. Ivor J. Davidson and Murray A. Rae (Farnham, UK: Ashgate, 2011), 155–75, 166. Accordingly, Davidson writes: 'Great care is needed in the articulation of this twofold reality [that the 'risen and ascended one acquires no status that is not his antecedently' and that his mission is the 'temporal outworking of the divine will to save']: the completeness of the Son's person and work on the one hand, his continuing temporal activity on the other. Much theology has stumbled at just this point, envisaging the futurity of the Son's inheritance as evidence that his current status (even his hypostatic identity) is somehow transient, or so pressing God's decision to define himself in temporality that the history of God's relations with creatures is seen as literally determinative of the divine essence' (166–7). Davidson insightfully concludes that because 'the outcome' of God's saving work 'is grounded in the sovereignty of God's triune commitment to embrace within his own perfection the fulfilment of creaturely reality' therefore any suggestion that this 'conclusion is uncertain' by conceptualizing the future as 'open' or 'incomplete in some literal sense for divine persons' means that such a view confuses 'being and time in such a way that the immanent Trinity is collapsed entirely into the economic' and that indeed fatally compromises 'the eternal fullness of God's life *in se*' (167).

100 *STI*, 196–201.

101 *STI*, 201.

meaning of heaven, and Ptolemaic and Copernican cosmology in order to stress that if Jesus has no body after the resurrection then we are in fact denying the resurrection itself as well as our own future with God. Also, as Thomas Aquinas believed, Christ embodied on the altar did not have to *travel* to get there (as in the Ptolemaic model), but by God's fiat the embodied Christ is simply both places at once, that is, in heaven and on the altar. Here Jenson follows and intends to correct the shortcomings of the Swabians who relied on a radically Cyrillean Christology. The question then is: 'Where is Christ's body, if it needs no spatial heaven and is not restricted in its presence by created spatial distances?'[102] Jenson's answer follows Paul and argues that the church 'is the risen body of Christ. She is this because the bread and cup in the congregation's midst is the very same body of Christ'; accordingly Christ's risen body is 'whatever object it is that is Christ's availability to us as subjects'.[103] Since the bread and cup are the objects of Christ's promised presence, we might thus locate him and respond to his word there. 'Sacrament and church are *truly* Christ's body for us' because he makes himself available to us through them. We are told that Jesus 'needs no other body to be a risen man, body and soul'.[104] Jenson finally decides cautiously that he can say that the tomb was empty because if it were not, then Jesus would have been merely a saint whose relics we are devoted to and not the living Lord.

There are at least two problems here. The first is that the New Testament appearance accounts suggest that Jesus had his own glorified body during the 40 days between the resurrection and the ascension.[105]

---

102 *STI*, 204.

103 *STI*, 205.

104 *STI*, 206. George Hunsinger notes that Jenson's thinking in this respect appears to be monistic since he 'strangely conflates the church with the actual (metaphysical) body of the risen Christ' as when he says 'the church is *ontologically* the risen Christ's human body' (Hunsinger, *SJT*, 195) referring to Jenson, *Systematic Theology II*, 213. Ivor J. Davidson gets the distinction just right maintaining that 'Resurrection and ascension mean genuine exaltation, actual enthronement of the formerly dead Jesus "far above" all created things (Eph. 1:21–2). But this occurs inasmuch as it is simply "not possible" for death to hold him (Acts 2:24)' (*Salvation's Destiny*, 165). All of this is enacted by the divine-human Son for us as an act of transcendence. Hence 'it is not the story of the Son's episodic journey towards majority' (*Salvation's Destiny*, 166).

105 Cf. Lk. 24:36f., Jn. 20:24 and *CD* III/2, 327, 330, 448.

This is important because it precludes confusion of Christ and the church and suggests that our own hoped for resurrection is grounded in what has already happened in the life of Jesus himself. As T. F. Torrance puts it:

> The resurrection of Christ in *body* demonstrated that the saving work of Christ on our behalf was fulfilled within the concrete reality of our actual human existence, and in such a way as to set it upon an entirely new basis in the regeneration or renewal of human being in the risen Lord ... Far from being just a promise for the future, it [Christ's bodily resurrection] is an evangelical declaration of what had already taken place in Christ, and in him continues as a permanent triumphant reality throughout the whole course of time to its consummation, when Christ will return with glory to judge the quick and the dead, and unveil the great regeneration (παλιγγενεσία) which he has accomplished for the whole creation of visible and invisible realities alike.[106]

Jenson's statement that 'God does in fact have a body, the body born of Mary and risen into the church and its sacraments',[107] compromises this distinction. It is Jesus Christ himself who is risen from the dead; he did not simply rise into the church and its sacraments. Jenson would probably be horrified to find himself in the same company as Elizabeth Johnson with this assertion. As noted earlier in Chapter 1, it is Johnson's contention that 'the body of the risen Christ becomes the body of the community'.[108] Jenson's view appears to be another version of Bultmann's reduction of the Easter history to the rise of faith, albeit one that substitutes the church and the sacraments for Jesus, true God and true man, who appeared to his disciples during the 40 days. Interestingly, while Jenson was critical of Barth for having an insufficient doctrine of the Spirit, Barth insisted that the church 'lives by the Holy Spirit and in faith' such that we are in the church 'on the strength of the fact that Jesus Christ is for us in eternity' and we 'are within in the Holy Spirit' and thus 'in faith'.[109] Hence, 'where the Holy Spirit is and therefore where faith is, there is the Church'. We are the church, Barth says, not when we try to be

---

106 Torrance, *The Trinitarian Faith*, 299.
107 *STI*, 229.
108 Johnson, *She Who Is*, 162.
109 *CD* II/1, 160.

it, but when through the Spirit and in faith we participate 'in the person and work of Jesus Christ'.[110] For Barth then the church

> lives literally and really only in Jesus Christ as its Head to which it is the body; or in Jesus Christ its heavenly body of which it is the earthly form. This is just as literally and really the case as the Holy Spirit in us is only the temporal presence of Jesus Christ Himself, or faith is only our relationship to Him ... [the church] is a totality in the manhood taken by Jesus Christ, in His heavenly body, crucified and transfigured in His resurrection but now existing in the glory of the Father. The Church is not another body. It is just the earthly form of this His own heavenly body, the manhood reconciled in Him and represented by Him above (and because above also below).[111]

The second problem is the fact that the Holy Spirit is noticeably absent in Jenson's thinking at this point. The result is that while we may describe the eucharist and the church as Christ's body in virtue of their unity with their heavenly head who is Christ himself, that cannot mean that these can be substituted for his own glorified (transfigured) body in heaven or his presence to us through the Holy Spirit uniting him to us through these earthly media. Any such substitution implies that Christ needs the church as the church needs Christ and detaches our hope from Christ's active mediation of himself. This again calls into question our own hoped-for resurrection which is proleptically experienced here and now.

One further point needs to be mentioned. In one sense, Jenson believes that one would not have perceived the uncanny phenomenon 'as the result of a resurrection unless one *recognized* it as someone one knew who had died'.[112] But this reasoning suggests that it is

---

110 *CD* II/1, 160.

111 *CD* II/1, 160. It would be hard to find a clearer expression of the unity and distinction between Christ and the church and between the risen Lord in his heavenly body and the church as his earthly body united with its heavenly head in faith through the Spirit. There is no confusion of Christ and the church in this understanding as there is in Jenson's understanding. Barth thus can firmly insist that Christian hope is a very specific hope which we have as we are 'seized' by Jesus himself. Barth says: 'He is the living man who as such is the future of the world and of every man, and the hope of the Christian. By His coming to His disciples after His resurrection in the revelation of the forty days He pointed to Himself as their hope and future' (*CD* IV/1, 117).

112 *STI*, 199.

we (or the disciples) who can believe in the resurrection because we or they are able to make the connection between the one event and the rest of Jesus's life. Yet this places the power of comprehension in human hands and misses the important point that what the disciples experienced went 'utterly against the grain'.[113] Since God was present as the man Jesus in the 40 days, they were empowered to become believers rather than unbelievers. The risen Lord himself therefore, rather than their powers of recognition, enabled their comprehension here.[114]

The Relation between Time and Eternity

This brings us to a consideration of God's being by exploring the relationship of time and eternity. Here Jenson notes that Greek philosophy has bequeathed to theology the false idea that God must be immune to time and that he must also be impassible and that modalism (locating God above time) and subordinationism (which makes the Father alone transcendent) preceded the Nicene solution.[115] The gospel contradicts both of these concepts and Jenson will solve this problem partially by following Thomas Aquinas and partially by following Gregory of Nyssa in order to understand eternity as 'God's temporal infinity'.

Consistent with his belief that the identity of the God of the gospel is not determined antecedently but only by the gospel story itself, Jenson understands authentic belief to mean that one is unconditionally open to the future, but not just any future, as Bultmann apparently held. It is to be open to 'a future determined as fellowship with Jesus'; thus, Jesus in his full historical reality 'is the Word of God in that he is the identity of the future opened by the Word of God … he is not the Word of God in isolation as himself, nor is he first word and then the particular Word of God … Jesus would not be the Word without the Resurrection'.[116]

Jenson thus follows Gregory of Nyssa to fill out Thomas Aquinas' notion of God as 'He who is' in a trinitarian way. Accordingly, in the first instance, the one God is the 'mutual life of Father, Son, and Spirit'. This being of God is 'a *going-on*, a sequentially palpable event, like a

---

113 *CD* III/2, 449.

114 For further discussion of this, see Molnar, *Incarnation and Resurrection*, esp. 33–4.

115 *STI*, 94ff.

116 *STI*, 171.

kiss or a train wreck'.[117] Second, 'that the Father is the Father, or that the Son is the Son, or that the Spirit is the Spirit, is other than and prior to the fact that God is'.[118] Third, Gregory thinks of the divine *ousia* in an anti-Greek way as the infinite. Thus what characterizes the Father, Son and Spirit is 'limitlessness'; 'what Father, Son and Spirit have from each other to be three identities of *God*, and what characterizes their mutual action *as* God, is limitlessness'.[119] While the Greeks could only envision an infinity using a spatial analogy and concluded that an infinite something would be nothing, Gregory's idea of God's deity is '*temporal* infinity. God is not infinite because he extends indefinitely but because no temporal activity can keep up with the activity that he is'.[120] While Aristotle's understanding of the infinite would imply that it lacked all boundaries, Gregory's idea was that the infinite would overcome all boundaries. The Arians, following Greek thinking, refused to call the *Logos* God because he acts and suffers. However, Gregory believed that precisely this activity qualifies the *Logos* to be God and suggested, according to Jenson, that: 'If they [the Arians] must divide eternity, let them reverse their doctrine and find the mark of deity in endless futurity ...; let them guide their thinking by what is to come and is real in hope rather than by what is past and old.' Thus, 'to be God is always to be open to and always to open a future, transgressing all past-imposed conditions'.[121] Interestingly, while Jenson appeals to Gregory's *Book I Against Eunomius* to advance this argument, the fact is that Gregory maintains that God's eternity consists *both* in his endlessness *and* in his being without beginning and so actually portrays the position that is adopted by Jenson as a choice one might make if one were confused about the triune God's eternity![122]

This then is the proper view of eternity: 'A religion', according to Jenson, 'is the cultivation of some eternity ...' and 'The biblical God's eternity is his temporal infinity'. Consequently, 'the true God is not

---

117 *STI*, 214.

118 *STI*, 215.

119 *STI*, 216.

120 *STI*, 216.

121 *STI*, 216.

122 Cf. Gregory of Nyssa, *Against Eunomius Book I*, §42 in *Select Writings and Letters of Gregory, Bishop of Nyssa*, trans. William Moore and Henry Wilson, *Nicene and Post-Nicene Fathers of The Christian Church* (Grand Rapids, MI: Eerdmans, 1988), 98.

eternal because he lacks time, but because he takes time'.[123] God is eternal 'because he is primally future to himself and only thereupon past and present for himself'. This is of a piece with Jenson's idea that the Spirit must liberate the Father and the Son for mutual relationship.[124] Thus, we finally have our full-blown definition of eternity: 'God is not eternal in that he adamantly remains as he began, but in that he always creatively opens to what he will be; not in that he hangs on, but in that he gives and receives, not in that he perfectly persists, but in that he perfectly anticipates'. God's eternity therefore consists in the fact that God 'is faithful to his commitments within time … Israel's God is eternal in that he is faithful to the death, and then yet again faithful'.[125]

Notice here that God's eternity is defined by his relationship with history instead of by his self-sufficient being as Father, Son and Spirit. Thus, Jenson actually believes that God is eternal '*because* he is triune'[126] and that God's whence (the Father) and whither (the Spirit), the origin and goal, do not fall apart because they are 'reconciled in the action and suffering of the Son'. If this is the case, then Jenson has allowed history and suffering to define God's supposed eternal and self-sufficient being as triune. Hence, he writes: 'the way in which the triune God is eternal, is by the events of Jesus' death and resurrection'.[127]

Here once again historical events that have meaning only because God *is* eternally the one who loves in freedom and who then acts freely for us within history are allowed to define God's being, eternity and nature. Hence we are told that:

> Consciousness is as such infinite … The Ego as which the Father finds himself is the Son. But the Son exists not at all for himself

123 *STI*, 217. It will be remembered that, as George Hunsinger has pointed out, Jenson's historicized and Hegelian thinking will not allow for God to be God before time and above time. So while Barth had a clear idea of God's time in simultaneity without opposition of past, present and future and as his pretemporal, supratemporal and posttemporal existence, Jenson will not allow for any idea that God's eternal time transcends time.

124 Cf. *STI*, 223.

125 *STI*, 217.

126 *STI*, 218.

127 *STI*, 219. This sort of thinking led Hunsinger to conclude rightly that for Jenson 'God's eternal being, therefore, is not "timeless". It is rather at once metaphysically determined by time's real distinctions (past, present, future), while yet also being superior to them. Because God's temporal infinity

and altogether for those for whom the Father intends him. Thus the Father's preoccupation with the Son, Jesus' intrusion into the outward flight of the Father's consciousness, does not restrict the Father's consciousness but is rather his consciousness's opening to its universal scope.[128]

Unfortunately, the implication here is that God is not eternally self-sufficient but is becoming who he will be because of his relations ad extra. This understanding of eternity appears to be more a projection of our self-consciousness onto the eternal than an accurate depiction of God's pretemporal, supratemporal and posttemporal existence.[129] Here both time and suffering are allowed to define the divine nature. If, however, a proper distinction between the immanent and economic Trinity had been made, then we could say that God's time is uniquely his and so is above and prior to our time and that when God suffered in Jesus Christ it was indeed a miraculous condescension that cannot be explained in terms of consciousness. Thus, it disclosed the nature of God as one who can suffer on our behalf while remaining one who does not suffer by nature. As T. F. Torrance notes, if we try to understand passibility and impassibility logically, then they cancel each other out – God must either be one or the other. However, if we understand them soteriologically, then we will see that God is both passible and impassible at the same time, just as he is human and divine at the same time.[130]

is teleological, God's being is teleological ... [God] is *not* eternal in that he adamantly remains as he began, *but* in that he always creatively opens himself to what he will be' (*SJT*, 182–3). This thinking Hunsinger identifies as a type of 'panentheistic historicism' (*SJT*, 183).

128 *STI*, 220.

129 For a careful and nuanced interpretation of Barth's understanding of the relation of time and eternity which avoids the pitfalls of Hegelian and processive thinking while showing how Barth's understanding of God's pretemporal, supratemporal and posttemporal existence is dictated by his understanding of the Trinity, see George Hunsinger, *Disruptive Grace*, chapter eight. Hunsinger himself is critical of Jenson noting that in his Hegelian thinking 'eternity, like time, is a flowing now ... that not only moves along with time but also requires time for its own self-actualization', 188.

130 Torrance, *The Trinitarian Faith*, 185. For a full discussion of how time and eternity might properly be understood in this way, see Molnar, *Faith, Freedom and the Spirit*, chapter 4, 'Origenism, Election, and Time and Eternity', 187–224. See also, Molnar, *Thomas F. Torrance: Theologian of the Trinity*.

Both these features are compromised here because Jenson insists that we must abandon any thought of fixed perfection in God and define God by futurity instead of keeping our eyes fixed on Christ himself who is the same yesterday, today and tomorrow.

We have seen that Robert Jenson's trinitarian theology offers a very clear illustration of the kinds of problem that arise for contemporary theologians when they do not formulate their understanding in relation to a clear doctrine of the immanent Trinity. Had Jenson been able to make a clear distinction between the immanent and economic Trinity, he would have been able to acknowledge God's freedom consistently by not suggesting that Jesus in his humanity as such is the revealer; that Jesus was not eternally incarnate but that he preexisted the incarnation as the *Logos asarkos* who was the eternally begotten Son of the Father; that the God who humbles himself on our behalf in the incarnation, cross and resurrection never was, is or will be dependent on events within history to become who he will be; that the resurrection does not in any sense constitute Jesus's eternal sonship, but rather it discloses who he was and is as the incarnate Son; that the resurrection is an event in Jesus's life on the basis of which he (the risen Lord) gives meaning to the faith of the disciples then and now; and finally that God's eternity is not defined by its relation to time but by who God the Father, Son and Spirit is in his pretemporal, supratemporal and posttemporal existence. We have also seen that Jenson is not alone holding these beliefs; both Bruce McCormack and Douglas Farrow follow him in different ways with their inability to acknowledge the continued importance of a *Logos asarkos* both for Barth and for contemporary theology.

Since a great deal of discussion has followed on issues related to my presentation of the importance of the doctrine of the immanent Trinity for Barth's entire theology, it will be useful here to explore in detail where some of these issues have led in the years since the publication of the first edition of this book. Thus, before exploring exactly how Rahner's thinking has shaped the present landscape, I will discuss a number of responses to my understanding of divine freedom explaining exactly how and why I think it is still important to acknowledge God's antecedent existence as crucial to a proper grasp of God's actions of love for us in history. Toward this we now turn.

Chapter 4

RECONSIDERING DIVINE FREEDOM

There is little doubt that, whatever difficulties may yet attend Barth's trinitarian doctrine,[1] he offered a very powerful understanding of God's relations with us and ours with God just because he based those actions

1 See, for example, George Hunsinger, 'Karl Barth's Doctrine of the Trinity, And Some Protestant Doctrines After Barth', in *The Oxford Handbook of The Trinity*, ed. Gilles Emery, O.P. and Matthew Levering, (New York: Oxford University Press, 2011), who suggests that while Barth's presentation of the doctrine 'was characteristically subtle, deep, and idiosyncratic' (294), there was nonetheless a weakness and that was that he paid insufficient 'attention (arguably) to the question of derivation' (296). Hunsinger believes that if Barth had done this then he would have stressed both reconciliation and worship since the doctrine arises because the church 'confesses the full deity of Jesus Christ' and this mystery 'is indispensable to the doctrines of revelation, reconciliation, and worship' (296). Perhaps most importantly, however, in this context it should be noted that for Hunsinger, Barth's 'later use and development of the doctrine did not depart from these basic outlines' (294), that is, the outlines he offered in *CD* I/1, 295–489. This assertion, which I regard as quite accurate, is ignored or obviated by those who believe that Barth either had two doctrines of the Trinity, one expressed in *CD* I/1 and another in *CD* IV/1 or that his trinitarian presentation needed to be revised in light of his later thinking, especially after his presentation of the doctrine of election. See, for example, Bruce L. McCormack, 'The Doctrine of the Trinity after Barth: An Attempt to Reconstruct Barth's Doctrine in the Light of His Later Christology', in *Trinitarian Theology after Barth*, ed. Myk Habets and Phillip Tolliday (Eugene, OR: Pickwick Publications, 2011), 87–117. Ignoring or obviating this important point, unfortunately, leads to very different interpretations of theologians such as Rahner, Moltmann, Pannenberg and Jüngel. Hunsinger is properly critical of these thinkers because he thinks Rahner's rule unwittingly threatened the relation of correspondence that Barth saw between the immanent and economic Trinity while the others just mentioned never managed to uphold Barth's view of correspondence either

ad extra on a positive consideration of who God eternally was and is.²
While many today still are unclear about this, there are others who are

(310). It is no accident then that McCormack mistakenly believes that Rahner's
axiom of identity does not collapse the immanent into the economic Trinity and
that the views of Moltmann, Pannenberg and Jüngel do not compromise Barth's
thinking either (Bruce McCormack, 'The Lord and Giver of Life: A "Barthian"
Defense of the *Filioque*', in *Rethinking Trinitarian Theology: Disputed Questions
And Contemporary Issues in Trinitarian Theology*, ed. Robert J. Woźniak and
Giulio Maspero [London/New York: T & T Clark, 2012, 238]). Hence, with
respect to the question of whether or not Rahner, Moltmann, Pannenberg
and Jüngel had finally collapsed the immanent into the economic Trinity in
some measure, McCormack says 'such a collapse is not true of Rahner himself
or any of the three Protestant theologians under consideration here' (238).
McCormack of course believes wholeheartedly in Rahner's axiom as long as it
is modified by Jüngel's idea that the immanent Trinity must be identified with
the economic at the point of Jesus's suffering and death. Among other things,
McCormack exhibits no knowledge of Rahner's wider thinking and of how his
theology of the symbol led him to problems in his Christology and in his view
of God's relations with the world in terms of mutual conditioning (see above,
Divine Freedom, Chapter 2, and below Chapters 5, 6 and 7). Also, he either
never noticed or chose to ignore Moltmann's explicitly stated aim to move
beyond Rahner's axiom of identity toward a view that asserts that the economic
Trinity has a retroactive effect on the immanent Trinity thus leading him
toward *Patripassianism* (see below, *Divine Freedom*, Chapter 8). Interestingly,
the position for which McCormack now argues, as he has reconstructed it in
light of his reading of Barth's later Christology, is amazingly similar to the views
of Moltmann. See Han-Luen Kantzer Komline, 'Friendship and Being: Election
and Trinitarian Freedom in Moltmann and Barth', *Modern Theology* 29:1, 1–17
(January) 2013.

2 This is why it is so important to recognize and to uphold the freedom
of God 'in himself and as such' precisely by recognizing and respecting
the importance of God's antecedent being and action as the ground of what
God does in history. George Hunsinger has gathered several of Barth's key
statements together helpfully to make the point that God's incomprehensibility
is not the equivalent of some agnostic assertion that God is ultimately
unknowable. Rather it is an assertion that 'there was more to the eternal God's
self-relationship than just his world-relationship' (*Reading Barth with Charity*,
158). Thus, 'the Logos *asarkos* is "real in God in a form which is concealed
from us and incomprehensible to us" (*CD* II/1, 357)' as 'the second mode of
existence ("person") of the *inner* divine reality *in itself* and *as such*' (*CD* III/

and remain clear in their thinking on this theme. For instance, in a recent article, John Webster writes: 'We do not understand the economy unless we take time to consider God who is, though creatures might not have been.'[3] Hence, 'the starting point for a Christian doctrine of creation, as for any Christian doctrine, is God in himself ... Only out of the sheer antecedent perfection of God's life *in se* can we feel the force of the concept of creation.'[4] This means that

> God is not one item in a totality, even the most eminently powerful item in the set of all things ... the creator can be conceived neither by thinking of him as in some fashion continuous with the world nor by conceiving of a purely dialectical relation between uncreated and created being; both ... make creation intrinsic to God's fullness. Yet the triune God could be without the world.[5]

In his recent book on the eternal generation of the Son, Kevin Giles agrees.[6] Adam Johnson focuses the question precisely when critically assessing the following remarks: 'For Barth, the beginning of all the ways and works of God, *and therefore of the identity of God*, is the self-giving of God in Jesus Christ.'[7] For Johnson the critical question concerns whether or not God's self-giving in Jesus Christ 'is in fact an

1, 50), (see *Reading Barth with Charity*, 158). This Logos is the Word in which God eternally speaks with himself and is conscious of himself for all eternity (*CD* III/2, 147). It is indispensable to understand Christology and the Trinity and thus for dogmatic reflection (*CD* III/1, 54). We have already referred to the important passage in *CD* IV/1, 52 where Barth insists that the *Logos asarkos* is necessary to recognize and uphold God's freedom. For Barth it is 'only because the triune God was already active in himself [that] he could also be active in the world' (*Reading Barth with Charity*, 9).

3 John Webster, 'Trinity and Creation', *IJST*, vol. 12, no. 1 (January 2010): 4–19, at 7.

4 Webster, *IJST*, 9.

5 Webster, *IJST*, 12.

6 See, for example, *The Eternal Generation of the Son: Maintaining Orthodoxy in Trinitarian Theology* (Downers Grove, IL: InterVarsity Press, 2012), 203–4.

7 Adam J. Johnson, *God's Being in Reconciliation: The Theological Basis of the Unity and Diversity of the Atonement in the Theology of Karl Barth* (New York and London: T & T Clark International, 2012), 54 cites Paul Nimmo's book, *Being in Action: The Theological Shape of Barth's Ethical Vision* (New York: T & T Clark, 2007).

accurate interpretation of Barth's thought: does the self-giving of God in Jesus Christ constitute the identity of God (with regards to the modes of God's being or his perfections), or does it simply specify his being and life in a new direction?[8] Johnson notes further that Barth made repeated claims, even in his later theology, that 'God would be triune without us' and that this should be taken to mean that election is not constitutive of God's triunity since:

> The election of Jesus Christ is not the beginning of God's being and therefore his being as Father, Son and Holy Spirit, but the beginning of the triune God's interaction with all that is not God ... The act of election is the act of God at the beginning of all things (*ad extra*) by a God who Himself has no beginning – and the nature of this act is first and foremost with regards to himself by willing to become Jesus Christ.[9]

We may also note that George Hunsinger, in his definitive article 'Election and the Trinity' and in his seminal book *Reading Barth with Charity*, offers a thoroughly convincing and detailed case in favor of understanding why it is important to hold, with Barth, that 'God would be no less God if He had created no world and no human being'.[10] Yves Congar clearly agrees when he writes: 'As the Fathers who combated Arianism said, even if God's creatures did not exist, God would still be a Trinity of Father, Son and Spirit, since creation is an act of free will, whereas the procession of the Persons takes place in accordance with nature, *kata phusin*.'[11] Bruce Marshall concurs when he maintains that while our human identities may 'plausibly be regarded as contingent ... it seems impossible that the identities of the divine persons could be contingent', because our existence is completely dependent on God's gracious acts of creation, incarnation, reconciliation and redemption,

8 Johnson, *God's Being in Reconciliation*, 54.

9 Johnson, *God's Being in Reconciliation*, 55.

10 See George Hunsinger, 'Election and the Trinity: Twenty-Five Theses on the Theology of Karl Barth' in *Modern Theology*, 179–98, 181ff. and chapter four of *Trinity and Election in Contemporary Theology*, ed. Michael T. Dempsey. See also Hunsinger, *Reading Barth with Charity*, 36f. et al. We will discuss some of Bruce McCormack's responses to Hunsinger later in this chapter.

11 Yves Congar, *I Believe in the Holy Spirit*, vol. III, *The River of the Water of Life (Rev 22:1) Flows in the East and in the West*, trans. David Smith (New York: Crossroad, 1997), 13.

and God is dependent on no one and nothing. Further, these are free acts of the triune God who might not have made this or any world. Hence, each person of the Trinity 'would be the person he is, the person with whom we are allowed to become acquainted in time, even if there were no creatures – nothing besides these three divine persons'.[12]

Finally, it is worth mentioning Thomas F. Torrance's helpful reminder that 'we do not say that God is Father, Son and Holy Spirit, because he becomes Father, Son, and Holy Spirit to us … he only becomes Father, Son, and Holy Spirit to us precisely because he *is* first and eternally Father, Son, and Holy Spirit in himself alone'.[13] Hence, 'The world needs God to be what it is, but God does not need the world to be what he is … the Creator was free not to create …'[14] And since God really does not need the world, we must say that 'the Fatherhood of God is in no way dependent on or constituted by relation to what he has created outwith himself'.[15]

Karl Barth's own thinking sums up the point rather nicely when he says:

> Why should God not also be able, as eternal Love, to be sufficient unto Himself? In His life as Father, Son, and Holy Spirit He would in truth be no lonesome, no egotistical God even without man, yes, even without the whole created universe … He wants in His freedom actually not to be without man but *with* him and in the same freedom not against him but *for* him …[16]

12 Bruce D. Marshall, *Trinity and Truth*, (Cambridge: Cambridge University Press, 2000), 262–3. Marshall goes on to assert that since Nicaea, theologians have 'uniformly insisted' that 'the identities of the three divine persons who freely give themselves to us in creation, redemption, and consummation are the same as they would be even if the three had not decided to create and give themselves to us', 264. See also Bruce D. Marshall, 'The Absolute and the Trinity', *Pro Ecclesia: A Journal of Catholic and Evangelical Theology*, vol. XXIII, no. 2 (Spring 2014): 147–64 and my response, 'A Response: Beyond Hegel with Karl Barth and T. F. Torrance', *Pro Ecclesia* (2014): 165–73.

13 Thomas F. Torrance, *The Doctrine of Jesus Christ* (Eugene, OR: Wipf and Stock, 2002), 107.

14 Thomas F. Torrance, *Divine and Contingent Order* (Edinburgh: T&T Clark, 1998), 34.

15 Torrance, *The Christian Doctrine of God*, 207.

16 Karl Barth, *The Humanity of God*, trans. Thomas Wieser and John Newton Thomas (Richmond, VA: John Knox Press), 50.

Earlier in his *Church Dogmatics* Barth wrote:

> We can certainly say that we see the love of God to man originally
> grounded upon the eternal relation of God, Father and Son. But as
> this love is already *free* and *unconstrained* in God Himself, so, too,
> and only then rightly, is it free in its realisation towards man. That is,
> in His Word becoming flesh, God acts with inward freedom and not
> in fulfilment of a law to which He is supposedly subject. His Word
> will still be His Word apart from this becoming, just as Father, Son
> and Holy Spirit would be none the less eternal God, if no world had
> been created.[17]

A key question in relation to Barth's Christology as interpreted by those
whom Hunsinger calls the 'revisionists' concerns whether or not the
later Barth retracted this statement or so qualified it that one could or
should no longer embrace it. My position is and will be that it is exactly
this statement that underwrites the strength of what Barth has to say in
his later Christology.[18] It is akin to this statement which appears later in
his *Church Dogmatics*:

> In the inner life of God, as the eternal essence of Father, Son and Holy
> Ghost, the divine essence does not, of course, need any actualisation.

17 *CD* I/2, 135, emphases mine. It is worth noting that in his doctrine of
creation Barth also states that God 'could have remained satisfied with the fullness
of His own being. If He had willed and decided in this way, He would not have
suffered any lack. He would still be eternal love and freedom. However, according
to His Word and work which we have been summoned to attest He has willed and
decided otherwise' (*CD* III/1, 69). Importantly, Barth insisted that 'the Word of
God is properly understood only as a word which has truth and glory in itself and
not just spoken to us. *It would be no less God's eternal Word if it were not spoken
to us*, and what constitutes the mercy of its revelation, of its being spoken to us,
is that it is spoken to us in virtue of the freedom in which God *could be "God in
Himself"* and yet He does not will to be so and in fact is not so, but wills to be
and actually is "God for us"' (*CD* I/1, 171–2, emphasis mine). This thinking is
repeated many times by Barth, for example, 'While He [God] could be everything
only for Himself (and His life would not on that account be pointless, motionless
and unmotivated, nor would it be any less majestic or any less the life of love), He
wills – and this is for us the ever-wonderful twofold dynamic of his love – to have
it not only for Himself, but also for us' (*CD* II/1, 280–1).

18 For a thorough discussion of this issue see Molnar, *Faith, Freedom and
the Spirit*, chapter six and Hunsinger, *Reading Barth with Charity*, chapter three.

On the contrary, it is the creative ground of all other, i.e., all creaturely actualisations. Even as the divine essence of the Son it did not need His incarnation, His existence as man ... to become actual. As the divine essence of the Son it is the predicate of the one God. And as the predicate of this Subject it is not in any sense merely potential but in every sense actual.[19]

Closely connected with these remarks by Barth is another important statement, namely, that:

The triune life of God which is free life in the fact that it is Spirit, is the basis of His whole will and action even *ad extra*, as the living act which He directs to us. It is the basis ... of the election of man to covenant with Himself; of the determination of the Son to become man, and therefore to fulfil this covenant ... of the atonement with its final goal of redemption to eternal life with Himself.[20]

Furthermore, speaking about how human love is grounded in God's love, Barth writes:

He reveals Himself as the One who, even though He did not love us and were not revealed to us, even though we did not exist at all, still loves in and for Himself as surely as He is and is God; who loves us by reason and in consequence of the fact that He is the One who loves in His freedom in and for Himself, and is God as such. It is only of God that it can be said that He is in the fact that He loves and loves in the fact that He is ... God loves, and to do so He does not need any being distinct from His own as the object of His love. If He loves the world and us, this is a free overflowing of the love in which He is and is God and with which he is not content, although He might be, since neither the world nor ourselves are indispensable to His love and therefore to His being.[21]

Questioning Barth's View of God's Freedom

The above cited very traditional statements about the freedom of God's love in himself and in the incarnation have been questioned as already

19 *CD* IV/2, 113.
20 *CD* IV/2, 345.
21 *CD* IV/2, 755.

noted in the previous chapter.[22] They continue to be questioned. For example, relying on Rowan Williams and Bruce McCormack, Benjamin Myers claims that Barth's doctrine of the Trinity offers not just one doctrine of the Trinity, but two.[23] And from this he concludes that 'God's being as God is constituted by God's self-determined relation to the human Jesus'[24] and ultimately that 'Jesus is not merely epistemologically significant, as the one who makes God known; *he is ontologically significant, as the one who (so to speak) makes God God*'.[25] All of this follows, he claims, from the fact that Barth's doctrine of God was radically changed with his doctrine of election in *CD* II/2, and that the doctrine of the Trinity that he presented in *CD* I/1 was formally based on revelation while the new doctrine presented in *CD* IV/1 was based on Jesus Christ as, in his mind, making God to be God! Now, from within any reasonable reading of Barth's *Church Dogmatics*, it should be quite obvious that these claims not only obviate God's freedom for us, but they destroy God's freedom as eternal Father, Son and Spirit precisely by making God's essence dependent on the historical existence of the man Jesus.

As can be seen from the several statements from Barth cited above, it is very clear that for him it is not Jesus who makes God God since God eternally exists as Father, Son and Holy Spirit and would have so existed even if God had never created the world.[26] Of course God did create the world and God did determine to become incarnate and

---

22 See Bruce L. McCormack, 'Grace and being: The role of God's gracious election in Karl Barth's theological ontology', *Orthodox and Modern*, 183–200, 193–4. This is a slightly altered version of his 'Grace and being: The role of God's gracious election in Karl Barth's theological ontology', which first appeared in *The Cambridge Companion to Karl Barth* ed. John Webster (Cambridge: Cambridge University Press, 2000), 92–110.

23 Myers, *Trinitarian Theology after Barth*, 121. As already noted, similar problematic assertions are made in the *Cambridge Companion to the Trinity*, ed. Peter C. Phan (Cambridge: Cambridge University Press, 2011), 'Karl Barth, reconciliation, and the Triune God', Peter Goodwin Heltzel and Christian T. Collins Winn, 171–91.

24 Myers, *Trinitarian Theology after Barth*, 130.

25 Myers, *Trinitarian Theology after Barth*, 130, emphasis mine.

26 George Hunsinger has compiled a full set of such statements and helpfully concludes that 'the documentary record shows that his [Barth's] position did not change' on this matter. See Hunsinger, *Modern Theology*, 181–2 and above, n. 2.

to reconcile and redeem the world. However, the God who did these things and remains eternally united with us in his Word and Spirit, did not *become* who he eternally was and is by virtue of those determinations to be God for us. As each of the theologians cited above properly recognize, any such viewpoint not only destroys God's freedom in himself; it abolishes any possibility of distinguishing God's actions from history as the sphere in which he acts for us. This is the danger embedded in the assumption that Barth 'historicized' God's being in light of the humiliation, death and resurrection of Jesus Christ because of an alleged radical change in his understanding of God that was supposed to have taken place in connection with his doctrine of election.

We will explore this thinking in more detail in a moment. For now it is important to ask: could the triune God, who freely and from eternity chose to be our creator, reconciler and redeemer, have been this God without us? Today we are told by a number of theologians that any such statement would embody a false idea of the divine freedom. As argued in the previous chapter, my contention is that it is important to realize that this statement is tied to an acknowledgment of the importance of the *Logos asarkos* for a proper trinitarian theology and for a proper Christology. As noted above, there certainly are dangers involved in affirming the *Logos asarkos* in the context of the doctrine of reconciliation because some theologians have done so precisely in order to advance a kind of natural theology that would speak of Christ's presence in history without attending to the fact that this presence can neither be seen nor understood apart from the historical Jesus who is and remains to all eternity the Word of God to us and for us. Nonetheless, it is crucial to recognize that the Word incarnate never ceased being who and what he was from all eternity as the Word: 'The Word is what He is even before and apart from His being flesh. Even as incarnate He derives His being to all eternity from the Father and from Himself, and not from the flesh.'[27] As noted above in Chapter 3, the Word exists in distinct forms. However, that does not mean he relinquishes one form for another when he becomes incarnate. It must be stressed here that Barth's words are not only completely opposed to the thinking advanced by Benjamin Meyers and those who think as he does, but they convey an insight which is lost in all historicized portrayals of the Trinity and Christology. They present us with a God who literally came into existence only for

27 *CD* I/2, 136.

the sake of creating, reconciling and redeeming the world. In other words, while professing to have overcome Hegel's pantheistic view of the God/world relation, anyone who would claim that Jesus makes God God has in fact embraced a mutually conditioning and mutually conditioned view of God's relations with us and thus has spoiled the true meaning of Jn 1:14.[28] Put another way, Barth wished to maintain that the *logos asarkos* was "the *terminus a quo*" while the *logos ensarkos* was the "*terminus ad quem*" of the incarnation without of course obviating the fact that there was a real union of natures in the incarnate Word.[29]

In spite of the fact that we have been told by some that he abandoned this view in *CD* II/2 and beyond, we can say that, in light of the evidence, Karl Barth certainly maintained these insights with respect to the freedom of God's love throughout his career. This chapter will build on Barth's understanding of faith as a human action that is grounded in God's freedom for us exercised in the incarnation and in the outpouring of his Holy Spirit.[30] As such it embodies a proper view of human freedom as grounded in and shaped by God's freedom for us. In this chapter, I begin by explaining exactly why it is still important to acknowledge that the God who is for us in Christ and his Spirit could have been God without us but freely chose not to. Here I will directly address once more the question of the proper relation between election and the Trinity. We have already discussed this issue in the last chapter. I do not intend to repeat all of that discussion here. However, I will develop the thesis that unless this statement continues to be made in a serious way and not just as a type of throwaway statement, then and to that extent God's actual freedom for us, which is the very basis of human freedom (the freedom of faith and thus the freedom of the life of faith), is lost because it comes to be described as in some sense dependent on what

28 For a proper understanding of how Jesus Christ should be understood as the subject of election, see George Hunsinger, *Modern Theology*, 182–3. For Hunsinger, the eternal Son 'is necessarily the eternal Son; he is only contingently *incarnandus*' (183). One cannot say that Jesus Christ is the subject of election, Hunsinger rightly maintains, without qualification. See also Hunsinger, *Reading Barth with Charity*, chapter two. Myers's statement certainly represents one that is made without qualification!

29 *CD* I/2, 169ff.

30 For a full discussion of faith in Barth's thinking see Molnar, *Faith, Freedom and the Spirit*, chapter one.

happens within history.[31] In other words, just as Barth wished to avoid any notion of a mutually conditioning relationship between the Word and the flesh assumed by that Word in the incarnation, so too must we avoid any idea in our Christology that the Word was not fully the Word prior to and apart from the incarnation. What Barth wanted to avoid of course was Luther's idea that just as Christ's human nature has its reality only in and through the Word, 'so too the Word only has reality through and in the humanity'.[32] In relation to this view Barth wondered whether such a position took sufficient account of 'the freedom, majesty and glory of the Word of God' in such a way that 'they are in no way merged and submerged in His becoming flesh'.[33] Hence,

> if the concept 'Word' and the concept 'flesh' are both taken seriously but are considered as *mutually conditioning* one another, is the statement of Jn. 1:14 an understandable statement at all? On the assumption of a *mutual conditioning* does it not mean that either the *vere Deus* or the *vere homo* is taken less than seriously, is in fact weakened down and altered in meaning?[34]

My answer to this question of course is yes, while the answer of those who claim that Barth's view of God's freedom changed after *CD* II/2 is to claim that Jesus's human history constitutes his being as the second person of the Trinity in some sense. As it relates to the doctrine of the Trinity, it is important to note here Barth's vital distinction in *CD* II/1 between God's primary and secondary objectivity. Those who misinterpret this distinction tend to argue for the mutually conditioning relationship that Barth consistently rejected.

Primary and Secondary Objectivity

As George Hunsinger has noted, Barth followed Luther in distinguishing between God's 'naked' and 'clothed' objectivity. The former referred

---

31 In *Faith, Freedom and the Spirit*, chapter six I argued that theologians who claim to accept the 'value' of the *Logos asarkos* but reject these insights of Barth's end up embracing the mutual conditioning that Barth consistently rejected between humanity and divinity as they are united in the Person of the incarnate Word.

32 *CD* I/2, 166.

33 *CD* I/2, 166–7.

34 *CD* I/2, 167, emphasis mine.

to 'God's direct objectivity to himself in his eternal self-knowledge as the Holy Trinity' so that the word 'naked' 'means no mediation by any creaturely object, and therefore alludes to the *logos asarkos*' while the latter referred to God's objectivity to us in and through history and in particular the history of Jesus Christ.[35] This is why Barth will say, for example, that: 'In their existence as apostles the secondary objectivity of the human appearing of Jesus Christ Himself is repeated. And hidden within this is the primary objectivity of God Himself, calling to faith, awakening faith, establishing and renewing faith, and with faith the knowledge of God – not by these men's own strength but by the power of the Holy Spirit communicated to them, in the freedom of grace.'[36] For Barth, 'The Reconciler, Jesus Christ, who in the Holy Spirit makes the knowledge of God real and possible, is also the Creator, from whom man can only proceeds as one who knows God.'[37] Primary objectivity then referred to the 'eternal, immanent, primordial, self-existent, and necessary' being of God in 'the *koinonia* of the Father with the Son and the *logos asarkos* in the Holy Spirit. This mode, which remains forever hidden from us, represents the Holy Trinity in its primary objectivity.'[38]

This is an excellent interpretation as it captures Barth's thought nicely. Barth thinks of God's primary objectivity as God in himself, the eternal Father, Son and Holy Spirit who in his self-knowledge and love is entirely self-sufficient and as such, in his free grace makes himself objective to us in and through secondary objects of created history without handing over his power to that history. Hence, Barth appropriately states that the

---

35 George Hunsinger, *Evangelical, Catholic and Reformed: Doctrinal Essays on Barth and Related Themes* (hereafter: *Evangelical, Catholic and Reformed*) (Grand Rapids, MI: Eerdmans, 2015), 52 referring to *CD* II/1, 16. This chapter largely re-presents Hunsinger's original article 'Election and the Trinity: Twenty-Five Theses on the Theology of Karl Barth' which appeared in *Modern Theology* in April 2008. Hunsinger helpfully notes that for Barth 'It is a matter of one and the same Holy Trinity in two simultaneous modes of existence' existing in a relationship 'governed by the Chalcedonian pattern' so that there is 'an inseparable unity, abiding distinction, and irreversible asymmetry in the relationship of the Trinity's eternal mode of existence with its historical mode of existence' (52).

36 *CD* II/1, 24–5.

37 *CD* II/1, 25.

38 Hunsinger, *Evangelical, Catholic and Reformed*, 52.

Messiah, the promised Son of Abraham and David, the Servant of Yahweh, the Prophet, Priest and King has appeared; and not only as sent by God, but Himself God's Son. Yet the Word does not appear in His eternal objectivity as the Son who alone dwells in the bosom of the Father. No; the Word became flesh. God gives Himself to be known, and is known [in his entirety or not at all] in the substance of secondary objectivity, in the sign of all signs, in the work of God which all other works of God serve to prepare, accompany and continue, in the manhood which He takes to Himself, to which he humbles Himself and which He raises through Himself.[39]

This explains why Barth unequivocally rejected what he called 'non-objective' knowledge of God; he did so because while God is objective to himself as Father, Son and Spirit within the immanent Trinity, he becomes objective to us in and through the mediation of created objects without surrendering his freedom, but exercising it. This is why Barth insists that God knows himself directly and we know him truly and fully, but indirectly as he makes himself known to us mediately through history and in particular through the history of Jesus himself. This is the knowledge of faith which takes place only by grace, that is, 'as His free gift, in the act of His grace' for which we can only pray and receive.[40]

Hunsinger gets this just right when he explains that God's 'secondary objectivity' is God's objective presence to us in history such that this presence is 'historical, economic, derivative, dependent, and contingent'; it is 'the *koinonia* of the Father with the Son as the *logos ensarkos* in the Holy Spirit'.[41] Thus Hunsinger rightly claims that 'we have noetic access to the Holy Trinity only through this mode, which represents its secondary objectivity'.[42] He goes on to make the point that we participate only indirectly through the incarnate Word in the *koinonia* of the eternal Father, Son and Spirit and that 'the *logos asarkos* becomes

---

39 *CD* II/1, 19–20.

40 *CD* II/1, 22.

41 Hunsinger, *Evangelical, Catholic and Reformed*, 52–3. Hunsinger is fully justified in linking the eternal Son with the *logos asarkos* by virtue of Barth's statement that the eternal Word who alone dwells in the bosom of the Father is not made known in this eternal objectivity that he has in the bosom of the Father, but only as the Word made flesh and then explaining the *logos ensarkos* as the embodiment of what Barth meant by God's secondary objectivity.

42 Hunsinger, *Evangelical, Catholic and Reformed*, 53.

the *logos ensarkos* without ceasing to be the eternal *logos asarkos* in God's relationship in and for himself to all eternity'.[43] The point here is this: Barth's distinction between primary and secondary objectivity clearly and consistently refers to God's eternal being as Father, Son and Holy Spirit who is objective to himself and knows himself without mediation and who freely chooses by grace to include us in his own self-knowledge and love by uniting us to himself in his incarnate Son and through his Holy Spirit. This distinction between primary and secondary objectivity, with its clear 'Chalcedonian pattern' is determinative for Barth's understanding of the immanent Trinity and the relation of the immanent and economic Trinity. Once God's primary objectivity is lost, weakened or obscured, then God's secondary objectivity and our true knowledge of God is lost. It no longer becomes possible to speak forcefully about who God is and what God is doing for us and with us in history. Barth classically expresses his point in this way:

> If it is true that God stands before man, that he gives Himself to be known and is known by man, it is true only because and in the fact that God is the triune God, God the Father, the Son and the Holy Spirit. First of all, and in the heart of the truth in which He stands before us, God stands before Himself; the Father before the Son, the Son before the Father. And first of all and in the heart of the truth in which we know God, God knows Himself; the Father knows the Son and the Son the Father in the unity of the Holy Spirit. This occurrence in God Himself is the essence and strength of our knowledge of God ... without God's objectivity to Himself there is no knowledge of God; without the truth of a primary objectivity of Him who reveals Himself to us there is no truth of His secondary objectivity in his revelation [*ohne Gegenständlichkeit selber keine Erkenntnis Gottes, ohne die Wahrheit einer primäre Gegenständlichkeit dessen, der sich uns offenbart, keine Wahrheit seiner sekundären Gegenständlichkeit in Seiner Offenbarung*]. But the primary objectivity of God to Himself is reality in His eternal being as Father, Son and the Holy Spirit.[44]

From what has been said, it is clear that the categories 'primary' and 'secondary objectivity' refer to the immanent and economic Trinity and as such include both God's self-knowledge and love as fellowship

43 Hunsinger, *Evangelical, Catholic and Reformed*, 53.
44 *CD* II/1, 48–9. *KD*, II/1, 53.

(*koinonia*). When, by grace through faith and revelation, we are enabled to know God, then, it is through fellowship or communion with God by being united with God through being united with Jesus's humanity as the humanity of the Word and also through the Holy Spirit enabling all of this. My reason for specifying this here is to make it clear that these categories do not just refer to our knowledge of God – they refer to God himself and only then to our knowledge of God. This important distinction is misunderstood when the 'revisionist' reading of Barth is in evidence. Let me give one brief example.

In his important book on Barth's understanding of the incarnation, Darren O. Sumner explicates God's relation to time by explaining his understanding of the distinction between God's primary and secondary objectivity in Barth noting the meaning of the terms explained above. He asserts that 'this distinction would appear to be closely related to the classical distinctions between Creator and creature . . . and between the immanent Trinity and the economic Trinity'.[45] But he immediately adds that 'we should not presume too quickly that Barth is distinguishing God's objectivity to Himself and to others in the same way as indicated by these other contrasts [the contrasts between the immanent and economic Trinity, being and act, and creator and creature]'.[46] As he presents his further understanding of Barth at this crucial juncture, Sumner fails to distinguish without separating God's eternal being and act as Father, Son and Holy Spirit from his actions *ad extra* as creator, reconciler and redeemer. This leads him to misinterpret what Barth was actually claiming.

Sumner rejects the traditional idea that God is revealed in the economy such that 'a primary objectivity ... stands prior to and apart from the act of its disclosure'.[47] This, however, is exactly the point that Barth was at pains to assert, as noted above. God's being and act does indeed stand prior to and apart from his free disclosure of himself in history; without that prior triune being and act, Barth claims that we would have no knowledge of God and indeed no relation of communion with God. Here Sumner confuses the immanent and economic Trinity because of his misconceived view of Barth's 'actualism'. He thus mistakenly concludes that 'because for Barth being and act are equally basic

45 Sumner, *Karl Barth and the Incarnation*, 126.
46 Sumner, *Karl Barth and the Incarnation*, 126.
47 Sumner, *Karl Barth and the Incarnation*, 127.

and interdependent concepts, we may say that – by virtue of God's freedom – the divine disclosure of Himself that takes place in the incarnation *determines* the sort of God He is in eternity'.[48] The problem here is
that Sumner makes no distinction between God's being and act in eternity (primary objectivity) and God's free being and act ad extra (secondary objectivity). That is the only way he could conclude that what
happens in the incarnation *determines* the sort of God he is in eternity.
For Barth, as we have just seen, our knowledge of God

> is bound to the Word of God as an event utterly undetermined by
> man but utterly determined by God as its object. God distinguishes
> Himself from man in this event. God also distinguishes this event
> from all other events. God's work is the medium of this event, and
> that in such a way that if this event comes to pass God is and remains
> the operator of His work.[49]

God is not determined as God by the incarnation. However, God does
disclose himself to us fully as the one who loves in the incarnation. This
problematic interpretation of Barth leads to a complete misunderstanding of his view of God's primary and secondary objectivity.

Sumner claims that for Barth this language 'must mean something
other than "God as He is in Himself" and "God as He reveals Himself
to creatures". In truth, this distinction has a strictly noetic function …
it serves to specify not how God *is* but how God is *known* … The distinction between primary and secondary objectivity is thus a corollary
of revelation, not of ontology'.[50] Sumner concludes that 'God's primary

48 Sumner, *Karl Barth and the Incarnation*, 127, emphasis mine.

49 *CD* II/1, 31. It is no accident that Sumner thinks 'Barth came to believe
that only Jesus – not an abstract Logos – may be confessed as the eternal Son and
Word of God' (*Karl Barth and the Incarnation*, 203) and that 'because God has
determined Himself for creatures, for incarnation and redemption, this event
is constitutive of the Son's identity' (204). By contrast, Barth insisted that: 'The
Son of God does not need His humanity as form needs matter … The Son of
God does not need any completion, any concretion, any form which perhaps he
lacks. He is not an abstraction which follows something real and is attained by
the interpretation of it … He is actual in Himself – the One who is originally and
properly actual. And as such He is true in Himself – the One who is originally
and properly true … He is the Creator and Lord of heaven and earth. And it is as
such that He makes His existence that of another', *CD* IV/2, 53–4.

50 Sumner, *Karl Barth and the Incarnation*, 127.

objectivity is simply God's self-knowledge, not His inner life, and so it is not flatly synonymous with divine immanence, or with the Creator's lack of creatureliness, or with metaphysical being that stands behind the act of revelation'.[51] While I certainly agree that God's act of revelation in his Word and Spirit disallows any idea of a 'metaphysical being that stands behind the act of revelation', since God in his primary objectivity meets us entirely or not at all in his revelation through the medium of history,[52] that cannot be taken to mean that God's primary objectivity refers only to our knowledge of God or only to God's self-knowledge and not to God himself. That very idea would pull the ground out from under our objective knowledge of God in Jesus Christ. Interestingly, part of the problem here seems to be Sumner's unwillingness to acknowledge, as Hunsinger rightly does, that God's primary objectivity refers only to the *Logos asarkos* and not to the *Logos ensarkos*. For this reason Sumner concludes that 'when God makes Himself known to us, He makes *Himself* known – and the identification of Christ's humanity as a medium of revelation does not preclude its inclusion in the identity of the eternal Son'.[53]

For Barth, however, Christ's humanity does not constitute the identity of the Son as seems to be the case for Sumner; rather the Son, in and through his humanity in the incarnation, enables us to participate in God's own self-knowledge and love through his grace and in faith. Hence for Barth,

> Revelation of God means that although as Father, Son and Holy Spirit God is self-sufficient in His own inward encounter – for otherwise He would not be God – He now encounters us ... It begins with the possibility of an *opus ad extra*, with the will and deed of God the Creator. God does not need a creature. He is an object to Himself. No other object can be an object to Him in the way that He is to Himself.[54]

This is why Barth insists that the objectivity of God is not 'naturally inherent in the objectivity of the creature instituted as a sacrament and used as such. It is not even present in the man Jesus merely by reason

---

51 Sumner, *Karl Barth and the Incarnation*, 127.
52 See *CD* II/1, 52.
53 Sumner, *Karl Barth and the Incarnation*, 128.
54 *CD* II/1, 57–8.

of the fact that this man exists, so that we can assure ourselves of it by assuring ourselves of the existence of this man.'[55] Here Barth maintains, in a way similar to his claim that Jesus in his humanity as such is not the revealer, that 'Jesus as such is always an enigma' and that if he also communicates God to us 'then it is thanks to His unity with the Son of God and therefore in the act of the revelation of the Son of God and of the faith in Him effected by the Holy Spirit.'[56] Thus it is the Son's identity that is disclosed in Jesus in the incarnation.

Unfortunately, Sumner's misinterpretation of Barth's understanding of God's primary and secondary objectivity leads him to claim that while early Barth might have rejected any notion of a mutually conditioning relationship between God and us in *CD* I/2, as noted above, the later Barth did indeed do so. However, this thinking once again undermines the positive point of Barth's consistent emphasis on God's antecedence as the enabling factor for our subsequent relations with God in grace and by faith. Even as Sumner attempts to explain his belief that in *CD* IV/2 Barth advances a notion of mutual conditioning, his own presentation of the evidence undermines his argument. First he argues that for Barth, in the incarnation 'the divine acquires a determination to the human, and the human a determination from the divine.'[57] Here Sumner claims that 'the divine essence of the Word is conditioned vis-à-vis its unity with the human.'[58] Yet that is not what Barth says here at all. He says that in his humanity the divine Son acquires a determination to be human and the human Jesus receives his determination *from* the divine. The fact that this is so excludes any idea of mutual conditioning between the divine and human natures in the incarnate Son.

Hence, even as Sumner attempts to explain what he takes to be the mutually conditioning relation that Barth was supposed to have advanced here, he contradicts himself arguing that 'God the Son remains the acting Subject, and the mutual determination of His essences is carefully delineated as irreversibly *from* the divine *to* the human. This is still a determination of the divine essence – but the active subject of that determination is not the humanity itself but the Word who acts to assume and unite.' Exactly. Barth clearly does not uphold a mutually conditioned relation between the Word and the flesh assumed by the Word; it is exactly the opposite – the flesh receives its determination from the

---

55 *CD* II/1, 56.

56 *CD* II/1, 56.

57 Sumner, *Karl Barth and the Incarnation*, 188 referring to *CD* IV/2, 70.

58 Sumner, *Karl Barth and the Incarnation*, 188.

action of the Word. Hence, as Sumner himself is forced to conclude from the 'textual Barth', 'Christ's divinity is therefore not conditioned *by* his humanity, strictly speaking, but by the event of their union – that is, by the Word's free decision for incarnation.'[59] Even this statement, however, is ambiguous because for Barth the Word is not determined or conditioned by the event of incarnation in the sense that God does not cease being God even as he becomes human in the man Jesus and acts as man for us during his ministry, life, death, resurrection and ascension.[60]

These assertions regarding the fact that Barth emphasized a genuine distinction in unity between the immanent and economic Trinity and rejected any notion of mutual conditioning between creator and creature are not meant to underwrite a view that sees God as aloof from us in his divinity; rather they are meant to underscore the fact that

---

59 Sumner, *Karl Barth and the Incarnation*, 188.

60 Additional evidence from *CD* IV/2 indicating Barth's continued rejection of a mutually conditioned relation between God and us can be seen in the following statements by Barth: (1) 'If what God willed and resolved from all eternity took place as an event between Himself and man in time, *this is not even partly conditioned* by an act of man, nor is it the outworking of a necessity which binds Himself to man and man to Himself, but it is the work of His own free initiative and act, of His grace. The divine act of humility fulfilled in the Son is the only ground of this happening and being. On this ground the unity achieved in this history has to be described, not as two-sided, but as founded and consisting absolutely and exclusively in Him. He is the One who did not and does not will to be the One He is – the eternal Son – without also being the Son of Man' (46–7, emphasis mine); (2) 'In Jesus Christ it is not merely one man, but the *humanum* of all men, which is posited and exalted as such to unity with God. And this is the case just because there has been no changing of God into a man; just because there was and is no creation of a dual existence of God and a man; just because there is only One here, "the Father's Son, by nature God," but this One in our human likeness, in the form of a servant (Phil. 2:7), in the likeness of sinful flesh (Rom. 8:3)' (49). Hence, 'Jesus Christ exists as a man because and as this One exists, because and as He makes human essence His own, adopting and exalting it into unity with Himself. As a man, therefore, He exists directly in and with the one God in the mode of existence of His eternal Son or Logos – not otherwise or apart from this mode', 49; (3) 'Where Jesus Christ is really known, there is no place for a monistic thinking which confuses or *reverses* the divine and the human ... The divine and the human work together. But even in their common working they are not interchangeable. The divine is still above and the human below. Their

the God who acts for us as creator, reconciler and redeemer is a God whose love for us on the cross and in the resurrection and outpouring of his Spirit in no way depends on us or on history in order to function effectively for us within history. Without this insight the specter of conditional salvation looms large in any consideration of the doctrine of reconciliation. All of this relates to the problems seen above in connection with those who advance some idea of a dependent deity. In light of what I have just written, and in light of everything said above, I think it should be clear why I do not believe that Barth ever would have countenanced the idea of such a deity. In this Chapter I hope to explain why those whose thinking compromises the reality of the *logos asarkos* in relation to the *logos ensarkos*, do so precisely because they have reduced God to who and what God is for us. In other words they have, in spite of their denials, collapsed the immanent into the economic Trinity.[61] As this chapter develops I will respond to various characterizations of the first edition of this book while developing the ideas just introduced.

Misinterpreting God's Freedom

Let us begin by considering Ben Myers's misguided interpretation of the view of divine freedom I presented in my first book on the Trinity. His thinking is hopelessly controlled by his confusion of the immanent and economic Trinity and of time and eternity from the start. Hence, with respect to the *Logos asarkos* he writes that his 'reading of Barth ... is antagonistic to the notion of a *Logos asarkos*, any moment at which God's identity was not already bound up with the human history of

relationship is one of genuine action' (116, emphasis mine); (4) speaking of the crucified and risen Lord in his transition to us as attested in the New Testament Barth refers to our objective being in Christ as 'objective truth'. However, he says that 'this truth is not satisfied with a purely objective form but demands also a subjective, pressing in upon us and our seeing and understanding and knowing' in order to determine 'our existence in light of it' (302). Then Barth insists that we can only accompany or follow or correspond to the 'original' and we cannot repeat it, 'just as on the other side it can only be a question of the reality and truth which are not in any way *conditioned* or evoked by, but themselves condition and sovereignly evoke, our accompanying and following' (303).

    61 See Molnar, *Faith, Freedom and the Spirit*, chapter five for how the thinking of Thomas F. Torrance helpfully avoids the pitfalls of those whose thinking is marked by the idea that God's relations with us are mutually conditioned.

Jesus'.[62] Myers's analysis is unacceptable in part because he ignores facets of Barth's thought that are present in the material he cites and this leads him to misunderstand Barth's thinking as well as the importance of the *Logos asarkos* for trinitarian doctrine. First, there is a hermeneutical issue over how to interpret Barth that arises because in the very same section Meyers refers to, Barth himself insisted that the *Logos asarkos* 'is the content of a necessary and important concept in trinitarian doctrine when we have to understand the revelation and dealings of God in the light of their free basis in the inner being and essence of God'.[63] Indeed, Barth insists that the second person of the Trinity 'in Himself and as such is not God the Reconciler. In Himself and as such He is not revealed to us ... He is not *Deus pro nobis*, either ontologically or epistemologically'.[64] Second, Barth goes on to note that since he is now considering the Mediator in connection with the doctrine of reconciliation, it is impermissible to return 'to the second person of the Trinity as such, *in such a way* that we ascribe to this person another form than that which God Himself has given in willing to reveal Himself and to act outwards'.[65] Myers either fails to notice or chooses to ignore the fact that even here Barth not only does not deny the reality of the *Logos asarkos* but rather insists that we cannot retreat to this notion in this context (of the doctrine of reconciliation) in a way that separates the form of revelation from the shape it has taken in the One Mediator. In other words he is opposing any use of a concept of the *Logos asarkos* to construct a natural theology, that is, an understanding of God that is not tied to the person and work of the Mediator. The problem with Myers's assertion that there is no moment at which God's identity is not bound up with Jesus is that it amounts to a denial of the preexistent Son who has his eternal being from the Father in the Spirit and necessarily exists as the one who freely decides to become incarnate and live out a life of perfect obedience for us. We cannot pry into the eternal life of the Godhead to know how it is that God exists prior to creation and incarnation other than by acknowledging, on the basis of revelation, that God always existed as Father, Son and Holy Spirit who

---

62 Myers, 'Election, Trinity, and the History of Jesus', 132.
63 *CD* IV/1, 52.
64 *CD* IV/1, 52.
65 *CD* IV/1, 52, emphasis mine.

loves in freedom. To speak of moments with respect to God's eternal life without clearly distinguishing God's unique eternal time from created time runs the risk of projecting the limitations of our time into God's eternal time.[66]

Here it is important to note that the risk becomes a disaster because Myers does not make the careful distinctions made by Barth himself. He claims not to deny the Son's preexistence while actually denying it because he has already confused time and eternity. Hence, he says that 'eternity here is not some anterior divine state that precedes the election of the human Jesus. The Son of God pre-exists precisely as a human being; the human history of Jesus of Nazareth is already the form of God's eternal being.'[67] What could this possibly mean? If Jesus's human history is 'already the form of God's eternal being', then God has no eternal being prior to this human history. Such a conclusion implies either that God never existed prior to the incarnation or that God was always incarnate. Both these choices mishandle Barth's thinking and leave Myers unable to acknowledge the basic truth of the incarnation as an act of free grace. It would of course be incorrect to think that God existed for a time and then decided to create, reconcile and redeem us. Such a view would falter because it attempts to understand God's eternity *by* created time instead of from itself as it has entered time and taken time into itself without any compromise of divine and human being and action. God's decision to elect us is indeed an eternal decision; but whenever that is taken to mean that God never existed without us, even in his pretemporal being and act, then and there the mystery of the Trinity is no longer respected and a rationalistic attempt to explain something that can only be acknowledged takes over. This was the point I tried to make when I asked in the first edition of this book: 'If God's election has always taken place, how then can it be construed as a decision; does it not then become a necessity?'[68] The question here concerned whether or not God

66 For a discussion of this issue see Molnar, *Faith, Freedom and the Spirit*, chapter four.

67 Myers, 'Election, Trinity, and the History of Jesus', 132.

68 See Molnar, *Divine Freedom*, 62. That I was correct in this reading of McCormack is supported by the fact that he later claimed that since God's being in his second mode of existence is a determination of God's electing to be God for us it 'is a decision which has never *not* already taken place. So there is no "eternal Son" if by that is meant a mode of being in God which is not identical with Jesus Christ' (*Orthodox and Modern*, 213–19). If, however, the eternal Son cannot exist

could have been God without electing us. The answer is no if and to the extent election is understood to be the ground of God's triunity. The point I was making was that God's triunity was and is eternally necessary while his electing us is eternally contingent as I explained later.[69] God could not not be Father, Son and Holy Spirit without ceasing to be God; but God could be the Father, Son and Holy Spirit without electing us. Nonetheless, out of sheer love, God eternally (but contingently) chose not be God without us.[70] Hence, God's election has always taken place, but the objects of his will ad extra are not ontologically necessary to God and God could have refrained from deciding thus and would have been no less the eternal God he was and is.[71] Still, election of us, even as an eternal act of God is new in a distinctive way.[72]

without being Jesus Christ, then that very assertion makes incarnation necessary to the divine being, and that undermines the divine freedom.

69 See n. 71 below.

70 Here I was following Barth's thinking that: 'We must guard against disputing the eternal will of God which precedes even predestination. We must not allow God to be subsumed in His relationship to the universe or think of Him as tied in Himself to the universe … we confess the eternal will of the God who is free in Himself, even in the sense that originally and properly He wills and affirms and confirms Himself', *CD* II/2, 155.

71 Scott R. Swain helpfully clarifies this point in *The God of the Gospel*, 161. Swain thinks Torrance's emphasis on the priority of the Father/Son relation over the creator/creature relation is correct but imprecise and that it would be better to speak of a distinction between 'objects of God's love that are "eternally natural/necessary"' and those that are '"eternally free/contingent" objects'. Torrance's thinking is indebted to Athanasius and makes more sense to me because it clearly suggests that God is necessarily Father, Son and Holy Spirit and would be even if he never had decided to create, reconcile and redeem the world. It also implies that God's actions ad extra are new actions that cannot be understood to be co-eternal with God, but must be understood as contingent on God's eternal decision to do something he had not previously done. This is why I have argued that there is a sense in which there is a 'before' and 'after' even in God's pretemporal eternity (*Faith, Freedom and the Spirit*, 198ff). Beyond that, we both agree that 'God eternally but contingently wills the *ad extra* objects of his will'. However, it is not clear to me what objects of God's love are natural and necessary in Swain's understanding. God's act of willing is eternal and necessary. However, the objects of God's love are his creatures and so they are, as we both agree, 'not ontologically necessary'.

72 See Molnar, *Faith, Freedom and the Spirit*, 198ff.

In this context, Myers is unable to acknowledge the incarnation as an act of free grace. In explaining his understanding of the Son's pre-existence, Myers cites Barth's thinking about the *incarnate Word* in connection with the doctrine of *reconciliation* and writes: 'For Jesus Christ – not an empty *Logos*, but Jesus Christ the incarnate Word … is the unity [of God and humanity] … That he is both … is something which belongs to himself as the eternal Son of God for himself and prior to us. In this he is the pre-existent *Deus pro nobis*.'[73] It must, however, be recalled that Barth also says that in himself and as such the eternal Son is not *Deus pro nobis* so that a distinction must be made between God's eternal existence as Son of the Father and his future (in God's eternal counsel) and actual existence as *Deus pro nobis*. Because Myers makes no such distinction, he reaches a number of bizarre conclusions. He says: (1) 'The second person of the Trinity is a human being – or rather, the divine-human history enacted in Jesus';[74] (2) The '*logos asarkos* … represents … "some image of God which we have made for ourselves"'; (3) 'from all eternity, there is really no "second person of the Trinity", but only the divine-human history of Jesus of Nazareth';[75] and finally, (4) 'God's deity is *constituted* – through God's own eternal decision – by the way God relates to this particular human being'.[76]

Each of these conclusions stands in conflict with the trinitarian doctrine that Barth espoused and that is central to the faith of the church. First, to simply say that the second person of the Trinity is the human Jesus is to confuse the doctrines of reconciliation and the Trinity. This statement is an obvious collapse of the immanent into the economic Trinity – one which Barth never countenanced, although he is to some extent responsible for readings that go astray because in volume IV of the *CD* he did indeed inappropriately read back elements of the economy into the immanent Trinity as I will note in a moment. Second, to suggest that for Barth the *Logos asarkos* is an image of an idol plain and simple, as an image of God we have made for ourselves, is to ignore the fact that it is so only when it is used to avoid knowing and relating with God through the reconciler, that is, the One Mediator. That would turn Jesus Christ, the incarnate Word into a Christ-principle used to validate some naturally known God. Third, once again this remark that from all eternity there is no second person of the Trinity must be taken to be a

---

73 Myers, 'Election, Trinity, and the History of Jesus', 132 citing IV/1, 53.

74 Myers, 'Election, Trinity, and the History of Jesus', 133.

75 Myers, 'Election, Trinity, and the History of Jesus', 133.

76 Myers, 'Election, Trinity, and the History of Jesus', 133, emphasis mine.

denial of the *homoousion* of the Father and Son. This opens the door directly to some form of Arianism as Kevin Giles never tires of reminding us. The statement, however qualified, that God's decision to relate to the human being of Jesus *constitutes* his deity actually is a contemporary embodiment of the Arian view that without the human Jesus, God would not be the triune God. All four of these ideas must be rejected.

This, however, is not the end of it. Based on these ill-considered notions, Myers offers his critique of the view of divine freedom that I advanced in the first edition of *Divine Freedom*. His thinking is therefore thoroughly confused and confusing. First, demonstrating a complete failure to understand that for Barth the basis of all that God does ad extra is his eternal act of being Father, Son and Holy Spirit, Myers says that Barth hints at a 'kind of self-limitation in God', not in Moltmann's sense, but 'in the sense of God's freedom to restrict God's own possibilities to one particular course of action'. Hence, Jesus's history 'functions as a kind of inner "necessity" for God, in as much as God is freely yet wholly self-determined towards this history'.[77] This statement is more than a little problematic because Barth explicitly and repeatedly asserts that God's being is subject to no inner or outer necessities. When he speaks of the incarnation as necessary it is only in light of the fact that that is what God decided to do in his gracious love and wisdom for us. In the sense that it is a *factual necessity* that can never be undone and that remains forever decisive for all history, it may be referred to as a necessity.[78] However, to suggest that Jesus's history functions as a kind of inner necessity *for* God is precisely to imply that God needs Jesus's history in order to exist. That is exactly the opposite of what Barth intended. Based on this confused notion of God's freedom Myers claims that the Barth of *CD* IV/1 'knows nothing of Paul Molnar's picture of a sublime divine freedom that stands behind history, with differing possibilities balanced evenly on the scales'.[79] This sort of statement is typical of Myers's caricatures and completely misses the point for which I argued in the first edition.

77 Myers, 'Election, Trinity, and the History of Jesus', 133.

78 For a superb explanation of the difference between a factual necessity and a logical necessity (which leads to determinism and to arbitrary ideas of God's relations with creation) see Torrance, *Divine and Contingent Order*, 22–3.

79 Myers, 'Election, Trinity, and the History of Jesus', 133. Interestingly, a check of the footnote for a reference to where I supposedly said this shows only a reference to my book with no page reference. That is because I never actually said this!

In the first edition of *Divine Freedom*, I argued that God is free both positively and negatively. That is, God is free as the only self-moved being within himself and because God remains God in his relations with us, he acts for us and in relation to us without becoming dependent on us but rather by effectively creating and maintaining fellowship with us in spite of and against our sin. Moreover, while I did insist, with Barth and Torrance, that God remains who he is as Lord of the universe even in his incarnate Word and as the risen, ascended and advent Lord, I never argued that God's freedom is to be equated with something that stands behind history with evenly balanced possibilities between a freedom for us and one that might be against us. Quite the contrary. The whole point of the first edition was based on the fact that, although God *could have* chosen to be God without us, he chose not to so exist and did in fact choose to create, reconcile and redeem us in his Word and Spirit. Without God's incarnation in Jesus Christ and without Jesus's resurrection from the dead we would have no genuine relations with God and no objective knowledge of God. So I argued that while the eternal God really exercised his freedom to be for us in Jesus Christ, that could never be taken to mean that God is wholly subsumed by the history of Jesus Christ as he must be if it is thought, with Myers, that ' "there is no second person of the Trinity", but only the divine-human history of Jesus'.

The following statements from Barth found in the first edition are decisive here:

> [God] does not need His own being in order to be who He is: because He already has His own being and is Himself ... If, therefore, we say that God is *a se*, we do not say that God creates, produces or originates Himself ... He cannot 'need' His own being because He affirms it in being who He is ... what can need existence, is not God Himself, or His reality, but the reality which is distinct from Himself.[80]

It should be stressed here that all views that suggest that God becomes triune in order to relate with us falter when weighed against this important statement by Barth because they always assert that God needed to give himself his triunity for his relations with us. Moreover, in *CD* IV/2 where Barth speaks about the inner relations of the Father, Son and Holy Spirit as a history in partnership, he also insists that:

---

80   *CD* II/1, 306. See also *CD* I/1, 354 where Barth insists that God does not need 'a Second and then a Third in order to be One . . .'

This history in partnership is the life of God before and above all creaturely life … His inner union is marked off from the circular course of a natural process as His own free act, an act of majesty … it is not subject to any necessity. The Father and the Son are not two prisoners. They are not two mutually conditioning factors in reciprocal operation. As the common source of the Spirit, who Himself is also God, they are the Lord of this occurrence. God is the free Lord of His inner union.[81]

Of course the force of this statement is meant to allow us to recognize that God is free, as God who loves, to enter into covenant relations with us without ceasing to be God.[82] As a humble God who experiences our alienation and judgment as the man Jesus, God can and does act in history in order to relieve our distress caused by sin. That is indeed what is revealed in his resurrection and ascension; but that cannot be taken to mean that God is *constituted* by this or that God needed to do this in order to be God or that God 'triuned' himself in order to relate with us.[83] Contrary to this, Myers claims that God's freedom for Barth 'is indeed a kind of necessity – but it is simply the necessity of God's own loving self-consistency. God is necessarily faithful to God's own

---

81 *CD* IV, 2, 344–5.

82 It is extremely important to remember at this point that for Barth, and rightly so, 'God is simple. This signifies that in all that He is and does, He is wholly and undividedly Himself. At no time or place is He composed out of what is distinct from Himself. At no time or place, then is He divided or divisible. He is One even in the distinctions of the divine persons of the Father, the Son and the Holy Spirit … the assertion of God's unity can be called the basic proposition of the doctrine of God's freedom. Being simple … God is incomparably free, sovereign and majestic. In this quality of simplicity are rooted, fixed and included all the other attributes of His majesty: His constancy and eternity, His omnipresence, omnipotence and glory. Nothing can affect Him, or be far from Him, or contradict or withstand Him, because in Himself there is no separation, distance, contradiction or opposition. He is Lord in every relationship, because he is the Lord of Himself, unconditionally One as Father, Son and Holy Spirit' (*CD* II/1, 445).

83 For this way of stating the matter see Kevin Hector, 'Immutability, Necessity and Triunity: Towards a Resolution of the Trinity and Election Controversy' *SJT*, vol. 65, no. 1 (2012): 64–81, 67. For a full discussion of Hector's most recent discussion of these issues see below, 162ff.

decision about what the divine identity will be like.'[84] Hence, in Myers's view, Jesus 'is *the* possibility, the free necessity of God's deity.'[85] This statement once again is confused and confusing.

In the section Myers cites from *CD* IV/1, when Barth writes of the 'inner necessity of the freedom of God and not the play of a sovereign *liberum arbitrium*' he is not suggesting that God is subject to history in the sense that there is no longer any Son of God or second person of the Trinity as such. Rather, he is saying that the condescension of the Son in his obedience to the Father acting as man for us is not the result of some arbitrary choice on God's part. What takes place in Jesus's humiliation and exaltation on our behalf is the 'divine fulfilment of a divine decree and thus an act of obedience.'[86] In light of the *fact* that God has chosen to be God in this way ad extra from all eternity, and has thus acted for us as the savior in this history, Barth is explaining why it is important to see that we do not have to do here 'with one of the throws in a game of chance which takes place in the divine being.'[87] It is, in other words, an act of divine 'self-humiliation ... as the presupposition of reconciliation.'[88] Here the all-important distinction between a factual necessity and a logical necessity is once again ignored by Myers. At this point, however, an issue arises in the thinking of Barth that we will not consider in detail here. That issue concerns whether and to what extent Barth illegitimately read back elements of the economy into the immanent Trinity and thus, against his own intentions, uncharacteristically introduced an element of subordination into the immanent Trinity. I have treated this in Chapter 7 of *Faith, Freedom and the Spirit* where I compared the thinking of Karl Barth to that of Thomas F. Torrance who, after a conversation with Barth late in his life, was asked by Barth to re-write those sections of *CD* IV that did not take due consideration of Jesus's ongoing high-priestly mediation and thus led him to introduce some problematic notions into his thinking.[89]

84 Myers, 'Election, Trinity, and the History of Jesus', 134.
85 Myers, 'Election, Trinity, and the History of Jesus', 134.
86 *CD* IV/1, 195.
87 *CD* IV/1, 195.
88 *CD* IV/1, 195.
89 See Thomas F. Torrance, *Karl Barth, Biblical and Evangelical Theologian*, (hereafter: *Karl Barth*), (Edinburgh: T & T Clark, 1990), 134–5 and then 206–7 for Torrance's thinking about the obedience of the Son as a priestly obedience effected for us in order to 'convert' us 'back to true and faithful sonship through his own obedient self-offering to the Father'.

Myers puzzlingly writes that 'God's freedom is not, as Molnar imagines, a mysterious abyss standing behind this event; rather it is fully realized in the event itself. This history is the form which God's freedom takes. And God's freedom *always already* takes this form, since Jesus is the content of God's eternal decision about who God will be.'[90] All of the confusion resident in Myers's original statement that Jesus makes God God is on display here. Instead of noting that God loves in freedom as the electing God who condescended to be the Judge judged in our place as Barth did, Myers argues that God's triune being is constituted by Jesus's history and thus that it is 'fully realized in the event itself' with the result that 'Jesus is the content of God's eternal decision about who God will be'. That would be a true statement except for one important thing, namely, Myers forgot to add that Barth here was referring once again to the incarnate Word or Son acting as our reconciler. So he should have written that Jesus is the content of God's eternal decision about who God would be *for us* and *for our salvation*; but he did not write that because from the very outset he had collapsed God's eternal sonship into his actions ad extra. It is at this point that Myers thinks my notion of the divine freedom must be resisted because, while he says it is a faithful interpretation of the Barth of *CD* I/1 as perhaps 'interpreted by T. F. Torrance, who shapes all Molnar's thinking about divine freedom and the immanent Trinity', still it embodies a type of thinking that is 'structured by a tight sequence of paired opposites: the priority of eternity over history, the objective over the subjective, of reality over experience, of God *in se* over God-for-us'.[91] And he claims

---

90 Myers, 'Election, Trinity, and the History of Jesus', 134.

91 Myers, 'Election, Trinity, and the History of Jesus', 134. The weakness of this analysis can be seen when one wonders exactly what Myers could possibly be affirming by rejecting the ideas that (1) eternity has priority over history; (2) the objective has priority over the subjective; (3) reality has priority over experience; and (4) God in se has priority over God for us. Both Barth and Torrance unfailingly maintained that God's relations with us were *irreversible* precisely in order to advance a realist view of theology, that is, one that allowed the unique object of the Christian faith to determine our subjective experiences of God in the economy. The content of these conceptions is not taken from metaphysics but from revelation in an attempt to think about God in faith and thus obediently without making God in his revelation dependent on or controlled by human experience or reflection. That is why Barth and Torrance insisted that God could be known only through God and that one could never

that the problem resident in interpreting God's freedom 'through the lens of these metaphysical categories becomes clear' when one sees 'how slight a place the human history of Jesus assumes in Molnar's thought' because 'the human Jesus stands in the shadow of an antecedent *logos asarkos*.'[92]

The real culprit, according to Myers, then is that in my thinking 'God's decision is overshadowed by the ominous possibility that God might have chosen otherwise.'[93] Hence, 'the real history of Jesus is eclipsed by the sublime divine essence, which stands ineffably behind time and history. Behind the divine decision stands some nameless essence.'[94] We are told that this idea is captured by my statement that 'if God's election has always taken place, how then can it be construed as a decision.'[95] Here, Myers finally exhibits his inability to comprehend the real point of affirming a *Logos asarkos*. It is not to assert that there is a God behind Jesus Christ since anyone reading the previous edition of this book could see quite easily that, with Barth and Torrance, I consistently opposed both ebionite and docetic forms of Christology and specifically argued against the idea of a 'nameless divine essence'; with

be a real theologian unless one adopted Hilary's maxim that words are subject to realities and not realities to words. For a discussion of this see Molnar, *Torrance: Theologian of the Trinity*, 35–6. Just consider the fact that theology would become mythology if experience assumes priority over reality; that the creature indeed would become the creator (the original sin) if history assumed priority over eternity; that subjectivism (mythology) would rule the day if the subjective had priority over the objective with the result that there never would be any true knowledge of God and of ourselves; and that if God for us assumed priority over God in himself, then we would inevitably have the God we want rather than, in the words of Colin Gunton, recognizing that in reality it is not the God we want who is the real God, but the God we are 'damn well going to get'! If one rejects this realist approach which I am advocating, then the only thing left is a theology of irrationality and of mythology rather than one that is obedient to the Word of God incarnate and active in Jesus himself. It is only such an approach that would lead to the preposterous idea that Jesus makes God to be God!

92 Myers, 'Election, Trinity, and the History of Jesus', 134.

93 Myers, 'Election, Trinity, and the History of Jesus', 134.

94 Myers, 'Election, Trinity, and the History of Jesus', 135.

95 Myers, 'Election, Trinity, and the History of Jesus', 135. See above, 116 for my discussion of this statement.

Torrance and Barth, I emphatically and consistently opposed any God behind the back of Jesus Christ while simultaneously insisting that the God who is for us in Jesus Christ became incarnate *without ceasing to be God* so that God could act for us in Christ effectively both from the divine and from the human side.

What is really at stake in this statement 'that God might have chosen otherwise' is the distinction between the God who eternally wills to be God for us with a freedom that expresses his eternal love as Father, Son and Spirit and the view that it is this decision for us that *determines* or *constitutes* God's triune being. With George Hunsinger, Karl Barth, T. F. Torrance and the others mentioned above I have plainly argued for the fact that God could have been God without us but *freely* chose not to, not because I think that Jesus's history can be 'reduced to one possibility among others, to be arbitrated by the indeterminate freedom of an unknowable divine essence',[96] but because the history that was actualized in Jesus as the obedient Son acting as our savior from the divine and human side was indeed the history of the one God acting for us in that particular way. In other words the statement that God could have been God without us but freely chose not to, enables one to recognize that God acting for us *as* the man Jesus cannot be reduced to what he does for us, as clearly happens in Myers's thinking when he claims that Jesus makes God God. That is the issue at stake here and it is lost when Myers's convoluted thinking is embraced. While Myers does say that he agrees with me that 'God does not contradict God's being when God enters into our history' and that he shares my 'unease with the way a thinker like Moltmann introduces rupture and discontinuity within the being of God, the real point of contrast concerns his view that 'the trinitarianism of IV/1 does not require any *logos asarkos* or any formalistic notion of divine choice in order to safeguard God's self-consistency'.[97]

In light of this discussion, then, the problem that I tried to highlight in the first edition of *Divine Freedom* and consistently thereafter, including the previous chapter of this edition is this: whenever the *Logos asarkos*, even in the restricted sense that Barth embraces it in *CD* IV/1 and elsewhere, is jettisoned as in the thought of Robert Jenson or others, so also is the actual divinity of the man Jesus. When that happens, an adoptionist or ebionite Christology looms large and God

---

96 Myers, 'Election, Trinity, and the History of Jesus', 135.
97 Myers, 'Election, Trinity, and the History of Jesus', 135–6.

the Son is then seen as dependent on history and merged with history in order to be God. However, that is an idea of divinity that is useless because it can no longer allow God the freedom that is and remains his alone before, above and within history as a God who really is free for us and thus whose actions can be conceptually distinguished from the processes of history.

Reconsidering the Divine Freedom

Now let me discuss a recent attempt to adjudicate the conflicts that have developed in recent years in connection with Bruce McCormack's thesis that Barth should have logically reversed the doctrines of election and the Trinity. A number of crucial issues should come clearly into view in this discussion. Kevin W. Hector argues, and I agree, that: 'It seems overwhelmingly likely ... that Barth would reject McCormack's claim about the logical priority of election to triunity.'[98] Nevertheless, he chooses to defend McCormack against charges of subordination-ism and modalism while embracing the general aims of his thesis. It might be helpful to the reader here if I summarize McCormack's thesis through the prism of Hector's presentation. First, he claims that for McCormack 'God determines to be triune as a result, as it were, of God's determination to be God-with-us.'[99] This misguided refrain follows from the logical reversal of the doctrines of election and the Trinity which is, as seen in the previous chapter, fundamental to McCormack's interpretation of Barth and his attempt to reconstruct Barth's doctrine of the Trinity. However, it is, as I pointed out in the previous chapter and on a number of other occasions,[100] extremely problematic, because while God determines himself for us in electing us, that does not mean

98 Hector, 'Immutability, Necessity and Triunity', 70.

99 Hector, 'Immutability, Necessity and Triunity', 64–5.

100 See Molnar, 'The Trinity, Election and God's Ontological Freedom: A Response to Kevin W. Hector' *IJST*, vol. 8, no. 3, 2006, 294–306 and 'Can the Electing God be God without Us? Some Implications of Bruce McCormack's Understanding of the Doctrine of Election for the Doctrine of the Trinity', *Neue Zeitschrift für Systematische Theologie und Religionsphilosophie*, vol. 49, no. 2, 2007, 199–222. These articles have been reissued in *Trinity and Election in Contemporary Theology*, ed. Michael Dempsey.

that he *thereby* gives himself his eternal being.[101] Why? Because a God who has to give himself his being is in reality limited by the fact that he *needs* to do that. God eternally is the one he is and simply affirms this in his eternal act of being Father, Son and Spirit. In Barth's words:

> The freedom in which God exists means that He does not need His own being in order to be who He is: because He already has His own being and is Himself ... this being does not need any origination and *constitution*. He cannot 'need' His own being because He affirms it in being who He is.[102]

There is a great deal at stake here because while McCormack claims he is only logically reversing election and the Trinity and not doing so in a chronological or ontological way, the fact remains that any such logical reversal changes the meaning of both doctrines. It does so most decidedly by always implying that God could not be God without electing us and that he therefore needs to give himself the being he would have for eternity in order to do so. This misses the all-important point stressed by both Barth and Torrance that God's eternal election of us and his subsequent acts of creation, reconciliation and redemption are acts of grace that express God's eternal love and plan for us. However they do not in any way constitute his eternal being. That is why Barth specifically rejected the idea that God's *aseity* could be referred to as an act of 'self-realisation' since 'the God who takes His origin from Himself or is *constituted* by Himself is in a certain sense limited by the possibility of His non-being and therefore He is not the free God'.[103]

---

101 George Hunsinger has demonstrated this with clarity. See, for example, 'Election and the Trinity: Twenty-Five Theses on the Theology of Karl Barth'. McCormack's response to Hunsinger 'Election and the Trinity: Theses in Response to George Hunsinger' *SJT*, vol. 63, no. 2 (2010): 203–24, never actually addresses the real question which concerns whether or not the position he espouses is Barth's. However, as Hector notes, McCormack admits that he has moved beyond Barth. The question I am raising concerns the fact that McCormack's main conclusions result precisely from this reversal. Therefore, for Hector to embrace his conclusions while rejecting this reversal, leaves him in a position where he is still unable to recognize and maintain the freedom of God's love.

102 *CD* II/1, 306, emphasis mine.

103 *CD* II/1, 305, emphasis mine. It is no accident, as we shall see, that McCormack simply rejects this thinking, because in his view Barth here was

There is a critical distinction here that is lost by McCormack and his followers and it is this: Following Thomas Aquinas, Barth insists that God's triunity is both a work of his will and his nature because in God nature and will are one. Hence, the begetting of the Son

> is not an act of the divine will to the degree that freedom to will this or that is expressed in the concept of will. God has this freedom in respect of creation – He is free to will it or not to will it … But He does not have this freedom in respect to His being God. God cannot not be God … He cannot not be Father and cannot be without the Son.[104]

It is extremely important to realize that this is not simply an insight of Thomas Aquinas. It was a pivotal insight also espoused by Athanasius as when he wrote: 'If He [the Word] be other than all things … and through Him the works rather came to be, let not "by will" be applied to Him …'[105] For Athanasius, because the Word is begotten from the Father's being, the Father 'did not counsel beforehand' about the Word, because it was in him that the Father makes all else that he counsels. Since the will of God is in his Word and his Word exists as begotten of the Father without beginning, any suggestion that the Word came into being by an act of will on the part of the Father would have to mean that 'the will concerning Him consists in some other Word, through whom He in turn comes to be; for it has been shewn that God's will is not in the things which He brings into being, but in Him through whom and in whom all things made are brought to be'.[106] Therefore, Athanasius argues that to say that the Son exists 'by will' must mean that whoever says such a thing, 'places times before the Son; for counseling goes before things which once were not, as in the case of all creatures'.[107] In other words any suggestion that the Son exists because of an act of will on the part of the Father has to imply that the Word could not

only on the way toward his new anti-metaphysical position that would no longer permit him to hold that God could have been triune without us.

104 *CD* I/1, 434.

105 Athanasius, *Contra. Ar.* III, 61 in *A Select Library of Nicene and Post-Nicene Fathers of the Christian Church*, trans. and ed. Philip Schaff and Henry Wace, *Volume IV, St. Athanasius: Select Works and Letters* (Edinburgh: T & T Clark, 1987), 427.

106 Athanasius, *Contra Ar.* III, 61.

107 Athanasius, *Contra Ar.* III, 61.

4. Reconsidering Divine Freedom

have co-existed with the Father as the one through whom the world was created.

Athanasius goes on to reject both the idea that the Son exists because of an act of will or because of some necessity within or outside of God.[108] Athanasius thought the very idea that the Son or Word could have come into existence by an act of will on the part of the Father to be both an 'unseemly' and a 'self-destructive' and even 'shocking' idea because God simply is who he is and this applies both to the Father and to the Word. Hence,

> He who is God not by will, has not by will but by nature His own Word. And does it not surpass all conceivable madness, to entertain the thought only, that God Himself counsels and considers and chooses and proceeds to have a good pleasure, that He be not without Word and without Wisdom, but have both? For He seems to be considering about Himself, who counsels about what is proper to His Essence.[109]

Athanasius answers that things 'originate' have come into existence by an act of will and favor, but not the Son because the Son is 'not a work of will, nor has come after, as the creation, but is by nature the own Offspring of God's Essence'.[110] He is himself, Athanasius says, 'the Father's Living Counsel, and Power, and Framer of the things which seemed good to the Father'.[111]

Athanasius concludes that it is blasphemous to say 'that will was in the Father before the Word ... for if will precedes in the Father, the Son's words are not true, "I in the Father;" or even if He is in the Father, yet He will hold but a second place, and it became Him not to say "I in the Father," since will was before Him in which all things were brought into being and He Himself subsisted'.[112] Finally, Athanasius asserts that it is madness to introduce 'will and consideration between' the Father and the Son. While Athanasius is very clear that God's nature is not at all opposed to his will because who and what God is is not opposed to his will, nonetheless it is one thing to say ' "Of will he came to be," ' because that implies that 'once He was not' and also that 'one might suppose that

---

108 See Athanasius, *Contra Ar.* III, 62.
109 Athanasius, *Contra Ar.* III, 63.
110 Athanasius, *Contra Ar.* III, 63.
111 Athanasius, *Contra Ar.* III, 63.
112 Athanasius, *Contra Ar.* III, 64.

the Father could even not will the Son'.[113] But Athanasius says that to claim that the Son 'might not have been' is

> an irreligious presumption reaching even to the Essence of the Father, as if what is His own might not have been. For it is the same as saying 'The Father might not have been good'. And as the Father is always good by nature, so He is always generative by nature; and to say, 'The Father's good pleasure is the Son', and 'The Word's good pleasure is the Father' implies not a precedent will, but genuineness of nature.[114]

For Barth, then, the begetting of the Son is a work of nature that 'could not not happen just as God could not not be God' but creation is an act of God's will 'in the sense that it could also not happen and yet God would not on that account be any the less God'.[115] In other words, there is an important distinction that Barth makes in *CD* II/1 that is fully in accord with the thinking of Thomas Aquinas and of Athanasius, that must be stressed here: 'There is, for example, the distinction between His willing of Himself and His willing of the possibility and reality of His creation as distinct from Himself'.[116] Strangely, McCormack claims that he is 'as convinced as [I am] that God need not have created this world; God might have chosen to create a different world or to have created no world at all'.[117] But nothing could be further from the truth. The logic of his thinking is such that, as Hector himself indicates, God *gave* himself the being he would have for all eternity as triune 'for the sake of creation, reconciliation and redemption'.[118] It is this very thinking that is at odds with the idea that God need not have created the world or might have chosen to create a different world or no world. The problem resides in McCormack's refusal to acknowledge that the God who might never have created at all, is indeed the very same triune God who meets us in the incarnate Word and in his Spirit. He claims that the issue here is not one of divine freedom, but that is exactly the problem. He says he questions whether or not anyone can 'know what God would have been without us, to know, in fact, how the

---

113 Athanasius, *Contra Ar.* III, 66.
114 Athanasius, *Contra Ar.* III, 66.
115 *CD* I/1, 434.
116 *CD* II/1, 590.
117 McCormack, *Orthodox and Modern*, 297.
118 Hector, 'Immutability, Necessity and Triunity', 65.

divine being would have been structured had God not determined to be God for us in Jesus Christ.[119] But this assertion rests on the premise that God structured his triunity in order to elect us or in the process of electing us. That premise, however, is incorrect because, as George Hunsinger rightly states:

> The Father does not eternally generate the Son for the purpose of pre-temporal election. If election were the purpose of the Son's eternal generation by the Father ... the Trinity would *necessarily* be dependent on the world ... the Son would be subordinated to an external end; and ... the Son would be object but not the subject of election.[120]

This thinking seems fully in accord with the views of Athanasius discussed above and would certainly be in accord with Barth's important statement: 'Of course, the fact that Jesus Christ is the Son of God does not rest on election.'[121]

McCormack is unable to accept this or to acknowledge the problem here because he claims that Barth's idea that God would exist as eternal Father, Son and Holy Spirit even without creation, reconciliation and redemption was something Barth affirmed from *CD* I/1 through *CD* II/1 'but that such a formulation is not finally compatible with the statement that "Jesus Christ is the electing God" '.[122] But this thinking leads to the strange conclusion that it is important to say that 'God could be God without us' in order to safeguard the divine freedom, but that any statement that God 'would have been this way or that way' is the result of 'unwarranted speculation' which necessarily opens 'a gap in material content between the immanent and economic Trinity – as Molnar does'.[123] I say this is strange because in the first edition of *Divine*

119 McCormack, *Orthodox and Modern*, 297.

120 Hunsinger, 'Twenty-Five Theses', *Modern Theology*, 192, emphasis mine. Compare this quite proper assertion to Bruce McCormack's problematic claim that 'the second "person" of the Trinity is the "one divine I" a second time, in a different form – a form which is constituted by the anticipation of union with the humanity of Christ,' 'Grace and Being', 104.

121 *CD* II/2, 107. I emphasized this point in 'Can the Electing God be God without Us?' *NZSTh*, 2007, 206.

122 McCormack, *Orthodox and Modern*, 297.

123 McCormack, *Orthodox and Modern*, 297.

Freedom I never opened a gap between who God is for us and who God is in himself. Instead, I consistently insisted, with Barth and Torrance, that what God is toward us, he is eternally in himself. I made it clear that for me that means that God is eternally the Father, Son and Holy Spirit – the one who loves in freedom and is free in his love. Therefore, I never had to make the incoherent assertion that God could be God without us but that we could not identify that God as the eternal Father, Son and Holy Spirit. To know the immanent Trinity from God's actions within the economy means precisely to know that the triune God who could have remained who he is in himself to all eternity freely chose not to do so. It is only on the basis of God's free grace and love which meet us in Christ and in his Spirit uniting us to Christ that we know this. Thus, from within a properly functioning doctrine of the Trinity it is impossible to speak of God at all unless one is speaking of the triune God precisely by thinking of the Father through the Son and by the Holy Spirit enabling that speech. So, to claim that one could say that God could be God without us without specifying who God is in his triunity, truly represents an exercise in unwarranted speculation. It is not thinking that is prompted by the Holy Spirit. It is not thinking within faith which itself is acknowledgment because it can only follow the revelation of God in Jesus Christ as an act of obedience that 'is not preceded by any other kind of knowledge'.[124] If it were knowledge of faith, one could never speak of God without referring to the Father, Son and Holy Spirit who is the one who loves in freedom in se and ad extra. It is exactly such reasoning that opens a gap in material content between the immanent and economic Trinity; a gap that is then closed by improperly reading back elements of the economy into the immanent Trinity and thus allowing history itself to condition and to define God's triunity. What we have here is simply another example of someone offering us a 'dependent deity'. Hence, when McCormack thinks of closing that imaginary gap, what he means is that God's actions ad extra actually must be understood to determine who God is ad intra. That is precisely the difficulty that I have identified and rejected by insisting, with Barth, that the God who meets us in history is the triune God who had and has no need of us but who nevertheless in his grace and love does not will to exist without us and therefore does not in fact exist without us. Greater emphasis on the deity of the Holy Spirit here and on the *homoousion* of the Spirit with the Son would prevent any attempt to introduce the notion of a dependent deity at this point.

124 See *CD* IV/1, 758.

But McCormack is so intent on pressing his claims here that he simply dismisses Barth's clear statements about God's freedom to have existed as the triune God without us in *CD* I/1, I/2 and also in II/1, many of which have been meticulously documented by George Hunsinger.[125] Here it is worth mentioning that McCormack claims that there are 'tensions' in Barth's thinking in *CD* II/1 such that Barth 'is able to speak of the work of reconciliation and redemption as a "fundamentally new work"'[126] and that this idea is something Barth later rejected, especially in *CD* IV/1.[127]

McCormack thus claims that in *CD* IV/1 Barth does not believe the incarnation 'is a new event in God when it happens in time'.[128] It is new to human beings because it is the revelation of what up to that point had been a mystery.

> But it is not new to God because it is the outworking in time of the eternal event in which God gave to himself the being he would have for all eternity. We have before us here another piece of significant evidence demonstrating that an important change has taken place within the bounds of the *Church Dogmatics*. In I/1 ... Barth insisted that the incarnation was a new event in God's life. In IV/1, he denies it.[129]

It is crucial, however, to understand that the text McCormack cites (*CD* IV/1, 193) does not support this reading of Barth at all. Barth never says

125 See, for example, 'Twenty-Five Theses', *Modern Theology* and *Reading Barth with Charity*. An especially good example, among many others, is found in Barth's distinction between God's primary and secondary objectivity as discussed in detail above. Hunsinger correctly notes that: 'For Barth, however, throughout the *Church Dogmatics* from beginning to end, God is seen as free not to have created the world, but he is not seen as free not to be himself, and therefore he is not seen as free not to be the Holy Trinity (to all eternity)', 'Twenty-Five Theses', 197. For a full discussion of how this relates to Barth's Christology and to the thought of Thomas F. Torrance and Robert W. Jenson, see Molnar, *Faith, Freedom and the Spirit*, chapter five, and Molnar, 'The Perils of Embracing a "Historicized Christology"' *Modern Theology*, vol. 30, no. 4 (2014): 454–80.

126 McCormack, *Engaging the Doctrine of God*, 234.

127 McCormack, *Trinitarian Theology after Barth*, ed. Habets and Tolliday, 109.

128 McCormack, *Trinitarian Theology after Barth*, ed. Habets and Tolliday, 108.

129 McCormack, *Trinitarian Theology after Barth*, ed. Habets and Tolliday, 108.

that the incarnation is an event in which 'God gave to himself the being he would have for all eternity'. He continues to insist that the incarnation is a free act of God, the Son assuming human nature into union with his divine being in time and history as he did in *CD* IV/2 as well: 'Even as the divine essence of the Son it did not need His incarnation, His existence as man ... to become actual. As the divine essence of the Son it is the predicate of the one God. And as the predicate of this Subject it is not in any sense merely potential but in every sense actual.'[130] And: 'The triune life of God which is free life in the fact that it is Spirit, is the basis of His whole will and action even ad extra, as the living act which He directs to us. It is the basis ... of the determination of the Son to become man ... of the atonement with its final goal of redemption to eternal life with Himself.'[131] In *CD* IV/1, Barth says that Jesus 'as the Son of God the Father and with God the Father the source of the Holy Spirit, united in one essence with the Father by the Holy Spirit ... is God. He is God as He takes part in the event which constitutes the divine being'.[132] Then he says:

> We must add at once that as this One who takes part in the divine being and event He became and is man. This means that we have to understand the very Godhead, that divine being and event and therefore Himself as the One who takes part in it, in the light of the fact that it pleased God – this is what corresponds outwardly to and reveals the inward divine being and event – Himself to become man. In this way, in this condescension, He is the eternal Son of the eternal Father.[133]

While Barth is clear that we must understand God in light of what he has done in the incarnation, there is no hint that he argues here that God 'gave himself' his being in an eternal event of incarnation.

What he did was give himself to the human race without ceasing to be God and so he could effectively reconcile us to the Father. He humbled himself 'all without giving up His own form, the *forma Dei*, and His own glory, but adopting the form and cause of man into the most perfect communion with His own, accepting solidarity with the

130 *CD* IV/2, 113.
131 *CD* IV/2, 345.
132 *CD* IV/1, 129.
133 *CD* IV/1, 129.

world'.[134] Furthermore, when Barth speaks of the mystery of the Word humbling himself for us, he does not say that in the incarnation God makes suffering and death to be essential to God.[135] Rather, he argues that God takes our suffering and death into his divine being in order to overcome these for us. If suffering and death were to be thought of as essential to God, then God himself would stand in need of redemption.[136] Beyond this, when Barth says that the humility in which God 'dwells and acts in Jesus Christ is not alien to Him, but proper to Him' and is thus not a 'novum mysterium' to God but only a 'novum mysterium' to us, he is clearly referring to the act of kenosis in which the Son did not grasp at equality with God but freely humbled himself for our benefit. This is not a new mystery to God because, Barth says, God does not become another God in condescending to give himself to us in this way. Rather he acts as the one he is from all eternity, that is, the eternal Father, Son and Holy Spirit, namely, 'the one God Himself in His true Godhead'.[137] There is no indication here that Barth intended to say that God gave to himself his eternal being in and by this event. It was rather the outworking of his eternal decision of love for us. Still, for Barth, this is a new act in that God was not always incarnate and God could well have existed without the incarnation if he had chosen to do so. Indeed God did not need to become incarnate in order to be the triune God.[138]

134 CD IV/1, 187.

135 Barth argues in fact that God's omnipotence is such that he 'can assume the form of weakness and impotence and do so as omnipotence, triumphing in this form', CD IV/1, 187. See also CD IV/2, 357 where Barth notes that the element of truth in the otherwise false position of Patripassianism is that it is 'God the Father who suffers in the offering and sending of His Son, in His abasement. The suffering is not His own, but the alien suffering of the creature, of man, which He takes to Himself in Him'. God does not here make suffering part of his nature. Indeed while God in his 'innermost being' is moved and stirred to compassion for us in our suffering – not 'in powerlessness' like us, but because God is 'open, ready, inclined ... to compassion with another's suffering and therefore to assistance', it is still the case that 'God finds no suffering in Himself' CD II/1, 370.

136 For more on this see the discussion of Moltmann's thinking below, Chapter 8, and Molnar, Pro Ecclesia, 'Beyond Hegel with Karl Barth and T. F. Torrance'.

137 CD IV/1, 193.

138 In addition to the important statements to this effect adduced above, it would be very instructive here to add Barth's remark: 'We must distinguish

Additionally, Barth's explication of God's omnipotence is said to be extremely problematic because Barth 'describes God's power as a power "over everything that He actually wills *or could will*".[139] This we are told allows Barth to distinguish between God's omnipotence and God's omnicausality and to insist that

> we must reject the idea that God's omnipotence and therefore His essence resolves itself in a sense into what God actually does, into His activity, and that it is to be identified with it. It is not the case that God is God and His omnipotence omnipotence only as He actually does what He does. Creation, reconciliation and redemption are the work, really the work of His omnipotence. He is omnipotent in this work ... He has not lost His omnipotence in this work. It has not changed into His omnicausality in this work, like a piece of capital invested in this undertaking, and therefore no longer at the disposal of its owner. The love with which He turns to us in this work, and in which He has made Himself our God, has not made Him in the least degree poorer or smaller. It has its power and its reality as love for us too in the fact that it continues to be free love, that God has bound and still binds Himself to us as the One who is able thus to bind Himself and whose self-binding is the grace and mercy and patience which helps us, because primarily He is not bound, because He is the Lord, because stooping down to us He does not cease to be the Lord, but actually stoops to us from on high where He is always Lord. He is wholly our God, but He is so in the fact that He is not our God only.[140]

McCormack claims that this thinking is both dangerous and that it trespasses 'against the very core of [Barth's] methodological commitments' since it opens the door 'to speculation with regard to what God could have done – thereby looking away from the limits set for us by God's self-revelation in Jesus Christ.'[141] Moreover, we are told that 'none of this was necessary. Barth could have upheld the divine freedom

between God as such and God in His purpose (decree). From eternity the Son (as God *and man*) exists in God. But until the incarnation this has not happened. Nevertheless, this must be made clear; otherwise you have a fourth member of the Trinity', *Table Talk*, 52.

139 McCormack, *Engaging the Doctrine of God*, 235, citing *CD* II/1, 522.
140 *CD* II/1, 527.
141 McCormack, *Engaging the Doctrine of God*, 236.

simply by insisting that the eternal act of Self-determination in which God chose to be God in the covenant of grace and to be God in no other way is itself a free act'.[142] Notice the way McCormack imposes his own thinking on Barth here. Barth was at pains to indicate that God is who he is both in himself and in his works, but God could never be reduced to what he does in his works ad extra. Because McCormack cannot agree with the distinction that led to that assertion, a distinction which is central to Barth's trinitarian theology, he reduces the divine freedom to what God actually chose to do in the economy by confusing God's choice to be God in the covenant of grace with God's eternal being as Father, Son and Spirit, with the result that he claims that God can be God in *no other way*. Put differently, McCormack clearly has moved beyond Barth by claiming that God's freedom exercised in his relations with us in the covenant must mean that God no longer has any existence in himself and thus apart from us. It is therefore no surprise that in quoting this text McCormack leaves out that last sentence which was crucial for Barth, namely, that God 'is wholly our God, but He is so in the fact that He is not our God only'.

That statement makes all the difference in the world. It does not lead Barth into abstract speculation about what God could have done, that is, into natural theology. It only leads him to acknowledge and assert the truth that the God who in fact meets us in his Word and Spirit could have remained perfectly God in himself without us but chose not to. That very distinction is lost by McCormack as when he writes, commenting on what he takes to be Barth's revised doctrine of the Trinity in *CD* IV/1, that: '*There is no longer any room left here for an abstract doctrine of the Trinity. There is a triune being of God – only in the covenant of grace.*'[143] When compared to what Barth says in *CD* II/1 it is obvious that Barth never would have made this statement because it overtly reduces God to his actions in the covenant of grace.[144]

---

142 McCormack, *Engaging the Doctrine of God*, 236.

143 McCormack, 'Election and the Trinity: Theses in Response to George Hunsinger', in Dempsey, 128, emphasis mine.

144 Importantly, Robert B. Price, *Letters of the Divine Word: The Perfections of God in Karl Barth's Church Dogmatics*, ed. John Webster, Ian A. McFarland and Ivor Davidson, T & T Clark Studies in Systematic Theology (London/ New York: T & T Clark, 2011), notices that McCormack's proposal that election should have logically preceded the Trinity in Barth's thought represents 'an overemphasis on the divine loving (God's love for us) and a compromising

That is exactly what Barth was trying to avoid, while simultaneously asserting that grace as God's free action is an action of the Lord who became incarnate for us and for our benefit, without, in the least, ceasing to be the Lord who has his freedom in himself and is not exhausted by what he does for us. McCormack's problematic thinking here is dictated by his belief that when Barth spoke of Jesus Christ *rather than* of the eternal Son as the subject of election this had to refer to the fact that God's 'eternal act of choosing to be God-for-us in Jesus Christ is the very act in which God *constitutes* himself as triune'.[145] This is meant to remind us that 'the Second Person of the Trinity is not the "eternal Son" in abstraction from the humanity he would assume. The eternal Son has a name and his name is Jesus. *Any talk of the eternal Son in abstraction from the humanity to be assumed is an exercise in mythologizing; there is no such eternal Son – and there never was.*'[146]

of the divine freedom' (11). More than that, Price astutely points out that 'for McCormack, God's eternal election logically includes the incarnation' (141) and that this position is in conflict with what Barth actually says, namely, that 'the incarnation is as such the confirmation of the triunity of God' (*CD* II/1, 515) and 'there is revealed in it [the incarnation] the distinction of the Father and the Son, and also their fellowship in the Holy Spirit' (*CD* II/1, 515). Price thinks that the many other statements about God's freedom that are in conflict with McCormack's thinking as it follows his logical reversal of election and triunity 'would appear too numerous to represent a mere inconsistency in Barth's thought' (142). The point is that for Barth 'what God does in time is … a function of what he is in eternity – not the other way round' (142). This, says Price, 'is one of the most basic themes of Barth's exposition' (142). According to Price: 'To claim that it is God's interaction with the created order which determines his immanent life is to run counter not merely to isolated inconsistencies or residual elements of classical theism in *CD* II/1, but to its entire flow of thought' (142). Price rightly concludes that 'McCormack's is a striking constructive proposal in its own right. But it encounters only resistance from Barth's doctrine of the divine perfections' (142). However, resistance is also evident in Barth's statement: 'The true and living God is gracious. He transcends Himself. He discloses and imparts Himself. He does this first in Himself, and then and on this basis to man in His eternal election and its temporal and historical fulfilment' (*CD* IV/3.1, 81). Here is another important instance of Barth basing God's eternal election in his triune being and act and not collapsing the former into the latter.

145 McCormack, *Engaging the Doctrine of God*, 218, emphasis mine.
146 McCormack, *Engaging the Doctrine of God*, 219, emphasis mine.

Here once more we see very clearly the results of McCormack's inability to distinguish without separating the immanent and economic Trinity as Barth had done. If there never was an eternal Son without Jesus, then the only option left is to assert that Jesus Christ, the God-man, is the subject of the incarnation itself, thus obviating both Jesus's true humanity and true divinity. This, because it eliminates Jesus's humanity by implying that it always existed instead of stating clearly that it only comes into existence at a particular point in time, and it undermines Jesus's true divinity as an authentic, definitive and essential existence that has its fullness in itself without respect to the humanity to be assumed.

Before ending this particular discussion it is worth noting that because Barth's most basic insights about the divine freedom made in *CD* II/1 cannot be reconciled with McCormack's basic thesis that election and the Trinity need to be logically reversed, since he believes it is in election that God gives himself his triune being, McCormack simply argues that these statements must be rejected. Hence, while Barth decisively disallowed any idea that God causes himself, by rejecting the thinking of Hermann Schell in *CD* II/1,[147] McCormack claims that Barth's remark that God's triune being 'does not need any origination and constitution'[148] 'cannot be redeemed and should be rejected.'[149] As is characteristic with McCormack, he admits that Barth does indeed reject the idea that God is the cause of himself but claims that 'the question must remain open as to whether his later Christology would allow him to continue to do so.'[150] Of course in McCormack's thinking this is not an open question; it is answered repeatedly by his own assertions in many contexts that God gives himself his being in the act of election – something Barth never approved and never would approve. In fact, as George Hunsinger writes: 'The notion that the eternal Son was constituted by pre-temporal election was something so bizarre, and obviously false, that Barth could see little point in pausing very long to refute it.'[151] Nonetheless, Hunsinger does cite a very relevant remark that Barth did make: 'Of course, the fact that Jesus Christ *is* the Son of God does not rest

---

147 See Molnar, 'Can the Electing God Be God Without Us?', *NZSTh*, 2007, for a discussion of this issue.

148 *CD* II/1, 306.

149 McCormack 'Election and the Trinity', 132.

150 McCormack 'Election and the Trinity', 133.

151 Hunsinger, 'Twenty-Five Theses', 195.

on election,'[152] and one which was noted above. Even here, McCormack alleges that at this early date Barth was ambivalent in rejecting Hermann Schell's thinking. Yet, even McCormack's own presentation shows that Barth was not at all ambivalent – he clearly rejected Schell's statement. However, he did want to honor Schell's 'special concern' which was to overcome 'the scholastic equation of God with the unmoved Mover of Aristotle'.[153] Barth wanted to overcome the static and unmoved God of Aristotle because he consistently argued that the triune God was in reality the only self-moved being since God was the living God.[154] Torrance, too, wanted nothing to do with the unmoved Mover of Aristotle.[155]

Schell may have intended that, but the way he went about overcoming Aristotle's view was unacceptable to Barth because the only way forward was on the ground of what God actually revealed in his Word and Spirit. It is only too clear from the context that McCormack wants to argue that God does take his origin from himself and that if Barth could have abandoned his rejection of that point, his thinking would have moved closer to the thinking of John Zizioulas. Indeed, for McCormack, 'God must give himself being eternally in the act in which he sets himself in relationship to Jesus Christ and, in turn, to the world'.[156] Neglecting the fact that Barth insisted that a God who had to give himself his being was limited by the fact that he needed to do this, McCormack simply asserts this point, which is the logical consequence of his having reduced the immanent to the economic Trinity, precisely by logically reversing the doctrines of election and the Trinity. Finally, according to McCormack, there are two other statements of Barth that must be rejected: (1) that ' "Jesus Christ has a beginning, but God has no beginning" (II/2, 102)', and (2) that ' "We know God's will *apart* from predestination only as the act in which, from all eternity and in all eternity, God affirms and confirms Himself" (II/2, 155)'. We are told: 'Once Barth makes his later Christology to be the epistemological basis for all that may be said of God, such an "apart from" becomes a complete impossibility'.[157] As George Hunsinger has shown, these kinds

---

152 Hunsinger, 'Twenty-Five Theses', 195–6, citing *CD* II/2, 107 with slight revision.

153 *CD* II/1, 305.

154 *CD* II/1, 268ff.

155 See, for example, Molnar, *Torrance: Theologian of the Trinity*, 50–1, 81, and 133.

156 McCormack, 'Election and the Trinity', 135.

157 McCormack, 'Election and the Trinity', 134.

of statements illustrate McCormack's uncharitable reading of Barth because McCormack ascribes inconsistency to him even though the textual Barth does not agree with McCormack's assumed position.[158] In my view it is wholly inappropriate simply to dismiss these crucial statements made by Barth that demonstrate that he had no intention of arguing that election determines or constitutes God's triunity simply because they don't fit the logic of one's own position.

An Attempt to Mediate the Disagreements

For now I wish to explore exactly why I think Kevin Hector fails to convince in his latest attempt to resolve the controversy. Following Jüngel, Hector says that in the act of creation God repeats ad extra 'the Father's eternal act of begetting the Son' while in reconciling us it is 'the Son's eternal act of reflecting the Father's love' that is repeated ad extra, and in mediating this reconciliation God repeats ad extra 'the Spirit's eternal act'.[159] While it is true that God draws us into his eternal relations through grace and faith, it is more than a little ambiguous to suggest that God is repeating his eternal acts of begetting and so on when he relates with us since in reality God is doing something new, new even for himself when he acts outside himself for us. Hector at least is able to acknowledge that God would still be Father, Son and Holy Spirit if he did not determine to be God with us, so that he would not then 'repeat' his being ad extra. However, he also makes the strange assertion that since Barth claims that God has determined to be with us, therefore, 'God has never been triune without appropriating creation to the Father, reconciliation to the Son and redemption to the Spirit'.[160] It is this very statement that demonstrates that, while Hector attempts to separate himself from McCormack's mistaken view that we cannot say that the triune God could have existed without us without being any less God, he cannot separate himself from the thinking that is singularly unable to distinguish without separating the immanent and economic Trinity. For if God has *never* been triune without appropriating creation, reconciliation and redemption to himself, then, what is being suggested is that God in fact never existed without the world! And that, once again,

158 See Hunsinger, *Reading Barth with Charity*, chapter one.
159 Hector, 'Immutability, Necessity and Triunity', 70.
160 Hector, 'Immutability, Necessity and Triunity', 70.

is the old Origenist error coming back to haunt modern theology.[161] Hector, like McCormack, is unable to distinguish clearly between God's internal and external actions. Things go downhill from here.

Hector proceeds to argue that both election and triunity are necessary to God in different ways. 'Triunity is necessary to God in an absolute sense, whereas election is not, since God could have been God without us.'[162] But his thinking is still caught in the web of the reasoning that equates triunity with election since he has already told us that God never exists as triune except in relation to us. So Hector maintains that while election is not absolutely necessary to God, it is '*volitionally* necessary'.[163] From where does Hector acquire this notion? He gets it from Harry Frankfurt and from his analysis 'of the phenomenon of love'. It is very clear that his analysis is based on an exploration of human love. That in itself is a major problem from Barth's perspective since he insisted that we could not come to a true understanding of God's love for us in Christ by examining human love. While humans need others to love, God does not; and in that sense God is truly free in a way that humans can never be. In any case, Hector argues that one's care for one's child means that one 'could not bring oneself to act cruelly towards him or her' and thus it must be the case that one's care of another 'imposes certain volitional necessities upon one, in the sense that one could not will otherwise'.[164] From this he concludes that necessities that are self-imposed rather than imposed from without do not compromise one's freedom: 'If I identify with this configuration of my will … then it follows that I am free with respect to it not because I could will otherwise, but precisely because this will is self-imposed.'[165] Applying this thinking to the doctrine of election, Hector reaches the following conclusions: (1) 'in electing to be with us, God identifies our interests as God's own and thus identifies with us'; (2) 'that God identifies wholeheartedly

---

161   For a full discussion of how Origenism hovers over this discussion of election and the Trinity, see Molnar, *Faith, Freedom and the Spirit*, chapter four, 'Origenism, Election, and Time and Eternity'.

162   Hector, 'Immutability, Necessity and Triunity', 71.

163   Hector, 'Immutability, Necessity and Triunity', 71.

164   Hector, 'Immutability, Necessity and Triunity', 72. There is an additional problem with this analogy as well since some parents clearly do not embrace this supposed 'volitional necessity' and do indeed harm their children. So some parents clearly do will otherwise for various reasons.

165   Hector, 'Immutability, Necessity and Triunity', 73.

with this identification'; (3) 'in so identifying, God has imposed certain volitional necessities upon Godself, the most important of which is that God has made this identity itself *necessary* to Godself'.[166]

A moment ago I pointed out that one could not understand God's free love by analyzing human love. That is and always remained Barth's view. As I pointed out in a 1989 article on Barth's doctrine of the Trinity, Barth's thinking on this matter stood in conflict with Jüngel's idea that we could only understand God's love by first inquiring into the nature of human love.[167] First, in electing to be with us God does not elect our interests as his own. Rather God elects our rejection of him, which is not in our best interest, precisely in order to love us by judging us in his Son and freely rectifying the human situation. So, in loving us, God does not just identify with us – he calls us into question in his Son and empowers us to love on the basis of his free and undeserved loving of us while we were still sinners. He is not bound to this by any necessity, but acts this way with a freedom that is unhindered by our self-will and opposition. Second, no necessity is placed on God when he acts graciously and lovingly and thus unconditionally toward us in sending his Son to be the Judge judged in our place. Barth never ceased insisting that our relations with God in his Word and Spirit never could be construed in terms of mutual necessity; any such thinking would at once deny and obscure the very meaning of grace as a free overflow of the divine love toward us. Third, and finally, the fact that God loves us in electing us simply cannot be construed as necessary to God without in fact making God dependent on this relation. That of course was bound to happen in Hector's analysis because there are such necessities imposed in all human relations. However, there are never any such necessities imposed on God because God's relations with us never were and never are necessary to God. There is an irreversible relation between God and us and any idea at all that our relations with God mean that election is necessary to him has not in fact escaped the logic that follows the idea that election is indeed the ground of God's triunity. So it turns out that even though Hector formally rejects McCormack's idea that election and triunity should be logically reversed, his thinking still advances all that follows from that mistaken reversal, since by embracing the fact that human love needs others to activate itself

---

166 Hector, 'Immutability, Necessity and Triunity', 73, emphasis mine.

167 Molnar, 'The Function of the Immanent Trinity in the Theology of Karl Barth: Implications For Today', *SJT*, vol. 42, no. 3 (1989): 367–99. See also below, Chapter 9.

and imposes necessities on those who love, his thinking compromises the fact that God himself acts with both inward and outward freedom in loving us. That, Barth rightly insists, is the very mark of divine love that enables us to distinguish it from human love, and that indeed is what makes God's love divinely effective in its movement toward us who are sinners in need of divine forgiveness.

Hector tries to ground this thinking in Barth's view that once God has determined to love us as he has, it is a necessity in light of the fact that it is a decision of God and therefore cannot be undone. Barth does indeed say that, but for Barth the all-important distinction here is between factual necessities and logical necessities. The former refer to facts that have been accomplished by God and so are what they are because God has freely executed them, and the latter refer to necessities imposed on God on the basis of which it is thought that God must conform to certain volitional or other necessities. Hector thus concludes that 'God has freely limited God's possibilities ... by ruling out the possibility of being otherwise than God-with-us'.[168] So, while still paying lip service to the idea that God could still be God without us, Hector concludes that 'properly speaking, God has no being-in-Godself apart from the covenant'.[169] It is clear from the context and from the texts Hector cites from the *CD*, that Barth wants to uphold the view that what God is toward us he is eternally in himself and so God is not other than who he is in the covenant; this of course is the view that I wish to embrace following both Barth and T. F. Torrance. However, Hector's thought has moved beyond this with the claim that God has no being apart from the covenant. It is that very claim that reduces God to what he does for us. This conclusion stands in stark contrast to Barth's continued insistence that God 'reveals Himself as the One who, even though He did not love us and were not revealed to us, even though we did not exist at all, still loves in and for Himself as surely as He is and is God'.[170] Hector's thought will not allow for this because he has erroneously introduced necessity into the divine loving and thus compromised the freedom of God's grace.

While Hector argues that his notion of volitional necessity is compatible with Barth's thinking, this last statement by Barth demonstrates that it is not. While Hector rightly insists that 'election is a *determination* of God's being rather than *constitutive* of it' he also says that 'there

168 Hector, 'Immutability, Necessity and Triunity', 74.
169 Hector, 'Immutability, Necessity and Triunity', 74–5.
170 *CD* IV/2, 755.

is no height or depth in which God is indifferent to this identification, such that God has no being-in-Godself apart from the covenant'.[171] Here what is given with the right hand is taken away with the left. Election is indeed a determination of God's being but that cannot mean that 'God has no being-in-Godself apart from the covenant'. When Barth spoke of the covenant of grace he meant that it was a freely established and freely maintained relation that God, who has his life in himself and could have maintained that life without us, freely chose to be God in communion with us. Still, God retains his life in himself even in his closest relations with us. That is the crucial point that is lost by Hector and those whose thinking is in the grip of an untheological understanding of the immanent Trinity in its relation with the economic. While I agree with Hector that 'God is unreservedly God-with-us', I think the idea of a volitional necessity collapses God's eternal being into his being for us and thus does not solve the problem he set out to solve.

Hector makes every effort to escape the errors that McCormack introduced by logically reversing the doctrines of election and the Trinity, but he seems unable to do so. So while he understands 'the eternal *logos* as *incarnandus*', he also asserts that the *logos* cannot be understood as ' "nothing but" *incarnandus*, since the Son could have been otherwise than *incarnandus* and since ... the Son maintains the being he would have had apart from the covenant'.[172] The problem embedded in this thinking is this: it is problematic to say that the Son maintains the being 'he would have had apart from the covenant' because that suggests that he never really had a preexistent being in himself and thus apart from the covenant and apart from the incarnation. Why does Hector not say that the Son maintains the eternal relation with the Father that he had before the creation of the world and thus also before the covenant? Why can he not say, with Athanasius and with T. F. Torrance, that while God was always Father and always Son, he was not always creator and he was not always incarnate? It seems that the answer is that his own thinking will not allow him to assert a genuine eternal existence of the Son who actually did in fact exist otherwise than *incarnandus* as the eternally begotten Son within the immanent Trinity who freely chose to love us in his electing grace, without needing to. The reason for this can be traced to his idea of a volitional necessity which causes him to think both that 'God has no being-in-Godself apart from the covenant' and

171 Hector, 'Immutability, Necessity and Triunity', 75.
172 Hector, 'Immutability, Necessity and Triunity', 76.

this implies that 'his being-incarnate is nothing other than that which he has been from all eternity'.[173] The obvious difficulty with this latter assertion is that if the Son has been incarnate from all eternity, then one cannot affirm, with Torrance and Barth, that while the Son was always the Son he was not in fact always incarnate. Such an idea compromises both Jesus's full humanity and full divinity, and the only way to avoid doing that, as I have consistently argued, is to acknowledge that the incarnation is something new even for God.

Having said this, however, it must be admitted that Hector seems to affirm the *logos asarkos* in the proper sense when he says that this refers to 'the Son's ownmost relation to the Father, a relation which he would have enjoyed even if God had not determined to be with us, and which he continues to enjoy even in determining to be with us'.[174] However, there also seems to be a serious instability in his thought. On the one hand he quite properly and graciously acknowledges that his prior interpretation of what I had said in the first edition of *Divine Freedom* about this issue was mistaken. He thought I was espousing the idea that God not only could have been God without us, but that 'God *remains* God without us' so that 'God remains isolated from election'.[175] Here we both agree that election is a *determination* of the *triune* God for us but not an act which *constitutes* God's triunity. However, on the other hand, his idea of a volitional necessity problematically leads him to go on to say that 'we should not accept Molnar's suggestion that "when a theologian claims that creation or humanity are in *any sense* necessary to God, that claim is a sure sign that the true idea of contingence has been lost and a logical necessity has been introduced"'.[176] Rejecting this idea, Hector nevertheless thinks he has done justice to the spirit of my affirmation that '"since God exists eternally as Father, Son and Holy Spirit and would so have existed even if he had never decided to create, save and redeem the world, his decision to be God for us could neither be deduced from his nature nor could it be seen as necessitated by any external constraint"' so that he has avoided my 'Hegelian scruples'.[177]

Unfortunately, as I have already indicated, I am not so sure that he has avoided a Hegelian outcome because his very idea of a volitional

---

173 Hector, 'Immutability, Necessity and Triunity', 75.
174 Hector, 'Immutability, Necessity and Triunity', 77.
175 Hector, 'Immutability, Necessity and Triunity', 77.
176 Hector, 'Immutability, Necessity and Triunity', 77.
177 Hector, 'Immutability, Necessity and Triunity', 77–8.

necessity causes just the problem I was seeking to avoid; it leads to statements that reduce God to what God does for us. This difficulty becomes especially clear when we see exactly how Hector attempts to defend McCormack's proposal against charges of subordinationism and from modalism, even though he properly acknowledges that McCormack's proposal is not compatible with Barth's position and thus 'should not be understood as an elaboration of Barth' but should be understood as his own 'novel contribution to contemporary trinitarianism'.[178] Here I must admit that both Hector and McCormack have been misled by Barth himself to some extent with the element of subordinationism that was left over in his doctrine of the Trinity and with his own problematic introduction of a type of subordinationism into the immanent Trinity in his discussion of the Son's subordination and eternal obedience in *CD* IV/1. I will not treat that issue in detail here because I have already discussed this elsewhere by comparing what T. F. Torrance says about the Son's obedience with what Barth says about that in *CD* volume IV.[179]

Here I would simply like to illustrate the problems embedded in Hector's defense of McCormack. Let us first address the issue of subordinationism. Hector notes that McCormack's proposal has been thought liable to this charge since he believes that the God who could have been God without us 'would not necessarily be triune'.[180] This idea could suggest that God might have been the Father without the Son and Spirit and thus that the Father alone would be God in the proper sense and that would imply subordinationism and thus an undoing of trinitarian doctrine at its heart. Hector offers two reasons why he thinks McCormack's trinitarian contribution is not subordinationistic. It will be worthwhile to examine these reasons very carefully.

First, Hector notes that we must 'distinguish subordination from subordinationism'.[181] This assertion already is ambiguous since, without a clear distinction, without separation, of the immanent and economic Trinity, such an assertion will necessarily end in subordinationism. Sure enough, Hector fails to make that distinction when he

---

178 Hector, 'Immutability, Necessity and Triunity', 78.

179 See 'The obedience of the Son in the theology of Karl Barth and of Thomas F. Torrance', *SJT*, vol. 67, no. 1 (2014): 50–69 and chapter seven of *Faith, Freedom and the Spirit*.

180 Hector, 'Immutability, Necessity and Triunity', 78.

181 Hector, 'Immutability, Necessity and Triunity', 78.

says that understanding the Son's eternal being from the economy of grace means that 'one may conclude that the Son's dependence upon the Father – even for his very being – does not compromise the fullness of his divinity'.[182] The results are catastrophic because he is led directly into several serious errors, the most important of which is that he concludes that the Son's being 'is contingent upon the will of the Father'.[183] Yet, it is that very belief that was firmly rejected at Nicaea and by later theologians who accepted the teaching of Nicaea in the interest of affirming the *homoousion* of the Son with the Father from all eternity. If the Son's being is contingent on the Father's will, then and to that extent, the Son would have to be conceptualized as needing to come into being and then God's triunity would have been conceptualized as a result of God's decision to elect us. At this point we are right back into the heart of McCormack's trinitarian proposal which, as we have been seeing, is extremely problematic! And the results here are disastrous. Instead of arguing that the Son is eternally begotten of the Father in the sense that the Father never existed and never could exist without the Son, Hector, following McCormack, maintains that 'the Son's being is not necessary in the same way that the Father's is, but this would not entail that the Son is less divine'.[184] Here it must be said very pointedly that if the Son's being is not necessary in the same way that the Father's is, then and to that extent, his true oneness of being with the Father has been denied. What is the evidence for this assertion by Hector? This appears in Hector's second point.

He argues that 'while McCormack's proposal may imply that the Son's being is not necessary in the way the Father's is, this does not necessarily entail that the Father could be the Father without the Son, since McCormack could claim that the (actual) Father's love for the Son *makes* the latter necessary'.[185] Exactly as written here, this is the perfect assertion of Arian subordinationism![186] If the Son's being needs to be *made* necessary by the Father's actual love for the Son and is not eternally what it is as a *unity of being* between the Father and the Son

182 Hector, 'Immutability, Necessity and Triunity', 79.

183 Hector, 'Immutability, Necessity and Triunity', 79. See my discussion above about why Athanasius forcefully rejected this idea in his arguments against the Arians.

184 Hector, 'Immutability, Necessity and Triunity', 79.

185 Hector, 'Immutability, Necessity and Triunity', 79.

186 See my discussion of Athanasius's position previously.

in the unity of the Holy Spirit such that it does not need to be made necessary, we already have a Son who 'once was not' necessary but had to and did become so. As seen earlier, this is exactly the thinking that Athanasius rejected in rejecting the twin ideas that the Son exists by an act of the Father's will or by any necessity within or outside of God. Things get even worse. We are told by Hector that 'the Father could not be the Father without the Son ... not because of some impersonal necessity imposed by the Son's being, but because the Father loves the Son wholeheartedly and therefore *wills* not to be God in any other way than with him by his side'.[187] The wording of this assertion is quite similar to McCormack's claim that election is the ground of God's triunity. It is simply wrong from a trinitarian standpoint because while the Son's being one with the Father is in no sense 'impersonal', it is nevertheless necessary in the sense that God the Father never was without his Son and never could have existed without his Son, while both Father and Son did exist prior to the existence of human history and could have continued to do so but chose not to.

In this thinking there is a confusion of the immanent and economic Trinity and the result is indeed a form of subordinationism. Insofar as the Son is thought to exist as a consequence of the Father's will or the Father's love, his *homoousion* with the Father has been negated. There is no way around this. Hector thinks that by saying that 'since the Father has never not loved the Son – just as he has never not loved us – so he has never been the Father without the Son and, in consequence of his love for the Son, *could* never have been the Father without the Son',[188] he is upholding the Son's uniqueness within the immanent Trinity. However, he has not done so because he here equates the Son's eternal existence with the Father's love of us. This is the ultimate confusion of the immanent and economic Trinity that I consistently and forcefully opposed in the first edition of *Divine Freedom* because it is just here that Hector is unable to maintain what he himself insisted was crucial to affirm, namely, that God the Father, Son and Spirit could have been fully God without us but *freely* chose not to. Here, because God needs to give himself his being, that is, because the Father needs to give himself his triune being by willing (loving) the Son, he could never be without the Son only insofar as he wills to love us eternally along with the Son. So when Hector argues that McCormack could say that the Son's

---

187 Hector, 'Immutability, Necessity and Triunity', 79, emphasis mine.
188 Hector, 'Immutability, Necessity and Triunity', 79.

necessity 'is a consequence not of his being, but of the Father's love'[189] therein we have a fully embodied Arian position;[190] it undercuts the full divinity of each of the divine persons so that while each is fully divine, there are not on that account three Gods but only one God in three persons and all subordination within the immanent Trinity is ruled out.[191] From the time of Nicaea it was crucial to assert the oneness in being of the Father and the Son in the eternal act of the Father's begetting the eternal Son. This act could not be confused with or made contingent on God's willed relations with us. Since McCormack's thinking does not operate apart from the idea that God's electing us is the ground of his triunity and God's triunity is the result of an act of will, this confusion becomes necessary and unequivocal. Hector's thinking clearly has not escaped from this difficulty. As already argued, I suspect that the reason for this is that he believes that God's relations with us can be understood

189 Hector, 'Immutability, Necessity and Triunity', 79.

190 Athanasius saw this point with great clarity when he argued that 'God is not as man; for men beget passibly, having a transitive nature, which waits for periods by reason of its weakness. But with God this cannot be; for He is not composed of parts, but being impassible and simple, He is impassibly and indivisibly Father of the Son' *Contra Ar.* 1. 28. Athanasius continues by noting that 'the Word is not begotten according to affection'. And that is because his eternal generation from the Father was eternal and not the result of an act of will (*Contra Ar.* 1. 29).

191 See, for example, T. F. Torrance's statement, following Epiphanius, that: 'There is no suggestion of any subordinationism in God, for whatever the Father is, this the Son is and this the Spirit is in the Godhead ... There never was when the Spirit was not' (*The Trinitarian Faith*, 222). Further, Torrance insists, following Athanasius, that 'there is a coinherent relation between the Holy Spirit and God the Son, just as there is a coinherent relation between the Son and the Father' (*The Trinitarian Faith*, 233). It is here of course that Torrance objected to the idea that it was the first person of the Trinity who was the 'sole Principle or Cause or Source of Deity' because this weakened Athanasius's view that 'whatever we say of the Father we say of the Son and the Spirit except "Father"' (*The Trinitarian Faith*, 241). That is why one must say that each of the divine persons is fully God and Lord such that the divine monarchy resides in the being of God as one and three. For a full discussion of this issue see Molnar, 'Theological Issues involved in the *Filioque*' in *Ecumenical Perspectives on the Filioque for the 21st Century* (London: Bloomsbury, T & T Clark, 2014), ed. Myk Habets, chapter three.

properly by introducing a volitional necessity into the divine being in eternity. They cannot.[192]

192 Unfortunately, the idea that creation is in some sense necessary for God has become more and more attractive to a number of contemporary theologians. For example, Kevin Diller mistakenly considers that divine '*self-causation*' and divine '*self-determination*' are the same, 'Is God *Necessarily* Who God Is? Alternatives for the Trinity and Election Debate', *SJT*, vol. 66, no. 2: 209–20 (2013), 214. Following Barth, I have rejected the idea that God gives himself his own being in willing himself and I have argued that God's self-determination in election is a determination freely willed by the triune God. Diller unfortunately equates election and triunity and so fails to maintain the fact that election is an eternally contingent act of the Trinity and is therefore not necessary to God. He writes that: 'Molnar argues that keeping the priority of election is necessary to maintain "God's freedom to have existed from eternity without us"' (215). Given the context, I suspect he meant to say that I argue that keeping the priority of triunity is important so that one could see that election is not necessary for God to be God. Still, aside from many problematic assertions, I simply note two that are important here: (1) Diller thinks election and triunity are mutually necessary so that 'in a sense' one could say they are 'grounded in each other' (215) so that one could also say they are 'mutually dependent' (218). Such a view does not escape the problem of making God's triunity dependent on his election of us. Saying that 'election is simply part of who God is' solves nothing and only makes matters worse. (2) Following distinctions he finds in Aristotle, Diller notes that McCormack's position seems to imply that creation is in some sense necessary. He proceeds to argue that in some sense creation is indeed necessary to God, that is, it is a 'necessary consequent of God's being' (216). This leads him to think that God's love is 'more significant or more at the heart of who God is than the fact that God is uncreated and almighty' (218–19). Yet, since God is One who loves in freedom, any view that prioritizes love over freedom or freedom over love has missed the truth of who God is. See my discussion of Robert B. Price's view above, n. 144. Beyond this, I think Barth's statement that 'what can need existence, is not God Himself, or His reality, but the reality which is distinct from Himself' (*CD* II/1, 306) is decisive here. There is no sense in which God needs us. Any such idea is at variance with the fact that all God's relations with us are acts of free grace. Walter Kasper states this quite clearly: 'If God needs the world in order to be able to be the one God, then he is not really God at all. The transcendence and freedom of God are perceived only if the world is not necessary for God to be himself', Walter Kasper, *The God of Jesus Christ*, 294, citing Gregory of Nazianzus.

Hector offers a final point of defense: those who favor Barth's proposal, as he understands it, are no better off than McCormack. Once again, the confusion of the immanent and economic Trinity is in evidence. First, he says that Barthians claim that God does not change in electing to be God for us; second, he claims that God's election of us means that the Father freely decides to do so and the Son accepts 'this determination as determining his very being'; and third, 'God's antecedent triunity must be characterised by a free decision of the Father which determines the very being of the Son'.[193] Here we have a major problem because God's determination to be God for us is indeed a self-determination, but for Barth, it is not a determination in the sense that in this act God gives himself his eternal triunity, while for McCormack that is exactly what it is. Crucially, when Barth speaks of Jesus Christ in this connection he is referring to the Son of God 'in His whole giving of Himself to the Son of Man, and the Son of Man in his utter oneness with the Son of God' as the realization of the decree which is the 'very first thing' done in the resolve of God 'which precedes the existence, the possibility and the reality of all His creatures'.[194] Here the Son is not the result of an eternal decision of the Father; rather God eternally exists in the act of being Father, Son and Holy Spirit, which does of course involve his decision. Yet, God is not the result of his decision, as noted earlier, because that is the error of those who believe God takes his origin from himself. Furthermore, God's eternal triune act also includes God's decisions, but the decision of God to act ad extra is eternally contingent while the decision to affirm his own eternal existence is eternally necessary in the sense that God could not will not to be the Father of the Son since God cannot come into conflict with himself. The upshot of all this is that the distinction between subordination and subordinationism is spurious – the subordination advanced here is nothing but subordinationism in modern guise.

Hector's defense of McCormack against modalism is no more successful than his attempted defense of McCormack against the charge of subordinationism. Hector begins his defense with respect to modalism by 'assuming that subordinationism is no longer an issue'.[195] While I have indicated why I think it still is an issue, it is worth listening to

---

193 Hector, 'Immutability, Necessity and Triunity', 79–80.
194 *CD* II/2, 157.
195 Hector, 'Immutability, Necessity and Triunity', 80.

his views on modalism just the same. He says: 'McCormack could claim that the God who elects to be with us, and so triunes Godself, is in fact the Father, and thereby acquit himself of the suspicion that the electing God is a "fourth" behind the three hypostases'.[196] That is the question. Can McCormack actually make this problematic assertion while avoiding both subordinationism and modalism? I have already indicated why I think his thinking cannot and does not avoid subordinationism. Here I will let Hector's own conclusion demonstrate why I think he does not escape from modalism either. Hector writes that 'while McCormack would still be unable in principle to say anything about what God would have been like if God had not elected to be God with us, he can say, unequivocally, that the actual God is wholeheartedly committed to us and has thus ruled out any other way of being God ...'.[197] This assertion is seriously problematic simply because any statement that in principle one could not say anything about what God would have been like without election necessarily introduces the specter of an unknown God behind the being of the eternal Trinity. Such an assertion in reality denies the very idea that Hector's article was meant to uphold, namely, that God would have been the one and only triune God even if he never decided to relate with us. That is the issue that is at stake in claiming that God 'triunes' himself in electing to be God for us. So while Hector thinks that McCormack's position can be acquitted of both subordinationism and modalism, his own conclusions demonstrate exactly the opposite. Moreover, as I have argued elsewhere, McCormack's Christology seems to open the door to a kind of modalism as well since he believes that: 'The second "person" of the Trinity is the God-man. So even in the act of hypostatic *uniting*, the "subject" who performs that action is the God-man, Jesus Christ in his divine-human unity.'[198] Yet, Karl Barth astutely noted that: 'We must distinguish between God as such and God in His purpose (decree). From eternity the Son (as God *and*

---

196 Hector, 'Immutability, Necessity and Triunity', 80. It is no accident that George Hunsinger asks: 'Is not revisionism's "God beyond the Trinity" just this sort of Hidden Fourth? [which Barth rejected as modalism in *CD* I/1, 355]' *Reading Barth with Charity*, 37. Their thinking on this subject Hunsinger thinks threatens 'to make the economic Trinity into something "foreign to God's essence"' *Reading Barth with Charity*, 38, referring to *CD* I/1, 382.

197 Hector, 'Immutability, Necessity and Triunity', 80.

198 See Molnar, *Faith, Freedom and the Spirit*, chapter five.

man) exists in God, but until the incarnation this has not happened. Nevertheless, this must be made clear; otherwise you have a fourth member of the Trinity.'[199]

Hector's attempt to defend the 'orthodoxy' of McCormack's position must be deemed a failure in light of his own stated position. Hector laments the fact that McCormack's proposal 'has been subjected to endless critique'.[200] Here I can only suggest that there may be some good theological reasons for that endless critique. Indeed, while Hector himself now realizes quite properly that McCormack's attempt to ground his proposal in the theology of Karl Barth is mistaken, he nonetheless demonstrates that his own thinking about God for us is in the grip of an untheological understanding of God in himself to the extent that he implicitly supposes that there is a right way to say a wrong thing. That is, he believes one could say, with McCormack, that God 'triunes' himself in electing us and that one could also say there is no other being of God than God for us. I have explained in detail why I think both those statements are problematic – the former statement undermines the eternal triune being of the three persons, while the latter reduces God's eternal triunity to his actions for us. Still, I do believe that there is no gap between God in himself and God for us because the God who eternally exists as Father, Son and Holy Spirit and thus as the one who loves in freedom, is the very same God who meets us in revelation and in his reconciling activity for us in created history. To put it another way, I would say that what God is toward us he is eternally in himself. However, that statement cannot be taken to mean that God in himself has now ceased to exist since God only exists for us. That is the problem that arises when it is thought that God can or does give himself his eternal triunity in an act that aims toward us. Before drawing this chapter to a close, let us discuss two other proposals in order to make clear exactly what I am affirming theologically and what I am rejecting.

Understanding God's Freedom and Love

Like Kevin Hector, Paul Dafydd Jones clearly and quite rightly opposes the idea that election constitutes God's triunity as when he writes that

199 *Karl Barth's Table Talk*, recorded and ed. John Godsey [Richmond, VA: John Knox, 1962], 52.

200 Hector, 'Immutability, Necessity and Triunity', 80.

'it would certainly be wrong to claim that "God's pretemporal decision of election actually gave rise to the Trinity" or that "the Holy Trinity is a function of God's pretemporal decision of election" '[201] since, as he again rightly argues, God's elective action is not required for God to be triune inasmuch as 'God does not stand under obligations of this kind'.[202] Nevertheless, his thinking is inspired by the basic moves made by McCormack in his actualistic reduction of the immanent to the economic Trinity, and to that extent, he is conceptually unable to maintain the sense of his initial insight, namely, that 'the Son's self-determination has its ground in the divine being who is complete in himself – "before" the incarnation'. Hence, he concludes incorrectly that 'God's triunity is distinguished, reaffirmed – perhaps even *intensified* – given the Son's self-determination to become and be the "electing God" and "elected human" '.[203] Jones recognizes that this is a 'risky' statement that 'stands at the farthest edges of interpretative propriety'[204] and yet his thought is driven in that direction when he again rejects McCormack's claim 'that election has logical priority over divine triunity' but grants 'that the eternal identity of the Son encompasses and, in a sense, is *constituted* by the concrete life of Jesus Christ'.[205]

Here the error embedded in McCormack's thinking continues to shape the thinking of Paul Jones in spite of his attempts to extricate himself from the idea that God needs the incarnation to be the God he eternally is. Jones wants to modify Barth's statement that the 'Word is what he is even before and apart from his being flesh' made in CDI/2,[206] in light of Barth's later Christology. He thus suggests,

201 Paul Dafydd Jones, 'Obedience, Trinity, and Election: Thinking With and Beyond the *Church Dogmatics*,' in *Trinity and Election in Contemporary Theology*, ed. Dempsey, 153.

202 Jones, 'Obedience, Trinity, and Election', 153.

203 Jones, 'Obedience, Trinity, and Election', 153–4. See Christopher R. J. Holmes, 'The Person and Work of Christ Revisited: In Conversation with Karl Barth', *Anglican Theological Review*, vol. 95, no. 1 (2013): 37–55, 47 where he writes 'we must not say with Jones that "God's action *ad extra* has ramifications for God's immanent being" '. Holmes sees the positive intentions of Jones, but rightly questions the thinking that suggests that God is in some way transformed by virtue of the incarnation.

204 Jones, 'Obedience, Trinity, and Election', 154.

205 Jones, 'Obedience, Trinity, and Election', 155, emphasis mine.

206 Jones, 'Obedience, Trinity, and Election', 152, citing *CD* I/2, 136.

against George Hunsinger's belief that the 'Son *qua* Son is *properly* defined without reference to his being *incarnandus*' and against his wish to distinguish the '*Logos*, the *Logos incarnandus*, and the *Logos incarnatus*', that 'the Son's becoming human has ontological ramifications for God ... God's elective self-determination bears back on God's eternal being'.[207] So it turns out that although Paul Jones makes every effort to recognize and to maintain God's internal and external freedom as the one who loves, he is conceptually unable to do so consistently precisely because he mistakenly argues that 'the incarnation, as an elective event of divine self-transformation, *intensifies* God's triune self-differentiation'.[208] This leads him into the misguided idea that we should think of the Son's life 'in terms of a beginning, a middle, and an end that, in a mysterious way, bears back on God's being'.[209] At this point, I think it is important to regard Barth's statement that 'Jesus Christ has a beginning, but God has no beginning'[210] as decisive because it is precisely in that statement that the distinction advocated by Hunsinger implies a distinction without separation of the immanent and economic Trinity.[211]

207 Jones, 'Obedience, Trinity, and Election', 152. It should be noted here that it is exactly this wish that led Jürgen Moltmann to move beyond Rahner's axiom of identity to insist that ' "the economic Trinity *is* the immanent Trinity, and vice versa." ... The thesis about the fundamental *identity* of the immanent and the economic Trinity of course remains open to misunderstanding as long as we cling to the distinction at all ... The economic Trinity not only reveals the immanent Trinity; it also has a retroactive effect on it', (Moltmann, *Trinity and Kingdom*, 151). It is this mutual conditioning that follows from the failure to distinguish the *Logos* as George Hunsinger has suggested we must.

208 Paul Daffyd Jones, *The Humanity of Christ: Christology in Karl Barth's Church Dogmatics* (London and New York: T & T Clark, 2008), 212.

209 Jones, 'Obedience, Trinity, and Election', 146.

210 *CD* II/2, 102.

211 Hunsinger clearly identifies this weakness in Jones's thinking. He believes that Jones's rhetoric, which could suggest that 'God's contingent properties serve to "transform" his noncontingent properties (like eternality, simplicity, impassibility, and immutability) into something essentially other than they were before' would be problematic as an instance of what Hunsinger refers to as the 'revisionist' 'doctrine of subsequence' which does not take into

As we shall see at the end of this chapter, it is precisely because McCormack rejects that statement by Barth that he is then led to conclude that God 'must give himself his being eternally in the act in which he sets himself in relationship to Jesus Christ and, in him, to the world' so that in that way there is 'no metaphysical gap between God's being and his acting.'[212] This is an idea that Jones wishes to

account the perfection and significance of God's antecedent triune existence, *Reading Barth with Charity*, 140. Nonetheless, Hunsinger believes that Jones's aim was to argue that 'for Barth God's non-necessary but freely chosen properties make a material difference for God' and that that would be a correct interpretation. Hunsinger does, however, maintain that Jones's substitution of the idea of 'divine *self-transformation*' in place of the 'revisionists' idea of *"self-constitution"* is unfortunate since it is just 'a variation on an unfortunate theme', *Reading Barth with Charity*, 141. However, Hunsinger demonstrates very clearly that one could and should understand God's 'contingent properties' as making a difference to God's identity 'by addition and self-qualification, not by essential transformation', 141. Thus 'by becoming human in Jesus Christ, God adds to himself a series of differentiae without changing in his formal constitution', 141.

212 'Theses in Response to Hunsinger', (ed.) Dempsey, 135. This whole idea that Barth opened a metaphysical gap between the immanent and economic Trinity earlier in the *Church Dogmatics* that needed to be closed is a ruse invented by those who confuse and reverse the actions of the immanent and economic Trinity. Thus, for example, Alan Lewis argues that Barth 'illogically' drove a wedge between the economic and immanent Trinity when he maintained that God could have remained satisfied with his own eternal glory, but chose not to (Alan E. Lewis, *Between Cross and Resurrection: A Theology of Holy Saturday* (Grand Rapids, MI: Eerdmans, 2001), 208ff. Lewis proceeds to argue that God needs the world, that God's nature needs perfecting and that God could not have done anything other than what he did in Jesus, 253, 210, 212ff. More on this will be said in a later chapter. See also David Lauber, *Barth on the Descent into Hell: God, Atonement and the Christian Life* (Aldershot: Ashgate, 2004) for an interesting critique of Alan Lewis's thinking. The truth of the matter is that Barth distinguishes God's being and act within the immanent Trinity and in the economic Trinity so that God's eternal act of being Father, Son and Spirit simply cannot be reduced to God's actions and works ad extra. It should be noted that this distinction is missing even from what McCormack says here. That affects one's view of time and eternity and of election and triunity.

advance without accepting McCormack's notion that God's triunity is constituted by his electing us; but as clearly seen, in Jones's ideas that the Son has a beginning, that the Son is transformed in the incarnation, and that God's triunity is intensified in his relations with us, he is clearly unable to distinguish consistently, without separating, God's internal and external actions. That is the problem that always follows from rejecting Barth's important recognition that God could have been God without us but freely chose not to. In this second edition of *Divine Freedom* I am therefore contending once again that it is always important to realize that God's being for us is in no way defined by, intensified by or limited by what he does for us in the economy. It is for that very reason that we can speak forcefully about divine and human freedom in light of reconciliation and redemption as Barth himself did when he powerfully insisted that our being as Christians and thus our freedom is not something we find in ourselves. For Barth, 'What we find in ourselves, what comes ringing mockingly back from these caves [in which we find ourselves at home] if we enquire, is the very opposite of the fact that we are Christians, the contradiction of our Christian freedom.'[213] Our freedom is the freedom to decide to live by the revelation of the risen Lord himself as the power of our own freedom; that cannot be explained, but must be accepted as a miraculous empowerment by the risen Lord himself through the power of his Holy Spirit. He enables us here and now to participate in his own conversion of human being back to God. In placing ourselves under the Word of God revealed in Christ we receive the power to be truly free: 'the freedom to appropriate as our own conversion the conversion of man to God as it has taken place in Jesus Christ; the translation of man from a state of disobedience to one of obedience; the freedom to keep to the fact, and orientate ourselves by it, that the alteration of the human situation which has taken place in Him is our own; the freedom, therefore, to set ourselves in the alteration accomplished by Him'.[214]

---

213 *CD* IV/2, 308.

214 *CD* IV/2, 304–5. This Barth says is 'the power, not to repeat the being of Jesus Christ and our being in Him, for this is not needed, nor is it fitting or even remotely possible, but rather … to see and understand and recognise it, making a response of love to the One who first loved us', *CD* IV/2, 305. This, according to Barth, is the power that becomes our own 'in whose operation we are motivated and impelled from within, of ourselves, to be in this freedom

It is crucial to realize at this juncture that a distinction between God's internal and external relations must be made. God's eternal sonship is not 'transformed' in his determination to be God for us in the incarnation, and then in his actually becoming incarnate and reconciling the world to himself in the life history of Jesus of Nazareth, and finally in his movement toward us as the risen Lord enabling us to live as part of the new creation in Christ. That is the very notion that Barth rejected and that certainly was rejected by Athanasius and others in the patristic era. The Word was not transformed in the incarnation, but became man in Jesus Christ without ceasing to be God in order to exist as the One Mediator between the Father and us. Barth's insistence on the distinction without separation of the immanent and economic Trinity was meant precisely to avoid the idea that God's own eternal being was intensified or transformed in the incarnation.[215] It is just his continued belief that God

and to use it as our own' (305). This calls us 'effectively' to 'decision in relation to what is said to us, to the freedom of that accompanying and following, of conversion' (305). This is the power of the resurrection which makes us free: 'In its operation we *are* free' (305). Barth goes on to explain that this power is not anything mechanical or organic within this world; it is rather the miraculous action of the power of Christ's own resurrection which enlightens us, frees us and always 'effects a clear and invincible joyfulness' since 'it is always joy to belong to this majestic and true man and to be able to cleave to Him' (311).

215 While Jones admits that Barth's earlier understanding of *kenosis*, as the Son joining human nature to his divine being is present in *CD* IV/1, he also claims that in *CD* IV/1 Barth argues that 'God wills that the incarnation should prove ontologically transformative for the divine Son' (Jones, *The Humanity of Christ*, 214). Even his citation from Barth's *Church Dogmatics* at that point in his argument does not seem to support his contention as Barth says of *kenosis* that this 'does not mean that God ceases to be himself as human, but rather that God takes it upon himself to be something quite other … than that which corresponds and befits his divine form, his co-equality with God' (*CD* IV/1, 180). Since Barth is here speaking of the incarnate Word and of the fact that his life lived for us is in reality God's action for us from the divine and human side, Barth is not suggesting that the Son is transformed in the incarnation but rather that the incarnate Word now exists as God and man for all eternity and thus is the One Mediator. See also *CD* IV/1, 135ff. and *CD* IV/2, 49–51.

did not need the incarnation for the Son's being to be actual that underscores this point (IV/2, 113).[216] This belief also underwrites our human freedom. Take away the Son's eternal freedom with the idea that God's being is 'transformed' in the incarnation and the *mystery* of revelation and reconciliation is undermined and these divine actions, which establish and maintain our human freedom as reconciled sinners, can no longer be seen as free acts of grace. Whenever Jesus's human history is erroneously thought to constitute his being as the eternal Son, there can be no doubt that God's actions ad extra on our behalf as the one who loves in freedom has been reduced to his actions ad extra. This was the key problem I sought to address in the first edition; it is surprising that the problem of reducing God to what God does for us has reappeared in the thinking of those who George Hunsinger calls the 'revisionists'. Hence, although this issue has now taken the form of a discussion of the relationship between election and God's triunity, the fundamental problem remains the same.

The Holy Spirit and Election

Before concluding this chapter, I think it might be helpful to explore very briefly one other proposal that has been offered in order to demonstrate one final time that whenever the logic embedded in the proposal to logically reverse election and triunity is at work, God's eternal being is made to be dependent on, and thus to that extent reduced to, what God does ad extra. Paul T. Nimmo believes that consideration of the Holy Spirit and of pneumatology have not received their proper due in this discussion. Seemingly uncommitted to what he calls a 'strong' rather than a 'weak' reading of Barth's view of this matter, the former referring to the opinion that Barth's thinking changed with *CD* II/2 and the latter referring to the belief that Barth continued to believe that the Trinity must precede election,[217] Nimmo immediately proceeds to endorse a 'strong reading' of Barth

---

216 See the discussion above.

217 See Paul T. Nimmo, 'Barth and the Election-Trinity Debate: A Pneumatological View', in *The Trinity and Election in Contemporary Theology*, ed. Michael T. Dempsey, 163.

claiming that: 'In a primal, eternal act, God determines and disposes over not only the being of the covenant partner, but also the very essence of God itself.'[218] We are told that while Barth was not always consistent in affirming God's 'self-constitution' in the act of election, nonetheless, based on two quotations Nimmo must embrace the 'strong reading'. When both quotations are read in context, however, they clearly refer, as Barth himself insists, to God's 'primal decision' not to 'remain satisfied with His own being in Himself' but to reach out 'to something beyond, willing something more than His own being. He willed and posited the beginning of all things with Himself'.[219] Barth goes on to say: 'Our starting-point must always be that in all His willing and choosing what God ultimately wills is Himself. All God's willing is primarily a determination of the love of the Father and the Son in the fellowship of the Holy Ghost.'[220] Hence, in willing something other than himself as the beginning of his ways and works ad extra, the content of that love cannot be anything other than something that is good and glorious, 'a glory which is *new* and *distinctive* and *divine*'.[221] Then he says that in God's 'primal decision', which in Barth's thinking definitely refers to the beginning of his ways and works ad extra, 'God does not choose only Himself. In this choice of self He also chooses another, that other which is man. Man is the outward cause and object of this overflowing of the divine glory. God's goodness and favour are directed towards him. In this movement God has not chosen and willed a second god side by side with Himself, but a being distinct from Himself.'[222]

Note clearly that Barth never says that God's triunity is constituted in his eternal election of us in this context. What he does say is that God *also* chooses us and he clearly suggests that this is something new even as an eternal act of the triune God. So when Barth also says 'the deity of God, the divinity of His love and freedom, being confirmed and demonstrated by this offering of the Father and this self-offering of the Son [in the covenant]' he can also say that 'this choice was in the beginning. As the subject and object of this choice, Jesus Christ

---

218 Nimmo, 'Barth and the Election-Trinity Debate', 165.
219 *CD* II/2, 168.
220 *CD* II/2, 169.
221 *CD* II/2, 169, emphasis mine.
222 *CD* II/2, 169.

was at the beginning. But He was not at the beginning of God, for God has indeed no beginning. But he was at the beginning of all things, at the beginning of God's dealings with the reality which is distinct from Himself.'[223] It is not surprising then that Nimmo writes: 'The election of God to be for humanity in Jesus Christ is eternal, an event that, Barth writes, "precedes absolutely all other being and happening" (II/ 2, 99).'[224] Stating the matter this way not only leaves out Barth's crucial qualification that nothing precedes his eternal triune being, but it fails to note that Barth here once again is speaking about the beginning of God's ways and works ad extra which is grounded in his eternal being and action as triune. He is saying that all God's works both internal and external depend on God's election. Election therefore 'precedes absolutely all other being and happening'.[225] But this 'all other being and happening' very clearly refers to the being and happening of all that is other than God. It does not refer to God's 'self-constitution' as Nimmo mistakenly thinks.

Whatever the merits of focusing on the Spirit as Nimmo suggests – and there are some very good and important points that he makes – the fact remains that his thinking is still encumbered by a mindset that refuses to acknowledge that God's eternal act of election is a free new action of God to do something that he had never done before, that is, to create, reconcile and redeem the human race and to do so in and through Jesus Christ. That is why Barth famously rejected the *decretum absolutum*. He did not want to detach God's love for us from Jesus Christ himself who is God acting from the divine and human side as the Judge judged in our place and therefore as the one who graciously elevates us into fellowship with himself.

A number of strange conclusions follow. First, Nimmo asks: 'Can there be, for Barth, in any sense an existence of the Spirit that does not have the existence of the community of God in view?'[226] Second, while he then cites a number of texts that support the 'weak reading', he insists that at crucial moments Barth's theology 'seems to point in an altogether different direction' and that is to the idea that

---

223 *CD* II/2, 101–2.
224 Nimmo, 'Barth and the Election-Trinity Debate', 165.
225 *CD* II/2, 99.
226 Nimmo, 'Barth and the Election-Trinity Debate', 172.

once obedience in a second mode of being of God is seen as being *both* the fulfillment of a decree and essential to the being of God, then the being of God itself in its Trinitarian modes of being is posited as being determined by the decree of election in which it is determined what God will be in time. In other words, election logically precedes the Trinity: the eternal act of election as an act of self-determination is primal and there is no triunity behind or without it.[227]

A careful reading of what is said here reveals exactly the confusion of the immanent and economic Trinity that Barth sought to avoid even in *CD* volume IV. Barth never holds that the existence of God in his second mode of being as the Son was the *result* of his eternal decree to be God for us without exception; if he had, he never could have asserted, even in *CD* volume IV, that the *Logos asarkos* was necessary in order to assert God's freedom in his actions ad extra in connection with the doctrines of the Trinity and of Christology.[228] It is a mistake to think that the Son's eternal relation to the Father could or should be seen as the fulfillment of the divine decree. What is fulfilled in the divine decree is the obedient condescension of the Son, in obedience to the Father, as God humiliating himself on our behalf in the incarnation, death and resurrection of Jesus Christ. What God is eternally in himself is the eternal Father, Son and Holy Spirit who could have been God without us but freely chose not to.

Moreover, it is imperative to hold, with Athanasius, that while God was always Father, he was not always creator and that while God was always the Son he was not always incarnate. Hence, creation and incarnation were new acts, new even for God. Consequently, what God is in time does not define who God is in eternity, even by way of anticipation. Rather, what God does in time, even by way of anticipation falls within the life of the eternal Trinity, but not in such a way that elements of the economy are indiscriminately read back into the immanent Trinity. In other words, one cannot confuse the order of the persons of the Trinity with their eternal being. Furthermore, Nimmo's question about whether there could be 'an existence of the Spirit that does not have the existence of the community of God in view' seems to imply that there would be no Holy Spirit without the community since the Spirit might

227 Nimmo, 'Barth and the Election-Trinity Debate', 173.
228 See *CD* IV/1, 52.

seemingly not exist without having the community in view.[229] This is surely not Barth's view of the Spirit.[230]

229 George Hunsinger thinks Nimmo misunderstood two crucial points regarding the Spirit in Barth's theology. Nimmo thinks that Barth would agree with his faulty proposal that we should think of the Holy Spirit as '"elected God" along with Jesus Christ' (*Reading Barth with Charity*, 85). Nimmo began his attempt to construct that thesis by first noting that one might parallel Barth's idea that the Son 'has no need of any special election' (*CD* II/2, 103) with a statement that 'the Spirit has no need of any special election' (Nimmo, 'Barth and the Election-Trinity Debate', 167). Nimmo then stated that while Barth 'did not avail himself of such a statement, it seems likely that he would offer his assent to it' (Nimmo, 'Barth and the Election-Trinity Debate', 167). Hunsinger, however, insists that 'nothing could be more unlikely than Barth's assenting to such a statement' (*Reading Barth with Charity*, 85) because it is both exegetically and dogmatically flawed; the main flaw being that 'the Spirit's task is to maintain in the economy what is already true in eternity: the undisturbed unity between the Father and the Son'. Hence, any idea that the Spirit could be considered 'elected God' in a manner similar to the Son might then suggest the idea somehow as 'elected God' the Spirit would be conceptualized as in 'competition with the incarnate Son's unique saving work. It is the Son who is elected while the Spirit plays a vital, though auxiliary, role in the accomplishment of revelation and reconciliation' (*Reading Barth with Charity*, 85–6). Then Hunsinger criticizes Nimmo's view of the Spirit because he allows no antecedent or independent trinitarian role for the Spirit such as the Spirit's being the eternal bond of love between Father and Son within the immanent Trinity (the point I am making here) and Hunsinger astutely concludes that for Nimmo 'the Spirit is viewed as exclusively or exhaustively world related. Because God has no antecedent inner life of his own, the Spirit has no place within it … the Spirit evidently has no purpose apart from helping to constitute God's being through the church. God the Holy Spirit's constitutive reason for existence is to be "enchurched"' (*Reading Barth with Charity*, 86). Hunsinger here points to the importance of the doctrine of the immanent Trinity for recognizing the proper function of the Spirit in the economy. This supports the argument both of the first edition of this book and this new edition. Nimmo's own statements about the Spirit, as we shall see in a moment, certainly make Hunsinger's conclusions quite credible. In a critical review of Hunsinger's book, Matthias Gockel ('How to Read Karl Barth with Charity: A Critical Reply to George Hunsinger' *Modern Theology*, vol. 32, no. 2 (April 2016): 259–67 claimed that Hunsinger had misrepresented Nimmo's position because Nimmo was only referring to the idea that the Spirit needed no special election when Nimmo said that it is likely Barth would agree. Gockel suggested that Hunsinger and Nimmo might have actually agreed about that statement, but Gockel missed Hunsinger's point. His point was that Barth would not agree with Nimmo's proposal that the Spirit could or should be thought of as the 'elected God' because there is no exegetical support for that. So Barth would in reality have rejected both ideas, from Hunsinger's perspective, namely, the idea that the Spirit needed no special election and the idea that the Spirit is the 'elected God'.

230 For an excellent short summary of Barth's actual position on the Spirit, see Hunsinger, *Reading Barth with Charity*, 84–8. See also Hunsinger,

I will not discuss Barth's belief that 'it belongs to the inner life of God that there should take place within it obedience'[231] in detail here since I have discussed this issue thoroughly elsewhere.[232] It will suffice here to point out that Barth's intention was to avoid any notion that what God did in humbling himself for us in the incarnation was an arbitrary act. It was instead an act of loving condescension that took place in accordance with his primal decision to be God for us in Jesus Christ. Hence, I do not believe that Barth intended to logically reverse the doctrines of election and the Trinity. Barth never says or even suggests that 'election logically precedes the Trinity' even in *CD* IV/1 when he speaks of a *prius* and a *posterius*, a super and subordination, and obedience in God. What I believe he intended to say was that the events that occurred in the economy fell within the eternal being of God himself and could not be held apart from God's being. However, I do believe that Barth incorrectly read back elements of the economy into the immanent Trinity causing much of the confusion here, such as the idea that God's second mode of being resulted from his electing us and that God's self-determination for us is the fulfillment of the divine subordination.

A third strange conclusion is offered by Nimmo. He believes that 'as the eternal determination to incarnation is part of the determination of the eternal being of the Son, so the mediating activity of the Spirit in time between Jesus Christ and the community of God is part of the eternal determination of the Spirit'.[233] Therefore, 'the temporal events of the covenant of grace in which the Spirit mediates between the Son and the community that is elect in him are *as fundamental to the being in action of the Spirit* as the mediating activity between the Father and the Son in the eternal life of the Trinity'.[234] The only way that this could be a true statement is if the immanent and economic Trinity is confused! The Holy Spirit is the Spirit of the Father and of the Son in eternity, that is,

'The mediator of communion: Karl Barth's doctrine of the Holy Spirit', in *The Cambridge Companion to Karl Barth*, ed. John Webster (Cambridge, Cambridge University Press, 2000), 177–94.

231 *CD* IV/1, 200–1.

232 See 'The obedience of the Son in the theology of Karl Barth and of Thomas F. Torrance', *SJT*, vol. 67, no. 1 (2014): 50–69 and chapter seven of *Faith, Freedom and the Spirit*. For George Hunsinger's view of this matter, see *Reading Barth with Charity*, chapter four, 'Two Disputed Points'.

233 Nimmo, 'Barth and the Election-Trinity Debate', 174–5.

234 Nimmo, 'Barth and the Election-Trinity Debate', 175, emphasis mine.

antecedently in God himself and simply cannot be reduced to what the Spirit does in the covenant of grace as implied in this remark. Indeed, when Nimmo claims that 'for Barth, the Trinitarian self-determination of God is a consequence of the primal divine decision of election',[235] this suggests once again that God would not and could not exist as triune without electing us.

Things get even more problematic when Nimmo develops his constructive proposals regarding the Spirit. Without acknowledging that Barth also insisted that the *Logos asarkos* had an important role in the construction of the doctrine of the Trinity and of Christology,[236] Nimmo simply claims that Barth rejects the concept and then concludes that 'one could say that the Spirit without reference to the temporal activity of mediation between Jesus Christ and the community can only ever be a conceptual placeholder'.[237] Such a statement is tantamount to implying that the Spirit has no antecedent eternal existence of his own in relation to the Father and Son! This stands opposed to Barth's statement that

> the reality of God which encounters us in His revelation is His reality in all the depths of eternity ... In connexion with the specific doctrine of the Holy Spirit this means that He is the Spirit of both the Father and the Son not just in His work *ad extra* and upon us, but that to all eternity – no limit or reservation is possible here – He is none other than the Spirit of both the Father and the Son. 'And the Son' means that not merely for us, but in God Himself, there is no possibility of an opening and readiness and capacity for God in man – for this is the work of the Holy Ghost in revelation – unless it come from Him, the Father, who has revealed Himself in His Word, in Jesus Christ, and also, and no less necessarily, from Him who is His Word, Jesus Christ, who reveals the Father.[238]

For Barth it was crucial to hold that:

> The Holy Spirit does not first become the Holy Spirit, the Spirit of God, in the event of revelation. The event of revelation has clarity and

---

235 Nimmo, 'Barth and the Election-Trinity Debate', 177.

236 See *CD* IV/1, 52 and the discussion of the *Logos asarkos* in Chapter 3 and earlier in this chapter.

237 Nimmo, 'Barth and the Election-Trinity Debate', 178.

238 *CD* I/1, 479–80.

reality on its subjective side because the Holy Spirit, the subjective element in this event, is of the essence of God Himself. What He is in revelation He is antecedently in Himself. And what He is antecedently in Himself He is in revelation.[239]

Indeed, 'Within the deepest depths of deity, as the final thing to be said about Him, God is God the Spirit as he is God the Father and God the Son.'[240] Finally, Barth insists that God the Spirit

is 'antecedently in Himself' the act of communion, the act of impartation, love, gift. For this reason and in this way and on this basis He is so in His revelation. Not *vice versa*! We know Him thus in his revelation. But he is not this because He is it in His revelation; because He is it antecedently in Himself, He is it also in His revelation.[241]

Take away or weaken the 'antecedently in Himself' and the Lordship of the Holy Spirit is lost. What is also lost is the distinction between the Holy Spirit and the human spirit such that once that happens it is no longer possible to distinguish God's actions enabling us to participate in God's own knowledge and love from our own. That is the end of theology! Here, with regard to the Spirit, it seems we must be called back to a proper understanding of the doctrine of the immanent Trinity once again.

Barth certainly never retracted any of these statements and does not even imply that the antecedent existence of the Spirit is only a 'placeholder' for what he says in the doctrine of reconciliation. Had he done so, he would have reduced God's eternal existence as Father, Son and Spirit to a conceptual placeholder for his descriptions of what God was supposedly doing in history. He never did that and never could without coming into conflict with his own understanding of God's love and freedom. In any case Nimmo proceeds to draw the unfortunate conclusions that follow when one reverses who God is in himself with who God is for us. He claims that 'there is simply no third person of

---

239 *CD* I/1, 466.
240 *CD* I/1, 466.
241 *CD* I/1, 470-1. Barth consistently insisted on the eternal existence of the Holy Spirit who proceeds from the Father and Son. See, for example, *CD* II/1, 48.

the Trinity *in abstracto*, no Spirit to be considered either in time or in eternity without the mediating activity between Jesus Christ and the community of God in view'.[242] He repeats once again that the idea of a Spirit 'without the community of God, a third person of the Trinity "as such" can only be a conceptual placeholder and cannot be the subject of independent inquiry'.[243] In the end Nimmo claims that he is following Barth, when in his Christology, Barth insists that 'the concept of Jesus' true humanity is therefore primarily and finally basic – an absolutely necessary concept – in exactly the same and not a lesser sense than that of His true deity'.[244] Thus, Nimmo thinks that this should mean that the 'actualistic enchurchment of the Spirit might also be considered primarily and finally basic to the ontology of that Spirit'.[245]

What he failed to note, however, is that for Barth, Jesus's humanity was absolutely necessary in virtue of the incarnation. It was not necessary in the sense that God needed that humanity in order to be God. Therein lies the difference of emphasis one will have whenever one fails to distinguish without separating the immanent and economic Trinity. Any claim that 'enchurchment' is basic to the 'ontology of the Spirit' has to suggest that the Spirit cannot really be the Lord and giver of life because he is the Spirit of the Father and Son in eternity, one in being with God, as the church is not. In light of God's grace we can and must say that God does not will to be without us; but that hardly means that the church defines the ontology of the Spirit, any more than Jesus's humanity makes Jesus to be the eternal Son of the Father in eternity! We have now come full circle from the point where Ben Myers did indeed argue that Jesus makes God to be God to the much more sophisticated and nuanced presentations of Kevin Hector, Paul Dafydd Jones and Paul Nimmo. All these positions have been developed in relation to the theology of Karl Barth after the publication of the first edition of *Divine Freedom*. It is hard to resist the conclusion that it is just as important today as it was in 2002 when the first edition appeared to call attention to the fact that a properly functioning doctrine of the immanent Trinity such as the one found in Barth's theology is indispensable to every attempt to discuss what God is doing in the economy. In the end,

242 Nimmo, 'Barth and the Election-Trinity Debate', 178.

243 Nimmo, 'Barth and the Election-Trinity Debate', 178.

244 Nimmo, 'Barth and the Election-Trinity Debate', 178, citing *CD* IV/ 2, 35.

245 Nimmo, 'Barth and the Election-Trinity Debate', 178.

it is just because so many contemporary theologians still marginalize that doctrine with its emphasis on the antecedent existence of the persons of the Trinity as the ground of what God does for us in history, that they then draw problematic assertions by dismissing or merely paying lip service to the *Logos asarkos* or historicizing the eternal Son or the Holy Spirit. What I have tried to show here is that whenever theologians think they can or must embrace the train of thought that follows from assuming that we can or should logically reverse the doctrines of election and of the Trinity, God's being in se inevitably is reduced to God's actions ad extra, and in some measure what we then have is a dependent deity; a deity whose very being is constituted, shaped or transformed by created history. However, a dependent deity is truly incapable of acting decisively for us in history as the living God actually does. That is why I continue to reject this sort of thinking as I did in the first edition of *Divine Freedom*.

Chapter 5

EXPERIENCE AND THE THEOLOGY OF THE TRINITY: HOW KARL RAHNER'S METHOD AFFECTS HIS UNDERSTANDING OF REVELATION, GRACE AND THE TRINITY

In this chapter, we shall discuss two questions concerning the doctrine of God in the theology of Karl Rahner that will shed light on the problems that we have already seen develop in the first four chapters regarding the way his trinitarian axiom functions for him and for others. These questions will illuminate some of the difficulties Rahner has bequeathed to contemporary trinitarian theology and in the end point a way toward a better understanding of the doctrine of the immanent Trinity and how it ought to function today. What is Rahner's understanding of God? On what is it based? In the process of answering these questions, we shall critically examine the relationship between the doctrine of God and Rahner's view of Christian revelation, focusing on the nature of his theological method. Analysis will proceed by comparing Rahner's method with the one advocated in this book, that is, one that allows the object of the Christian faith rather than transcendental experience to shape one's conception of divine and human freedom. It is hoped that by this comparison the problem that we saw develop in relation to Rahner's Christology will be seen more clearly as it stems from his starting point for thinking about God.

In *Foundations of Christian Faith* chapter 2, 'Man in the Presence of Absolute Mystery', *Theological Investigations*, Volume 4, 'The Concept of Mystery in Catholic Theology', and *Theological Investigations*, Volume 11, 'The Experience of God Today', Rahner develops his doctrine of God from his concept of absolute mystery which is drawn from human experience of reality according to his transcendental method. As we shall see, this method itself establishes the foundation for answering the first question. In answering the second question it is important to carefully examine the foundation and determining element for any concept of God and of the creature's relation with God. The following issues will also have to be discussed: the nature of and need for Christian revelation, the role of faith and the kind of relation that exists between the creator God and creatures in Rahner's thought. I shall discuss how Rahner deals with the free grace of God's revelation and presence in history while fusing creaturely self-transcendent experience with grace and revelation according to his transcendental method. To the extent that such fusing perceives the reality of God according to the constructs of natural theology, it eliminates any practical need for revelation and faith in the triune God as the only true God. As noted previously, this is puzzling in light of the fact that Rahner has been very influential in renewing trinitarian theology today. What I hope to show in this chapter is that the starting point for Rahner's transcendental method [human experience] is the very factor that causes irreconcilable conflicts for a theology (such as Rahner's) which claims to be a theology based on revelation.[1]

1 This is no doubt a complex and difficult issue because Rahner virtually equates what he calls 'transcendental revelation' with his view of the 'supernatural existential'. Owing to this, some argue that Rahner should not be seen as a 'foundationalist' and if he is not then, so the argument goes, his theology might be read independently of his philosophical presuppositions. On that basis, it is then presumed that his concept of the *Vorgriff* could be seen within a strictly theological context, and it would thus make theological sense. The question I am raising here is whether or not the very attempt to speak of Christian revelation in its identity with Jesus Christ the revealer can bring in any idea of a preapprehension of being (*Vorgriff auf esse*), which is assumed to be the being of the Christian God at all, without detaching revelation from Christ and locating it within general human experience which is simply thought to be 'graced'. There is no question that Rahner thinks that is possible, but I am arguing that Barth explicitly opposed such thinking because he refused to detach grace and revelation from God's Word and Spirit at any point in his reflections. This will explain why I think their methods are fundamentally irreconcilable as they stand. For the nonfoundational reading of Rahner, see Karen Kilby, 'Philosophy, theology and foundationalism in the thought of Karl Rahner', *SJT*, vol. 55, no. 2 (2002), 127–40. Kilby thinks that the tensions in Rahner's early and later theology and between his embrace of 'pluralism' together with his 'transcendental theology' can be overcome if his theology is just seen as one possible approach in 'a certain set of circumstances' (139). This can be accomplished, she thinks, only if 'it does in fact decouple Rahner's theology from his early philosophical works', that is, 'if Rahner is not read as grounding his theology on an independently known universal

This chapter will then present the problems noted in Chapter 2 in more detail and tie them more precisely to Rahner's understanding of God. Ultimately, the problem with Rahner's trinitarian theology is that his actual theological method does not bear the mark of his stated intentions, which were to begin thinking about the God–world relation from the economic Trinity, which *is* the immanent Trinity. In this chapter, I will not highlight Rahner's distinctive positive contributions to contemporary trinitarian theology. These have been well documented by others.[2] My intention here is to highlight the fact that his

experience of God ... but is rather read as grounding his understanding of the nature of universal human experience in a particular theology' (139). In my view, this distinction solves nothing because my question concerns whether or not Rahner's theology, which all agree, begins with transcendental experience, allows Jesus Christ in his uniqueness to be the sole starting point, criterion and conclusion for what he says theologically about God, revelation, faith and grace. The questions that I raise in this chapter from the theology of Karl Barth help show the differences between a theological method such as Rahner's which claims that natural theology and revealed theology mutually condition each other and Barth's which claims an unequivocal priority for revelation and grace such that neither of these realities can be ascribed to people's experiences without detaching revelation and grace from the Giver of revelation and grace, namely, Christ himself. That, to me, is the central issue that at present divides Rahner from Barth. In the end, Kilby thinks that 'Rahner's conception of the human being is best judged, then, not by the questionable arguments he offers for it, or not mainly by these, but by its fruit in the whole of his thought', *Karl Rahner*, Fount Christian Thinkers, Series (ed.) Peter Vardy, (London: Fount Paperbacks an Imprint of HarperCollins, 1997), 14. Exactly! A theology that leads to the idea that self-acceptance is identical with accepting Christ is one that has gone wrong because it methodologically undercuts the *need* for Christ as the starting point and exclusive criterion for its reflections.

2 See, for example, John Thompson, *Modern Trinitarian Perspectives* (New York: Oxford University Press, 1994), 21–3 and more critically, 26ff.; C. M. LaCugna, *God for Us*, 210ff.; Ted Peters, *GOD as Trinity: Relationality and Temporality in Divine Life*, (hereafter: *Trinity*) (Louisville, KY: Westminster/ John Knox Press, 1993), 96ff.; Colin E. Gunton, *The Promise of Trinitarian Theology* (1991), 10, 32f.; Thomas F. Torrance, *Trinitarian Perspectives: Toward Doctrinal Agreement* (hereafter: *Trinitarian Perspectives*) (Edinburgh: T & T Clark, 1994), 78ff.; David F. Ford, ed., *The Modern Theologians: An Introduction to Christian Theology in the Twentieth Century*, vol. I, (Oxford: Blackwell, 1989), 183–204; Stanley J. Grenz and Roger E. Olson, *20th Century Theology: God &*

reliance on the human experience of self-transcendence as an interpretative tool and his subsequent use of symbolic theology to articulate his view of the trinitarian actions ad intra and ad extra create more problems than they solve. Later, in Chapter 7, I will try to make this difficulty more precise by comparing Rahner's understanding of God's self-communication (an expression which Colin Gunton has correctly noted suggests emanationist overtones)[3] with T. F. Torrance's understanding of the same category. It will become clear that while Torrance sees Rahner's axiom as a potential path toward unity between Reformed and Roman Catholic theology, he also interprets the axiom differently just because he will not allow experience the same hermeneutical function as Rahner does. Torrance accepted Rahner's axiom of identity, but he also believed that Rahner had introduced a logical necessity into the doctrine of the Trinity.[4] By that, Torrance meant that Rahner had

the World in a Transitional Age (Carlisle, UK: The Paternoster Press, 1992), 237–54; Leo J. O'Donovan, S.J., ed., *A World of Grace: An Introduction to the Themes and Foundations of Karl Rahner's Theology* (hereafter: *A World of Grace*) (New York: Crossroad, 1981); William V. Dych, S.J., *Karl Rahner*, and Herbert Vorgrimler, *Understanding Karl Rahner: An Introduction to His Life and Thought* (New York: Crossroad, 1986); Karen Kilby, *Karl Rahner: Theology and Philosophy* (London and New York: Routledge, 2004); Patrick Burke, *Reinterpreting Rahner: A Critical Study of His Major Themes* (New York: Fordham University Press, 2002); *The Cambridge Companion to Karl Rahner*, ed. Declan Marmion and Mary E. Hines (Cambridge: Cambridge University Press, 2007).

3 See Colin E. Gunton, *The Promise of Trinitarian Theology, Second Edition*, xix.

4 Thomas F. Torrance, *Trinitarian Perspectives*, 79ff. It is important to see that Torrance had some serious reservations about Rahner's theology because on occasion Torrance's approval of Rahner's axiom is incorrectly taken as unequivocal. See, for example, Burke, *Reinterpreting Rahner*, (75, n. 4) where he claims that for Torrance 'Rahner's and Barth's trinitarian theology are united in this axiom'. That was only true for Torrance if and to the extent that Rahner's thinking began exclusively with the economic trinitarian self-revelation as Barth did. Torrance himself expressed deep reservations about Rahner's approach saying that 'Rahner is found expressing the Economic Trinity as immanent, that is, as it is in God, in such way that it prescinds from God's free self-communication' *Trinitarian Perspectives*, 79. One of the key points demonstrated in this chapter and forcefully in Chapter 7 is that, although Rahner's axiom *could* function that way, for Rahner it did not in reality do so, as he explicitly and consistently does not begin and end his thinking with Jesus

allowed his abstract thought rather than God's trinitarian self-revelation (self-communication) to shape what he had to say about the Trinity. In his 1996 book on the Trinity, Torrance very clearly distinguishes the immanent and the economic Trinity and seems to move further away from unqualified acceptance of Rahner's axiom.[5]

Rahner's analysis of experience is profound and has been useful for many in describing the creature's relation with the creator. *However*, as long as it is thought that our self-transcending experiences provide a point of departure for knowing the true God, Christian theologians will always have difficulty actually distinguishing God from their ideas about God.[6] This problem was discussed earlier in relation to the

Christ himself as the sole determining factor of what he says about God and us. See also David Coffey who thinks that Torrance conceptualizes Rahner's view of self-communication in an essentially positive way and thus as the basis for agreement between Catholic and Evangelical theology (as represented by Barth), *The Cambridge Companion to Rahner*, 110. One of the points that will be established in Chapter 7 will be how very different Torrance and Rahner actually are in the way they interpret God's self-communication precisely because Rahner detaches that self-communication conceptually from Jesus Christ himself while Torrance and Barth unambiguously reject all such moves for good theological reasons.

5 See Torrance, *The Christian Doctrine of God*, (108–9). Thus, 'when we rightly speak of the oneness between the ontological Trinity and the economic Trinity, we may not speak of that oneness without distinguishing and delimiting it from the ontological Trinity ...' (109).

6 Karen Kilby argues that 'Rahner may be committed to the idea that theology is secondary to a more fundamental experience, but this is itself a theological commitment', *Karl Rahner: Theology and Philosophy*, 98. On Kilby's 'nonfoundationalist' reading of Rahner this means that even though such experience is prior to theology, it is still 'methodologically, in the order of Rahner's argument, secondary' (98). The fundamental question that I am raising in this book is whether or not Rahner's 'theological commitment' is or even can be construed as exclusively determined by who God is in Jesus Christ, in Barth's sense, once it is presented in terms of a *Vorgriff auf esse* (a preapprehension of being), a supernatural existential and as a universal element in our transcendental experience of ourselves. The chief indicator that Rahner's theological commitment is in fact driven by our experience of ourselves rather than by God's actual self-communication in grace, is the simple fact that he thinks of natural theology and revealed theology as well as Christology and anthropology as mutually conditioning and mutually

thinking of Gordon Kaufman and Sallie McFague and it was shown how their thinking has resolutely influenced the theology of Catherine LaCugna and Elizabeth Johnson. It is my contention that the point of departure for knowing the reality of God was and remains God's own *free* self-manifestation in his historical interventions within the realm of experience. As we shall see, contrary to those such as Catherine LaCugna, Anne Carr and Elizabeth Johnson who use experience as a source for theology, this very point is what Rahner seeks to uphold, but his method causes him to be inconsistent. While Rahner would insist that this historical intervention is what happened in Israel, in Christ and in the Church, his method cannot allow him to hold consistently that the only point of departure for knowing the *truth* about our experiences is the Word of God revealed and active in Christ and the Spirit. We have already contrasted this aspect of Rahner's method with Barth's analysis and rejection of Ebionite and Docetic Christology with a view toward seeing how and why Barth refused to ground theology in experience, even though he knew that without experience of the Word and Spirit there could be no theology at all. For Rahner, by comparison, true knowledge of God is simultaneously ascribed to the grace of God and to our *innate* knowledge of absolute being. This claim is actually indebted to the Cartesian method and, as we shall see, it causes numerous problems for a theology such as Rahner's that claims to be a theology of revelation.

Concerning Rahner's doctrine of God, then, we return to the opening questions: What is it? On what is it based? Following Rahner's own outline in *Foundations of Christian Faith* these questions can only be answered together by tracing the development of his own logic based on the transcendental experience of our 'horizon'. Rahner's doctrine of God begins from the assumption that an experience of one's 'horizon' is an experience of God, and this assumption dictates what it is. Therefore, in Rahner's thought, these two questions cannot in fact be separated. Rahner provides no other foundation for this assumption than the idea

conditioned. This leads him to believe that self-acceptance is the same as accepting Christ and that love of neighbor and love of God are in reality identical when they are not. For a discussion of how this thinking affects his view of the resurrection of Jesus in particular, see Molnar, *Incarnation and Resurrection* and Chapter 7. For a discussion of how this thinking affects his view of love of God and neighbor, see Molnar, 'Love of God and Love of Neighbor in the Theology of Karl Rahner and Karl Barth' *Modern Theology*, vol. 20, no. 4 (October 2004), 567–99.

that we humans must think and act in light of this horizon. Instead of pointing beyond the circle of human experience to show us that he has spoken about a reality which totally transcends it, he directs us back to our experiences. While Rahner knows that God is totally transcendent, his method ascribes even to the philosopher a knowledge of God which would follow a recognition of God's grace revealed in Christ.[7] So, instead of consistently allowing the unique object (Jesus Christ) encountered by theologians in their experiences of faith to be the norm of his theological ontology, Rahner holds that being as experienced within and without the Bible is 'graced'.

In this book I am arguing that a properly grounded theology begins and ends in faith. Such a theology would allow God the freedom to be the originator as well as the one who completes the process of true knowledge. This is where a consistent trinitarian theology would allow for the fact that it is in, by and through the power of the Holy Spirit that such knowledge as a human act takes place through our participation in Christ's new humanity.[8] This would explain why theology has been described as *fides quaerens intellectum.*[9] *Faith* in the triune God would be a necessary prerequisite to philosophical reflection for this kind of theology. For Rahner it must be said that, in all three pieces under consideration, the

7 This very well may be based on his theological commitment, but the question concerns whether or not one can speak of the Christian God in this way. My answer is that the only way to speak accurately about the Christian God is on the basis of revelation and in faith, both of which point us away from our experience (transcendental or other, including so-called prethematic experiences which include the *Vorgriff*) toward Christ through his Holy Spirit. Therefore, Rahner's theological commitment is indeed mutually conditioned by his natural theology just as he told his readers in *TI* I, 98: 'the revealed Word and natural knowledge of God mutually condition each other'. His thinking bears this out as he also claims that 'the *a priori* transcendental subjectivity of the knower on the one hand and the object of knowledge (and of freedom) on the other are related to one another in such a way that they *mutually condition* one another' *TI* 11, 87. I am arguing that *any idea* of mutual conditioning between who Jesus is as the Word and what he says and does for us and our acknowledgment of that Word or response to it compromises the sovereignty of grace and the very meaning of theology as faith seeking understanding.

8 For a sustained discussion of this idea, see Molnar, *Faith, Freedom and the Spirit*, chapters one and two.

9 Perhaps the most renowned theologian to use this expression was Anselm. Karl Barth's book titled *Anselm: Fides Quaerens Intellectum Anselm's Proof of*

word faith rarely appears.[10] The idea that the truth of human knowledge is determined *solely* by the object of the Christian faith, as it was for Barth and for T. F. Torrance, would be unworkable in his approach. In fact, in addition to the positive features of Rahner's identification of the immanent and economic Trinity, this axiom also leads him to synthesize the Christian God with the idea of God drawn from the self-transcending experiences of Christians.[11] Accordingly, what determines truth is the idea of God drawn from the experience of one's *term*, that is, absolute being.[12] Rahner's method presumes that the Christian doctrine of the

the *Existence of God in the Context of his Theological Scheme* (Richmond: John Knox, 1960) displays a continued interest in this expression as it relates to theological method.

10 See, for example, Karl Rahner, 'The Concept of Mystery in Catholic Theology' *TI*, vol. 4, 36–73, at 60. Where Rahner does mention faith, the meaning of the word is defined by his transcendental method. Thus, its biblical meaning is distorted. Since Rahner deduces the meaning of faith from the 'primordial mystery' which everyone always experiences (our term or whither or absolute being) he thinks that we must understand biblical faith too as pointing to this experience and not to something outside it. This, of course, distorts the very meaning of biblical faith, since what determines truth for Rahner is our experience of our 'whither' and faith in *it* as something that is always present. What determines truth for Paul (whom Rahner cites here) is the risen Lord *alone*. For Paul, faith is true faith when it points to Him *alone*. Cf., for example, 1 Cor. 12:3. This might explain why Rahner can make the peculiar claim that 'the knowledge of man's resurrection given with his transcendentally necessary hope is a statement of philosophical anthropology even before any real revelation in the Word' *TI* 17, 18. One could say that Rahner is making this philosophical statement only because of his theological commitments. That may be so, but a theological commitment that would lead one to assert knowledge of Christ's resurrection without knowing specifically about his resurrection and its significance for faith and hope is one that has confused the object of Christian faith and hope with the human experiences of faith and hope.

11 Rahner, 'The Concept of Mystery', 70–1. For more on the dogmatic problems involved in this identification, see Paul D. Molnar, 'Can We Know God Directly? Rahner's Solution from Experience', in *Theological Studies* (hereafter: *TS*), vol. 46, no. 2 (1985): 228–61, 230ff. and 248ff.

12 See, for example, Rahner, 'The Concept of Mystery', 49 where Rahner writes: 'We begin ... with the finite spirit's transcendence, which is directed to absolute being.' Rahner calls this 'whither' of transcendence God in *TI* 4, 50. On this point see also *TI* 11, 'The Experience of God Today' 149–65, 149–53ff.

Trinity confirms this experience and the knowledge derived from it. In this chapter I hope to show that wherever this assumption is at work, a proper theology of revelation cannot be held consistently and a clear distinction between philosophy and theology cannot be attained. The obvious implication then is that a clear distinction between the immanent and economic Trinity is jeopardized as well.

God

Rahner's presupposition for knowing God precludes dependence on the *free* revelation attested in scripture at the outset. Since he is a being who is 'entrusted into his own hands and always in the hands of what is beyond his control',[13] Rahner assumes that the human person is 'a being oriented towards God'.[14] Probably no one would deny that we are all, in some sense, in the hands of what is beyond our control. However, the fact that there are always things in life we cannot control neither proves that there is a God nor that we are oriented to this God rather than opposed to him. By this assumption, Rahner is compelled to describe knowledge of God as an orientation of human being according to his transcendental method. The meaning of the term 'God', for Rahner, is neither taken from scriptural revelation nor from dogmatics but from 'this orientation to mystery'.[15] Accordingly, 'We inquire therefore into man, as the being who is orientated to the mystery as such, this orientation being a constitutive element of his being both in his natural state and in his supernatural elevation.'[16] This is why, for Rahner, 'At this point theology and anthropology necessarily become one'[17] and knowledge of God represents human explication in reflection of 'what is already present in [our] transcendentality'.[18] As noted earlier, Rahner

---

13 K. Rahner, *FCF*, 44. See also *TI* 4, 52 where Rahner writes: 'The Whither of transcendence is at no one's disposal'; *TI* 11, 151 expresses the same idea. By experiencing himself this way man is placed into 'that mystery which reduces us to perplexity, which controls us and is not controlled by us'. For more on this see *FCF*, 42.

14 *FCF*, 44. See also *TI* 4, 49 and *TI* 11, 153.

15 *FCF*, 44.

16 *TI* 4, 49.

17 *FCF*, 44.

18 *FCF*, 44. This same idea is repeated frequently. See, for example, *TI* 4, 50: 'All conceptual expressions about God, necessary though they are, always

works out the logic of this insight in his Christology: 'And if God himself is man and remains so forever, if all theology is therefore eternally an anthropology ... man is forever the articulate mystery of God.'[19] This leads him to conclude that 'anthropology and Christology mutually determine each other within Christian dogmatics if they are both correctly understood.'[20]

stem from the unobjectivated experience of transcendence as such: the concept from the pre-conception, the name from the experience of the nameless.' See also *TI* 4, 57 and *TI* 11, 149 where Rahner writes: 'The so-called proofs of God's existence ... are possible ... only as the outcome of an a posteriori process of reasoning as the conceptual objectification of what we call the experience of God, which provides the basis and origin of this process of reasoning.' Thus, for Rahner, the task is to 'reflect upon an experience which is present in every man' (*TI* 11, 150–1) and 'we can only point to this experience, seek to draw another's attention to it in such a way that he discovers within himself that which we only find if, and to the extent that we already possess it' *TI* 11, 154. See also *FCF*, 21: 'The knowledge of God is always present unthematically and without name, and not just when we begin to speak of it. All talk about it, which necessarily goes on, always only points to this transcendental experience as such, an experience in which he whom we call "God" encounters man ... as the term of his transcendence.' For Rahner's explanation of his method, see *FCF*, 24–39.

19 *TI* 4, 'On the Theology of the Incarnation', 116.

20 *TI* 9, 'Theology and Anthropology', 28. In his response to the first edition of *Divine Freedom* and in an attempt to argue that his reading of Rahner brings Rahner much closer 'methodologically to Barth's sense of the immanent Trinity which preserves the priority of grace', Jeffrey Hensley claims that there may be a viable way to understand anthropology and Christology as mutually determined (conditioned) within Christian dogmatics, 'Trinity and freedom: A response to Molnar', *SJT*, vol. 61, no. 1 (2008): 83–95, 89. He objects to my contrasting Rahner's statement to Barth's rather unequivocal view that 'there is a way from Christology to anthropology, but there is no way from anthropology to Christology' (*CD* I/1, 131 and *CD* III/2, 71) cited on p. 163 of the first edition and in Chapter 6. He claims that these quotations 'do seem to cut against [his] reading of Rahner', but only until we qualify this with Rahner's statement that 'if they are both correctly understood'. Here he missed the whole point of my book because of his attempted 'non-foundational' reading of Rahner in order to bring him closer to Barth. He says anthropology is incorrectly understood if it is thought to be foundational to Christology. I agree, but then he concludes that 'the mutually determining relationship they can have only exists when

christology is given primary place in the [order] of being and knowing. What then is mutually determined is the way in which both anthropology and christology are explicated,' Hensley, *SJT*, 89. Hensley further claimed that the context within which the Word is heard (anthropology) 'does not determine *a priori* the account of the Word heard' (89). However, as we have been seeing throughout this book, Rahner does not and indeed cannot give unequivocal priority to the Word in its identity with Jesus Christ just because he believes that natural knowledge of God and revealed knowledge are mutually conditioned as well. Indeed Rahner explicitly refuses to begin his thinking exclusively with Jesus Christ as the revelation of God in history and instead begins with 'man' and thus equates revelation with our 'transcendentality'. The telltale sign of this mistake is his belief that self-acceptance is the same as accepting Christ. My argument in the book and in my response to Hensley: 'What does it mean to say that Jesus Christ is indispensable to a properly conceived doctrine of the immanent Trinity?' *SJT*, vol. 61, no. 1: 96–106 (2008) was that there is no right way to understand anthropology and christology as mutually conditioned since any such view obviates the priority of grace in its identity with Jesus Christ at the outset (100). Rahner's own thinking repeatedly bears that out as when he searches for an a priori doctrine of the God-man. Hensley's abstruse claim that they are mutually determined in explication solves nothing because for Barth the only way to understand anthropology is through christology and this could never be explained in a way that suggests that these are mutually determined without ascribing grace to us in some Pelagian sense. There is of course an inherent conflict in Rahner's own thought. On the one hand, he claims that one would only search for that a priori doctrine after one had encountered Jesus. On the other hand, he also claims that his searching christology (the human search for a savior with or without encountering Jesus) is the basis for understanding christology and operates without an encounter with the concrete historical Jesus (*FCF*, 212). My argument, following Barth and Torrance, is that the very idea that one could or should search for an a priori doctrine of the God-man is an obvious attempt to bypass Jesus in his uniqueness in order to understand him from some standpoint other than from himself. So, once again, a nonfoundational reading of Rahner does not save him from both inconsistency and from undermining Christ's uniqueness as the *first* and *final* Word in theological reflection. The very fact that for Rahner, Jesus is not both the *first* and the *final* Word in his theology places his thinking in direct opposition to Barth's since Barth insisted that 'if in the sphere of faith and the Church man as such has the offices of herald and advocate, if in this sphere the assertion of his possibility and aspirations can become a particular concern of his own, which can enter into a variously ordered relationship of reciprocity or even concurrence with the concern for the assertion of revelation … Jesus

Now, if God is truly free even in his relations with us ad extra, then Rahner's claim that knowledge of God is always present in our human striving for 'being as such',[21] illustrates the problem implicit in any attempt to harmonize reason and revelation according to his method. According to such presuppositions our very nature forces us to continually transcend our present experience toward something beyond. While there is no reason to doubt this experience, any claim that such experiences involve true knowledge of God compromises the freedom of the Christian God; for this God is especially free in relation to such necessary strivings. In this book I am contending that this difficulty can be solved only by revelation and that it will only be exacerbated by ascribing a solution simultaneously to reason and to revelation.

Rahner begins analyzing the term 'God' by considering human experience, and concludes: 'The mere fact that this word exists is worth thinking about.'[22] What does the word mean? 'The present form of the word reflects what the word refers to: the "ineffable one" the "nameless one" who does not enter into the world we can name as part of it ... it expresses the whole in its unity and totality ... It means that which really is wordless.'[23] Thus, Rahner writes that 'the word "God" which no longer refers by itself to a definite, individual experience, has assumed the right form to be able to speak to us of God'.[24]

For Rahner, the term 'God' signifies the 'single whole of reality' and 'the single whole' of human existence.[25] This is a significant insight, for it leads Rahner to conclude that: 'If the word "God" really did not exist, then neither would those two things exist anymore for man, the single whole of reality as such and the single whole of human existence in the mutual interpenetration of both aspects.'[26]

Christ is no longer understood as the only sovereign Lord, but must, as the man Jesus Christ ready for God, divide His kingdom with the man ready for God whom natural theology affirms it can know and discuss ... He [Jesus] no longer speaks the first and last word, but only at best an additional word' (*CD* II/1, 163).

21 *FCF*, 35.
22 *FCF*, 45.
23 *FCF*, 46. For the same idea see, for example, *TI* 4, 50–51ff. and *TI* 11, 157, 160.
24 *FCF*, 46.
25 *FCF*, 47–8.
26 *FCF*, 47–8.

The word God 'asks about reality as a whole and in its original ground'.[27] Rahner does not rigorously distinguish between the reality of God and the word God, perhaps because in his view, symbolic reality and its expression condition one another. The fact that the word exists gives it a reality all its own. 'This word exists, it belongs in a special and unique way to our world of language and thus to our world. It is itself a reality, and indeed one that we cannot avoid.'[28] Indeed, 'We should not think that, because the phonetic sound of the word "God" is always dependent on us, therefore the word "God" is also our creation. Rather it creates us because it makes us men.'[29] What creates us and makes us human? Apparently it is the synthetic word-reality which is 'the totality of the world and of ourselves'.[30] 'This real word confronts us with ourselves and with reality as a whole, at least as a question. This word exists. It is in our history and makes our history. It is a word.'[31] Rahner continues, 'It is our opening to the incomprehensible mystery ... it is itself the final word before wordless and worshipful silence in the face of the ineffable mystery.'[32]

27 *FCF*, 49. Since Rahner believes this, he identifies ontology with natural theology and natural knowledge of 'absolute being' with knowledge of God, *TI* 4, 52. For more on this point see *TI* 1, 79–148, 'Theos in the New Testament', esp. 81–3 and 133. Compare to Rahner, *Hearers of the Word* (hereafter: *HW*), trans. by Michael Richards (New York: Herder & Herder, 1969), 8ff. and 53–68.

28 *FCF*, 50 and *TI* 11, 160.

29 *FCF*, 50. How or why a word can create us is not explained; but, in another context, Rahner suggests that key words have the power to create and recreate us. See *TI* 8, 219ff. Rahner believed we must seek unifying words which enable us to conjure up the truth of the original unity revealed in Christ. This original unity of course is already part of the structure of human being in accordance with assumptions concerning the original unity of knower and known. Rahner writes: 'Such key-words do exist, with their power to adjure, to epitomise and to unify' (220). He notes that the Logos was probably one of these words but that we must always search for new key words. 'But woe betide that age which no longer possesses any word imbued with a quasi-magical force of this kind to epitomise all in one!' (220). For a similar discussion that categorizes these key words as primordial words, see *TI* 3, 323ff. Rahner's intention in both contexts was to apply this thinking to the Sacred Heart, and this thinking may be a clue to what he means here.

30 *FCF*, 50.

31 *FCF*, 51.

32 *FCF*, 51 and *TI* 11, 160.

Knowledge of God

For Rahner, then, knowledge of God is really inseparable from one's transcendental experience of the world. It is a posteriori in the sense that it 'is an a posteriori knowledge from the world'.[33] This is what Rahner describes elsewhere as categorical knowledge of revelation.[34]

On this view, 'man's basic and original orientation towards absolute mystery', constitutes an experience of God.[35] This experience is a 'permanent existential of man as a spiritual subject'.[36] Any conceptual proof for God is therefore simply a reflection on this 'orientation towards mystery'.[37] What proves the existence of God here is the fact 'that speaking of God is the reflection which points to a more original, unthematic and unreflexive knowledge of God'.[38] Of course Rahner thinks this way because, in addition to categorical revelation, he presumes the existence of what he calls transcendental revelation, which refers to our direct experience of the ontology of God himself via the incarnation and grace. For Rahner, it is God's quasi-formal self-communication to creatures which accounts for our ' "entitative" divinization,' that is, 'a transcendental divinization of the fundamental subjective attitude, the ultimate horizon of man's knowledge and freedom, in the perspective of which he accomplishes his life'.[39] This, for Rahner, is the human grace given supernatural existential. Thus, the *visio beatifica* is the direct apprehension of God, given by God himself. In reality it is no different than the object of our initial human dynamism of spirit which recognizes being in general; hence, Rahner describes grace as 'an inner, objectless though conscious dynamism

---

33 *FCF*, 52.

34 See Karl Rahner and Joseph Ratzinger, *Revelation and Tradition*. Quaestiones Disputatae, 17, trans. by W. J. O'Hara (New York: Herder & Herder, 1966), 13–21. For a similar idea see also *HW*, 114–15. See also *FCF*, 153ff.

35 *FCF*, 52 and *TI* 4, 42ff., 49ff., and *TI* 11, 155–6. Rahner appeals to the *Vorgriff* (prior or preapprehension) as the factor which guarantees this, *TI* 11, 155. On this point see also *HW*, 53–68, esp. 59. See also 66–7. Cf. also Karl Rahner, *Spirit in the World* (hereafter: *SW*), trans. by William Dych, S.J. (New York: Herder & Herder, 1968), 142–4 and 156ff.

36 *FCF*, 52 and *TI* 4, 49ff.

37 *FCF*, 52 and *TI* 11, 152ff.

38 *FCF*, 52.

39 *Revelation and Tradition*, 16.

directed to the beatific vision.'[40] This insight leads to his explanation of the creator/creature relationship in terms of a quasi-formal alteration in the knowing subject.[41] It is Rahner's quasi-formal explanation of the creator/creature relationship that goes beyond the traditional distinction between nature and grace and ascribes true knowledge of God directly to human beings in their self-knowledge. That is why Rahner feels free to describe God's grace as a conscious dynamism of the creature whereas in fact, if one were to distinguish nature and grace clearly, one could never describe any creaturely activity as anything more than a creaturely activity.[42] This is a serious issue that is usually not addressed by those who defend Rahner without noticing this difficulty.

40 *TI* 4, 61.

41 See for example *TI* 4, 65–67ff., 54, 61 and also *TI* 1, 319–46. 'Some Implications of the Scholastic Concept of Uncreated Grace' 328–31. See also *FCF*, 118ff. and Chapter 5 where Rahner works out the logic of this theory of quasi-formal causality and the change in the structure of the creature, esp. 149. See also Paul D. Molnar, *TS* (1985), 240ff. for a critique of this thinking.

42 This is why it can be said from within Rahner's perspective that 'Grace, therefore, is experienced, though not as grace, for it is psychologically indistinguishable from the stirrings of human transcendentality' (Stephen Duffy, 'Experience of Grace', in *The Cambridge Companion to Karl Rahner*, ed. Marmion and Hines, 48). From this it follows that 'nature is in continuity with and positively open to grace' (51). Such thinking puts the lie to the idea that Rahner's method as it stands can be harmonized with Barth's method because the difference here between Rahner's thinking and Barth's is enormous, and this has decisive implications for one's understanding of faith. Since, for Barth, grace is and remains identical with God's action in Christ, and since the gift, namely, God's self-communication, cannot be separated in any sense from the Giver (Christ himself and his Spirit), Barth would never accept the idea that grace is indistinguishable in any sense from human transcendentality. Moreover, Barth would consider the idea that nature is in continuity with grace Pelagian in origin and outcome because what we learn from faith in the crucified and risen Lord is that nature is fallen (opposed to God's grace and in need of reconciliation). Thus human beings are not positively open to grace but only become open when the Holy Spirit actualizes reconciliation in them by enabling belief in Christ himself and not in their horizon, which is assumed by Rahner to be indistinguishable from the mystery of God himself.

Thus, for example, Leo J. O'Donovan, S.J. simply assumes that Rahner's quasi-formal explanation of the operation of God's redemptive grace preserves this distinction.[43] It does not in fact even recognize it. Of course the real problem here which O'Donovan fails to address is whether one can describe creation after the fall as intrinsically open to God at all without becoming Pelagian in one's doctrine of God. Also, James A. Wiseman, O.S.B. joins Rahner in following Ignatius,[44] who believed in 'an experience of God which … is not identical with a verbalized, conceptual knowledge of God. In the Exercises, Ignatius wants to lead one to nothing else besides this experience.'[45] However, that is precisely the problem. While knowledge of God is not reducible to concepts, it cannot be had without them.[46] Appeals to mystical experience do not help, to the extent that such claims factually bypass the *need* for Jesus Christ and for faith in him to understand God, revelation and grace. This is Rahner's chief problem and it does indeed stem from his mystical theology.

Further, Walter Burghardt, S.J. has suggested that, because Rahner's argument for direct knowledge of God is grounded in mysticism and because it is not comprehensive knowledge, his thinking is not in conflict with scripture and tradition which I believe clearly distinguish God and creatures in a way that Rahner does not.[47] Of course not all mysticism confuses our self-knowledge with knowledge of God. Each

---

43 Leo J. O'Donovan, S.J. 'A Journey into Time: The Legacy of Karl Rahner's Last Years,' *TS*, vol. 46, no. 4 (1985): 621–46, 626.

44 James A. Wiseman, O.S.B. ' "I Have Experienced God": Religious Experience in the Theology of Karl Rahner', *American Benedictine Review*, March, 1993.

45 Wiseman, 'I Have Experienced God', 52.

46 This, of course, shed light on another crucial issue that divides Rahner from Barth as well as from Torrance. Barth and Torrance unequivocally and rightly reject any sort of nonconceptual or nonobjective knowledge of God while Rahner's method and theology is built on the idea that all people have unthematic or prethematic knowledge of God based on their transcendental experiences of their 'horizon' or of the 'whither' of transcendence. For a discussion of nonconceptual and nonobjective knowledge and why it is a problem, see Molnar, *Faith, Freedom and the Spirit*, 61–81 and *Torrance: Theologian of the Trinity*, 33–4 and 172.

47 See Walter J. Burghardt, S.J., *Long Have I Loved You: A Theologian Reflects on His Church* (New York: Orbis Books, 2000), 189ff.

case would have to be evaluated individually. Unfortunately, however, Burghardt includes Gregory of Nyssa, Hildegarde of Bingen and Julian of Norwich together without regard for the fact that some of what they write may truly be problematic just because it seeks a direct knowledge of God, that is, a knowledge of God that bypasses the need for Jesus Christ and his Holy Spirit. In addition, we have shown in detail in this present chapter and will again show in Chapter 7 that Rahner's assumption that God can be known (however imperfectly) as the term of our transcendental dynamisms, leads him to compromise his own insistence that the God who meets us in experience is truly free. No doubt these Rahnerian insights are indebted to mysticism, but that hardly validates them. In addition, Rahner is led by his method to understand God as the nameless and as we are seeing, it is this very idea that fosters the agnosticism that collapses the immanent into the economic Trinity and opens the door to pantheism and dualism. Finally, a comparison of Rahner and Torrance (Chapter 7) will show quite clearly that Rahner's failure to *begin* and *end* his theology with Jesus Christ himself as the One Mediator, leads him to argue that self-acceptance is acceptance of God and that our experience of hope determines the true meaning of the resurrection for us.[48] Yet, any true Christian mysticism would have to assert that we must look away from our self-experience to Jesus himself and see our lives hidden with Christ in God precisely because the

---

48 One of the reasons that Rahner thinks this way is because he assumes that 'God's grace (and Christ's) is … present in everything as the mysterious essence of the whole of elective reality, with the result that it is not easy to strive after something without being concerned in one way or another with God (and Christ). A man may accept his existence and his humanity (this is not easy to do) in silent patience and perhaps without any verbal formulation which explicitly refers to the Christian revelation, or better still in faith, hope and love (or whatever he may call these virtues), as the mystery that is hidden in the mystery of eternal love and gives birth to life in the womb of death. The man who accepts his life in this way is in fact assenting to something to which he entrusts himself as to what is immeasurable, because God has filled it with the immeasurable, in other words, with himself, in letting the Word become flesh. Even if he does not know it, that man is giving assent to Christ', Karl Rahner and Wilhelm Thüsing, *A New Christology* (New York: The Seabury Press/Crossroad, 1980), 16–17. For Rahner: 'If a man freely accepts himself as he is, even with regard to his own inner being whose basic constitution he inevitably has not fully grasped, then it is God he is accepting' (*TI* 16, 67).

truth of the resurrection must come to us from outside the circle of our transcendental experience. It must come from the risen Lord himself in the power of his Holy Spirit and thus through faith that is directly related to him as he is attested in the New Testament.

In keeping with his method then, Rahner insists that knowledge of God does not mean knowledge of something new coming from without but that 'we are oriented towards God'.[49] Since 'this original experience is always present' everyone already knows God as he or she knows himself or herself.[50]

> This unthematic and ever-present experience, *this knowledge of God which we always have* ... is the permanent ground from out of which that thematic knowledge of God emerges ... in philosophical reflection ... we are only making explicit for ourselves what we already know implicitly about ourselves in the depths of our personal self-realization.[51]

Thinking in this way, Rahner assumes that revelation has its existence in one's consciousness and is indeed subject to the structures of the knowing subject.[52] This leads directly to the idea that knowing ourselves means knowing God.[53] For Rahner, 'experience of *God* constitutes the enabling condition of, and an intrinsic element in, the experience of self'. Therefore, 'the experience of self is the condition which makes it possible to experience God' and 'the personal history of experience of the self is the personal history of the experience of God'.[54] It is Rahner's concept of the luminosity of being which allows him to think this way.[55] Rahner writes of revelation that it is

49 *FCF*, 53, *TI* 4, 54, 61, 65–67ff., and *TI* 11, 156.

50 *FCF*, 53. See also *TI* 11, 155, 161.

51 *FCF*, 43, emphasis mine. Also, 21ff. and *TI* 11, 154–5.

52 'It [revelation] has its existence in man's own conscious thought and hence is subject to the *a priori* structure of human knowledge' (*TI* 11, 91, 'Reflections on Methodology in Theology').

53 See *TI* 11, 154 and *TI* 13, 122–32, 'Experience of Self and Experience of God,' esp. 124ff.

54 *TI* 13, 125.

55 See *HW*, 39 and 43 and *TI* 4, 49. For Rahner, there is an original unity between knowing and being. See, for example, *FCF*, 149ff. for more on this idea of luminosity.

a modification of our transcendental consciousness produced permanently by God in grace. But such a modification is really an original and permanent element in our consciousness as the basic and original luminosity of our existence. And as an element in our transcendentality ... it is already revelation in the proper sense.[56]

As we have seen earlier and will see again later, it is precisely this belief that makes it virtually impossible for Rahner to adhere to his stated goal of reflection on God from the economic trinitarian self-communication of God in Christ.[57]

At this crucial stage in the development of Rahner's doctrine of God it is clear that while Rahner believes God is *free*, his method of synthesizing natural and revealed theology causes him to believe that any attestation of God's existence stems from an experience of ourselves. This methodological assumption compromises God's independence in relation to human experience and reflection. Thus, 'The meaning of all explicit knowledge of God in religion and in metaphysics ... can really be understood only when all the words we use there point to the *unthematic experience* of our orientation towards the ineffable mystery.'[58]

---

56 *FCF*, 149.

57 See also *FCF*, 132 for more on this. While Rahner insists that our experiences must be distinguished from the being of God, this thinking makes such distinction more than a little difficult.

58 *FCF*, 53, emphasis mine. This same idea is expressed in *TI* 4 using the category of the 'whither', 50ff. and again in *TI* 11, 149 and 150. For example, Rahner writes: 'But surely both together, the initial *experience* and the subsequent reflection, make it justifiable to speak of the "experience of God" today' (150, emphasis mine). Cf. also *TI* 11, 159 where Rahner writes: 'What is meant by God is to be understood *on the basis of this experience*' (emphasis mine). 'This experience is no mere mood, no matter of mere feeling and poetry carrying no conviction ... For it is present irremovably, however unacknowledged and unreflected upon it may be, in every exercise of the spiritual faculties even at the most rational level in virtue of the fact that every such exercise draws its life from the prior apprehension [*Vorgriff*] of the all-transcending whole which is the mystery, one and nameless. It is possible to suppress this experience, but it remains' (*TI* 11, 159). All that Rahner has offered here to support his belief that it is the Christian God, as an independent entity confronting us, that he has recognized, is our *experience* of ourselves in relation to our innate apprehension of an all-transcending whole.

According to his method, this is the *foundation* for the doctrine of *God.* Everyone has an experience of a horizon that cannot be controlled which Rahner calls an experience of the reality of the transcendent God. Thus, when one is oriented toward what philosophy recognizes as mystery or absolute being it legitimately can be assumed that one is speaking about the scriptural God. Eventually Rahner claims that this 'being' is identical with the immanent Trinity.[59]

According to this description we do not have to wait upon God to reveal himself at particular historical moments because it is assumed that this orientation to 'mystery', which orientation and mystery can be adequately described by the metaphysician, and therefore what 'we call God'[60] *is* truly the *totally other,* the God of Christianity present to us in history in the incarnation of the Son in the humanity of Christ and through the Holy Spirit.

Now, how can Rahner say that God is truly transcendent and free and that both philosophers and theologians know him in this way? In other words, the obvious question here is: if God is really transcendent in the sense discussed earlier, then why does he not transcend this orientation, experience and definition as well? While Rahner would say it is this particular God we know, his very method renders such a God totally unknowable.[61] Indeed Rahner's presupposition is that *no reality*

59 *TI* 4, 71–2. Why? Because 'the three mysteries, the Trinity with its two processions and the two self-communications of God *ad extra* in a real formal causality corresponding to the two processions, are not "intermediate mysteries"'. They are not something provisional and deficient in the line of mystery which comes *between* the perspicuous truths of our natural knowledge and the absolute mystery of God, in so far as he remains incomprehensible even in the beatific vision. Nor are they as it were mysteries of the beyond … behind the God who is for us the holy mystery' (*TI* 4, 72). Obviously this is all true for Rahner because he really believes that what natural theology calls God and what Christians call God are one and the same thing. This, because of the luminosity of being. In fact, of course, the only way this could be true is if God were *not free* but subject to the a priori structures of the knowing subject. See also, *TI* 4, 228. It is just this position that is exploited by Elizabeth Johnson as seen earlier.

60 *FCF*, 54.

61 Cf. *TI* 11, 159. Our *Vorgriff* would not innately correspond with it. See *SW* where Rahner maintains that if God is an 'absolutely "unknown," something "coming from without" in every respect, [he] is not knowable at all to a human subject according to Thomistic principles' (182). Such a God would not be subject

at all, including God, transcends the limit of experience accessible to the metaphysician. Such a reality, says Rahner, could never be known.[62] Thus, in spite of Rahner's own awareness that he should not deduce the incarnation and grace from the abstract notion of God's absolute proximity as the holy mystery,[63] the fact is that being in general is the limit

to the a priori structures of the human mind since there would in fact be no original unity between knower and known. This insight would wreck Rahner's concept of luminosity as applied to God. Rahner could not hold his important insight that humanity is (via the *species impressa*) entitatively assimilated to God, *TI* 1, 327–8. His entire theory of *quasi-formal* causality is based on this insight. Rahner cannot actually maintain a real distinction between philosophy and theology because of this. So in his philosophy of religion he maintains that we cannot prejudge whether revelation has occurred, *HW*, 173–4. This view apparently affirms the freedom of God's revelation as unmerited and incalculable grace, but how do we know of this grace? Because, Rahner says, we must reckon with God's silence. Here is Rahner's problem. There cannot possibly be a *real* divine silence on this view since Rahner has already presupposed that his philosophy of religion, by which he knows this silence, is a 'condition that is itself created by God's speaking' *HW*, 174. The fact that this is not a real possibility for God is confirmed by Rahner's belief that if God did not speak, we humans by nature could hear at least his silence, *HW*, 16, 172, 175. This confusion of course invalidates any real distinction between what philosophy discovers as revelation and what the Christian believes is God's free revelation.

62 *FCF*, 67. Being in general is the limit of all knowledge for Rahner: 'Our proposition about the comprehensibility of being in itself did indeed arise from the fact that in the first question about being every possible object of cognition is already anticipated under the aspect of being in general. There can, therefore, be no existent thing that does not automatically and objectively fit into the context of being in general. For this very reason every thing is comprehensible' *HW*, 96. The translation offered in *Hearer of the Word: Laying the Foundation for a Philosophy Religion*, trans. Joseph Donceel, ed. and intro. Andrew Tallon (New York: Continuum, 1994) does not materially differ from this earlier translation by Michael Richards. It reads: 'Our statement about the intelligibility of being in itself derived from the fact that, always and also in the first question about being every possible object of knowledge is already viewed by anticipation under the general aspect of being as such. Hence there can be no being that does not, by itself, positively range itself in the context of being as such' (78). The same ideas are expressed in *FCF*, 24ff.

63 *TI* 4, 72.

of Rahner's doctrine of God. God's being cannot transcend this. Of this 'being' we humans always do have a 'prior apprehension' (*Vorgriff*) against which we interpret our experiences.

So while Rahner the theologian insists that God is *free*, Rahner the philosopher assumes that the *true source* of our knowledge of God is 'the transcendental experience of our orientation towards the absolute mystery'.[64] In fact, because experience of orientation is the determinant here, Rahner's approach cannot imagine God actually existing *apart* from human experience: 'we can speak of God and the experience of God ... only *together*'.[65] Thus, 'a radical distinction between a statement about "God in himself" and "God for us" is not even legitimate'.[66] Rahner quite properly wished to overcome separating the treatises on the one God and on the triune God, but part of the reason for his identifying the immanent and economic Trinity is because he cannot conceive of the permanence of the humanity of Christ in any other way, and because our 'experience of the incarnation and grace'[67] make it impossible for the being of God which we know by reflecting on ourselves to be different from the being of God revealed. Had Rahner's starting point been God's economic trinitarian self-revelation, it is possible that he might have avoided introducing a mutually conditioned understanding of divine and human relations; it is just because he conceives the 'identity' of the immanent and economic Trinity in light of his understanding of God as 'holy mystery' based on our transcendental experience that he allows our experience within the economy to condition revelation and grace.

Since the starting point for knowledge of God is our experience of 'mystery',[68] Rahner describes a 'more original unity'[69] among (1) natural

---

64 *FCF*, 54 and *TI* 11, 159–60ff.

65 *FCF*, 54. Also *TI* 11, 159 and *TI* 4, 50–1. This follows from his belief that being and knowing form an original unity. Thus, 'the question as to the ultimate cause of the possibility of subsisting-in-oneself is thus identical with the ultimate cause' *HW*, 57.

66 *FCF*, 54–5. This is why Rahner insists on identifying the immanent and economic Trinity and vice versa, *TI* 4, 70–2. On any other view we would have a merely formal reconciliation of natural and revealed theology, that is, of 'one and three' *TI* 4, 71.

67 *TI* 4, 68 and 72.

68 *TI* 11, 155.

69 *FCF*, 56.

theology, (2) revealed theology and (3) knowledge of God attained from 'experience of existence', perhaps from mystical experience or visions.[70] This derives from historical experience itself, and knowledge of it 'contains *elements* which subsequent theological reflection will appeal to as *elements* of grace and revelation'.[71] Moreover, 'Everything which we say here about knowledge of God ... refers to a more original experience'.[72] Rahner says this is not 'natural philosophical knowledge of God', though in part it is.[73] His point is that this experience of mystery (God) is what he will appeal to as the validation of his doctrine of God.[74]

Revelation – Grace

To the extent that Rahner includes grace and revelation as 'elements' in our experience, it is impossible to distinguish clearly between philosophy and theology, reason and revelation, and ultimately between nature and grace. Thus, for Rahner, 'There is no knowledge of God which is purely natural'.[75] This is true for Rahner because 'grace pervades the essence of man from his very roots with divine influence, and thereby gives him the possibility of acting positively for his own salvation, and so implants in him a free and active tendency towards his own consummation'.[76] It is precisely because the creature is endowed with this modality that 'the difference between "inner and outer" break down at this point. The orientation towards the self-bestowal of God as most radically different from the creature is the innermost element of all in it'.[77]

Thus, for Rahner's descriptions of experience, 'it is no great loss if the analysis of man as *potentia oboedientialis* is not a "chemically pure" presentation of pure nature but is mixed up with trace elements from actual nature, and hence from its state of grace'.[78] Since Rahner

---

70 *FCF*, 55.

71 *FCF*, 56, emphasis mine.

72 *FCF*, 56.

73 *FCF*, 56.

74 *TI* 4, 53–4.

75 *FCF*, 57.

76 *TI* 10, 273–89, 'Immanent and Transcendent Consummation of the World', 280.

77 *TI* 10, 281.

78 *TI* 4, 165–88, 'Nature and Grace', 187; also *TI* 9, 28ff. See also *FCF*, Chapter 4.

maintains that nothing but this 'holy mystery' by which a person always lives 'even where he is not conscious of it'[79] is the *true* God, Rahner concludes that 'Grace and the beatific vision can only be understood as the possibility and the reality respectively of the immediate presence of the holy mystery as such'.[80] 'Grace ... makes God accessible in the form of the holy mystery and presents him thus as the incomprehensible.'[81] Hence, for Rahner, even God's grace cannot be different than the 'absolute being' we all know and experience and define as God based on our self-experience.

Grace and glory for Rahner manifestly mean that we cannot control the horizon of our own existence. It may well be that we cannot control our horizon, but this uncontrollability hardly means we have seen or recognized grace as an act of a God existing independently of this experience. From all this Rahner concludes that knowledge of God 'has always been familiar to us' and indeed is 'self-evident'.[82] Furthermore, 'Mystery is already there with the very essence of the natural and supernaturally elevated being of man.'[83] It is clear that, having insisted that the being of God conform to what natural theology discovers as God on the basis of experience, Rahner *must* insist that *grace*, that is, knowledge of God revealed, is present all along 'with the very essence of the natural ... essence of man'. Thus, there is no real distinction between nature and grace at this point. Indeed, as we have already seen, Rahner finally concludes that grace is 'an inner, objectless though conscious dynamism directed to the beatific vision'.[84] The beatific vision is a term that Rahner applies to the highest possible description of an immediate experience of God.[85] Grace then, for Rahner, is not defined *only* as the free *charis* of God revealed in Jesus,[86] but also as our *orientation* toward

79 *TI* 4, 54, 'He would not be God if he ceased to be *this* holy mystery.'

80 *TI* 4, 55.

81 *TI* 4, 56.

82 *TI* 4, 57; also *TI* 11, 161.

83 *TI* 4, 59.

84 *TI* 4, 61.

85 For more on Rahner's notions of obediential potency and supernatural existential with critical analysis, see Chapter 6. In that chapter it is argued that it is precisely Rahner's theology of the symbol that causes the problem here.

86 Cf. Ex. 33:19, Mt. 10:8, Rom. 11:5f., Eph. 1:5f. Grace is the incomprehensible *free* gift of God's turning to the creature that we cannot merit. It implies forgiveness of sin. See also Ex. 34:9, Rom. 5:20 and Ps. 103:8f.

'the immediacy of God'.[87] This means nothing other than our 'orienta-tion towards absolute mystery'.[88] '*We call this orientation grace* and it is an inescapable existential of man's whole being.'[89]

This clear synthesis of nature and grace is no mere accident of Rahner's thought. It is the unavoidable consequence of his method. At one and the same time he believes he can know the scriptural God, revelation and grace and also deduce their meaning from the experience of 'not being at one's disposal'.[90] This, he assumes, is an experience of 'mystery' which he terms the experience of God.[91] So he thinks that when we experience our inability to control all this we are actually experiencing God.[92] 'The transcendence in which God is already known … may not be understood as an active mastering … of God himself … By its very nature subjectivity is always a transcendence which listens, which does not control.'[93]

Rahner then makes his distinction between nature and grace iden-tical with the distinction between our finiteness (being grounded in mystery) and the experience that this is not at one's disposal. This is described as the 'unity between transcendence and its term'.[94] The *term* or goal of this orientation or transcendence Rahner calls God: 'God is present as the asymptotic goal, hidden in itself, of the experience of the limitless dynamic force inherent in the spirit endowed with knowl-edge and freedom.'[95] It could have 'a thousand other names'.[96] It could

87 *FCF*, 57.

88 *FCF*, 52 and *TI* 4: 61ff.

89 *FCF*, 57, emphasis mine, and also 25 and 34.

90 *FCF*, 57-9, 43 and 75-6. See also *TI* 11, 156. See also *TI* 4, 52 where Rahner writes: 'The Whither of transcendence is at no one's disposal' and *TI* 4, 53: 'For the Whither … the nameless being which is at the disposal of none and disposes of all … we can call "holy" in the strict and original sense.'

91 *TI* 4, 54. 'If man himself is therefore to be understood as the being of the holy mystery, it also follows that *God* is present to man *as* the holy mystery.'

92 *TI* 11, 156, 160 and so on.

93 *FCF*, 58. This would have been a strange insight, especially for the Johannine community or for Paul to accept in view of the fact that the problem of sin suggests just the opposite, that is, since the fall and apart from dependence on Christ, humanity will always try to control God in various ways.

94 *FCF*, 58. This is an exact rendering of the ontological principle of luminosity as Rahner has understood this.

95 *TI* 11, 153; see also 156, *FCF*, 59-60, *TI* 4, 62 and *TI* 13, 123.

96 *FCF*, 60. At this point in his reflections, it really makes little difference to Rahner what we name him since the term God refers to an experience on the

be ' "absolute being" or "being in an absolute sense" ' or the ' "ground of being" which establishes everything in original unity'.[97] Rahner calls it 'the holy mystery'.[98] His ultimate goal is to show that the *term* or source of our transcendence is 'identical with the word "God" ... We must first describe the experience and the term *together* before what is experienced can be called God'.[99] From this series of presuppositions it is perfectly logical for Rahner to conclude that God is experienced whenever we experience our *term*, horizon or the nameless and indefinable. Rahner contends that because the horizon (the *term* of transcendence) is infinite, it is not only not at our disposal, but it cannot be given a name.[100] In this way Rahner attempts to preserve God's freedom and transcendence.

There is, however, a very serious and frequently overlooked problem with this position. If it were truly impossible to name this *term* – if it [the term] were truly transcendent and free – then it actually could not be conceptualized. Rahner, however, does name this term of experience the 'nameless'. It should be noted clearly that the idea of the 'nameless' serves a very definite function in his thought from the very beginning. It is our *experience* of our *horizon* which *is* the basis, foundation and norm of knowing God. Thus, this *term* is not really unnameable. It can indeed be categorized – but as that in human experience which is not at our disposal.

This is an extremely significant point. Since Rahner conceives creator and creatures under the dialectically necessary umbrella of an original unity between knower and known (horizon, term, nameless, mystery), his presuppositions disallow a God who is free in the scriptural sense described earlier, or in the sense understood by Karl Barth and Thomas

---

basis of which that which we all experience (the term) is what 'we call God' (*TI* 11, 159).

97 *FCF*, 60.

98 *FCF*, 60, *TI* 4, 53.

99 *FCF*, 61, emphasis mine.

100 *TI* 4, 37, 42, 53, 60. 'The name God is the nameless infinity' (*TI* 4, 6). God, for Rahner, is 'the all-transcending whole which is the mystery, one and nameless' (*TI* 11, 159). Indeed, Rahner believes that if the term 'God' was ever forgotten, 'we should still constantly, though silently be encompassed by this nameless mystery of our existence, judging us and endowing us with the grace of our ultimate freedom, and we would discover the ancient name for it anew' (*TI* 11, 160).

F. Torrance. So when Karl Rahner describes what is wrong with pantheism and dualism in a Christian doctrine of God, he is unable to escape the pantheist dilemma. Against dualism Rahner writes:

> The difference between God and the world is of such a nature that God establishes and is the difference of the world from himself, and for this reason he establishes the closest unity precisely in the differentiation. For if the difference itself comes from God, and, if we can put it this way, is itself identical with God, then the difference between God and the world is to be understood quite differently than the difference between categorical realities … God to be sure is different from the world. But he is different in the way in which this difference is experienced in our original, transcendental experience. In this experience this peculiar and unique difference is experienced in such a way that the whole of reality is borne by this term and this source and is intelligible only within it. Consequently, it is precisely the *difference* which establishes the ultimate unity between God and the world . . .[101]

If, however, God *alone* establishes and maintains the world in existence, then the *difference* between God and creatures must be grounded in *God alone*. Then it could not be said that 'God … is the difference of the world from himself', since, as other, he alone establishes and maintains the world in its difference without ceasing to be God. Then, Rahner would have to admit that we truly cannot experience our radical dependence on God simply by experiencing our horizon since we are identical with our horizon and not with God. Thus, to experience our distinction and union with our *term* may be necessary, but it is not necessarily an experience of God. In fact, according to the scriptural view and the view I am espousing in this book, nothing in creation is identical with God. So, in a Christian doctrine of God where the method was dictated by this fact, one would have to acknowledge a continuing difference of *essence* between creator and creatures. This would mean that faith in the creator would be necessary to perceive and maintain a clear and sharp distinction here without falling into pantheism or dualism. Rahner makes many distinctions since he knows that the Christian God is free and he knows that he must maintain the distinction between creator and creature, but he makes no such distinction and cannot because,

101   *FCF*, 62–3, emphasis mine.

according to his method, he assumes that God and human beings are already *one in intellectu*. Thus, while Rahner insists that God is free to be silent, his method causes him to describe a God who is not *really* free to reveal himself or not.[102] Indeed, for Rahner, 'God is the most radical, the most original, and in a certain sense the most self-evident reality'.[103] The important point here is that Rahner's definition of mystery is an ontological definition of our human relation with our horizon, which horizon is necessary as the condition of conceiving or experiencing anything.[104] This *term* is *mystery* because, logically enough, it is 'nameless'

102 See also *TI* 6, 71–81, 'Philosophy and Theology', 75. Rahner writes that Revelation 'presupposes as a condition of its own possibility the one to whom this revelation remains unowed'. Also *HW*, 168. Rahner writes that 'there would be no word of God were there no one who was at least intrinsically capable of hearing it'. See also *HW*, 92 where Rahner writes: 'In virtue of his nature as spirit, man constantly and essentially hears a revelation from God.' Since, for Rahner, revelation occurs as a transcendental necessity of man's spirit which includes grace Rahner even writes that 'revelation occurs of necessity', *HW*, 93; see also *HW*, 20, 94–6 and 147ff. See also *FCF*, 172. While Alan Torrance, *Persons in Communion: Trinitarian Description and Human Participation*, (hereafter: *Persons in Communion*), (Edinburgh, T & T Clark, 1996), believes that Rahner does not hold that 'the human being is created to be the free and creative co-condition of the event of communication' (268) the truth is that Rahner's transcendental method has built into it the principle of mutual conditioning with the result that Rahner continually sees our relation with God as one of mutual conditioning. For more on this see Paul D. Molnar, *Karl Barth and the Theology of the Lord's Supper: A Systematic Investigation* (New York: Peter Lang, 1996) chapter 2 and n. 112.

103 *FCF*, 63 and *TI* 4, 57.

104 For more on this see *HW* 66–7 where Rahner writes: 'A revelation from God is thus possible only if the subject to whom it is supposed to be addressed *in himself* presents an *a priori* horizon against which such a possible revelation can begin to present itself in the first place'. Thus, 'God does not for his part initiate the relationship; he is already implicit in the openness of this relationship' (*HW*, 66, n. 9). Put another way, for Rahner: 'We are forever the infinite openness of the finite for God' *Hearer of the Word* (Donceel), 53 and 'A divine revelation is possible only if we ourselves, the subjects to whom it is addressed, offer it an *a priori* horizon within which something like the revelation may occur' (53). This, of course, is why Rahner maintains that we by nature can come to terms with revelation and can perceive it (*TI* 1, 83). This, because the whole of nature has always been 'imbedded' in a supernatural context (*TI* 1, 81). Obviously that

and 'not at our disposal'.[105] This *term* or mystery cannot be defined, even by the *Vorgriff*, Rahner insists. However, the conflict, which I have tried to illustrate here, is that *he has already defined it* conceptually by the terms 'nameless', 'horizon', 'condition of the possibility', 'absolute being' and 'holy mystery'. This inconsistency is traceable to Rahner's starting point for his doctrine of God as noted earlier, that is, one's unthematic experience of the absolute. He is unwilling to begin his transcendental method solely by acknowledging the normativity of the scriptural revelation. Instead, Rahner insists that this *term* is not only a *mystery* which can be described philosophically; but it is a 'holy' mystery which we must worship.[106] This synthesis of the object of philosophy and of theology represents the conflict of his method once again. It becomes even clearer when Rahner's thought is compared with Kant.

Rahner and Kant

Rahner neither wishes to ignore Kant's critique of Pure and Practical Reason nor does he wish to leave us purely on the level of ideas. So,

is why, for Rahner, natural knowledge of God and theological knowledge based on revelation cannot contradict each other.

105 *FCF*, 64–5. Obviously Rahner did not just invent this idea. He got this from the fact that 'man experiences himself as being at the disposal of other things, a disposal over which he has no control', *FCF*, 42. Now this experience can hardly be disputed, but as a proof of the reality of God who *transcends such an experience* it presupposes what is not proven and is thus inadequate. This inadequacy follows from Rahner's method. He thinks he has discovered the being of God by examining our experience of our term. Thus, he writes that 'there is and can be only *one* proof: in the whole questionable nature of man seen as a totality' *TI* 9, 127–44, 'Observations on the Doctrine of God', 140. See also (*TI* 11, 149). Of course, the positive position I am espousing is that only God can prove himself and that he does so in his Word and Spirit. Recognition of this precludes identifying God as the term of our transcendental dynamisms. The difficulties involved here will become even clearer when we compare Rahner's thinking with the thinking of T. F. Torrance in Chapter 7.

106 *FCF*, 66. See also *TI* 4, 61 and 67. On 67 Rahner writes: 'We can therefore affirm at once with certainty that the two mysteries of incarnation and grace are simply the mysteriously radical form of the mystery which we have shown to be the primordial one, from the point of view of philosophy of religion and also of theology: God as the holy and abiding mystery.'

he insists that all of this is not just something going on in the human mind *because* if this were true then we 'would lose all connection with the original experience.'[107] Does this assertion really overcome Kant and actually refer us to God (a true transcendent other independent of us who then actually exists in relation to us precisely in his otherness)? Does this assertion point to anything *beyond* a regulative idea drawn from practical reason (the human experience of self-transcendence)? I do not see how these questions are answered by this assertion. In faithfulness to his method Rahner *assumes* that the universality of the experience proves that it cannot be just an idea. 'For this term is what opens up and makes possible the process of transcendence. Transcendence is borne by this term, and this term is not its creation.'[108] Yet, on the crucial question of what *proves* that this *idea* of a *term* determining the validity of our experiences, actually corresponds with a real and true 'being', a *Ding an sich* (in the case of trinitarian theology an immanent Trinity), Rahner passes over the *question* and assumes that because we cannot describe our experience without this idea of a term or horizon – it must be real.

So, while Kant asked metaphysicians to prove this connection between idea and reality, Rahner simply *assumes* it and by making that assumption he never really answers him. Thus, Rahner concludes: 'The affirmation of the reality of the absolute mystery is grounded for us, who are finite spirits, *in the necessity with which the actualization of transcendence as our own act is given for us*.'[109] Because the foundation for and validation of knowledge of God is a 'self-validating' experience

107 *FCF*, 67 and *TI* 11, 159–60.

108 *FCF*, 67 and *TI* 11, 160.

109 *FCF*, 67, emphasis mine. The foundation for all of this in Rahner's thought is what was described earlier as the luminosity of being. Since Rahner assumes an *original unity* of the knowable and its cognition (*HW*, 40–1), he argues that they 'must derive from a single origin' 41. Thus, the problem of objectivity for Rahner is solved by his assumption of this original unity between subject and object, which necessarily must be deduced from the knowing subject. It is precisely on the basis of this insight that Rahner develops his notion of the preconcept (*Vorgriff*) (*HW*, 53–68) as part of a person's subsisting-in-himself which is self-validating. Rahner assumes it is self-validating because of his supposition of the original unity between knower and known. If you do not have a self-validating experience then you simply cannot know what he is talking about, according to him. Hence, 'We must experience here what mystery is, or we shall never understand its true and perfect sense' *TI* 4, 53.

of one's horizon, Rahner, once again, does not conceptualize any independent freedom for God.

> The basic and original knowledge of what 'being' is comes from this act of transcendence, and it is not derived from an individual existent which we know. Something real can encounter us only in knowledge, and to state that there is something real which is a priori and in principle inaccessible to knowledge is a self-contradictory statement.[110]

According to his method that must be so, but the only way this can be true is *if* people *innately* possesses knowledge of every possible reality. Yet this possession is just what Kant called into question. If God is not an individual existent that we *can* know, then there is no real knowledge of God in his uniqueness and otherness as one who loves. Indeed if he is not an *existent* that is truly *inaccessible* to human insight, then he is not a real transcendent other at all; since he is accessible necessarily and always as we must affirm him as the term of all our transcendental acts.

It should be stressed that by assuming that knowledge of God is a universal experience of human beings as they are, Rahner has obviated any real transcendence or freedom for God *independent* of what human experience ascribes to him. Thus, while it is clear that Rahner has profoundly indicated that we cannot leave the sphere of experience and reflection to know the transcendent God, he has not shown that knowledge of God is a *free* human response of faith to God's confrontation of his creatures in Christ and the Spirit as expressed in scripture; a human response that is begun, upheld and completed through our human participation in Christ's new humanity and thus in the life of the Trinity. Rather, 'In the act of transcendence the reality of the term is *necessarily* affirmed because in this very act and *only* in it do we experience what reality is.'[111] Here is the crux of the matter. It is here that the creature either *needs* God, grace, revelation and faith or has them as part of his or her ontology; in which case, theology will never escape the appearance of re-defining God, revelation, grace and faith as elements which can be seen and described without the *need* to choose between a strict philosophical and theological method. It is just this thinking that

---

110 *FCF*, 67 and *TI* 11, 150. On 160 of *TI* 11 Rahner insists that this kind of God does not exist today.

111 *FCF*, 68. emphasis mine. Cf. also *TI* 11, 155–6, 159.

allows Rahner to apply his ontology of the symbol to the immanent and economic Trinity, with damaging results, as we shall see in Chapter 6.

Pantheism

The hallmark compromise of the divine freedom sought by the *creatio ex nihilo* is the fact of *mutual conditioning* which determines Rahner's thought in significant ways. For Rahner there can be no God without creatures as there can be no creatures without God. This is because Rahner identifies knowledge of God with the necessity of affirming our horizon. Again, Rahner would certainly insist that God is free precisely because he is nameless; but the question I have raised here is whether the term of our experience which Rahner has described truly is nameless. For if it were, God would then be inaccessible to human insight and that would be the most that anyone could assert without explicitly relying on revelation. We would not be able to know him by experiencing ourselves. As I have suggested earlier, however, Rahner's method begins precisely by naming the nameless because he assumes that there is an original *unity* between knower (creature) and known (God). 'We have discussed both the holy mystery, which exists absolutely and which we call by the familiar name "God," and our transcendence to this holy mystery together. In the original unity of this transcendental experience, the two are *mutually dependent* on each other for their intelligibility.'[112]

Indeed they are, but what has Rahner described here? According to his own presuppositions he has described our original experience

---

112 *FCF*, 68. For an example of Rahner's statement regarding proofs for the existence of God, see *FCF*, 69 where he writes: 'That which does the grounding is itself grounded, as it were, and what is present in silence and without a name is itself given a name'. Since Rahner thinks this way he actually maintains that 'God confers on man the power to make a genuine answer to his Word, and so makes his own further Word dependent upon the way in which man does in fact freely answer' (*TI* 1, 111). This follows again from his assumption that 'in any act of cognition it is not only the object known but also the knowing subject that is involved' (*TI* 11, 87). Indeed: 'It [knowledge] is dependent not only upon the object, but also upon the essential structure of the knowing subject ... they *mutually condition* one another' (*TI* 11, 87), emphasis mine. See also *TI* 4, 49 and *HW*, 39–41, 43. As noted earlier, this reasoning certainly calls into question Alan Torrance's belief that Rahner did not espouse such a view of co-conditioning by creatures, n. 102.

of our unity with the one and all of created being. We do not have to believe in the God of scriptural revelation to describe this mutually dependent relation. Thus, this description of God does not actually result from faith in the triune God seeking understanding, but from a synthesis of faith and understanding. In order to describe the Christian God there would have to be a clear statement that his particular *freedom* precludes the idea that he can be described in revelation and grace as mutually dependent in this way. Faith in the creator means knowledge of one who *freely* acts *for us*. This implies that he is dependent on no one and nothing *to be* and to be our God ad extra. It is this blurring of the distinction between philosophy and theology that influences Rahner's own perception of, and application of, his axiom that the immanent and economic Trinity is identical. Instead of allowing the immanent Trinity to determine the content of our experience of God in the economy, Rahner projects our experience of our *term* which takes place within history, into the immanent Trinity and in that way reunites the treatises on the One and triune God.

Rahner's identifying knowledge of God with the necessity of affirming one's horizon then prevents him from speaking of God as an individual existent confronting people at specific points in history. Yet this is exactly the kind of act that any realistic, scripturally based theology grounded in grace and revelation must affirm. Otherwise the theologian would run the risk of allowing an agnosticism to lead toward pantheism and dualism. In that way, although such a theologian might strongly affirm the importance of thinking about God from the economic trinitarian actions ad extra, such a theologian would have in fact grounded his or her thinking in a prior idea of God. Whereas in scripture God is the Lord of Israel and the one who is revealed in the events of the cross and resurrection, for Rahner he is the 'inconceivable and incomprehensible single fullness of reality. This fullness in its *original unity* is at once the condition of the possibility both for knowledge and for the individual thing known objectively.'[113] Thus, the proofs for the existence of God express this experience of union and distinction between oneself and the ground of this experience, that is, the *term* (horizon).[114] The metaphysical principle of causality itself comes from the same experience.[115] Hence, this principle too proves to Rahner that in his analysis

113 *FCF*, 69.

114 *FCF*, 70.

115 *FCF*, 70. Rahner insists that causality should not be interpreted as in the natural sciences but in terms of experience of our term.

of the experience of transcendence and its term he has truly described the creator/creature relationship. Yet this is possible because Rahner has actually synthesized both creator and creature under a metaphysical notion of being drawn from an experience of 'absolute being'.[116] So, all proofs of God spring from this 'same transcendental experience'.[117]

Analogy of Being

Rahner also re-defines the analogy of being using the transcendental method. We do not learn about God 'from something which does not have much to do with God'.[118] Since 'transcendental experience is the condition which makes possible all categorical knowledge of individual objects, it follows from the *nature of transcendental experience* that the analogous statement signifies what is most basic and original in our knowledge'.[119] Thus, for Rahner, *analogy* cannot mean a similarity between two utterly different beings (creator and creature) which do not exist in an original ontological *unity*. It must mean 'the tension between a categorical starting point and the incomprehensibility of the holy mystery, namely, God. We ourselves, as we can put it, exist analogously in and through our being grounded in this holy mystery which always surpasses us'.[120] Here, as elsewhere, Rahner appears to maintain divine and human freedom by distinguishing our categories (human freedom) from the holy mystery which always surpasses us (divine freedom). However, inasmuch as this 'holy mystery' has already been categorized as part of the *very structure of created being and mutually determined* by our experience of it, the problem of how to envision God's freedom remains. If this holy mystery is the creator God existing utterly in himself and in whom we can only *believe*, then it cannot logically be described as the necessary *term* against which all human knowledge takes place, that is, the metaphysical idea of absolute being. This assumption by Rahner allows him to think he can describe God as the absolute instance of a general principle of being. Thus, when Rahner defines God as person he writes: 'The statement that "God is a person"

---

116 *FCF*, 71.
117 *FCF*, 71.
118 *FCF*, 72.
119 *FCF*, 72, emphasis mine.
120 *FCF*, 73.

... is true of God only if, in asserting and understanding this statement, we open it to the ineffable darkness of the holy mystery.'[121] When asked where our philosophy receives its content Rahner would say: 'from our historical experience.'[122] Consequently, while he intends to do a theological ontology, his method leads him to make the experience of self the foundation, norm and source of understanding God, revelation and grace.[123]

This of course is the major predicament that Rahner has bequeathed to contemporary trinitarian theology, so that those theologians who have unequivocally accepted his axiom are led to shape God according to their experiences of faith rather than allowing God the freedom to determine what can and cannot be said about him. We have already illustrated how this problem has affected the thought of Catherine LaCugna and Elizabeth Johnson, and we will see in the next chapter that this thinking leads Ted Peters, in his important book on the Trinity, to ground his knowledge of the Trinity in an experience of the 'beyond and intimate' rather than exclusively in God's actions ad extra in Christ and the Spirit.[124] Here it is important for contemporary theologians to

121 *FCF*, 74.

122 *FCF*, 74.

123 *FCF*, 75. None of this is contradicted in *TI* Volume 4 or Volume 11. Both articles 'The Concept of Mystery' and 'The Experience of God' insist on the same point.

124 David Coffey, in his book *Deus Trinitas: The Doctrine of the Triune God* (hereafter: *Deus Trinitas*) (New York: Oxford University Press, 1999), uses our transcendental experiences of knowledge, love and goodness to understand the knowledge, love and goodness of the triune God. In so doing, he reads a pneumatized Rahnerian theological anthropology back into the New Testament and so compromises the person and work of Christ as well. For a critical discussion of his thinking, see Paul D. Molnar '*Deus Trinitas:* Exploring Some Dogmatic Implications of David Coffey's Biblical Approach to the Trinity' in *Irish Theological Quarterly* (*ITQ*), vol. 67, no. 1 (Spring 2002), 33–54. Coffey unhesitatingly adopts Rahner's view that love of God and neighbor are identical, or in Rahner's words 'the love of God and love of neighbor are one and the same thing' (*TI* 6, 233), because Coffey envisions Jesus as a model of human personhood and concludes that the experience of human love not only discloses the nature of God's love but is at one and the same time always love of God (*ITQ*, 46ff.). It leads him to think that 'love of neighbor is the primary act of the love of God' (47) when in reality the primary act of loving God is loving the Father through union with Christ as enabled by the Holy Spirit.

see that it is Rahner's transcendental method that prevents him from being faithful to his own trinitarian insights. This will become clearer in Chapter 7 when I try to spell this out more precisely by comparing his understanding of God's self-communication with that of T. F. Torrance.

The rest of Rahner's doctrine of God simply works out the logic of this 'transcendental' reflection on experience. 'Man implicitly affirms absolute being as the real ground of every act of knowledge … and affirms it as mystery. This absolute … which is always the ontologically silent horizon of every intellectual and spiritual encounter with realities, is therefore always infinitely different from the knowing subject.'[125] While this may be true, I would say we cannot therefore leap to the conclusion that this absolute being is the Christian God. For in a Christian

Love of neighbor follows from that primary act, which is a free human action enabled by God's loving us, and freeing us to love him in his Son who loved us while we were still sinners. Among the strange ideas advanced by Coffey are that (1) 'we should expect divine persons to be subsistent relations because that is what human persons are' (49); (2) our relation to the Father 'is essentially the same as for Christ, except that it lacks the radicality present in his case' (35, referring to *Deus Trinitas*, 43 and 82); (3) 'the divinity of Christ is not something different from his humanity; it *is* the humanity' (35); (4) 'the love of the Father with which he generates the Son can only be his self-love, not his love for a Son who according to the taxis (and to put the matter crudely) does not yet exist' (39, referring to *Deus Trinitas*, 49); and finally, because he rejects Barth's interpretation of Jn. 1:14 as basic and as referring to Christ's metaphysical sonship, Coffey makes the bizarre assertion that Barth's Christology is Arian because he thinks that Barth introduced contingency into the eternal relations of the Trinity (*Deus Trinitas*, 20). Clearly, Coffey confused Barth's idea of God's self-determination to be God for us with the idea that for Barth 'the Father who freely determines himself might just as easily have decided not to do so' (*Deus Trinitas*, 20). Thus, he thinks Barth held that the Son was 'contingently generated' and that, in this regard, his thinking could be compared to Arius. What is stunning here is that Coffey's own assertion that the Father's love existed before the Son is itself an explicitly Arian perspective. To claim that for Barth the Son only existed contingently simply misses the point that for Barth Father, Son and Spirit exist necessarily and not contingently because Barth insisted that God is free in relation to us but is not free not to be the eternal Father, Son and Spirit (Cf. Chapter 4, 162f. and n. 125). See also *ITQ* 67 (2002) 375–8 for Coffey's response to me and *ITQ* 68 (2003) 61–5 for my response to him.

125 *FCF*, 77 and also *TI* 4, 50.

doctrine of God we speak of one who is of a completely different being and nature than the absolute being conceivable as the 'single whole of reality' and we cannot speak of the Christian God in abstraction from his Word and Spirit.

Creatio ex nihilo

At this point in his discussion in *Foundations of Christian Faith*, Rahner explains the creation 'out of nothing'.[126] It is a clear expression of the fact that for the Christian theologian creation can in no sense be seen or described as necessary to God without denying God's freedom. However, the conflict between philosophical and theological presuppositions surfaces here once again. Although Rahner intends to maintain God's freedom in se and in revelation, and though he states this eloquently, he does not realize that his method, which distinguishes us from God by distinguishing us and our *term*, cannot actually preserve the freedom he describes as a theologian. So while he writes: 'God does not become dependent on the world, but remains free vis-a-vis the world and grounded in himself,'[127] his thinking does not bear that out consistently. Attempting to preserve human and divine freedom, Rahner says that God does not become an object of categorical knowledge, which knowledge always involves mutual necessity between cause and effect and presumably leads to the definition of causality envisioned by natural science but which is inapplicable here.[128] Thus, Rahner is faced with the problem of explaining how we (in our categories) actually know God while maintaining his freedom. Instead of turning to the God of scriptural revelation, he answers from his method by saying that God is the '*absolutely distant term* of the transcendence within which an individual finite thing is known'.[129] This answer demonstrates again the logical and theological problem involved in synthesizing natural and revealed theology as in the following dilemma.

Either Rahner may argue that we have no innate and reliable categorical knowledge of the triune God since he is free. This would preserve creaturely and divine freedom and point us to revelation and

126 *FCF*, 78.
127 *FCF*, 78.
128 *FCF*, 70.
129 *FCF*, 78, emphasis mine.

thus to God's economic trinitarian action as that which authenticates our concepts. Our concepts would be limited and would point beyond that limited range only when God intervened to enable it; but then, of course, Rahner would have to maintain that we have *no real knowledge* of God by reflecting on ourselves apart from scriptural faith in the triune God. *Or* he may argue that knowledge of our *term* (which of course has to involve categories – the nameless being a category too) is *real knowledge* of God; in which case he has in fact denied his own description of God's freedom. However, he cannot *logically* argue both that God is *free* (that we have no categories for him) *and* that we know him as the 'term' of our spiritual dynamism. What is it that leads Rahner to believe he has maintained God's freedom here? Clearly, it is the idea that God is the *horizon* we all experience necessarily as that which is 'not at our disposal'.[130] So, by conceptually making this 'term' not just remote but 'absolutely distant' Rahner believes he is maintaining the freedom of the Christian God. The problem here is that no matter how distant this *term* may be, Rahner and any philosopher can still describe it (categorically) as the holy mystery, absolute being, the nameless or as Rahner himself stated 'by a thousand other names', and indeed as the creator God of Christianity, without ever believing in the triune God. Insofar as this is thought possible, the *freedom* of God implied by the Christian *creatio ex nihilo* recedes into the background since the transcendental method *must claim* a true knowledge of God as part of an experience of one's horizon. Whenever this assumption is the starting point of a doctrine of God, Christian revelation, which sees the scriptural word as its only norm for truth (because Christ alone is the eternally begotten Son of the Father), becomes more a conclusion than a starting point for reflection. We have already seen the christological difficulties caused by this methodology in Chapter 2. Once this happens it is hard to see why we would *need* Christian revelation in any practical way, except perhaps as that which confirms our own self-experience.

Categorical – Transcendental Revelation

By removing knowledge of God from the realm of the categorical and placing it into the realm of experience Rahner posits an original

---

130 See *TI* 11, 159–60.

unity between creator and creatures.[131] Thus, this cannot be understood without an experience of freedom and responsibility. At this point Rahner applies his method to the scriptural understanding of God, revelation and grace. We know God 'in a transcendental experience in which the subject ... is experienced as being borne by an incomprehensible ground ... the absolute mystery which is not at our disposal ... Creatureliness, then, always means both the *grace* and the mandate to preserve and to accept that tension of analogy which the finite subject is.'[132]

The same procedure takes place in *Theological Investigations* Volume 4, 'The Concept of Mystery in Catholic Theology', and again in Volume 11, 'The Experience of God Today'. The results reveal once again how difficult it is to describe revelation and grace as free acts of God calling for faith seeking understanding once it is assumed that experience can be a starting point equal to scripture in this matter.

The transcendental method excludes the idea that a special inconceivable act of God within experience is the sole source of truth. Thus, the key to interpreting lectures two and three of *Theological Investigations*, Volume 4, 'The Concept Mystery ...' is to realize that what dictates Rahner's view of incarnation, grace and glory and his identifying the immanent and economic Trinity is not a special inconceivable act of God. It is not the revelation of something previously hidden as it might be in scholastic school theology. Rather it is the fact that he believes each of these represents the radical proximity of God to creatures in their self-transcending experiences. That is why Rahner's distinction between nature and grace, reason and revelation and philosophy and theology can be perfectly clear in one description and become quite obscure in another. Each of these 'supernatural' mysteries is understood by Rahner as a truth confirming one's unity and distinction with absolute being (mystery – term – horizon) which one always experiences. Thus, incarnation, grace and glory are not truths that reveal something totally from beyond the sphere of human experience. Rather they simply confirm that the holy mystery is *indeed* always present as the *term* of our experience is present.

Consequently, the immanent Trinity is identical with the economic Trinity and God's radically close relation with creatures can only be

---

131 *FCF*, 79. This is the more 'primordial unity of the spirit' he presumes exists and defines in *TI* 4, 38ff.

132 *FCF*, 80, emphasis mine.

expressed in terms of quasi-formal causality.[133] While Rahner the theologian insists that truth is grounded in the triune God, in Christ and in grace, he is led increasingly away from a specifically Christian interpretation of those concepts as he applies his method. The operative principle of his method asserts that theological and philosophical truth can be known from one's experience of and interpretation of oneself. The problem here is that the triune God, Christ and grace tend to become instances of his general transcendental principles.

> The experience of God to which we have appealed ... is not necessarily so a-Christian as appears at first sight. On the contrary ... it is precisely Christianity which makes real this experience of God in its most radical and purest form, and in Jesus Christ achieves a convincing manifestation of it in history ... This experience of God ... really constitutes the very heart and centre of Christianity itself and also the ever living source of that *conscious manifestation* which we call 'revelation.' ... Through this experience of God Christianity itself simply achieves a more radical and clearer understanding of its own authentic nature. For in fact in its true essence it is not one particular religion among others, but rather the sheer objectivation in history of that *experience* of God which exists everywhere in virtue of God's universal will to save all men by bestowing himself upon them as grace ...[134]

Why should Christianity and not other religions possess this objectivity? If the experience of God exists everywhere as this statement indicates, then why should Christian experience be any more authentic than any other religious experience? Of course Rahner intends to preserve Christianity's uniqueness, but again his method explains that uniqueness as an instance of his general principle of being applied to human experience. Consequently, as a Christian theologian, Rahner maintains that Christianity is the 'pure form' of an experience of God, which all religions describe. Yet, this creates more problems than it solves. For if truth is contingent on anyone's experience of God then any statement that Christianity is the 'purest' expression of religious experience can only make it appear that Christian experience is somehow inherently better than other religious experience, which it is not.

---

133 See Molnar, *TS*, 1985, 240ff., 245–8ff. for more on this problem.
134 *TI* 11, 164, emphasis mine.

The problem which I have tried to present in this chapter and throughout this book surfaces here once more. Any attempt to explain the objective uniqueness of Christianity by pointing to our subjective experience interpreted philosophically or religiously will always describe grace and God's universal will to save as properties of creaturely being. Yet if scriptural faith and revelation are normative, then it is clear that the objective uniqueness of revelation never resides in anyone's religious experience, but in the uniqueness of the Christian God acting ad extra in free revelation and free grace. Rahner's argument would have been more convincing had he held that a Christian's experience is not one among others because it is tied to Christ alone. Instead he argues that it is not one among others because it is a more radical form of what everyone experiences. This thinking opens the door not only to a form of Ebionite Christology as discussed earlier and to a form of degree Christology that will be discussed later, but it gives the unfortunate impression that Christ's uniqueness itself is somehow the result of the community's projection of its own self-experience onto the man Jesus.

Thus, Rahner believes that Jesus is a 'convincing manifestation' of our self-experience in history. Yet, if this is so, it is hard to know why he was crucified and not installed as king of Israel or heralded as the solution to the philosophical problems of the Greeks.[135] If Rahner's norm here had been the word of God revealed, he would have realized that Jesus (as truly God and truly human) brings us all what we, in our religious experiences *cannot* procure for ourselves, that is, God's inconceivable act of revelation and salvation manifested in his life, death and resurrection. The prophets and apostles were witnesses to that truth. Also, he would have realized that describing this self-sufficient revelation of a *free* God as a 'conscious' or unconscious manifestation in ourselves compromises the very objectivity he sought to maintain. Instead of presenting Christianity as the purest or most radical form of religion, he would have been more able to show that *everyone*, including Christians, depends always on God's *free grace* for salvation and for objective verification of these truth claims. Christians cannot point to any religious experience or set of experiences as the pure or true form of religion any more than anyone from another religion can do it. This, because God's grace *alone* makes 'religion' true existentially and theoretically. Thus,

---

135 Cf., for example, 1 Cor. 2:8.

Christians are those who actively live this truth, namely, their justification by faith.[136]

Rahner's conclusion really goes beyond the limits of theology to the extent that the principles of his method dictate the solution to this problem. It is this predicament that causes major difficulties when he himself works out the implications of his trinitarian axiom. He writes:

136 Cf. Acts 11: 26. The word Christians was first used at Antioch to refer to the disciples who accepted the teaching of the apostles. Rahner's difficulty here is that he assumes that God's 'universal will to save' is identical with grace as a constitutive element in human experience. It really is not. As long as grace is conceptualized in this way there can be no clear distinction between God's will and human experience which, in fact, is not structurally altered by the incarnation as Rahner thinks. Humans exist in *relation* to God's salvific act in Christ and the Spirit – not in identity with it. Barth's critique of religion (Christianity included) and his understanding of the truth of the Christian religion in *CD* I/2, 280–361 is predicated on the freedom of grace understood in this way. For a discussion of how and why Barth insisted that we cannot know the truth of the Christian religion by means of an analysis of religious experience but only through revelation in its identity with the action of God in his Word and Spirit, see Molnar, '"Thy word is truth": the role of faith in reading scripture theologically with Karl Barth' *SJT*, vol. 63, no. 1 (2010): 70–92. A slightly edited version of this article was published as "'Thy Word is Truth': The Role of Faith in Reading Scripture Theologically with Karl Barth" in *Thy Word is Truth: Barth on Scripture*, ed. George Hunsinger (Grand Rapids, MI: Eerdmans, 2012), 151–72. The contrast between Rahner and Barth can be most clearly expressed by noting that 'Rahner saw the diversity of religions as stepping stones to the fullness of expression in explicit Christianity' (Jeannine Hill Fletcher, 'Rahner and religious diversity', 235–48, at 242 in *The Cambridge Companion to Karl Rahner*, ed. Marmion and Hines). By contrast, Barth insisted that we, as sinners, render God who is truly present to us and for us in Jesus Christ, innocuous in religion and piety by turning to a 'supreme being' which tolerates us instead of surrendering ourselves to Jesus Christ; hence in our avoidance of Jesus as the only one who makes the Christian religion true (since no religion, including the Christian religion, is true in itself), we actually avoid God himself whose presence and claim on us in Christ we find to be offensive. In Barth's thinking, when we come face to face with the will of God in this man, we also come 'to the frontier which [we] can cross only if [we] will give up [ourselves] and [our] congenial deities and find God and [ourselves] in this Other' (*CD* IV/2, 407).

It is, therefore, a task precisely for Christianity itself to point ever anew to this basic *experience of God*, to *induce* man to discover it within himself, to accept and also to avow his allegiance to *it* in its verbal and historical objectivation; for, in its pure form and as related to Jesus Christ as its seal of authenticity, it is precisely this that we call Christianity.[137]

Is it now the task of Christians to point out to other Christians and non-Christians that they can achieve knowledge of God in this way and that their allegiance is to their experiences of 'absolute being' which being can well be explained as a universal human manifestation without *faith* in Jesus and the Spirit and thus without need of a strictly theological method that begins in faith as it is specifically tied to Jesus himself and enabled through union with him conceptually and existentially and only thus seeks understanding?[138] Again, it is another question entirely whether Christianity is the 'pure form' of *this experience* at all since Christ actually points us away from any existential or conceptual self-reliance to complete dependence on him. Thus I would say that biblical revelation is at variance with Rahner's conclusion as we are told that *we cannot really achieve knowledge of the true God* in this way since we *are* dependent *only* on the One Mediator – to whom *alone* we owe allegiance.[139] Or in other words, we must think from a center in God and not from a center in ourselves, if we are to think in accordance with the revelation of God in Jesus Christ.

Mediated Immediacy

Returning to *Foundations of Christian Faith*, Rahner assumes once again that 'grace' and God's 'self-communication' are embedded in the world

---

137 *TI* 11, 164–5, emphasis mine.

138 For a full description of what this might look like, see Molnar, *Faith, Freedom and the Spirit*, esp. Chapter 8, 'A Theology of Grace: Living in and from the Holy Spirit', 355–418. See esp. 386–7 for how Barth's understanding relates to Rahner's view of grace as bringing about an entitative modification of human nature itself in the form of a 'supernatural existential'.

139 See, for example, Eduard Schweizer, *Jesus*, trans. David E. Green (Atlanta: John Knox Press, 1971), 89–90. This self-reliance is exactly what was advocated in Gnosticism.

of experience,[140] and recognizing that leads to the truth of the Christian doctrine of God. It is worth examining this final assertion by Rahner of how to find God in the world using the transcendental method.

Rahner has established two things thus far in *Foundations*: (1) 'As ineffable and incomprehensible presupposition, as ground and abyss, as ineffable mystery, God cannot be found in his world'. This is his way of insisting that God is *free*; (2) yet all religion, including the Christian religion, 'declares phenomena existing within our experience as definite and exclusive objectifications and manifestations of God'. This is his way of insisting that we, as creatures, can know God. Examples of these phenomena, Rahner suggests, are the pope (as vicar of Christ) and Jesus himself; 'in this way God as it were appears within the world of our categorical experience'.[141]

In relation to this theological problem, namely, that God is the ineffable silent term of all knowledge and that religion claims a categorical knowledge of God, Rahner proposes his theory of 'mediated immediacy'.[142] This theory basically articulates the unity and distinction between ourselves and our horizon or term as discussed earlier. The conflict between reason and revelation is evident since at one and the same time Rahner affirms indirect knowledge of God through created symbols and experiences and *direct knowledge* of and experience of God through grace and revelation. It is, of course, this latter affirmation which I believe is excluded by God's freedom (*creatio ex nihilo*). While Rahner holds the *creatio ex nihilo* as any Christian theologian would, his philosophical and theological explanations of it categorize grace and revelation as elements within human consciousness – as existentials of human beings as they exist in the world. The reason he thinks this way is that within his system it is completely impossible to conceive of God

---

140 *FCF*, 87. It is on this basis that some Rahnerians assert that 'because created spirit is boundless thrusting toward being, nature is in continuity with and positively open to grace' (Stephen Duffy, 'Experience of grace' in *Cambridge Companion to Rahner*, 43–62, at 51). Indeed, for Rahner we are told that 'Grace permeates our experience' so that 'Nature is not nor has it ever been pure nature' (51). For Barth, of course, revelation discloses to us that we are closed to God's grace and self-communication as they meet us in the crucified and risen Jesus, and that we can only become open as the Holy Spirit actualizes in us the objectively completed event of reconciliation that took place for all in Jesus.

141 *FCF*, 82.

142 *FCF*, 83ff.

acting in the incarnation, grace and glory while remaining absolutely other than the creature as the naturally known efficient cause.[143]

Thus, when God acts (imparts himself) in the incarnation, grace and glory, this *must* take place via quasi-formal causality[144] because this signals the kind of entitative divinization of the transcendental subjective attitude necessary for Rahner's natural theology. Quasi-formal causality means that 'God imparts himself immediately of himself to the creature.'[145] In Rahner's mind there is a certain necessity involved here: 'God as his own very self *must* penetrate into the non-divine region of the finite.'[146] This, because the triune God can be none other than the *holy mystery* Rahner discovered as efficient cause from his philosophy of religion (natural theology).

As efficient cause, God creates another. God does not act this way in relation to creation. He is 'formal' cause acting in creation. The problem here, however, is that the creator God is not merely a naturally known efficient cause. In fact the creator God, as efficient cause, is no less than the efficient cause acting in the form (creation); but, Rahner cannot conceive of such a God and such a transcendent divine action on and in the creature. This is because he insists that revelation of the immanent Trinity cannot contradict the fact that the absolute holy mystery (the efficient cause) is the reality of God revealed. Thus, for Rahner, there is *no triune God transcending the concept of mystery* drawn from the *experience* of one's *term*, that is, the nameless. That is why, in his trinitarian doctrine, Rahner can only conceive of God in his proper reality as the unoriginated origin, while in the incarnation, grace and glory we apparently meet something less than this, that is, the Real Symbol (Christ).[147]

As an example of Rahner's difficulty here, consider this statement taken from his article 'The Concept of Mystery in Catholic Theology':

> It is simply contradictory that something should belong completely to the order of creation, by being created, and still belong to the strictly divine order, by being strictly supernatural. Supernatural

---

143 *TI* 4, 66–72.

144 *TI* 4, 67.

145 *TI* 4, 66.

146 *TI* 4, 67, emphasis mine.

147 *TI* 4, 221–52, 'The Theology of the Symbol', 228ff. and 237–41. More will be said about the problematic nature of Rahner's symbolic understanding of the trinitarian actions later in this chapter and again in the next chapter.

reality and reality brought about by the divine self-communication of quasi-formal, not efficient type, are identical concepts.[148]

This is a clear and *necessary synthesis* of *supernatural* and *natural reality* which must follow from Rahner's *method*. Rather than thinking of God's grace as his incomprehensibly *free act on* and *in* the creature – the act of the efficient cause (the creator) – Rahner thinks of it as the quasi-formal alteration of the knowing subject, that is, the reality 'brought about' by God's immediate communication of himself to the creature in grace and glory. In fact, this is a denial that the incarnation is a mystery of faith as 'Scholastic' theology saw it. Yet isn't that the very mystery of our faith, that is, that Jesus, being *true God* and *true man*, belongs to the creaturely sphere and yet is truly supernatural – *no less God* than the creator – the efficient cause? Isn't the real problem of knowing God truly solved *only* by the fact that in Jesus we have the revelation of the Father (efficient cause) *only* because God has acted and does act freely (grace) on our behalf in Jesus and the Spirit?[149]

Yet, if Christian revelation means that God *freely* reveals himself in and through history without becoming dependent on history, then we really have no *direct* knowledge of God and any such claim would make our experience more than human or God less than transcendent in order to explain incarnation, grace and glory. The main point of a theology that is faithful to revelation and is based on the New Testament is that we, as creatures, can know God truly when our thinking in faith points to and participates in his sovereign intervention in history (by grace). Sign and thing signified, though seen as related in faith, would not be synthesized. While Rahner continually insists on the distinction between sign and reality, he also synthesizes them to the extent that grace and revelation [what is signified] cannot transcend being in general which we experience and know from philosophy.[150] The New

---

148   *TI* 4, 67.

149   For Rahner's explanation of quasi-formal causality, see also *TI* 1, 329ff. and *FCF*, 119–20ff.

150   See *TI* 4, 234–5 where Rahner writes: 'They [the principles of symbolic ontology] arise because the concept of being is "analogous", that it, [*sic*] it displays the various types of self-realization of each being, and being in itself, and hence also the concept and reality of the symbol are flexible. But because these are necessarily given with the general concept of beings and being – as the "unveiled" figure of the most primordial "truth" of being – the symbol shares this "*analogia entis*" with being which it symbolizes.' Rahner's explanation of God,

Testament view seems closer to the concept of mystery which Rahner rejects as Scholastic 'school theology', since he believes that this view maintains that mystery is obscured and veiled and only accessible to *faith*.[151] Rahner cannot go along with this because, for him, *ratio* is a spiritual entity of absolute transcendence and therefore is the very faculty by which the presence of *mystery* is assured.[152] That is why Rahner asserts that God (as unknown) is included essentially in every act of cognition.[153] The comprehensive concept of mystery which Rahner has in mind[154] derives from his consideration of humanity in its natural and supernaturally elevated state as 'oriented toward mystery as such'.[155] This analysis follows from his method. It asserts that we humans can have a self-validating experience of God, and in that assertion the *real need* to depend on God's special intervention into history either in Israel, Christ or the Church, or by awaiting the coming of the Holy Spirit, can no longer be stated with the same clarity and consistency as in the New Testament and in the tradition. For our orientation already contains what scripture and the tradition claim we can only receive as *free gift*.

Rahner clearly recognizes the problem here and states that God could be said to play an indirect role as the 'primordial ground' of experience. Or, he says, a person might worship nature as divine or make scientific truth the answer thinking in this fashion. Nonetheless, despite the fact that 'it is very difficult to distinguish clearly here between nature and supernatural grace in their mutual relationship'[156] this can be called 'natural religion'. Here Rahner turns to Christian revelation again to explain God's transcendence and immanence. He says that categories such as sacrament, church, revelation and scripture only point

Christ, Church and sacrament all bear the mark of this thought. For him 'the symbol is the reality, constituted by the thing symbolized as an inner moment of moment of itself, [*sic*] which reveals and proclaims the thing symbolized, and is itself *full of the thing signified*' *TI* 4, 251, emphasis mine. This is why he thinks there is a mutual causal connection between the sacramental signs and God's grace, 240. See also Karl Rahner, *The Church and the Sacraments*, Quaestiones Disputatae 9, trans. W. J. O'Hara (New York: Herder and Herder, 1968), 38.

151 *TI* 4, 38–40.
152 *TI* 4, 41.
153 *TI* 4, 41ff., 49–50.
154 *TI* 4, 48ff.
155 *TI* 4, 49.
156 *FCF*, 85.

to the 'transcendental presence of God'. How can he describe these in terms of 'mediated immediacy'? His answer is clear. If God is to remain infinite while encountering us in religion 'then this event must take place on the basis of transcendental experience as such'. This means that this presence must be a modality of this relationship. Since transcendental experience of absolute being allows for an immediacy of God, it must be true. Again, Rahner is consistent in his method by holding that Christian categories do not point to specific interventions of God in history which can be seen only in faith. Rather, they point to the 'modality of this transcendental relationship'.[157]

Of course, for Rahner, this modality is our supernatural existential, which he frequently describes in terms of quasi-formal causality. This explanation is ultimately traceable to his philosophy of the symbol, which assumes fusion and mutual dependence of sign and thing signified.[158] But, in connection with his doctrine of God, this means 'immediacy' to God 'must be embedded in this world to begin with'.[159] This follows because he has already assumed that experience of our *term* (God – the single whole of reality – absolute being) is an innate experience of creatures. Thus, religion simply is a moment in and modality of our transcendental and 'mediated immediacy to God'. But what kind of God can be known *directly* by knowing the medium (religion) and God *embedded* in the religious medium? A God who 'as the transcendental ground of the world has from the outset embedded himself in this world as its self-communicating ground'.[160] Rahner clearly intends to say that the Christian God has been involved with the world since the very beginning; but as he explains how we interpret experience of the Christian God according to his method, he cannot really conceive of a God truly existing independently of the world (i.e. an immanent Trinity).

The significance of all this highlights the problem I have sought to clarify in this chapter and throughout this book. As our self experience is both starting point and norm for the question of God and his activity in the world, Rahner believes that the 'categorical presence of God' is

157 *FCF*, 85.

158 See, for example, *TI* 4, 236–42 and above. Also *TI* 4, 228ff. See also Molnar, 'Can We Know God Directly?' and *Karl Barth and the Theology of Lord's Supper* for more on this.

159 *FCF*, 87.

160 *FCF*, 87.

simply the religious subject objectivating his or her religious experiences. As such they (categories-objectivations) perform a 'valuable role'. Actually, 'the role indeed really belongs to those phenomena in themselves'.[161] This attempt to speak of a God who is and remains *free* in the scriptural sense or in the realistic theological sense advanced by Barth and Torrance ascribes too much to created phenomena. It assumes that all religious experience points to the reality of God insofar as it points to the horizon (*term*) of human experience. This is the very assumption that causes Rahner to compromise the scriptural and the traditional distinctions between God (the true God) and his *free* grace and idols and existentials which might lead us away from the true God and not toward him. Rahner concludes his treatment in *Foundations* by defining God's intervention in history with an example of what validates our 'good idea' which we think corresponds with God's intervention.

> The moment I experience myself as a transcendental subject in my orientation to God and accept it, and the moment I accept this concrete world in which ... the absolute ground of my existence unfolds historically for me and I actualize it in freedom, *then* within this subjective, transcendental relationship to God this 'good idea' [his intervention] receives objectively a quite definite and positive significance.[162]

Perceptively, Rahner asks what is to prevent me from calling *anything* an *intervention* of God arguing in this fashion. His answer is: 'Why, then, may this not be the case?'[163] How this question is actually answered can be a matter of no small concern both to philosophers and theologians.

Following the position for which I have argued, that is, that the God of scripture, the triune God, is truly *free* even in his involvement in human experience, we would have to say that this may not be the case because God himself is not in any way *dependent* on anyone or anything to be God in himself or God for us ad extra. This insight would preclude arguing, as Rahner does, that our orientation to God contributes

---

161 *FCF*, 88. Cf. also *TI* 4, 221–52. Symbols must have this function for Rahner because being and appearance are intrinsically and essentially related so that one cannot really exist without the other. See 230ff. All of this is true for Rahner because he believes that symbols possess an 'overplus of meaning' (225).

162 *FCF*, 88, emphasis mine.

163 *FCF*, 89.

objectively to the positive significance of our ideas about his intervention in history. The only way Rahner's insight could be true is if the
Christian God were in fact 'embedded' in the world as a 'ground of
being' recognizable by the metaphysician and the philosopher of religion as well as by the theologian, whose thinking occurs from within
the biblical faith.

This is not to say that God cannot be conceptualized as a 'ground of
being'. Obviously, insofar as we all actually depend on God for our being
he is the 'ground of being'. The question raised here is what specific object
determines the truth of our metaphysical concept of God's being? If it
is the immanent Trinity acting ad extra in Christ and the Spirit, then
it is my contention that we cannot actually begin thinking about him
outside of faith in the Father, Son and Spirit. This would mean that we
could not begin thinking about God truly as the 'ground of being' prior
to an acknowledgment of the unique being of God revealed in Christ
and the Spirit. Any attempt to define God as the 'ground of being' before
believing in the immanent Trinity and without allowing the economic
Trinity to determine what is said, might lead directly to the conclusion
of the Deists, that is, that Christ is unnecessary really to know God.[164]
Interestingly, the position, which I am questioning here, is exactly what
must be stated in a philosophy of symbolic reality.[165] It is just this idea
which obscures philosophical and theological investigation.

164 Etienne Gilson, *God and Philosophy* (New Haven: Yale University
Press, 1979), 104–5ff.

165 See Molnar, 'Can We Know God Directly?' 238ff. and 251ff. See also
Karl Barth and the Theology of the Lord's Supper, esp. chapters 2 and 4. See *TI*
4, 225ff. Rahner believes that 'in the long run everything agrees in some way
or another with everything else' (225). Thus, for Rahner, symbols are related
essentially to what is symbolized and the two are intrinsically and mutually
dependent. All of this is true because what is symbolized 'passes over into the
"otherness" of the symbol' (240). In other words, in a symbolic philosophy,
signs and things signified are embedded in one another in such a way that no
clear and sharp distinction between them can be made. Clearly, this cannot
apply to knowledge of God who is and remains different from the creature
in his encounter with creation. This symbolic thinking is exactly what leads
to Rahner's insistence on a quasi-formal explanation of the creator/creature
relationship once again 245ff. The whole problem here centers on the fact that
in a Christian doctrine of God – God is and remains ontologically different
from his creatures even in the incarnation, grace and glory. There is in fact no

The philosopher can indeed bypass Christ and attempt to know God. He or she may always discover a 'supreme being', but that is the most that can be discovered thereby. The theologian of revelation cannot bypass Christ (and by implication the Old and New Testaments) and attempt to know God. Thus, he or she will know that the unity and Trinity of the Christian God would preclude any attempt to define God as a supreme being without allowing Christ and the Spirit the sole freedom to determine the truth of the concept. Then a 'deliberate and sharp' distinction between the immanent and economic Trinity would be maintained since it would be very clear that the being of God revealed (the immanent Trinity) actually transcends and is different from the being of God recognized by the philosopher apart from biblical faith (supreme being recognized as the term of our experiences of self-transcendence).

Since he is faithful to his method (attempting to harmonize natural knowledge of God with revealed knowledge) Rahner is actually unable to resolve this theological problem. Thus, he must maintain that *what* is categorized, that is, 'the holy mystery', is not conceptually beyond the religious phenomena which, in themselves, are supposed to convey God's grace. On this view the theological question of how we really know that this or that 'concept' of God's intervention is *true* is left ambiguous. For Rahner, of course, the answer resides in his *assumption* that transcendental experience of one's horizon is a real experience of *God* simply because people experience themselves this way, and their experiences are self-validating. Thus, what 'we call' God and his intervention ultimately depends not on God *alone* but on God as well as the strength of our transcendental experiences. I am arguing that this mutual coordination of God's action in history with our historical self-experience compromises the unique objectivity and freedom of God envisioned by the scriptural revelation and recognized and upheld in a properly conceived doctrine of the immanent Trinity.

Furthermore, this assumption by Rahner actually subverts the real need for Christian revelation as an independent source of truth coming to us from something other than our self-experience. One does not *need* to believe in God's special presence in history in his Word and Spirit if one already possesses this truth in the experience of his or her orientation toward the absolute, which absolute may well have

original ontological unity between creator and creatures as there must be for a symbolic ontological explanation of absolute being in relation to finite being.

little or nothing to do with the eternally triune God of Christianity.[166] In Rahner's doctrine of God then we are told that we need this God, but his method ends exactly where it began, that is, with our human experience of ourselves which we 'call' God.[167]

This leads to his theory of anonymous Christianity in which he spells out the implications of this position by maintaining that everyone can know and experience what Christians know and experience in faith simply by having these transcendental experiences.[168] Rahner's position that Christianity is present in everyone in an incipient state[169] simply confirms the fact that he is consistent in carrying through the logic of his method. If he did not say this he would have to deny that we could know God by knowing our *term* and that grace and God's self-communication are embedded in creation. Ultimately, he would have to deny his theory of luminosity and his philosophy of symbolic reality. Since human being is already changed ontologically (obediential potency and supernatural existential) in virtue of the incarnation, Rahner believes that people do not have to hear about Christ to be Christians. Rather, in deciding for or against themselves they already decide for or against God and Christ.

The problem with anonymous Christianity is the same problem that is apparent in Rahner's doctrine of God. He never really shows us that we are believing in and knowing anything that truly transcends us and exists in reality apart from our experience and interpretation of that experience. Thus, God, grace, revelation and faith are simply qualities of human experience interpreted philosophically and theologically for Rahner. As long as that is the case we really do not need to believe in Jesus and the Spirit *before* knowing the true God. As long as this is the case we shall never answer the theological question of whether what we 'call' God, grace, revelation and salvation are *true* as realities coming to us from a real God independent of us, that is a God who retains his

166 See, for example, Gilson, *God and Philosophy*, 105ff. and Ludwig Feuerbach, *The Essence of Christianity*, 50–8. The god of the Deists (cf. Gilson) and the god of Feuerbach are not the Christian God but an apotheosis, a mythological human invention.

167 See *FCF*, 53–4 and Rahner and Weger, *Our Christian Faith*, 13 and 25.

168 See, for example, *TI* 12, 161–78, 'Anonymous Christianity and the Missionary Task of the Church'. On 161 many additional references to Rahner's treatment of this topic of anonymous Christianity are given.

169 *TI* 12, 164.

own inner life even in his closest connections with us as these occur as God relates with us and enables us to relate with him in and through his incarnate Word and the outpouring of the Holy Spirit. For Rahner, we do not really *need* the grace of God revealed in Christ to explain 'reality' to ourselves and others. God merely confirms our transcendental experiences and our interpretations of them. Thus, for Rahner, everyone is a believer whether he or she knows it or not. This, simply because everyone has unthematic experiences of absolute being in order to continue to exist meaningfully in the world.[170]

Such thinking leads to speculation like that of the 'questioner' who poses for Rahner the assertion in *Our Christian Faith* 'that everyone who lives their world-view with determination and commitment will find that this world-view proves true'.[171] In fact the answer to the question of which 'world-view' is true cannot be answered by examining anyone's determination and commitment to it. This is the predicament of Rahner's method; that is, he begins and ends his thought about truth with the determination and commitment of one's transcendental experiences. Rahner also insists that a person is a believer in the 'unreflected core of her existence' as long as she loves, is loyal and committed to the truth.[172] The problem with this assertion, however, is that on his presuppositions Rahner cannot tell us whose version of 'truth' is really true since we can in fact know the truth without knowing Christ. That is because what actually determines the truth of his doctrine of God is our reflection on this 'unreflected core of existence'. For this reason, belief in God for Rahner, means belief in mystery or human existence or reality as a whole. It cannot mean belief in the Christian God who transcends humanity and confronts people who experience him in judgment and grace according to the Old and New Testaments. It is obvious that one can live and be committed in fact without acknowledging the truth of Christianity. Paul's analysis of his own position in Galatians and Romans would provide a good example of this.[173]

170 On this see *TI* 7, 211–66, 'The Eucharist and Our Daily Lives', 223. Rahner writes: 'There may be many who face up to life bravely ... yet who do not regard themselves as believers at all. But ... in their calm acceptance of their lives they actually achieve, implicitly and in principle, what the conscious and professed believer does explicitly.'

171 Rahner and Weger, *Our Christian Faith*, 19–20.

172 Rahner and Weger, *Our Christian Faith*, 12–13.

173 Cf. also *TI* 6, 231–49, 'Reflections on the Unity of the Love of Neighbour and the Love of God,' 232 and 238ff. It is interesting to note that Moltmann

Although Rahner certainly wished to present a more open view of salvation in his theory of anonymous Christianity, the net effect renders Christianity less rather than more necessary. This, because the pivotal factor which determines the truth of Christianity on this view is to have significant human experiences, beginning with the experience of our horizon. Any real dependence on Christ in the New Testament sense would demand faith and action with respect to him alone.

To sum up, we have seen *what* Rahner's doctrine of God states and we have seen that it is *based* on 'transcendental experience'. I have contended that this starting point compromises God's *freedom* and the consequent *need* to *believe* in the *triune* God *before* being able to make sense of the creator/creature relationship. Further, I have contended that this leads to Rahner's synthesis of nature and grace and to the idea that God's free grace and free revelation can be described as 'elements' or modalities by the philosopher of religion as well as the theologian.

In the context of our presentation of a contemporary doctrine of the immanent Trinity, it is extremely important that we note the ambiguity in Rahner's thought here. On the one hand, Rahner has reshaped contemporary theology in a positive way by insisting that we begin thinking about God from the economic Trinity which *is* the immanent Trinity. Most contemporary theologians would certainly agree with this. On the other hand, however, Rahner's transcendental method, which begins with experience instead of with an acknowledgment of Jesus, the Word incarnate as the sole way to the Father, leads him to think about the immanent and economic Trinity in categories drawn from his philosophy of the symbol. This in fact means that it is God as defined by our self-experience that Rahner portrays instead of God uniquely revealed in Christ. This is certainly not what Rahner intended,

too accepts a version of Rahner's 'anonymous Christianity' when he asks with Rahner: 'Are there "anonymous Christians" outside Christianity in the world? There are: they are the poor, the hungry, the thirsty, the sick and the imprisoned of Matt. 25 whom Christ declares to be his "brothers and sisters", whether they are Christians or not. There are the children of Matt. 18 to whom Jesus promises the kingdom, whether they believe or not. So there are also "anonymous Christians" where deeds of mercy and justice are done to them' Jürgen Moltmann, *History and the Triune God: Contributions to Trinitarian Theology* (hereafter: *History and the Triune God*), trans. by John Bowden (New York: Crossroad, 1992), 122. For further discussion of this issue in Moltmann, see Paul D. Molnar, 'Karl Barth and the Importance of thinking Theologically within the Nicene Faith', *Ecclesiology*, vol. 11 (2015): 153–76, 173–4.

but it is unfortunately where his method unwittingly led him. We will explore this predicament more deeply in the next chapter by showing how Rahner's method of beginning theology from self-transcending experience leads to difficulties in Christology and trinitarian theology. By comparing the way the doctrine of the immanent Trinity functions in the theology of Karl Barth with a number of prominent contemporary theologians who tend to follow Rahner's method rather than Barth's, I hope to show more clearly why a proper doctrine of the immanent Trinity could have allowed Rahner and others to take human experience seriously without making it the starting point and thus the norm for their trinitarian reflections. To this we now turn.

Chapter 6

CAN A METAPHYSICAL PRINCIPLE OF RELATIONALITY BE SUBSTITUTED FOR THE RELATIONS OF THE IMMANENT TRINITY? KARL BARTH AND THE CURRENT DISCUSSION

In this chapter we shall explore several factors that indicate how a number of contemporary theologians, such as Eberhard Jüngel, Catherine LaCugna, Jürgen Moltmann, Wolfhart Pannenberg, Ted Peters and Karl Rahner either fail to think through the implications of a doctrine of the immanent Trinity or, by merely paying lip service to the doctrine, allow some principle rather than God to define the meaning of relationality.[1]

1 This chapter is an argument against one of the most basic premises of what is called 'social trinitarianism', that is, the idea that human experiences of relationality can or should be used as a basis for understanding the Holy Trinity. As stated several times, this book advances the idea that no experience can or should be the starting point for knowing God because any experience of the triune God in faith immediately implies that it is God and not any experience of ours (including Christian experience of course), that dictates who God is in se and ad extra. As I indicated in chapter two of *Two Views on the Doctrine of the Trinity*, ed. Jason S. Sexton and Stanley N. Gundry (Grand Rapids, MI: Zondervan, 2014), 69–95, referring to the position of Ted Peters, any assumption that 'relationality' as a 'social psychological concept' could 'unlock newer understandings of the divine life' necessarily moves away from the revelation of God in his Word and Spirit and toward a general idea of relationality exactly in such a way that relationality, as we experience it, becomes the subject and God the predicate. In reality, however, a properly conceived doctrine of the immanent Trinity would always point in the opposite direction. This chapter will explore these issues once again illustrating the kinds of inappropriate positions that follow when a properly functioning doctrine of the immanent Trinity is marginalized, as happens frequently in 'social trinitarianism'. For an interesting discussion of 'social trinitarianism', see Gijsbert van den Brink, 'Social Trinitarianism: A Discussion of Some Recent Theological Criticisms' *IJST*, vol. 16, no. 3 (July 2014): 331–50. While van den Brink rightly recognizes that one

This chapter will not involve an exhaustive treatment of the thought of each theologian; instead the focus here will be on how their thinking relates both to the theology of Karl Barth and to a proper doctrine of the immanent Trinity. Here, with the help of Barth's theology, we shall explore some of the problems that result from allowing relationality, abstractly understood, instead of the triune God as understood in faith and through revelation, to dictate trinitarian thinking. I also hope to show more precisely, with particular focus on his theology of the symbol, the kinds of difficulties that Rahner has bequeathed to modern trinitarian theology. Hopefully this will lead us closer to a contemporary doctrine of the immanent Trinity, that is, one that recognizes that the doctrine of the Trinity is indeed a statement about who God is as the eternal Father, Son and Holy Spirit and as the one who loves in freedom. Only when this is recognized and accepted in faith can one speak within the Nicene faith of who this particular God is for us in the economy without separating God from us, but also without collapsing God's eternal being and action into his actions for us. Without such a clearly articulated doctrine of the immanent Trinity theologians will have a difficult, if not impossible time distinguishing and relating without confusing divine and human action.

We have already noted in Chapter 1 that the purpose of a doctrine of the immanent Trinity, broadly speaking, is to recognize, uphold and respect God's freedom. We also noted that Karl Barth insisted that the

---

of the great weaknesses of 'social trinitarianism' is the danger of projection and while he notes the danger of tritheism, he still seems to think that positions such as that espoused by LaCugna are helpful even though he himself says that in going beyond Rahner, her thinking ended in a 'near-assimilation' of *oikonomia* and *theologia*. Her thinking was discussed earlier at length and will be discussed again in this chapter to illustrate how and why LaCugna is unable to maintain either divine or human freedom just because her starting point for trinitarian reflection was the experience of salvation. From this, relationality as generally understood, replaces the unique trinitarian relations revealed in Christ and through the Spirit, as the criterion for her theological reflections, with disastrous results which are then carried forward by Ted Peters and others. Her agnosticism with respect to the immanent Trinity leads her to confuse divine and human being and action and at times to separate them as well. In connection with 'social trinitarianism', it is worth mentioning Barth's terse reaction to this approach when he said: 'Modernism has no Doctrine of the Trinity. The notion of a "Social Trinity" is fantastic!' (Godsey, *Table Talk*, 50).

doctrine of the Trinity was not merely a description of salvific events but a statement about the eternal Father, Son and Spirit as the one who enables the events of salvation and redemption. Hence, for Barth trinitarian doctrine or trinitarian thinking could not displace God as the foundation of true knowledge, since God's action in revelation is not a dogma, view or principle but the actual Word of God working ad extra as creator, reconciler and redeemer. Our position therefore has been that knowledge of God takes place from Jesus Christ through the power of his Holy Spirit and consequently it must be sought in and from a center outside us, that is, from a center in God acting for us. It must be sought and found objectively in Christ and subjectively through the Holy Spirit and therefore in faith and by grace.

While Christian theologians agree that the doctrine of the immanent Trinity should uphold God's freedom, we have already seen that the way many today employ trinitarian categories leads from agnosticism to monism and/or dualism and thus compromises divine and human freedom. We have also seen that most modern theologians adopt Rahner's axiom of the identity of the immanent and economic Trinity in some form, even if only to move beyond it, to speak about God's involvement with the world. However, I have suggested that this axiom, with its vice versa, tends to compromise divine and human freedom by seeing our human relationship with God as one of mutual conditioning. It is apparent that some confusion and reversal of the creator/creature relationship results both in Rahner's own thought with his assertion of a mutually conditioning and mutually conditioned relation between anthropology and Christology and between natural theology and revealed theology. I am suggesting that this occurs not only in his thought, but in the thought of others who uncritically accept his axiom along with its vice versa. With this in view, we noted earlier that several indications of such a reversal today are: (1) the trend toward making God, in some sense, dependent on and to that extent indistinguishable from history; (2) the lack of precision in Christology which leads to the idea that Jesus, in his humanity as such is the revealer; (3) the failure to distinguish the Holy Spirit from the human spirit; (4) a trend, following Rahner, to begin theology with experiences of self-transcendence.[2] Up

2 For an almost classic case of a contemporary theology that allows Rahner's transcendental method to define the terms of discussion in exactly the wrong way, see *Trinitarian Theology as Participation* by Frans Josef Van Beeck, S.J. in *The Trinity: An Interdisciplinary Symposium on the Trinity*, ed. Stephen T. Davis, Daniel Kendall, S.J. and Gerald O'Collins, S.J. (Oxford: Oxford University Press, 1999).

to this point we have seen the marks of one or another of these difficulties in the works of a number of prominent contemporary theologians and we have suggested that a proper doctrine of the immanent Trinity could serve to overcome these difficulties. While the doctrine is not to be constructed in order to avoid these difficulties, it is necessary as a statement of and recognition of God's freedom that does indeed lead away from them. In other words, while a proper understanding of the doctrine of the immanent Trinity acknowledges the importance of God's triune relations as the free basis of his actions as creator, reconciler and redeemer, we must insist that relationality abstractly understood, and thus as defined by our human relational experiences, does not define God. Therefore, we cannot use either the doctrine of the immanent or the economic Trinity to validate a general principle of relationality.

That a doctrine of the immanent Trinity should function this way is not always clearly recognized today. For instance, Colin Gunton appraises C. M. LaCugna's *God for Us* as 'a polemic against the doctrine of the immanent Trinity' and wonders whether her approach 'finally escapes the pantheism which results from any attempt to bring God and the world too close'.[3] I agree with Gunton that the doctrine upholds divine and human freedom. However, I believe pantheism does not *just* follow an attempt to bring God and the world too close; it follows, as Barth clearly saw, from an attempt to see this closeness in abstraction from the immanence God has freely established by grace in Jesus Christ.

> If the freedom of divine immanence is sought and supposedly found apart from Jesus Christ, it can signify in practice only our enslavement to a false god ... the Church must ... see that it expects everything from *Jesus Christ*, and from Jesus Christ *everything*; that He is unceasingly recognized as the way, the truth, and the life (Jn. 14.6) ... The freedom of God must be recognised as His own freedom ... as it consists in God and as God has exercised it. But in God it consists in His Son Jesus Christ, and it is in Him that God has

3 Colin Gunton, Review of Catherine LaCugna, *God for Us*, *SJT*, vol. 47, no. 1 (1994): 136–7. Gunton suggests greater distinction between the economic and immanent Trinity in *The Promise of Trinitarian Theology*, 137ff. Thompson, *Modern Trinitarian Perspectives*, argues with clarity and subtlety for the *unity* and *distinction* of the economic and immanent Trinity (25ff.) and opposes grounding the doctrine in philosophy or anthropology.

exercised it ... If we recognise and magnify it, we cannot come from any other starting point but Him or move to any other goal.[4]

For LaCugna

> Economy and theology are two aspects of *one* reality: the mystery of divine-human communion ... There is neither an economic nor an immanent Trinity; there is only the *oikonomia* that is the concrete realization of the mystery of *theologia* in time, space, history and personality ... [economic and immanent mislead because] *Oikonomia* is not the Trinity *ad extra* but the comprehensive plan of God reaching from creation to consummation, in which God and all creatures are destined to exist together in the mystery of love and communion ... *theologia* is not the Trinity *in se*, but, much more modestly and simply ... the mystery of God with us ... The life of God is not something that belongs to God alone. *Trinitarian life is also our life* ... The doctrine of the Trinity is not ultimately a teaching about 'God' but a teaching about *God's life with us and our life with each other.*[5]

Any thinking which makes the twin claims that 'Trinitarian life is also our life' and that 'The doctrine of the Trinity is not ultimately a teaching about God' demonstrates that such thinking is unwilling and/or unable to distinguish God in se from God acting ad extra. Just because of this, such thinking inevitably invites pantheism and dualism because it refuses to see the distinction in union between God and creatures in and through the union established and maintained in Jesus himself, in whom divinity and humanity are united without mixture, separation or confusion.[6] For such problematic thinking, unfortunately, God

---

4 *CD* II/1, 319–20.

5 LaCugna, *God for Us*, 222–24 and 228.

6 In this statement, I am deliberately following George Hunsinger's notion of a 'Chalcedonian pattern' because a proper view of divine and human relations begins and ends with the kind of relation that was established and is maintained by God in and through the hypostatic union. For more on this notion see Chapter 3, n. 74. A particularly clear example of Barth's Chalcedonian thinking can be seen in his discussion of God's omnipresence: 'God is Himself this man Jesus Christ, very God and very man, both of them unconfused and unmixed, but also unseparated and undivided, in the one person of this Messiah and Saviour.

is no longer the subject acting toward us and for us from within history but becomes little more than the content of our experiences of love and communion projected onto what is uncritically assumed to be the divine being. Clearly, the expression 'God's life with us' depicts an apotheosis unless it *first* refers to God in himself; and the way LaCugna conceives the doctrine prevents this as she thinks the mystery of God revealed is

> the mystery of persons in communion who embrace death, sin, and all forms of alienation for the sake of life [while the Spirit transforms us so] 'we become by grace what God is by nature', namely, persons in full communion with God and with every creature ... The life of God – precisely *because* God is triune – does not belong to God alone.[7]

Here, persons in communion are substituted for Jesus Christ and the Lordship of the Holy Spirit is transformed into a necessary attribute of creatures; such a view represents an all too common confusion of the Holy Spirit with the human spirit. In this venue it is thought that because God is triune, he must be in communion with all creatures and his life cannot be uniquely his. Here, love in general defines God's love and displaces his freedom:

> Love by its nature is outgoing and self-giving ... Divine self-sufficiency is exposed as a philosophical myth ... [Thus God's love] spills over into what is other than God, giving birth to creation and history ... we become by grace what God is already by nature, namely self-donating love for the other ... To be God is to be the Creator of the world.[8]

This is what cannot be said about any other creature, even any prophet or apostle' *CD* II/1, 486. As we shall see shortly, her view of Jesus disallows his genuine eternal preexistence, and thus his divinity when she claims that 'His person, as the achievement of truly divinized human nature is in this sense [that he lived, died and was raised to eternal life] eternal', *God for Us*, 317. This could be characterized as a dualistic view in that she will not allow Jesus to be God acting for us and so separates his true divinity from his true humanity.

    7 LaCugna, *God for Us*, 1. Cf. also 354.

    8 LaCugna, *God for Us*, 353–5. While LaCugna knows that blurring the distinction between creator and creature also compromises God's freedom, grace and self-sufficiency and while she thinks her position avoids all of this as when she notes that 'creation is the result of divine freedom, not metaphysical

To suggest that 'To be God is to be the Creator' overtly absorbs God's eternal being and action into God's creative function and in that way completely loses the meaning of the doctrine of the Trinity which, in the first instance, points to the eternal being of God as one who loves in

necessity' (355), her confusion of the immanent and economic Trinity leads to numerous other conflicting statements that do not just deny God's freedom to exist self-sufficiently even while in closest relations with his creation, but obliterate it. For example, she is unable to clearly distinguish the missions from the processions as when she writes: 'The images of "begetting" and "spirating" express the fruitfulness or fecundity of God who is alive from all eternity as a dynamic interchange of persons united in love. The temptation is to think that all of this happens "inside" God. Rather, *the eternal begetting of the Son and the breathing forth of the Spirit take place in God's economy'* (354). This leads to the rather emanationist idea that God's love for us is not a free expression of grace ad extra, but something that 'spills over', thus giving rise to creation. Hence, 'The centrifugal movement of divine love does not terminate "within" God but explodes outward; God gives rise to the world just as God gives rise to God' (354–5). The failure to distinguish between the freedom of God's love within the eternal (immanent Trinity) and the economic Trinity (God acting ad extra) in these remarks, and the idea that God simply explodes outward, make it impossible to maintain with Gregory of Nyssa, whom she cites in this context, that creation is an act of God's will and not simply the result of an involuntary explosion outward! Even as she appeals to Gregory for this insight, her own language so lacks precision that it is impossible to distinguish creator and creature in her thought in any consistent or reliable way. Thus she says 'the world is begotten (created) out of the will of God and thus the world is not of the divine substance' (355). But even this image of the will of God is confused because she equates the terms *begotten* and *created* which carry within themselves a clear distinction between creation as the result of an *act* of will and the Son's being begotten of the Father which is not the result of an act of will on God's part. The world is not in fact begotten 'out of the will of God' as LaCugna maintains, but *by* the will of God. The former image cannot distinguish the substance of creation from the creator as something that is contingent on God's will. That is why she erroneously claims that 'Creation is indeed the fruit of divine love and freedom. But to be the Creator, that is, to be in relation to creation as the Creator, is not a relation added on to the divine essence, ancillary to God's being. To be God is to be the Creator of the world,' and concludes that 'the world is not created *ex nihilo* but *ex amore, ex condilectio*, that is, out of divine love' (355). This is in fact a classically pantheist mode of thought.

freedom as Father, Son and Holy Spirit and would have so existed even without creation.[9]

Elizabeth T. Groppe defends LaCugna's theology saying that she never intended to question the reality of the immanent Trinity, even though she believed the language of immanent and economic was 'imprecise'. Yet Groppe goes on to write that: 'Ultimately LaCugna rejected a theology of God in se not because of Kant or any other philosophical development but rather because of God's revelation in creation, covenant, Incarnation and the gift of the Holy Spirit.'[10] That, however, is the problem – she did indeed reject a theology of God in se (that is of the immanent Trinity) precisely because she reduced the immanent to the economic Trinity as I and many others believe. Groppe also defends LaCugna against the charge of pantheism. Unfortunately, as already noted, while LaCugna (and Groppe following LaCugna) make statements affirming God's freedom and transcendence, these are called into question by their subsequent thinking as I have been arguing. In one context LaCugna overtly reduces God to what God does in the economy. In another she affirms God's freedom and transcendence. If God is really free in acting for us, then God cannot be rightly recognized if it is thought that God is 'absolutely immanent' without remainder as LaCugna recommends when she writes: 'God is Absolute Mystery not because God remains locked in other-worldly transcendence, but because the transcendent God becomes also absolutely immanent.'[11] While we all agree that God does not remain locked in 'other-wordly transcendence', the telltale sign that, in following LaCugna's thought, Groppe herself also has embraced a pantheist conceptuality that confuses divine and human love can be seen quite clearly in her own

---

9 As will be seen in Chapter 8, Etienne Gilson very rightly traced this confused understanding of God back to Descartes's misbegotten natural theology.

10 Elizabeth T. Groppe, 'Catherine Mowry LaCugna's Contribution to Trinitarian Theology,' *TS*, vol. 63, no. 4 (2002): 730–63, at 748.

11 LaCugna cited in Groppe, 757. If God truly remains God even in closest union with us, then God is absolutely transcendent because God needs no other to be who God is. But God is not absolutely immanent in history because such a view would in reality reduce the immanent to the economic Trinity without remainder. That is why Barth affirmed the *Extra Calvinisticum* insofar as it held that God continued to rule the world as Lord even though he was fully incarnate in Jesus – but not so without remainder.

espousal of a series of remarks from a 14th-century Flemish mystic Jan van Ruusbroec to express the kind of communion she and LaCugna envision between us and God. These remarks clearly demonstrate both a confusion of the Holy Spirit with the human spirit and a confusion of divine and human love – the very problems Groppe thinks she and LaCugna have avoided.

'These two spirits, that is, our spirit and God's Spirit, cast a radiant light upon one another and each reveals to the other its countenance. This makes the two spirits incessantly strive after one another in love. Each demands of the other what it is, and each offers to the other and invites it to accept what it is. This makes these loving spirits lose themselves in one another. God's touch and his giving of himself, together with our striving in love and our giving of ourselves in return – this is what sets love on a firm foundation. *This flux and reflux make the spring of love overflow, so that God's touch and our striving in love become a single love*.'[12]

Role of Experience

Why this confusion? Because LaCugna begins with experience and then interprets doctrine: 'The only option is for Christian theology to start afresh from its original basis in the *experience* of being saved by God through Christ in the power of the Holy Spirit.'[13] God's freedom

12 Cited in Groppe, *TS*, 757, emphasis mine.

13 LaCugna, *God for Us*, 3, emphasis mine. While I freely admit that experience and doctrine must indeed be properly coordinated, it is misguided to suggest that the original basis for Christian theology is in our experience of being saved. Any genuine experience of salvation would necessarily point away from itself to its true basis in God's action ad extra, that is, an action of the Father, Son and Holy Spirit in light of which our experience makes sense. Stanley Grenz clearly expresses the view that I am contesting: 'LaCugna is convinced that the salvation experience reveals the mystery of God' (*Rediscovering the Triune God*, 155). In my view the salvation experience does not reveal God since only God can do that. In addition, Veli-Matti Kärkkäinen rightly concludes that 'the end result of LaCugna's program is the collapse of the immanent Trinity into the economic' since 'for LaCugna it is the *experience* (of salvation) that serves as the ground [of authenticity in theology]' *The Trinity*, 191. With the exception of the fine chapter on the Trinity and Preaching by

can no longer be conceived as autonomy and self-sufficiency but must be understood as 'the contemplation of the divine *oikonomia*'.[14] God must be seen as one who *needs* and cares for us and is thus not immune to our suffering.

But, according to Barth, the original basis of Christian theology is God himself acting objectively for us in Christ and subjectively within us by the Holy Spirit; his starting point for learning 'the lofty but simple lesson that it is by God that God is known ... was neither an axiom of reason nor a datum of experience. In the measure that a doctrine of God draws on these sources, it betrays the fact that its subject is not really God.'[15] It is the deity of the Holy Spirit which creates faith. Despite criticism that his theology is not eschatological enough, Barth argues:

> This being of ours is thus enclosed in the act of God ... we cannot as it were look back and try to contemplate ... this being of ours as God's redeemed ... To have the Holy Spirit is to let God rather than our having God be our confidence ... it lies in the nature of the *regnum gratiae*, that having *God* and our *having* God are two very different things ... We believe our future being. We believe in an eternal life

Marguerite Shuster, and a number of the patristic chapters, there is a tendency in *The Trinity: An Interdisciplinary Symposium on the Trinity* to see the doctrine of the Trinity as a description of experience rather than a description of the immanent Trinity, which takes place in and through experience.

14 LaCugna, *God for Us*, 169. Cf. also 397–8: 'The God who does not need nor care for the creature, or who is immune to our suffering, does not exist ... person, not substance is the root (radix) of all reality ... the idea of person as self-sufficient, self-possessing individual ... is perhaps the ultimate male fantasy. Classical metaphysics, the effort to ascertain what something is "in itself", is perhaps the ultimate projection of masculinity.' While the errors of individualism are well known and well documented, this hardly means that the effort to find out what something is in itself is always a projection. Once again, LaCugna's thinking is thoroughly inconsistent since she simultaneously claims that: 'It would make no sense to say that God "needs" the world in order to be God' (355). The problem of course is that her emanationist thinking compels this inconsistency. The point here is that a God who needs the world in any sense is in fact dependent on the world for his being and thus needs creation in order to be God. This issue is discussed in detail in Chapter 4 in connection with Kevin Hector's idea of 'volitional necessity'.

15 *CD* II/ 2, 3.

even in the midst of the valley of death. In this way, in this futurity, we have it … the assurance of faith means concretely the assurance of hope … The man we know does not live an eternal life. This is and remains the predicate of God, of the Holy Spirit … Both [becoming rich in God and poor in ourselves] become our experience … But we do not have the divine and spiritual riches and the divine and spiritual poverty in our experience [because] God remains the Lord even and precisely when He Himself comes into our hearts … The deity of the Holy Spirit is thus demanded.[16]

Recognizing God's actual freedom led Barth to direct us away from our experiences and ideas toward God himself who certainly is for us, but as the sovereign God.

When we ask questions about God's being, we cannot in fact leave the sphere of His action and working as it is revealed to us in His Word. God is who He is in His works. He is the same even in Himself, even before and after and over His works, and without them. They are bound to Him, but He is not bound to them. They are nothing without Him. But He is who He is without them. He is not therefore, who He is only in His works. Yet in Himself He is not another than He is in His works. In light of what He is in His works it is no longer an open question what He is in Himself … there is no possibility of reckoning with the being of any other God, or with any other being of God, than that of the Father, the Son and the Holy Spirit as it is in God's revelation and in eternity.[17]

---

16 *CD* I/1, 462–5. Cf. also *CD* I/2, 249.

17 *CD* II/1, 260–1. This important statement by Barth underscores the importance for him of the immanent Trinity and the need to recognize that God is who he is in perfect love and freedom before he relates with us and would be this God even if he had never decided to do so. This undercuts those actualistic views that suggest that such passages as this can no longer be held as decisive in light of Barth's doctrine of election. The problem here is clearly recognized by Alan Torrance, 'The Trinity', *Cambridge Companion to Barth*, 90 n. 28. Bruce McCormack thinks that Alan Torrance is mistaken because 'he makes the perichoretic unity of God to be an event that is indeed *anterior* to the differentiated reality of God encountered in his work in the world' and that Torrance was wrong to cite part of this passage to support his view (*Orthodox and Modern*, 220–1). Yet, as I have been arguing throughout this book, unless

God is supremely and utterly independent of creation and is not subject to the limitation of created being which

> cannot affirm itself except by affirming itself against others ... [God is also free] to be present with that which is not God, to communicate Himself and unite Himself with the other and the other with Himself, in a way which utterly surpasses all that can be effected in regard to reciprocal presence, communion and fellowship between other beings.[18]

God then is not a prisoner of his transcendence and so is for us; but he is the *only divine subject* and so he cannot become the predicate in a sentence in which the subject is relationality as defined through an ontology which comprehends both human and divine experience. Certainly the notion of a divine subject is slippery and can be understood in a Hegelian way which leads to pantheism and modalism. However, Barth does not so use this concept because by it he asserts God's sovereignty and lordship in relation to the world and within the world (as just explained). He continually bases his analysis in the antecedent being of the Father, Son and Spirit refusing to define eternity *by* time,[19] affirming that who Jesus

God's being and act as Father, Son and Spirit exists as an event that is *anterior* to God's free revelation of himself to us, then the immanent Trinity will indeed be collapsed into the economic Trinity. The proof that it is so collapsed in McCormack's thinking is clearly visible in his remark that there was 'something improper' about Barth's affirmation in *CD* IV/1, 52 that the *Logos asarkos* was not the Reconciler and not revealed to us and that this *Logos asarkos* was necessary for theologians to recognize the freedom of the trinitarian God's grace; hence McCormack tellingly asks: 'For when has God ever been anything other than God the Reconciler?' (*Orthodox and Modern*, 220). The answer that both George Hunsinger and I have given is that God was eternally Father, Son and Holy Spirit in pretemporal eternity and thus his pretemporal being and act could not be reduced to his action for us as the Reconciler, as insinuated in this question. As argued earlier, God does not give up his being as *Logos asarkos* but is free to act as *Logos incarnandus* and *Logos incarnatus* without relinquishing his eternal being which is inaccessible to us apart from the incarnate Word. For a full discussion of this difficulty, see Molnar, *Faith, Freedom and the Spirit*, 307–12.

18 *CD* II/1, 313. Cf. also *CD* II/1, 326–7.
19 Cf. *CD* I/1, 384–489 and *CD* II/1, 611ff.

is as Son does not arise from history but from an act of divine lordship,[20] and he opposes Schleiermacher because

> [he saw in Christ] the preservation 'of the receptivity implanted in human nature from the beginning and continuously evolving, a receptivity which enables it to take up into itself such an absolute potency of the God-consciousness' ... The Word of God is not seriously regarded by him as the Subject of the redeeming act, but as one of the factors in the world-process.[21]

20 Cf. *CD* I/1, 426–7. '"Begotten of the Father before all time" means that He did not come into being in time as such ... That the Son of God becomes man and that He is known by other men in His humanity as the Son of God are events, even if absolutely distinctive events, in time ... *But their distinction does not itself derive or come from time* ... because the power of God's immanence is here the power of His transcendence, their subject must be understood as being before all time, as the eternal Subject,' emphasis mine.

21 *CD* I/2, 134–5 and 150ff. Barth insisted that the incarnation takes place in the freedom of the eternal Word and therefore does not rest on any inner or outer *necessity* (*CD* I/2, 136ff.). It is a miracle which, if it could be explained, would no longer be a miracle. When Barth speaks of God as person he emphasizes that 'Precisely in His Word God is person' (*CD* I/1, 139), namely, Jesus as the Word is not a thing or an object; but a 'free subject' even 'in respect of the specific limitations connected with its individuality' (138); to be a real person then is to be a 'really free subject' (139), a 'knowing, willing, acting I' (*CD* II/1, 283ff.). Here we may note that new difficulties have arisen in recent theology because some are trying to rehabilitate Schleiermacher's thinking with the claim that Barth mistakenly criticized him in a number of ways and that their concerns were really quite similar. See Bruce L. McCormack, 'Barth's Critique of Schleiermacher Reconsidered', *Theological Theology: Essays in Honour of John Webster* (ed.) R. David Nelson, Darren Sarisky and Justin Stratis (London/New York: Bloomsbury, T & T Clark, 2015), 167–79. Thus, McCormack speaks of the 'real tragedy of Barth's critique [of Schleiermacher]' because 'it serves to conceal from us just how much Barth owes to Schleiermacher' (177). According to McCormack, one of the things he owes to Schleiermacher can be seen in the fact that: 'Both believe that a relation to the world is made "essential" to God by the eternal activity in which He has His own being' (177–8). Beyond this McCormack recommends Schleiermacher's Christology which is quite obviously a 'degree' Christology over against Barth's criticism that such Christology undermines the truth that Jesus was truly divine and truly human (173ff.). For another view of Schleiermacher, which notices the genuine

Footnote 21 (*cont.*)

differences between Schleiermacher's view of Christ and salvation and Barth's view, see George Hunsinger, 'Schleiermacher and Barth: Two Divergent Views of Christ and Salvation', *Evangelical, Catholic and Reformed: Doctrinal Essays on Barth and Related Themes* (Grand Rapids, MI: Eerdmans, 2015), 146–68. Hunsinger's assertions that for Schleiermacher Christ's person did not exist before the 'Redeemer appeared on earth'; 'that the person of the Redeemer nevertheless came into being by the will and counsel of God from before all time'; that for Schleiermacher, 'the person of the Redeemer' was 'a perfect human creature who was brought into being out of nothing' all suggest that 'for Schleiermacher as for Arius, the Son was a mutable creature, and there was a time when he was not' (150). Hence, against McCormack's claim that 'the spontaneous activity which flowed from Jesus' perfectly potent God-consciousness in the posture of receptivity' as experienced by his disciples 'is yet another confirmation of Schleiermacher's belief in the deity of Jesus Christ' [McCormack, 'Barth's Critique Reconsidered' (175)], Hunsinger maintains that Schleiermacher rejected 'any Nicene belief in the Redeemer as the true, eternal God' and indeed Schleiermacher 'also insisted that there were no trinitarian distinctions within the eternal Godhead' (150). Thus, in contrast to McCormack's view that Schleiermacher's idea that Christ was the second Adam and more powerfully God-conscious than all others illustrated his belief in Christ's deity, Hunsinger firmly notes that 'Jesus is certainly the Redeemer for Schleiermacher, just as he is the second Adam. But the one thing that he most certainly is not is the Lord. Lordship cannot be ascribed to Jesus qua Jesus because Jesus qua Jesus is nothing but a human being, even if the most perfect and dignified of human beings' (152). This 'degree' Christology (with its similarity to Nestorian thinking) means that Barth's concern to maintain Christ's true deity and humanity still is thoroughly opposed to the approach of Schleiermacher which does not in fact begin and end with who Jesus was and is as the Lord, that is, as God himself acting for us *as* the man Jesus. Hunsinger mentions what he calls the 'panentheistic cast' of Schleiermacher's thought – a panentheistic view that Barth categorically rejected (152, n. 13). This is extremely important because Barth never held the view nor would he 'that a relation to the world is made "essential" to God by the eternal activity in which He has His own being'. God's relation to the world is contingent and thus completely dependent on God in his otherness – it is not essential to God. Such a view would have to mean that God could not have existed without a relation to the world. Moreover, the idea that a relation to the world was made essential to God in an eternal action 'in which He has His own being' clearly suggests that God never could have existed without the world and thus the two are co-eternal. What is the essential difference then between Schleiermacher and Barth? It is, says Hunsinger, 'that

Jürgen Moltmann misunderstands Barth here. When Barth suggested that, to escape an eschatological onesidedness, he should let 'the doctrine of the immanent Trinity function as an expository canon for the proclamation of the lordship of Jesus Christ', Moltmann responded:

> I must admit that in studying *CD* at these points I always lost my breath. I suspect you are right but I cannot as yet or so quickly enter into this right. Exegetical friends … have forced me first of all to think through eschatologically the origin, course, and future of the lordship of Christ. In so doing I thought I could so expound the economic Trinity that in the foreground, and then again in the background, it would be open to an immanent Trinity. That is, for me the Holy Spirit is first the Spirit of the raising of the dead and then as such the third person of the Trinity.[22]

But Barth was suggesting that the Holy Spirit is first the third person of the Trinity and then the Spirit of the raising of the dead; thus, God's sovereignty and the certainty of our hope could never become dependent on historical events but would be disclosed in and through them.

Moltmann now abandons the conceptual framework which includes immanent and economic Trinity because such 'distinctions derive from general metaphysics, not from specifically Christian theology. They grasp the mystery of God merely exoterically, not esoterically, and are therefore at most applicable to God's relation to the world generally, but not to the inner self-distinctions in God himself.'[23] He believes that for Barth and Rahner 'the unity of God precedes the triunity' and that Barth left us with no immanent Trinity existing independently. Yet the very fact that Barth refused to allow God's being and act to be defined outside God's own actions in Christ and the Spirit and refused to see God's relations with us as mutually conditioned shows exactly the opposite. So while Moltmann finds the presence of the Spirit 'in God's *immanence* in human experience, and in the *transcendence* of human beings in God' he frees theologians from the need to believe in

Barth affirmed Nicaea whereas Schleiermacher rejected it' (153). In these ideas one can clearly see that the differences between the 'revisionists' discussed earlier and the more traditional reading of Barth as a Nicene theologian have very far-reaching consequences indeed.

22 *Karl Barth Letters 1961–1968*, 348.

23 Jürgen Moltmann, *The Spirit of Life A Universal Affirmation* (Minneapolis, MN: Fortress Press, 1993), 343 n. 38 and 290.

Jesus Christ through the power of the Holy Spirit. The human spirit 'is self-transcendently aligned towards God'.[24] By thus claiming for experience what Barth affirmed only God can give in ever new acts of freedom, Moltmann fails to distinguish consistently the Holy Spirit from the human spirit, misunderstands God's freedom and believes because 'God is in all things, [and] ... all things are in God ... Every experience of a creation of the Spirit is hence also an experience of the Spirit itself'.[25] Instead, Barth stressed that

> we have always to take in blind seriousness the basic Pauline perception of Colossians 3.3 which is that of all Scripture – that our life is our life hid with Christ in God. With Christ: never at all apart from Him, never at all independently of Him, never at all in and for itself. Man never at all exists in himself [but] in Jesus Christ and in Him alone; as he also finds God in Jesus Christ and in Him alone.[26]

As we have seen throughout this book, pantheism and dualism threaten whenever theology begins with experience. It is a mark of LaCugna's pantheism that she cannot find God in Jesus Christ except insofar as he humanly embodies 'divinization'. Thus, 'His person, as the achievement of truly divinized human nature is in this sense [that he lived, died and was raised to eternal life] eternal'.[27] This pantheistic perspective allows the dualistic idea that Jesus is not fully God acting for us *as* man. Instead, LaCugna holds that the human Jesus embodies God's economic relatedness to us in the Spirit and to that extent is the Christ. She seeks to rehabilitate some form of subordinationism arguing that Jesus finds his origin in God and that subordinationism 'is not always the same as Arianism; the monarchy of the Father necessarily entails at least an economic, if not an ontological, subordination of the Son'.[28] An

24 Moltmann, *The Spirit of Life*, 7.

25 Moltmann, *The Spirit of Life*, 34–5.

26 *CD* II/1, 149.

27 Cf. LaCugna, *God for Us*, 317n. 143 and 296.

28 LaCugna, *God for Us*, 119. She misunderstands Barth's theology as modalist, claiming he says that God was one subject existing in 'three modes of revelation, as Father, Son and Holy Spirit' (252). For Barth, revelation is threefold ad extra because God who *is* Father, Son and Spirit in eternity has freely acted in revelation as God for us. Like Rahner, she equates God's original being (unity) with the unoriginate, which she equates with the Father. For a

ontological subordination of the Son, however, means that he cannot be *homoousion* with the Father and the Spirit. Rahner's axiom and method have been influential here and have led some to believe that experience is actually a source for theology.[29] Yet, as seen earlier, Barth firmly held that while experience and reason receive their true meaning from God alone in his revelation, which is also an act of reconciliation, which unites him with us and us with him, he also insisted that in the measure that a doctrine of God draws on reason and experience, instead of allowing for the fact that God can be known only through God, its subject matter is not really God at all. Barth clearly saw the issue:

> All Subordinationism rests on the intention of making the One who reveals Himself ... the kind of subject we ourselves are ... Subordinationism finally means the denial of revelation, the drawing of divine subjectivity into human subjectivity, and by way of polytheism the isolation of man ...[30]

proper defense of Barth against the charge of modalism, see George Hunsinger, *Disruptive Grace*, 191. Hunsinger rightly notes that modalism 'means that the trinitarian *hypostases* are merely manifestations of God in history, but not essential distinctions within the eternal Godhead itself' (191). Barth, however, 'repeatedly states that the living God would have been an eternal communion of love and freedom between the Father and the Son in the unity of the Holy Spirit, whether the world had been created or not. Nothing could be farther from modalism ... modalism can be charged against Barth only out of ignorance, incompetence, or (willful) misunderstanding' (191).

29 Cf. Anne Carr 'Theology and Experience in the Thought of Karl Rahner', in *Journal of Religion*, vol. 53 (1973): 359–76, at 359 and Chapter 1. Ellen Leonard, 'Experience as a Source for Theology', in the Proceedings of the Annual Convention of *The Catholic Theological Society of America* (1988): 44–61 believes that 'It is the task of theology to revision God in the light of contemporary experience', 56. Without necessarily being influenced by Rahner, Gordon D. Kaufman thinks that this is the main function of theology. Cf., for example, Gordon D. Kaufman, *God the Problem* (Cambridge, MA: Harvard University Press, 1972), 24 and Kaufman, *Method*, 8. William V. Dych believes that neither God nor scripture can be starting points for theology today but rather 'our shared human existence', in *A World of Grace*, ed. O'Donovan, 3.

30 *CD* I/1, 381. This firm rejection of any ontological subordination was always clear in Barth's theology, but he did obscure this somewhat when he read back elements of the economy such as Christ's obedience to the Father in his

Using Rahner's theology as a point of departure, but rejecting his Thomistic view of theology as the science of God, LaCugna welcomes Eberhard Jüngel's view that 'the economic doctrine of the Trinity deals with God's history with [humanity], and the immanent doctrine of the Trinity is *its* summarizing concept.'[31] However, if the doctrine is seen this way, then the freedom of God to unite himself with creatures in a manner which surpasses communion between others who are not God (Barth's view) is compromised by the need to affirm itself against others, that is, God might only have as much freedom as our experiences allow. Agnostic modalism follows: 'An immanent trinitarian theology … cannot be an analysis of what is "inside" God, but a way of thinking and speaking about the structure or pattern of God's self-expression in salvation history'; and as noted in Chapter 1, LaCugna argues that

condescension to be God for us into the immanent Trinity. For a full discussion of this issue, see Paul D. Molnar, 'The obedience of the Son in the theology of Karl Barth and of Thomas F. Torrance' *SJT*, vol. 67, no. 1 (2014): 50–69. See also Molnar, *Faith, Freedom and the Spirit*, chapter seven.

31 LaCugna, *God for Us*, 224, 211, 222. Cf. Molnar 'The Function of the Immanent Trinity', *SJT* (1989), 396 and Chapter 8. Bruce McCormack, *Orthodox and Modern*, thinks that Jüngel's attempt to maintain the distinction between the immanent and the economic Trinity in this way suggests that 'the "immanent Trinity" is regarded (in Hegelian fashion) as a "summarizing concept"' (256). Hence McCormack reads Jüngel as suggesting that '"The death of Jesus Christ … *forced* a differentiation between God and God"' (256). The immanent Trinity then simply describes what happened in the economy and thus 'God's historicity' as 'God's being in coming' (256). 'The immanent Trinity' then in McCormack's view, here 'addresses the capacity of God to undertake that which occurs economically' (256). The problem is that this thinking leads to the idea that the resurrection 'was the fulfillment of God's eternal being *as love*' (257); indeed, according to McCormack, it transformed the separation of the Son from the Father which occurred on the cross with the 'emergence of a new relation … at which the being in coming of God had aimed eternally'. In Barth's thinking God's being as love does not need to be fulfilled in what he does for us in his love. Rather, the resurrection expresses his free grace as a self-sufficient act of fulfilling the purposes of his love in the incarnation. The Father and Son were not separated in the event of the cross, but remained at one even in Jesus's experience of God-forsakenness. A separation of Father and Son would have disrupted the eternal oneness in being between the persons of the Trinity.

there *may* be distinctions in God, but not necessarily, since we have no 'transeconomic perspective' from which to know.[32] While Jüngel says nothing like this, he unintentionally opens the door to this kind of thinking by accepting Rahner's axiom without hesitation and by the way he states the function of the doctrine.[33]

32 LaCugna, *God for Us*, 225, 227. 'The immanent Trinity is not transhistorical, transempirical, or transeconomic ... to speak about God in immanent trinitarian terms is nothing more than to speak about God's life with us in the economy ... an immanent theology of God is an inexact effort to say something about God *as God is revealed in the economy* ... Speculating about the immanent Trinity is a kind of discernment ... a way to speak about the nature of God *with us* in the economy ... Because the essence of God is permanently unknowable as it is in itself, every attempt to describe the immanent Trinity pertains to the face of God turned toward us' (229–30). Hence, LaCugna believes, 'It would be better *if* the interrelationships of divine persons were located not in an intradivine sphere but in the mystery of the economy – which is where God exists anyway' (369). While it is certainly true that every attempt to say something about the immanent Trinity begins with the 'face of God turned toward us', our knowledge of that very God is indeed knowledge of who God is in eternity. That is what is lost in LaCugna's analysis. Thus, her agnosticism at this point leads her to assert later on that 'God's existence is grasped in relationship to us; we do not know God "in Godself" or "by Godself"' (334). This is because within 'a relational ontology being is found always in being-with-another; thus it is impossible to say what something is by-itself or in-itself' (334). Here her relational ontology disallows the very thing that I am claiming, with Barth and Torrance, is absolutely essential if it is the triune God that we are referring to when we speak about the Trinity. For a positive understanding of God's freedom in se and ad extra, see Christopher R. J. Holmes, *Revisiting the Doctrine of the Divine Attributes: In Dialogue with Karl Barth, Eberhard Jüngel, and Wolf Krötke* (New York: Peter Lang, 2007), 50ff. Strangely, Karen Kilby is cited by Gijsbert van den Brink as arguing for a type of agnosticism similar to LaCugna when she maintains that there is no need to assume that the doctrine of the Trinity provides 'a deep understanding of the way God really is' ('Social Trinitarianism' *IJST*, 344). This, even though she also quite properly opposes projectionism (338).

33 Cf. Eberhard Jüngel, *God as the Mystery of the World: On the Foundation of the Theology of the Crucified One in the Dispute between Theism and Atheism*, trans. by Darrell L. Guder (hereafter: *God as the Mystery of the World*) (Grand Rapids, MI: Eerdmans, 1983), 392, 316f. Cf. also Molnar, *SJT*,

Theological Agnosticism

LaCugna's agnostic view is not grounded in the incarnate Word and, as seen in Chapter 1, is similar to the agnostic views of Sallie McFague and Gordon Kaufman. LaCugna asserts that history shows that to argue on the basis of a transeconomic perspective must mean that we leave the economy behind; then the doctrine has no bearing on our life of faith. Certainly we cannot leave the economy behind without such an effect, but that hardly means we *must* leave the economy if we argue on the basis of God's inner trinitarian life. With Schoonenberg, she claims that the question of whether God would be trinitarian apart from salvation history 'is purely speculative and cannot be answered on the basis of revelation'.[34]

Yet it is precisely on the basis of revelation that Barth believed we *must* answer this question or succumb to subjectivism, pantheism, panentheism (which is worse than pantheism)[35] or dualism just because of an agnostic inability to perceive that the truth of revelation hinges on the fact that God is in revelation what he is in himself. Hence,

---

vol. 42, no. 3: 390–98, Thompson, *Modern Trinitarian Perspectives*, 32f., 58ff. and Chapter 8. See also Holmes, *Revisiting the Doctrine of the Divine Attributes*, 124ff.

34   LaCugna, *God for Us*, 227; also, 334. For more on Schoonenberg's thinking in this regard, see Molnar, *Faith, Freedom and the Spirit*, 209ff.

35   *CD* II/1, 312. 'The mythology of a merely partial and ... selected identity of God with the world, which under the name of panentheism has been regarded as a better possibility than undiluted pantheism, is really in a worse case than is that of the latter.' This, because it must mingle God with something else idealistically or materialistically and it leads either to materialism or to spiritualism. See also, *CD* II/1, 562 where Barth says that pantheism and panentheism manifest a false understanding of 'the freedom of God's will' which 'excludes' all views that see the relation between God and 'the reality distinct' from God 'as a relation of mutual limitation and necessity'. Both these problematic views think of the existence of 'this other reality' as something that 'belongs in some way to the essence and existence of God Himself'. As mentioned earlier in n. 20, this view by Barth puts the lie to the idea that he would agree with Schleiermacher in supposing that God's relation to the world was made 'essential' to God. In reality, Barth believed that 'God is one in the fullness of His deity and constant in its living vigor. He does not therefore acquire fullness and life from his relation to creation. He has it in Himself before all creation and every relation to it' (*CD* II/1, 592).

It is not true, then that the father-son relation is itself originally and properly a creaturely reality. It is not true that in some hidden depth of His essence God is something other than Father and Son. It is not true that these names are just freely chosen and in the last analysis meaningless symbols, symbols whose original and proper non-symbolical content lies in that creaturely reality. On the contrary, it is in God that the father-son relation, like all creaturely relations, has its original and proper reality.[36]

---

36 *CD* I/1, 432. Cf. also *CD* II/1, 324ff., 286f. and Torrance, *The Trinitarian Faith*, 71, 133 and 246. This is an enormously important point for two reasons: (1) our understanding of God as Father and Son is not based on our choice of symbols which we could then change; and (2) any attempt to understand God in his unique being and act as Father and Son from our human experiences of fathers and sons will never be based on the revelation of God in Christ but always on us and to that extent will represent an attempt to know God without God by bypassing revelation in its identity with Jesus Christ. This second choice is indeed the one taken by those who make relationality the subject and God the predicate in their thought. An especially clear case of such thinking can be seen in the statement that 'if divine persons are relations, as I have been arguing, we use motherly language specifically on those occasions when we are involved in relationships in God that make it apt for us to call on God as mother', Paul S. Fiddes, *Participating in God: A Pastoral Doctrine of the Trinity* (Louisville, KY: Westminster John Knox Press, 2000), 94. Fiddes can say this because for him 'God is the name for an event or happening of relationships in which we are engaged' so that 'human "life-in-relationship" is our best way into a vision of God as Trinity', Paul S. Fiddes, 'Relational Trinity: Radical Perspective', *Two Views on the Doctrine of the Trinity* (Grand Rapids, MI: Zondervan, 2014), 159–85, 160. In this thinking relationality displaces God who *IS* the eternal Father, Son and Holy Spirit because he is and not because we have experimented with our symbols to speak of experiences of relationality that we think are experiences of God. If Barth is right and I think he is, then there is no way into a vision of God that is possible apart from a specific engagement with Jesus Christ himself and his revelation of God the Father through the power of his Holy Spirit and thus in faith which is tied to him alone and not to any or all our experiences of relationality. This thinking would explain why Fiddes can so uncritically respond to Barth's view of the immanent Trinity claiming that 'the projection of the immanent Trinity as a self-sufficient divine grouping from which man is, or even might be, absent is sheer speculation; this is not actually how God has manifested himself', *The Creative Suffering of God* (Oxford: Clarendon Press, 1988), 122. The immanent

Further, speaking of the fact that authority in the Church reflects the authority of God in his revelation, Barth writes: 'This is just as certain as that fatherhood is found first not on earth but in heaven, not among men but in God Himself.'[37] Nonetheless, LaCugna suggests that: 'A theology of the immanent Trinity does not refer to "God as such apart from relationship to us" but to "God revealed in Christ and the Spirit." '[38] Substituting her 'relational ontology' for an 'ontology of substance' she argues that:

> What makes God to be God, is to be the Unoriginate yet Originating person who by virtue of love of another brings about all that exists. Now it is impossible to say exactly and definitively what this personal *ousia* of God is, because this would entail explaining both what it means for God to be Unoriginate Origin ... and what it means for divine persons *to be* in communion with every creature. What God *is* remains unspeakable.[39]

LaCugna's two crucial errors can be seen at work here. First, unable to distinguish God from creatures, she argues that as originating person God is in relation to us simply because God loves another. Which other is she referring to? Is it the Father's love for the Son or is it God's love of creatures? Here a clear conceptual distinction must be made to avoid pantheism. LaCugna fails to make such a distinction because she is not thinking of God on the basis of revelation but of God incorporated into

Trinity for Barth is not a 'projection' or a 'grouping' but who God eternally is in his unique relations as Father, Son and Holy Spirit, the one who loves in freedom and is free in his love. The very idea that we could never be absent from those eternal relations obviates God's eternal freedom because it suggests that God never existed or could have existed without us. So it is entirely wrong to say that God is manifested as one who was never without us; God existed without us as the one who eternally willed to be with us and is with us in his Word and Spirit in the freedom of his grace and not in the form of relations which we might imagine are divine relations. Without this proviso we could mistakenly say, with Fiddes, that the world and we are 'necessarily included' in God's inner relations because the ' "for us" is included in whatever is meant by the eternal begetting of the Son by the Father. There can be no self-sufficient, self-contained society of the Trinity, for God has not chosen to be in that way' (123). All of this thinking clearly reduces the immanent to the economic Trinity.

37 *CD* I/2, 587.

38 LaCugna, *God for Us*, 227.

39 LaCugna, *God for Us*, 334.

her relational ontology that views the Trinity as a description of persons (divine and human) in communion. Second, it is precisely her agnosticism that allows her to substitute her arbitrary relational ontology for an ontology shaped by the nature and activity of God revealed in Christ through the Holy Spirit and recognized in faith. Since she believes we do not know what God is, she clearly does not think of God as the eternal Father, Son and Spirit. Rather, God can be described by many metaphors because of his incomprehensibility.[40] Of course this is why she, like McFague and many others, names God mother or Godself.[41] But this view is fatal to faith and theology, not because it seeks to join our knowledge of God in se to God's actions for us, but because it dissolves God's aseity into his being for us and thus leaves us with no God existing a se. As already noted, LaCugna *says* she endorses a God existing a se[42] but merely pays lip service to such a God and so concludes: '*The life of God does not belong to God alone.*'[43] Indeed,

---

40 See Catherine Mowry LaCugna, 'God in Communion with Us', in *Freeing Theology: The Essentials of Theology in Feminist Perspective*, ed. LaCugna, (San Francisco: HarperSanFrancisco, 1993), chapter four.

41 LaCugna, *God for Us*, 18. While she believes it is appropriate to name God Mother, she will avoid the distracting name Father and use God and Godself. Her 'agenda' is ultimately to refer merely to God with us rather than 'probing an intradivine realm ("God *in se*")' (n. 7). Yet she also believes that Mother expresses better than Father the deep physical bond between God and creation (303). Both Roland Frye and Robert Jenson have pointed out the gnostic and polytheist connotations in speaking of God as Mother or Godself. Cf. Kimel (ed.), *Speaking the Christian God*, 17ff. and 95ff.

42 LaCugna, *God for Us*, 221, 228, 321–2, 355. See also the Review Symposium on *God for Us* in *Horizons*, vol. 20, no. 1 (1993): 127–42 at 139 where LaCugna responds to criticism indicating that she thinks abandoning the language of 'economic' and 'immanent' will lead to greater precision (!) and that this does not imply that she does not 'believe in the immanent Trinity'. The problem of course with this particular belief is that she insists that her relational ontology must take the place of any notion of self-sufficiency for God. This leads directly to her confusion of God and the world. Our view of God is certainly one that is relational but our concept of relation is dictated by God's free relations in se and ad extra. In other words, the Christian God is and remains self-sufficient even in his actions on our behalf. Unless that is true, the content of the concept of God is nothing more than a description of our necessary relations with others within the sphere of creation.

43 LaCugna, *God for Us*, 354.

Christian orthopraxis must correspond to what we believe to be true about God: that God is personal ... ecstatic and fecund love, that God's very nature is to exist toward and for another. The mystery of existence is the mystery of the *commingling* of persons, divine and human, in a common life, within a common household ... Our relationship to others, which is indistinguishable from our relationship to Jesus Christ, determines whether we are or are not finally incorporated into God's household.[44]

It is just this commingling which Barth insisted Chalcedon sought to avoid. She does not simply reject a doctrine of the immanent Trinity but, as seen in Chapter 1, uncritically emulates Gordon Kaufman who sees it as a symbol reflecting the threefold structure of Christian experience which we cannot say is internal to God because we have no access to

this innermost essence ... in history or revelation; and anything said about it is pure speculation. About the trinitarian structure of God's being-in-revelation, however, we can speak with confidence, because this is the only way to conceive what *is* given directly in Christian revelation.[45]

Any distinction between the immanent and economic Trinity is thus a 'pseudo-distinction'.

Since the symbol 'God' represents *our* ultimate point of reference for unifying our experiences, Kaufman, as seen in Chapter 1, embraces both a naïve pantheism and a form of self-justification:

The symbol 'God' suggests a reality, an ultimate tendency or power, which is working itself out in an evolutionary process ... The symbol 'God' enables us to hold this whole grand evolutionary-historical sweep together ... God – this whole grand cosmic evolutionary movement – is giving birth, after many millennia, to finite freedom and self-consciousness in and through our human history, in *us* ... .[46]

---

44 LaCugna, *God for Us*, 383–4, emphasis mine. By comparison, for Barth, 'Revelation remains identical with Christ and Christ remains the object of Christian faith, even though He lives in Christians and they in Him' (*CD* I/2, 118).

45 Kaufman quoted in LaCugna, *God for Us*, 226.

46 *TNA*, 43f.

This leads to a dualism which represents Jesus's eternal sonship as the product of Christian triumphalism rather than a reality which Christians acknowledge and describe. Salvation cannot come in one individual because this is not in keeping with contemporary pluralism or self-understanding which are dictated by modern biological and evolutionary theories. Moreover, according to Kaufman, belief in Jesus's eternal sonship reifies who Jesus is, instead of seeing him as a symbol of human self-sacrifice.[47] God and Christ are symbols we construct in order to create a better society; they help us relativize, humanize and liberate society; thus God's sovereignty is fundamentally irrelevant today and theology 'serves human purposes and needs, and it should be judged in terms of the adequacy with which it is fulfilling the objectives we humans set for it.'[48] Hence salvation 'comprises all the activities and processes within human affairs which are helping to overcome the violence and disruptions and alienations'.[49]

Similarly, instead of saying that Christ empowers us to live a life of love and communion with others, LaCugna believes that '*Entering into divine life therefore is impossible unless we also enter into a life of love and communion with others*.'[50] Indeed, 'According to the doctrine of the Trinity, God lives as the mystery of love among persons' and we should ask 'what forms of life best enable us to live as Christ lived.'[51] Yet if this is the case, we neither need Christ nor can we distinguish nature and grace; thus we create the forms of life which correspond to the patterns of relationality we glean from scripture. Not surprisingly, she thinks that 'the vocation and mission of *every* member of the church [is] to become Christ.'[52] Barth was very clear on this important issue: 'The relation between Jesus Christ and His church is, therefore, an irreversible relation. Whatever the glory and authority of the church may be, the glory and authority of Jesus Christ are always his own.'[53]

---

47 *TNA*, 50–6. For the Christological implications of this thinking, see Chapter 2. See also, Molnar, 'Myth and Reality', *Cultural Encounters* (2005) for more on this.

48 *TNA*, 19.

49 *TNA*, 57.

50 LaCugna, *God for Us*, 382.

51 LaCugna, *God for Us*, 378.

52 LaCugna, *God for Us*, 402. As noted in Chapter 1, Elaine Pagels has shown that this was a Gnostic but not a Christian belief.

53 *CD* I/2, 576. For Barth of course the church is the 'earthly-historical' form of the risen and ascended Christ's presence in history but it cannot be confused

The doctrine of the immanent Trinity should be a true understanding of who the transcendent God who is immanent in Christ and the Spirit in virtue of his transcendence is. It is necessary to know, even though it can be known only through revelation and even though we do not know God as God knows himself. Without this knowledge, agnosticism, pantheism and dualism become possible and compromise our understanding of God as Father, Son and Holy Spirit. God then becomes only a conceptual construct *of* our *experiences* in the economy rather than God himself acting in the economy as one who enables our human freedom. For Barth,

> The God of whom we speak is no god imagined or devised by men. The grace of the gods who are imagined or devised by men is usually a conditional grace ... and not the true grace which gives itself freely ... man's imagined grace is usually directly offered and accessible in some way to him and can be rather conveniently, cheaply, and easily appropriated.[54]

Thus human freedom is absolutely bound up with the fact that: 'If the Son therefore shall make you free, you shall be free indeed' Jn. 8:36.[55]

God and Relational Ontology

Ted Peters provides yet another perspective, and it is deeply influenced by the thought of Catherine LaCugna. In part, this will explain why

---

or equated with him as the living Lord and head of his body on earth. Thus, he writes that 'there is indeed correspondence, but no parity, let alone identity' between the church and Christ. 'Even in its invisible essence it is not Christ, nor a second Christ, nor a kind of extension of the one Christ ... it is His body, His earthly-historical form of existence. It is indeed in the flesh, but it is not, as He is, the Word of God in the flesh, the incarnate Son of God' (*CD* IV/3.2, 729). For an important discussion of Barth's ecclesiology, see Kimlyn J. Bender, *Karl Barth's Christological Ecclesiology* (Eugene, OR: Cascade Books, 2013).

54 Barth, *Evangelical Theology*, 152. Since this is so, we cannot say with LaCugna that participation in God's life is conditional on our entering into love and communion with others. The latter activity obviously follows our union with Christ. But union with Christ is not conditional on our love of others. God's grace is unconditional. There is no conditional salvation envisioned in this relationship.

55 Cf. *CD* II/2, 589ff. Cf. also *CD* IV/1, 744–5 and IV/2, 129, 496.

his theology exhibits problems similar to those of LaCugna and how his failure to understand the function of the doctrine of the immanent Trinity in the theology of Karl Barth contributed to this. Although Colin Gunton was quite critical of LaCugna's approach, he found much of Peters's presentation acceptable and only briefly complained that Ted Peters did not sufficiently ground his insights in a doctrine of the immanent Trinity;[56] this, despite the fact that Peters regards LaCugna's trinitarian theology as a 'real jewel'.[57] Since Peters believes that the point of trinitarian theology is to help us conceptualize God's work as creator and redeemer, he also believes that we need not assume that the three persons of the Trinity must be 'identical or equal in nature'. This, because 'the notion of one being in three persons is simply a conceptual device for trying to understand the drama of salvation that is taking place in Jesus Christ'.[58] With LaCugna, Peters thus advocates the chiastic model of emanation and return, according to which 'there is neither an economic nor an immanent Trinity'[59] since he thinks, with LaCugna, that 'by collapsing the distinction between the immanent Trinity and the economic Trinity, the inner life of God no longer belongs to God alone'.[60] Therefore, making no distinction between God's internal and external relations, Peters believes that God is personal since he is necessarily one who is in relationship with other persons. He thus analyzes Jüngel's adaptation of Rahner's axiom to advance the question and argues that if we then ask what is the status of God's relationality, we are caught in a dilemma. Either we insist that God is a se and not dependent on the world or that God's relations ad extra make God dependent on the world. According to Peters, Jüngel resolved this by affirming that 'relationality already exists within the divine being, already within the immanent Trinity'.[61] In an important digression, Peters argues that Jüngel has difficulty reconciling his position that God's being is in becoming with Luther's concept of paradox, which asserted that God's

56 Colin E. Gunton, Review of Ted Peters, *GOD as Trinity*, *Theology Today*, vol. 51, no. 1 (1994): 174–6.

57 Peters, *Trinity*, 122ff. While we have shown that she never even perceived God's freedom as Barth understood it, he believes that she 'extends the Barthian insight into practical spirituality' (123).

58 Peters, *Trinity*, 70.

59 Peters, *Trinity*, 125.

60 Peters, *Trinity*, 125.

61 Peters, *Trinity*, 91 and 143.

power is revealed under its opposite which is weakness; Peters believes that Barth and Jüngel removed Luther's paradox by arguing that 'Jesus' weakness and humility are not said to be opposed to divinity. Rather, they are *constitutive* of divinity'. From this Peters concludes that 'God is in the process of becoming Godself through relationship with the temporal creation'.[62]

Barth, however, argued that God was self-revealed and self-concealed (the only self-moved being);[63] thus revelation includes our

62 Peters, *Trinity*, 92, emphasis mine.

63 *CD* II/1, 268–69. Two extremely important points follow from this assertion: (1) God exists 'in the unity of spirit and nature' (267). To deny this, Barth says, would be to deny to God his ability to act, decide, to have a history – there would be no creation, redemption, revelation, reconciliation and 'of course, no eternal witness of the Son through the Father, no eternal procession of the Holy Spirit from the Father and the Son, no inner life of God' (267). (2) Barth therefore rejects false 'spiritualising' (which denies to God his nature as an acting personal subject precisely as the eternal Father, Son and Spirit), as well as 'false realism' which attempts to balance spirit and nature as well as 'inner and outer . . . in such a way that their relationship is treated as symmetrical and reversible' (268). God is thus not an 'It' nor a 'He' 'like a created person' but an 'I who knows about Himself, who Himself wills, Himself disposes and distinguishes, and in this very act of His omnipotence is wholly self-sufficient' (268). Importantly, Barth concludes by saying: 'In this formula we are simply interpreting the triune being of God as Father and Son in the unity of the Holy Spirit proceeding from both. This being as such and in its entirety is the being, the *essentia*, of the Godhead, and whatever else we may have to say about it will have to be understood as a definition of this being' (268). In this sense we must say that 'God is Spirit' (Jn. 4:24). From this it follows for Barth that as the only self-sufficient and self-moved being (since we are moved by others and God is not) God can act effectively for us: 'God's revelation draws its authority and evidence from the fact that it is founded on itself *apart from all human foundations*. God's commandment, God's grace and God's promise have a unique force because they are without reference to human strength or weakness. God's work is triumphant because it is not bound to our work, but precedes and follows it in its own way, which may also be the way of our work' (271, emphasis mine). These actions of God ad extra and for us are all compromised if 'we think of God's being as unmoved' or 'if we think of it as anything other than self-moved' (271). When Barth emphasizes that God is his decision here he does not mean to reduce God to his actions *ad extra*; he only means to stress that his acts and decisions are sovereign, free, living and therefore divinely effective just

sinful secularity without implying that God was in the process of becoming who he would be through relationship with the world.[64] By the revelation of the glory of the Lord through Christ's humiliation, death and resurrection, God demonstrated an eternal power as Father, Son and Holy Spirit that did not accrue to him in or from his relations with the world. This was God's positive freedom.[65] Peters inaccurately claims to be following Barth's original insights when he mistakenly criticizes Jüngel for thinking that 'because God is self-related, God can be world-related'.[66] He trades on an ambiguity in Jüngel's thought that can be avoided only by seeing God as the subject of both his external and internal relations. Barth reminds us:

> [God] does not need His own being in order to be who He is: because He already has His own being and is Himself ... If, therefore, we say

because they are the actions of the one and only being who 'exists absolutely in its act' (271). However, that act is the act of the eternal Father, Son and Holy Spirit and not the act of one who becomes this in his decision to relate with us as the 'revisionists' falsely think. That is why Barth insists that 'originally and properly there is no other beside or outside Him' (271). All of this is lost when, with LaCugna and Peters the distinction between the immanent and economic Trinity is abandoned. So instead of offering a confused assertion such as that 'trinitarian life is our life' Barth instead asserts that 'our quality of life can never be confused with His, or compared or contrasted with it as commensurate'. For Barth, 'The validity of every further statement about God, as a statement about the living God, depends on the avoidance of this confusion, or this comparison and contrast, between His life and ours' (272).

64 Cf. *CD* II/1, 324 and *CD* IV/2, 346–7.

65 *CD* II/1, 314ff. For Barth, 'the one God in His three modes of being corresponds to the Lord of glory. As it is of decisive importance to recognise the three modes of being, not only economically as modalism does, but, according to the seriousness of the divine presence and power in the economy of His works, as modes of being of the one eternal God Himself, so it is equally important to understand that God in Himself is not divested of His glory and perfections, that He does not assume them merely in connexion with His self-revelation to the world, but that they constitute His own eternal glory' (326–7).

66 Peters, *Trinity*, 93ff. As can be clearly seen in n. 63 previously and elsewhere in this book, Barth emphatically argues that it is only because God exists in sovereign freedom in his internal relations as Father, Son and Spirit that he can be world related *as* God in freedom and not in dependence on the world.

that God is *a se*, we do not say that God creates, produces or originates Himself ... He cannot 'need' His own being because He affirms it in being who He is ... what can need existence, is not God Himself, or His reality, but the reality which is distinct from Himself.[67]

Indeed in God himself there is history in partnership:

God was never solitary ... [but is] the Father's eternal begetting of the Son, and the Son's eternal being begotten of the Father, with the common work which confirms this relationship, in which it takes place eternally that the one God is not merely the Father and the Son but also, eternally proceeding from the Father and the Son, the Holy Ghost ... This history in partnership is the life of God before and above all creaturely life ... His inner union is marked off from the circular course of a natural process as His own free act ... it is not subject to any necessity. The Father and the Son are not two prisoners. They are not two mutually conditioning factors in reciprocal operation. As the common source of the Spirit, who Himself is also God, they are the Lord of this occurrence. God is the free Lord of His inner union.[68]

---

67 *CD* II/1, 306. See also *CD* I/1, 354 where Barth insists that God does not need 'a Second and then a Third in order to be One'.

68 *CD* IV/2, 344–5. Here one can see Barth's continued stress on distinguishing without separating the immanent and economic Trinity later in the *Church Dogmatics*. Importantly, when Barth asserts that God is Lord of his inner union, he does not mean that God therefore constitutes himself as triune by anticipating his relations with us. He means that God is not a prisoner of his freedom in eternity and thus God can relate with us effectively as Father, Son and Holy Spirit because that is who he is as the one who loves in freedom from all eternity and it is that God who elects us from all eternity in his Son, Jesus Christ. Barth here stresses that in God there is history in partnership because 'God was never solitary'; thus any such individualist thinking is rejected here because 'God was always Partner. The Father was the Partner of the Son, and the Son the Father ... the closed circle of the knowing of the Son by the Father and the Father by the Son which according to Mt. 11:27 can be penetrated only from within as the Son causes man to participate in this knowledge by his revelation' (344). This, according to Barth is the life of the immanent Trinity. We have access to this life only as the Son acts through his Holy Spirit to draw us into this partnership. Since God is thus Lord of his inner union as Spirit Barth says: 'This means that before all earthly history, yet also in it, He is the One who

Free from limits, conditions or restrictions, as one who is self-grounded and self-moved from his own center, God is not even, as it were, subject to himself (though he is self-limited):

> God has the prerogative to be free without being limited by His freedom from external conditioning, free also with regard to His freedom, free not to surrender Himself to it, but to use it to give Himself to this communion and to practise this faithfulness in it, in this way being really free, free in Himself.[69]

Hence God can and will be conditioned, but as a manifestation of his inner freedom and not in abandoning this;[70] as God remains lord of his life we must acknowledge who he is in se and ad extra.

is also for us (in His own history) transition, mediation and communication, and therefore the One who creates and gives life, the answer and solution to our problem. It is He Himself who does this, and He does it out of His own most proper being. *He is always active in Himself in His action among us.*' From this, Barth insightfully concludes that: 'The triune life of God, which is free life in the fact that it is Spirit, is the basis of His whole will and action even *ad extra*, as the living act which He directs to us' (345, emphasis mine). As they have lost this all-important emphasis, Peters and LaCugna have also lost the ability to speak decisively and clearly about God *acting* in history for us. Here Barth's thinking is thoroughly antithetical to the 'revisionist' thinking discussed in Chapter 4. In *CD* II/1, Barth insists that in his relation to us God 'is not fulfilling a kind of function necessary to Himself' but is acting freely since God is not 'the slave of His own immutable life' but the one who freely 'controls His own immutable life' (547).

69 *CD* II/1, 303.

70 See *CD* II/1, 303 and 314. 'God is free to be and operate in the created world either as unconditioned or as conditioned. God is free to perform His work either within the framework of what we call the laws of nature or outside it in the shape of a miracle' (314). Barth is not arguing here for a woeful idea of mutual conditioning between God and us; it is an argument for the fact that God is really free to act as he did in Jesus Christ such that God 'is free to be wholly inward to the creature and at the same time as Himself wholly outward'. Indeed God can 'be eternal also in our finitude' (315). Hence, even though God limits himself to a particular time and place in the incarnation, that does not mean that he needs the world and us to be who he is in himself and for us. Thus, 'The existence of the world is not needed in order that there should be otherness for Him. Before all worlds, in His Son He has otherness

Because Peters, following Pannenberg and Jenson here, neglects this important insight, he thinks that God is dependent on history to become who he will be. He rejects any *Logos asarkos* and describes Jesus as having to attain his eternal sonship in the future.[71] These insights

in Himself from eternity to eternity. But because this is so, the creation and preservation of the world, and relationship and fellowship with it, realised as they are in perfect freedom, without compulsion or necessity, do not signify an alien or contradictory expression of God's being, but a natural, *the* natural expression of it *ad extra*' (317). For a very interesting explanation of how God can be conditioned without implying that his actions in history are conditional on our response, see Barth's discussion of and rejection of Louis de Molina's *scientia media* (*CD* II/1 569ff.). His main objection of course is to the idea that for God's grace to be effective for us, our co-operation is necessary. He rejects the idea that God's will and action for us are conditional on what we do because they are accomplished and real for us exclusively in Christ. He argued that while the Thomists objected to this Jesuit thinking (that autonomous creatures 'constitute a riddle for the divine knowledge ... and God can read it only as this solution is given by the creature'), in the end they did not decisively overcome it because their thinking did not begin and end exclusively with the will of God that was and is decisively active and fulfilled in Christ himself. Nonetheless, he did say that the Thomists were right to reject this view as 'blasphemous' since 'the creature which conditions God is no longer God's creature, and the God who is conditioned by the creature is no longer God' (580). Over against this thinking, Paul Fiddes, commending his type of panentheism, believes that 'we can conceive of God as desiring that creation should contribute to God's satisfaction, bliss and fulfillment of purposes, without supposing that God's existence is dependent on anything but God's self' (*Two Views*, 108). This is an amazing statement in light of the fact that he also says on the same page that panentheism requires 'that in some sense God's eternal being is dependent on the development of history' but that 'his own existence is not' (108). This distinction without a difference illustrates that panentheism, as Barth claimed, is really worse than pantheism because it does indeed make God's being (which includes his existence) dependent on something other than God without realizing it and thus obliterates his free love of us that establishes and maintains human freedom in Christ alone.

71 See, for example, Peters, *Trinity*, 134ff. and 180. When Peters depicts Barth's understanding of God's eminent temporality as the simultaneity of past, present and future he misses Barth's point, that is, that God's time is not subject to the limitations and sin connected with our time. Instead he says: 'Barth goes on to insist that the eternal life of God is dynamized by the temporal actuality

compromise God's self-sufficiency and tend toward dualism partially because Peters's starting point for trinitarian reflection is experience rather than revelation. In fact he equates Christian experience in the Church with special revelation[72] and argues that:

> Relationality – a social-psychological concept ... is becoming the key for unlocking newer understandings of the divine life ... The trinitarian life is itself the history of salvation ... the fullness of God as Trinity is a reality yet to be achieved in the eschatological consummation.[73]

Grounding his doctrine of the Trinity on 'revelation and Christian experience' allows relationality and temporality as we experience these to become the subject with God the predicate. Hence the Trinity becomes a reality yet to be achieved instead of our future hope grounded in Jesus Christ who is the same yesterday, today and tomorrow in virtue of God's constancy. It is no accident that Barth insisted that God was at peace and never in conflict with himself,[74] while Peters, following

of the world' (149). So Peters wonders 'why we need to maintain simultaneity of past, present and future' at all. Thus, 'God's eternity is gained through the victory of resurrection and transformation' (175). For Barth, of course, God does not have to gain his eternity – he already has and is it in freedom. Peters believes his thinking is not captive to a metaphysical principle and that 'It is God who defines what divinity is' (145); yet if God depends on history then history defines God. All this confusion follows Peters's collapse of the immanent into the economic Trinity following LaCugna.

72 Peters, *Trinity*, 214. Following Rahner, he thinks that logical or analytic explanations of scripture must 'always refer back to the origin from which they came, namely the experience of faith that assures us that the incomprehensible God is really ... given us ... in ... Christ and the Spirit' (98) and thus mistakenly believes that the doctrine of the Trinity primarily refers to the experience of the 'beyond and intimate' (19). It is this experience of the beyond and intimate that becomes the norm for his trinitarian thinking. For more on this see Molnar, 'Experience and Knowledge of the Trinity in the Theology of Ted Peters: Occasion for Clarity or Confusion?', *Irish Theological Quarterly*, vol. 64 (1999): 219–43.

73 Peters, *Trinity*, 15–6. Cf. also 9, 78, 82. Following Hegel he believes that God is in the process of constituting himself and this includes God's saving relationship to the world.

74 *CD* II/1, 492–503.

Hegel, believes that God 'undergoes self-separation' and therefore needs an 'eschatological reunion'.[75]

Peters claims to find a further dilemma in Jüngel's position. Rejecting tritheism, Barth had opposed using the word person to describe Father, Son and Spirit and spoke of God's *ousia* as the person of God. If Jüngel follows Barth and affirms that God is personal in the divine substance then God would be only one person and would need the world in order to be personal; any correspondence between the immanent and economic Trinity would collapse. However, if Jüngel describes Father, Son and Spirit as 'a community of terms defined by their relations',[76] he could establish a correspondence between God in se and ad extra but would risk tritheism. Yet, this 'dilemma' is itself contrived, since for Barth, God is simultaneously one and three – not one and then three or three and then one;[77] and God is the subject of his own *ousia*. He does not equate person and substance as a modalist would, but uses person to express God's freedom in se and ad extra;[78] his entire theology, chiefly

75 Peters, *Trinity*, 16, 81–2. Cf. also 83–4.

76 Peters, *Trinity*, 95.

77 Cf. *CD* I/1, 349–52. God's *ousia* 'is not only not abrogated by the threeness of the "persons" but rather that its unity consists in the threeness of the "persons"' *CD* I/1, 349–50. Many think that for Barth God's oneness has priority over his threeness. Thus, Colin Gunton: 'As Pannenberg has written, the weakness of Barth's theology of the Trinity is that God's unity is seen as the *ground* of his threeness, rather than the *result*', 'The triune God and the freedom of the creature' in *Karl Barth: Centenary Essays*, ed. S. W. Sykes, [hereafter: *Karl Barth*], [Cambridge: Cambridge University Press, 1989], 60). For Barth, God is simultaneously one and three; neither threeness nor oneness comes first. Thus, 'the point from the very first and self-evidently is both the oneness of God and also the threeness of God, because our real concern is with revelation, in which the two are one' (*CD* I/1, 352).

78 Thomas F. Torrance, *Trinitarian Perspectives*, thinks that God can be properly seen as three persons and 'the infinite and universal Person' 97f. This would seem to correspond with what Barth means here although John Thompson is critical of Torrance calling this a 'difficult, even dubious suggestion' while still expressing in his own words what he sees as the positive point that Torrance wanted to make, namely, that 'God has in himself "a fullness and communion of personal being" and is at the same time "creatively personalising or person-constituting, in his activity toward us through the Son and in the Spirit", *Modern Trinitarian Perspectives*, 148. For a full explanation of exactly what Torrance meant by this and how he avoided any sort of modalism or tritheism, see Molnar, *Torrance: Theologian of the Trinity*, 203–4.

the divine perfections, illustrates that this is the particular freedom of the Father, Son and Holy Spirit.

> God's perfect being is the one being of the Father, the Son and the Holy Spirit. It is only as this that it has the perfection of which we have spoken ... What makes it divine and real being is the fact that it is the being of the Father, the Son and the Holy Spirit ... Here there is always one divine being in all three modes of being, as that which is common to them all. Here the three modes of being are always together ... We can never have one without the others. Here one is both by the others and in the others, in a *perichoresis* which nothing can restrict or arrest, so that one mode is neither active nor knowable externally without the others.[79]

Peters says Jüngel did not initially commit himself to either position; but he later followed Barth by rejecting the philosopher's deity as 'simple, transcendent, immutable, eternal, *a se* ... a God who is in-and-for-himself'. Thus the dilemma (pantheism or tritheism) is a pseudo-problem because the philosopher's God is not the one revealed in Jesus Christ, and so Peters asks:

> Why not just go all the way and affirm a God whose personhood is itself being constituted through God's ongoing relation to the creation? ... Why is it necessary that God be related to himself *ad intra* before becoming related to the world *ad extra*? Why does Jüngel feel constrained to depict God in terms of unrelated relatedness?[80]

Since God 'becomes personal through relationship with the other just as we do', Peters proposes that God's incarnate dealings with the world are part of an 'ongoing process of divine self-definition', and that by unequivocally accepting Rahner's axiom Jüngel may have abandoned

---

79 *CD* II/1, 659–60. Regarding God's pretemporality, supratemporality and posttemporality, Barth argued: 'There is just as little place for ... rivalry here as between the three persons of the Trinity, whose distinction is really ... the basis of these three forms ... there is in God both distinction and peace' (639). For those who would restrict themselves to *CD* I/1 for an understanding of Barth's doctrine of the Trinity, it is important to recall that Barth himself said: 'The more explicit development of this concept [of the essence of God] must be reserved for the doctrine of God' (*CD* I/1, 349). It is in II/1 that that development is offered.

80 Peters, *Trinity*, 95f.

his 'grip on a God of unrelated relatedness'. Hence, Peters pursues a trend found in Pannenberg, Moltmann and Jüngel as they head toward or beyond Rahner's axiom (rule),[81] claiming that 'the relationality God experiences through Christ's saving relationship to the world is constitutive of trinitarian relations proper. God's relations *ad extra* become God's relations *ad intra*'.[82]

However, this conclusion illustrates that Ted Peters never actually understood the importance of the doctrine of the immanent Trinity in Barth's theology. From revelation, Barth asserted that history, including God's sovereign actions in history on our behalf and our life of faith, do not define who God is in eternity but reveal who God is precisely by coming into conflict with our various philosophies. The idea that God's relations ad extra will become God's relations ad intra indicates a confusion and reversal of reason and revelation which follows if Christ is not seen as God's grace and if faith and revelation become the products of human experience in the form of a relational ontology, rather than the way we participate in God's truth by God's own self-sufficient act. For Barth, we can be certain about who God is and about our creation, reconciliation and redemption as each divine action, which includes history in a real relationship with God, is seen as grounded in God's eternal primary objectivity and not directly in the realm of secondary objectivity.

> If we wish to state who Jesus Christ is … we must also state or at least make clear – and inexorably so – that we are speaking of the Lord of heaven and earth [when speaking of the Word of Jn. 1.14], who neither has nor did have any need of heaven or earth or man, who created them out of free love and according to His very own good pleasure, who adopts man, not according to the latter's merit, but according to His own mercy, not in virtue of the latter's capacity, but in virtue of His own miraculous power. He is the Lord who … never ceases in the very slightest to be God, who does not give His glory to

---

81 Cf. esp. Peters, *Trinity*, 128–45.

82 Peters, *Trinity*, 96. Having completely lost the distinction between God's internal and external relations, Peters uses trinitarian categories to describe the experience of the beyond and intimate and concludes that the absolute becomes related through the incarnation and that the related becomes absolute eschatologically (146ff., 182ff.). For more details on this issue see Molnar, 'Experience and Knowledge of the Trinity in the Theology of Ted Peters'.

another. In this, as Creator, Reconciler and Redeemer, He is a truly loving, serving God. He is the King of all kings just when He enters into the profoundest hiddenness in 'meekness of heart'.[83]

As seen above, Thomas F. Torrance adopts this same position by saying that we must think from a center in God and not from a center in ourselves.[84] This important insight is missing from Ted Peters's presentation; thus he believes that God's relations with us in creation, reconciliation and redemption will determine the nature of God ad intra. This reversal of God and the world obliterates the distinction between the immanent and economic Trinity. Thus he believes that God becomes personal through relationships as we do and ignores the *Deus non est in genere* which, for Barth, precludes a higher unity between God and us which might explain his unique freedom and love.

> If they [creatures] belong to Him and He to them, this dual relationship does not spring from any need of His eternal being. This would remain the same even if there were no such relationship. If there is a connexion and relatedness between them and Him, God is who He is in independence of them even in this relatedness. He does not share His being with theirs. (*Er teilt sein Sein nicht mit dem ihrigen*). He does not enter with them into a higher synthesis. He does not mingle and blend Himself with them. He does not transform Himself into them. Even in His relationship and connexion with them He remains who He is.[85]

83 *CD* I/2, 133.

84 Cf., for example, Thomas F. Torrance, *The Trinitarian Faith*, 52f. and 'The Christian Apprehension of God the Father', in *Speaking the Christian God*, ed. Kimel, 123.

85 *CD* II/1, 311 (*KD* II/1, 350). Cf. also 187, 310. Speaking of the incarnation as an act of God's free love Barth said that 'while this event as a happening in and on the created world makes, magnifies and enhances the glory of God outwardly; inwardly it neither increases nor diminishes His glory, His divine being. For this is neither capable nor in need of increase or decrease. God did not and does not owe this happening to the world or to us any more than He did creation or the history of salvation ... It was not the case, nor is it, that His being necessitated Him to do it' (*CD* II/1, 513–14). Jesus Christ did not surrender or curtail his divinity in his self-concealment and self-offering but was divine in it showing his freedom to be humiliated on our behalf (*CD* II/1, 516ff). By

Positively, against agnosticism (even a future oriented one), we may have firm knowledge of our relationship with God; negatively, this knowledge cannot be achieved by relying on our own knowledge and existence (experience), as in making a relational ontology the subject with God the predicate. Panentheism and pantheism require this mutual dependence just because and to the extent that they do not advert to the *Deus non est in genere*. They fail to acknowledge that while 'no created beings are in fact so independent of each other that in spite of this relative mutual independence they have not also to some extent a certain mutual interdependence ... God confronts all that is in supreme and utter independence'.[86] Hence, the tendency to see God as a dependent deity misses God's essential freedom and expresses an apotheosis via agnosticism, monism and dualism; thus God will not be completely who he is becoming until salvation is complete:

> The immanent Trinity is consummated eschatologically, meaning that the whole of temporal history is factored into the inner life of God. God becomes fully God-in-relationship when the work of salvation – when the economic Trinity – is complete.[87]

Yet the critical insight which ought to be retrieved from Barth's theology is that God's freedom signifies that he is a se but not as defined by any philosophical principle. Ted Peters mistakenly supposes that *any* notion that God is a se must arise from philosophy whereas God's positive and negative freedom derive only from his own unique being and act as Father, Son and Spirit who loves in freedom. Moltmann and Pannenberg also incorrectly criticize Barth for this. However, for Barth,

> God is ... independent of everything that is not He. God is, whether everything else is, or is not, whether it is in this way or some other. If

contrast Peters believes that 'God ceases to be God – or, at least, what we might assume to be God – in order to become human and die' (*Trinity*, 13); God needs history to be relational.

86 *CD* II/1, 311.

87 Peters, *Trinity*, 181. Jesus is not the sole norm for Peters's understanding the Trinity; it is also our experience of the beyond and intimate as already mentioned. Thus Jesus must gain his divinity and the Holy Spirit must find his divinity by accomplishing community between Father and Son and with the world (*Trinity*, 180–1).

there is something other, it cannot precede God, it cannot place God in dependence upon itself . . .[88]

God is free in himself – before and apart from his freedom from conditioning ad extra: 'The fact that in every way He is independent of all other reality does not in itself constitute God's freedom but its exercise. It does not constitute His divinity, but He is divine in it.'[89] God does not need his own being but freely affirms himself in being.

This is a crucial ingredient of a doctrine of the immanent Trinity which disallows the mutual dependence intrinsic to created being but which is inapplicable to God's living and loving. It enables us to affirm that God's pretemporal, supratemporal and posttemporal freedom is the foundation for a theology of creation, reconciliation and redemption which does not overemphasize the past, the present or the future in order to grasp the mystery of Christ and the Spirit. Such overemphases indicate that no clear conception of the immanent Trinity was at work in Peters's thought in the first instance and that, in order to avoid these conclusions, which are tantamount to Feuerbach's reduction of theology to anthropology, we need a doctrine of the immanent Trinity which affirms the freedom of God's love in such a way that, once that is truly acknowledged by us, it will prevent us from espousing this kind of confusion and reversibility of history and eternity. I am not suggesting here that we construct a doctrine in order to prevent this reversal but that construction of such a doctrine is necessary in order to say who God is as the eternal Father, Son and Spirit. Then we may recognize that God is fully who he is without needing to submit to a metaphysical principle of relationality or temporality ad intra or ad extra. Only if we recognize this truth as the ground of salvation history may we see and preserve the freedom of God's grace, without which we have the pantheist conclusion that God will be who God is when salvation is complete. From this follows the dualist view that Jesus somehow is becoming the eternal Son (and thus is not this already – even before Easter) and that the economic Trinity is only eschatologically the immanent Trinity. Such thinking emerges to the extent that the deity of the Holy Spirit has been displaced by the experience of faith at the outset.[90]

88 *CD* II/1, 308.

89 *CD* II/1, 307f.

90 This is why Peters can say: 'As the Holy Spirit, God becomes so inextricably tied to our own inner self that the line between the two sometimes seems to us blurred' (*Trinity*, 19).

Christological Implications

How might the doctrine of the immanent Trinity clarify what Barth considered one of the hardest problems in Christology: does Jesus's humanity as such reveal his divinity?[91] For Barth, the incarnation was not a principle but an act whose terminus a quo is 'God in Himself' and whose terminus ad quem is 'man in himself'; thus 'the Word of God is properly understood only as a word which has truth and glory in itself and not just spoken to us'.[92]

> Revelation as such is not relative. Revelation in fact does not differ from the person of Jesus Christ nor from the reconciliation accomplished in Him ... we are saying something which can have only an intertrinitarian basis in the will of the Father and the sending of the Son and the Holy Spirit, in the eternal decree of the triune God, so that it can be established only as knowledge of God from God ... [revelation] has no basis or possibility outside itself [and] can in no sense be explained in terms of man and man's situation ... It is Jesus Christ Himself who here speaks for Himself and needs no witness apart from His Holy Spirit and the faith that rejoices in His promise received and grasped.[93]

Barth rejected the idea that Jesus's humanity *as such* disclosed his divinity because, as we have already seen, God's act of revelation involves both a veiling and an unveiling: 'Mystery is the concealment of God in which He meets us precisely when He unveils Himself to us, because He will not and cannot unveil Himself except by veiling Himself'. Since the form (sinful secularity) must be distinguished from the content we have a paradox; that is, 'a communication which is not only made by a ... phenomenon, but which must be understood ... in antithesis to what the phenomenon itself seems to be saying'. Only the Word can fulfill this paradox, while in other paradoxes, communication and form can be 'dissolved from a superior point of vantage'. Creaturely reality is an 'unsuitable medium' because 'it does not correspond to the matter but contradicts it. It does not unveil it but veils it'.[94]

91 Cf. *CD* I/1, 323.
92 *CD* I/1, 171.
93 *CD* I/1, 17–20.
94 *CD* I/1, 163–6. Cf. also *CD* II/1, 287.

Knowledge of God takes place indirectly and in faith without denying the secularity of the form of revelation. This is a miracle because what is revealed is actually concealed by the reality in which it takes place. There is neither a pure nature distinct from our fallen nature, nor can human reason grasp the mystery of God apart from Christ or without Christ 'in creaturely reality'. We can neither go behind the secularity to a God in himself nor can we identify God in himself with this sphere. 'If God's Word is revealed in it, it is revealed "through it," of course, but in such a way that this "through it" means "in spite of it". The secularity proper to God's Word is not in itself and as such transparent.' God's self-communication has a twofold indirectness: creatureliness and sinfulness. God's Word has really entered our sinful secularity making it 'an authentic and inalienable attribute of the Word of God itself. Revelation means the incarnation of the Word of God'. We can neither evade this secularity nor rely on it to reveal; due to sin 'we have no organ or capacity for God'.[95]

Responding to Gogarten, Barth asks: 'What would "God for us" mean if it were not said against the background of "God in Himself"?' God's love for us is 'unmerited and free' and must always be discussed against the background of God in himself; 'what constitutes the mercy of its revelation, of its being spoken to us, is that it is spoken to us in virtue of the freedom in which God could be "God in Himself" and yet He does not will to be so and in fact is not so, but wills to be and actually is "God for us"'. A sharp distinction between the immanent and economic Trinity follows: ' "God for us" does not arise as a matter of course out of the "God in Himself" ... it is true as an act of God, as a step which God takes towards man and by which man becomes the man that participates in His revelation.' Our human becoming is conditioned by God, but God

> is not conditioned from without, by man. For this reason – and we agree with Gogarten here – theology cannot speak of man in himself, in isolation [*Isolierung*] from God. But as in the strict doctrine of the Trinity as the presupposition of Christology, it must speak of God in Himself, in isolation [*Isolierung*] from man.[96]

---

95 *CD* I/1, 166, 168.

96 *CD* I/1, 171–2. This important statement of course is not an argument for the isolation of God from us as though God chose to remain God without us; it is rather an argument that: 'The love which God has in Himself as the

Thus we must seek and find the immanent Trinity 'in the *humanitas Christi*' as Luther did since 'we do not see and have directly'. Identifying God in himself and God for us would allow an *analogia entis* which neither takes seriously the incarnation nor our sinful secularity.

Barth rejected the idea that Jesus's humanity as such revealed his divinity because this idea would obliterate Jesus's pretemporal existence as the eternal Word and so would obscure the truth of the incarnation as an act of God and God's existence within time. The Chalcedonian formulation of the two natures, unmixed and not identical, distinguished but not separated, followed from a distinction of the kind just described. Identifying the immanent and economic Trinity would give us an axiom by which we could actually avoid both the need for faith and the need to admit that:

> God's presence is always God's decision to be present ... God's self-unveiling remains an act of sovereign divine freedom. To one man it can be what the Word says and to another true divine concealment ... In it God cannot be grasped by man or confiscated or put to work. To count on it is to count on God's free loving-kindness, not on a credit granted once and for all, not on an axiom to which one may have recourse once and for all, not on an experience one has had once and for all ... [Hence] even Christ's humanity stands under the caveat of God's holiness, i.e., that the power and continuity in which the man Jesus of Nazareth was in fact the revealed Word ... consisted here too in the power and continuity of the divine action in this form and not in the continuity of this form as such. As a matter of fact even Jesus did not become revelation to all who met Him but only to a few ... Revealing could obviously not be ascribed to His existence as such. His existence as such is indeed given up to death, and it is in this way, from death, from this frontier, since the Crucified was raised again, that He is manifested as the Son of God.[97]

Since God remained throughout the divine subject of the incarnation,[98] incarnation did not befall him, but was his own act in union with the

triune God has also turned and manifested itself in freedom outwards. It did not have to do this. It would not have been any less love if it had not done so. But it has done so' (*CD* II/1, 476). Without these inflections, God's activity within creation will always be confused with creation itself.

97 *CD* I/1, 321, 323.
98 Cf. *CD* I/2, 131ff. Cf. esp. *CD* II/1, 516ff. and IV/2, 46.

Father and the Spirit. This detail, which is noticeably absent from contemporary Christology, especially Spirit Christologies, enabled Barth to avoid agnosticism, pantheism and dualism in his Christology and doctrine of election and elsewhere.

Barth, Pannenberg and the Meaning of Revelation

Comparing Barth and Pannenberg should clarify the issue. For Barth, Jesus Christ is the Son who reveals and reconciles us to the Father. The dogma of the Trinity adds to scripture the interpretation that Jesus can reveal and reconcile because 'He reveals Himself as the One He is'. Apart from revelation and reconciliation, Jesus Christ already was in himself the Son or Word of God. Against an agnosticism which equates God's incomprehensibility with a higher essence of God in which there is no Son or Word, in which God exists with a different name, or no name (Johnson, McFague and LaCugna think God can be named mother while Rahner thinks of God as nameless and wordless) Barth argues that revelation and reconciliation have eternal validity because 'God is God the Son as He is God the Father'; the eternity and glory of God especially reflect this. This interpretation arose from the incomprehensible truth that creation and reconciliation are equally divine works based on the 'unity of the Father and the Son … we have to accept the simple presupposition on which the New Testament statement rests, namely, that Jesus Christ is the Son because He is'. As already seen in Chapter 2, all thinking about Jesus and thus about God *must* begin here. The dogma of the deity of Christ springs from this insight which can neither be proven nor questioned epistemologically; it refers to Christ's eternal 'antecedent' existence as Son or Word and is not a 'derivative statement' but a basic statement. Theology must begin with Jesus, the Word just because he is and his incarnate being in *no way* derives its meaning from anyone or anything else. As a *derivative* statement acquired from experiences of self-transcendence which include the experience of Christ and the Spirit, the doctrine of the Trinity then explains, in varying degrees for Johnson, Kaufman, LaCugna, McFague, Moltmann, Peters, Rahner and others, the content of Christian experience instead of God in se. While this dogma is not found in scripture, it properly refers to the true and eternal deity of Christ seen in his work of revelation and reconciliation. 'But revelation and reconciliation do not create His deity.'[99]

99 *CD* I/1, 414–15 and *CD* II/1, 625ff.

Failure to acknowledge Christ's true and eternal deity compromises the truth of revelation and reconciliation. Here Barth's concept of the *Logos asarkos* is important. As discussed in Chapter 3, he believed that the *Logos asarkos* was necessary because God acting for us must be seen against the background of God in himself who could have existed in isolation from us but freely chose not to. He rejected a *Logos asarkos* in his doctrine of creation if it implied a 'formless Christ' or 'a Christ-principle' rather than Jesus who was before the world with God as the Word; he rejected it in connection with reconciliation if it meant a retreat to an idea of God behind the God revealed in Christ; but he still insisted that it had a proper role to play in the doctrine of the Trinity and in Christology. In stark contrast, as we saw earlier, Robert Jenson rejects such a concept while others simply pay lip service to it or collapse it into the *Logos incarnandus*, because history rather than God acting in history was determining their thinking at that point; Jenson himself was trying to reconcile God's freedom with Rahner's axiom as it stands (with the vice versa).[100] Ted Peters follows Jenson's thinking in this matter. As I have argued earlier and elsewhere, while Bruce McCormack claims to uphold the reality of the *Logos asarkos* prior to the incarnation, his historicized Christology leads him to effectively deny the reality of the *Logos asarkos* as when he writes, commenting on what he takes to be Barth's 'revised' doctrine of the Trinity in *CD* IV/1 that: '*There is no longer any room left here for an abstract doctrine of the Trinity. There is a triune being of God – only in the covenant of grace.*'[101] Such thinking results from the problematic idea that:

100 As noted earlier, Jenson believes that such a concept prevents the procession of the Son from being the same as Jesus's mission. Indeed it does; precisely in order to prevent God's eternal freedom from being confused with his freedom for us. Again, I am not arguing here for a separation of Jesus's humanity and divinity but for the fact that, unless his mission is seen against the background of his being *in se* before the world was, then his deity will be equated with or seen as the outcome of history. We have already seen how this thinking leads Jenson and Peters to displace the immanent Trinity from their thinking about the historical Jesus and the Spirit and thus to argue for an immanent Trinity that will exist eschatologically. That is why Jenson substitutes Christ's resurrection for God's *ousia* and that is why Pannenberg thinks that Christ's resurrection constitutes his sonship.

101 McCormack, 'Election and the Trinity: Theses in Response to George Hunsinger' (ed.) Dempsey, 128, emphasis mine. See Chapter 3, 110ff. for a full discussion of this.

If, in Jesus Christ, God has elected to become human, then *the human history of Jesus Christ is constitutive of the being and existence of God in the second of God's modes* to the extent that the being and existence of the Second Person of the Trinity cannot be rightly thought of in the absence of this human history.[102]

As discussed in Chapter 3, Barth refused to discredit Christ's antecedent existence precisely because his deity could not be recognized without distinguishing between the Son of God in himself and in his actions for us. Without a clear acknowledgment of this distinction there could be no recognition of the freedom of grace either. While Pannenberg emphasizes the need to grasp Christ's eternal sonship,[103] and neither opposes the importance of the dogma nor advocates detaching the 'for us' from Christ's antecedent existence, he differs from Barth regarding this distinction. Similarly, Peters and LaCugna do not overtly deny the 'antecedently in himself', insofar as they argue that this is needed to secure our understanding of salvation and redemption. *However*, their thinking about Christ's eternal sonship is, in Barth's words, in the grip of an 'untheological speculative understanding of the "for us" '.[104] That is the issue. Since Christ's antecedent existence precludes an untheological understanding here, it must be acknowledged first. Several implications follow.

First, failure to hear this as the *basis* of our grasp of God's being for us turns his being for us into 'a necessary attribute of God. God's being is then essentially limited and conditioned as a being revealed, i.e., as a relation of God to man'.[105] Revelation and reconciliation are no longer

102 McCormack, *Orthodox and Modern*, 223, emphasis mine. For a discussion of these issues, see Molnar, 'The Perils of Embracing a "Historicized Christology"', *Modern Theology*, vol. 30, no. 4 (October) 2014: 454–80 and *Faith, Freedom and the Spirit*, Chapters 3 and 5.

103 For example, Pannenberg, *Systematic Theology 2*, 370ff.

104 *CD* I/1, 420.

105 *CD* I/1, 421. See Molnar, 'The Function of the Immanent Trinity' *SJT* (1989) and Chapter 8 for a discussion of how this problem manifests itself in the theology of Jürgen Moltmann. Moltmann conceives Christ's antecedent existence in terms of suffering love, which is more blessed in giving than in receiving, and so sees God's actions in history as necessary attributes of God. Indeed as Stanley Grenz notes, for Moltmann: 'God is not immutable. Insofar as the historical event of the cross constitutes God's eternal being, God not only

seen as acts of grace since God's nature is to forgive and human nature must have a God who forgives. This is what happened to LaCugna and Peters. Instead of the triune God *freely* acting for us *within* history, we are told that 'trinitarian life is our life', that it does not belong to God alone, and that God can *only* exist for us; this is why Peters mistakenly criticized Jüngel and Rahner for asserting that God is self-related before being related to the world. These views exhibited a tendency seen in the Christologies of Pannenberg and Rahner to make God dependent on history. Pannenberg believes Barth failed to ground the doctrine of the Trinity in revelation but that Rahner made progress with his thesis of identity, although by keeping the Father transcendent, he did not go far enough; he should have seen that the Father 'has made himself *dependent* upon the course of history'.[106] Therefore, the truth that Jesus is the Son of God depends on contingencies within history: "The statements are true if the conditions hold.'[107] Hence, 'the Easter event is not merely the basis of the knowledge that Jesus of Nazareth even in his earthly form was the eternal Son of God, but also *decides* that he was this by giving retrospective confirmation'.[108] Pannenberg's belief that Jesus's human self-distinction from the Father is the ground of his divine Sonship virtually eliminates any genuine preexistent sonship:

> The eternal Son is first ... an aspect of the human person ... Hence self-distinction from the Father is constitutive for the eternal Son. [Indeed] the difference between Father and Son in God's eternal essence, *depend* upon, and take place in, the fact that God as Father is manifest in the relation of Jesus to him ... [Furthermore] The self-distinction of the Father from the Son is not just that he begets the Son but that he hands over all things to him, so that his kingdom and *his own deity are now dependent upon the Son*.[109]

affects the world but is also affected by the world and above all by humankind' (*Rediscovering the Triune God*, 78). Peters agrees with this aspect of Moltmann's thought.

106 Wolfhart Pannenberg, *Systematic Theology, Volume 1*, trans. by Geoffrey W. Bromiley (Grand Rapids, MI: Eerdmans, 1991), 327–9, emphasis mine; and 296.

107 Pannenberg, *Systematic Theology 1*, 56.

108 Pannenberg, *Systematic Theology 1*, 331, emphasis mine.

109 Pannenberg, *Systematic Theology 1*, 310–13, 322, emphasis mine. Cf. also *Systematic Theology 2*, 391.

Barth's positive conception of freedom neither requires nor permits this internal and external dependency which inevitably obscures grace. According to Pannenberg, while the Father is neither begotten nor sent, 'the designation "Father" might well involve a *dependence* of the Father on the Son and *thus* be the basis of true reciprocity in the trinitarian relations'.[110] While we will stress, against Rahner, that there should indeed be true mutuality between the Father and Son within the Trinity, here *true reciprocity* does not express the *free* mutual relatedness of Father, Son and Spirit and thus cannot be a reliable basis for our human freedom. Instead, it follows the introduction of history into the Godhead in such a way that, in some sense, history determines the outcome of the Father's relation to the Son within history. God is no longer the free subject of his own internal and external relations: 'the divine essence overarches each personality' such that 'love is a power which shows itself in those who love ... Persons do not have power over love. It rises above them and thereby gives them their self-hood ... This applies especially to the trinitarian life of God.'[111] Here it appears that love is the subject, God's freedom to love is the predicate and God's love for us is conditional. Having said this, it is important to realize, as I have previously stated, that while Pannenberg does indeed insist on God's freedom 'and upon the fact that his eternity is not grounded in the

---

110 Pannenberg, *Systematic Theology 1*, 312, emphasis mine.

111 Pannenberg, *Systematic Theology 1*, 430 and 426-7. Barth helps us to see the problem with this remark because he insists that God's love is his personal action in himself and for us. Therefore, it cannot be conceptualized correctly as a power over which he has no control. That would deny his free Lordship over his own inner life. Hence, Barth insists that when we consider the fact that God is love as stated in 1 Jn. 4, this must be understood 'personally: He is the One who loves' (*CD* II/1, 286). This is neither childish, naïve nor anthropomorphic. Rather, 'the personal way in which Holy Scripture speaks corresponds absolutely and exclusively to the fact that God is not something, but someone' (*CD* II/1, 286). God thus is the 'person' who 'surpasses all our concepts and ideas of person' and thus as personal God can act, know and will and love in himself and do so freely (*CD* II/1 283-7); on this basis God can be gracious and is gracious and merciful toward us. Thus, 'God's act is His loving. It is His blessedness in so far as it is His essence even apart from us. But He wills to have this same essence, not merely for Himself alone, but also, having it for Himself, in fellowship with us. He does not need us and yet he finds no enjoyment in His self-enjoyment' (*CD* II/1, 283).

historical process [e.g. *Systematic Theology I*, 367, 376–7] his method will not allow him to maintain the character of this insight … [A] God who depends upon the course of history is in fact conditioned by the outcome of history; his freedom is compromised.'[112]

Second, failure to recall that the Son of God for us is 'antecedently the Son of God in Himself' means failure to recognize that theology is knowledge of a 'divine act' (knowledge of faith); its terminus a quo and terminus ad quem is the actual stepping forth of God from his inaccessibility. This influenced Barth's doctrine of analogy which stressed that God is by nature hidden from human insight and that there are no analogies which are true in themselves. Today, instead of seeing God stepping forth from his inaccessibility to meet us, many see God's being as somehow *inherent* in the world process so that God's eternal sonship becomes the product of certain historical events, rather than their

---

112 Molnar, 'Some Problems with Pannenberg's Solution to Barth's "Faith Subjectivism"', *SJT* 48 (1995), 331. Indeed Pannenberg quite rightly does not wish to collapse the immanent into the economic Trinity and even criticizes Robert Jenson for not making a distinction necessary to maintain the priority of the immanent over the economic Trinity. He also criticizes Jenson for rejecting the *Logos asarkos* outright noting that if Jenson holds that the Son's eternal 'birth from the Father' has priority over his temporal history, 'it is difficult to see how the notion of *logos asarkos* can still be rejected', Wolfhart Pannenberg, 'Eternity, Time and the Trinitarian God' *Trinity, Time, and Church: A Response to the Theology of Robert W. Jenson* (ed.) Colin E. Gunton (Grand Rapids, MI: Eerdmans, 2000), 62–70, 68. Regarding the priority of the immanent Trinity Iain Taylor, *Pannenberg on the Triune God* (London/New York: T & T Clark/Continuum, 2007), notes Pannenberg's inconsistency, 42–4. Taylor's important book will be discussed in more detail shortly. Here it is necessary to stress that he thinks that while Pannenberg did indeed wish to uphold God's freedom, still 'his making God's deity dependent on the establishment of the kingdom on earth does tie the hands of the trinitarian God *in se*' (42). He helpfully cites two important texts to show that on the one hand Pannenberg rightly wanted to say what I have indicated Barth and Torrance also said, namely, that 'God is the same in his eternal essence as he reveals himself to be historically' (42 citing Pannenberg, *Systematic Theology I*, 331); and, on the other hand, Pannenberg's thinking led him also to say improperly that 'the progress of events *decides* concerning his deity as well as the deity of the Son' (42, again citing Pannenberg, *Systematic Theology I*, 329). As we shall see, Taylor believes at this point that Pannenberg's thinking is not trinitarian enough.

presupposition, inner meaning and concluding goal. Analogies are thus considered true in themselves just as Jesus, in his humanity as such, is thought to reveal God. All theologians assert God's incomprehensibility but many do not allow Jesus Christ, the incarnate Word to govern their conception of God's incomprehensibility from *beginning* to *end*. We have been exploring this difficulty at length in this book and its significance today cannot be stressed too strongly.

Third, restricting the task of theology to understanding Christ in his revelation would mean that the criterion for this understanding would 'have to be something man himself has brought'; Jesus will be called the Son of God 'on the basis of our value judgment',[113] and Ebionite or Docetic Christology will result. The christological and trinitarian implications of this important insight were discussed earlier in Chapter 2. Interestingly, Pannenberg now approaches Christ's deity by not considering the divine nature 'in isolation'. This must be discovered, according to Pannenberg, 'in his human reality'. As seen earlier in Chapter 2, his eternal sonship

> precedes his historical existence on earth and must be regarded as the creative basis of his human existence. If the human history of Jesus is the revelation of his eternal sonship, we must be able to perceive the latter in the reality of the human life. The deity is not an addition to this reality. It is the reflection that the human relation of Jesus to God the Father casts on his existence, even as it also illumines the eternal being of God.[114]

However, if the human history of Jesus is the revelation, then how do we distinguish, and why must we acknowledge a preexistent divine sonship as the creative basis for our present insights? Since Jesus's deity is here conceived as 'the reflection that the human relation of Jesus to God the Father casts on his existence' there can be neither a clear distinction between an act of God coming into history in Jesus, nor a need to believe in Jesus's sonship from the outset,[115] since it is

---

113 *CD* I/1, 421.

114 *Systematic Theology 2*, 325. Chapter 10 concerns the deity of Christ.

115 That is why Pannenberg explains that today we cannot begin Christology by acknowledging Jesus's uniqueness as the Word (beginning with the incarnation as a presupposition) and argues that this must first be established (*Jesus – God and Man*, 279, 34; see Molnar, *Incarnation and*

already an aspect of his humanity; it is an insight which comes from the community as a retroactive perception based in history itself. His deity can neither be the free subject of the incarnation nor can it be equated with his eternal sonship as it *is* from eternity; his sonship is first an aspect of his humanity and then, because of the historical event of the resurrection, becomes what it was supposed to have been.

Pannenberg seems to maintain both the eternal reality of Jesus's humanity[116] and that 'the assuming of human existence by the eternal Son is not to be seen as the adding of a nature that is alien to his deity. It is the self-created medium of his extreme self-actualization *in consequence* of his free self-distinction from the Father, that is, a way of fulfilling his eternal sonship.'[117] But to see the humanity this way means it cannot be distinguished from his deity as the medium in and through which God acts toward us and for us within our humanity and we can hardly avoid concluding that the Son needed to become incarnate to actualize his eternal sonship if this is described as 'his extreme self-actualization *in consequence* of his free self-distinction from the Father';[118] this obscures the incarnation as the merciful act of condescension on the part of God for us (grace).[119] It is no accident that Pannenberg frequently substitutes Jesus's message for his person. Indeed, 'In the debate about the figure of Jesus it is of decisive importance that we should not put his person at the center. The center, rather, is God, the nearness of his rule, and his

Resurrection, 264ff.); it is why he explicitly seeks a historical Jesus behind the biblical texts (*Basic Questions in Theology*, 1, 149); it is also why in contrast to Barth, Pannenberg espouses a two-stage Christology based on his Christology from below which cannot do justice to the uniqueness of Christ in his true divinity and true humanity (see Molnar, *Incarnation and Resurrection*, 282–88).

116 *Systematic Theology* 2, 367, n. 126.

117 *Systematic Theology* 2, 325, emphasis mine.

118 This is a crucial point that is missed by Kent Eilers, *Faithful to Save: Pannenberg on God's Reconciling Action* (London/New York: Bloomsbury, T & T Clark, 2011), 39ff.

119 Pannenberg's thinking is echoed by many today. The problem here is that the incarnation is not a *consequence* of Jesus's free self-distinction from the Father as the Son within the eternal Trinity because that self-actualization was who God was and is and would have been even without the incarnation. Incarnation rather is a consequence of God's free decision to relate with us as he has elected to do in Jesus Christ; that election is indeed the beginning of God's ways and works ad extra.

fatherly love.'[120] For Barth, there is no debate about the figure of Jesus. He *is* the Son in whom we are confronted with a decision to accept him for who he is, that is, the kingdom of God which is present and future, or to seek the ground of revelation in someone or something else. For Pannenberg, Jesus's appearance in history involved a claim 'that needed divine confirmation'[121] which the community saw in his resurrection. For Barth his claim was grounded in his being as the Son who could forgive sins; hence the power of the resurrection was not absent from Jesus's earthly life since this power is that of God's presence in his person and work.[122] This is why Barth rejected two-stage Christology[123] while Pannenberg believes: 'Only the Easter event determines what the meaning was of the pre-Easter history of Jesus and who he was in his relation to God.'[124] This lack of precision implies that Jesus's identity is in some sense dependent on the community: 'Only by way of the relation of Jesus to the Father can we decide how and in what sense he himself may be understood to partake of deity, namely, as the Son of this Father.'[125] Yet this is not our decision at all; we may only accept him as he was and is. Since Jesus Christ is the power and wisdom of God

120 Pannenberg, *Systematic Theology 2*, 335. Cf. Barth, 'We cannot say that Jesus did not act in His own right, but in the name of another, namely God ... He acts in the name of God, and therefore in His own name' *CD* III/2, 62.

121 Pannenberg, *Systematic Theology 2*, 337.

122 *CD* II/1, 605–6. 'He, the crucified One, is the power of God (1 Cor. 1:24). Note that He not only has this power but that in His existence He Himself is it. He certainly has it as well ... the epitome and sum of all the power He enjoys as given and active in Him by God is the fact that God in His power raised Him from the dead (1 Cor. 6:14; 2 Cor 13:4).' Following (Acts 2:24) Barth says: 'He is the One for whom it was impossible that the resurrection from the dead should not take place. This was only His declaration as the Son of God, and therefore as the possessor of the power of His Father which he gained by this event, according to Rom. 1:4. He did not have to become this. He is from the very beginning the possessor of "the power of an endless life" (Heb. 7:16) ... Jesus Christ is not merely the bearer and executive of a power of God which is given Him but which is not originally and properly His. On the contrary, Jesus Christ has the power of God because and as He Himself is it.'

123 Cf. Barth, *Evangelical Theology*, 29–30. Cf. also *CD* I/1, 459–60. For a discussion of two-stage Christology, see Molnar, *Incarnation and Resurrection*, 3, 282–88.

124 Pannenberg, *Systematic Theology 2*, 345.

125 Pannenberg, *Systematic Theology 2*, 326.

we must really keep before our eyes God's reconciliation along with His revelation ... it is actually to those who are called ... that He is what He is, God's power and wisdom ... the Logos by whom all things have come into being ... we have to be saved and therefore to have faith if we are to recognise this δύναμις θεοῦ at the very point at which alone in all ages it can be recognised ... We cannot gain this key ourselves. We can only receive it.[126]

In his important and very insightful book on Pannenberg's theology Iain Taylor sees this issue very clearly and offers a proper way beyond it. He thinks that the problem in Pannenberg's thought relates to his 'failure to observe a distinction that is present in other christologies, namely that although Christ's identity is revealed *in* his human nature, it is not *in virtue of* it'.[127] He rightly notices that for Pannenberg

---

126 *CD* II/1, 607.

127 Taylor, *Pannenberg on the Triune God*, 204. I have argued against the idea that the resurrection can or should be seen as the basis of Jesus's eternal sonship and also against Pannenberg's idea, taken from Heidegger with some modifications, that it is only in the experience of anticipation of the end that we can recognize the truth of who God is. Grasping truth, according to the experience of anticipation, leads Pannenberg both to the idea that Christian theologians must allow the God recognized by philosophers to determine the truth of what they say and then to the ideas that the Father depends on the Son, that God is dependent on the outcome of history, that Jesus's message rather than his unique being as God and man is the object of the biblical faith and that knowledge of God and of the totality of reality mutually condition one another. See Molnar, 'Some Problems with Pannenberg's Solution' *SJT*. My argument was misunderstood by F. LeRon Shults because, following Pannenberg, he mistakenly believes that there should be a mutually conditioning relationship between anthropology and theology. Shults missed the point of my article which was that Pannenberg was mistaken in supposing that it was necessary 'to abandon the assumption that *the reality of God is a presupposition* for dogmatics from the very outset' (*Systematic Theology 1*, 45, emphasis mine). My argument was that theology must always begin and end in faith in the incarnate Word because he was and is the reality of God who encounters us in Jesus Christ now through his Holy Spirit and through the power of the risen Lord himself. Abandoning the reality of God as presupposition has to mean that that presupposition becomes something else – and that something else is, for Pannenberg the experience of anticipation which is assumed to be an experience of God as the

'there is either an epistemological basis in Jesus' history, in particular his resurrection insofar as it is accessible to general historical investigation' for understanding Jesus's identity, 'or a foundation in Christian

'true infinite'. That assumption is the problem. Shults mistakenly thinks I missed Pannenberg's critique of Barth first because Pannenberg thought that for Barth acknowledging God in faith meant bypassing experience. I understood Pannenberg's critique quite well in fact. However, I rejected it because Barth was right to insist that acknowledgment of God involved recognition of God (the triune God); but that recognition came only in faith that allowed the Trinity to determine one's idea of God. Pannenberg certainly did not do that since he explicitly claimed that 'the natural theology of the philosophers' was a 'criterion for judging whether any God could be seriously considered the author of the whole cosmos' (*Systematic Theology 1*, 68f.). Second, Shults claimed that Pannenberg's charge of subjectivism against Barth was 'aimed at his inability to argue intersubjectively with a proponent of some other religious claim' (F. LeRon Shults, *The Postfoundationalist Task of Theology: Wolfhart Pannenberg and the New Theological Rationality* (Grand Rapids, MI: Eerdmans, 1999), 13. Shults did not explain this, but if it means that one can reach a knowledge of the truth of who the triune God is by arguing with others on the basis of religious claims, then once again he missed my point completely and missed Barth's point as well. One cannot reach a true understanding of religion by means of comparing intersubjective truth claims because the truth of the Christian religion is grounded exclusively in the revelation of God in Jesus Christ and rests therefore on its being justified by grace and faith which are tied to Christ himself as the only one who makes religion true. Again, my point was that Barth appealed to this objective reality of revelation while Pannenberg appealed to a modified version of Heidegger's notion of anticipation (*SJT*, 335, 330), and that led him to conclude that 'the various experiences of revelation ... do not have God as their direct content' (*Systematic Theology 1*, 243) and thus 'Talk about an action of God ... must begin with *experience* of the connections in the course of world history and not with the thought of a divine subject' (*Systematic Theology 1*, 388). Such an assertion subverts the need for faith in Christ as the revelation of God in history at the outset. Shults concluded that I never defined 'subjectivism' whereas I made it clear that subjectivism referred to any attempt to establish objective knowledge from within acts of a human subject, including acts of knowledge, faith and anticipation. For Barth revelation was objectively present in Christ and subjectively through his Holy Spirit and no anticipation of anything within the realm of creation can lead to knowledge of that particular revelation – only God could do that and that was a miracle because it could not be explained from the human side.

experience.[128] However, Taylor opts for another option, 'namely that the epistemological basis is the Trinity itself, God himself in the person of the Son. The ontological basis is also the epistemological basis, i.e. the eternal Son who alone sustains and directs Christ's person and his knowability.'[129] This is a crucial point and it is the point that I expressly tried to make in my criticisms of Pannenberg. Taylor gets this just right.

He says that for Pannenberg, those approaches to Christology from above that are problematic are those 'that do not allow an irreducible epistemological basis in Christ's human history per se, i.e., those that cannot be justified in terms of that history and do not necessarily rest on it.'[130] He argues for a different approach 'that Pannenberg's method excludes ... That is, that Jesus' uniqueness and significance is to be understood in virtue of the Trinity'[131] and not on the basis of an analysis of his history. Here Taylor cites *Divine Freedom* to make his point: ' "Christ's humanity draws its meaning from the immanent Trinity and not from history"; ' consequently, 'It is *in virtue of* the Trinity, since it is the strength of the trinitarian action alone and not of a corresponding human strength that is the key to Jesus' identity and how we come to know him.'[132] Taylor astutely points out that while Pannenberg offers a substantial doctrine of the Trinity, insisting that one cannot collapse the immanent into the economic Trinity as he believed Robert Jenson was in danger of doing; this particular important distinction which one would have expected to see in such a consistent doctrine is missing at the very places one might look for it.[133]

The question then is this: has Pannenberg recognized and presented Christ's eternal sonship accurately if he believes recognition of this 'self-revelation' still 'requires arguments for the historicity of his resurrection' as its 'epistemological basis.'[134] My answer here is no because one cannot know Christ as the true Son of the Father apart from the Son's own act enabling such knowledge which can only take place in faith enabled by the Holy Spirit and thus through acknowledgment in the

---

128 Taylor, *Pannenberg on the Triune God*, 204.

129 Taylor, *Pannenberg on the Triune God*, 204.

130 Taylor, *Pannenberg on the Triune God*, 111.

131 Taylor, *Pannenberg on the Triune God*, 111.

132 Taylor, *Pannenberg on the Triune God*, 111. See Molnar, *Divine Freedom* (first edition), 280.

133 Taylor, *Pannenberg on the Triune God*, 112.

134 Taylor, *Pannenberg on the Triune God*, 112; also 114–15.

sense described by Barth. This is why I have followed Barth in rejecting the idea that Jesus is the revealer in his humanity as such.

Taylor again sees this correctly, since he rightly claims that Pannenberg is mistaken in trying to find Jesus's uniqueness directly in his humanity as such. First, he says, 'it lacks exegetical foundation'.[135] Thus, 'Christ's uniqueness and significance are not explained by means of the Trinity'. Pannenberg, Taylor asserts, 'requires a part of Christ's significance that is to be found not in trinitarian terms, but solely in human terms. Yet none exists'.[136] This is an extremely important insight and it follows from the fact that Pannenberg does not allow his own Christology to be shaped consistently by who Jesus was and is as the eternal Son, begotten of the Father before all worlds. The second criticism concerns the fact that for Pannenberg, Christ's authority 'is not something he already possesses in his person, but it is granted to him by the course of this earthly life ... Christ's authority is to be discerned, not first of all in his person, but in his message, miracles and especially the resurrection, all of which confer authority on him as the Messiah of God'.[137] Taylor rightly claims that none of this corresponds with the witness of the New Testament since in Mk. 1:22 his authority is not conferred on him 'by his life and work, but is revealed through them' since 'he is already "the one having authority"'. Jesus's miracles do not enable him to receive glory but instead reveal the glory he already had'.[138] In sum, the real problem with Pannenberg's theology is his method because it allows the Trinity to 'fall from view when Pannenberg is dealing with how one comes to know God, when he deals with faith, the basis of christology and the doctrine of revelation and what one might call his theological method'.[139]

135 Taylor, *Pannenberg on the Triune God*, 205. Taylor notes that the Gospels are very clear 'from the very outset that the significance of this one (Jesus) is the coming into time of Almighty God, whether it be by accounts of incarnation in the virgin's womb, prologue or reference to Christ as the "Lord" of the OT' (205).

136 Taylor, *Pannenberg on the Triune God*, 206. With this I fully agree once again. Indeed, at this point Taylor also criticizes Pannenberg for adopting a view of '"mutual conditioning" in his doctrine of creation' (206, n. 34).

137 Taylor, *Pannenberg on the Triune God*', 206. Here, once again, we are in agreement as I have criticized Pannenberg for substituting Jesus's message for his person.

138 Taylor, *Pannenberg on the Triune God*, 206.

139 Taylor, *Pannenberg on the Triune God*, 206.

Iain Taylor's question is an important one and it concerns why Pannenberg's Christology is trinitarian 'ontologically' but not 'epistemologically'. So he asks: 'If, as Pannenberg says, Christ's person and being have their basis in the free, gracious self-presentation of the triune God and can only be rightly understood as such, why is this not also the case for how we *come to know him*?'[140] In this book and elsewhere, I have suggested that the reason for this is because he refuses to begin his thinking about Jesus the way Barth began, that is, by acknowledging his uniqueness as the Son or Word who alone can disclose to us the true meaning of who God is and who we are. It is he alone who validates the truth of the Christian religion; nothing we can offer from the human side can do this without displacing God himself from the center.

As important as these issues are, there is an even more important problem with Pannenberg's thinking, as noted previously and that concerns his idea of a dependent deity. Ted Peters curiously thinks that Pannenberg's 'point of embarkment is practically identical to Barth's method of analysis'.[141] As we have been seeing, however, it is anything but identical to Barth's method just because Pannenberg will not begin and end his reflections by allowing Jesus to be the epistemological and ontological criterion for all that is said about God, revelation and faith. Peters maintains that: 'Pannenberg believes that the reciprocity in the relationship of the divine persons makes room for the constitutive significance of the central events of salvation history for the Godhead of God.'[142] Peters believes that the work of the Spirit 'dynamically realizes the kingdom of God in this world' such that for Pannenberg this means that 'Without this kingdom, God could not be God. The existence of God as Trinity depends upon the future of God's coming kingdom.'[143] Peters argues that for Pannenberg, since each of the persons of the Trinity is dependent on the others, one cannot suppose that Christ's suffering and death do not take place 'within the life of God proper'. In Peters's view this means that 'the divinity of the eternal God is in the process of being determined and defined in the historical events of Jesus' destiny. The eternal nature of God is at least in part dependent upon temporal events'.[144]

140 Taylor, *Pannenberg on the Triune God*, 119.
141 Peters, *Trinity*, 135.
142 Peters, *Trinity*, 135.
143 Peters, *Trinity*, 135.
144 Peters, *Trinity*, 137.

Stanley Grenz offers an interesting summary of Pannenberg's approach to the Trinity. He maintains that Pannenberg elevates history as central 'in the prolegomenon to his trinitarian theological proposal' and to his view 'of the proper theological starting point' for theology. Since truth is provisional, Grenz says, 'the unfolding of Christian theology cannot assume the reality of God'.[145] Just these assumptions, I have argued, invalidate Pannenberg's attempt to present God first as one who is known via some unthematized knowledge that is not shaped explicitly by the trintiarian self-revelation; only then does he turn to the Trinity. This accounts for the proper criticism of Iain Taylor. This also illustrates that Pannenberg and Barth were separated by an almost unbridgeable chasm since Barth believed one had to begin dogmatics by allowing the reality of God in Christ to determine one's thinking from the outset while Pannenberg believed that Barth needed to abandon this idea.[146] Grenz also notes that Pannenberg criticized Barth for positing 'a God who is ultimately a single subject, rather than three persons'.[147]

Of course, given the development of Barth's thinking in this book, it is clear that while Barth did insist that God was a single subject, since God is one even as he exists eternally as Father, Son and Holy Spirit, still for Barth, God eternally exists in three modes of being *as* one divine subject. As noted several times already, Barth never played off God's oneness against his threeness but always thought of God's oneness in and as his existence as Father, Son and Holy Spirit. So to suggest that when Barth employed the imagery of a single divine subject that he was advocating oneness 'rather than' the three persons demonstrates a clear misunderstanding of Barth's theology. Grenz proceeds to summarize many of the key aspects of Pannenberg's theology noting what he calls 'Pannenberg's principle', which affirms that 'God's being is his rule' since for Pannenberg 'God's deity, is linked to divine rulership over the world'.[148] This leads him to spell out Pannenberg's idea of a dependent deity: 'The self-distinction of the Father from the Son is not just that he

145 Grenz, *Rediscovering the Triune God*, 92.

146 See Molnar, 'Some Problems with Pannenberg's Solution', 317 and Pannenberg, *Systematic Theology 1*, 44–5 where he accuses Barth of theological subjectivism because he decided to begin his theology with God himself. My article explains why I think that Pannenberg is mistaken in this and why he himself falls into a kind of subjectivism in the process of trying to 'correct' Barth.

147 Grenz, *Rediscovering the Triune God*, 95.

148 Grenz, *Rediscovering the Triune God*, 96.

begets the Son but that he hands over all things to him, so that his kingdom and his own deity are now dependent upon the Son.'[149] This mutual
dependency is not limited to the economy Grenz notes, but is also present within the divine life. My point in bringing this up here is to stress
once again that any idea of mutual conditioning or dependency of God
on history in reality strips God of his eternal freedom as the one who
loves. It undermines a properly functioning doctrine of the immanent
Trinity. Grenz captures my main objection nicely when he mentions
that 'Molnar voices a concern shared by many critics, when in comparing Pannenberg to Barth he writes: "While Pannenberg also insists that
only God can reveal God, his method incorporates our philosophical
knowledge into revelation in such a way that God becomes dependent
upon the processes of history."'.[150] One of the more important difficulties is that this thinking leads Pannenberg to believe that God's eternal
being is in some sense constituted by what happens in history. As Grenz
correctly maintains, Pannenberg 'argues that the historical missions of
Jesus and the Holy Spirit as sent into the world by the Father are *constitutive* of not only the eternal character of the three persons but also *of
their very deity*'.[151] They are not.

Samuel M. Powell helpfully distinguishes Pannenberg's innovation
here from traditional trinitarian theology as advocated by Barth when
he writes:

> For Pannenberg, the historical relations are in fact determinative of
> the eternal character of the persons. God is not, for Pannenberg, one
> thing in eternity and another in history. The Trinitarian persons are
> what they are because of their mutual relations in salvation history
> ... Pannenberg proposes that the relations not only distinguish the
> persons but also constitute them in their deity ... In Pannenberg's
> view, Jesus is the Son precisely because he proved himself obedient
> to the Father. His subordination to the Father not only identifies him
> as the Son, but also constitutes him as the Son.[152]

---

149 Grenz, *Rediscovering the Triune God*, 97.

150 Grenz, *Rediscovering the Triune God*, 103.

151 Grenz, *Rediscovering the Triune God*, 105, emphasis mine.

152 Samuel M. Powell, *The Trinity in German Thought* (Cambridge:
Cambridge University Press, 2001), 238. See esp. here Pannenberg, *Systematic
Theology 1*, 310–11. It is of course one thing to say that what God is toward us
in the economy God is in himself and quite another to suggest that what God

It also leads Pannenberg to think that God is in some sense dependent on history just because his idea of futurity also shapes his thinking. Let me briefly explain why this is such a problem by referring to a few remarks made by George Hunsinger.

Let me conclude this section noting that in his estimation 'Pannenberg's doctrine of the Trinity involved a more complex [than Moltmann's] eschatology along with a similar suggestion that in some sense God existed in codependency with the world'.[153] He thinks that Pannenberg 'abandoned the idea of God's absolute perfection and

is in the economy constitutes who God is in himself. The former position is clearly that of Barth and Torrance as already mentioned. The latter is a view that becomes possible when history is allowed to determine who God is in eternity. Interestingly, Pannenberg wants to make that first statement and denies that the trinitarian God can be seen as the result of history (*Systematic Theology 1*, 331). However, there is certainly enough ambiguity in the idea that Jesus is retroactively the Son for all eternity to raise some questions here. His clear remark that 'The eternal Son is first, however, an aspect of the human person' hence, 'self-distinction from the Father is constitutive for the eternal Son in his relation to the Father' (310); and belief that 'the difference between Father and Son in God's eternal essence depend upon, and take place in, the fact that God as Father is manifest in the relation of Jesus to him' (311); together with his clear statement that 'the self-distinction of Jesus from the Father is constitutive for the fact that even in the eternal God there must be a counterpart to the Father, i.e., the Son' (311); all say otherwise. Indeed, Powell asks whether or not Pannenberg here has fallen into adoptionism and concludes that he has not because he did not claim that the man Jesus became the Son by his obedience. Instead, he says, 'the relation of Son to Father is, for Pannenberg, eternally a relation characterized by obedience and submission; Jesus is *the* Son because his life was one of complete submission to the Father' (Powell, *The Trinity*, 239). A crucial question that must be asked, however, in connection with this last statement concerns whether or not Pannenberg, like Barth, has improperly read events in the economy (obedience) back into the immanent Trinity at this point causing the kinds of problem that I discuss in 'The obedience of the Son in the Theology of Karl Barth and of Thomas F. Torrance' *SJT*, vol. 67, no. 1 (2014): 50–69. What sense does it make to say that Jesus is the Son *because* his life was one of complete submission? That life of submission in the economy was freely willed as an act of not grasping at equality with the Father and condescending to become one with us for our salvation. That presents a rather different image than Pannenberg's thinking here.

153 Hunsinger, 'Karl Barth and Some Protestant Theologians', 311.

unqualified self-sufficiency' since for him 'The perfection of God's essence was somehow subsequent, contingent, and teleological rather than (as for Barth) antecedent, necessary, and primordial.'[154] He thinks that for Pannenberg the immanent Trinity becomes 'a function of the economic Trinity'.[155] While Hunsinger notes that Pannenberg did not eliminate all antecedence or aseity from God, he was unable to affirm these in an unqualified sense as Barth had done as when he wrote that: '"Even in his deity ... God has made himself dependent on the course of history." '[156] While Pannenberg did assert that 'the trinitarian God is complete in himself prior to his relation to the world',[157] he also claimed that 'with the creation of the world God's deity and even his existence become dependent on the fulfilment of their determination in his present lordship'.[158] Hunsinger judges that: 'Whatever else this startling claim may mean, it implies that after creating the world God was ontologically diminished and could not retrieve himself without retrieving the world. God had subjected his deity and even his existence, if only provisionally, to a nexus of cosmological contingencies, obscurities, and imperfections.'[159] Hunsinger captures Pannenberg's thought accurately by noting that he had historicized eternity and then 'subjected it to an eschatological scheme' so that 'God's essence was under construction by the three persons of the Trinity' with the result that 'once God becomes enmeshed in history (by creating the world), the essence of the eternal Trinity is determined, and effectively constituted, by the historical actions of the Trinitarian persons. God's Trinitarian essence (*ousia*) is eternal only by way of its fulfillment in the absolute future (which is indeed the only absolute in this scheme).'[160] God's unity therefore is realized only in relation to the world and to that extent does not have an existence independent of history. Moreover, in this scheme, 'the immanent Trinity is determined and effectively constituted by the economic actions of the three persons by virtue of their

154 Hunsinger, 'Karl Barth and Some Protestant Theologians', 311.

155 Hunsinger, 'Karl Barth and Some Protestant Theologians', 311.

156 Hunsinger, 'Karl Barth and Some Protestant Theologians', 311, referring to *Systematic Theology 1*, 329.

157 Pannenberg, *Systematic Theology 1*, 391.

158 Pannenberg, *Systematic Theology 1*, 390.

159 Hunsinger, 'Karl Barth and Some Protestant Theologians', 311–12.

160 Hunsinger, 'Karl Barth and Some Protestant Theologians', 312.

teleological consequences'.[161] These are apt critical judgments by which we may end our discussion of Pannenberg's thinking. It is clear from this presentation that, instead of consistently recognizing and maintaining the freedom of God in eternity and in history, Pannenberg has undermined key aspects of the doctrine of the immanent Trinity, as recognized and explicated by Barth. He has done so just because of his view of history and his idea of futurity which are largely shaped by his view of anticipation that was taken over from Heidegger and modified according to Pannenberg's own agenda.

Karl Rahner's Christology: Does Jesus's Humanity as such Reveal?

Let us conclude this chapter by returning now to Rahner's thought and noting some problems with Rahner's Christology which indicate more precisely why I think his axiom cannot be given unqualified agreement. Part of the difficulty, as we shall see, is that Rahner allows his analysis of human relations to shape his understanding of God's being and action. His philosophy and theology of the symbol cause him to compromise God's freedom in se and ad extra. Formulating his axiom, Rahner considers three difficulties: (1) that the incarnation might not be a certain instance of the identity of the immanent and economic Trinity; (2) that any divine person could have become incarnate and so there would be no connection between the missions and the intratrinitarian life; and (3) how to interpret Christ's human nature (which concerns us here): 'is the humanity of the Logos merely something foreign which has been assumed or is it precisely that which comes into being when the Logos ex-presses himself into the non-divine?'[162] Should we start from a known human nature or one more clearly revealed by the incarnation? Should not human nature be explained through the 'self-emptying, self-utterance of the Logos himself?' On the surface, Barth and Rahner are at one affirming that true humanity and true deity can be understood only through the Logos becoming incarnate. However, they are actually far apart because Rahner's thought is governed by his philosophy of symbolic expression and because he begins with transcendental experience.

---

161 Hunsinger, 'Karl Barth and Some Protestant Theologians', 312.
162 Rahner, *Trinity*, 31, n. 27.

Barth and Rahner and those who follow Rahner's transcendental method are in conflict over the role of experience in theology. As seen in the previous chapter, it is out of our transcendental experience of the absolute which Rahner calls the 'mystery, one and nameless'[163] that we come to know God. Our self-knowledge is the condition for this possibility. Unthematic experience and knowledge of God are part of the very structure of our divinized subjective orientation toward mystery and 'the meaning of all explicit knowledge of God in religion and in metaphysics … can really be understood only when all the words we use there point to the *unthematic experience* of our orientation towards the ineffable mystery'.[164] Hence revelation (God's self-communication to creatures) is

> a modification of our transcendental consciousness produced permanently by God in grace. But such a modification is really an original and permanent element in our consciousness as the basic and original luminosity of our existence. And as an element in our transcendentality … it is already revelation in the proper sense.[165]

Why is this the case? Because, as we have already noted in Chapter 4,

> The three mysteries, the Trinity and its two processions and the two self-communications of God *ad extra* in a real formal causality corresponding to the two processions, are not 'intermediate mysteries'. They are not something provisional and deficient in the line of mystery which comes between the perspicuous truths of our natural knowledge and the absolute mystery of God … Nor are they as it were mysteries of the beyond … behind the God who is for us the holy mystery.[166]

---

163 *TI* 11, 159. Cf. Rahner, *FCF*, 44 and *TI* 4, 50 where Rahner writes: 'All conceptual expressions about God, necessary though they are, always stem from the unobjectivated experience of transcendence as such: the concept from the pre-conception, the name from the experience of the nameless.' This thinking plays a decisive role in Rahner's view of the incarnation. Our spiritual movement helps us appropriate the ancient Christologies: 'For no understanding is possible anywhere if what is understood remains fixed and frozen and is not launched into the movement of that *nameless mystery* which is the vehicle of all understanding' (*TI* 4, 106, emphasis mine).

164 *FCF*, 53.

165 *FCF*, 149. For LaCugna 'Revelation is the experienced self-communication of God *in* the history of salvation,' *God for Us*, 318.

166 *TI* 4, 72.

All this rests on a supernatural existential which means that 'it belongs to the very essence of concrete human nature to be called to grace, to be able to find God in the particularities of all history ... the history of salvation and revelation are coextensive with the history of the human race'.[167] Thus, 'the offer and the possibility of grace is given with human nature itself as ... historically constituted ... the supernatural existential wants to affirm something about the reality of grace, namely, that it is a constituent part of our historical human existence'.[168] However, for Grenz and Olson:

> The supernatural existential is a highly unstable concept. If the theologian emphasizes the universal aspect denoted by the term *existential*, the concept may easily fall into intrinsicism and become little more than another religious a priori like Schleiermacher's God-consciousness. If one puts forward the supernatural aspect, the supernatural existential may easily fall into extrinsicism and become little more than another theological assertion about the transcendence of God's self-revelation ... [supernatural existential] is highly ambiguous and of dubious value in solving the dilemma of transcendence and immanence in contemporary Christian theology.[169]

I agree. The universal aspect allows many who follow Rahner to claim that God's universal offer of salvation is given in transcendental experience rather than exclusively by God's Word in its identity with Jesus Christ and his Holy Spirit. This has affected the theological landscape today perhaps more than any of Rahner's other insights. As seen previously, this thinking could lead to the feminist belief that we creatures make the symbol God function and therefore we should reconstruct the symbol in order to help achieve equality between men and women. However, this thinking can also lead to the view that our love of neighbor is itself, as such, love of God and thus could undermine our genuine need for revelation by ascribing grace to our human experiences of love.[170]

---

167 Dych, *A World of Grace*, 13.

168 Dych, *Karl Rahner*, 36–7.

169 Grenz and Olson, *20th Century Theology: God & the World in a Transitional Age*, 246–7.

170 See David Coffey, *Deus Trinitas*, for a clear example of this position. See also Chapter 5, n. 124.

In any case, Rahner contrasts his 'neo-Chalcedonism' with a 'pure-Chalcedonism'[171] for which 'the human as such would not show us the Logos as such ... he would show himself only in his formal subjectivity'. Then the human nature, as already known to us, logically and ontologically but not temporally ('that which is not trinitarian') is what is assumed in the incarnation. However, then the Logos would not have 'stepped outside his intra-divine inaccessibility and shown *himself through* his humanity and *in* his humanity'. We could not say: 'He who *sees* me, sees *me*. For when we glimpse the humanity of Christ as such, we would in reality have seen nothing of the subject of the Logos himself, except at most his abstract formal subjectivity'. How then do we interpret the ἀσυγχύτως (unmixed) of Chalcedon? Following his principles of symbolic ontology Rahner affirms that the subject (Logos) expresses *itself* in the humanity; thus the relation between the Logos and the assumed human nature is

> more essential and more intimate. Human nature in general is a possible object of the creative knowledge and power of God, because and insofar as the Logos is by nature the one who is 'utterable' (even into that which is not God) ... [When the Father freely empties himself] into the non-divine ... that precisely is born which we call human nature [which is not something] from behind which the Logos hides to act things out in the world. From the start it is the constitutive, real symbol of the Logos himself ... [Thus] man is possible because the exteriorization of the Logos is possible ... what Jesus is and does as man reveals the Logos himself; it is the reality of the Logos as our salvation amidst us ... here the Logos with God and the Logos with us, the immanent and the economic Logos, are strictly the same.[172]

The humanity is posited as the Logos' own way of positing himself. While Rahner's intention is to see our humanity as created and restored in Christ and not to foster a 'lifeless identity', this statement certainly seems to suggest that Jesus's humanity is the Logos present among us.

---

171 Rahner, *Trinity*, 31 n.27. In *TI* IV, 124–5, Rahner refers to this as both 'Neo-Chalcedonism' and 'Neo-Chalcedonianism' in reference to a book by H.-J. Schulz, 'Die "Höllenfahrt" als 'Anastasis"', *ZKT* 81 (1959) 1–66.

172 Rahner, *Trinity*, 31–3.

At least one Rahnerian actually interprets Christ's humanity as his divinity under the rubric 'theandric'.[173]

Also, confirming this reading of Rahner, Joseph H. P. Wong explains that, when Christ's humanity is thought of as the very expression of the Logos, the idea is conveyed that 'the symbol not only renders the symbolized present, but is its very reality'.[174] This makes it impossible to distinguish either Christ's divinity and humanity or the immanent and economic Trinity. Here Rahner applies his notion of quasi-formal causality and believes that the doctrine of the Trinity can be properly grasped only 'by going back to the history of salvation and of grace, to our *experience* of Jesus and the Spirit of God, who operates in us, because in them we really already possess the Trinity itself as such'.[175]

But here Rahner's symbolic ontology has caused more problems than it solves. He believes that 'all beings are by their nature symbolic, because they necessarily "express" themselves in order to attain their own nature' and that 'the symbol strictly speaking (symbolic reality) is the self-realization of a being in the other, which is constitutive of its essence'. God is the supreme instance of this. Thus, 'Being *as such*, and hence *as* one (*ens* as *unum*), for the fulfillment of its being and its unity, emerges into a plurality – of which the supreme mode is the Trinity'.[176]

---

173 See David Coffey, *The Theandric Nature of Christ*, in *TS*, vol. 63, no. 2 (September, 1999), 405–31, 411 ff. Thus he writes: 'For Rahner, human nature, though created, is potentially divine, and in the case of Christ actually so' (412). It is important to note that Coffey's belief that Christ's human nature as 'theandric', that is, 'human in a divine way, or, equally, divine in a human way' is 'inevitable once human nature is defined in terms of orientation to God' (413). Such a definition, as we have seen, is intrinsic to Rahner's transcendental method and from my point of view it necessarily confuses nature and grace and reason and revelation.

174 Joseph H. P. Wong, *Logos-Symbol in the Christology of Karl Rahner* (Rome: Las-Roma, 1984), 193. Cf. also *TI* 4, 251 and 239. Similarly, Peters, *Trinity*, presses Rahner's axiom 'to its extreme consequence' 192; thus 'the loving relationship between the Father and the Son within the Trinity *is* the loving relationship between the Father and Jesus … [hence] when we look at Jesus we see the real thing [the Son]', 22.

175 Rahner, *Trinity*, 40, emphasis mine.

176 *TI* 4, 224, 234 and 228.

> All activities, from the sheerly material to the innermost life of the Blessed Trinity, are but modulations of this one metaphysical theme, of the one meaning of being: self-possession, subjectivity. 'Self-possession', however, is itself realized through a double phase: a flowing outwards, an exposition of its own essence from its own cause – an *emanatio*, and a withdrawing into itself of this essence ...[177]

The 'mysterious unity of transcendence through history and of history into transcendence' has its 'roots in the Trinity, in which the Father is the incomprehensible origin and the original unity, the "Word" his utterance into history, and the "Spirit" the opening up of history into the immediacy of its fatherly origin and end'.[178] However, according to the doctrine of the Trinity, God is not first origin and original unity as Father. The unity of God is the unity of the Father, Son and Holy Spirit.

Here Rahner's metaphysics, which states that being as one emerges into a plurality for the fulfillment of its being, leads him to compromise the simple fact on which Barth's theology stands. For Barth, there is no knowledge of God's oneness if it does not take place through and in Jesus Christ, the Son, by the power of the Holy Spirit at the start. For Rahner, one knows God's oneness whenever one recognizes a supreme one transcending the many, whatever name is given to this reality.[179] This leads both toward subordinationism and to Rahner's belief that the Trinity does not reveal anything that contradicts our natural knowledge of God. In the end Rahner has no difficulty equating self-acceptance with acceptance of Christ[180] and saying that 'man is the event of God's absolute self-communication'.[181] However, this 'universalism' shows that Rahner's starting point was transcendental experience as explained previously, rather than God's act in Christ and the Spirit. More will be said about this in the next chapter. Here it is important to note that Rahner's idea that the Word is God's utterance into history allows no clear distinction between the Word's internal

177 *HW*, 49.

178 Rahner, *Trinity*, 47.

179 Cf. *TI* 1, 91, *FCF*, 60, and *TI* 11, 153–6. As seen in Chapter 5, the term 'God' refers to an experience on the basis of which that which we all experience (the term of our transcendental orientations) is what 'we call God'.

180 Cf. *TI* 4, 119. This leads to Rahner's anonymous Christianity and encourages the idea that love of God and neighbor are finally identical.

181 *FCF*, 126ff.

utterance and external expression. Rahner speaks of humanity in general as coming into existence when God expresses his Word into the void; as seen earlier in Chapter 2, he conceives the hypostatic union at least in part as Jesus's human self-transcendence into God and this blurs the very fact which, for Barth, would preserve a clear distinction between nature and grace.

For Rahner a 'symbol renders present what is revealed' and is 'full of the thing symbolized'.[182] Hence Christ's human nature *as such* discloses the Logos.[183] Yet, since this is exactly what Barth denied in order to affirm both a true humanity and a true divinity in Christ, he clearly distinguished between Christ and our need for him in a way that Rahner cannot. For Rahner, Christ's human nature is the real symbol (expression) of God (the unoriginate) in the world.[184] It comes about as God expresses himself into the void. However, while Rahner indeed insists that God is free and not subject here to a 'primal must', God's freedom actually is compromised. According to Scripture it was by the Holy Spirit that Mary conceived Jesus and not by a symbolic expression into the void. The former suggests a miraculous act of Lordship *for us*; the latter a natural process. Faithful to his symbolic ontology, Rahner concludes both that God's act of positing the Logos results in its exteriorization and that the human nature is full of the unoriginate (God). The appearance (humanity) allows God to be present while being full of the reality symbolized.[185] Conceived in this way it is difficult, if not impossible, to claim that the Son is the subject of this event: 'what happened to Jesus on earth is precisely the history of the Word of God himself, and a process which *he* underwent'.[186] From this Rahner draws two problematic conclusions: *First*, 'the creature is endowed, by virtue of its inmost essence and constitution, with the possibility of being assumed'. Therefore, 'the finite itself has been given an infinite depth and is no longer a contrast to the infinite'. *Second*,

> God's creative act always drafts the creature as the paradigm of a possible utterance of himself. And he cannot draft it otherwise ... The immanent self-utterance of God in his eternal fullness is the

182 *TI* 4, 239 and 251.
183 *TI* 4, 239ff. and Rahner, *Trinity*, 32–3.
184 *TI* 4, 115.
185 *TI* 4, 237. Cf. also 225 and 231.
186 *TI* 4, 113.

condition of the self-utterance of God outside himself, and the *latter continues the former.*[187]

All of this follows from Rahner's understanding of God's love as 'the will to fill the void'.[188] Had he kept to a clear doctrine of the immanent Trinity (which he believed was important) then he could have said consistently that God loves in freedom as the Father, Son and Spirit and thus could and did create in freedom. Instead he argues that creation is the continuation of God's immanent self-utterance and presumes that there is a void which God wishes to fill by means of creation and incarnation. Yet, the doctrine of creation implies that before creation nothing but God, as Father, Son and Spirit existed – no void existed simultaneously with God. God's freedom is so conditioned by creation that, as seen in the previous chapter, Rahner believes that grace presupposes nature as a condition of its own possibility.[189]

Of course Rahner insists that God's expression ad extra is *free*. However since, according to his symbolic ontology, 'All beings must express themselves' God can express himself outwardly only 'because God "must" "express" himself inwardly'.[190] Thus, when Rahner describes the incarnation as the continuation of God's inner symbolic movement ad extra, he conceptually compromises God's freedom to have existed without becoming incarnate. He extends symbolic expression beyond Jesus to all humanity in their acts of self-transcendence just because he believes, as already noted in Chapter 5, that 'in the long run everything agrees in some way or another with everything else',[191] and that what is symbolized passes 'over into the "otherness" of the symbol'.[192] Moreover,

---

187 *TI* 4, 115, emphasis mine and 117. 'God has taken on a human nature, because it is essentially ready and adoptable' (110); human nature 'when assumed by God as *his* reality, simply arrived at the point to which it always strives by virtue of its essence' (109). For Barth, 'human nature possesses no capacity for becoming the human nature of Jesus Christ' (*CD* I/2, 188). When it is assumed by God in Christ it receives a new point of departure toward which it could no longer strive by virtue of its essence which is affected by sin.

188 *TI* 4, 115–17.

189 'Grace exists … by being the divinising condition [of the person], and hence presupposes and incorporates into itself the whole reality of this person as the condition of its own possibility' (*TI* 6, 73).

190 *TI* 4, 236.

191 *TI* 4, 225.

192 *TI* 4, 240.

when he describes creation as 'a continuation of the immanent constitution of "image and likeness"', he claims that an encounter with the man Jesus is not only an encounter with but knowledge of the Logos.[193]

Rahner then says what Barth insisted could never be said, that is, 'If God wills to become non-God, man comes to be ... And if God himself is man and remains so forever, if all theology is therefore eternally an anthropology ... man is forever the articulate mystery of God.'[194] There is and can be no clear distinction between Christ and us here. It is thus perfectly logical for Rahner to understand love of neighbor 'in the direction of a radical identity of the two loves' and say that 'the love of God and the love of neighbour are one and the same thing'. Thus:

> Wherever a genuine love of man attains its proper nature and its moral absoluteness and depth, it is in addition always so underpinned and heightened by God's saving grace that it is also love of God, whether it be explicitly considered to be such a love by the subject or not ... this is the direction in which the understanding of the thesis of identity as it is meant here leads ... wherever man posits a positively moral act in the full exercise of his free self-disposal, this act is a positive supernatural salvific act ... wherever there is an absolutely moral commitment of a positive kind in the world ... there takes place also a saving event, faith, hope and charity ...[195]

---

193 *TI* 4, 236–9, Rahner, *Trinity*, 32–3.

194 *TI* 4, 116.

195 *TI* 6, 233, 236–7, 239. For more on this see Molnar, 'Love of God and Love of Neighbor in the Theology of Karl Rahner and Karl Barth' *Modern Theology*, vol. 20, no. 4 (October 2004), 567–99. On this issue Thomas F. Torrance offers some intriguing and helpful advice: 'True love of others is generated in the heart of the believer by the Holy Spirit; but the Holy Spirit operates in that way in and through us as our eyes are fixed unselfishly on the Lord Jesus Christ' *The Doctrine of Jesus Christ*, 89. By this he means that in the incarnation God has loved us and does love us in his movement toward us in Christ as an act of grace to reconcile us with himself. On that basis we are freed to love God spontaneously and therefore 'we cannot really love our neighbours by trying to love them ... To cultivate Christian personalities [by attempting to get to God through ethical actions of love] is nothing short of a secret cult of self! ... [it is] to start from ego-centricity, to cultivate a refined form of selfishness' (89). This occurs because one has failed to allow one's behavior to be shaped by God's selfless movement toward us in the Incarnation. This is important because it revealingly leads Torrance to say that: 'I cannot love God through loving my

Therefore, 'Christology is the end and beginning of anthropology ... this anthropology, when most thoroughly realized in Christology, is eternally theology,'[196] and 'for all eternity such an anthropology is really theo-logy.'[197] Indeed, 'anthropology and Christology mutually determine each other within Christian dogmatics if they are both correctly understood.'[198] For Barth, this reversibility of Christ's divinity and humanity and mutual conditioning compromises theology's foundation in the immanent Trinity because 'there is a way from Christology to anthropology, but there is no way from anthropology to Christology.'[199] From what was said previously, we can see that many who follow Rahner's basic insights have used this thinking to argue that there should no longer be any clear distinction between the immanent and economic Trinity. Rahner never intended to say what they say and in fact he affirmed God's sovereignty.[200] Unfortunately, however, his symbolic logic leads to what others have concluded and to inconsistencies in his own position.

neighbor. I can love my neighbor truly and only through loving God. To love God through loving my neighbor is to assert that the Incarnation is not a reality, the reality it is, that relation to God is still a mediated one. To love God through my love to my neighbor is to move toward God. It does not know a movement of God toward man' (88–9). For Torrance, unless Christ himself is central and thus unless we love God in Christ and thereby recognize that our love of neighbor is a by-product of the fact that God has loved us in him while we were still sinners and freed us to love our neighbors, we will be relying on ourselves instead of on Christ. In this light, any claim that love of neighbor is already love of God, without explicitly recognizing God's love for us in Christ, will always mean a self-centered attempt to justify and sanctify ourselves. It will in the end confuse love of God with love of neighbor. That is why Torrance rejects what he calls the cultivation of Christian personalities – it is a form of 'anthropocentricity' that bypasses the need for Christ as the one in whom we are justified and sanctified.

196   *TI* 4, 117.

197   *TI* 1, 185.

198   *TI* 9, 28.

199   *CD* I/1, 131 and *CD* III/2, 71. As noted in n. 194, Torrance holds a view quite similar to Barth's view that there is no mutually conditioning relationship between anthropology and theology. It is at this point that one may see very clearly why Jeffrey Hensley's attempt to harmonize Barth and Rahner on this point, as discussed earlier, fails completely.

200   Rahner, *Trinity*, 36–7 and *TI* 4, 112.

Here, contemporary trinitarian theology is still in turmoil because the question has ceased to be: what is God, *as God*, saying to us in the humanity of the Word and in our humanity by the Holy Spirit uniting us to this Word in faith? The questions have become: how can we make the Trinity a doctrine which is alive so that it reflects our experiences of faith and incorporates relationality and temporality into the divine life? Or how can relationality which was given dogmatic status in the doctrine of the Trinity enable *us* to reconceive God in order to create a society of persons existing in freedom and equality? Or how can we recognize that our relations with others are already our relations with and participation in the relations of the Trinity? This is the kind of self-designed irrelevance which follows an inability to speak first about God *as* God the Father, Son and Holy Spirit and then, on that basis, about our relations with God, other creatures and the world in light of revelation and faith.

Interestingly, Rahner's axiom is meant to affirm that the 'Trinity of salvation history, as it reveals itself to us by deeds, is the "immanent" Trinity.'[201] However, since symbols are necessary (and thus condition the expressive reality – God) and since they are full of the reality symbolized, they have the power to render present what is revealed. There literally cannot be any clear distinction between Christ's humanity and divinity at exactly the point where a precise analysis of one of Christology's hardest problems could clarify the meaning of revelation, reconciliation and redemption. For Rahner all of these become explicable, first in and by our transcendental experiences and then through the doctrines. Therefore, when Barth spoke eschatologically, he argued:

> Let us be clear that ... we are again speaking of the Second Coming of *Jesus Christ*. Christian Eschatology is different from all other expectations for the future, whether they be worldly or religious or religious-worldly, in that it is not primarily expectation of something, even if this something were called resurrection of the flesh and eternal life, but expectation of the *Lord*.[202]

---

201 Rahner, *Trinity*, 47.

202 Karl Barth, *Credo*, 166–7. Underestimating Jesus's lordship followed from depreciating the foundation of the community in his resurrection and a failure to perceive the 'consolation of the Holy Spirit in whose work the community may find full satisfaction at every moment in its time of waiting' *CD* III/2, 509.

When Rahner speaks of hope he equates our transcendental experience with grace and revelation; he does not *start and end* his thinking with Jesus's actual resurrection and second coming.

> If one has a radical hope of attaining a definitive identity and does not believe that one can steal away with one's obligations into the emptiness of non-existence, one has already grasped and accepted the resurrection in its real content ... The absoluteness of the radical hope in which a human being apprehends his or her total existence as destined and empowered to reach definitive form can quite properly be regarded as grace, which permeates this existence always and everywhere. This grace is revelation in the strictest sense ... this certainly is revelation, even if this is not envisaged as coming from 'outside'.[203]

Rahner's axiom 'provides us with a methodical principle for the whole treatise on the Trinity. The Trinity is a mystery whose paradoxical character is preluded in the paradoxical character of man's existence.' Rahner explores human self-transcendence assuming that we have an obediential potency for revelation and a supernatural existential which identifies revelation and grace with our transcendental dynamisms. However, these very assumptions blur the distinction between nature and grace. Consequently, while Rahner is materially correct to assert that no theology can deny in principle that the doctrine of the missions is a starting point for the doctrine of the Trinity and that without this, one cannot avoid 'the danger of wild and empty

203 Rahner and Weger, *Our Christian Faith*, 110–11. In *TI* 17, 16 Rahner begins his analysis of Jesus's resurrection saying: 'It is possible to enquire about Jesus' resurrection today ... only if we take into account the whole of what philosophy and theology have to say about man. Here we must start from the assumption that the hope that a person's history of freedom will be conclusive in nature ... already includes what we mean by the hope of "resurrection" ... this hope must include knowledge of what is really meant by resurrection.' For Rahner, 'the knowledge of man's resurrection given with his transcendentally necessary hope is a statement of philosophical anthropology even before any real revelation in the Word' (18). By the time Rahner appeals to grace and scripture they can only describe something which everyone already knows and experiences without faith in Christ and the Spirit. We shall analyze in more detail how Rahner allows this transcendental experience of hope to define his understanding of grace, revelation and the resurrection in the next chapter.

conceptual acrobatics',[204] he compromises the free basis of the missions in God's pretemporal eternity by applying his symbolic ontology to the incarnation.

So he maintains two critical insights which Barth's doctrine of the immanent Trinity resisted. He makes it possible to equate Jesus's humanity as such with the power of the Word, thus providing an explanation of Christianity which circumvents Jesus's deity and the need for faith in him *before* thinking about God, salvation, grace, revelation and even resurrection.[205] And he argues that everyone has an obediential potency and a supernatural existential which can also be starting points for grasping the Trinity. This ends in the universalism which Barth consistently rejected by refraining from agnosticism, pantheism and dualism. Rahner can thus say that 'the mystery of the Trinity is the last mystery of our own reality, and that it is experienced precisely in this reality'.[206] This statement is not as far removed from the positions of LaCugna and Peters as one might at first glance assume. So when Ted Peters criticizes Rahner for still wanting to maintain an essential Trinity prior to the economy, there is a mixture of truth and error. Rahner knew quite well that without a real immanent Trinity the freedom of God would be compromised. In this respect his thinking certainly is in harmony with Barth, Jüngel and Torrance. However, the logic of his symbolic ontology allows for no such free existence of God to be determinative. In this respect his thinking was ahead of his time, because he was already allowing history to condition God's own being and action in the ways noted earlier. Here then is the real basis for the difficulties that can be seen in contemporary trinitarian theology insofar as it has been shaped by Rahner's axiom. My suggestion in this book is that Barth's doctrine

204 Rahner, *Trinity*, 47–8.

205 Torrance, *Trinitarian Perspectives*, reflecting the views of a 1975 Colloquium on Rahner's doctrine of the Trinity, notes this and other problems in Rahner's view, 79, 82, 91, even though he also presents Rahner's positive contributions to the discussion. Interestingly, David Coffey, *Deus Trinitas*, makes this christological error (equating Jesus's divinity with his humanity) the centerpiece of his trinitarian theology. Catherine LaCugna, *The Trinitarian Mystery of God* in *Systematic Theology: Roman Catholic Perspectives*, 151–192 (ed.) by Francis Schüssler Fiorenza and John P. Galvin (Minneapolis, MN: Fortress Press, 1991), writes: 'The divinity of Christ lies in his perfect humanity, which is why he can be seen as the perfect fulfillment of our own humanity' (188).

206 Rahner, *Trinity*, 47.

of the immanent Trinity could help us perceive and actually avoid these difficulties and thus present a doctrine of the Trinity which truly sees human freedom established on the basis of and not in abstraction from God's eternal sovereign freedom.[207]

One contemporary theologian who does indeed establish human freedom on the basis of God's eternal sovereign freedom is Thomas F. Torrance. In the next chapter we shall therefore compare the thought of T. F. Torrance with Karl Rahner with a view toward seeing how exactly they agree and differ in their respective views of God's self-communication in Christ. This will show that while Rahner's axiom of identity can provide a non-controversial way of seeing that the economic Trinity is and should be the ground of our understanding of the immanent Trinity and that the two cannot be separated, it also can lead to a serious compromise of both divine and human freedom. Such a compromise would occur if the starting point and conclusion of one's reflections were someone or something other than the One Mediator, Jesus Christ.

207 For a discussion of what this might look like today, see Molnar, *Faith, Freedom, and the Spirit*, esp. chapters one and eight.

Chapter 7

KARL RAHNER AND THOMAS F. TORRANCE: GOD'S SELF-COMMUNICATION IN CHRIST WITH SPECIAL EMPHASIS ON INTERPRETING CHRIST'S RESURRECTION

Karl Rahner and Thomas F. Torrance have made enormous contributions to twentieth-century theology. Torrance is quick to point out that Rahner's approach to trinitarian theology which begins with God's saving revelation (the economic Trinity) and pivots 'upon God's concrete and effective self-communication in the Incarnation' does indeed have the effect that Rahner intended. First, it reunites the treatises *On the One God* and *On the Triune God*. This opens the door to rapprochement between systematic and biblical theology and binds the New Testament view of Jesus closer to the Church's worship and proclamation of the triune God. Second, it opens the door to rapprochement between East and West by shifting from a more 'abstractive' scholastic framework to one bound up with piety, worship and experience within the Church. Third, it opens the door to rapprochement between Roman Catholic theology and Evangelical theology 'especially as represented by the teaching of Karl Barth in his emphasis upon the self-revelation and self-giving of God as the root of the doctrine of the Trinity'.[1]

This chapter will explore how the notion of self-communication functions in the theology of Torrance and Rahner with a view toward seeing how, where and why they agree and disagree about the meaning of this important concept. There is no doubt that self-communication is a central category for each theologian. Despite the fact that it could have emanationist overtones, as noted earlier, the concept itself enables both Torrance and Rahner to fashion contemporary explanations of the Trinity, grace, incarnation and revelation which are intended to function in the three ways just noted. In fact, self-communication is, in many contexts, simply another term for self-revelation.

---

1 Torrance, *Trinitarian Perspectives*, 78.

I shall have to limit myself by addressing one key issue, namely, how consistent are Rahner and Torrance in beginning their theologies with God's economic trinitarian self-communication? In other words, how successful is each theologian in keeping the treatises *On the One God* and *On the Triune God* together without allowing some prior concept of God to determine the truth of his theological reflections? We shall concentrate on their respective methodologies by focusing on how each theologian interprets the resurrection. It is hoped that this comparison will lead to a clearer understanding of how a proper doctrine of the immanent Trinity might function today.

Several important features that structure T. F. Torrance's view of God's self-communication can be noted. First, the *homoousion* which stresses the *enousios* Logos (that the Logos is internal to God's being) is central.[2] Thus, 'Everything hinges on the reality of God's *self*-communication to us in Jesus Christ ... so that for us to know God in Jesus Christ is really to know him as he is in himself'.[3] Second, his theological realism implies that theology must be both devout and scientific.[4] It must be

---

2   Torrance, *The Trinitarian Faith*, 72–3, 130–1 and 311. Cf. also Thomas F. Torrance, *The Christian Doctrine of God*, 129. See also Kang Phee Seng, 'The Epistemological Significance of Ὁμοούσιον in the Theology of Thomas F. Torrance' *SJT*, vol. 45, no. 3 (1992), 341–66, 344ff. For a brief but good biographical and theological introduction to Torrance's theology, see Alister E. McGrath, *Thomas F. Torrance: An Intellectual Biography* (Edinburgh: T & T Clark, 1999). For more on the function of the homoousion in the theology of T. F. Torrance, see Molnar, *Torrance: Theologian of the Trinity*, chapters 2 and 4.

3   T. F. Torrance, *Reality and Evangelical Theology* (Philadelphia: The Westminster Press, 1982), 23. Kang, *SJT*, helpfully explains that for Torrance: 'All human knowing of God which takes the path from man to God, instead of following the way of the incarnation of the homoousial Son from God to man, simply speaks of God by speaking of man in a loud voice or thinks of God's Being as the extension of man's being to infinity, and thus is but an irreligious, mythological projection into the Holy of holies out of the depth of man's creative spirituality and zealous piety' (352). One example of what Kang says is rightly to be rejected here is the thinking of James Mackey who believed that 'the movement, as far as the human spirit is concerned, is always from below upward, from human experience in and of this world to intimations of divinity' (353). Such a conclusion is only possible, Kang rightly argues, when the epistemological significance of the homoousion is ignored; thus what is ignored is the truth that it is only by God that God is known (354).

4   Torrance, *The Trinitarian Faith*, 51.

devout in the sense that for Athanasius, as seen earlier in Chapter 1, it is 'more godly and true to signify God from the Son and call him Father, than to name God from his works alone and call him Unoriginate'.[5] It must be scientific in that 'scientific knowledge was held to result from inquiry strictly in accordance with the nature (κατά φύσιν) of the reality being investigated, that is, knowledge of it reached under the constraint of what it actually and essentially is in itself, and not according to arbitrary convention (κατά θέσιν)'.[6] This theological realism attempts to recognize truth for what it is by thinking after the truth itself. This scientific method is not unique to theology but because theology is under the compulsion of a unique object it certainly knows what cannot be known in other scientific endeavors.[7] For instance, science can neither observe the event of creation itself nor that of the resurrection because we would have to be able to get behind creaturely processes to observe them and that is impossible.[8] Still, in the overlap between natural sciences and religion, as we shall see, Torrance believes there is room for a new kind of natural theology. Third, the relation between subjectivity and objectivity must neither compromise the object nor the subject. Therefore to know God, our thinking must have a point of access in God himself and in our creaturely existence, but this in no way compromises Torrance's belief that only God can reveal God. Torrance frequently opposes subjectivism and dualism while seeking a unitary theology – not a monistic or agnostic theology – but one which respects human subjectivity while finding the true meaning of human subjectivity in a center in God and not in itself. This helps him overcome a particularly thorny issue for modern theology that we have highlighted throughout this book. He argues that we cannot read back our ideas and experiences into God if we are to have a proper theology and that the controlling factor is and remains Christ's active mediation of himself through the Holy Spirit and thus through the Bible, the Church and its sacraments. Arius was the prime historical example of someone

5 Torrance, *The Trinitarian Faith*, 49 and *The Christian Doctrine of God*, 117.

6 Torrance, *The Trinitarian Faith*, 51. See Thomas F. Torrance, *Christian Theology and Scientific Culture* (New York: Oxford University Press, 1981), 27, 29. Cf. also *The Christian Doctrine of God*, 206.

7 Cf. Torrance, *Christian Theology and Scientific Culture*, 8 and *Reality and Evangelical Theology*, 30–1.

8 Cf. Thomas F. Torrance, *Space, Time and Resurrection* (Grand Rapids, MI: Eerdmans, 1976; reissued Edinburgh: T&T Clark, 1998), 77.

who failed to think scientifically about God precisely because he did not think from a center in God.

Therefore, for Torrance, the all-important point of his theology is that we have a point of access in God and in creaturely existence in the incarnation which is God's self-communication to us: 'Jesus Christ himself, then, is the hearing and speaking man included in the Word of God incarnate.'[9] Torrance relies on Hilary of Poitiers for his belief that: 'The very centre of a saving faith is the belief not merely in God, but in God as Father, and not merely in Christ, but in Christ as the Son of God, in him, not as a creature, but as God the Creator, born of God.'[10] Therefore, when we come to God as Father through the Son, our knowledge is 'grounded in the very being of God and is determined by what he essentially is in his own nature.'[11] Since it is in Jesus Christ that we may truly know this God then we may thus know him in a way that is godly and precise. For Torrance, then, the *lex orandi* and the *lex credendi*, piety and precision, godliness and exactness belong together.[12]

Like Rahner, Torrance believes that 'created intelligibility ... by its very nature is open to God and points beyond itself to God',[13] but Torrance does not believe that an inferential argument can be developed from that created intelligibility to God's uncreated intelligibility and so he consistently opposes building a 'logical bridge' between the world and God or between our thoughts and God's being.[14] Although

9 Torrance, *Reality and Evangelical Theology*, 88. For Torrance 'it is specifically in Jesus Christ, the incarnate Son, that God has communicated himself to us ... Thus it is only in him who is both ὁμοούσιος with the Father and ὁμοούσιος with us, that we may really know God as he is in himself' (*The Trinitarian Faith*, 203).

10 Hilary cited in Torrance, *The Trinitarian Faith*, 53.

11 Torrance, *The Trinitarian Faith*, 53.

12 Cf. Torrance, *The Trinitarian Faith*, 43.

13 Thomas F. Torrance, *The Ground and Grammar of Theology* (Charlottesville: University Press of Virginia, 1980; reissued Edinburgh: T&T Clark, 2001, 99). See also Thomas F. Torrance, *God and Rationality* (London: Oxford University Press, 1971; reissued Edinburgh: T&T Clark, 2001, 186). Torrance gives an excellent account of how this openness is to be understood through the Holy Spirit in Chapter 7. For a discussion of Torrance's view of the Spirit and human knowledge of God, see Molnar, *Faith, Freedom and the Spirit*, Chapter 2.

14 Torrance, *The Ground and Grammar of Theology*, 99 and 75ff., 79, 81, 86. Torrance regards Anselm's argument as a scientific one rather than a logical

Torrance believes there is a role for natural theology, he grants it no independent status in relation to positive theology. Like Rahner, Torrance seeks to integrate 'so-called natural theology and so-called revealed theology' indicating that

> natural theology has its natural place in the overlap between theological and natural science where they operate within the same rational structures of space and time and have in common the basic ideas of the unitary rationality of the universe – its contingent intelligibility and contingent freedom, contributed by Christian theology to natural science . . .[15]

one. Within this method intelligibility and being are not separated, but created intelligibility operates under the compulsion of God's uncreated intelligibility. Cf. also *Reality and Evangelical Theology*, 24.

15 Torrance, *The Ground and Grammar of Theology*, 100 and 107. While Colin Gunton agrees with Torrance that parallel rationalities may be found in the sciences of God and of created realities and that 'created and uncreated intelligibility' may be viewed together, he prefers to maintain a distinction between natural theology and 'a theology of nature' rather than speaking, with Torrance, of a transformed natural theology. See Colin E. Gunton, *A Brief Theology of Revelation* (Edinburgh: T & T Clark, 1995), 63. This makes sense since traditional natural theology is understood as a knowledge of God from nature, whereas Torrance's 'transformed natural theology' operates within the ambit of revelation and is thus a knowledge of nature from revelation based on faith and grace. Unfortunately, however, that is not the full story because Torrance's 'new natural theology', is said to differ from traditional natural theology, because it attempts to relocate natural theology within the sphere of revelation by not detaching it from its material content (Thomas F. Torrance, *Reality and Scientific Theology* [Eugene, OR: Wipf and Stock, 2001], 59). This leads him to claim that his new natural theology is natural to the object of faith, namely, the triune God. This creates problems because, according to Barth a theology that is faithful to the revelation of God in his Word and Spirit (the triune God), is in reality no longer a natural theology, but a theology of grace based on revelation. So it really is a confusion of categories for Torrance to suggest that such knowledge is a 'new natural theology'. Clearly, what he intends to suggest is that grace does not destroy nature but fulfils nature in its proper relation with God, but again that very notion is built on a theology of revelation. Beyond that, Torrance does seem to espouse certain elements of the old natural theology when he considers the relation of theology and science, even though he consistently rejects or excludes such thinking in

Footnote 15 (*cont.*)

his dogmatic theology. So, in a less than careful moment he argues that an independent natural theology (one detached from revelation which he and Barth rejected) misses the mark 'by abstracting his [God's] existence from his act, and so by considering one aspect of his being apart from other aspects' (Torrance, *Karl Barth*, 151). This statement suggests that natural theology does actually know an 'aspect' of God's being whereas for Barth it does not, simply because one either knows God fully in his entire being as Father, Son and Holy Spirit or one does not (*CD* II/1, 51). Moreover, there are residual elements of the old natural theology embedded in Torrance's own thinking, for example, while Torrance believes the universe cannot provide an answer to its ultimate intelligibility, he also says 'it does more than raise a question for it seems to *cry silently* for a transcendent agency in its explanation and understanding' (*Reality and Scientific Theology*, 58) and he argues that we cannot coerce God by our questions, 'rather does He coerce us by this silence or emptiness to listen to Him' (Torrance, *Theological Science* [New York: Oxford University Press, 1978, 47]), 101). Further, he claims that the unpredictability and lawfulness of nature 'may be regarded as something like the signature of the Creator in the depths of contingent being' (Torrance, *Divine and Contingent Order*, 73). These remarks seem to be in conflict with Torrance's own conviction that, while God can reveal himself through nature, that does not mean that an examination of nature can actually produce reliable knowledge of God (Torrance, *The Trinitarian Faith*, 78). Barth believed that natural theology in any form is of no service to the church at all because it always bypasses Christ, the Word of God, in order to know God. For a full discussion of this matter, see Paul D. Molnar, 'Natural Theology Revisited: A Comparison of T. F. Torrance and Karl Barth', *Zeitschrift für dialektische Theologie* 1 (2005): 1–31, *Incarnation and Resurrection*, 83–7 and *Torrance: Theologian of the Trinity*, 93–9. In his *Theology in Transposition: A Constructive Appraisal of T. F. Torrance* (Minneapolis, MN: Fortress, 2013), Myk Habets notes three major views of natural theology in Torrance studies: (1) Alister McGrath's view that Torrance's theology 'sponsors a natural theology that functions in an apologetic way'; (2) that Torrance's theology is 'consistently Barthian and allows no place for a traditional natural theology at all, even though Torrance was at times inconsistent with these intentions (Paul Molnar)'; and finally (3) that Torrance consistently spoke of natural theology in a way that 'we would normally speak of a theology of nature' so that there is no inconsistency in his thought (Elmer M. Colyer and W. Travis McMaken)', 85–6. Habets offers a fourth way, namely, 'one that seeks to bring natural and theological sciences into dialogue, which allows for a soft apologetic role to natural theology, and yet, one that does not

Torrance, however, insists on the irreversibility of the creator/creature relation and of our knowledge and God's being and act.[16] Finally, Torrance insists that God's being and act are indeed one ad intra and ad extra; thus God can be known only out of God himself[17] and what God is toward us in Christ and the Spirit, he is eternally in himself.[18] This last point, of course, is where Rahner and Torrance agree about the immanent and the economic Trinity. Like Rahner, Torrance maintains that God was free to create or not.[19] He also insists that creation does

Footnote 15 *(cont.)*

allow any strictly logical bridge to God from unaided human reason on the basis of natural revelation. I also contend that Torrance was less than clear or consistent in his use of and development of his transposed form of natural theology' (86). This is an intriguing suggestion, but it may be that Torrance was doing no more than attempting to demonstrate that human reason needs an explanation that it cannot provide for itself whenever those residual elements of the old natural theology appeared in his discussion of theology and science. It is certainly the case that he has no interest in engaging in apologetics unless it is a kind of apologetics that operates exclusively within faith. That is why I indicated that he would never accept the approach offered by Alister McGrath who turns to Pannenberg to present a 'public theology' that appeals to those with or without faith in the Christian God [see Alister E. McGrath, *A Scientific Theology: Volume I Nature* (Grand Rapids, MI: Eerdmans, 2001), 264–305]. McGrath argues that the apologetic value of a 'legitimate natural theology' will allow us to see that 'the Christian evangelist will have a number of "points of contact" for the gospel within the created order' (299), and he believes that all acts of understanding are based on some pre-understanding (298) so that 'the human mind possesses the capacity to recognize this work of creation as such, and to draw at least some reliable conclusions concerning the nature and character of God from the created order' (299). Torrance unequivocally rejects all three of these ideas in his theology, *Torrance: Theologian of the Trinity*, 95.

16 Torrance, *The Ground and Grammar of Theology*, 67, *The Christian Doctrine of God*, 18ff. and 158, and *The Trinitarian Faith*, 49, 76 and 82.

17 Cf. for example, Torrance, *The Trinitarian Faith*, 52 and 207, *The Christian Doctrine of God*, 11, 13ff., 22 and 74 and *God and Rationality*, 72, 176.

18 Cf. for example, Torrance, *The Trinitarian Faith*, 71, 130, *The Christian Doctrine of God*, 8, 92, 158, 237 and Torrance, *Reality and Evangelical Theology*, 14, 141. These are only a few of the many places where this insight is stressed.

19 Torrance, *The Trinitarian Faith*, 52, 90–3, 105 and *The Christian Doctrine of God*, 207.

not take place through an inner compulsion in God's being.[20] Further, Torrance emphasizes that the Gift and the Giver are one in Christ and the Spirit. Thus, he understands grace in a way that does not ascribe God's (onto-relational) personal actions directly to created being and in a way that does not detach God's actions in history from the being of his Word and Spirit.[21] Both theologians also agree that there should be dialogue between science and theology.

Torrance's View of the Resurrection

A brief but not exhaustive exploration of Torrance's understanding of Christ's resurrection should allow for an interesting comparison of the two theologians and will illustrate that each of the above-mentioned factors is at work in his theology of the resurrection. Torrance begins by noting that in his last conversation with Barth the two theologians agreed (1) that natural theology had a place within positive theology; and (2) on the importance of the resurrection of the body when speaking of Christ's resurrection from the dead. Thus, for Torrance, there should be a proper natural theology, that is, one that does not create a chasm between God and the universe and then try to bridge that chasm without allowing its knowledge to be shaped by the content of Christian revelation. Such a natural theology can neither be independent nor antecedent to 'actual or empirical knowledge of God upon which it is then imposed'.[22] Torrance therefore rejects any a priori understanding

20 Torrance, *The Trinitarian Faith*, 93 and Torrance, *The Ground and Grammar of Theology*, 66.

21 See Torrance, *The Trinitarian Faith*, 138, 140f., 201, 215, 222 and 297, *The Christian Doctrine of God*, 63 and *Theology in Reconciliation*, 131ff. where Torrance stresses that Christ's real presence (*self*-communication) in the Eucharist is grounded in God's real presence to himself. Cf. also Thomas F. Torrance, *Theology in Reconstruction* (London: SCM Press, Ltd, 1965), 182f. For Torrance's onto-relational notion of persons (divine and human), see *The Christian Doctrine of God*, 102ff., 124, 133, 157 and 163 and *Reality and Evangelical Theology*, 42ff. The ontic relations of the three divine Persons in the one God 'belong to what they essentially are in themselves in their distinctive *hypostases*'. Thus, relations among persons belong to what they are as persons. See also Molnar, *Torrance: Theologian of the Trinity*, 61–3.

22 Torrance, *Space, Time and Resurrection*, 1.

of God as he has actually communicated himself to us in the economy and argues that the resurrection should be the starting point for scientific theology.

> *The raising of the Christ* is *the* act of God, whose significance is not to be compared with any event before or after. *It is the primal datum of theology, from which there can be no abstracting*, and the normative presupposition for every valid dogmatic judgment and for the meaningful construction of a Christian theology.[23]

As such it cannot be derived from empirical reflection and is 'established beyond any religious *a priori*'.[24] Torrance thus insists that the resurrection is *utterly unique* and therefore it, like the incarnation, conflicts with our prior knowledge and belief about God by forcing itself on our minds as an ultimate event whose truth was and is identical with the transcendent truth of God. This is why Jesus was an offense to the Jews and folly to the Greek. Based on prior beliefs and knowledge, Jesus's resurrection 'was deemed to be utterly incredible'.[25] While one 'may (or will be able to) observe the resurrected actuality of Jesus Christ' as a new creation within the old order, it must be known in accord with its own nature and out of itself.[26] Torrance thus argues that the order of redemption intersects with the order of creation in the resurrection so that 'the basic structure of what emerges in the Easter event is absolutely new: a reality which is not only entirely unknown to us but entirely unknowable in terms of what we already know or think we know, and knowable through a radical reconstruction of our prior knowledge'.[27] For Torrance, the very idea that the act of resurrection is an interruption of the laws of nature assumes that creation and resurrection can be observed a posteriori or predicted a priori and fails to recognize that it, like Jesus himself (as God and man), is *utterly unique*. It is a creative act of God within nature and cannot be grasped in the same way that we formulate natural laws since natural laws only express connections immanent in nature. The resurrection did not arise from history and is not a natural process that can be observed as such. 'Just

---

23 Torrance, *Space, Time and Resurrection*, 74.

24 Torrance, *Space, Time and Resurrection*, 74 and 175ff.

25 Torrance, *Space, Time and Resurrection*, 17.

26 Torrance, *Space, Time and Resurrection*, 78.

27 Torrance, *Space, Time and Resurrection*, 175.

as in justification the law was not destroyed but established, so in the resurrection time is not annihilated but recreated, for it is taken up in Christ, sanctified in his human life and transformed in his resurrection as man.'[28] Christ's ascension refers us back to the historical Jesus as the place where we may know the immanent Trinity.[29] In the ascension Torrance argues:

> Our human nature in Jesus Christ is exalted to the right hand of God. But even with the resurrection itself it is made clear that in Jesus Christ man is assumed into the divine life embodied in him. The relation of Jesus Christ to God is unique, for he is God the Son in the unity of the Holy Trinity, but the reconciliation of our human nature in him implies a reconciliation or oneness with God which is not identity, yet a real sharing in the union of the incarnate Son with the Father, through a sharing not only in his human nature but in the life and love of God embodied in him.[30]

This means also that it is precisely as the incarnate Son that Jesus is risen and therefore he is 'not simply the Word of God addressed to man, but answering word of man addressed to God in the unity of his one Person.'[31] Jesus Christ then, in this perspective, is 'the actualization of the Truth of God among us in such a way that it creates its own counterpart in us to itself' such that God's truth and our truth are one in him. He is thus 'the bridge between the reality of God and the realities of our world.'[32] This is an important point. We have seen how some contemporary theologians, already discussed, think that because we cannot and indeed ought not attempt to reach beyond creation in an attempt to know God, therefore they supposed that we could only speak with certainty about the economic Trinity. Some then suggested that we could say little or nothing about the immanent Trinity. In opposition to such thinking, Torrance believed that if our concepts were not shaped by who God is in his internal relations (the relations of the immanent Trinity) then we could not know God truly at all. Here

28 Torrance, *Space, Time and Resurrection*, 98.

29 Torrance, *Reality and Evangelical Theology*, 37 and *Space, Time and Resurrection*, 128ff.

30 Torrance, *Space, Time and Resurrection*, 70.

31 Torrance, *Space, Time and Resurrection*, 71.

32 Torrance, *Space, Time and Resurrection*, 71.

Torrance explains exactly how we can and must know the immanent Trinity within creation (without attempting to transcend it) by referring to the resurrection. He says of Jesus that:

> He is thus the centre in our midst where the Reality and Word of God are translated into human reality and word and where we human beings may know and speak of God without having to transcend our creaturely forms of thought and speech. It is in and through Jesus Christ therefore that we creatures of space and time may know God the Father, in such a way as to think and speak truly and validly of him, even in such a way that the forms of our thought and speech really terminate objectively on God himself in his own ultimate Being and Reality. Apart from the resurrection we could not say this.[33]

What Torrance means by this of course is that without the resurrection we would finally be cut off from God such that we would in reality be unable to know God as he is in himself. It is in him that God has forged such a unity between us and himself that we can be certain that our concepts have a genuine objective referent in God himself: 'The whole epistemic function of the incarnation thus comes to its complete fruition in the resurrection of Christ in the fullness of his humanity.'[34] For Torrance, the resurrection of Christ is 'the pledge that statements about God in Jesus Christ have an objective reference in God, and are not just projections out of the human heart and imagination'.[35]

Since Christ's resurrection is utterly unique, Torrance argues that the kingdom did not come by the processes of history. If it had, there would have been no need for Christ's resurrection.[36] There was nothing comparable in the Old Testament and it is dominant in the New Testament as a supernatural miraculous event which could not be explained from the human or natural side. Christ was not only raised bodily from the dead but was appointed Messiah. Indeed, Jesus's birth and resurrection are linked and his whole life is a miracle. Jesus's resurrection also has corporate implications: we receive immortality from him. Unbelievers are affected since they will be judged by Jesus, but only believers will enjoy the fruit of the resurrection. The New Testament does not first

---

33 Torrance, *Space, Time and Resurrection*, 71.
34 Torrance, *Space, Time and Resurrection*, 71.
35 Torrance, *Space, Time and Resurrection*, 72.
36 Torrance, *Space, Time and Resurrection*, 28.

focus on individual resurrection but on God's covenant mercies and on Christ's resurrection, which can only be understood in faith because it exists in a transformed context which it brought about. Jesus appeared only to believers. Therefore one must dwell in it to grasp it. It will appear differently inside and outside of the community.[37]

Torrance opposes any non-cognitive or non-conceptual or what is sometimes called implicit faith as a form of dualism which disjoins God from the world and permits no knowledge of God as he is in himself.

> Even though God transcends all that we can think and say of Him, it still holds good that we cannot have experience of Him or believe in Him without conceptual forms of understanding – as Anselm used to say: *fides esse nequit sine conceptione.*[38]

He would thus oppose an application of the historical critical method which separates the empirical and the theoretical or the dogmatic and factual such as might happen if someone refused to accept the commission of the risen Lord as part of the original tradition coming from Jesus.[39] What Torrance rejects is the kind of source, form or redaction criticism that operates with the assumptions of 'observationalism and phenomenalism. Thus they assume that theoretical elements can only have a later origin and have to be put down to the creative spirituality of the early Christian community rather than to Jesus himself.'[40] If the facts presented in the New Testament are taken out of their theological contexts they are mutilated and can no longer be properly conceived. Torrance, like Rahner, wishes to see fundamental theology and dogmatic theology unified. However, he insists that Christ must be the starting point and that this excludes an a priori knowledge of the resurrection because such a priori knowledge is not actually scientific. This is precisely why he rejects Bultmann's view of the resurrection.

He argues that Bultmann's view, that the objective form of incarnation, atonement, resurrection and ascension resulted from unscientific mythologizing based on an unscientific world-view, is unacceptable because it ignores the fact that early Christians were well aware of the *conflict* between the gospel and the prevailing world-view. Rather, it is Bultmann's own dualist and scientifically antiquated world-view that

---

37 Torrance, *Space, Time and Resurrection*, 32–7.
38 Torrance, *God and Rationality*, 170.
39 Torrance, *Space, Time and Resurrection*, 7.
40 Torrance, *Reality and Evangelical Theology*, 80.

allowed him to mythologize the New Testament and 'then "demytholo-gize" it in terms of his own mistaken exaltation of self-understanding, which transfers the centre of reference away from the action of God in the historical Jesus to some spiritual event of "resurrection" in man's experience'.[41]

41 Torrance, *Space, Time and Resurrection*, 17–18, n. 25. Cf. also *Reality and Evangelical Theology*, 82. For an interesting analysis of Bultmann, see *God and Rationality*, Chapter 3, *Cheap and Costly Grace*. Torrance writes: 'whenever we take our eyes off the centrality and uniqueness of Jesus Christ and His objective vicarious work, the Gospel disappears behind man's existentialized self-understanding, and even the Reality of God Himself is simply reduced to "what He means for me ..."' (60). Torrance offers a thorough and profound analysis and critique of Bultmann in *Incarnation: The Person and Life of Christ* (ed.) Robert T. Walker (Downers Grove, IL: InterVarsity Press, 2008), 274–96 tracing his ultimate error to his separation of ideas from reality and fact existing in space and time. Instead of allowing for a real incarnation of God in space and time in Jesus and a real objective resurrection of Jesus from the dead, Bultmann conceptualized these events as mythological interpretations of the historical Jesus that needed to be demythologized. The result was that for him 'the saving event is not an independent objective act of God out there, in the historical Jesus made on my behalf, but simply encounter, a subjective experience in my own heart – the saving event is my acceptance of the challenge of the word, and my decision' (280). In a misguided attempt to rehabilitate Bultmann from the critique of Barth, Torrance and others, Benjamin Myers, 'Faith as Self-Understanding: Towards a Post-Barthian Appreciation of Rudolf Bultmann' *IJST*, vol. 10, no. 1 January 2008, 21–35 claims that Bultmann's intention was always 'to maintain the utter *singularity* and *distinctiveness* of the reality of God' (31). Yet, in spite of the many references to Bultmann's *Jesus Christ and Mythology*, Myers left out points of Bultmann's own thinking which completely subvert his intention to speak of the 'reality of God'. First, Bultmann claims that 'the facts of redemption constitute the grounds of faith, but only as perceived by faith itself' [Rudolf Bultmann, *Jesus Christ and Mythology* (New York: Charles Scribner's Sons, 1958), 72]. This remark very clearly places the power of knowing redemption not in the redeemer but in our perception of faith. In that way it undermines any objective knowledge of the reality of God. That explains why Bultmann can suppose that 'we can dispense with the objective form in which they [the events of Jesus' life] are cast' [Rudolf Bultmann, *Kerygma and Myth: A Theological Debate* (ed.) Hans Werner Bartsch (New York: Harper Torchbooks, 1961), 'New Testament and Mythology', 1–44, 34]. In his view, we use mythological language regarding resurrection and Jesus's sonship to express

Footnote 41 (*cont.*)

his meaning for us. Second, the problem here becomes acute with Bultmann's own assertion that 'the ground and object of faith are identical. They are one and the same thing, because *we cannot speak of what God is in Himself but only of what He is doing to us and with us*' (*Jesus Christ and Mythology*, 73, emphasis mine). Such an assertion not only undermines the possibility of genuine knowledge of the reality of God, but illustrates the point of this book once again, namely, that we really cannot say anything true about the Christian God acting for us unless we are enabled by God himself (and not our faith) to know God as the eternal Father, Son and Holy Spirit, that is, as God in himself! Ignoring this problem, Myers simply follows Bultmann claiming that: 'If we were to speak objectively of God, we would need to place ourselves *outside* God, to view God from a distance' (30). Thus, in his estimation 'it is only in order to affirm God's reality that Bultmann so emphatically denies God's "objectivity"! It is in order to *distinguish* between God and humanity that he so carefully seeks to *correlate* God and humanity' (31). Myers thus affirms Bultmann's view that true knowledge of God as articulated by John Macquarrie should be expressed as follows: '"A purely subjective and a purely objective understanding are alike abstractions from the self-world correlation which alone makes possible any understanding whatsoever' (31). He also follows Gerhard Ebeling arguing that speaking 'about God and speaking about the whole of reality are not two entirely different matters, but mutually condition each other' (32). It should be self-evident by now why this kind of thinking must be rejected. It must be rejected simply because we know in faith that true knowledge of God comes about for us only through God himself, that is, by the Holy Spirit enabling our knowledge of God's primary objectivity in and through God's secondary objectivity by which he encounters us mediately through other created objects chosen by him to reveal himself to us. In particular, it means that God makes himself known objectively in and through the incarnate and risen Lord. Nowhere in this article does the author address the fact that Bultmann claimed that if the resurrection was indeed a historical event additional to the cross then it could be 'nothing else than the rise of faith in the risen Lord, since it is was this faith which led to the apostolic preaching' (Bultmann, *Kerygma and Myth*, 42). In this remark the objective reality of the risen Lord himself is marginalized and replaced by the faith of the disciples, once again undermining both the historicity and the objectivity of God's actions within the sphere of secondary objectivity by which he makes himself known to us as the eternal Trinity. Unsurprisingly Bultmann claims that 'the saving efficacy of the cross is not derived from the fact that it is the cross of Christ: it is the cross of Christ because it has this saving efficacy' (43). This thinking does not acknowledge the power of salvation which resides

Torrance insists that his critically realist theology will avoid fundamentalism and extreme realism. It will not argue that scripture is impregnated with changeless divine truth that can be authoritatively interpreted and it will think about realities through thoughts rather than thinking only thoughts themselves. One's thoughts therefore must be controlled by God's self-communication as Father, Son and Holy Spirit.[42] Torrance rejects Neo-Protestant dualism which might lead to historicizing the scriptural material by searching for raw facts without penetrating to understand what it says out of its own dynamic processes. Torrance dismisses what he calls a kind of Q fundamentalism which supposes an earliest layer of the New Testament message from which it will think. Theology is interested in the different layers of tradition only as they are correlated and controlled by God's self-revelation. We cannot say then exactly how ideas are related to the realities we experience because it is an ontological relation that eludes formalization. Yet it is only in that relation that we can know. Theology must dwell within the semantic relations of the New Testament so that one's mind may apprehend the realities intended and be shaped by God's objective self-communication in Christ. This is why Torrance insists that the resurrection must be interpreted historically *and* theologically. A merely theological view would end in mythology and Docetism while a merely historical view would not take account of Jesus's uniqueness from the start and would be neither open minded nor scientific.[43]

How then does Torrance understand subjective and objective realities in connection with the resurrection? Our thinking must be

in Christ and his unique atoning actions for us as the incarnate Son. Instead it places the power of salvation in us. So it is very difficult to see how anyone with a clear idea of who God is in himself and for us could agree with Myers that 'Bultmann's doctrine of faith has a great deal to offer theology today' (Myers, *Faith as Self-Understanding*, 33).

42 Torrance, *Space, Time and Resurrection*, 9f. See Torrance, *God and Rationality*, 170ff. Torrance believes the Holy Spirit creates our capacity for God; is not mutually correlated with us; is essentially in God as is the Son and enables us to participate in the Father and Son without ceasing to be Lord: 'As the Spirit of Truth He is the self-communication and the self-speaking of the divine Being dwelling within us who renews our minds, articulates God's Word within our understanding, leads us into all truth, so that through the Spirit we are converted from ourselves to thinking from a centre in God and not in ourselves, and to knowing God out of God and not out of ourselves', 174.

43 Torrance, *Space, Time and Resurrection*, 94.

governed by or shaped and informed by 'the self-evidencing force and intrinsic significance of their [the biblical reports] objective content, i.e. the self-revelation and self-communication of God through Jesus Christ and in the Holy Spirit'.[44] This is different from logical inferences empty of ontological content. What makes scripture transparent then is the divine light that shines through. Torrance is very consistent arguing this position. For example, in *Reality and Evangelical Theology* he opposes fundamentalism and liberalism precisely because each approach to scripture, in its own way, fails to acknowledge that the truth of God's self-communication is and remains grounded in God himself and not in the media through which God interacts with us.[45] Thus fundamentalism makes the Bible a 'self-contained corpus of divine truths in propositional form' and fails to acknowledge the identity of being between what God is toward us in Jesus Christ and what he is in himself.[46] Fundamentalism refuses to see that God's self-communication is his free continuous act which must be given and received and whose content is God himself. Liberalism stumbles at the identity of God and his revelation by denying the deity of Christ and assimilating the Spirit of Christ to the human spirit. It is thus 'thrown back upon the autonomous religious reason to provide the ground on which all that is claimed to be divine revelation is to be considered';[47] this detaches Christ from God and Christianity is then detached from Christ.

Finally, the theologian must interpret scripture within the frame of objective meaning that gave rise to the layers of the apostolic tradition. There was an integration of the self-proclamation of Christ with the apostolic proclamation of him which had an impact on the early church and they should not be separated. Therefore, as Torrance notes, Jesus was not a Christian since a Christian is saved by him. For that reason theology is not concerned with Jesus's private religious understanding of God but with his vicarious life and activity through which we know the God and Father of Jesus Christ as redeemed sinners.

Most importantly, the context of objective meaning here for the theologian 'is bound up with the incarnation of the Son of God to be

---

44 Torrance, *Space, Time and Resurrection*, 11.
45 Torrance, *Reality and Evangelical Theology*, 85–8, 90.
46 Torrance, *Reality and Evangelical Theology*, 17–18.
47 Torrance, *Reality and Evangelical Theology*, 15.

one with us in our physical human existence' so that in and through his vicarious life and passion he could 'redeem human being and creatively reground it in the very life of God himself, and therefore it is also bound up with the resurrection of Jesus Christ in body, or the physical reality of his human existence among us'.[48] In the resurrection, God's incarnate and redeeming purpose is triumphantly fulfilled. Owing to this any abstraction from the incarnation, life, death and resurrection leaves scholars unable to find the unity of scripture.

Therefore, it is clear that for Torrance an *objective* self-disclosure took place which was the basis for Christianity and that the incarnation and resurrection still force themselves in the same way on our minds today.[49] Indeed, for Torrance, the resurrection accounts must be accepted in their own settings in Israel which had a non-dualistic view of reality (as against Hellenic, Gnostic or mystic views). Since Christians did not separate the humanity from the incarnate Son and spoke of bodily resurrection they rejected Docetism and adoptionism. This led to a radical revision in the concept of God. Judaism in fact refused to go forward with the Church by accepting the implications of the resurrection, that is, that God himself was directly and personally present in the passion and resurrection of Jesus. The resurrection therefore destroyed the dualist view of God's relation with the world. In fact the root of the doctrine of the Trinity is formed here because resurrection of the body implies a knowledge which participates in Christ's being and life as already described. Torrance's realist view of the resurrection then stresses that God acts within space and time; that our thinking must be faithful to the nature of the event and that we must develop radically different notions of space and time in accordance with this. In other words the resurrection must be seen in light of Christ's divine-human natures; in fact his own uniqueness is what makes the resurrection credible. Since the resurrection is the other side of the cross, our humanity is sanctified in *his* life of obedience; his healing and

---

48 Torrance, *Space, Time and Resurrection*, 13. For Torrance, following Athenagoras, 'If there is no resurrection, human nature is no longer genuinely human' 81–2. Without this, theology collapses into moralism, existentialism and subjectivism. Unless Jesus actually rose, then the power of sin and death and nonbeing remain unbroken. 'Everything depends on the resurrection of the body, otherwise all we have is a Ghost for a Savior' (87).

49 Torrance, *Space, Time and Resurrection*, 18. Cf. Torrance, *The Christian Doctrine of God*, 46f.

forgiving as well as his death and resurrection are bound up with who he is in relation to the Father. Important here are the notions 'enhypostasis' and 'anhypostasis'.

Christ remained passive in the sense that he did not use his divine power to avoid temptation and the cross (this corresponds to the anhypostatic element); he experienced a real death in submitting to the Father's judgment and was so powerless that he had to be raised up by God himself. This was a vicarious act of Jesus for us, and it was thus positive and creative, since the resurrection was the Father's justification of our humanity; this corresponds to the 'enhypostatic' element in the incarnation. While our humanity is indeed sanctified, it is sanctified in *his* life of free obedience. The hypostatic union implies a living and dynamic union which ran through his whole life. Therefore atonement cannot be separated from Christ, its 'Agent'.[50] The subject of the resurrection then is

> a divine-human subject, and therefore we have a unique happening defined by the nature of the unique Agent. Other human agents were involved in the life of Jesus ... but because we have here a different Subject, the Son of God incarnate in human existence ... we have to understand the inner movement of his history in a way appropriate to his nature – that applies to his birth, to the whole of his life, and to his resurrection ...[51]

---

50 Torrance, *Space, Time and Resurrection*, 42–55.

51 Torrance, *Space, Time and Resurrection*, 94. Thus both the ideas of the virgin birth and the empty tomb were not invented but forced themselves on the early Church against its current beliefs (56). Since the resurrection of our human nature is the goal of the atonement, Torrance can also say, in light of the concepts of 'perichoresis' and 'enhypostasis', that 'the resurrection also means that the steadfastness of the Son of Man is such that it held on its way in utter obedience to the Father in the spirit of holiness in the midst of judgment, death and hell, and in spite of them, so that he raised himself up from the dead in perfect Amen to the Father's Will, acquiescing in his verdict upon our sin but responding in complete trust and love to the Father. The resurrection is the goal of the steadfast obedience of the Son of Man in answer to the steadfast love of the Father ... the resurrection is the complete Amen of the Son to the Father as of the Father to the Son ... It is with the resurrection that the *I am* of God is fully actualized among us – the *Ego eimi* of God to man, of God in man, and so of man in Christ to God' (67–8).

It must be accepted or rejected on its own ground, but it confronts us with a self-communication of God which lays claim to our commitment. This is not an act of blind faith because it is the subjective pole of commitment to objective reality.[52] Torrance advocates what he calls repentant thinking because it is thinking which must yield to God's self-revelation which is clearly not to be found first within experience but first in Jesus Christ and then in experience. There is no reason to separate the two, but there is every reason to see that the meaning of experience is illuminated by the *historical events* of incarnation, atonement, resurrection and ascension: God's own self-revelation thus prevents us from grounding our beliefs in faith. The only proper ground of faith then is the reality to which it is correlated as its objective pole. Bultmann clearly reduced the objective to the subjective pole by collapsing the Easter event into the disciples' experience of faith. It is clear that this thinking is a consistent outworking of Torrance's pivotal insight that theology must think from a center in God and not in ourselves. Even though Torrance explains that knowledge arises from experience and, in his view, through intuition,[53] he is very clear that 'evangelical experience' depends on Christ's self-communication and ultimately on the Son's mutual knowing and loving relation with the Father for intelligibility. Thus, experience is controlled from a center in God and must be open and completed beyond itself in the Word and Spirit.[54]

Here the notion of self-communication functions in the incarnation and resurrection constituting the intelligible constitutive ground of Christian faith so that in and through these events the 'Word of truth' from God himself is communicated to us. Since Jesus Christ himself is

---

52 Torrance, *Space, Time and Resurrection*, 18–19.

53 For an explanation of what he means by this see Molnar, *Torrance: Theologian of the Trinity*, 34, 326–7.

54 See Torrance, *The Christian Doctrine of God*, 83–111. David Fergusson presents a very helpful analysis of the relation between the resurrection and faith by showing how the traditional view that is grounded in scripture sees the resurrection as an event in the life of Jesus that gives meaning to faith rather than as an event that is created within or realized by the believer. Cf. 'Interpreting the Resurrection' in *SJT*, vol. 38, no. 3 (1985): 287–305. For an extended discussion of how Fergusson's important distinctions function in the thought of Barth, Torrance, Rahner and other prominent contemporary theologians, see Molnar, *Incarnation and Resurrection*. Chapters 1 through 4 deal with Barth, Rahner and Torrance.

that ground and authority there is no extraneous ground.[55] The incarnation and resurrection are ultimate and carry their own authority in themselves. As such they call for intelligent commitment and belief. In this sense theology is faith seeking understanding.[56] As God became man in Christ, our knowledge is grounded in the internal being and reality of God. The resurrection has stripped death and evil of their force and the union between God and man established in Christ remains valid beyond death; Christ is and remains Lord of time as a man of his time. The truth of these events can be seen as all-embracing miracles. Hence they cannot be *verified* or *validated* on any other grounds than those they themselves provide. Since acts of God include nature, they can be investigated but can in fact only be explained from grounds in God. Thus, the incarnation and resurrection are not to be seen as interruptions of the natural order or infringements on its laws but as a restoration of order within nature where it had been damaged.[57]

Unless we accept the resurrection as part of God's self-revealing activity in history and as an ultimate belief we will try to account for it in terms of ordinary experience and then it will appear as self-contradictory and meaningless.[58] For Torrance we must think through self-critically the relation of this ultimate belief in relation to others such as creation, incarnation and the love of God; we should grasp the significance of Christ's humanity for understanding the gospel and its message of salvation in relation to the ascension and second coming as well. All of this will reflect on our understanding of the resurrection. If we hold a view of the ascension in which Jesus's humanity is 'swallowed up in the Spirit or Light of the eternal God, or a concept of the

55 Torrance, *Space, Time and Resurrection*, 20.

56 Cf. Torrance, *Theology in Reconstruction*, 163ff. Thus, 'There is no authority for believing in Jesus outside of Jesus himself' (121) and 'Justification by grace alone tells us that verification of our faith or knowledge on any other ground, or out of any other source, than Jesus Christ, is to be set aside' (163).

57 Torrance, *Space, Time and Resurrection*, 22–3.

58 Torrance, *Space, Time and Resurrection*, 25. In this regard it would be worth comparing the thinking of Roger Haight to the thinking of T. F. Torrance in order to see how and why Haight held that belief in the resurrection does not necessarily entail that a body was no longer in the tomb and that resurrection primarily refers to our faith and hope and not to an event in Jesus's life that gives meaning to ours. See Paul D. Molnar, 'Incarnation, Resurrection and the Doctrine of the Trinity: A Comparison of Thomas F. Torrance and Roger Haight', *IJST*, vol. 5, no. 2 (July 2003): 147–67.

eschatological future which has little more material content to it than that somehow the future is more real than the past or the present, and in which the humanity of the advent Christ is replaced by "hope",[59] then we have a Docetic view of the resurrection. The human realism of our view of the resurrection, ascension and second coming then will affect our view of the historical and risen Jesus Christ himself.

The fact that the resurrection will look different to those who believe and are affected by its transforming impact does not imply that the evidence for the resurrection is only the evidence of belief. The resurrection is rather an objective event that includes those for whom it has taken place. Thus for St. Paul, 'we have already been raised up before God in him: to what has objectively taken place in him there is a corresponding subjective counterpart in us which as such belongs to the whole integrated reality of the resurrection event'; but this does not mean that Christ's resurrection 'can simply be identified with or resolved into that counterpart'.[60] Anything less or other than the resurrection of Christ's body would deny that in his humanity we have an *objective* act of God in time and space. Redemption would then collapse as well. Torrance therefore regards acceptance of the empty tomb as crucial.[61] The union of God and man which began in the incarnation and occurred throughout Jesus's incarnate life was fully and finally achieved in the cross and resurrection. Our human nature is in fact restored in Christ. That was the goal of the atonement. Reconciliation becomes eternally valid because Jesus is the resurrection and the life – it is identical with his person. Our human nature is now set within the Father/Son relation.

Since Christ himself is the bridge between the reality of God and the world – we must emphasize once more that it is here (in him) that we may speak of God without having to transcend creaturely speech and thought.[62] This is why Torrance argues that theological statements direct us to what is new and beyond our language and cannot contain it; while concepts must retain their creaturely content, we cannot claim to lay hold of divine reality by them.[63] Yet they must be employed in an act of

---

59 Torrance, *Space, Time and Resurrection*, 26.

60 Torrance, *Space, Time and Resurrection*, 38–9.

61 Torrance, *Space, Time and Resurrection*, 66. Cf. also Torrance, *Reality and Evangelical Theology*, 37.

62 Torrance, *Space, Time and Resurrection*, 68–71.

63 Cf. Thomas F. Torrance, *Space, Time and Incarnation* (London: Oxford University Press, 1978); reissued Edinburgh: T&T Clark, 1997), 20f.

objective intention in which creaturely content is not ascribed to God as such but becomes the medium of transcendental reference to him. Thus, theological concepts are essentially open, that is, they are closed on our side but open on God's side.[64] This is why Torrance rejects a container notion or the receptacle notion of space and time; such a notion would not be able to maintain the positive point that, in Christ, God himself became man without ceasing to be God. It would inevitably suppose that if Christ was truly human, then he could not continue to exist simultaneously as the Lord of creation, that is, the Son of God would have emptied himself into a containing vessel.[65] Grace is not contained in the sacraments and thus handed on by means of them. It is identical with Christ's own action as the incarnate, risen and ascended Lord who was and is present within space and time as the reconciler through the Holy Spirit and will return at the second coming to complete our redemption. This then is how Torrance maintains the integrity of divine and human freedom specifically in his analysis of the resurrection.

Rahner's View of the Resurrection and the Transcendental Method

Now let us see Rahner's view of the resurrection and how it relates to his theological method. In Rahner's view:

> Although we ourselves may always remain dependent on the testimony of the first disciples in order to be able to connect our experience of the spirit explicitly and by name specifically with Jesus, we may nevertheless say with confidence that wherever and

64 Cf. Torrance, *God and Rationality*, 170ff., *Space, Time and Resurrection*, 131f.

65 Torrance, *Space, Time and Resurrection*, 123ff. See esp. Torrance, *Space, Time and Incarnation*, for a detailed discussion of how the container and receptacle notions of space and time have caused problems for theology and why these notions were firmly rejected by Nicene theologians who insisted that God's relations with us in time and space were his creative relations and so were not constrained by created time and space. For a full discussion of the wide-ranging implications of embracing the problematic concepts of the container or receptacle view of space and time in theology, see Molnar, *Incarnation and Resurrection*, 90–6 and *Torrance: Theologian of the Trinity*, 124–35.

whenever we experience the unshakeableness of our own hope of a final victory of our existence, there takes place, perhaps anonymously, that is, without reference to the name of Jesus, an experience that he is risen. For this power of the spirit that we experience in this way as life's victorious defiance of all forms of death is the power of the Spirit which raised Jesus from the dead and thereby displays its victorious power to the world in history.[66]

It seems clear that Rahner has made a number of important assumptions here. First, he believes with the rest of Christendom, that we today are dependent on the biblical witness in order to know about Jesus's resurrection and its significance in our lives today. Second, he assumes that wherever anyone has an unshakeable hope of some kind of life after death, then they have already had an experience that Jesus is risen through the power of the Spirit. Now this makes no sense at all, unless it is understood from within Rahner's transcendental method as described in Chapter 5. It will be recalled that this method was and is intended to make sense of the traditional doctrines of Christianity such as Christology, the Trinity, faith and the resurrection (among others) to contemporary people without falling into Monophysitism or mythology and indeed without in any way compromising the traditional doctrines or God's freedom.

However, clearly there is a difference between Torrance and Rahner here. How indeed can one claim even an anonymous experience of the Holy Spirit and of Jesus's resurrection without knowing about Jesus explicitly through the witness of the apostles first? While it may be possible for someone to have such an experience without knowing exactly what it implies, it is impossible to have an experience that Jesus is risen anonymously, that is, without knowing about Jesus's own resurrection and its significance for us (without faith in the risen Lord). Here we shall briefly analyze why Rahner reaches this conclusion and its implications for his appeal to the economy to know God, revelation, faith and grace. At the end of the previous chapter we already saw that Rahner attempted to explicate Christian hope first by appealing to transcendental experience and then by connecting that experience with Jesus in order to interpret doctrine. Hence, for Rahner:

If one has a radical hope of attaining a definitive identity and does not believe that one can steal away with one's obligations into the

66 Rahner and Weger, *Our Christian Faith*, 113.

emptiness of non-existence, one has already grasped and accepted the resurrection in its real content … The absoluteness of the radical hope in which a human being apprehends his or her total existence as destined and empowered to reach definitive form can quite properly be regarded as grace, which permeates this existence always and everywhere. This grace is revelation in the strictest sense … this certainly is revelation, even if this is not envisaged as coming from 'outside'.[67]

In these two statements Rahner has ascribed the power of the resurrection to us in our experience of hope and has described grace and revelation as part and parcel of those same experiences. How can he possibly escape subjectivism and universalism once he has taken these positions? How can he possibly distinguish nature and grace, reason and revelation and ultimately God's self-communication from our own self-experience and/or self-acceptance? Certainly it is obvious that such an inability collapses theology into anthropology and leaves him in the very position he designed his theology to avoid.

A large part of the answer to these questions can be found in Rahner's transcendental method. We will not explore this method in detail here since that was already done in Chapter 5. Instead, we will recapitulate those aspects of his intentions and method that bear on the present discussion. Rahner is famous for his desire to overcome a merely formal approach to theology. He wanted to incorporate fundamental theology (that area of theology which deals with the most basic introductory questions such as revelation, faith, authority, the ways of knowing God and the nature and task of theology itself)[68] into dogmatic theology so that the justification of one's belief today would not be detached from the material content of theology.[69] He wanted 'to give people confidence from the very *content* of Christian dogma itself that they can believe with intellectual honesty'.[70] Thus, Rahner sought a closer unity between fundamental theology and dogmatic theology. The concept of mystery does not hinder this because mystery does not describe something senseless and unintelligible but the 'horizon of human existence which

67 Rahner and Weger, *Our Christian Faith*, 110–11.

68 Richard P. McBrien, *Catholicism Completely Revised and Updated* (San Francisco: HarperSanFrancisco, 1994), 1240.

69 *FCF*, 11ff.

70 *FCF*, 12.

grounds and encompasses all human knowledge'.[71] Theological science actually is 'the "science" of mystery'.[72] Hence, creatures have a positive affinity, given by grace, to the Christian mysteries of faith which he conceptualizes as our obediential potency and supernatural existential. The former refers to our openness to being (as spirit in the world) and as such it refers to our openness to God's self-communication, at least as a possibility. 'This potency is ... our human nature as such. If the divine self-communication did not occur, our openness toward being would still be meaningful ... we are by nature possible recipients of God's self-communication, listeners for a possible divine word'.[73] The latter refers to

> a basic structure which permeates the whole of human existence; it is not a localized part or region of our being, but a dimension pertaining to the whole. Our being in the world, or our being with others, could serve as examples ... this existential ... is not given automatically with human nature, but is rather the result of a gratuitous gift of God ... Because of the supernatural existential, grace is always a part of our actual existence.[74]

71 *FCF*, 12. See Karl Rahner, 'Reflections on Methodology in Theology' in *TI* 11, 101ff. and *TI* 4, 36–73. Such thinking leads Stephen J. Duffy to think 'because created spirit is boundless thrusting toward being, nature is in continuity with and positively open to grace' ('Experience of grace', 51). Indeed such thinking leads Daniel Donovan to say 'there is no purely natural experience of human life. Ours is a world that is permeated by grace' ('Revelation and faith', *Cambridge Companion to Karl Rahner*, 83–97, 87).

72 *TI* 11, 102.

73 John P. Galvin, 'The Invitation of Grace', in *A World of Grace*, ed. O'Donovan, 64–75, 72.

74 Galvin, 'The Invitation of Grace', 71–3. This idea leads Stephen J. Duffy to say 'no purely natural order has ever existed' ('Experience of grace', 47). The irreconcilable conflict in Rahner's thought discussed in Chapter 5 is present in Duffy's thinking because he adopts Rahner's idea of transcendental revelation which is not 'restricted to Israel and the Christ event' but rather is 'co-extensive with history's sweep' (47). Hence, on the one hand we are told that 'categorical revelation', that is, specific conceptual knowledge of historical events (special revelation) such as the Incarnation is required to know 'not only of the fact but of the very possibility of graced existence' (47). However, on the other hand, any necessity for knowing God's particular revelation or self-communication

The Christian mysteries that Rahner has in mind include 'the self-communication of God in the depths of existence, called grace, and in history, called Jesus Christ, and this already includes the mystery of the Trinity in the economy of salvation and of the immanent Trinity'.[75]

In order to bring fundamental theology and dogmatic theology closer, Rahner also wishes to avoid 'a too narrowly Christological approach'. Thus he writes: 'It is not true that one has only to preach Jesus Christ and then he has solved all problems. Today Jesus Christ is himself a problem' as 'the demythologizing theology of the post-Bultmann age' has shown. Hence, 'we cannot begin with Jesus Christ as the absolute and final datum, but we must begin further back than that'.[76] In this way, Rahner lays the foundation for his transcendental method which he then develops in order to overcome both the secular loss of God's transcendence and in order to present a view of God's immanence which will not compromise his transcendence. In fact, Rahner frequently seeks to preserve both God's transcendence and human freedom by arguing that human freedom and human dependence on God 'vary in direct and not in inverse proportion'.[77] How then does Rahner get to his position on the resurrection?

First, as seen in Chapter 5, he believes that there is a relationship of mutual conditioning between subject and object in knowledge. A transcendental line of inquiry 'raises the question of the conditions in which knowledge of a specific subject is possible in the knowing subject himself'. Thus,

> In any act of cognition it is not only the object known but also the subject knowing that is involved. It is dependent not only upon the

---

in Jesus Christ and through his Holy Spirit is completely undermined when he also maintains that 'transcendental revelation is the *condition of the possibility* of a response to categorical revelation' (47). In this context, that would mean that one would not have to know anything about Christ's actual resurrection from the dead to know about the resurrection as revelation and its meaning for us because the determining factor would be our anonymous experiences of transcendental hope which, for Rahner, are already revelation inspired by grace (and grace is part of our human existence as given so that grace itself is not and cannot be identical exclusively with the Giver of grace, namely, Jesus Christ).

75 *FCF*, 12.

76 *FCF*, 13.

77 *FCF*, 79. See also *TI* 5, 12.

distinctive characteristics of the object, but also upon the essential structure of the knowing subject … The *a priori* transcendental subjectivity of the knower … and the object of knowledge … are related to one another in such a way that they mutually condition one another . . .[78]

Moreover, 'The philosophical question as to a particular object is necessarily the question as to the knowing subject, because *a priori* the subject must carry with it the limits of the possibility of such knowledge. Thus the "transcendental" structures of the object are already determined *a priori*.'[79] Knowledge is thus not simply a posteriori. 'Man can only find and retain what he encounters in history if there is an *a priori* principle of expectation, seeking and hope in man's finding and retaining subjectivity.'[80] Indeed, as we have already seen, for Rahner revelation exists within the realm of human thought and is subject to the a priori structures of human knowledge since God becomes a constitutive principle of the subject who hears the word which is more than a word about God. The condition that makes this hearing possible in the human subject is God himself through his self-communication. He upholds this act as an intrinsic principle.[81] Hence,

the transcendental experience of the expectation of one's own resurrection, an experience man can reach by his very essence, is the horizon of understanding within which and within which alone something like a resurrection of Jesus can be expected and experienced at all. These two elements of our existence, of course, the transcendental experience of the expectation of one's own resurrection, and the experience in faith of the resurrection of Jesus in salvation history, mutually condition each other.[82]

78   *TI* 11, 87.
79   *TI* 9, 34.
80   *TI* 17, 47.
81   *TI* 11, 91–2.
82   *FCF*, 273–4. Cf. also *TI* 17, 16ff. Thus, for Rahner: 'We might now formulate the proposition that the knowledge of man's resurrection given with his transcendentally necessary hope is a statement of philosophical anthropology even before any real revelation in the Word. But we should have to counter this by saying that, at least initially, the elucidation of man's basic hope as being the hope of resurrection was in actual fact made historically through the revelation of the Old and New Testaments' (18). This last statement

As a result of this mutually conditioning relationship, it is perfectly logical for Rahner to believe that 'we do not learn something which is totally unexpected and which lies totally outside of the horizon of our experience and our possibilities of verification' when we hear the witness of the apostles regarding the resurrection.[83]

Second, using the ideas of formal and quasi-formal causality, Rahner believes that God has made himself an intrinsic principle of human transcendentality. Rahner very clearly does not want to say that God inserts himself into the chain of secondary causes 'as one cause among them' but still he argues, as we have already seen, that God's presence in time and space is 'embedded in this world to begin with'. This allows him to identify God's immediacy to us as a 'moment in and a modality of our transcendental and at the same time historically mediated immediacy to God'.[84] His positive point is to avoid seeing grace as a thing standing between God and us and to see it as does Torrance, as God's personal trinitarian action.

> The one God communicates himself in absolute self-utterance and as absolute donation of love. Here is the absolute mystery revealed to us only by Christ: God's self-communication is truly a *self*-communication. He does not merely indirectly give his creature some share of himself *by* creating and giving us created and finite realities ... In a *quasi-formal* causality he really and in the strictest sense of the word bestows *himself*.[85]

Like Torrance, Rahner argues that the 'giver himself is the gift'. However, for Rahner, 'God in his absolute being is related to the created existent in the mode of formal causality, that is, that he does not originally cause

---

shows that even Rahner's understanding of the scriptural view of revelation is largely determined by what is experienced in transcendental experience. Thus, in order to experience the fact that Jesus is alive, 'He (the Christian) has only to accept believingly and trustingly his own transcendental hope of resurrection and, therefore, also be on the look out, implicitly or explicitly, for a specific event in his own history, on the basis of which his hope can be believed in, as something that has been realised in another person' (19). Indeed, 'the "facts" of Jesus' resurrection must simply be determined in the light of what we have to understand by our own "resurrection"' (20).

83 *FCF*, 275.

84 *FCF*, 86–7.

85 Rahner, *Trinity*, 36. Cf. also *FCF*, 120ff., *TI* 1, 307, 329ff., 343ff. and *TI* 4, 175ff.

and produce something different from himself in the creature, but rather that he communicates his own divine reality and makes it a constitutive element in the fulfillment of the creature.' Indeed the basis for this assertion is 'found in the transcendental experience of the orientation of every finite existent to the absolute being and mystery of God'.[86] For Rahner then, 'the term "self-communication" is really intended to signify that God in his own most proper reality makes himself the inner-most constitutive element of man'.[87] Thus, 'God's offer of himself belongs to all men and is a characteristic of man's transcendence and his transcendentality … God's self-communication in grace, as a modification of transcendence … cannot by simple and individual acts of reflection … be differentiated from those basic structures of human transcendence.'[88] This leads Rahner to wonder:

To put it in biblical terms: if God as he is in himself has already communicated himself in his Holy Spirit always and everywhere and

86 *FCF*, 121. Cf. also *FCF*, 44. The same idea is frequently repeated. See for example *TI* 4, 50 where Rahner writes: 'All conceptual expressions about God, necessary though they are, always stem from the unobjectivated experience of transcendence as such: the concept from the pre-conception, the name from the experience of the nameless.' See also *TI* 4, 57 and *TI* 11, 149 where Rahner writes: 'The so-called proofs of God's existence … are possible … only as the outcome of an *a posteriori* process of reasoning as the conceptual objectification of what we call the experience of God, which provides the basis and origin of this process of reasoning.' Thus, for Rahner the task of theology is to 'reflect upon an experience which is present in every man' (*TI* 11, 150–1). Since this is so theology means 'we can only point to this experience, seek to draw another's attention to it in such a way that he discovers within himself that which we only find if, and to the extent that we already possess it' (*TI* 11, 154). See also *FCF*, 21 where Rahner writes: 'The knowledge of God is always present unthematically and without name, and not just when we begin to speak of it. All talk about it, which necessarily goes on, always only points to this transcendental experience as such, an experience in which he whom we call "God" encounters man … as the term of his transcendence.' For Rahner's explanation of his method, see *FCF*, 24–39. All of this was discussed at length in Chapter 5.

87 *FCF*, 116.

88 *FCF*, 129. This is why Stephen J. Duffy can say that for Rahner 'Grace, therefore, is experienced, though not as grace, for it is psychologically indistinguishable from the stirrings of human transcendentality' ('Experience of grace', 48).

to every person as the innermost center of his existence, whether he wants it or not, whether he reflects on it or not, whether he accepts it or not, and if the whole history of creation is already borne by God's self-communication in this very creation, then there does not seem to be anything else which can take place on God's part.[89]

Rahner's solution to this difficult problem is to suggest that transcendence itself has a history, 'and history is in its ultimate depths the event of this transcendence.'[90] However, the obvious question that arises here is how can Rahner avoid having transcendental experience actually define what he finds within history? Rahner himself argues: 'There is never a salvific act of God on man which is not also and always a salvific act of man. There is no revelation which could take place in any other way except in the faith of the person hearing the revelation.'[91] These are indeed strange assertions because they certainly seem unable to distinguish clearly objective historical events from the subjective experiences of faith and salvation. Ultimately such an inability would lead to a blurring of the Christian message precisely by implying that salvation could be equated with our self-experience and moral behavior – two things which Rahner clearly does not want to do; but can he avoid it?

On the one hand, Rahner argues that our supernaturally elevated orientation toward immediacy and closeness to God 'must be characterized as real revelation throughout the whole history of religion and of the human spirit'. This is not merely a natural revelation. 'This transcendental knowledge, which is present always and everywhere in the actualization of the human spirit in knowledge and freedom, but present unthematically, is a moment which must be distinguished from verbal and propositional revelation as such.' On the other hand,

---

89 *FCF*, 139.

90 *FCF*, 141.

91 *FCF*, 142. This thinking leads one Rahner scholar to say 'there can be no revelation in the full sense of the term without faith' Donovan, 'Revelation and faith', 86. It is of course one thing to say that people can only hear the Word of revelation in Christ through faith, given by the Holy Spirit. However, it is quite another to suggest that in faith creatures as subjects have a 'certain connaturality with its object [God]' (86). Then, unfortunately, revelation itself is conditioned by faith in the sense that it is not fully what it is in and of itself even without our faith.

as we have already noted in Chapters 5 and 6 in connection with his Christology, he argues that

> it deserves nevertheless to be characterized as God's self-revelation. This transcendental moment in revelation is a modification of our transcendental consciousness produced permanently by God in grace. But such a modification is really an original and permanent element in our consciousness as the basic luminosity of our existence. And as an element in our transcendentality which is constituted by God's self-communication, it is already revelation in the proper sense.[92]

Ultimately, 'God's self-revelation in the depths of the spiritual person is an a priori determination coming from grace ... it is not something known objectively, but something within the realm of consciousness.'[93] As seen in Chapter 5, it is through his notion of quasi-formal causality that Rahner understands transcendental revelation as 'a transcendental divinization of the fundamental subjective attitude, the ultimate horizon of man's knowledge and freedom, in the perspective of which he accomplishes his life.'[94] This is our grace-given supernatural existential which itself is the beginning of the *visio beatifica* in this life. As God's self-communication to the creature then, this revelation cannot be confined to words. It must also be the giving of grace, that is, 'an inner, objectless though conscious dynamism directed to the beatific vision.'[95] The beatific vision is the direct apprehension of God, given by God, which is in reality no different from the object of our initial dynamism of spirit which discerns being in general. Hence,

> In his intellectual and transcendental dynamism, Maréchal considers man (as spirit, i.e. in his 'nature') in the inmost heart of his being as '*desiderium naturale visionis beatificae*' – to use the words of St Thomas. This desire is conditional and so there is no necessity for the actual call to the vision by grace. But it is a real longing for the absolute being and one which is present in every spiritual act as its

---

92 *FCF*, 149.

93 *FCF*, 172.

94 Rahner and Ratzinger, *Revelation and Tradition*, 16.

95 *TI* 4, 61.

raison d'être ... it is the *a priori* condition of all knowledge where a finite object is grasped.[96]

From this insight he proceeded to describe grace as noted earlier (as an element in human being) and concluded that:

> The experience of God to which we have appealed ... is not necessarily so a-Christian as appears at first sight. On the contrary ... it is precisely Christianity which makes real this experience of God in its most radical and purest form, and in Jesus Christ achieves a convincing manifestation of it in history ... this experience of God ... really constitutes the very heart and centre of Christianity itself and also the ever living source of that *conscious manifestation* which we call 'revelation' ... through this experience of God Christianity itself simply achieves a more radical and clearer understanding of its own authentic nature. For in fact in its true essence it is not one particular religion among others, but rather the sheer objectivation in history of that *experience* of God which exists *everywhere* in virtue of God's universal will to save all men by bestowing himself upon them as grace.[97]

But, as seen in Chapter 5, the problem with this reasoning is that once this supposition is made, creatures may then rely on their experiences, whether religious or not, to lead them to the truth which Christians believe.

Here we have recapitulated the most basic dilemma of Rahner's theology. On the one hand, he insists on God's freedom and that in this freedom God has communicated himself and not some intermediary to creatures for their salvation. On the other hand, while he insists on the centrality of Christ, as the unsurpassable medium of revelation and salvation, his transcendental method ascribes what is supposed to be grounded in Jesus's history to the length and breadth of human history. Thus, while Rahner insists that transcendental experience needs history and is not just self-defining, history itself has no genuine independent bearing on transcendental experience. In other words, they mutually condition each other. This thinking leads Rahner to believe that eternity is 'imbedded in the time of freedom and responsibility' so that any

---

96 *TI* 4, 169.
97 *TI* 11, 164. Some emphases mine.

radically good moral decision is an experience of the eternity promised in the resurrection.[98]

Third, as we have just seen, Rahner accepts an a priori unthematic knowledge of God, Christ, revelation, faith and hope and it is to these that he appeals apologetically in order to speak to people within and outside the Church by connecting this experience and non-objective knowledge with the historical events of revelation and salvation. Thus, Rahner treats the theology of the death and resurrection of Jesus Christ first by establishing

> the intellectual presuppositions of the core of that original experience of Jesus as the Christ, and then the core of this original experience itself. This experience is the original, indeducible and first revelation of Christology which is then articulated and interpreted more reflexively in the 'late' New Testament and in the official teaching of the church.[99]

After stating that Jesus's death and resurrection must be seen together and that Jesus's death was a death into the resurrection and that the empty tomb, although not necessarily disputed, cannot by itself testify to the resurrection, Rahner insists that Jesus's resurrection means salvation and acceptance by God. Then, attempting to avoid an idealist misunderstanding of the fact that Jesus's person and cause are one, Rahner argues that

> if the resurrection of Jesus is the permanent validity of his person and his cause, and if this person and cause together do not mean the survival of just any person and his history, but mean the *victoriousness* of his claim to be the absolute saviour, then *faith* in his resurrection is an intrinsic element of this resurrection itself. Faith is not taking cognizance of a fact which by its nature could exist just as well without being taken cognizance of.[100]

---

98 *FCF*, 272. This thinking is confirmed in the following remark: 'Any serious moral choice, any such choice that engages us at the deepest level of our being, involves inevitably an acceptance or rejection of the Holy Mystery and its offer of itself to us in grace' Donovan, 'Revelation and faith', 94.

99 *FCF*, 265.

100 *FCF*, 267.

Indeed Rahner does not simply say that faith is necessary to understand or to participate in the power of the resurrection. Rather he says that 'it is only in this faith that its own [the resurrection] essential being is fully realized'. It is in this sense that Rahner asserts that

> Jesus is risen into the faith of his disciples. But this faith into which Jesus is risen is not really and directly faith in this resurrection, but is that faith which knows itself to be a divinely effected liberation from all the powers of finiteness, of guilt and of death, and knows itself to be empowered for this by the fact that this liberation has taken place in Jesus himself and has become manifest for us.[101]

By the time Rahner insists that it is primarily faith in Jesus's resurrection that gives us hope for our own resurrection, he has already connected them in such a way that Jesus's own resurrection cannot be fully what it is without our faith in our own future.

At this point Rahner turns to our transcendental experience of hope to make sense of the resurrection and argues that an act of hope in one's own resurrection takes place as a transcendental necessity either as freely accepted or rejected. Resurrection thus is not an assertion which could not be known in hope from a primordial understanding of the human, but is an expression which promises our abiding validity. It includes the whole person and not just one's body in a dualistic sense. Of course, Rahner believes that we are more successful in actually objectifying our self-understanding here in light of an experience of Jesus's resurrection, since the circle between transcendental and categorical experience is operative everywhere. For Rahner, 'This transcendental hope in resurrection is the horizon of understanding for experiencing the resurrection of Jesus in faith.'[102] This hope necessarily seeks historical confirmation.

The result is that Rahner appeals to the profession of faith in Galatians 1:8ff. as a 'global experience' which both Christians and non-Christians have, and believes that there should be an apologetic Christology not only for believers, but for those outside. We should presume that those outside the Christian sphere are persons of morally good will who therefore exist 'in the interior grace of God and in Christ' and that they have 'said an interior, unreflexive yes to Christ'. Therefore,

101 *FCF*, 268.
102 *FCF*, 269.

in fundamental theology, Christology cannot simply construct faith in Christ (both the *fides quae* and the *fides qua*, the act and the content of faith) in a 'purely reflexive and synthetic way and by scientific retort'. It follows that a Christian must accept 'the "Christology" which he is living out in his life: in the faith of the church, in the cult of its risen Lord, in prayer in his name, and by participating in his destiny ... The profession of faith in Gal. 1:8ff. is still valid *for this global experience*.'[103]

Making no clear distinction between those who have heard the gospel and those who have not, Rahner believes that Christology in fundamental theology can turn in three ways to this 'global understanding of existence which is already "Christian" because of antecedent grace', and that this would work out reflexively one part of 'transcendental Christology'. What do all three of these have in common? They have in common 'the supposition that if a person accepts his existence resolutely, he is really already living out in his existence something like a "searching Christology." These appeals do not try to do anything but clarify this anonymous Christianity somewhat.'[104] For Rahner, Jesus Christ must be the one for whom this search is being made. However, there is no disguising the fact that the main function of the historical Jesus, for Rahner, is to link our prior unthematic experiences and beliefs to an event in history which then is thought to validate our transcendental experience.

From here Rahner appeals to love of neighbor, to a readiness for death and to hope in the future and concludes that: (1) wherever any one radically loves his or her neighbor, he or she is already living as a Christian;[105] (2) wherever anyone affirms present and future reality as the ground of

---

103 *FCF*, 294, emphasis mine.

104 *FCF*, 295. This is why, in addition to the traditional Christology, Rahner advocates what he calls 'existentiell Christology' and concludes that an anonymous Christian has a real and existential relation to Christ 'implicitly in obedience to his orientation in grace toward the God of absolute, historical presence and self-communication. He exercises this obedience by accepting his own existence without reservation' (306).

105 Here it is important to recall a point that was made in Chapter 6, n. 194, namely, that for Torrance 'I cannot love God through loving my neighbour. I can love my neighbour truly and only through loving God. To love God through loving my neighbour is to assert that the Incarnation is not a reality, the reality it is, that relation to God is still a mediated one. To love God through my love to my neighbour is to move toward God. It does not know a movement of God

existence, that person already affirms a 'hoped-for death which is of such a nature that it reconciles the permanent dialectic in us between doing and enduring in powerlessness;' (3) wherever anyone hopes for a future reconciliation between what we are and what we should be or want to be, then one can rely on that hope to understand both the meaning of the incarnation and of the resurrection. This is in fact the horizon within which these events can become meaningful.[106] Finally, Rahner appeals to what he calls the searching memory that is intrinsic to all faith. Memory does not just refer to a past event; Rahner believes (following Plato and Augustine), that it can be related to something not yet found and this coheres with the whole problematic of transcendental experience and history. Thus, we can find and retain something which encounters us in history 'only if there is present in the finding and retaining subjectivity of man an a priori principle of expectation, of searching, of hoping ... we can call this a priori principle "memory".'[107]

It is Rahner's transcendental method then that explains how he can appeal to our own hope as the horizon within which Jesus's resurrection can be understood as the foundation for Christian theology. Ultimately, it is because Rahner conceives of faith, grace and revelation as elements within our transcendental experience that he can appeal to universal human experience in his attempt to make Christian faith credible in a secularized world. However, it is just here that he is led to believe that the resurrection is not fully realized without the disciples' faith and that Jesus is risen into the faith of the disciples and indeed into our faith insofar as the beginning of the Christian faith is identical with the unthematic knowledge of God which everyone implicitly has in each transcendental act. With respect to his understanding of the resurrection in particular, this leads Rahner to believe that 'we can never adequately separate this "for us" aspect of the risen Lord from

---

toward man' (*The Doctrine of Jesus Christ*, 88–9). For Torrance, Christ himself is central and thus we must love God in Christ and thereby recognize that our love of neighbor is a by-product of the fact that God has loved us in him while we were still sinners and freed us to love our neighbors. In this perspective, any claim that love of neighbor is already love of God even if it does not explicitly recognize God's love for us in Christ, will always mean a self-centered attempt to justify and sanctify ourselves. It will, in the end, confuse love of God with love of neighbor.

106 *FCF*, 294ff.
107 *FCF*, 319.

the "in himself" aspect of him ... I do not even know whether one who has been glorified has a head. I have no positive grounds for denying it, but ultimately speaking I do not know it, and, moreover, it is a matter of indifference.'[108] It is clear that from within Torrance's perspective any conception of the risen Lord must be very clear in distinguishing Jesus himself as risen from the dead and interacting with the disciples and us as the ascended and coming Lord. Indeed any idea that the risen Lord might not have a head would very clearly indicate an inability to allow Jesus in his full bodily existence as the glorified Lord to be the determining factor in one's thinking. It is Rahner's method, unfortunately, that causes him to be unable to distinguish between God's specific actions in history within the history of Jesus himself and the faith of those who respond to him. Thus, Rahner can say:

> There is such a thing as Easter faith ... It is present first in the disciples of Jesus, and the witness which they bear to their Easter experience ... It may be that we of today cannot draw any clear distinction within the Easter event as understood here between Easter itself (precisely the fact of the risen Christ) and the Easter experience of the disciples ... In the case of Jesus' disciples their Easter faith and their Easter experience (their belief and the grounds for that belief) are already blended into each other indissolubly.[109]

This blending of the Easter experience with the object of faith (the risen Lord) results from Rahner's method and is shaped by the fact that he believes that anthropology and Christology mutually condition each other; but this thinking undercuts the fact that it is the risen Lord himself and him alone who enables the faith of Christians. Taking this seriously would mean that Rahner would have to give up his idea of an anonymous experience of the resurrection just as he would have to surrender his idea of anonymous Christianity. Both ideas confuse grace and revelation in their identity with Jesus Christ with our experience of ourselves. Finally, Rahner's major difficulty comes to light in his belief that it is not the risen Lord in himself and him alone who justifies our belief in him. Rather, he believes that 'the credibility of this historical witness ("the Lord is risen indeed") is itself sustained by the transcendental expectation of resurrection which is inherent in man's basic attitude. It is because (whether he explicitates it to himself or not)

108 *TI* 11, 210.
109 *TI* 7, 164.

he entertains a hope for himself ... that he has "ears" to hear this witness to an historical fact.'[110]

Conclusion

First, it is clear that Torrance and Rahner are at one in wishing to unite fundamental and dogmatic theology and in affirming that God's self-communication in Christ and the Spirit is decisive. Second, it is clear that they both believe that knowledge of God should make sense to contemporary people and that revelation and grace should be seen as God's personal presence in the historical and risen Christ and not as a thing that can be detached from God, Christ or the Spirit. Third, it is clear however, that they both disagree methodologically even though they both affirm the need to reunite knowledge of the one God and the triune God by focusing on the economy; the central issue concerns how to relate experience to the economy.

Torrance rejects building a logical bridge from experience to revelation without necessarily denying that we have the kind of experiences that Rahner describes as transcendental experiences. However, Rahner insists that such a bridge must be built for apologetic reasons. This is the very foundation for his 'searching Christology' and his appeal to the experience of the nameless, and this disagreement leads to very different notions of revelation, grace, faith and of the resurrection itself.

Rahner advocates an unthematic ever present universal knowledge of God, Christ, revelation, faith, grace and hope which is related to historical Christianity in a mutually conditioning way. He appeals to this a priori structure of the knowing subject in its intrinsic connection with history to discover the meaning of the resurrection in particular. This, because subjective and objective knowledge are intrinsically and mutually related. Thus, the resurrection cannot be its own validation, but can and must be validated from *transcendental experience* which validates all theological knowledge. This inhibits a clear distinction between nature and grace, reason and revelation, philosophy and theology, creator and creatures, the

---

110 *TI* 17, 16. For a full discussion of how Rahner's method affects his understanding of the incarnation and resurrection and for a comparison of his view with the views of Barth and Torrance, see Molnar, *Incarnation and Resurrection*, chapters one through four. The critical comparison is given in chapter four.

economic and immanent Trinity, Christ's bodily resurrection and our faith in him. It leads Rahner to conclude that acceptance of hope (in the form of our transcendentally necessary hope) can be equated with acceptance of Christ's resurrection, even without having heard the gospel.

It leads him to argue that the apostolic message of the resurrection is not totally unexpected but like revelation itself, it is something people necessarily are already searching for in history itself. Hence, for Rahner 'we do not learn something which is totally unexpected and which lies totally outside of the horizon of our experience and our possibilities of verification'.[111] It finally leads him to conclude that one can accept or reject the resurrection by accepting or rejecting one's transcendental experience of hope. Indeed he even argues that if one were to reject the 'apostolic experience of this resurrection in Jesus' this would only incur guilt if it also involved rejecting one's transcendental experience of hope.[112] This is the corollary to his attempt to understand love of God and neighbor 'in the direction of a radical identity of the two loves' and his belief that 'the love of God and the love of neighbour are one and the same thing'.[113] That is why, as seen in Chapter 6, Rahner concludes that

> wherever a genuine love of man attains its proper nature and its moral absoluteness and depth, it is in addition always so underpinned and heightened by God's saving grace that it is also love of God, whether it be explicitly considered to be such a love by the subject or not …

111 *FCF*, 275. For a discussion of this in detail, see Molnar, *Incarnation and Resurrection*, 59ff. By contrast, for Torrance the resurrection is a miracle that is inexplicable from the human side. As a miracle, the resurrection is connected to the virgin birth so that 'the whole life of Jesus is to be regarded as downright miracle, the raising up of the Saviour and Servant out of the dry ground' as an act of God drastically altering the world in those events by 'inaugurating a new creation' which was 'quite unexpected' from the human side (*Space, Time, and Resurrection*, 33–4). For Torrance, one could think accurately about something that is totally new exclusively from the new reality itself, which for him, meant that Jesus and his resurrection could only be understood as ultimates which have their own authority in themselves and cannot be verified from a point outside themselves or cannot be verified or validated "on any other grounds than those which they themselves provide" (*Space, Time, and Resurrection*, 22).

112 *FCF*, 277–8.

113 For a comparison of Barth and Rahner on love of God and love of neighbor, see Molnar 'Love of God and Love of Neighbor in the Theology of Karl Rahner and Karl Barth', *Modern Theology*, 567–99.

wherever there is an absolutely moral commitment of a positive kind in the world ... there takes place also a saving event, faith, hope and charity ...[114]

It is no accident then that Rahner begins his Christology from below by answering the question of what is really experienced, witnessed and believed with Jesus's resurrection by asserting that 'a knowledge "in faith" of the "metaphysical" divine sonship of this Jesus may not be already presupposed'.[115]

By comparison, Thomas F. Torrance refuses to build a logical bridge from the experience of self-transcendence to the God revealed in Christ and by the Holy Spirit and because of this he insists that revelation is and remains identical with God's actions in the historical Jesus who died, rose, ascended and is present now in the power of the Holy Spirit. He further insists that it is utterly inconceivable and indeed it stands in conflict with our prior knowledge of God and secular understanding; it calls for a constant re-thinking of our theology in relation to Christ's real presence within the structures of space and time. Moreover, he insists that, according to his idea of scientific method, subject and object are not mutually conditioned even though they are inseparably related by the grace of God. Consequently, for Torrance, the resurrection is its own validation and any attempt to validate it from what Rahner describes as transcendental experience amounts to the creature using his or her own experience and language to redefine God's eternal being manifested in time and space. Therefore, Torrance could never agree that self-acceptance is acceptance of God, grace and revelation in reality. In fact Torrance rejects this kind of thinking as unscientific, because it operates from a center in ourselves while scientific theology ought to refer us back to Christ as the center. Torrance insists that it is Christ's uniqueness as the eternal Son of God who became man that dictates the utter uniqueness of the resurrection as the objective pole of our subjective knowledge which cannot be rightly understood without allowing the empirical correlates of that unique event such as the empty tomb and his appearances to structure what is said about the resurrection. As it happens then, the entire difference between Rahner and Torrance is methodological with extensive consequences for all aspects of theology. Torrance begins and ends his understanding of the resurrection and of

114   *TI* 6, 233, 236–7, 239. Cf. *FCF*, 295.
115   *FCF*, 279.

God's self-communication with Christ as presented in the Bible. Rahner considers such a starting point too narrowly christological. However, it is just this choice by Rahner that inhibits him from consistently turning to the economy, as he certainly intended to do, for the verification of his theology and leaves him exposed to the very subjectivism (and intrinsicism) he believes he has overcome.

What then are the prospects for Reformed and Roman Catholic dialogue concerning the proper interpretation of God's self-communication in Christ? Based on what has been said in this chapter and throughout this book, the answer, I suggest, is to be found in a clearer doctrine of the immanent Trinity which will not separate Christ and creatures but will also not detach the trinitarian self-communication from Christ's active mediation of himself to us through the power of the Holy Spirit and within the historical structures of space and time. It seems clear from what has been said earlier that Reformed and Roman Catholic theology are already one in their desire to unite fundamental and dogmatic theology by starting theology more consistently from God's economic trinitarian actions within history.

In this regard, David Tracy offers an illuminating discussion that insists, on the one hand, that 'a Christian theological understanding of God cannot be divorced from the revelation of God in Jesus Christ'.[116] Here, as I have just indicated, Reformed and Roman Catholic theologians agree, at least formally; but, on the other hand, in accordance with his view of natural theology, Tracy proceeds to find reasons of credibility and intelligibility within human experience in order to correlate what was supposedly found in Jesus Christ with that natural knowledge. Precisely in that way he follows Rahner and compromises his own assertion that 'the Catholic theological understanding of God is, therefore, grounded in the self-revelation of God in Jesus Christ'.[117] In addition to Jesus Christ he turns to 'ontologies of relationality' supplied by process theology and feminist theology. Instead of allowing his notion of relationality to be dictated by the trinitarian relations freely revealed in the history of Christ himself, his abstract notion of human relationality conceived as love, defines God's love. In the end he argues that: 'A relational model of human perfection is clearly a more adequate one for understanding divine perfection than either an ancient individualist or

---

116 David Tracy, 'Approaching the Christian Understanding of God', in *Systematic Theology: Roman Catholic Perspectives*, ed. Schüssler Fiorenza and Galvin, 133–48, 133.

117 Tracy, 'Approaching the Christian Understanding of God', 139.

modern autonomous one.'[118] While most modern theologians agree in rejecting individualism and a false Cartesian autonomous view of persons, the problem here is that instead of allowing his analogies for God to be drawn from Christ himself and thus to be understood within faith, Tracy grounds his theology of God 'in the revelation of God in Jesus Christ' *and* in 'the quest for God that *is* the ultimate meaning of all the classic limit-experiences and limit-questions of human beings'.[119] This dual grounding of theological knowledge repeats Rahner's error precisely by ascribing revelation and grace to human experience, while simultaneously insisting that Christian knowledge of God should be grounded in Christ. Such knowledge, as we have just shown in this chapter, cannot possibly be grounded in Christ as the first and final word shaping our knowledge of God because its starting point and norm is and remains our limit-experiences and what can be gleaned from those.

What has emerged then up to this point in our effort to construct a contemporary doctrine of the immanent Trinity is that any such doctrine must be grounded consistently in the economic Trinity in an *irreversible* way. Further, such a doctrine must respect the fact that revelation is a completely new and unexpected divine action and thus cannot be equated with any sort of transcendental experience, any aspect of transcendental experience or with what might be inferred from such transcendental experience. It is certainly not a description of our experience of faith, but instead is a description of who God is who meets us in our experience of faith. Consequently, thinking about human freedom must find its basis in God's freedom for us which was and is exercised in Christ and the Spirit. As a result of this, a clear doctrine of the immanent Trinity will reflect our need to begin and end our theological reflections with Jesus Christ himself, simply because he is our only access to the Father.

In the next chapter we shall explore the theology of Jürgen Moltmann with a view toward seeing even more precisely why it is important to perceive and maintain the irreversible noetic and ontic relation between creator and creatures disclosed in the history of Jesus Christ. Moltmann is ambiguous about the concept of experience and so he introduces a mutually conditioned view of divine and human relations that consistently compromises both God's freedom in se and ad extra. His theology provides an exceptionally clear instance of what happens when theologians are inconsistent in affirming a properly conceived doctrine of the immanent Trinity. To his theology we now turn.

---

118 Tracy, 'Approaching the Christian Understanding of God', 145.
119 Tracy, 'Approaching the Christian Understanding of God', 146.

Chapter 8

THE FUNCTION OF THE TRINITY IN JÜRGEN MOLTMANN'S ECOLOGICAL DOCTRINE OF CREATION

In this book I have accepted Barth's basic theological insight regarding the relationship between the immanent and the economic Trinity that 'a deliberate and sharp [*bewußt und scharf*] distinction between the Trinity of God as we may know it in the Word of God revealed, written and proclaimed, and God's immanent Trinity, that is, between "God in Himself" and "God for us," between the "eternal history of God and His temporal acts,"' must be maintained in order to avoid confusing and reversing the role of creator in relation to creature both theoretically and practically.[1] As seen earlier, this insight will not allow the vice versa associated with Rahner's axiom of identity because, for Barth, theology can only take place as acknowledgment, that is,

> Jesus Christ Himself lives in the message of His witnesses ... [thus] experience of His presence ... does not rest on man's act of recollection but on God's making Himself present in the life of man [hence] it is acknowledgment of His presence ... the life of man, without ceasing to be the self-determining life of this man, has now its centre, its whence, the meaning of its attitude, and the criterion whether this attitude really has the corresponding meaning – it has all of this outside itself, in the thing or person acknowledged.[2]

---

1 *CD* I/1, 172. *KD* I/1, 179. Barth's point is crucial: the person who participates in revelation does so only on the basis of God's free action so that on our side it is 'conditioned from without, by God, whereas God in making the step [towards us] by which the whole correlation is first fashioned is not conditioned from without, by man' (172).

2 *CD* I/1, 206–8.

We have seen that this issue of confusing and reversing the roles of creator and creature is a burning issue in contemporary theology as it was in the fourth century, when Athanasius opposed the Arian attempt to define God by human experience. My contention is that a contemporary doctrine of the immanent Trinity will help theologians recognize and maintain both divine and human freedom by stating with clarity that God's freedom in se as the eternal Father, Son and Holy Spirit exists outside of and apart from our experience of faith and salvation. By recognizing that God did not and does not need to act mercifully toward us ad extra, even as he in fact did so and does so in his Word and Spirit, we recognize the freedom of grace. To that extent our trinitarian theology stands on the unshakeable ground which is the very presence of God in his Word and Spirit, and to that extent also trinitarian theology cannot displace God's present action as its sole determining criterion. This is why Barth insists that 'we must know God as the One who addresses us in freedom, as the Lord, who does not exist *only* as He addresses us, but exists as the One who establishes and ratifies this relation and correlation, who is also God before it, in Himself, in His eternal history'.[3] This is not just a statement we find early in the *Church Dogmatics* as Barth reiterates this much later when he writes that 'God loves us by reason and in consequence of the fact that He is the One who loves in His freedom in and for Himself, and is God as such'.[4]

The work of Jürgen Moltmann provides an interesting and important illustration of a prominent contemporary theologian who accepts Rahner's axiom of identity and then attempts to move beyond it in a theologically inappropriate way. It is hoped that by analyzing certain of Moltmann's key insights in relation to Barth's understanding of the union and distinction of the immanent and economic Trinity, more light will be shed on the problems and potential solutions as we work toward a contemporary doctrine of the immanent Trinity. Then it is hoped that a look at how the Trinity functions in Moltmann's ecological doctrine of Creation will clarify matters even further.

As noted previously, Moltmann now has moved beyond the language of immanent and economic to understand the Trinity. Nonetheless, key differences between Moltmann and Barth early on suggested that the problematic element in Moltmann's theology would be his failure to recognize and maintain God's freedom. Such failure, as we have seen,

---

3 *CD* I/1, 172.
4 *CD* IV/2, 755.

means that human freedom itself becomes threatened to the extent that it is not truly grounded in an act of God that is independent of our human experiences of suffering, love and freedom.[5] In fact Barth was concerned that Moltmann had subsumed 'all theology in eschatology'.

> To put it pointedly, does your theology of hope really differ at all from the baptized *principle* of hope of Mr. Bloch? What disturbs me is that for you theology becomes so much a matter of principle (an eschatological principle) ... *Would it not be wise to accept the doctrine of the immanent trinity of God?*[6]

Barth hoped that Moltmann would 'outgrow' this 'onesidedness', but Moltmann's 'panentheism', which starts from experience and reconstructs theology in process terms, cannot allow for 'an immanent Trinity in which God is simply by himself, without the love which communicates salvation'.[7] Thus, Moltmann must 'surrender the traditional distinction between the immanent and the economic Trinity', and affirm

5 Christopher Holmes, '"A Specific Form of Relationship": On the Dogmatic Implications of Barth's Account of Election and Commandment for His Theological Ethics' in *Trinity and Election in Contemporary Theology*, ed. Dempsey, 182–200 stresses the importance of recognizing God's freedom as the basis of human freedom and thus emphasizes that it is crucial not to reduce the immanent to the economic Trinity with the idea that 'God's being is actualized and completed only with respect to creation' (198).

6 *Karl Barth Letters*, 175, some emphases mine.

7 Moltmann, *Trinity and Kingdom*, 151. George Hunsinger rightly recognizes that Moltmann 'rejected any strong distinction between "God for us" and "God in himself"' since for Moltmann 'they were two sides of the same coin. God's eternity was not an independent realm over against history. It was rather the transcendent dimension of history. In a broadly Hegelian way, what Moltmann proposed was the "historicization of eternity". Time and eternity were objectively constituted by their mutual relations in "dialectical identity"' ('Karl Barth and Some Protestant Theologians' *Oxford Handbook of the Trinity*, 311). Hence, for Moltmann the immanent and economic Trinity 'form a continuity and merge into one another' (311 and *Trinity and Kingdom*, 152). Curiously, Thomas R. Thompson '*Interpretatio in bonem partem:* Jürgen Moltmann on the Immanent Trinity' in *Theology as Conversation: The Significance of Dialogue in Historical and Contemporary Theology*, eds Bruce L. McCormack & Kimlyn J. Bender (Grand Rapids, MI: Eerdmans, 2009), 159–78, thinks Moltmann's statements regarding the immanent Trinity can be rescued from Barth's

Rahner's thesis that 'the economic Trinity *is* the immanent Trinity, and vice versa' ... The thesis about the fundamental *identity* of the immanent and the economic Trinity of course remains open to misunderstanding as long as we cling to the distinction at all ... The economic Trinity not only reveals the immanent Trinity; it also has a retroactive effect on it.[8]

As seen previously and as we shall see in detail throughout this chapter, Moltmann uncritically employs the principle of mutual conditioning and eliminates any need to conceptualize a God truly independent of creatures. Any real notion of Lordship applying to God's love revealed in Christ is simply reinterpreted by the experience of suffering drawing God into the vicissitudes of creation itself.[9]

To avoid any such synthesis of experience and the Word of God, Barth insisted that theology could not begin with experience and re-define God's 'antecedent' existence if the criterion for that theology were Christ.[10] As seen earlier, all Christian theologians claim Christ as their criterion; yet unless in Christ there is an immanent Trinity which is *recognizable* and in *no way dependent* on anyone or anything else, and unless that truth is what is perceived and applied in faith, the whole positive point of theology is missed.[11]

critique. However, what Thompson demonstrates is nothing more than that Moltmann pays lip service to God's freedom. He offers nothing to show how the mutual conditioning embedded in Moltmann's 'trinitarian thinking' by virtue of his embrace of panentheism, which leads him beyond Rahner's 'axiom' by arguing that the actions of the economic Trinity have a retroactive effect on the immanent Trinity, is at all compatible with a genuine recognition of God's freedom in se. Moltmann's statements that God needs the world and that God cannot find bliss in his eternal self-love simply do not bear the mark of having allowed God's free love to shape what he says about the God/world relation.

8 Moltmann, *Trinity and Kingdom*, 160.

9 See Chapter 1.

10 See, for example, *CD* I/1, 119. Cf. also 193 and esp. 198ff., 'The Word of God and Experience'. See also, *CD* I/1, 414–15.

11 Walter Kasper, for example, *The God of Jesus Christ*, mistakenly thinks that the views of Barth and Rahner are the same here, 273–4. Compare *CD* II/1, 308–9. For a comparison of the thinking of Karl Barth, Walter Kasper and Elizabeth Johnson, see Molnar, 'Barth and Contemporary Roman Catholic Theology' in the *Oxford Handbook of Karl Barth*, eds Paul Dafydd Jones and Paul T. Nimmo, forthcoming.

Moltmann clearly begins his trinitarian theology from experience: 'God suffers with us – God suffers from us – God suffers for us: *it is this experience of God that reveals the triune God.*'[12] Methodologically his thinking invariably moves from the general to the particular and this influences his view of Christ and of the Trinity in several ways. First, Moltmann accepts natural theology as a necessary prolegomenon to theology.[13] Second, he attempts to deduce the meaning of creation not *only* from the traditional doctrine,[14] but from nature as well as from a *direct* knowledge of God. Third, Moltmann literally cannot distinguish creatures from the creator in any recognizable way. Thus, he argues that, although *creatio ex nihilo* means God is *free*, still God makes *room* within himself by fashioning the nothingness from which he then creates the world.[15] In the supposed existence of God before the world, God is in fact *conditioned* by this withdrawal within. While Barth maintains that God makes space for creation, he insists on a doctrine of the immanent Trinity and asserts that time, experience and created space dictate nothing here, while Moltmann consistently defines God *by* the experiences creatures have of suffering, nothingness and death.[16]

While experience is important for Barth, the norm for truth is and remains revelation. Following Thomas's insight that *Deus non est in genere*,[17] Barth argues that God cannot be classified with other 'supreme ideas' such as freedom and immortality and then known; this, because his *esse* really is his *act*. Therefore, 'no self-determination of the second partner [the creature] can influence the first, whereas the

12 Moltmann, *Trinity and Kingdom*, 4, emphasis mine.

13 See Moltmann, *Creation*, chapter three. It is not a real immanent Trinity that defines truth here but a Trinity based on 'the saving experience of the cross', Moltmann, *Trinity and Kingdom*, 161.

14 Moltmann, *Creation*, 72ff.

15 Moltmann, *Creation*, 86–94 and *Trinity and Kingdom*, 37ff. and 108ff. A God who makes nothingness in order to create and then makes this part of his being is not the Christian God. Following Irenaeus and Athanasius, T. F. Torrance astutely notes that 'creation of the universe out of nothing does not mean that God created the universe out of some "stuff" called "nothing", but that what he created was not created out of anything' (*The Trinitarian Faith*, 99). See also n. 91 below.

16 See, for example, Moltmann, *Creation*, 27ff. and 97–103, and *Trinity and Kingdom*, 97 and 99ff.

17 *Summa Theologica*, qu. 3, art. 5, and *CD* II/1, 187–90, 310 and 445–7.

self-determination of the first, *while not cancelling the self-determination* of the second, is the sovereign predetermination which precedes it absolutely'.[18] The very being of the Christian God revealed thus excludes *any* pantheistic or panentheistic attempt to define his relation with creatures.

Rejecting this idea of lordship, Moltmann begins his panentheistic re-conception of the Trinity from experience and insists that we *can* explain the *how* of the trinitarian self-revelation by perceiving that God *needs* to suffer in order to love.[19] This is, of course, in contrast to the important insight stressed in the last chapter, namely, that for Barth and T. F. Torrance the *how* of the trinitarian self-revelation remains a mystery. Ignoring this limit that Barth and Torrance insisted on, Moltmann argues that 'God "needs" the world and man. If God is love, then he neither will nor can be without the one who is beloved'.[20] This applies

18 *CD* II/1, 312, emphasis mine.

19 Moltmann, *Trinity and Kingdom*, 19ff., 32ff., and 197, and *Creation*, 13ff. and 108ff.

20 Moltmann, *Trinity and Kingdom*, 58. See Moltmann, *Creation*, where he understands human likeness to God 'as a relationship of fellowship, of mutual need and mutual interpenetration' (258). Part of the difficulty here concerns the fact that Moltmann thinks he can apply *perichoresis* as it is understood in connection with the inner trinitarian relations to our relations with God. For an informative critical analysis of Moltmann on his use of *perichoresis*, see Randall E. Otto, 'The Use and Abuse of Perichoresis in Recent Theology' *SJT*, vol. 54, no. 3 (August 2001): 366–84. According to Stanley Grenz, Leonardo Boff 'maintains that rather than being a reality totally distinct from God, the world is the receptacle for God's self-communication, and hence it belongs to the history of the triune God' (Grenz, *Rediscovering the Triune God*, 125–6). For Boff, then, '*perichoresis* cannot be limited to the intra-trinitarian relations but denotes the relationship between God and the world as well' (126). This confusion regarding *perichoresis* was also embedded in the thought of LaCugna, as seen earlier with her view of the divine dance. While Boff follows Moltmann, he thinks from the economic Trinity and rightly wishes to maintain the fact that God in himself is the Trinity and thus affirms the immanent Trinity, *Trinity and Society*, trans. Paul Burns (Maryknoll, NY: Orbis, 1988), 96. Unfortunately, however, his thinking departs radically from traditional trinitarian theology which maintains that only the Word became incarnate and not the Holy Spirit or the Father. Boff maintains that there is a 'personal (hypostatic) self-communication to the Virgin Mary' (210) and that 'the Holy Spirit, coming down on Mary, "pneumatized" her, taking on human form in her, in the same

to the Father's relation with the Son and to creation: 'Creation is a part of the eternal love affair between the Father and the Son.'[21] While Barth carefully excluded *any* notion of necessity from both the immanent and economic Trinity, Moltmann, as we shall see shortly in more detail, believes that the Father *necessarily* generates the Son;[22] he plays off God's nature and will which, as Barth correctly insisted,[23] is impossible in a Christian doctrine of God. Moltmann's God cannot exist without the world since 'the idea of the world is already inherent in the Father's love for the Son.'[24] For Barth, as seen earlier in his debate with Gogarten, 'theology cannot speak of man in himself, in isolation from God. But as in the strict doctrine of the Trinity as the presupposition of Christology, *it must speak of God in Himself in isolation from man*.'[25]

manner as the Son who, in a personal and unmistakable manner, set up his tent amongst us in the figure of Jesus of Nazareth' (210–11). While Boff notes that this is not 'official church teaching', he thinks it is a valid 'theological hypothesis' (211). Grenz, however, notes that 'many critics find themselves put off by Boff's heightened Mariology' (*Rediscovering the Triune God*, 129) and rightly explains that 'a supposed incarnation of the Spirit in Mary not only produces a Mariology that goes beyond the teaching of his church but also suggests an adoptionist Christology that appears to stand outside the historic teaching of the church as a whole' (129–30).

21 Moltmann, *Trinity and Kingdom*, 59.

22 Moltmann, *Trinity and Kingdom*, 167. 'The generation and birth of the Son come from the Father's *nature*, not from his will. That is why we talk about the *eternal* generation and birth of the Son. The Father begets and bears the Son out of the *necessity* of his being', emphasis mine. As we shall see, Moltmann distinguishes 'the world process and the innertrinitarian process' by saying that in God necessity and freedom coincide, (106–7). Yet, because he has confused the immanent and economic Trinity, God also needs to create and give himself away since love must move toward another. This also affects his view of time and eternity. Cf. *Creation*, 112–18.

23 *CD* II/1, 546–7.

24 Moltmann, *Trinity and Kingdom*, 108.

25 *CD* I/1, 172, emphasis mine. The point here is not that God continued to exist in 'isolation' from us; rather it is that the God who elects to be in relationship with us is and remains who he is in himself even in his closest relations with us. As Barth succinctly put it, the God 'who addresses us in freedom, as the Lord, who does not exist only as He addresses us, but exists as the One who establishes and ratifies this relation ... is also God before it, in Himself, in His eternal history' (*CD* I/1, 172).

While Moltmann sees the need to maintain belief in creation from nothing and in the Trinity, it is certainly not the person and work of Christ which *alone* determines truth. Thus, he holds, contrary to Barth's view, that there are analogies that are true in themselves and that can lead to a knowledge of the trinitarian God. For this reason *perichoresis* does not describe a trinitarian *circumincessio*, which would preclude *any* natural knowledge of the Christian God, but rather is a principle by which he both separates[26] and synthesizes God's being and act.[27] Barth rejected both tritheism and modalism just because we cannot comprehend the immanent Trinity as such by grasping the *opus Dei* ad extra.[28] By contrast, Moltmann's whole theology is dominated by the principle of mutual conditioning.[29] Thus, we have no way of distinguishing *what*

26 See Moltmann, *Creation*, 16ff., 57–60 and 206ff. While Barth insisted that the oneness and threeness of God are one (*CD* I/1, 352 and 469) Moltmann's thinking tends toward tritheism, *Trinity and Kingdom*, 86. Walter Kasper, *The God of Jesus Christ*, notes the 'danger' of tritheism in Moltmann's theology, 379, n. 183. Stanley J. Grenz and Roger Olson, *20th Century Theology*, conclude that Moltmann has overemphasized God's immanence and that this 'resulted in his outright denial of monotheism and possible fall into the heresy of tritheism' (*20th Century Theology*, 184). With respect to Moltmann's belief (discussed later) that there has never been a Christian tritheist, George Hunsinger remarks: 'If this is true then one can only conclude that Moltmann is vying to be the first. Despite the evident scorn with which he anticipates such a charge, *The Trinity and the Kingdom* is about the closest thing to tritheism that any of us are ever likely to see', *The Thomist*, vol. 47 (1983): 129–39, 131. See also Hunsinger, 'Karl Barth and Some Protestant Theologians', 311.

27 Moltmann, *Creation*, 258ff. This leads to his mistaken criticism of Barth for modalism (56ff.) and nominalism. These criticisms rest on his failure to see that the oneness and threeness of God is dictated by Christ and not by experience.

28 Moltmann holds that there has never been a 'Christian tritheist', *Trinity and Kingdom*, 243, n. 43. Yet Adolf von Harnack, *History of Dogma*, trans. by Neil Buchanan, (New York: Dover Publications, 1961), vol. 3, 90, and vol. 6, 82 and 101 cites several. Marcion was also named as a tritheist in a letter of Pope St. Dionysius *circa* AD 260.

29 See, for example, *Creation*, 206. Also, 'We have understood human likeness to God in this same context of the divine perichoresis ... as a relationship of fellowship, of *mutual need* and mutual interpenetration', (258, emphasis mine). See also 266 and *Trinity and Kingdom*, 106ff. and 148ff. For more on this see

is being *affected* by us in our experience. This reversal of predicates, which follows *identity*, is precisely why Barth rejected panentheism as worse than pantheism.[30]

Moltmann accepts Rahner's axiom of identity because God *must* communicate the love of salvation. While Barth maintains a 'deliberate and sharp' distinction between creation and covenant by insisting that creation is the external basis of the covenant but not the condition of its possibility (as Balthasar and Rahner assume), Moltmann confuses both with the very being of God and assumes that creation and incarnation are necessary to God as they are for the creature.[31]

Indeed, 'As the Father of Jesus Christ, he is almighty *because* he exposes himself to the experience of suffering, pain, helplessness and death. But what he *is* is not almighty power; what he *is* is love. It is passionate, passible love that is almighty, nothing else'.[32] Hence, following C. E. Rolt, Moltmann writes: 'The sole omnipotence which God possesses is the almighty power of suffering love ... Rolt then goes on to deduce the eternal divine nature from Christ's passion. What Christ, the incarnate God, did in time, God, the heavenly Father, does and *must do* in eternity'.[33] Thus,

> God *has to give himself completely; and it is only in this way that he is God. He has to go through time; and it is only in this way that he is eternal* ... He has to be man and nothing but man; and it is only in this way that he is completely God ... 'It was necessary for God to be Man, for only so could He be truly God.'[34]

Jürgen Moltmann, *History and the Triune God*, 133 where Moltmann states that 'the mystery of creation is best grasped philosophically by panentheism'.

30 *CD* II/1, 312–13 and 562. See also Chapter 6, n. 35. Karl Rahner also accepts a modified doctrine of panentheism in Karl Rahner and Herbert Vorgrimler, *Theological Dictionary*, ed. by Cornelius Ernst (New York: Herder and Herder, 1965), 333–4.

31 Moltmann, *Trinity and Kingdom*, 56ff., 99ff., 106ff., 159–61 and 167–8.

32 Moltmann, *Trinity and Kingdom*, 197, emphasis mine.

33 Moltmann, *Trinity and Kingdom*, 31, emphasis mine.

34 Moltmann, *Trinity and Kingdom*, 32–3, emphasis mine. Thus, for Moltmann, the incarnation means for God 'an increase of his riches and his bliss' (121). By contrast, of course, as noted earlier in connection with the thinking of Ted Peters, for Barth the incarnation meant: 'While this event as a happening in and on the created world makes, magnifies and enhances the glory of God outwardly, inwardly it neither increases nor diminishes His glory,

For Barth, God *freely* re-affirms himself in eternity and in time; for Moltmann, 'God must, therefore pass through time to attain his eternal being ... In order to be completely itself, love has to suffer ... Through openness and capacity for suffering, the divine love shows that it is life's pre-eminent organizing principle in the deadly conflicts of blind natural forces.'[35]

All of this leads Moltmann to Unamuno's panentheistic confusion of history and eternity: 'A God who cannot suffer cannot love either ... only that which suffers is divine'.[36] This clear projection of human love and suffering into the eternal Godhead manifests the mutual conditioning associated with all human love and suffering; it cannot, however, describe the trinitarian God as free in himself or in revelation in a way which definitively overcomes suffering. This God cannot even *freely* act since 'It is not through supernatural interventions that God guides creation ... Seen in terms of world history, the transforming power of suffering is the *basis* for the liberating and consummating acts of God'.[37] By this reasoning, which has identified the immanent and economic Trinity in light of the cross of Christ, God cannot overcome suffering since suffering itself is the *principle* which encompasses his very being and love.

His divine being. For this is neither capable nor in need of increase or decrease. God did not and does not owe this happening to the world or to us any more than He did creation or the history of salvation ... It was not the case, nor is it, that His being necessitated Him to do it' *CD* II/1, 513–14.

35 Moltmann, *Trinity and Kingdom*, 33–4. Barth specifically rejects this thinking in *CD* II/1, 304–6.

36 Moltmann, *Trinity and Kingdom*, 38. Moltmann appears to modify his view of panentheism in *Creation* by ascribing to the creature's self-transcending movements the indwelling Creator Spirit, 103. The only change, however, is that the Spirit is now the principle of infinity which 'imbues every finite thing ... with self-transcendence' (101). Indeed the Spirit is part of the structure of creation (212). Creation is seen as evolving toward God (Chapter 8) and God is necessarily related to it (207, 213). Barth consistently rejected both of these views by rejecting Pelagianism and panentheism.

37 Moltmann, *Creation*, 211. Moltmann cites Teilhard's view as an adequate account of this. Barth correctly rejected Teilhard de Chardin's gnostic pantheism several times. Cf. *Karl Barth Letters*, 116f. and 119f. and Eberhard Busch, *Karl Barth*, trans. by John Bowden (Philadelphia: Fortress Press, 1976): 'Teilhard de Chardin is an almost classic case of Gnosticism', wrote Barth (487).

We have seen how Moltmann's panentheistic understanding of the Trinity is in conflict with Barth's theology and how Moltmann's view that the economic Trinity has a retroactive effect on the immanent Trinity reflects the kind of mutual conditioning inherent in human experience, but absent from the triune God who loves in freedom. Now let us explore how Moltmann's understanding of the Trinity functions in his ecological doctrine of creation with a view toward seeing how this problem of mutual conditioning really does compromise God's freedom precisely because of Moltmann's failure to make a proper distinction between the immanent and the economic Trinity.

According to Moltmann,

> In the 1930's, the problem of the doctrine of creation was knowledge of God. Today the problem of the doctrine of God is knowledge of creation. The theological adversary then was the religious and political ideology of 'blood and soil', 'race and nation'. Today the theological adversary is the nihilism practised in our dealings with nature. Both perversions have been evoked by the unnatural will to power . . .[38]

Moltmann's ecological doctrine of creation sees God's Spirit '*in* all created beings'. In order to understand this, Moltmann has interwoven the first three articles of the Apostles' creed in a trinitarian sense in order to 'develop a pneumatological doctrine of creation. This doctrine of creation . . . takes as its starting point the indwelling divine Spirit of creation'.[39] This thinking, Moltmann hopes, will provide a more holistic philosophy of nature. The word ecology means

---

38 Moltmann, *Creation*, xi.

39 Moltmann, *Creation*, xii. Among other things this thinking eventually leads to these conclusions: first, 'The Spirit is the principle of evolution' *Creation* (100); second, 'The Spirit is the holistic principle . . . he creates interactions, . . . co-operation and community [and] is the "common Spirit of creation"'; and third, 'The Spirit is the principle of individuation'. Therefore 'self-preservation and self-transcendence are two sides of the process in which life evolves. They are not mutual contradictions. They complement one another' (100). Moltmann can even say: 'Through his Spirit God is also present in the very structures of matter. Creation contains neither spirit-less matter nor non-material spirit; there is only *informed* matter' (212).

'the doctrine of the house'. Moltmann's point is that if we see creation only as God's 'work' such a doctrine will make little sense, but 'if we understand the Creator, his creation, and the goal of that creation in a trinitarian sense, then the Creator, through his Spirit *dwells in* his creation as a whole, and in every individual created being, by virtue of his Spirit holding them together and keeping them in life'.[40] As the inner secret of creation is this indwelling of God, the purpose of Shekinah (God's indwelling) is 'to make the whole creation the house of God'.[41] To this theological side of the doctrine of creation there corresponds an anthropological side, that is, existence can become a home only if the stresses and strains between human beings and nature are overcome in a viable 'symbiosis'.

Moltmann sees his 'ecological doctrine of creation' as corresponding to his social doctrine of the Trinity presented in *The Trinity and the Kingdom*. In that work, as we have just seen, Moltmann attempted to reconceive the Trinity panentheistically in terms of 'relationships and communities' and 'out of the doctrine of the Trinity'.[42]

> By taking up panentheistic ideas from the Jewish and the Christian traditions, we shall try to think *ecologically* about God, man and the world in their relationships and indwellings. In this way it is not merely the Christian *doctrine* of the Trinity that we are trying to work out anew; our aim is to develop and practise trinitarian *thinking* as well.[43]

---

40 Moltmann, *Creation*, xii.

41 Moltmann, *Creation*, xiii. In connection with the notion of Shekinah (90ff.) Moltmann advocates the kabbalistic tradition of Judaism which he adopts from Isaac Luria with its divine *zimzum* (God's self-limitation); the essential problem with this doctrine is that its pantheistic and emanationist understanding of creation obliterates the traditional distinction between God and the world by making nothing the condition of the possibility of God's action ad extra (cf. *Trinity and Kingdom*, 109ff. and above n. 15). Thus, for example, Moltmann writes: 'God withdraws into himself in order to go out of himself. He "creates" the preconditions for the existence of his creation by withdrawing his presence and his power … Nothingness emerges' (*Creation*, 87). For Moltmann, 'The doctrine of the Shekinah is the logical result of making God's pathos the starting point' (*Trinity and Kingdom*, 30).

42 Moltmann, *Trinity and Kingdom*, 19.

43 Moltmann, *Trinity and Kingdom*, 19–20.

Such thinking avoids Kant's view that 'nothing whatever can be gained for practical purposes, even if one comprehended it [the doctrine of the Trinity]';[44] it also avoids starting from a general concept of one divine substance because then 'natural theology's definition ... becomes a prison for the statements made by the theology of revelation'.[45] Such a doctrine of the Trinity would disintegrate into 'abstract monotheism'. Moltmann compares this to what he believes is Thomas Aquinas's idea that when we abstract from the trinitarian Persons 'what remains for thought is the one divine nature. It is this ... which is in general to be called "God", not the three Persons, or only one of them'.[46] Finally, Moltmann hopes to avoid Hegel's idea of God as absolute subject, that is, one subject – three modes of being; here the trinitarian concept of person is replaced by mode of being and in Moltmann's view this leads to modalism, that is, 'to the reduction of the doctrine of the trinity to monotheism'.[47] Neither a 'return to the earlier Trinity of substance' nor adopting a more modern 'subject' Trinity are viable options; instead he suggests that we refrain from beginning with God's unity, as he notes has been the custom in the West, and commence 'with the trinity of the Persons and ... then go on to ask about the unity'. What then emerges is 'a concept of the divine unity as the union of the trinity'.[48] In his doctrine of creation he is presenting 'the corresponding ecological doctrine of creation'.[49] In both works Moltmann suggests that we 'cease to understand God monotheistically as the one, absolute subject, but instead see him in a trinitarian sense as the *unity* of the Father, the Son and the Spirit'.[50]

In the rest of this chapter we hope to show how this thinking leads Moltmann to re-interpret the doctrines of the Trinity and of creation. In addition we hope to show that the choice between monotheism and trinitarianism as Moltmann conceives it is neither required nor possible when the triune God is recognized as the one God who does not surrender his deity in his actions ad extra. Indeed, I believe that one can say it is as the one absolute subject that God creates and maintains

44 Moltmann, *Trinity and Kingdom*, 6.

45 Moltmann, *Trinity and Kingdom*, 17.

46 Moltmann, *Trinity and Kingdom*, 16.

47 Moltmann, *Trinity and Kingdom*, 18.

48 Moltmann, *Trinity and Kingdom*, 19.

49 Moltmann, *Creation*, 2.

50 Moltmann, *Creation*, 2. *Trinity and Kingdom*, chapter 1.

the world in existence through the Son and the Spirit without being a Hegelian as long as there is a clear distinction drawn between the immanent and the economic Trinity. Since God remains God, therefore it would have to be God alone who is and remains the *only* divine subject in the encounter with creatures. His actions would never become dependent on those of his creatures, since such a view is workable only if divine and human being are confused and one falls directly into the Feuerbachian dilemma. Here I intend to explore Moltmann's method and conclusions regarding the God-world relation with a view toward assessing whether and to what extent his revision of the traditional doctrines clarifies or obscures the being of God the creator, the Lord and Giver of life of the familiar Nicene Creed. This should lead to a clearer vision of the function of the immanent Trinity today. We have already seen that Moltmann reacted against the way the doctrine of the immanent Trinity functioned for Karl Barth. Now we will see Moltmann's alternative in more detail and evaluate it in the context of our discussions developed so far in this book.

Method and Problem

Moltmann contends that traditional theology has emphasized duality, that is, creation *and* redemption, creation *and* covenant, necessity *and* freedom, nature *and* grace. Accordingly, in his view, grace presupposes and perfects nature but does not destroy it. Moltmann says this is captured by Rahner's phraseology 'that anthropology is "deficient christology" and christology is "realized anthropology"'.[51] He believes that the second part of the proposition fails to distinguish 'grace and glory, history and new creation, being a Christian and being perfected' and has led to 'triumphalism', that is, 'the glory which perfects nature is supposed already inherent in the grace'.[52] While I agree with Moltmann that triumphalism must be avoided, I shall suggest here, against his view, that 'triumphalism' would follow only if the *glory*, which perfects nature, is supposed to be somehow inherent in nature or some synthesis of nature and grace. In other words there would be a problem with this position only if nature and grace were not clearly distinguished and then united.

---

51 Moltmann, *Creation*, 7.
52 Moltmann, *Creation*, 7.

Moltmann recommends that we say that grace does not perfect nature, but prepares nature for eternal glory. Thus, as Christ's resurrection is the beginning of the new creation of the world we must speak of nature and grace in a 'forward perspective' in light of the 'coming glory, which will complete *both nature and grace*'.[53] The dualities will no longer be defined over against one another; rather 'they will be determined in all their complex interconnections in relation to a third, common to them both'.[54] That third is conceived by Moltmann as the *process* common to both and when this is seen then, he believes, we will have a reconciliation of opposites such as freedom and necessity, grace and nature and finally covenant and creation. It is of course this common process which I believe identifies God with creation and thus fails to distinguish the above-mentioned dualities in the long run. Among many problems which result from this thinking is the idea that Christ's lordship is provisional; it will be complete only in the kingdom of glory when the Son transfers the, as yet, incomplete kingdom to the Father.

> With this transfer the lordship of the Son ends ... it means the consummation of his sonship ... all Jesus' titles of sovereignty – Christ, kyrios, prophet ... – are *provisional* titles, which express Jesus' significance for salvation in time. But the name of Son remains to all eternity.[55]

Moltmann also contends that:

> Without the difference between Creator and creature, creation cannot be conceived at all; *but this difference is embraced and comprehended by the greater truth* which is what the creation narrative really comes down to, because it is the truth from which it springs: *the truth that God is all in all.* This does not imply a pantheistic dissolution of creation in God; it means the final form which creation is to find in God.[56]

The problem, however, is that if the difference is embraced in this way then one could argue, as Moltmann does, that since God and creatures

---

53 Moltmann, *Creation*, 8, emphasis mine.
54 Moltmann, *Creation*, 8.
55 Moltmann, *Trinity and Kingdom*, 92.
56 Moltmann, *Creation*, 89, emphasis mine.

mutually co-exist, therefore the kingdom of glory arises from the history of suffering which, according to the kabbalistic doctrine of creation, God makes part of himself in order to create and in order to redeem; it follows that redemption then cannot be viewed as a free new act of God in creating a new heaven and a new earth. Thus, 'It is from the apotheosis of the Lamb that the kingdom of glory comes into being.'[57] This differs from John's gospel which traces the origin of Jesus's glory to his relation with the Father as one who was full of grace and truth as the Word who was God (Jn. 1:1, 1:14–18). Believers in the Word incarnate would see God's glory while those who refused to believe did so because they 'look to each other for glory and are not concerned with the glory that comes from the one God' (Jn. 5:43). The kingdom of glory in Moltmann's view comes into existence from within history and cannot be identical with God's self-sufficient glory revealed in the cross and resurrection. Since God 'enters into his finite creation . . . he also participates in its evolution'; hence 'God and the world are then involved in a common redemptive process'. God participates in the world's pain; thus 'we need God's compassion and God needs ours'. Finally, 'God himself becomes free in the process . . . even God himself will only be free when our souls are free.'[58] While Moltmann says God does not act out of deficiency of being,[59] it is precisely here that God's being is indeed deficient by virtue of his need for redemption, glory and freedom. This thinking results from Moltmann's conviction that: 'The trinitarian concept of creation integrates the elements of truth in monotheism and pantheism' by enabling us to 'find an integrating view of God and nature which will draw them both *into the same vista*. It is only this that can exert a liberating influence on nature and human beings.'[60]

The question which is being raised here then is whether there can be a process common to both nature and grace, freedom and necessity and so on, which encompasses them and determines their present and future meaning without obliterating the distinction between God and the world. For Moltmann this process is both possible and necessary because his theological starting point is a version of panentheism

---

57 Moltmann, *Creation*, 90.

58 Moltmann, *Trinity and Kingdom*, 39. Moltmann asks: 'Does God really not need those whom in the suffering of his love he loves unendingly?' (53). For the same idea, see *Creation*, 82ff.

59 Moltmann, *Trinity and Kingdom*, 23.

60 Moltmann, *Creation*, 98, emphasis mine.

which maintains that we cannot cling to any distinction between the immanent and the economic Trinity. Thus, 'The economic Trinity not only reveals the immanent Trinity; it also has a retroactive effect on it'[61] principally because, in the words of Unamuno, as seen earlier, 'A God who cannot suffer cannot love either … only that which suffers is divine.'[62] Hence,

> *Christian panentheism* … started from the divine essence: Creation is a fruit of God's longing for 'his Other' and for that Other's free response to the divine love. That is why the idea of the world is inherent in the nature of God himself from eternity. For it is impossible to conceive of a God who is not a creative God. A non-creative God would be imperfect … if God's eternal being is love, then the divine love is also more blessed in giving than in receiving. *God cannot find bliss in eternal self-love if selflessness is part of love's very nature.*[63]

Moltmann rejects identifying the world process with God as he believes that this took place in the speculative theology of the nineteenth century arguing that: 'In order to understand the history of mankind as a history *in* God, the distinction between the world process and the inner-trinitarian process must be maintained and emphasized.'[64]

---

61 Moltmann, *Trinity and Kingdom*, 160.

62 Moltmann, *Trinity and Kingdom*, 38.

63 Moltmann, *Trinity and Kingdom*, 106, emphasis mine.

64 Moltmann, *Trinity and Kingdom*, 106–7. See also *Creation*, 103, where Moltmann explains that the German Romantics such as Goethe have turned people into indifferentists with their pantheism. He believes that he has overcome this by saying 'everything is not God; but God is everything'; but all he actually has done is rejected a simple pantheistic identification of God's Spirit with matter and identified this instead with 'the overriding harmony of the relations' which he finds at work in history and nature (*Creation*, 103). We have here a more complex 'relational' identity which can discern 'future transcendence, evolution and intentionality', but it is still an identity and not a relationship between essentially distinct beings, that is, creator and creatures. It is interesting to note that later Moltmann presents a somewhat different view of Goethe by espousing what he calls the 'true pan-entheism' that he finds in Giordano Bruno and Goethe, *History and the Triune God*, 164.

Yet, given the fact that it is impossible to conceive of a God who is not creative and who cannot find bliss in his eternal self-love, the question arises as to whether, in this reasoning, there can be an inner-trinitarian process distinct from that trinitarian thinking which defines God's love as selflessness and which then insists that God cannot have existed without being the creator. The problem here is captured succinctly by Etienne Gilson in his analysis of Descartes's natural theology: 'Now it is quite true that a creator is an eminently Christian God, but a God whose very essence is to be a creator is not a Christian God at all. The essence of the true Christian God is not to create but to be. "He who is" can also create, if he chooses; but he does not exist because he creates ... he can create because he supremely is.'[65] According to Gilson, Descartes's 'stillborn God' was 'the God of Christianity reduced to the condition of a philosophical principle' and that 'the most striking characteristic of such a God was that his creative function had integrally absorbed his essence'.[66] Despite the fact that objections could be raised to Gilson about how the nature of 'He who is' is to be conceived (i.e. does God supremely exist merely as an act of existence whose essence is to be or as the triune God who knows and loves himself in the freedom of transcendence which is his alone?), the question he raises here is decisive.[67] It concerns the fact that God is free and does not need to create in order to be God. It concerns the distinction between the eternal being of God and his free, but real relations with the world.

Necessity and Freedom

Moltmann certainly recognizes and actually seeks to avoid this problem when he writes:

> The later theological interpretation of creation as *creatio ex nihilo* is therefore unquestionably an apt paraphrase of what the Bible means by 'creation'. Wherever and whatever God creates is without any preconditions. *There is no external necessity which occasions his*

---

65 Gilson, *God and Philosophy*, 88.

66 Gilson, *God and Philosophy*, 89.

67 This is the gist of Moltmann's objection to Thomas Aquinas's view of the Trinity as 'one divine substance;' he calls this 'abstract monotheism' as we saw earlier.

creativity, and no inner compulsion which could determine it. Nor is
there any primordial matter whose potentiality is pre-given to his
creative activity, and which would set him material limits.[68]

However, his pantheism causes him to ascribe an inner compulsion to
God's nature which he himself recognizes the *creatio ex nihilo* intended
to exclude. Hence in answering this question Moltmann writes: 'If we
lift the concept of necessity out of the context of compulsive necessity
and determination by something external, then in God *necessity* and
freedom coincide; they are what is for him axiomatic, self-evident. For
God it is axiomatic to love, for he cannot deny himself. For God it is
axiomatic to love freely, for he is God.'[69] Therefore, God is not 'his own
prisoner' and remains true to himself.

The only problem with this reasoning is that it constrains Moltmann
to suppose that in loving the world God is 'entirely himself'.[70] This means
that, since he cannot but will the good, he has no choice in 'communicating himself' to his creation. Thus, God's own self-determination is
'an essential *emanation* of his goodness'.[71] This view follows Moltmann's
hermeneutical presupposition which is that 'the eternal origin of God's
creative and suffering love' must include 'God's free self-determination,
and *at the same time* the overflowing of his goodness, which belongs
to his essential nature'.[72] This synthesis of God's act (of will) and being

68 Moltmann, *Creation*, 74. See also 75, 'The world was created neither out
of pre-existent matter nor out of the divine Being itself.' This why he rejects
Tillich's understanding of creation (80). Moltmann thinks Tillich's abolition
of the divine self-differentiation from creation is the monism and pantheism
Christians must reject (84).

69 Moltmann, *Trinity and Kingdom*, 107.

70 Moltmann, *Trinity and Kingdom*, 55. See also *Creation*, 83. This
supposition follows from his method and it is worth noting the striking
similarity between his conclusion and the view of the incarnation offered by
Ludwig Feuerbach, that is, 'there is nothing more in the nature of God than
in the incarnate manifestation of God ... The Incarnation ... is therefore no
mysterious composition of contraries' (Feuerbach, *The Essence of Christianity*,
56). 'The love of God to man is an essential condition of the Divine Being: God
is a God who loves me – who loves man in general' (57).

71 Moltmann, *Trinity and Kingdom*, 54, emphasis mine.

72 Moltmann, *Trinity and Kingdom*, 54, emphasis mine. It is this 'at the
same time' that is the heartbeat of all pantheism. For instance, Meister Eckhart
proposed that 'at the same time and once and for all, when God existed and

resulted from Moltmann's belief that the Gnostic and Neoplatonic doctrine of emanation contained 'elements of truth which are indispensable for a full understanding of God's creation'.[73] In his resolute unwillingness to exclude emanationism and pantheism decisively Moltmann is led to believe that he can reconcile freedom and necessity in relation to the Trinity and creation without compromising the traditional doctrines. Perhaps he would be horrified to find himself in the company of Augustine in this predicament. Appropriately perceiving the need for a clear decision at this point Gilson put the matter this way:

> In short, as soon as Augustine read the *Enneads*, he found there the three essentially Christian notions of God the Father, of God the Word, and of the creation. That Augustine found them there is an incontrovertible fact. *That they were not there is a hardly more controvertible fact.* To go at once to the fundamental reason why they could not possibly be there, let us say *that the world of Plotinos and the world of Christianity are strictly incomparable; no single point in the one can be matched with any single point in the other one,* for the fundamental reason that their metaphysical structure is essentially different.[74]

when He generated His Son, God coeternal, and coequal to Himself in all things, He also created the world' in Clarkson, S.J., et al. (tr. and ed.) *The Church Teaches*, 147. This pantheistic viewpoint was rejected in 1329 based on the *creatio ex nihilo* which excluded the idea that both creation and creator were eternal. It is not particularly surprising that Moltmann cites Meister Eckhart in support of his panentheism (which as noted earlier is really worse than pantheism): 'only if we have a concept of God with a trinitarian differentiation ... can we say with Meister Eckhart that all is "from God", all is "through God", all is "in God" ... [indeed] It seems to me that Giordano Bruno is returning at the end of this age as the herald of a new "paradigm" for a world in which human beings can survive in organic harmony with the Spirit of the universe' (*History and the Triune God*, 164). Curiously, David Tracy thinks that Meister Eckhart's thinking might prove useful for contemporary trinitarian theology, see 'Trinitarian Speculation and the Forms of Divine Disclosure' in Davis, Kendall, S.J., and O'Collins, S.J. (eds), *The Trinity: An Interdisciplinary Symposium on the Trinity*, 290f.

73 Moltmann, *Creation*, 83.

74 Gilson, *God and Philosophy*, 48–9, emphases mine.

In his trinitarian doctrine, as noted earlier, Moltmann concludes that:

> From eternity God has desired not only himself but the world too ... That is why the idea of the world is already inherent in the Father's love for the Son ... The *Logos* through whom the Father has created everything, and without whom nothing has been made that was made is only *the other side of the Son*. The Son is *the Logos* in relation to the world. The Logos is *the Son* in relation to the Father.[75]

In connection with this problem, Thomas Aquinas clearly insisted that:

> There are two reasons why the knowledge of the divine persons was necessary for us. It was necessary for the right idea of creation ... *saying that God made all things by His Word excludes the error of those who say that God produced things by necessity*. When we say that in Him there is a procession of love, we say God produced creatures not because he needed them, ... *[and] that we may think rightly concerning the salvation of the human race, accomplished by the Incarnate Son, and by the gift of the Holy Ghost*.[76]

By contrast, in Moltmann's thought, it certainly appears that if God is not his own prisoner he is certainly the prisoner of love which by its very nature *must* freely create another in order to be true to its own nature. For Moltmann, selflessness is the essence of love and that selflessness must apply to God's free love as well as creaturely love.[77]

---

75 Moltmann, *Trinity and Kingdom*, 108.

76 *Summa Theologica*, pt. 1, qu. 32, art. 1, emphasis mine. In this thinking Thomas is in accord with Athanasius who, as we have noted in Chapter 1, argued correctly and powerfully that 'it would be more pious and true to indicate God from the Son and to call him Father than to name him from his works alone and to say that he is unoriginated'. Not indicating God from the Son leads, among other things, to a false idea of creation. It led Arius to think of Christ as a work of the Father.

77 Moltmann, *Trinity and Kingdom*, 28; this idea is essential to the doctrine of the Shekinah. Since Moltmann cannot conceive of creation as an expression of God's omnipotence – God had to empty himself of this to create (*Creation*, 88) – he argues that it is God's nature to will the good and since he cannot deny this, therefore in loving the world 'he is entirely himself'. Consequently, it is implied that it would be evil for God not to create since creation means 'communicating himself' and freedom is not freedom to choose but simple

Consequently, God is not free to create or not but must, in his very essence be described as creative love. Here and in Moltmann's often repeated idea that for God 'not to reveal himself and to be contented with his untouched glory would be a contradiction of himself',[78] as well as in this passage just cited, there can be no distinction between God's eternal self-sufficient love as Father, Son and Spirit and his free will to create a world distinct from himself. Rather he writes: 'The generation and birth of the Son come from the Father's *nature*, not from his will. That is why we talk about the *eternal* generation and birth of the Son. The Father begets and bears the Son out of the *necessity* of his being.'[79] Thus, for Moltmann, there can be no distinction between God's eternal self-sufficient love as Father, Son and Spirit, and his free will ad intra and ad extra in his act of creating a world distinct from himself. This is significantly different from the kind of careful distinction mentioned by Athanasius. Rejecting Patripassianism and Sabellianism it was held that

> those who irreverently say that the Son has been generated not by choice or will, thus encompassing God with a necessity which excludes choice and purpose, so that He begat the Son unwillingly, we account as most irreligious and alien to the Church; in that they have dared to define such things concerning God, beside the common notions concerning Him, nay, beside the purport of divinely inspired Scripture. For we, knowing that God is absolute and sovereign over Himself, have a religious judgment that He generated the Son voluntarily and freely; yet ... we do not understand Him to have been originated like the creatures or works which through Him came to be.[80]

'undivided joy in the good'. Hence, 'Love is a self-evident, unquestionable "overflowing of goodness" which is therefore *never open to choice at any time*' (*Trinity and Kingdom*, 55, emphasis mine). If God could 'choose' not to create it would in fact be an evil choice since overflowing goodness has no 'free choice'; this for Moltmann would imply arbitrariness or the possibility of a different God than the one he has described.

78 Moltmann, *Trinity and Kingdom*, 53.

79 Moltmann, *Trinity and Kingdom*, 167.

80 Athanasius, *Select Works and Letters* in *A Select Library of Nicene and Post-Nicene Fathers*, trans. and ed. by Philip Schaff and Henry Wace, vol. 4, (New York: Charles Scribner's Sons, 1903), *Epistle of Athanasius Concerning the Arian Bipartite Council held at Ariminum and Seleucia*, 463, part 2, no. 26.

The eleventh Council of Toledo (675) formulated the matter carefully as follows: 'He is the Son of God by nature not by adoption; and we must believe that God the Father begot him not through his will and not of necessity, for there is no necessity in God nor does the will precede wisdom.'[81] Following this tradition, Karl Barth argued that: 'The eternal generation of the Son by the Father tells us first and supremely that God is not at all lonely even without the world and us.'[82]

The consequences of this reasoning cause Moltmann to argue that God's freedom cannot mean that he is without obligation to creation since 'the self-communication of his goodness in love to his creation is not a matter of his free will'.[83] Moltmann dissolves God's will to act into what he describes as his essential nature arguing that 'his will *is* his essential activity'. Thus, 'God is not entirely free when he can do and leave undone what he likes; he is entirely free when he is entirely himself. In his creative activity he is wholly and *entirely* himself. He loves the world in the surrender of his Son with the very same love which he *is*, from eternity to eternity.'[84] Moltmann's failure to distinguish the immanent and economic Trinity then leads him to be unable to distinguish between God's being and act, nature and will, as well as creation and redemption at this crucial point.[85]

If, as Moltmann believes, the idea of creation is already inherent in the Father's necessary love of the Son, where is the distinction between God's free love and the necessary creation of a reality distinct from him to be drawn? If the Son is the Logos in relation to the world as Moltmann says, then is he not the Logos apart from the world in himself? Are we dealing with two different Logoi here; one who exists as God the Son and another who exists as the soul of

---

81 Clarkson et al. (trans. and ed.), *The Church Teaches*, 128.

82 *CD* I/1, 139.

83 Moltmann, *Creation*, 82.

84 Moltmann, *Creation*, 82–3.

85 Thus, instead of seeing creation and redemption as two distinct actions of the one God, for Moltmann, redemption refers to a future when 'God's creation and his revelation will be one' *Creation*, 287–8. 'The goal of this history [of consummation] is not a return to the paradisal primordial condition. Its goal is the revelation of the glory of God ... this ... represents the fulfillment of the real promise implanted in creation itself', (*Creation*, 207). Obviously a redemption that is implanted in creation (even as a promise) cannot be conceived as a free, new action of the triune God.

the created world? Has Moltmann here not introduced the world into the Godhead as the other side of the Son just because he has already introduced suffering into the Godhead as part of God's loving nature when he wrote, in accordance with the doctrine of the Shekinah, that creation is traced to a dichotomy in God so that there is a 'rift which runs through the divine life and activity until redemption'?[86] Moltmann is led to argue not only that God ' "needs" the world and man', but that the relation between the Father and Son 'is necessary love, not free love'.[87]

In his concept of the Son as the Logos in relation to the world Moltmann is unable to maintain what the traditional doctrine of the Trinity intended to assert, that is, that God's eternal Word is *identical* with God himself and thus the only begotten Son of the Father is identical with the Word through whom God creates.[88] However, if this is the case then it is impossible to conclude that the Father bears the Son out of necessity, for his love is only necessary insofar as it is his free self-affirmation in which he is subject to no necessary determinations from within or without as Moltmann himself believes the doctrine of *creatio ex nihilo* proposed. Any such necessity would make the love of God subject to a higher law encompassing his actual free love. That higher

86   Moltmann, *Trinity and Kingdom*, 30.

87   Moltmann, *Trinity and Kingdom*, 58. See Daniel Castelo, 'Moltmann's dismissal of divine impassibility: Warranted?' *SJT*, vol. 61, no. 4 (2008): 396–407 for an important discussion that links Moltmann's dismissal of divine impassibility to his method which employs suffering to understand who God is in a way that undermines the importance of recognizing God's sovereignty as the one who loves; in other words, Moltmann abandons 'a notion of the immanent Trinity'. This leads to his panentheism which opens the door to the idea that God needs the world (401–2).

88   Athanasius wrote: 'For since the Word is the Son of God by nature proper to His essence, and is from Him, and in Him, as He said Himself, the creatures could not have come to be, except through Him … He is the Father's Will' (Athanasius, *Select Works and Letters*, *Against the Arians, Discourse II*, 18, 364). Thomas Aquinas, following Augustine, wrote that 'Word and Son express the same' in order to avoid any idea that either term merely referred to a property of his which might lead to the idea that we were dealing with a being who was not fully divine. *Summa Theologica* pt. 1, q. 32, art. 2. Following this tradition Karl Barth wrote: 'In the vocabulary of Trinitarian doctrine God's Son cannot be differentiated from God's Word' (*CD* I/1, 137).

law of course would be accessible as a philosophical principle to which God himself was subject.

Here we reach the heart of the matter. For if the immanent Trinity as known from within the economy is the norm for the truth of our concepts of God as it should be, then the trinitarian actions ad extra would remain normative for any interpretation of present and future meaning; these could not be deduced from a panentheistic principle of suffering love discovered in a relational metaphysics and then applied to revelation.[89] Rather we would have to acknowledge, as Thomas Aquinas himself did following Augustine, that 'by faith we arrive at knowledge, and not conversely'.[90] A Christian doctrine of the Trinity therefore would derive its meaning from God in se acting ad extra and not from the realm of history accessible to the philosopher as such. It is my belief that because Moltmann attempts to conceive God's nature and suffering in creation in a single perspective in which both are on their way toward redemption that he incorporates need, nothingness, suffering and death directly into the nature of God.[91] In this way, he compromises his own

89 Thus Moltmann argues against a Cartesian 'subject' metaphysics and an Aristotelian 'metaphysics of substance' saying: 'Both can only be done away with by means of a relational metaphysics, based on the mutual relativity of human beings and the world' (*Creation*, 50). The norm for his thinking is a relational metaphysics dictated by the relativity of people and the world and not the freedom of God revealed in his Word and Spirit and acknowledged in the *creatio ex nihilo*. Hence, Moltmann's hermeneutical presupposition is that he can 'find a new interpretation of the Christian doctrine of creation in light of the knowledge of nature made accessible to us by evolutionary theories' (*Creation*, 205). Thus, his norm is not revelation but revelation interpreted from the perspective of mutual indwellings and developments he believes he has discovered in nature and history.

90 *Summa Theologica*, pt. 1, q. 32, art. 1.

91 Thus he is led to argue as noted earlier that: 'It is not through supernatural interventions that God guides creation ... Seen in terms of world history, the transforming power of suffering is the *basis* for the liberating and consummating acts of God' (*Creation*, 211). Creation traditionally was distinguished from salvation with the idea that creation was good but went wrong. Salvation was a free new action of God by which God negated the spheres of sin and evil which arose in opposition to his good will and were to be destroyed ultimately in the death and resurrection of Jesus Christ (*Athanasius's Orations Against the Arians*, in *The Trinitarian Controversy, Sources of Early Christian Thought*, trans. and ed. by William G. Rusch, [Philadelphia: Fortress Press, 1980], Book 1,

understanding of the *creatio ex nihilo* and is led to re-define the immanent Trinity by the history of the economic Trinity. In the remainder of this chapter I will restrict myself to indicating the reason why I think this happens to Moltmann and why it leads him both into the modalism he criticizes in Rahner and Barth and into tritheism.

Method and the Freedom of God

Since his understanding of the Trinity does not come only from the triune God acting ad extra but from a synthesis of human and divine experience, Moltmann does not distinguish clearly between human experience of the created realm and God's being and action in his Word and Spirit. Thus, he argues against Schleiermacher that:

> If one were only to relate the experience of God to the experience of the self, then the self would become the constant and 'God' the variable. It is only when the self is perceived in the experience which God has with that self that an undistorted perception of the history of one's own self with God and in God emerges.[92]

Accordingly, Moltmann assumes that Schleiermacher actually has described God by speaking of our feeling of absolute dependence and concludes that experience does not merely refer to our experience of God but to 'God's experience with us'.[93] In neither case, however,

---

41, 104–5). By contrast, Moltmann contends that nihil is a 'partial negation of the divine Being, inasmuch as God is not yet creator. The space which comes into being and is set free by God's self-limitation is a literally God-forsaken space. The *nihil* in which God creates his creation is God-forsakenness, hell, absolute death' (*Creation*, 87). The result of making the *nihil* something, rather than the symbol that God is truly free in relation to all that is distinct from him and dependent on him, is the incorporation of *nihil* itself directly into the Godhead. We have here the dualism that Moltmann himself intends to reject. God-forsakenness, hell and absolute death are part of God before creation. Ultimately Moltmann can conceive of creation only as an emanation of the divine being because according to the doctrine of the *zimzum*, creation refers to a shrinkage process in God himself and then to his 'issuing' outside himself (*Creation*, 87 and *Trinity and Kingdom*, 109–10).

92 Moltmann, *Trinity and Kingdom*, 4.

93 Moltmann, *Trinity and Kingdom*, 4.

has he shown that he is speaking of the Christian God who factually transcends all of our experiences even as he makes himself known; Moltmann merely assumes that Schleiermacher's reduction of the Trinity to abstract monotheism can be overcome with the counter question: 'how does God experience me'?[94] However, the fact remains that neither Schleiermacher nor Moltmann have shown that they are speaking of the Christian God whose being and action cannot be grounded in experience at all without compromising the distinction between God and the world. This has serious methodological consequences for the relationship between philosophy and theology.

Having blurred the distinction between human experience and God's experience at the outset, Moltmann argues that the more we come to understand God's experience, the closer we come to the perception that

> the history of the world is the history of God's suffering. At the moments of God's profoundest revelation there is always suffering: the cry of the captives in Egypt; Jesus' death cry on the cross; the sighing of the whole enslaved creation for liberty. *If a person once feels the infinite passion of God's love which finds expression here, then he understands the mystery of the triune God.* God suffers with us – God suffers from us – God suffers for us: *it is this experience of God that reveals the triune God* ... Consequently fundamental theology's discussion about access to the doctrine of the Trinity is carried on today in the context of the question about God's capacity or incapacity for suffering.[95]

Here, where we return to where this chapter began, Moltmann leaps to the assumption that an experience of suffering is not only an experience of God but also knowledge of the Trinity. This doctrinal foundation leads him to redefine both the immanent and economic Trinity by the experiences of suffering love which he discovers both in God and creatures. We have already seen that, on the one hand, this procedure compromises God's freedom with the emanationism which Moltmann himself rejects, and on the other hand, it compromises the freedom of grace with the claim that creatures have the inherent capacity for the divine and that both nature and grace are in need of completion in the kingdom of glory. He ignores the crucial point that unless God's glory

94 Moltmann, *Trinity and Kingdom*, 3.
95 Moltmann, *Trinity and Kingdom*, 4–5, emphasis mine.

is already inherent in his grace (i.e. his free creation and subsequent intervention in history in Israel, in Christ and in the Church), then it can no longer be seen as the glory of God who is and remains factually self-sufficient because he does not create, reconcile and redeem out of need but out of his free love.

Following this logic, Moltmann argues that it is not enough to say that God allows Christ to suffer or that in Christ we see the 'sufferings of God who cannot suffer'.[96] To understand correctly the suffering of the passionate God, Moltmann believes that we should start 'from the axiom of God's passion'[97] rather than the traditional view which asserts God's apathy. Moltmann therefore re-interprets the apathetic axiom to say that 'God is not subjected to suffering in the same way as transient, created beings'. Since 'God does not suffer out of deficiency of being, like created beings' he remains 'apathetic;' yet 'he suffers from the love which is the superabundance and overflowing of his being. In so far he is "pathetic."'[98] It is this same reasoning which later leads Moltmann to explain that 'God and the world are related to one another through the relationship of their mutual indwelling and participation: God's indwelling in the world is divine in kind; the world's indwelling in God is worldly in kind. There is no other way of conceiving the continual communication between God and the world.'[99] However, the crucial question which remains unanswered in this reasoning is whether the divine indwelling is *essentially* other than that of the world? Or are they mutually dependent and therefore identical?

Here Moltmann turns to Origen who asks: 'And the Father Himself ... does he not suffer in a certain way? ... Even the Father is not incapable of suffering'[100] and concludes that 'The suffering of love does not only affect the redeeming acts of God outwards; it also affects the trinitarian fellowship of God in himself.'[101] Moltmann classifies apathetic theology with monotheism declaring that we can only talk of 'God's

96 Moltmann, *Trinity and Kingdom*, 22.

97 Moltmann, *Trinity and Kingdom*, 22.

98 Moltmann, *Trinity and Kingdom*, 23.

99 Moltmann, *Creation*, 150.

100 Moltmann, *Trinity and Kingdom*, 24. Even Origen does not seem to have gone as far as Moltmann, for he also stated that God the Father 'suffers ... becoming something which because of the greatness of his nature He cannot be, and endures human suffering for our sakes' (*Trinity and Kingdom*, 24).

101 Moltmann, *Trinity and Kingdom*, 24.

suffering in trinitarian terms' by starting from God's passion *rather than* from his apathy; he seeks to develop a doctrine of *theopathy* by appealing to those rare theologians who started from 'God's passion and not from his apathy'.[102] His sources are the doctrine of Shekinah, Spanish mysticism, Russian-Orthodox philosophy of religion and the Anglican idea of sacrificial love, and what does he discover?

1. According to Moltmann (following Abraham Heschel) it is the divine passion (not his apathy) which 'is God's freedom. It is the free relationship of passionate participation'.[103] Here we may note that in this definition of divine freedom God's apathy, which Moltmann said it was necessary to affirm, is immaterial for this definition of freedom. This is no accident, because as we saw earlier, there is a common term which determines the nature of both freedom and necessity in such a way that God cannot really be free *as* he loves but must be free in accordance with the superior concept of fellowship or self-humiliation which is intrinsic to all selfless and suffering love, that is, pathetic love.

2. Here Moltmann adopts the doctrine of the Shekinah and grounds this in Jewish mysticism. Ultimately, he is led by this analysis to define love according to the explanation offered by the Spanish mystic Unamuno as noted earlier. This becomes the foundation for his redefinition of trinitarian fellowship and of God's sabbath relationship with creation. Indeed Moltmann argues that if Shekinah is viewed 'as God in person, then it is necessary to assume a profound self-differentiation in God himself'.[104] Whereas the traditional doctrine of the Trinity was a development of thought corresponding to a differentiation between the Father and the Son in the unity of the Holy Spirit which took place before creation in time, in Moltmann's thinking the differentiation arises from and is seen as necessary in light of the Jewish mystical assertion that God must have, before all worlds, included nothingness as well as creation in his very being. In part, this idea leads Moltmann to the dualism he theoretically rejects.

3. This thinking guides Moltmann to Franz Rosenzweig's mystical interpretation of creation and redemption. Here it becomes clear

102 Moltmann, *Trinity and Kingdom*, 25.

103 Moltmann, *Trinity and Kingdom*, 25.

104 Moltmann, *Trinity and Kingdom*, 28.

that while Moltmann explicitly and consistently rejects pantheism and emanationism, he is compelled by the logic implied in this thinking to maintain the essential insights of both pantheism and of emanationism in his doctrines of the Trinity and of creation. In order to overcome pantheism and emanationism Moltmann simply says that his panentheism is compatible with these Christian doctrines without being able to show how. He argues here that mysticism bridges the gap between '"the God of our fathers" and "the remnant of Israel with the help of the doctrine of the Shekinah"'.[105] First, God's descent to his people and his dwelling among them 'is thought of as a divorce which takes place in God himself. God himself cuts himself off from himself, he gives himself away ... he suffers with their sufferings'.[106] Second, 'God ... by suffering [Israel's] fate with her, makes himself in need of redemption. In this way, in this suffering, the relationship between God and the remnant points beyond itself'.[107] Third, God's unity is defined as a 'Becoming Unity. And this Becoming is laid on the soul of man and in his hands'.[108] In this analysis we begin to glimpse what Moltmann means by the kingdom of glory. As God himself now *needs* redemption from the division in his own being, so the kingdom of glory is that oneness which is becoming in the soul of the person who experienced suffering in the exile and experiences suffering even now, but who is looking forward to the time when God will be 'all in all' in an age of future harmony which has already begun in the form of his own acts of goodness here and now.

4. We have seen that Moltmann's basic methodological presupposition is that there is a common element beyond any antithesis between nature and grace and freedom and necessity which, when understood, will resolve our unnatural will to power and enable us to see that we are all really in God and that God is in us. Appealing to the Anglican idea of eucharistic sacrifice he writes:

> One basic concept runs through the whole literature on the subject: the necessity of seeing the eucharistic sacrifice, the cross on Golgotha and the heart of the triune God together, *in a single perspective*. The immediate occasion for developing the power

105 Moltmann, *Trinity and Kingdom*, 29.
106 Moltmann, *Trinity and Kingdom*, 29.
107 Moltmann, *Trinity and Kingdom*, 29.
108 Moltmann, *Trinity and Kingdom*, 29.

of God's suffering theologically was the apologetic necessity for providing a reply to Darwin's theory of evolution. In what sense are we to understand God's almighty power?[109]

The key point here is that Moltmann honestly believes that the historical event of the cross and the heart of the triune God can be understood together in a single perspective. If they can, then there is no distinction between the immanent and economic Trinity. There is no God independent of the world; there is only a God who can be seen from within the world's perspective as one who is subject to suffering love. The perspective (whether conceived relationally or not) would dictate the nature of God's love and freedom and to that extent would become that which is truly 'almighty'. Here, God can no longer be free in the traditional sense, that is, in the sense that he does not exist as one who stands in need.

The Cross

Thinking this way, Moltmann turns to C. E. Rolt, as noted earlier, in order to redefine God's almighty power in light of the cross and several key points which correspond exactly with the kabbalistic understanding of creation emerge.[110]

1. 'The sole omnipotence which God possesses is the almighty power of suffering love ... This is the essence of the divine sovereignty.'[111] Here, suffering love (pathos) is that which is almighty; thus any idea that God could love in a way that does not involve suffering is eliminated at the outset. This affects everything that Moltmann says in his doctrine of the Trinity and of creation; it leads him finally to argue that the Holy Spirit's suffering is identical with the world's suffering.

> The Spirit ... is God himself. If God commits himself to his limited creation, and if he himself dwells in it as 'the giver of life', this presupposes a self-limitation, a self-humiliation and a self-surrender

---

109 Moltmann, *Trinity and Kingdom*, 31, emphasis mine.

110 Moltmann, *Creation*, 86ff.

111 Moltmann, *Trinity and Kingdom*, 31. Hence, Moltmann, citing Studdert Kennedy, goes so far as to say 'God, the Father God of Love, is everywhere in history, but nowhere is He Almighty' (35).

of the Spirit. The history of suffering creation, which is subject to transience, then brings with it a history of suffering by the Spirit who dwells in creation.[112]

Moltmann also believes that God's Spirit is identical with the cosmic spirit; thus he writes: 'If the cosmic Spirit is the Spirit of God, the universe cannot be viewed as a closed system. It has to be understood as a system that is open – open for God and for his future.'[113] With these conclusions it seems clear that Moltmann's presuppositions cause him to ignore the problem of sin and to blur the distinction which the traditional doctrines correctly sought to maintain. Athanasius, for instance, deliberately rejected the idea that the cosmic Spirit could be equated with God's Spirit in this way.[114] While Moltmann seeks to avoid Stoic

112 Moltmann, *Creation*, 102.

113 Moltmann, *Creation*, 103. Thus, he believes that 'the freedom towards God of the human being … is as unbounded as God's capacity for passion and patience', *Trinity and Kingdom*, 30. He holds that 'As God's image, men and women are beings who correspond to God, beings who can give the seeking love of God the sought-for response, and who are intended to do just that' (*Creation*, 77). Where is the need for repentance, grace and the Holy Spirit here?

114 Torrance, *The Trinitarian Faith*, 201ff. presents the matter with great clarity especially as it relates to Athanasius's theology. Athanasius, for example, 'would have nothing to do with any attempt to reach an understanding of the Spirit beginning from manifestations or operations of the Spirit in creaturely existence, in man or in the world' (201). Athanasius also 'turned sharply away from any conception of the Logos as a cosmological principle (or of *logoi spermatikoi*, "seminal reasons", immanent in the universe) occupying an intermediate status between God and creation' (201). 'Athanasius developed the doctrine of the Spirit from his essential relation to the one God and his undivided co-activity with the Father and the Son, and specifically from his inherence in the being of the eternal Son' (201). In this way Athanasius preserved the unity of the Trinity by arguing that: 'The Father does all things through the Word and in the Holy Spirit' (202). In addition, 'The Holy Spirit does not bring to us any independent knowledge of God, or add any new content to God's self-revelation' (203). 'Thus, knowledge of the Spirit as well as of the Father is taken from and is controlled by knowledge of the Son' (203). From the outset of Moltmann's doctrine of creation this cannot be done because he actually equates God's Spirit, which is supposed to be *ex se* with the cosmic Spirit arguing that *this cosmic Spirit* acts in us; this follows his refusal to distinguish the immanent and economic Trinity.

Pantheism as did Calvin and Barth,[115] he is led by his method to say what neither Calvin nor Barth would say, that is, that the cosmic Spirit is the Holy Spirit and that, after the fall, creation is inherently open to God.

2. When Moltmann follows Rolt and attempts to deduce the eternal divine nature from Christ's passion he asserts, as noted previously, that: 'What Christ, the incarnate God, did in time, God, the heavenly Father, does and must do in eternity.'[116] Here we have a specific avowal of modalism which cannot distinguish the Father and the Son in eternity and so concludes that as Christ suffered in time so the heavenly Father does and *must* do this in eternity.

Whereas the tradition rejected Patripassianism in order to stress the *eternal* distinction between the Father and Son (independent of creation), so that we might perceive the freedom of God's action in Christ, Moltmann, following Rolt, collapses the actions of the economic Trinity into the being of the Father in eternity by arguing that

> the surrender of the Son for us on the cross has a retroactive effect on the Father and causes infinite pain ... God's relationship to the world has a retroactive effect on his relationship to himself – even though the divine relationship to the world is primarily determined by that inner relationship. The growth of knowledge of the immanent Trinity from the saving experience of the cross of Christ makes this necessary. *The pain of the cross determines the inner life of the triune God from eternity to eternity.*[117]

The trinitarian doctrine of the Church does not admit that the Father suffers from eternity to eternity simply because the Father almighty sends his Son for the purpose of salvation as a free gift of grace. Here the distinction between the Father and Son is an eternal one which is not defined by the historical events which took place in time. Still, the Father is not remote from the suffering of the Son on the cross since there is a *perichoresis* between the Father and the Son. Nonetheless, the events in time receive their meaning from God's free will actualized

---

115 Moltmann, *Creation*, 12.

116 Moltmann, *Trinity and Kingdom*, 31.

117 Moltmann, *Trinity and Kingdom*, 160–1, emphasis mine.

in those occurrences. Moltmann cannot say this because his method insists that Christ's suffering and the love of the immanent Trinity can be understood in a 'single perspective' which encompasses them both. It is an interesting fact that while Moltmann charges both Rahner and Barth with modalism they explicitly reject the modalist idea that the Father suffers.[118] Both Rahner and Barth recognized that to make suffering part of the nature of the eternal God (who existed before all worlds) would be to make God powerless to act as our savior (in history). Thus, for example, replying to a question indicating that Balthasar and others had criticized him for not having a sufficient *theologia crucis* Rahner states:

> In Moltmann and others I sense a theology of absolute paradox, of Patripassianism, perhaps even of a Schelling-like projection into God of division, conflict, godlessness and death. To put it crudely, it does not help me to escape from my mess and mix-up and despair if God is in the same predicament ... the classical teaching on the Incarnation and the theology of the hypostatic union ... must include, even while avoiding Patripassianism (a suffering and dying of God the Father), a meaningful and serious statement to the effect that *God* died ... [but] it is for me a source of consolation to realize that God, when and insofar as he entered into this history as into his own, did it in a different way than I did. From the beginning I am locked into its horribleness while God – if this word continues to have any meaning at all – is in a true and authentic and consoling sense the God *who does not suffer*, the immutable God, and so on.[119]

118 Karl Barth, *CD* I/1, 397. Other references in Moltmann's *Trinity and Kingdom* to the Father suffering are 31, 35, 59, 81 and 83. Moltmann's criticisms of Barth and Rahner can be seen in *Trinity and Kingdom*, 143ff.

119 *Karl Rahner in Dialogue: Conversations and Interviews 1965–1982*, ed. by Paul Imhof and Hubert Biallowons, trans. by Harvey D. Egan (New York: Crossroad, 1986), 126–7. Moltmann attempts an answer to Rahner's objection in *History and the Triune God*, 123–4. It is evident from Moltmann's reply that while he asserts that God enters our suffering in a divine way, his explanation of this completely discounts any impassibility on the part of God and to that extent misses the point that Rahner was trying to make, that is, that God in Christ is both passible and impassible and that we don't have to choose one over the other. Strangely, Rahner himself went on to say that maybe his own account of the cross might be inadequate and that a closer look at such a theology was needed to see whether or not it 'was binding for Christians', asserting that

In his doctrine of the Trinity Barth explained that:

> One can say very definitely that any systematising of the one-sidedness [of the trinitarian relations] such as is found in part in ancient Modalism (e.g., in the form of Patripassianism) is absolutely forbidden, since it would mean the dissolution of the triunity in a neutral fourth. The eternity of the fatherhood of God does not mean only the eternity of the fellowship of the Father with the Son and the Spirit. It also protects the Father against fusion with the Son and Spirit ... [this] would also be incompatible with any serious acceptance of the biblical witness which makes the Father and the Son one in their distinction.[120]

Barth also captured the positive point regarding God's action ad extra mentioned by Rahner indicating that:

> It is not at all the case that God has no part in the suffering of Jesus Christ even in His mode of being as the Father. No, there is a *particula veri* in the teaching of the early Patripassians. This is that primarily it is God the Father who suffers in the offering and sending of His Son, in His abasement. The suffering is not His own, but the alien suffering of the creature, of man, which He takes to Himself in Him. But He does suffer it in the humiliation of His Son with a depth with which it never was or will be suffered by any man – apart from the One who is His Son ... This fatherly fellow-suffering of God is the mystery, the basis, of the humiliation of His Son; the truth of that which takes place historically in His crucifixion . . .[121]

'Perhaps it is possible to be an orthodox Nestorian or an orthodox Monophysite. If this were the case, then I would prefer to be an orthodox Nestorian' (*Rahner in Dialogue*, 127).

120 *CD* I/1, 397–8.

121 *CD* IV/2, 357. For an illuminating discussion of why it is important to understand that God is both passible and impassible and that this can be understood only on the basis of soteriology and not logically since logically God could be either the one or the other but not both, see Molnar, *Torrance: Theologian of the Trinity*, 146–59. See also Bruce D. Marshall, 'The Absolute and the Trinity' *Pro Ecclesia*, vol. XXIII, no. 2 Spring 2014, 147–64 and Molnar, 'A Response: Beyond Hegel with Karl Barth and T. F. Torrance', 165–73. George Hunsinger offers a particularly important and instructive discussion of how Barth understood that the incarnation involves God suffering such that

In this analysis there remains a clear distinction between the Father and the Son and between the Father's suffering as a mystery grounded in the immanent Trinity and the creature's suffering which, while not part of God's nature, is experienced by God for the salvation of creatures.

3. After indicating that the sacrifice of love on the cross was neither simply a reaction to sin nor a *free decision* of God's will, Moltmann argues that it is part of love's nature to be capable of suffering. 'Self-sacrifice is God's very nature and essence.'[122] This insight later leads Moltmann to what he considers the following harmonious balance between the Reformed doctrine of decrees and Tillich's emanationism: God's 'divine life flows into his resolve, and from that resolve overflows to his creatures'.[123] This ultimately persuades Moltmann to argue that creation itself becomes part of God's nature in his sabbath rest.[124]

'God suffered in his divine nature without ceasing to be essentially impassible. God suffered in one sense without ceasing to be impassible in another' (*Reading Barth with Charity*, 147. Cf. 146–55). As against the kind of thinking advanced by Moltmann, Hunsinger rightly notes that for Barth, 'If God had not remained impassible in his sufferings and eternally alive in his [Christ's] death, neither sin nor death would have been destroyed (II/1, 400)' (146). Barth did not restrict the suffering only to Christ's human nature but, as noted, held that God suffered in his divine nature, but without ceasing to be divine; through the unity of divine and human natures in the incarnate Son the sufferings endured by Christ in his human nature were 'mediated to his divine nature by which they were eternally destroyed' (154). Closer to Gregory Nazianzen than to Cyril on this point, Barth did not vacillate 'about whether God could suffer in his divine nature' as Cyril apparently did. Instead, Hunsinger insightfully notes, for both Gregory and Barth 'the transcendent element in Christ's sufferings and death was the consuming fire of the divine life. The mystery of the divine nature in Christ was such that it became passible without ceasing to be impassible – and through impassibility prevailed' (154–5). These last comments are strikingly similar to the position explicated by T. F. Torrance in his *The Trinitarian Faith*, 184–5.

122 Moltmann, *Trinity and Kingdom*, 32.

123 Moltmann, *Creation*, 85.

124 Moltmann, *Creation*, 278ff. Thus, he asserts that God's sabbath 'does not spring from God's activity; it springs from his rest. It does not come from God's acts; it comes from his present Being' (282). Consequently, 'The human sabbath' becomes 'the rhythm of eternity in time' (287). While the tradition held that God's Being and Act are one in order to preserve God's freedom, Moltmann

Openness to the World

Rolt's thinking leads to a view of the Trinity which is 'open' toward the world and, as noted at the beginning of this chapter, this means that:

> Love *has* to give, for it is only in the act of giving that it truly possesses, and finds bliss. That is why God *has to give himself*; and he cannot possess himself apart from this act of serving. God has to give himself completely; and it is only in this way that he is God. *He has to go through time*; and it is *only* in this way that he is eternal ... *He has to be man and nothing but man*; and it is only in this way that

argues that God is directly present in his sabbath and can be equated with 'a transcendent encompassing milieu' and a 'transcendent future into which it is evolving' (204) such that the evolution of history as it transcends itself 'points towards the forecourt of an inviting and guiding transcendence' which can be called ' "God" ' (205). Hence, for Moltmann, the world is 'open to God' as its 'encompassing *milieu*' (205). God, Moltmann says, 'is its extra-worldly *forecourt*, into which it is evolving. God is the origin of the new possibilities out of which its realities are won' (205–6). Indeed God is not only 'open to the world' but God 'encompasses the world with the possibilities of his Being, and interpenetrates it with the powers of his Spirit. Through the energies of his Spirit, he is present in the world and immanent in each individual system' (206). He concludes that it 'is therefore impossible to think of this world-transcendence of God unless we think simultaneously of his world-immanence; and it is equally impossible to conceive of God's evolutive immanence in the world without his world-transcendence. The two are mutually related. It is only if we perceive the this-worldliness of God that we can usefully talk about a divine presence beyond the world; and the reverse is equally true' (206). This thinking is clearly a construct of natural theology with the idea that God can be envisaged vaguely as a 'transcendent milieu' and as part of the evolutionary process with the implication that the world is evolving toward God. None of this takes adequate account of the problem of sin and evil and of the need to recognize that God does not 'interpenetrate' creation but is present in history in his Word and Spirit in free actions which simply cannot be equated with movements of the evolutionary process as implied in this thinking. It is clear from this reasoning that God's transcendence of the world cannot mean that God is or could be God without the world. That is the problem of pantheism rearing its ugly head at this point in spite of the fact that Moltmann thinks he has overcome pantheism with this particular reference to God's transcendence.

he is completely God ... 'It was necessary for God to be Man, for only so could He be truly God.' ... In order to be completely itself, love has to suffer.[125]

In his creation doctrine this leads Moltmann to conclude that God's descent to human being and his dwelling among them is to be conceived as a 'division which takes place in God himself. God cuts himself off from himself. He gives himself away to his people. He suffers with their sufferings'.[126] Thus,

> God the Spirit is also the Spirit of the universe, its total cohesion, its structure, its information, its energy. The Spirit of the universe is the Spirit who proceeds from the Father and shines forth in the Son. *The evolutions and the catastrophes of the universe are also the movements and experiences of the Spirit of creation.*[127]

Further, Moltmann writes that it is 'one sided to view creation only as the work of "God's hands" ... something ... to be distinguished from God himself. *Creation is also the differentiated presence of God the Spirit*, the presence of the One *in* the many'.[128] Consequently, 'men and women correspond to the Creator in their very essence' and 'God enters into the creatures whom he has designated to be his image'.[129] In this thinking, where is the distinction between the Holy Spirit and the spirit of the universe to be found? Where is the distinction between Christ as the image of the unseen God and sinful creatures who *need* reconciliation to be found? If it cannot be found, how is our unnatural will to power to be overcome?

Moltmann's analysis explicitly negates God's freedom in the interest of stressing the fact that suffering (the historical suffering of Christ)

125 Moltmann, *Trinity and Kingdom*, 33.

126 Moltmann, *Creation*, 15. See also 86ff.

127 Moltmann, *Creation*, 16, emphasis mine.

128 Moltmann, *Creation*, 14, emphasis partially mine.

129 Moltmann, *Creation*, 77–8. Later Moltmann claims that 'the goal of creation is the revelation of the glory of God' and this 'represents the fulfillment of the real promise *implanted* in creation itself' (207, emphasis mine). Is the promise implanted in creation or is it a promise which remains identical with the Word in its identity with Jesus who is present in the power of his Spirit as the coming Lord?

defines the nature of both God's freedom and love. Clearly, there is and can be no distinction here between time and eternity[130] or between God's eternal begetting of his Son in the unity of the Holy Spirit and his free (gratuitous) actions ad extra. Rather, God's creative and salvific functions have integrally absorbed his essence. We have here a prototypical compromise of God's freedom as expressed in the Bible and in the tradition. It is no longer the case that the one God is the single transcendent subject of his actions in his Son and Spirit. Rather, his transcendent being and action is defined by his need to be man, his need to suffer and his need for another outside himself. Moltmann's own explanation of God's freedom leaves him in a logical and theological dilemma. Either he may argue that God really is subject to no internal or external necessities; then he would have to reject his own panentheist interpretation of the Trinity and of creation because the Christian God who loves is intrinsically free both in nature and will. Or he may argue that God is subject both to internal and to external necessities. Then he would have to reject the biblical and traditional view of creation and of the Trinity, but he cannot logically hold both positions at once. Yet that is exactly what he attempts to do, because it is of the very nature of panentheism to conceive of the God-world relation from within a process common to both God and creatures, nature and grace, freedom and necessity and into which these opposites are resolved by becoming an original perichoretic unity.

Panentheism cannot admit that God could have existed without a world but freely chose not to, that nature is not in itself open for grace but needs grace in order to become open, and that God's freedom excludes the idea that he exists because of any internal or external necessity. It would not be inaccurate to say that in Moltmann's theology, as in so many others that we have already explored, relationality is the subject and God is the predicate instead of the other way around. Thus, he argues that the doctrine of the two natures does not refer to 'two metaphysically different "natures." It is an expression of his exclusive *relationship* to the Father, by reason of his origin, and his inclusive *relationship* of fellowship to his many brothers and sisters. His *relationship* to God is the relation of God's own Son to his Father. His *relationship* to the world is the relationship of the eldest to his brethren.'[131] The fact

130 Moltmann, *Creation*, 287.
131 Moltmann, *Trinity and Kingdom*, 120, emphasis mine. In connection with the Spirit, Moltmann attempts to overcome pantheism and to improve

is that the doctrine of the two natures does refer to two metaphysically distinct natures or it does not convey the same meaning as Chalcedon at all. For the man Jesus was both truly God and truly human as the One Mediator. However, since Moltmann conceives the incarnation as the cessation of God's omnipotence,[132] he is forced to substitute for the reality of Jesus, *vere Deus* and *vere homo*, the perichoretic relationship inherent in suffering love itself. This thinking causes the difficulties in both the doctrines of the Trinity and of creation which we have been exploring in this chapter.

Tritheism

Since God cannot be a single subject of his actions ad extra Moltmann at times is actually led to describe three subjects: 'we interpreted salvation history as "the history of the Son" of God, Jesus Christ. We understood this history as the trinitarian history of God in the concurrent and joint workings of the three subjects, Father, Son and Spirit.'[133] In considering the meaning of revelation in relation to Gal. 1:15 Moltmann contends that 'God reveals his Son ... God does not reveal "himself". He reveals "his Son". The Son is not identical with *God's self*. He is a subject of his own.'[134] In his creation doctrine Moltmann claims that: 'The Spirit also acts as an independent subject ... each subject of the Trinity possesses his own unique personality.'[135] Also, in the kingdom of glory Moltmann believes that: 'The kingdom of God is therefore transferred from one divine subject to the other; and its form is changed in the process. *So God's triunity precedes the divine lordship.*'[136] Finally, Moltmann argues

panentheism arguing that 'It is not the elementary particles that are basic ... but the overriding *harmony of the relations* and of the self-transcending movements, in which the longing of the Spirit for a still unattained consummation finds expression. If the cosmic Spirit is the Spirit of God, the universe cannot be viewed as a closed system' (*Creation*, 103, emphasis mine). Here, Moltmann's concept of relationality leads to the confusion of the Holy Spirit with the movements of creation once again.

132 Moltmann, *Trinity and Kingdom*, 118–19 and *Creation*, 88. Consequently, 'God becomes omnipresent', *Creation*, 91.

133 Moltmann, *Trinity and Kingdom*, 156.

134 Moltmann, *Trinity and Kingdom*, 86.

135 Moltmann, *Creation*, 97.

136 Moltmann, *Trinity and Kingdom*, 93, emphasis mine. Moltmann also writes of the divine persons that: 'They have the divine nature in common; but

that: 'On the cross the Father and the Son are so deeply separated that their relationship breaks off.'[137]

Here his modalism returns to haunt him. For God's lordship is the lordship of the God who is simultaneously one and three. Previously, Moltmann argued that God's unity is the unity of his tri-unity and that he would investigate God's threeness and then proceed to ask about his unity; from this it follows that:

> The unity of the Trinity cannot be a monadic unity. The unity of the divine tri-unity lies in the *union* of the Father, the Son and the Spirit, not in their numerical unity. It lies in their *fellowship, not in the identity of a single subject.*[138]

Moltmann thus logically concludes that the kingdom of glory can be incomplete and changes when transferred from one subject to another. Among other things such a change would mean that Jesus is not always Lord but becomes and ceases to be Lord in time and as time reaches its fulfillment. This is why Moltmann explicitly redefines the meaning of Lordship arguing that, since Christ's Lordship is purely economic, the trinitarian formulas are baptismal and that this must be the case because 'the history of the Son ... is not a completed history'.[139] As 'Christ himself is not ... as yet complete' Moltmann believes that 1 Cor. 15:28 means that: 'The divine rule was given by the Father to the Son through Christ's resurrection' and that: 'In the final consummation it will be transferred from the Son to the Father. "The kingdom of the Son" will then become the kingdom of glory ... in which God will be all in all.'[140] These assertions of course are precisely what led to the charges of tritheism noted earlier. Intimately connected with this are the problems of adoptionism and subordinationism.[141]

---

their particular *individual nature* is determined in their relationship to one another ... The three divine Persons exist in their particular, unique natures as Father, Son and Spirit in their relationships to one another, and are determined through these relationships' (172, emphasis mine).

137 Moltmann, *Trinity and Kingdom*, 82.

138 Moltmann, *Trinity and Kingdom*, 95, some emphases mine.

139 Moltmann, *Trinity and Kingdom*, 90.

140 Moltmann, *Trinity and Kingdom*, 92.

141 This is why Moltmann argues that for Paul the title Son is not a christological title of sovereignty (*Trinity and Kingdom*, 87–8) while the *New*

The result of this reasoning is that Moltmann cannot describe God as free to choose to relate with us; rather the Father generates the Son by necessity[142] and 'the love of the Father which brings forth the Son in eternity *becomes* creative love ... Creation proceeds from the Father's love for the eternal Son'.[143] This reasoning leads Moltmann actually to change the creed which speaks of the Father begetting the Son in eternity in an utterly unique way that decisively excludes introducing gender into the Godhead. He argues that the Son's procession from the Father 'has to be conceived of both as a begetting and as a birth ... this means a radical transformation of the Father image; a father who both begets and bears his son is not merely a father in the male sense. He is a motherly father too'.[144] Moltmann's panentheism here overcomes both a 'patriarchal' monotheism of power and lordship and what he calls matriarchal pantheism with this 'bi-sexual' understanding of the Trinity. This, he believes, is the radical rejection of monotheism.[145] But the fact is that by *adding* the notion of birth to the notion of begetting in the way he has Moltmann compounds the problem by incorporating bi-sexual images into the Godhead whereas there ought to be none at all.[146]

Jerusalem Bible (New York: Doubleday, 1986) states correctly that for Paul the title Son (as in Rom. 9:5d) implied a strictly divine significance (60, n.d). Moltmann actually believes he has avoided all subordinationism and yet makes the conspicuous subordinationist assertion that: 'Through the incarnation of the Son the Father acquires a twofold counterpart for his love: his Son and his image ... This means an increase of his riches and bliss' (*Trinity and Kingdom*, 121. See also n. 34 above). For a specific discussion of Moltmann's Christology, see Molnar, 'Moltmann's Post-Modern Messianic Christology: A Review Discussion', *The Thomist*, 56 (1992): 669–93.

142 Moltmann, *Trinity and Kingdom*, 167. Cf. also 58.

143 Moltmann, *Trinity and Kingdom*, 168.

144 Moltmann, *Trinity and Kingdom*, 164.

145 Moltmann, *Trinity and Kingdom*, 165.

146 Cf. for example *Athanasius's Orations Against the Arians*, in *The Trinitarian Controversy*, ed. Rusch, Book 1, 21, 84: 'if God is not as man (for he is not), it is not necessary to attribute to him the characteristics of man', also 86 'God begets not as men beget but as God begets. God does not copy man. Rather, we men, because God rightfully and alone truly is the Father of his Son, have been named fathers of our own children'. That is, God the Father's unique begetting of his only Son transcends *any* such attempt to define his essence in terms of male or female sexuality. Cf. also Roland M. Frye, 'Language for God and Feminist Language: Problems and Principles', *SJT* (1988), 444 and the discussion of this

Moltmann makes the same mistake in his doctrine of creation arguing that while *creatio ex nihilo* means a calling something into existence without precondition, creation is also determined by God's withdrawal within. Thus the doctrine must mean that God creates 'by letting-be, by making room, and by withdrawing himself. The creative making is expressed in masculine metaphors. But the creative letting-be is better brought out through motherly categories.'[147] The problem here is that the use of masculine or motherly categories is irrelevant to the issue of whether, in the trinitarian and creation doctrines, the Bible intended to present us with the idea that creation ought to be understood as emanation or as the incomprehensible work which could be properly understood through faith in the Son. Then it could not be explained at all by arguing that God's love means incorporation of Nothingness into the inner being of the Trinity and subsequently arguing that creation results from that negation. That is precisely the mythology that the *creatio ex nihilo* was originally designed to protect against. Even more important, however, is the fact that Moltmann distorts the fact that references to God the Father in the Bible and in the tradition were not references to maleness or femaleness as they were in pagan and Gnostic religions.[148] Moltmann's suggestion that we correct our unnatural will for power by including feminine characteristics within the Godhead therefore amounts to a re-definition of God's immanent Trinity using bisexual imagery drawn from human experience. As seen earlier in Chapter 1, Christians rejected this kind of thinking not because they were trying to impose patriarchal power models on others but in the knowledge that God is not as we are, that is, creatures who are sexually limited.

Since Moltmann compromises God's freedom to choose, he argues that: 'Freedom arrives at its divine truth through love. Love is a self-evident, unquestionable "overflowing of goodness" which is therefore *never open to choice at any time*. We have to understand true freedom as being the self-communication of the good.'[149] In Moltmann's synthesis of freedom

issue in Chapter 1. See also, Thomas F. Torrance, 'The Christian Apprehension of God the Father', Kimel (ed.), 120–43 and Paul D. Molnar, 'Introduction to the Second Edition of Thomas F. Torrance's *The Christian Doctrine of God, One Being Three Persons*' (London: Bloomsbury T & T Clark, 2016), ix–xxxi, xx.

147 Moltmann, *Creation*, 88.

148 Cf. Frye, 'Language for God and Feminist Language', *SJT*, (1988), 444 and Chapter 1.

149 Moltmann, *Trinity and Kingdom*, 55.

and love we find the necessary emanation of the divine goodness which the traditional doctrines intended to protect against. This then is clearly the pantheistic emanationism which was necessary to Moltmann's understanding of God's love from the outset; here there is and can be no actual distinction between the Father begetting the Son and the act of creation ad extra resulting from a new decision and act on the part of God. It is this thinking which leads quite logically to the idea that 'the Son's sacrifice ... on Golgotha is from eternity already included in the essential exchange of the essential, the consubstantial love which *constitutes* the divine life of the Trinity'.[150] This leads Moltmann to believe that God's love is

> literally ecstatic love: it leads him to go out of himself and to create something which is different from himself but which none the less corresponds to him. The delight with which the Creator celebrates the feast of creation – the sabbath – makes it unequivocally plain that creation was called into being out of the inner love which the eternal God himself *is*.[151]

This emanationist interpretation of creation envisions God's mysterious and miraculous act of *creatio ex nihilo* not as an *act* of God's free *will* and decision expressing his being as the one who loves but as a coming into being out of the inner love which God is as one who suffers.

We have returned to where we began. Can we understand and maintain God's freedom as implied in the doctrines of creation and of the Trinity if we believe that the traditional dualities can be transcended in a common being which they are said to share now or in the future? Since God is and remains distinct from creatures, even as he suffers for them in the cross of Christ, I have argued that Moltmann's belief that God needs creatures is an idea necessary to his panentheist reinterpretation of freedom but excluded from the perception of faith. Moltmann cannot maintain the freedom of God because he believes that 'the so-called "sovereignty" of the triune God ... proves to be his sustaining fellowship with his creation and his people'.[152]

> Here the social analogy applies to the divine fellowship which is formed through the mutual indwelling of the Father in the Son, and

---

150 Moltmann, *Trinity and Kingdom*, 168, emphasis mine.
151 Moltmann, *Creation*, 76.
152 Moltmann, *Creation*, 241.

of the Son in the Father through the Spirit. Here it does not mean the Fatherhood or the Sonship; it means the community within the Trinity. It is the *relations* in the Trinity which are the levels represented on earth through the *imago Trinitatis*, not the levels of the trinitarian *constitution*.[153]

The problem with this reasoning is that Moltmann believes that he can speak about the trinitarian relations *without* speaking about the essential constitution of the Trinity *as* Father, Son and Spirit by which we know of these relations. The only way this can be done is if the unity of the Trinity is conceived modalistically as a neutral fourth (fellowship/relationship) which can be appropriated apart from any specific reference to the Father, Son or Spirit acting ad extra.[154] The purpose of this chapter has been to indicate why I think this cannot be done.

As seen in Chapter 6, Ted Peters adopted the views of Catherine LaCugna in order to present his relational understanding of the Trinity. Ted Peters mistakenly believes that Moltmann is not guilty of tritheism because 'tritheism has never been a genuine temptation for Christian faith'.[155] Still, he believes that 'the essence of Moltmann's position is that when it comes to divine action we have three subjects, or *loci*, of activity, not one'.[156] Thus, Peters believes that Moltmann's 'social doctrine of the Trinity' that 'begins with the plurality and only then asks about the unity'[157] actually avoids tritheism although, in the end, Peters thinks that Moltmann may end up with a 'divine nominalism' that may or may not consist of a 'single infinite Godhead composed of three finite gods'.[158] In the end, however, Peters believes that Moltmann has drawn

---

153 Moltmann, *Creation*, 241.

154 This faulty thinking results from Moltmann's rejection of the traditional doctrine of appropriation. 'Contrary to the Augustinian tradition, it is not that the work of creation is only "*appropriated*" to the Father, though being actually the work of the whole Trinity. On the contrary, creation is actually a product of the Father's love and is ascribed to the whole Trinity' (*Trinity and Kingdom*, 112). We have seen what Moltmann means by this.

155 Peters, *Trinity*, 103. We have noted earlier that Harnack cites several tritheists and that George Hunsinger thinks Moltmann is as close to a tritheist as one could get.

156 Peters, *Trinity*, 104.

157 Peters, *Trinity*, 104.

158 Peters, *Trinity*, 109.

out 'some of the implications of the seriousness with which Karl Barth viewed God's interaction with world history ... Echoing Hegel, he says the Trinity achieves its integrative unity principally by uniting itself with the history of the world ... God's unity is not simply an original unity.'[159]

However, of course that is exactly the problem that I have highlighted throughout this book. A proper trinitarian theology must begin thinking from a center in God as this has been manifested in Jesus Christ and through the Holy Spirit. Such a starting point will immediately lead one to acknowledge that we begin neither with plurality *nor* with unity, but with the triune God who is simultaneously one and three.[160] Therefore, it will be evident that in a Christian doctrine of God we are dealing with one divine subject precisely because God is one, but that one divine subject is the eternal Father, Son and Spirit and therefore God's unity

159 Peters, *Trinity*, 110. On this point see J. Matthew Bonzo, *Indwelling the Forsaken Other: The Trinitarian Ethics of Jürgen Moltmann* (Eugene, OR: Pickwick, 2009), 63, 80ff.

160 Lewis Ayres, *Nicaea and its Legacy: An Approach to Fourth-Century Trinitarian Theology* (New York: Oxford University Press, 2004), 52, 384, decisively debunks the idea that Eastern theologians began thinking of the Trinity with the three persons and moved toward the divine unity while Western theologians began with the divine unity and moved toward the three persons of the Trinity. See also Paul D. Molnar, 'Was Barth a pro-Nicene theologian? Reflections on Nicaea and its legacy' *SJT*, vol. 64, no. 3 (2011): 347–59. Ayres's interesting critique of contemporary theology for not engaging Nicaea sufficiently is appropriately critical of Rahner as 'an excellent example of the way that Hegelian and idealist dynamics can become fundamental in a thinker otherwise "committed" to credal principles that push in very different directions' (410). Importantly, Ayres notes that Rahner moves beyond analogies compatible with a pro-Nicene position just because of his idealist position in a number of ways. One such way was to begin 'not from any analysis of the isolated individual but from the experience which results from God's action in history, from a knowledge of the movement of the human spirit in history, its transcendence and openness towards the future' (411). Ayres criticizes Rahner for paving the way for 'the sort of pluralistic accounts [of the economic Trinity] found in such figures as Catherine LaCugna' (412) and criticizes Kasper's emphasis on 'the gratuity of the Father's gift to the Son and Spirit rather than focusing on a model of the Father as essentially Father, being God in the eternal and defining act of sharing' (412).

can neither be perceived nor known apart from faith in his Son, and without the operation of the Holy Spirit. Father, Son and Spirit are not three subjects, just because God is essentially one and three and never is one first or three first. While Peters acknowledges that Moltmann comes close to eliminating the need for the immanent Trinity, he nevertheless believes that he does not 'totally conflate the two' and concludes that 'for Moltmann there finally can be only one Trinity, the economic Trinity ... the immanent Trinity is the product of pious imagination, an abstraction from the concrete economy of the divine life that is actualized in history'.[161] Having said this, Peters reveals once again his own basic failure to understand Barth's theology and his inability to comprehend the practical significance of acknowledging God's freedom as the basis of human freedom. He claims that Moltmann carries through on Barth's attempt to allow history in some sense to dictate God's unity, but as we saw earlier, nothing could be further from the truth. Since Barth's thinking was shaped by an actual acknowledgment of the freedom of the immanent Trinity disclosed in the economic Trinity, he consistently refused to allow history to dictate the divine unity. He certainly did not think that the immanent Trinity was the projection of our imagination. Nor did he think of the immanent Trinity merely as an abstraction. He repeatedly appealed to the fact that God eternally exists as Father, Son and Holy Spirit and thus as the one who loves in freedom and is free in his love with the result that all God's actions within history and in relation to the world are acts of grace that are neither hindered in their effectiveness by our opposition (sin) nor dependent on us to be effective for us.[162]

---

161 Peters, *Trinity*, 107–8.

162 Stanley Grenz helpfully summarizes the main critiques of Moltmann's trinitarian theology noting that Gerald O'Collins observed that Moltmann's stress on the cross and resurrection as events within the immanent Trinity 'may be confusing the intradivine life with the story of human salvation even to the point of "imprisoning" God in the world's becoming' (*Rediscovering the Triune God*, 85). John Thompson rightly observed that 'there is a serious lack of an ontological dimension in his [Moltmann's] trinitarian formulations' which 'borders on tritheism' (*Modern Trinitarian Perspectives*, 51). He also noted that Moltmann 'ties God to his relationship to the world and makes the world a contributory factor to the ultimate nature of God. God is therefore not Father, Son and Holy Spirit without this relationship and reciprocity between himself and the world. This is a position that cannot ultimately be maintained

Footnote 162 (*cont.*)

since it fails to give proper expression to the abiding perfections of the triune God' (51). If Thompson is right, and I think he is, then Grenz's attempts to defend Moltmann's thinking about the relationship between the immanent and economic Trinity, also fail to see the seriousness of the problems embedded in Moltmann's position. While Grenz says that for Moltmann 'the immanent Trinity appears to collapse into the economic Trinity, out of which it arises' (*Rediscovering the Triune God*, 86), he calls attention to Moltmann's statements that doxological statements are drawn from the experience of salvation 'about the transcendent conditions which make the experience possible' and thus 'arrive at that experience's transcendent ground' they do not 'go speculatively beyond it [the experience of salvation]' (*Trinity and Kingdom*, 153). With these statements Moltmann asserts, in his own way, that '*Statements about the immanent Trinity must not contradict statements about the economic Trinity*' and '*Statements about the economic Trinity must correspond to doxological statements about the immanent Trinity*', seemingly making some sort of distinction between the immanent and economic Trinity. This leads Grenz to conclude that with Moltmann's view that the future has ontological primacy, he is in some sense able to maintain a distinction so that the immanent will not be collapsed into the economic. Grenz concludes by saying that 'sufficient ambiguity lies within Moltmann's innovative proposal to lend support to the charge that he has tied the immanent Trinity too closely to the historical process' (87). Still, Grenz thinks that Moltmann's 'futurist ontology which he finds at the heart of the biblical view of history as well as in the philosophy of Ernst Bloch may serve to exonerate him from the charge that he had reduced the triune God to the historical process' (88). This wavering is unfortunate since it is precisely Moltmann's panentheistic perspective that finally and decisively leads him to the many statements noted in this chapter that rather overtly state that God cannot be God without the history of suffering which he thinks defines the eternal relations of the Trinity from beginning to end. Here I conclude, with George Hunsinger, that Moltmann's panentheism does not escape the mutual conditioning between God and history that always obliterates both God's freedom in se and ad extra: 'The great problem with panentheism, from the standpoint of Christian theology, has always been either that it seems to make God ultimately responsible for whatever evil there is in the world, or else that it seems to regard God and the world as somehow inherently conditioned by one another, thereby obliterating the divine freedom implicit in the biblical witness to God as Creator and Lord. In working out his new position, which he [Moltmann] openly acknowledges as "panentheism", Moltmann unfortunately manages to escape neither of these liabilities' (Review

In the next chapter we shall explore the work of two important theologians who also claim to be indebted to Barth, while moving beyond what they perceive to be Barth's modalist tendencies and other limitations believed to be associated with Barth's *analogia fidei*. Unlike Jürgen Moltmann, Ted Peters and Catherine LaCugna, the theologians we are about to consider not only do not ignore or deny the need for a proper doctrine of the immanent Trinity, but actually insist on it. How then can the work of Alan Torrance and Eberhard Jüngel help us toward a positive understanding of divine and human freedom that takes seriously our inclusion by grace in God's own internal relations? What are the strengths and weaknesses of their critiques of Barth's theology? These are the questions that will be considered in the next chapter.

of *Trinity and Kingdom*, The *Thomist*, 47 (1983) 129–39, 133). With respect to Moltmann's take on the doctrine of creation discussed earlier, Hunsinger astutely concludes that: 'Moltmann's proposal of a cosmically impoverished Creator is as unabashed as it is biblically remote' (134). Indeed, after noting Moltmann's many statements that God is both free and that God needs the world, Hunsinger rightly concludes that: 'Having espoused the panentheistic notion that God inherently needs the world, Moltmann's ambivalent attempt to Christianize it is simply not convincing' (135). In this chapter I have shown why it is not convincing.

Chapter 9

PERSONS IN COMMUNION AND GOD AS THE MYSTERY OF THE WORLD: ALAN TORRANCE, EBERHARD JÜNGEL AND THE DOCTRINE OF THE IMMANENT TRINITY

We have argued that a 'deliberate and sharp' distinction between the immanent and economic Trinity will be necessary in order to stress that creation, reconciliation and redemption are not necessities grounded either in transcendental experience, suffering or love or some principle of relationality or of communion. Positively stated, the practical acknowledgment of God's internal freedom means that human freedom must continually find its basis and meaning outside itself and in God himself, that is, in God's external freedom exercised in his Word and Spirit on our behalf.[1] Karl Barth's theology is helpful here because his theological thinking always left room for the fact that only God himself could be the proof that is necessary for theology to succeed.[2] Thus, when Barth spoke of faith he said:

> Not, then as experience is faith faith, i.e., real experience, even though it is certainly experience. Or, the act of acknowledgment is not as such acknowledgment of the Word of God. Nor is it this in

1 For a discussion of how and why the contemporary trend to confuse the processions of the immanent Trinity with the missions of the Son and Spirit in the economy and how this relates to the problem of 'Origenism', see Molnar, *Faith, Freedom and the Spirit*, chapter 4. Thus, it is important to recall, with Thomas F. Torrance and Karl Barth, that there is and must be a priority of the Father/Son relation over the creator/creature relation; without recognizing this consistently, the freedom of God's grace is obscured.

2 See, for example, *CD* I/1, 264 where Barth notes that the Bible must speak and we must hear saying: 'If it is asked with what right we say this, we answer: By no right that we have and claim for ourselves, but by the right that proves itself to be such in the event of faith when it occurs.'

virtue of any perfection with which it is performed. It is the Word, Christ, to whom faith refers because He presents himself to it as its object, that makes faith faith, real experience. Let it be clearly understood: because He presents Himself to it as its object. For faith is not faith by the mere fact that it has or is a reference – it might well be in reality a pointless reference to an imagined object.[3]

The real basis of faith, then, is the Word of God, Christ 'given to us as the object' and acknowledged as such. When Barth spoke of analogy he said:

If there is a real analogy between God and man – an analogy which is a true analogy of being on both sides, an analogy in and with which the knowledge of God will in fact be given – what other analogy can it be than the analogy of being which is posited and created by the work and action of God Himself, the analogy which has its actuality from God and from God alone, and therefore in faith and in faith alone?[4]

When he rejected the doctrine of the *vestigia* in connection with his denial that there could be a second root of the doctrine of the Trinity, he wrote: 'Revelation would not be revelation if any man were in a position to advance and to establish against others the claim that he specifically speaks of and from revelation. If we know what revelation is, even in deliberately speaking about it we shall be content to let revelation speak for itself.'[5] For Barth, then, 'what God says to us specifically remains His secret which will be disclosed in the event of His actual speaking.'[6] All of this thinking illustrates that for Barth our knowledge of God is 'an event enclosed in the mystery of the divine Trinity'.[7]

It is important to note that for Barth knowledge was not merely a matter of viewing and conceiving God correctly, or obediently. Even

3 *CD* I/1, 230.
4 *CD* II/1, 83.
5 *CD* I/1, 346–7.
6 *CD* I/1, 143.
7 *CD* II/1, 181. Since God is known 'only by God' Barth maintains that 'even as an action undertaken and performed by man, knowledge of God is objectively and subjectively both instituted by God Himself and led to its end by Him'; this is the case 'because God the Father and the Son by the Holy Spirit is

though such knowledge involves correct knowledge of God, which takes place only through God himself, it includes the determination of our entire being without compromising our human self-determination.[8] This is why Barth insists that we are taken up into the life of the immanent Trinity and that anything we say about knowledge of God 'consists in the fact that we speak also and first of this event [that takes place in the mystery of the Trinity on high]. But we are now speaking of the revelation of this event on high and therefore of our participation in it.'[9] As seen in Chapter 2, Barth insisted that the starting point and conclusion of theological reflection must be Jesus Christ himself and no one and nothing else. This starting point clearly separates Barth from Rahner and, as we shall see, it is Alan Torrance's failure to see the depths of this difference that leads him to think that Rahner made explicit the problems that were implicit in Barth's theology, because their theologies were so similar.

This chapter will not be an exhaustive treatment of the theology of Alan Torrance and Eberhard Jüngel. It will focus instead on some of their positive contributions toward a contemporary doctrine of the immanent Trinity; just as in the next chapter we shall explore the thought of Colin Gunton toward that same end. However, in both chapters we will also call attention to several important aspects of

its primary and proper subject and object' (204). This means of course that this knowledge, which involves our human action, takes place only because 'God does not wish to know Himself without Himself giving us a part in this event in the grace of his revelation' (204). Consequently, 'we have to do with God Himself, and we have to do with Him in a matchless and incontestable certainty grounded on the faithfulness of God Himself' (205). Therefore, applying once again his distinction between God's primary and secondary objectivity, Barth insists that 'secondarily and improperly' we are 'included in this event in the height, in the being and essence of God, so that God is now the object not only of His own cognition, but also of that of man ... in the same way as this may be said of other objects of man's cognition ... For if this is not the case he does not know God. *Knowledge of God is then an event enclosed in the bosom of the divine Trinity*' (205, emphasis mine). A similar statement is made in *CD* I/2, 247: 'According to Scripture everything which can be, everything which is either objectively or subjectively possible in relation to revelation, is enclosed in the being and will and action of the triune God.'

8 See *CD* I/1, 207–8 and 246f.

9 *CD* II/1, 181.

Barth's theology that figure less prominently in their theologies and could, if properly employed, help to strengthen their arguments for a suitably conceived doctrine of the immanent Trinity. I have chosen to explore the thinking of these important theologians because each of them sees the significance of a doctrine of the immanent Trinity in a way that many of those discussed earlier do not. Each of these theologians is critical of Barth's theology in different ways, even though each supports Barth's basic recognition of God's freedom. It is hoped that by critically exploring the nature of some of their key criticisms and some of their proposed solutions a clearer understanding of the nature and function of a doctrine of the immanent Trinity will emerge.

Alan Torrance, Persons in Communion

The most important positive point to be gained from Alan Torrance's book, *Persons in Communion*, is that a proper understanding of the immanent Trinity will lead to a perception that humanity is included in a relationship with God by grace in such a way that our human participation within the Trinity excludes any Pelagianism or extrinsicism. The strength of this position is that, since our inclusion in God's trinitarian life is grounded in God's own freedom exercised for us in Jesus's own life, death, resurrection and ongoing high priestly mediation, it is certainly not something that remains external to us on the one hand, and on the other hand, it has an unshakeable and unassailable foundation – a foundation that is not at all dependent on our sinful human action to be beneficial to us. According to Torrance's doxological or worship model we participate in the priesthood of Christ through worship. This model directs us

> to that event of triune communion which is conceived not as a 'mode of being' to be appropriated or taken on by the human subject, but as the gift of sharing in the life of the Second Adam as it is constitutive of the New Humanity – of sharing in and living out of *his* life lived in place of ours (his worthship), *his* continuing and vicarious priesthood (his worship) and in *his* union and communion with the Father in the Spirit.[10]

10 Torrance, *Persons in Communion*, 324.

This is not to be seen as a task (as Moltmann mistakenly appears to do with Pelagian results) but as a gift: 'our worship is the *gift of participating, through the Spirit, in what Christ has done and is doing for us in his intercessions and communion with the Father*'.[11]

By contrast, according to Torrance, Moltmann sees worship as a task which we must perform and this compromises the freedom of grace with the result that the emphasis in worship falls on our activity rather than on the fact that our activity has been and is included by God in Christ's activity on our behalf. Torrance believes that Moltmann's 'Pelagian interpretation of worship results from a near collapse of the "immanent" Trinity into the economic Trinity' which is brought about in part by his 'adoption of a form of panentheism that fails adequately to distinguish between God's time and created temporality'.[12] Thus, in Torrance's view, Moltmann undermines a proper emphasis on God's transcendence in the event of doxological participation and in the end historicizes God by

'cementing' God into the process of the human struggle ... Moltmann fails to appreciate the extent to which participation in God's intra-divine glory requires to be described as a participation on the part of the human person in the transcendent triune Life. Doxological participation is an event of *grace* – a concept which barely features in Moltmann's theology – and not, therefore, of any natural human response or innate capacity.[13]

Part of Torrance's argument here is aimed at countering Rahner's notion of a supernatural existential as well. But Torrance's positive interest is to assert that worship is an 'event of "theopoietic" *koinonia*, which is both "in Christ" and "through the Spirit", and one, therefore, in which the Kingdom of God is "in a manner" actually and freely *present* – and not merely future, as Moltmann seems to suggest'.[14] God's unconditional grace requires human worship, but human worship is a gift of participating in Christ's high priesthood because he alone offers the required worship on our behalf. This act of worship, which Torrance

---

11 Torrance, *Persons in Communion*, 311. This interpretation is indebted to his father, James B. Torrance, as he notes on the same page.

12 Torrance, *Persons in Communion*, 311–12.

13 Torrance, *Persons in Communion*, 313.

14 Torrance, *Persons in Communion*, 313.

calls 'worthship' 'denotes the form of communion with God required by God's grace' and it includes 'epistemic truthfulness'. Accordingly, theological epistemology is grounded in doxological participation rather than the other way around.[15]

Torrance clarifies his positive point further by analyzing and criticizing C. M. LaCugna's position. Like Moltmann, she 'falls into a Pelagian tendency in her conception of salvation'[16] and because she fails to appreciate the importance of the Nicene *homoousion* 'she is led to what tends to be a synergistic conception of human fellowship with the Trinity'.[17] In short, like Moltmann, there is little room in LaCugna's analysis for what God has done and is doing. The emphasis falls on what we do. While Torrance believes that Moltmann and LaCugna were correct to tie the doctrine of the Trinity to worship, he believes that neither of them allowed the object of worship, that is, Christ himself to determine what they had to say. Hence in Torrance's mind, 'the primary end of the sacraments [is] the discovery of our righteousness as it is "included" by grace within the righteousness of God in Christ, and the liberation to live in the light of the fact that we have been made righteous in and through the vicarious faithfulness of Christ'.[18] According to Torrance, LaCugna misunderstands both *orthodoxy* and *orthopraxis* because she failed to understand the 'dynamic of grace'.

What then is the positive dynamic of grace that Torrance espouses? For Torrance, 'The event of grace does not stop where the free human response begins; it includes precisely that human response to the extent that the human response is completed on our behalf in Christ. Grace relates not only to the anhypostatic movement, but to the enhypostatic movement as well.'[19] For Torrance even the desire to do God's will is given us in Christ 'as we are brought to participate in *his* human life and live "out of" the vicarious worship (as this includes the totality of human "worthship") provided in him by the Spirit *on our behalf* – and where we are thereby recreated to live *out of* this event of grace in all its *objectivity*'.[20]

15 Torrance, *Persons in Communion*, 313 n.15.

16 Torrance, *Persons in Communion*, 316.

17 Torrance, *Persons in Communion*, 317.

18 Torrance, *Persons in Communion*, 318.

19 Torrance, *Persons in Communion*, 318–19.

20 Torrance, *Persons in Communion*, 319.

This is the ultimate positive point that Torrance wishes to convey in his book, namely, that we are drawn by grace into the communion of the trinitarian relations by the Spirit and so we are recreated, with the result that it is Christ living in us who enables our thinking and action in such a way that our thinking and action are not obliterated or confused with the divine action (as in the thought of Moltmann and LaCugna) but upheld and brought to completion in Christ. In Torrance's words: 'We are brought to live "out of" Christ by the Spirit in such a way that "we are no longer under the supervision of the law." '[21] This means that it is not our ethical behavior that establishes or maintains communion with God, but God himself. We are made righteous through Christ's faithfulness and it is this righteousness that is given in Christ. The true dynamics of grace then involve our human movement toward God that is

> realised in and through the Son and which constitutes, through a parallel movement of the Spirit, the ground of our communion in the divine life. This means that the trinitarian relations *ad intra* are to be conceived as open to us as creatures. It is this free and dynamic opening to humanity of the divine communion that constitutes worship as the transforming possibility for humanity – where worship is conceived as the gift of participating in the human priesthood of the Son through the presence of the Spirit.[22]

Except for the fact that worship tends to displace Christ's present action as Lord in relation to us, Torrance's thinking here is important. He clearly achieves what Rahner himself intended with his axiom of identity, namely, a proper integration of our human activity, especially in worship with the Father, Son and Holy Spirit. He does so in such a way that grace is recognizable as grace and is therefore not confused with some universal aspect of our transcendental experience. In fact, as we shall see, Torrance is properly critical of just this aspect of Rahner's thought. In opposition to those who would assume that transcendental

---

21 Torrance, *Persons in Communion*, 320. This important thinking is related to and expressed nicely by James B. Torrance, *Worship, Community & the Triune God of Grace* (Downers Grove, IL: InterVarsity Press, 1996), 20ff. in what he calls the trinitarian view of worship as opposed to what he calls a unitarian view where the emphasis falls legally on what we do instead of Christ's intercession as the One Mediator for us, enabling us to worship the Father through the Spirit.

22 Torrance, *Persons in Communion*, 323.

theology is the only possible way to understand the significance of the Trinity today, Alan Torrance shows quite plainly that a trinitarian theology that is actually grounded in God's freedom for us must continually look away from itself and toward Christ as its objective ground. Subjectively, such a theology will be actualized in and through the Holy Spirit uniting us to Christ's own worship and faithfulness. This thinking is surely in accord with Thomas F. Torrance's crucial insight that we must think from a center in God rather than from a center in ourselves, if our thinking about God and humanity is to be accurate and true. This simple Athanasian insight, with its profound implications, is the theme of this book. A trinitarian theology that does not in fact think from a center in God (a center that can only be given by God in Christ and through the Spirit) is bound to end in some form of agnosticism. Such a theology will then find it necessary to fill the void in knowing God with its own fabrications. As documented earlier, this will inevitably lead both toward monism (pantheism) and toward dualism (the separation of God from Christ with Pelagian or extrinsicist results).

Barth, Torrance and the Limits of Trinitarian Thinking: 'Revelation Model' or 'Communion Model'?

While Torrance's positive position is exactly where a theology that is properly cognizant of the doctrine of the immanent Trinity should lead, the road he takes to get to this conclusion is not completely without its potholes. Torrance is very critical of Barth for choosing 'modes of being' rather than person to describe the 'members' of the Trinity and because he believes that Barth's so-called 'revelation model' obscures the fact that communion is intrinsic to our knowledge of God and our relation with God. Still, he sees himself only modifying Barth's theology and not rejecting it. Let us discuss these important issues briefly.

We have just noted that for Barth our knowledge of God is 'an event enclosed in the mystery of the divine Trinity'. By this Barth meant to assert that: 'Knowledge of God ... as the knowledge of God which is objectively and subjectively established and led to its goal by God Himself, the knowledge of God whose subject and object is God the Father and the Son through the Holy Spirit, is the basis – and indeed the only basis – of the love of God which comes to us and the praise of God which is expected of us.'[23]

---

23 *CD* II/1, 180.

Hence, 'even as an action undertaken and performed by man, knowledge of God is objectively and subjectively both instituted by God Himself and led to its end by Him; because God the Father and the Son by the Holy Spirit is its primary and proper subject and object'.[24] Barth asserts that God gives 'us a part in this event in the grace of His revelation'.[25] For this reason we may proceed with assurance and without skepticism, but we must remember that God is hidden. Still, God is an object of our cognition because he chooses to make himself so and for that reason Barth again insists that 'knowledge of God is then an event enclosed in the bosom of the divine Trinity'.[26] Reinterpreting the doctrine of appropriation Barth insists that knowledge of the unity of God's essence and work

> will not lead us beyond revelation and faith, but into revelation and faith, to their correct understanding … In no sense does God's unity mean the dissolution of His triunity … the unity of their work [i.e. that of the Father, Son and Holy Spirit] is to be understood as the communion of the three modes of being along the lines of the doctrine of 'perichoresis' … according to which all three, without forfeiture or mutual dissolution of independence, reciprocally interpenetrate each other and inexist in one another . . .[27]

Owing to this, in Barth's mind, 'the Triune is the subject of the *opus ad extra indivisum*'.[28]

Barth's belief that our knowledge of God is an event enclosed within the Trinity is significant, because it seems to me to discredit Alan Torrance's most important criticism of Barth's theology, namely, that his 'revelation model' obscures the importance of our communion with God. Barth himself would have been unhappy with the whole idea of models because, in his view, one does not choose a 'revelation model' or a 'communion model' or a 'doxological model' in order to explicate the meaning of the doctrine of the Trinity. Rather, for Barth, such knowledge was and must remain based on the knowledge of God revealed in and by Christ himself, as the Word incarnate. We are, as Barth noted, led into revelation

24 *CD* II/1, 204.
25 *CD* II/1, 204.
26 *CD* II/1, 205.
27 *CD* I/1, 396.
28 *CD* I/1, 396.

and faith by the knowledge of the triune God and not beyond revelation and faith. As seen earlier, this obviated any opening toward Ebionite or Docetic interpretations of revelation. That is exactly why Barth understood our knowledge of God as an event enclosed in the mystery of the Trinity. Such knowledge could only take place in acknowledgment precisely because God is the one who initiates, sustains and completes our knowledge of him. This is especially true in Christology where Barth insisted that Jesus was not the revealer in his humanity as such. For Barth then, revelation was not just informational. Revelation was and is identical with Jesus Christ, and as such revelation meant and means that we are included in God's own self-knowledge, love and fellowship by grace.[29] Important also is Barth's insistence that when we really know God with our views and concepts, because God enables such knowledge by taking us up by his grace and determining us to participate 'in the veracity of the revelation of God', then: 'In all his impotence he becomes a place where his honour dwells – not his own, but God's. As a sinner he is justified.'[30] This is what makes our knowledge of God true without us, against us and yet as our own knowledge and thus to that extent through us. 'By

29 For Barth, 'Jesus *is* the revelation of the Father and the revelation of the Father *is* Jesus. And precisely in virtue of this "is" He is the Son or Word of the Father'. Barth insists that the apostolic thinking about Jesus 'always ended with the knowledge of Christ's deity because it had already begun there' (*CD* I/1, 412). However, none of this is under our control: 'The knowability of the Word of God stands or falls, then, with the act of its real knowledge, which is not under our control' (*CD* I/1, 224). Real knowledge of God must find its assurance not in itself but in the Word of God so that 'His assurance is his own assurance, but it has its seat outside him in the Word of God . . .' (*CD* I/1, 224–5). Barth applies the same thinking to the doctrine of justification insisting that the proposition that we sinners are made righteous by God in Christ does not prove that this is so. Only God in his act 'can speak of His grace in such a way that every contradiction and misunderstanding is excluded' (*CD* II/2, 757). The doctrine cannot do this. Only God's miraculous act can do this. 'This act of divine proof is the resurrection of Jesus Christ. The resurrection alone is decisive for the truth that, as sinners before God, we are pronounced righteous . . . If the resurrection of Jesus Christ is simply the revelation of the faithfulness of the Father and the Son, which persists in the judgment to which he was subjected [on Golgotha], it is also the revelation of the faithfulness which persists in our judgment' (*CD* II/2, 758).

30 *CD* II/1, 213.

the grace of God we may view and conceive God and speak of God in our incapacity.'[31] However, the fact that this happens means that we have a positive relationship with God himself 'one in which there exists a real fellowship (*Gemeinschaft*) (communion) between the knower and his knowing on the one hand and the known on the other. If it is regarded as negative, and this fellowship is denied, God is not revealed to man. His grace is not grace. Man's faith is not faith.'[32]

Here I agree with George Hunsinger who observes that Alan Torrance 'fails to appreciate the inseparability Barth establishes between "knowledge" (*Erkenntnis*) and "fellowship" or "communion" (*Gemeinschaft*) throughout his theology, not only centrally in II/1 but as early as I/1'.[33] Hunsinger cites an important text in *CD* I/1 that bears repeating here. For Barth the intra-divine fellowship of the Holy Spirit is the basis of the fact that

> there is in revelation a fellowship in which not only is God there for man but in very truth – this is the *donum Spiritus sancti* – man is also there for God ... in this fellowship in revelation which is created between God and man by the Holy Spirit there may be discerned the fellowship in God Himself, the eternal love of God: discerned as the mystery, surpassing all understanding, of the possibility of this reality of revelation; discerned as the one God in the mode of being of the Holy Spirit.[34]

31 *CD* II/1, 213.

32 *CD* II/1, 224; *KD* II/1, 252. Again Barth writes: 'What He establishes (creates) (*stiftet*) with the revelation of His knowledge is fellowship (*Gemeinschaft*) (communion) between Himself and us' (*CD* II/1, 547; *KD* II/1, 615–16).

33 Hunsinger, *Disruptive Grace*, 144, n. 20. In fact it is important to realize that Barth himself connected his thinking in *CD* I/1 with the thinking he would advance in *CD* II/1 and II/2 as when he wrote: 'The more explicit development of this concept [of the essence of God] must be reserved for the doctrine of God' (*CD* I/1, 349).

34 *CD* I/1, 480. Important also is Barth's remark that reconciliation is another name for the revelation of God miraculously coming to us in spite of human darkness: 'To the extent that God's revelation as such accomplishes what only God can accomplish, namely, restoration of the fellowship of man with God which we had disrupted and indeed destroyed; to the extent that God in the fact of His revelation treats His enemies as His friends; to the extent that in the fact of revelation God's enemies already are actually his friends, revelation is

Again, this is part of what Barth meant when he insisted that knowledge of God is an event enclosed within the mystery of the Trinity. In contrast to the widespread agnosticism discussed earlier, Barth insisted that God reveals his innermost essence to us by revealing his name (as Father, Son and Spirit) to us. Since God's being and act are one and God's eternal essence is 'His act as Father, Son and Holy Spirit'[35] Barth argues that:

> God is He who, without having to do so, seeks and creates fellowship between Himself and us. He does not have to do it, because in Himself without us ... He has that which He seeks and creates between Himself and us ... He wills to be ours, and He wills that we should be His. He wills to belong to us and He wills that we should belong to Him ... He does not exist in solitude but in fellowship. Therefore what He seeks and creates between Himself and us is in fact nothing else but what He wills and completes and therefore is in Himself. It therefore follows that as He receives us through His Son into His fellowship with Himself, this is the one necessity, salvation, and blessing for us, than which there is no greater blessing – no greater, because God has nothing higher than this to give, namely Himself.[36]

Everything here turns on the perception of grace. Barth's insistence that theology must begin and end with Jesus Christ himself reflected his belief that grace is God's unmerited and free act of mercy on our behalf. Hence, even in the context of the ethical question, Barth refused to relegate theology to a separate sphere and then allow for an independent ethics. He was thus led to ask of those who sought to separate theological and philosophical ethics:

> Outside and alongside the kingdom of Jesus Christ are there other respectable kingdoms? Can and should theology of all things be content to speak not with universal validity, but only esoterically? ...

itself reconciliation. Conversely reconciliation, the restoration of that fellowship ... can only have the form of the mystery which we describe as revelation' (*CD* I/1, 409).

35 *CD* II/1, 273.
36 *CD* II/1, 273–5.

as if Jesus Christ had not died and risen again; as if we could *salute the grace of God*, as it were, and then go our own way . . .[37]

By this Barth meant to stress that God both veils himself and unveils himself in revelation without surrendering his prerogative. This meant that our inclusion in revelation was not demanded by God's essence or by ours; yet we could ignore it only at our peril. It has its free basis in the fact that God really is for us specifically in Christ and by the Spirit. For Barth:

> Hearing man, as the object of the purpose of the speaking God, is thus included in the concept of the Word of God as a factual necessity, but he is not essential to it. He is not, as I most astonishingly stated on p. 111 of the first edition, 'co-posited' in it the way Schleiermacher's God is in the feeling of absolute dependence. If he is co-posited in it with factual necessity, this is God's free grace.[38]

This is why it is important to realize that, when Barth puzzled over the term 'person' and finally chose mode of being instead of person, he was not arguing on the basis of an agnostic position as Torrance seems to think.[39] Rather he was stressing that no word can make conceivable to us what only God can reveal according to his promise fulfilled in Christ. Thus, in *CD* II/1, Barth emphasizes that we do indeed know God's inner nature as Father, Son, and Spirit – as the One who loves in freedom. Importantly, Barth uses the word person to stress that God is a 'knowing, willing, acting subject' in relation to us.[40] Barth rejects the word person only in the sense that it connotes the idea that three subjects might be acting in relation to us.[41] In fact, Barth did not 'want

---

37 *CD* II/2, 526, emphasis mine. For an important and helpful discussion of grace and law in Barth's thinking, see Gerald McKenny, *The Analogy of Grace: Karl Barth's Moral Theology* (Oxford: Oxford University Press, 2010), 180–96. For Barth, McKenny says: 'In Jesus Christ, God has accomplished the good in our place, realizing it as the human good, and it is only on this ground that God claims us – not as a God to whom we are forced to submit or as one who completes an economy of desire but as the God in whom we *may believe*' (184).

38 *CD* I/1, 140.

39 Torrance, *Persons in Communion*, 229f.

40 See *CD* II/1, 284ff.

41 *CD* II/1, 297.

to outlaw the concept of person or to put it out of circulation'.[42] Instead, he argued that those who want to use it can do so only because they don't have a better concept to replace it with. In effect, Barth uses the word person to denote God's personal essence as the one divine subject, while speaking of his acts as Father, Son and Spirit as modes of being. Alan Torrance himself admits that God is both one person and three persons: 'Theologically speaking, *koinonia* ... allows us to speak simultaneously of the person (singular) of God and the persons (plural) of the Trinity'.[43] Torrance says that the term 'person' is not absolutely necessary: 'there is no "absolute" need to use the term "person" with respect to the members of the Trinity'.[44] However, the point here is simply this: Torrance's choice of the term person led him to find the continuity of revelation in communion and then in revelation. Barth's choice led him to allow his notion of communion to be dictated by Christ himself and so argued that human inclusion in revelation is not integral to revelation, but is a factual inclusion that cannot imply priority of one over the other because God, who seeks and creates fellowship (communion) with us, is already God who is complete in himself. It may also be noted that Barth continually insisted that it is God the Father, the Son and the Holy Spirit who defines trinitarian thinking. Hence, his thought about the 'members' of the Trinity was rigorously dictated by the *act* of God denoted in scripture, namely, the actions of the Father, Son and Spirit as the One who loves in freedom. Torrance's criticism that ' "modes of being do not love at all. Hence they cannot love each other" '[45] is easily answered since for Barth modes of being were not abstractly defined, but were identified with the personal activities of the God who *is* one *as* the Father, Son and Holy Spirit.[46] For this

42 *CD* I/1, 359.

43 Torrance, *Persons in Communion*, 256–7.

44 Torrance, *Persons in Communion*, 335.

45 Torrance, *Persons in Communion*, 116.

46 Thus, Barth can write: 'It is not, of course, to satisfy a law of love, nor because love is a reality even God must obey, that He must be the Father of the Son. The Son is the first in God and the Spirit the second in God, that is, as God is the Father of the Son, and, as Father, begets the Son, He also brings forth the Spirit and therefore the negation of isolation, the law and the reality of love. Love is God, the supreme law and ultimate reality, because God is love and not *vice versa*' (*CD* I/1, 483). Indeed, 'The love which meets us in reconciliation, and then retrospectively in creation, is real love, supreme law and ultimate reality, because God is antecedently love in Himself: not just a supreme principle of the

reason there is in God a unique knowledge, love and mutuality and God loves creatures by freely creating, saving and redeeming them in and through his Word and Spirit. What Barth is clearly able to maintain is the identity of God's essence in his act of being Father, Son and Holy Spirit. What Barth is clearly seeking to avoid is any attempt to find the root of the doctrine in anyone or anything other than revelation, namely, God's Word and Spirit, the actions of God for us as creator, reconciler and redeemer.

Still, in order to accentuate his point that we cannot comprehend the divine essence, even when we know God in accordance with his revelation, Barth insists that we cannot explain the *how* of revelation; this, because when we know it, such knowledge itself is a miracle – it is an act begun, upheld and completed by God alone and hence can only be accepted and not explained. A miracle that could be explained, in Barth's estimation, would not be a miracle. Thus, 'the knowledge of God's Word is no other than the reality of the grace of God coming to man, whose How as a reality is as hidden from us as God Himself is'.[47] For Barth then, it is because the incarnation itself is grounded in God's inner being and act, that we can neither explain *how* God can be and remain totally transcendent and free and yet simultaneously become man,[48] nor *how* God can be revealed yet hidden, nor *how* God can be triune.[49] Indeed for Barth the purpose of Chalcedon and the two natures doctrine was not to control this mystery of Christ but to state it. Thus, our knowledge of the immanent Trinity (God in se) is indirect knowledge; it takes place only in acknowledging the supremacy of God's action ad extra in Christ. This respects Gregory of Nyssa's insistence that the *how* of the two natures is beyond our understanding; nevertheless, 'Its being an event (its γεγενῆσθαι) is beyond question for us'.[50]

> What it [the Church] sees directly is only the little child in His humanity; it sees the Father only in the light that falls upon the Son,

relation of separateness and fellowship, but love which even in fellowship wills and affirms and seeks and finds the other or Other in its distinction, and then in separateness wills and affirms and seeks and finds fellowship with it' (*CD* I/1, 483–4).

47 *CD* I/1, 227.

48 *CD* I/1, 476–7. This applies also to election (*CD* II/2, 20ff.) and to knowledge of God's hiddenness and wisdom, *CD* II/1, 184 and 510ff.

49 *CD* I/1, 367.

50 *CD* I/2, 126.

and the Son only in this light from the Father. This is the way, in fact, that the Church believes in and recognises God in Christ ... to all visual appearance He is literally nothing but a human being ... This is the place of Christology. It faces the mystery. It does not stand within the mystery. It can and must adore with Mary and point with the Baptist. It cannot and must not do more than this. But it can and must do this.[51]

Since God is really veiled in his revelation we do not stand within the mystery of revelation.

Here there is a fundamental disagreement over the limits of language. For Alan Torrance 'the communion event ... constitutes revelation'.[52] However, with communion as the subject, there is very little room in Alan Torrance's analysis for God to think, decide and act in relation to us. Rather we are said to participate in a 'communion event'. In fact for Torrance

it is indeed appropriate to speak of a *vestigium creaturae in trinitate* with respect to the trinitarian event of Self-revelation. God's Self-identification in Christ, within the created order, commits us to, indeed *demands* of us, the affirmation that the created order, to the extent that it is integral to this event, is indeed taken into the event of the triune Being of God with us.[53]

For Torrance this implies that our speech about God can take place because God creates and sustains

by the Spirit, an essential *continuity* here in such a way that our affirmation of the personhood of Christ becomes at one and the same time the affirmation of the second person of the Triunity ... What is implied here is what one might term a *creative continuity* which involves a semantic continuity grounded in a divine dynamic which takes the form of the redemptive commandeering of our terms and grammar to the extent that in Christ's 'becoming' our language or semantic thought forms 'become' integral to the reconciling and atoning dimension of the Christ event.[54]

51 *CD* I/2, 125.
52 Torrance, *Persons in Communion*, 230.
53 Torrance, *Persons in Communion*, 209.
54 Torrance, *Persons in Communion*, 210.

In what sense is the created order integral to the event of revelation if it is included factually by grace? Where does Torrance find that continuity? He clearly wishes to find it in Christ; but it would appear that because he thinks our 'adoption in Christ and participation through the Spirit must be essential elements of an interpretation of revelation',[55] he goes beyond the limit recognized by Barth. For Torrance we are brought by the Spirit 'epistemically and semantically to *indwell* the triune life as created human beings and, thereby, to participate in created ways in the Son's eternal communion with the Father. As this happens the fully human semantic means of this indwelling are *interiorised* within us, becoming constitutive of our personhood.'[56] Can one really say that the semantic means of Christ's indwelling become constitutive of our personhood? What would happen to our *need* for a present action of God to constitute our personhood if this is thought to be true? Barth argued that no theological construction had the wherewithal to effect knowledge of God. Torrance says the same thing, that is, 'Semantic at-one-ment is realised in Christ alone and is not a property of our language'.[57] However, it is not always clear that this remains true precisely because Torrance finds the continuity between God and creatures in semantic thought forms that he believes have become integral to the Christ event. As we shall see shortly, similar difficulties arise when Torrance relies on Jüngel to speak of God's love overflowing and of the fact that 'love heightens and expands' God's own being 'in such great self-relatedness still more selflessness and *thus* overflowing';[58] we will have to ask whether or not he has tried to explain what really remains a mystery even when it is revealed. Can God be 'more selfless'?

All this leads Torrance to find a continuity between our language and Christ's act that no longer must seek its veracity in a present act of God's Word and Spirit. Instead, the continuity is sought and found, following John Zizioulas, in his 'establishing the primacy of communion over revelation'.[59] Accordingly, 'his [Zizioulas'] discussion offers support for interpreting revelation in the context of a proper appreciation of the divine communion and human participation ... rather than the other way round'.[60] However, this conclusion leads exactly to a compromise of

55 Torrance, *Persons in Communion*, 104.
56 Torrance, *Persons in Communion*, 354.
57 Torrance, *Persons in Communion*, 369.
58 Torrance, *Persons in Communion*, 281.
59 Torrance, *Persons in Communion*, 304.
60 Torrance, *Persons in Communion*, 305.

the freedom of grace from within Barth's theology because, for Barth, revelation is precisely our inclusion in the event of fellowship (communion) that is internal to God made possible by God's free action ad extra in the history of Jesus Christ and through the Holy Spirit. In Barth's thinking one could never claim that communion has priority over revelation, precisely because it is only in and through revelation as reconciliation that we know of and participate in the eternal communion of his only begotten Son through the Holy Spirit in the first place. Since God's being and act are one, revelation and communion are equally important for us. To allow divine communion *and* human participation to become the subject of the predicate revelation would mean a failure to recognize grace as grace.

This difficulty is compounded by the fact that Torrance adopts LaCugna's rather imprecise assertion that ' "God by nature is self-expressive, God seeks to reveal and give Godself ..." and that "This is consistent with the biblical images of a God who is alive, who is ineluctably oriented 'otherward', who is plenitude of love, grace and mercy overflowing." '[61] Where is the necessary distinction between the immanent self-expression of God in freedom and his free action ad extra here? Both are clearly blended together in the thought of LaCugna, so that the overflowing nature of God coalesces with creation, incarnation and redemption. The freedom of grace is thus lost. While Torrance properly rejects LaCugna's understanding of grace, he nevertheless says that

> the grammar of this *other-ward* orientation is realised in a dynamic of communion that, by the Spirit, completes the other-ward or anhypostatic dynamic in a *consequent* "in-ward" dynamic ... it corresponds to the enhypostatic dynamic in the incarnation whereby the "*ex-pressive*" nature and giving of God is completed in a bringing of humanity to participate in the life of God ...[62]

Here, LaCugna's failure to distinguish the immanent and economic Trinity marks Torrance's belief that God's expressive nature *needs* to be completed in bringing humanity to participate in the life of God.

However, here, Barth had the better idea. He insisted that God's expressive nature needed no completion, even though God willed and wills not to be without us. This specific recognition of God's freedom

---

61 Torrance, *Persons in Communion*, 108.
62 Torrance, *Persons in Communion*, 108.

is the difference between acknowledging grace and saluting it in this context. In Barth's words:

> In the inner life of God, as the eternal essence of Father, Son and Holy Ghost, the divine essence does not, of course, need any actualisation. On the contrary, it is the creative ground of all other, i.e., all creaturely actualisations. Even as the divine essence of the Son it did not need His incarnation, His existence as man and His action in unity with the man Jesus of Nazareth, to become actual. As the divine essence of the Son it is the predicate of the one God. And as the predicate of this Subject it is not in any sense merely potential but in every sense actual.[63]

Perhaps the entire difficulty here stems from the fact that communion, with the idea that person is more fundamental than being itself, is allowed to define both divine and human nature, and to that extent, it is allowed to supplant revelation.[64] Instead of respecting the fact that the *how* of God's triunity cannot be explained, Torrance seems to have explained this mystery *as* communion, even though he is aware that there can be no second root for the doctrine of the Trinity. Thus, 'the communion of the Trinity as such constitutes the *arche* and *telos* of all that is. It provides the hermeneutical criterion of all that has existence'.[65] However, is it not the Trinity as such – God himself who constitutes this *arche* and *telos*? If so, then while communion is an important factor, as Torrance rightly believes, it cannot be substituted for God himself as an acting subject in his relations with us. Torrance objects to Barth's view of God as a single subject asserting that such a notion is not required for Christian monotheism;[66] but the fact is that unless God is seen as the only acting divine subject in relation to us, there is the continual danger of confusion and reversal of divine and human predicates. While

---

63 *CD* IV/2, 112.

64 Barth once made an interesting remark that the NT always appeals to revelation saying that: 'There are only two kinds of theology: one that begins with revelation, a lot of others that begin elsewhere. The whole doctrine of the Trinity is simply an attempt to explain this beginning' (Godsey, *Table Talk*, 53). He made this remark in the context of rejecting Ebionite and Docetic Christology.

65 Torrance, *Persons in Communion*, 258.

66 Torrance, *Persons in Communion*, 220.

Torrance accepts Barth's view that *Non sermoni res, sed rei sermo subiectus*,[67] he also follows Jüngel, Wittgenstein and the Hintikkas to argue that 'the realities of human existence, the social semantics of divine communication and the integration of language and thought are such that the *res* and *sermo* actually participate in each other in the revelation event in such a way that the language of God-talk ceases to be extrinsic to the revelation event itself'.[68]

This thinking could suggest just the kind of mixture of medium and reality that Barth tried to avoid since only God could effect true human speech about God and God is not dependent on or mixed with the media he uses to accomplish this communication and fellowship. This is precisely why Barth refused to think of Christ's humanity *as such* as revelation and rejected any sort of *direct* knowledge of God. God did not hand over his free act of revelation as a veiling and an unveiling to the form of revelation; and Barth decisively rejected dualism:

> There is no place for a dualistic thinking which divides the divine and the human, but only for a historical, which at every point, in and with the humiliation and exaltation of the one Son of God and Son of Man ... is ready to accompany the event of the union of His divine and human essence ... In the work of the one Jesus Christ everything is at one and the same time, but distinctly, both divine and human ... it never becomes indistinguishable ... there is no place for monistic thinking which confuses or reverses the divine and the human ... in their common working they [the divine and human] are not interchangeable. The divine is still above and the human below. Their relationship is one of genuine action.[69]

So the ultimate question that arises here is whether or not the 'continuity' which Torrance seeks and finds in the notion of communion (relying on Zizioulas and the fact that God 'commandeers' human language) allows the notion of communion to displace God's miraculous (and thus incomprehensible) action in the present as the *sole* support on which theology takes its stand. Does trinitarian *thinking* grounded in communion supplant God's own *act* here?

---

67 *CD* I/1, 354.
68 Torrance, *Persons in Communion*, 261.
69 *CD* IV/2, 115–16.

Torrance argues for a reconstructed *analogia entis* that would allow God creatively to commandeer human language – 'a commandeering grounded in a continuity established by God which is, therefore, *from* the divine *to* the human and which is to be found in that divine communion present with us in and through the human Jesus as the one who grounds, sustains and constitutes the Body of Christ'.[70] Further, Torrance says: 'Revelation, or what I would prefer to term "epistemic atonement", is thus an event of provisional, participatory communion within the intra-divine communion.'[71] While Barth is here accused of offering a too literalistic interpretation of metaphors, it is interesting to observe that Alan Torrance has here failed to distinguish revelation as God's act in Christ and the Spirit from our epistemic participation in this event. With respect to the Holy Spirit, Barth insisted correctly that 'statements about the operations of the Holy Spirit are statements whose subject is God and not man, and in no circumstances can they be transformed into statements about man'.[72] By contrast, it appears that communion, rather than God's miraculous *act*, establishes revelation in Torrance's thinking, with the result that revelation itself is subordinated to communion. While Torrance here argues that the human Jesus grounds, sustains and constitutes the Body of Christ, Barth more accurately saw that 'in itself and as such the humanity of Jesus Christ is a predicate without a subject'.[73] By stressing that the Word or Son is or remains subject of the events of incarnation, reconciliation and redemption in his actions ad extra, Barth had clear, consistent and accurate insights on these matters which have unfortunately become blurred in contemporary theology, because it is thought that in some sense Christ is the revealer in his humanity as such. Thus, Barth rejects the idea that 'omnipotence and therefore divinity accrue to the human essence of this man as such ... rather ... in the existence of this man we have to reckon with the identity of His action as a true man with the action of

---

70 Torrance, *Persons in Communion*, 229. See also (364), where Torrance says that 'Revelation is an event of "communication-within-communion", where the impetus and semantically generative "control" in this event is the human Jesus as he mediates (enhypostatically) our participation in the triune life of God'.

71 Torrance, *Persons in Communion*, 223–4.

72 *CD* I/1, 462.

73 *CD* IV/2, 102.

the true God. The grace which comes to human essence is the event of this action.'[74]

One Divine Subject

Before focusing on Torrance's view of the identity of the immanent and economic Trinity, let us discuss briefly how Barth's understanding of God as the one divine subject relates with Torrance's view of the matter. Together with Moltmann, Torrance, as already noted, sees Barth's use of this expression as a problem: 'Moltmann has argued that Barth "uses a non-trinitarian concept of the unity of the one God – that is to say, the concept of the identical subject." '[75] Pannenberg makes a similar criticism: 'Barth subordinated his doctrine of the Trinity to a pre-Trinitarian concept of the unity of God and his subjectivity in revelation.'[76] Torrance, of course, accepts this criticism since he believes

---

74 *CD* IV/2, 99.

75 Torrance, *Persons in Communion*, 216, referring to Moltmann's *Trinity and Kingdom*, 144.

76 Pannenberg, *Systematic Theology 1*, 299. Importantly, Pannenberg corrects Cremer's idea of God's love with the idea of the true infinite and concludes that 'God himself is characterized by a vital movement which causes him to invade what is different from himself' (400). Here Pannenberg compromises God's freedom, since the God who actually loves in freedom is not caused by anything to create, reconcile and redeem the world; he is the free *divine subject* of these events. Furthermore, this thinking leads directly to the modalism Pannenberg theoretically rejects: 'the divine essence overarches each personality' (430) and 'love is a power which shows itself in those who love ... Persons do not have power over love. It rises above them and thereby gives them their self-hood ... This applies especially to the trinitarian life of God' (426f.). Barth could avoid these ambiguities because he consistently saw God the Father, Son and Holy Spirit as the sole acting divine subject in relation to us. It is worth noting here that Iain Taylor called attention to John Webster's proper criticism of Pannenberg for tending to describe God 'as subject to some impersonal process' saying that there is a striking absence 'of language of holiness as willed relation' in Pannenberg's discussion of the relation of the 'true Infinite' with the world along with a failure to distinguish properly the fact that God is not opposed to the world but to sin. In line with the point I have just made, Webster notes that 'Pannenberg's talk of the "essence of God as Spirit" which expresses "the fact that

that Barth's thinking has a modalist tinge and operates with a logically derived idea of God's unity as Lord (in a Hegelian manner) rather than with a concept that derives from communion.

Yet, as just stated, the truth is that for Barth the one divine subject that he envisions throughout the *CD is* the Father, Son and Holy Spirit, that is, the one who is three and loves in freedom: 'We are speaking of the knowledge of God whose subject is God the Father and God the Son through the Holy Spirit.'[77] In virtue of the eternal *perichoresis* of the Father, Son and Spirit, there is neither knowledge of God's oneness nor participation in that oneness unless it takes place in and through Christ by the action of the Holy Spirit. So Barth's concept of the one divine subject is clearly derived from and subordinate to God's actions in his Word and Spirit – God's actions in relation to us, even his condescension to act as our reconciler and redeemer remain acts of God in virtue of the fact that all the works of the Trinity ad extra are indivisible.

Curiously, Torrance relies once more on LaCugna here who says ' "theological reflection on the nature of God is inseparable from [the] theology of grace, theological anthropology, christology, pneumatology, and ecclesiology".'[78] Here, however, I think that Torrance is led astray by LaCugna's own inability to see that while trinitarian theology arises from an encounter with God in the economy, it cannot be reduced to a theology *of* the economy as she clearly does. While soteriology is important for understanding the Christian God, the doctrine of the Trinity cannot be reduced to a hermeneutical device for comprehending salvation. Yet, as we have seen, that is exactly how LaCugna and Peters construe the doctrine. Hence on the very page cited by Alan Torrance, LaCugna says that 'the referent for the immanent Trinity is not "God *in se*", or "God's essence as it is in itself" '.[79] When LaCugna and Peters say that reflection on God's nature is inseparable from reflection on grace and theological anthropology they clearly confuse God with the economy. It is one thing to say that our understanding of God

the transcendent God himself is characterised by a vital movement which causes him to invade what is different from himself and to give it a share in his own life" moves in a rather different direction'. Taylor concludes that this difficulty may indicate 'how the structure of the true Infinite can be ill suited to the character of the trinitarian God' (Taylor, *Pannenberg on the Triune God*, 57).

77 *CD* II/1, 181.

78 Torrance, *Persons in Communion*, 216.

79 LaCugna, *God for Us*, 231.

has a bearing on these other aspects of theology, but it is quite another to say they are inseparable and that therefore the continuity of revelation prohibits any genuine recognition of God in se. Alan Torrance certainly does not accept this aspect of LaCugna's thought. However, given the fact that she completely fails to recognize grace as grace and therefore fails to recognize the true freedom of God that sustains Barth's theology, why then would Torrance think she can offer a valid critique of Barth's theology? Alan Torrance's goal was to provide a more integrated theology than he found in Barth; but did he not, at least in part, surrender God's subjectivity to a notion of divine communion and human participation in the process?

Barth is criticized by Torrance for focusing on revelation at the expense of focusing on worship and communion. Yet, Barth insisted in *CD* I/1, and throughout the *CD* that prayer was an essential ingredient in proper theological reflection. For him, theology that takes place in faith cannot judge itself and cannot finally decide 'what is or is not true in dogmatics' even though it is the task of dogmatics to critically examine its thought and speech about God. This, because this decision is

> always a matter of the divine election of grace. In this respect the fear of the Lord must always be the beginning of wisdom ... The act of faith, which means, however, its basis in the divine predestination, the free act of God on man and his work, is always the condition by which dogmatic work is made possible but by which it is also called in question with final seriousness ... Humanly speaking, there is no way to overcome this fundamental difficulty ... We simply confess the mystery which underlies it, and we merely repeat the statement that dogmatics is possible only as an act of faith, when we point to *prayer* as the attitude without which there can be no dogmatic work.[80]

80 *CD* I/1, 21–3, emphasis mine. Barth carries through on this insight consistently. See, for example, *CD* I/1, 227, 231f. Barth insists that: 'It is precisely ἐν πνεύματι that we shall be ready ... to turn from ourselves to God and to pray to Him, not to contemplate God and manipulate Him ... only the man who seeks everything in God prays to Him ... only the man who seeks nothing in himself seeks everything in God' (*CD* I/1, 465). See also *CD* II/1, 512 where Barth insists that prayer is essential for faith. Perhaps most emphatically, Barth concludes *CD* II/2, by once again directing us to the certainty of our justification and sanctification as these have taken place in Jesus Christ for us (771ff.). The certainty of our sanctification and therefore of our conversion to

Torrance is certainly correct to call attention to the fact that, in his sacramental theology, Barth failed to emphasize Christ's high priestly

God then cannot be found in us: 'In all the heights and depths of our life, even our Christian life, we look in vain for our true sanctification for God as it is already impregnably and irrevocably accomplished' (775). Any attempt to find our 'new birth' in ourselves is just another form of 'self-sanctification'. Indeed whoever trusts 'in their own conversion and new birth, in their walk before God as an element of biography, ascribing credibility and the force of witness to a supposed "pneumatic actuality" in the sphere of experience, and thus trying to live in faith in themselves ... will know nothing of the death of the old man and the life of the new' (775–6). This, because it is only in Jesus Christ himself, the good shepherd that we find and have 'the completed fact of our sanctification, the fulfilled and realised purpose of God in God's judgment, just as He is also its presupposition and its execution' (777). Since it is in him that 'God has seen each human person from all eternity' (778); because 'He is the Word that was in the beginning with God. He is, therefore, the Word that is true of every man' (778); he therefore is our sanctification for eternal life and thus 'Jesus Christ is our sanctification because we are what we are only in relation to Him ... He is the life of our life' (778). Faith in him thus means acceptance and confirmation of this fact – it is not something we can create or even something we can complete because our faith adds nothing to him but only confirms and accepts the fact that we are holy in him. Only his voice, as the voice of the good shepherd, can make us free; we do not have this freedom in ourselves; but when he does make us free for faith in him 'every other choice but obedience [to him] is cut off ... Only as we listen to other voices can we think that we can choose between good and evil ... We can be disobedient only as we are not free' (779). Faith in Christ therefore 'gives glory to its object, to Jesus Christ as man's sanctification; [faith] wills to live only as an echo of His call, but live a full life by His call ... As Jesus Christ calls us and is heard by us He gives us His Holy Spirit in order that His own relationship to His Father may be repeated in us ... life in the faith irresistibly awakened and indestructibly granted by the call of Jesus Christ is as such life in the Holy Spirit' (780). Indeed, 'Since the life of repentance is life in the Holy Spirit, we shall take care not to confuse it with our own spiritual life, putting our trust in things – our own experiences or acts – which do not merit it and cannot justify ... From this standpoint we can only realise afresh that the required life in repentance, and therefore in conversion, consists in prayer. We are converted when we hear the call of God and respond to it, calling upon it in thankfulness and worship and intercession' (780–1). When this happens and thus when 'we join in this prayer in this communion [with Jesus Christ], the One who teaches us to pray in this way Himself intercedes with the Father for us in the Spirit. He Himself is the pledge that we do not pray in vain' (781).

mediation and our human inclusion in God's triune life.[81] However, I think Torrance is mistaken to trace that error to an Apollinarian tendency that can be discerned in *CD* volume One.[82] Instead, I think this is an inconsistency that could be corrected by retrieving Barth's repeated emphasis on the fact that theology must begin and end its reflections in faith by acknowledging that Jesus Christ is its only possible starting point. It is just this starting point that is obscured when it is thought that 'the prayer life of Jesus "as observed by the disciples and the early church, is a suitable empirical basis for the apostolic discernment of triunity"'.[83] It is not Jesus's prayer life as observed by the early church that is the starting point for the apostolic preaching, but Jesus himself who is the Lord, the Word of God incarnate – he alone and precisely now as the risen and ascended Lord is the suitable empirical basis for the apostolic discernment. The moment the weight of emphasis shifts

81 Yet, see John Webster, *Barth's Ethics of Reconciliation* (Cambridge: Cambridge University Press, 1995), who believes that T. F. Torrance's criticism of Barth's later baptismal theology is an example of misplaced anxiety about Barth's 'sacramental dualism' and that Torrance's own emphasis on Christ's vicarious humanity is similar to what Barth often says. Further, Webster believes the real divergence here concerns the fact that Torrance obscures the covenantal character of God's relation with humanity 'by his exclusive stress upon the vicarious character of Jesus' being and activity in relation to humanity. In Torrance's account of the matter, Jesus' humanity threatens to absorb that of others; in Barth's account, Jesus' humanity graciously evokes corresponding patterns of being and doing on the part of those whom it constitutes' (171). The reason I mention this here is because Alan Torrance follows the line of T. F. Torrance's critique of Barth on this issue. Still, Webster himself notes that 'Barth's separation of Spirit-baptism from water-baptism may still be made unnecessarily sharply' (172). As noted in an article titled 'The Importance of the Doctrine of Justification in the Theology of Thomas F. Torrance and of Karl Barth' *SJT*, vol. 70, no. 1, forthcoming, I believe that T. F. Torrance's view of Christ's vicarious humanity does not in reality 'absorb that of others'. Among other things Torrance follows Barth and says for instance that 'it is not through setting aside our subjectivity, but on the contrary through positing it, and making it free and spontaneous, and fully responsible, that God establishes the possibility of man's knowledge of Him' (*Theological Science*, 47).

82 Torrance, *Persons in Communion*, 193.

83 Torrance, *Persons in Communion*, 360.

away from him, as seen above, the danger of Ebionite and Docetic Christology becomes real.[84]

Alan Torrance then believes that Barth's theology rests 'on a prior *concept of divine freedom*' and that, to that extent, his thinking displays an internal inconsistency.[85] Yet, we have seen earlier that Barth's thinking consistently allows for the fact that the truth of dogmatics can and must be received continually by an act of the triune God; this act frees us for obedience, the obedience of faith, which allows only the object of faith, namely, Jesus Christ, through the power of his Holy Spirit to be the sole source and enabling condition of our true knowledge of and communion with God. Barth consistently recognizes the miraculous nature of our knowledge of God as an event enclosed within the mystery of the Trinity by refusing to explain the *how* of our knowledge of God, the *how* of revelation or the *how* of the trinitarian relations. While Barth can be seen as internally inconsistent with respect to the sacrament, I do not think he was internally inconsistent with respect to knowledge of God and human participation in the life of the Trinity.[86]

Rahner's Axiom of Identity and Participation in the Life of the Trinity

Alan Torrance's view of Rahner's axiom of identity is instructive in this regard. In a positive sense, Torrance sees Rahner's axiom as re-uniting the treatises on the One God and on the Trinity and as leading to a concept of grace that is more personal and directly tied to the trinitarian actions ad extra. However, in another more negative sense, Torrance notes that it is puzzling that Rahner thought he could integrate these insights with his 'transcendental anthropology'. This attempted

---

84 Interestingly, Barth once noted with respect to Christology, that 'Fundamentalism is docetic. Modernism is ebionitic. Bultmann combines both: his disinterest in the historical Jesus leads to Docetism; his notion that we believe only because of the faith of the Apostles is Ebionitism' (Godsey, *Table Talk*, 53).

85 Torrance, *Persons in Communion*, 48.

86 For a groundbreaking and instructive work on the Lord's Supper that moves beyond Barth's inconsistency with respect to the sacrament, see Hunsinger, *The Eucharist and Ecumenism*.

integration and Rahner's Kantian presuppositions lead Torrance to say that 'both seem to be arguably incompatible and, at the very least, made superfluous by the implications of his identification of the immanent and economic Trinities!'[87] According to Torrance, 'there is a great deal in Rahner's discussion that echoes similar themes in Barth's discussion.'[88] In fact, Torrance believes that Moltmann was right to assert that Rahner's exposition of the doctrine of the Trinity was quite similar to Barth's.[89] He unfortunately accepts LaCugna's erroneous judgment that Barth and Rahner could not break away from a Cartesian starting point because God was understood as a single divine subject.[90] As just noted, for example, the single subject that Barth has in mind is not a solitary Cartesian subject, but the unique subject who *IS* Father, Son and Holy Spirit and who can only be known in faith by acknowledging the deity of Christ himself through the power of the Holy Spirit. Since this particular subject is therefore also the object of our thought, that object cannot then be the human subject. That is why Barth insists that

> The impregnable basis of faith, the assurance of faith by God's revelation, depends on whether this basis, not just at the beginning but in the middle and at the end too, is sought in God alone, and not anywhere else, not in ourselves. Grace is the Holy Spirit received, but we ourselves are sinners. This is true. If we say anything else we do not know the deity of the Holy Spirit in God's revelation.[91]

Therefore I believe that the similarities are mainly formal. But, as noted in Chapters 5 and 6, Rahner's axiom arose and took shape in the context of his philosophy and theology of the symbol. This has a bearing on the fact that, for all their formal similarities, Barth and Rahner are not

87 Torrance, *Persons in Communion*, 265.

88 Torrance, *Persons in Communion*, 267.

89 Torrance, *Persons in Communion*, 245.

90 Torrance, *Persons in Communion*, 240. In fact Barth opposed Cartesian thinking throughout the *CD*. See esp. *CD* I/1, 41, 172ff., 195ff., 214ff., *CD* I/2, 286 and *CD* III/1, 356–65. Barth thought of God as one divine subject in accordance with God's antecedent *triune* existence as God encounters us in revelation. As noted earlier, it is because LaCugna obliterates the distinction between the immanent and economic Trinity that she mistakenly believes that Barth thought of God's triunity only as arising in connection with revelation.

91 *CD* I/1, 466.

really close at all in their trinitarian theologies mainly because Rahner does not in reality allow Jesus Christ himself in his uniqueness to be the sole determining factor in his understanding of theology from *beginning* to *end* and at all points along the way.

As seen earlier, Rahner interprets anthropology and Christology as mutually conditioned; Rahner thinks that our natural knowledge of God and revealed knowledge mutually condition each other; Rahner starts his theology with transcendental experience and defines God as the nameless; Rahner understands the trinitarian self-expression in terms of symbolic necessity; for Rahner, God's self-communication is part of human experience in the form of a supernatural existential. In spite of their formal similarities, then, these views are completely antithetical to Barth's thinking. Perhaps most importantly, Rahner thinks he can look within us in our experiences of faith to understand who God is and who we are while Barth always insists that this cannot be done because our lives are in fact 'hidden with Christ in God' (Col. 3:3).[92] For Barth,

92 Travis Ables, 'The Grammar of Pneumatology in Barth and Rahner: A Reconsideration' *IJST*, vol. 11, no. 2 (April 2009), 208–24, offers a confusing attempt to relate Rahner's thinking to Barth's by, as he puts it, 'to some extent' following Karen Kilby's position discussed earlier. Using her attempt to read Rahner as a nonfoundationalist as his *exclusive* criterion, and totally ignoring the detailed arguments presented in the first edition of *Divine Freedom* where I demonstrated the weaknesses of Rahner's theology of grace and revelation because Rahner consistently identified these with our experiences of ourselves, Ables mistakenly claimed that I assumed that 'Rahner's philosophy is controlling the theological decisions at *every point*' (216, emphasis mine). This assertion ignored the actual argument presented because I regularly argued that Rahner the theologian asserted God's freedom and the freedom of grace. However, I demonstrated that his theology was inconsistent and his conclusions were more than a little problematic precisely because of his method, which he himself insisted began by exploring the conditions of the possibility for understanding God, salvation, revelation (self-communication) and grace. Indeed, even his understanding of the Trinity, using his philosophy and theology of the symbol, caused great difficulties for him because it embodied a principle that could be seen in every aspect of his thinking, namely, that there was a mutually conditioning relationship between Christology and anthropology; between knower and known; between grace and nature; between natural theology and revealed theology and so on, that affected his thinking in many problematic ways. Thus, in response to Karen Kilby's analysis and to Jeff Hensley's attempt to read Rahner and Barth as holding similar positions

Footnote 92 (*cont.*)

because he claimed that both maintained the priority of Christology in their thinking, I explained with clarity, consistency and with substantial evidence that any theology (Rahner's included) that leads to the idea that self-acceptance is the same as accepting God and Christ was utterly opposed to Barth's theology from start to finish. So, no matter how close some of their formal assertions may be, for Ables to argue that, based on a theology of the Holy Spirit, Rahner and Barth can be seen to be quite close is as wrong as it is amazing. If one seriously compared Rahner and Barth with regard to their pneumatologies, the first thing that would be seen is that Rahner's epistemology is not shaped by the action of the Holy Spirit uniting us to Christ in any consistent way. That is why he argues that all knowledge of God develops from an experience of the nameless. In reality all knowledge of the triune God must begin and end with Jesus Christ himself and neither with our experiences of him nor with our ideas about God drawn from some other source than what Christ himself revealed. All of this was simply ignored by Ables, as it was misunderstood by Hensley before him. There is no need to rehash my responses to Hensley and Kilby which were presented previously and in other writings, as noted earlier. Here I simply mention Ables's misconstrual of Barth's theology and of mine.

Unaware of the real questions raised in my book, Ables unwisely asserts that 'Rahner understands the simple point that there is no God other than the one we experience, and that experience must be accounted for rigorously, if dialectically, in our speech about God' (216). Which God would that be referring to? Is it the nameless, silent incomprehensible one or is it holy mystery, who therefore can go by many names? Is it the triune God who alone is the true God and who simply cannot be known by reflecting on our experiences? None of this is addressed by Ables. Rather, he assumes that: 'It is therefore on the grounds of the conditions of the construction of a graced subjectivity that Rahner and Barth tack most closely together in their pneumatological thematizations' (221). Yet, from the perspective of Barth's theology, this is an impossible assertion simply because Barth never espoused anything close to Rahner's idea of a 'graced subjectivity' in order to thematize his understanding of the Spirit. Ables claims that he is following Barth and Rahner in displacing 'the epistemological focus of modern theology' so as to ensure that 'it is the being of God itself that is the object of knowledge' as well as 'the principle of that knowledge' and then concludes that Barth would agree 'virtually *in toto*' with the following Rahnerian assertion about God, namely, that it is ' "knowledge in the primary sense [as] the presence of mystery itself. It is being addressed by what no longer has a name, and it is relying on a reality which is not mastered but is itself the master' " (221–2).

of course, we cannot begin theology with experience without falling into Ebionite or Docetic Christology and thus failing to understand the mystery of revelation; for Barth, natural theology must be conditioned by revealed theology and not vice versa; for Barth, there is no way from anthropology to Christology and no way from man to God, except in Jesus Christ, and this fact is recognized through revelation itself; for Barth, God is not nameless and therefore cannot be known at all from the experience of the nameless; God has in fact revealed his name as Father, Son and Holy Spirit and thus there is no knowledge of God's oneness unless it takes place through the Son and in the Spirit; for Barth, theology must *begin* and *end* its reflections in faith – faith which is itself grounded in and created by God himself – even though it is itself a fully human act of self-determination; for Barth, as for T. F. Torrance, God's self-communication is identical with Jesus Christ himself and therefore cannot be detached from him and located in transcendental experience without compromising grace itself – Jesus Christ's divinity therefore cannot be circumvented by a method which would bypass him in any way; and finally for Barth, God's self-communication cannot be understood in terms of symbolic necessities because God is not subject to any sort of metaphysical necessities (including the necessity

Claiming that Barth had much to say about the '*mystery* of revelation', Ables asserts that he 'might simply point out that we can never get away from the name of Jesus Christ just at this point', concluding that he is 'not certain that Rahner would disagree, *pace* Molnar' (222, n. 35). Here is the nub of Ables's misreading of Barth and of my book: Barth would not simply point this obvious fact out to Rahner; he would explain that it is impossible to think accurately about revelation, grace, faith, the Trinity or Jesus himself unless one's thinking is shaped by who Jesus was and is from the outset. If Rahner would agree that 'we can never get away from the name of Jesus Christ' in discussing the mystery of revelation, why would he claim (as he does) that he cannot start his theology exclusively with Jesus Christ? Why would he espouse the many other views noted earlier (anonymous Christianity, for instance), that clearly are not shaped by the name of Jesus Christ? Put simply, any idea that the mystery of God is nameless demonstrates unequivocally that such thinking does not in reality rely on the name of Jesus but on the experience of the nameless. So if Rahner then *says* that he agrees with Barth, that would be nothing more than a gratuitous remark with no substance. That was the problem that I discussed in my book. Ables never even noticed that; perhaps because he was so committed to reading Rahner in the manner he proposes.

of relationality or communion) – God is the free subject of his inner life and of his expressions ad extra.[93] Perhaps Alan Torrance's assessment and criticism of Rahner's theology would have been stronger had he discussed the decisive implications of Rahner's supernatural existential and his symbolic ontology for his understanding of the Trinity. In my opinion he could have avoided implying that communion is the subject and God the predicate by insisting both that God is the sole divine subject and that God includes us in his own divine communion by grace, faith and revelation.

One final point needs to be discussed here. This concerns Torrance's understanding of Rahner's axiom of identity. According to Torrance, Rahner's denial of mutuality within the Trinity raises the question of how committed he really is to 'the two-way identification of the immanent and economic Trinities and what the hypostatic union specifically involves with respect to the unique *hypostasis* of the Son'.[94] Following Thomas F. Torrance, Alan Torrance clearly believes that Rahner has introduced a logical necessity of thought and so disjoins the immanent and economic Trinity, and that is why Rahner mistakenly disallows true mutuality within the immanent Trinity. For T. F. Torrance that mutuality is most clearly expressed in Matt. 11:27 and parallel passages.[95] Alan Torrance traces Rahner's erroneous view to what he calls a linear view of revelation as communication. But, as seen earlier, Rahner's error is due to his failure to allow Christ himself to be the *starting point* and *conclusion* of his theological reflections. While it may very well be true that Rahner's individualistically conceived notion of self-expression on the part of God leads him to deny mutuality within the immanent Trinity, that notion itself is thoroughly determined by his philosophy and theology of the symbol. So, the real problem in Rahner's analysis,

---

93 That is why, as seen in Chapter 6, Barth insisted that: 'The Father and the Son are not two prisoners. They are not two mutually conditioning factors in reciprocal operation. As the common source of the Spirit, who Himself is also God, they are the Lord of this occurrence. God is the free Lord of His inner union' *CD* IV/2, 345. This is precisely what led him to insist also that we must not confuse our life in the Holy Spirit enabling us to live as Christians 'with our own spiritual life' by 'putting our trust in things – our own experiences or acts – which do not merit it and cannot justify' (*CD* II/2, 780).

94 Torrance, *Persons in Communion*, 276.

95 See, for example, T. F. Torrance, *The Trinitarian Faith*, 58f., *The Christian Doctrine of God*, 57ff., 61f., 77f. and *Trinitarian Perspectives*, 91f.

from my perspective, is the fact that he refused to begin thinking about God, revelation, grace and faith exclusively and consistently from Jesus Christ himself and instead began with the human experiences of faith and hope in the form of our experiences of self-transcendence.

In Torrance's view, Rahner's identification of the immanent and economic Trinity becomes a mere formalism of the type he sought to avoid because Rahner 'fails to work out the implications for his two-way identification of the immanent and economic Trinities of the distinction between the *Deus ad intra* and *Deus ad extra*, and vice versa'.[96] What is needed, accordingly, is 'a more radical identification of the immanent and economic Trinities'.[97] Torrance is unhappy with the term 'immanent' because it suggests a 'static' concept of God in himself. He prefers the expression *Deus ad intra* because he believes this is more dynamic and it leads to the kind of distinction that allows for reference to the divine economy as applied both to the *Deus ad intra* and the *Deus ad extra*. Hence, for Torrance:

> The culmination of the divine mission (*ad extra*) will be participation in the divine life (*ad intra*), and the ground and impetus of the mission *ad extra* is the eternal dynamic *ad intra*. Consequently, the apotheosis of the divine *telos* requires to be defined with respect to the economic Trinity *ad intra*. This is not an *identification*, as it only takes place in the light of the divine freedom and, therefore, presupposes both an ontologically prior (and, indeed, from the human perspective historically prior) movement *ad extra* and also a radical distinction – though not disjunction – between the divine and the human.[98]

However, that is one of the key questions being considered in this book. How can one argue for a more radical identification of the immanent and economic Trinity, if in fact they must be distinguished because our encounter with the immanent Trinity takes place in and through the economy by grace, through faith and revelation? Isn't it precisely Rahner's *vice versa* in his trinitarian axiom that has been the bane of contemporary theology? It must be remembered that in Rahner's thought the symbol (Christ's humanity) is full of the thing symbolized (Christ's being as

---

96 Torrance, *Persons in Communion*, 278.
97 Torrance, *Persons in Communion*, 278.
98 Torrance, *Persons in Communion*, 279–80.

the Logos) and the symbol renders present the thing symbolized because there is a mutually causal relation between the two. As we have seen repeatedly, it is this conceptual scheme that makes it factually impossible for Rahner to recognize and to maintain the priority of faith, grace and revelation in the sense that Barth insisted was necessary. That is why his identification of the immanent and economic Trinity actually led him to compromise God's freedom in the ways discussed earlier. Those contemporary theologians who have adopted his axiom and gone beyond it by making it more radical have compromised the divine freedom even more than Rahner, by obliterating our relation to a real immanent Trinity. They have in fact made the immanent Trinity nothing more than a description of our own experiences within the economy of salvation.

Alan Torrance considers it a flaw in Barth's theology that he failed to affirm 'the identity of the immanent and economic Trinities'.[99] Yet, Barth would agree completely with Alan Torrance's main thesis which is also the thesis of T. F. Torrance, namely, that *'what God is eternally and antecedently in himself he is toward us* and *what God is toward us he is eternally and antecedently in himself*.[100] However, for this sentence to make any sense it would have to be made in the context of a 'deliberate

---

99 Torrance, *Persons in Communion*, 222.

100 Torrance, *Persons in Communion*, 222, emphasis in original. Interestingly, Bruce L. McCormack, *Karl Barth's Critically Realistic Dialectical Theology: Its Genesis and Development 1909–1936*, (Oxford: Clarendon Press, 1995), notes, in connection with Barth's *The Göttingen Dogmatics*, that for Barth 'there can be no distinction in content between the immanent Trinity and the economic Trinity' (352). McCormack also notes, correctly, that because God is the subject, object and content of revelation, 'Barth was rejecting any view which would seek to establish a continuity between revelation and human thinking and feeling' (353). Finally, in McCormack's view: 'However true it may be that the immanent Trinity and the economic Trinity are identical in content, the distinction between them is nevertheless valid and necessary ... Barth's identification of the economic and immanent Trinities has strictly anti-metaphysical significance. He was seeking to show that it is possible to speak of the being of God *in se* on the basis of revelation alone' (357–8). Importantly, George Hunsinger maintains that for Barth there was a correspondence between the immanent and economic Trinity, but not a 'dialectical identity' as he helpfully explains in relation to the *Logos asarkos* and the *Logos ensarkos* when he maintains that there is an 'asymmetrical' and thus an 'irreversible' relation between them, so that he can say these two forms of the 'divine Logos ...

and sharp' distinction between the immanent and economic Trinity – one for which Alan Torrance himself argues, in spite of his suggestion that what is needed is a more radical identification. In my view, what is really meant here, is that the more consistently one begins and ends one's reflections with the economic trinitarian self-revelation (Christ himself) as this is opened to us in and by the Holy Spirit, then the more clearly will it be realized that we are indeed drawn into the life of the immanent Trinity, because of God's special new direct and unforeseen actions in our favor. Or to put it another way, God neither remains remote from us in Christ and the Spirit (dualism) nor does God become dependent on us by virtue of his free actions of creation, reconciliation and redemption (monism). As T. F. Torrance notes: 'God is at once the Subject and the Object of revelation, and never the Object without also being the Subject. This interlocking of the Being and the Act of God in his revelation excludes the possibility of there being any other revelation.'[101] Hence, God who is and remains free in himself, can for that very reason, in the pure overflow of love and goodness, which is not subject to any law of love or goodness, relate with us as Barth once indicated:

> His presence in the life and being of the world is His personal and therefore actual presence expressed in continually new forms according to His sovereign decisions ... God is free to be and operate in the created world either as unconditioned or as conditioned. God is free to perform His work either within the framework of what we call the laws of nature or outside it in the shape of miracle ... He is

are dynamically related by a pattern of asymmetrical priority, indissoluble unity, and abiding distinction' (*Reading Barth with Charity*, 57–60, 161–2); a '"unity-in-distinction"' rather than a '"dialectical identity"' ("Karl Barth and Some Protestant Theologians", 312, also *Reading Barth with Charity*, 124–5). Hunsinger would agree that it is the immanent Trinity that we meet in the economy since what God is toward us he is in himself; but he would also argue that one cannot confuse or reverse God's primary and secondary objectivity. That confusion obviously took place in the thinking of McCormack when he claimed that the only Trinity there is, is in the covenant of grace, as discussed earlier. For Hunsinger, it is and remains vital to recognize that: 'Not even the human Jesus was necessary to God's eternal self-existence as the Holy Trinity' (312) because God's relationship to Jesus and through him to the world was one of 'self-repetition, not self-realization' (312).

101 Thomas F. Torrance, *The Christian Doctrine of God*, 22.

free to maintain as God His distance from the creature and equally free to enter into partnership with it, indeed, to lift the creature itself, in the most vigorous sense, into unity with His own divine being, with Himself. God is free to rule over the world in supreme majesty and likewise to serve in the world as the humblest and meanest of servants, free even to be despised in the world, and rejected by the world ... This is how He meets us in Jesus Christ.[102]

Alan Torrance turns to Eberhard Jüngel for his understanding of God's love and mutuality.[103] However, as noted earlier, to the extent that Jüngel departed from Barth's insistence that we can only know God's love from the love of God revealed in Christ, there is a certain ambiguity in Jüngel's thinking that replicates itself in the thinking of Alan Torrance. Jüngel sees the immanent Trinity as a summarizing concept for the dealings of the economic Trinity with us. Nevertheless, if this is the case, then Barth's insistence that human experience cannot set the paradigm for what can and cannot be said about God *in se* and *ad extra* is compromised. With this in mind let us briefly compare Jüngel and Barth on this specific point. I will make no attempt to present an exhaustive analysis of Jüngel's complex, imaginative and subtle thought here. I will restrict myself to analyzing how Rahner's axiom affects his theology and how that relates to the need to formulate a contemporary doctrine of the immanent Trinity. It is important to note that I completely agree with Jüngel against Ted Peters that God must be understood as relational and loving prior to and apart from his actions in relation to us or what is thus understood will not be the Christian God at all. Here, however, I would like to explore one fine point of a difference in methodology that will illuminate some of the difference between Barth and other contemporary theologians over the function of the immanent Trinity; a difference that could be resolved with a clearer articulation of a doctrine of the immanent Trinity that avoids reducing our understanding of God *in se* to God in his actions *ad extra*.

Eberhard Jüngel

While Karl Barth approved Eberhard Jüngel's work, he noted that Grover Foley had questions about his doctrine of analogy.[104] Despite

---

102 *CD* II/1, 314–15.
103 See Torrance, *Persons in Communion*, 274, 281f.
104 *Karl Barth Letters*, 71.

some criticisms of Rahner, Jüngel's belief that his thesis that: 'The "economic" Trinity is the "immanent" Trinity and the "immanent" Trinity is the "economic" Trinity'[105] 'should be given unqualified agreement'[106] affects his theology. For Rahner, as seen earlier, 'the immanent Trinity is strictly identical with the economic Trinity and vice versa'.[107] As we have already seen, his transcendental method explains dogmatics from our experience of the 'nameless' which 'we call' God;[108] thus any real *freedom* for God in his immanent divine life is discounted because the 'nameless' is not really identical with the immanent Trinity which cannot be known from such an experience since the immanent Trinity transcends any such experience.[109] As we have also seen, while Alan Torrance would agree that Rahner has not taken proper account of God's inner freedom, he does not trace this predicament to the foundations of Rahner's method as I have. Among the problems discussed earlier, this thinking can also reduce the church to a cultural institution using Christian categories to arrange its own existence. While Moltmann, LaCugna and many others have certainly fallen prey to this kind of thinking, and Jüngel largely escapes it, Karl Barth actually wrote to Rahner about this in March, 1968:

> Last Sunday I heard you on radio Beromünster, at first with pleasure … In the end and on the whole, however, I was completely stunned. You spoke much and very well about the 'little flock,' but I did not hear a single 'Baa' which was in fact authentically and dominatingly of the little sheep of this flock, let alone could I hear the voice of the shepherd of this flock. *Instead, the basic note was that of a religious sociology and the other favorite songs of what is supposed to be the world of modern culture.* In the way you are speaking now, so some fifty years ago Troeltsch was speaking of the future of the church

105 See, Rahner, *The Trinity*, 22. See Molnar, 'Can We Know God Directly?' in *TS*, 1985, and Chapters 5, 6 and 7 for how this thesis affects his thought.

106 Eberhard Jüngel, *God as the Mystery of the World*, 369–70.

107 Karl Rahner, 'Theology and Anthropology' *TI* 9: 28–45, 32. See also *TI* 9, 127–44, 'Observations on the Doctrine of God in Catholic Dogmatics', 130.

108 See, for example, Karl Rahner, 'The Concept of Mystery in Catholic Theology' in *TI* 4, 36–73 at 50ff., 'Reflections on Methodology in Theology' in *TI* 11, 68–114 and Karl Rahner, *FCF*, chapters 1 and 2. For a critique, see Molnar 'Is God Essentially Different From His Creatures?' in *The Thomist*, 1987 and Chapter 5.

109 See Molnar, 'Can We Know God Directly?', 1985, 254ff.

and theology. Get me right: I am not speaking a word against the seriousness of your personal faith and what I write is not even remotely meant to be an anathema. But, take it from me, our Neo-Protestants were and are in their own way pious and even churchly people.[110]

Barth's criticism of Neo-Protestantism and of modern method was neither arbitrary nor uncritical,[111] but rests, as I have argued in this book, on his 'deliberate and sharp' *distinction* (without separation) of the immanent and economic Trinity as it was necessitated by the being of God revealed in Christ. We have already seen how Barth's theology illustrates this distinction and how Rahner's axiom, with its *vice versa* compromises this important distinction, especially with his conception of mutual conditioning. Let us see how Rahner's axiom, which is given unqualified agreement by Eberhard Jüngel, affects Jüngel's understanding of God's love.

More than Moltmann and Pannenberg, Eberhard Jüngel struggles with the implications of Barth's method. Jüngel clearly accepts Barth's method[112] but modifies Barth's view that what people experience as love *is* actually contradicted by the love of God revealed in Christ,[113] with the idea that God's love 'may not contradict *what people experience as love*'.[114] For Barth there could be no compromise here because, while humans *need* others to love, God does not; any other view might ascribe either undue independence to creatures (who live by grace) or assume that God *necessarily* creates and loves us.[115] While Jüngel intends to say that human experiences of love cannot be equated with experiences of hatred and isolation, he modifies Barth's method here.

Since all understanding must be perceived in 'contexts'[116] Jüngel understands God not just from revelation but from the linguistic and existential *contexts* of philosophical and theological assertions. Here

110 *Karl Barth Letters*, 287–8.

111 See Bruce L. McCormack, *Divine Revelation and Human Imagination: Must We Choose Between the Two?*, *SJT*, vol. 37, no. 4 (1984), 431–55 for a fine analysis of Gordon Kaufman's misplaced criticisms.

112 Jüngel, *God as the Mystery of the World*, 163ff., 317, 376–7.

113 See esp. *CD* II/1, 272–85.

114 Jüngel, *God as the Mystery of the World*, 315, emphasis mine.

115 *CD* II/1, 282.

116 Jüngel, *God as the Mystery of the World*, for example, 14, 17, 32–3, 165 and 317.

experience seems to set the conditions; thus, where there is a genuine experience of gratitude there is an experience of the God who is 'more than necessary'[117] and therefore 'the invisibility of God is rather to be interpreted on the basis of the experience of acquaintance with God. Within the context of that experience, the truth that no one has ever seen God gains its ultimate precision'.[118] However, once again, a crucial question posed earlier arises here once more: does truth come from the miraculous intervention of God into our experience or from experience and understanding of the context? While Jüngel appears to adopt Barth's method – 'Obviously the being of the triune God is not to be deduced from the logic of the essence of love' – he cannot hold this position consistently and so he also says that 'even the understanding of the trinitarian history as the history of love presupposes a pre-understanding of love. This pre-understanding may well be corrected or made more precise if the task is to identify God and love.'[119]

Instead of allowing Christ *alone* to dictate the meaning of God's love in 1 Jn. 4, Jüngel agrees with Barth that God's act must clarify its meaning. But, thinking within a 'christological context',[120] he believes that he can provide a 'better understanding, when we first ask generally what love is'.[121] Here revelation can only change the meaning of

117 Jüngel, *God as the Mystery of the World*, 33. This is a 'miraculous experience' apparently because it cannot be deduced or induced from other experiences. It results from an event called 'the revelation of God'. Both his definition of miracle and of revelation, however, are quite different from Barth's. Against Pannenberg, Jüngel wrote: 'God, then, is first encountered where he allows himself to be experienced as the one who gives. That is precisely what I call revelation' (17, n. 6).

118 Jüngel, *God as the Mystery of the World*, 376–7. Similar statements are made in Eberhard Jüngel, *The Doctrine of the Trinity God's Being is in Becoming*, trans. by Horton Harris (hereafter: *The Doctrine of the Trinity*), (London: Scottish Academic Press, 1976), 52–60, 82ff. and 104. See also Eberhard Jüngel, *God's Being is in Becoming: The Trinitarian Being of God in the Theology of Karl Barth*, trans. with a new intro. by John Webster (Grand Rapids, MI: Eerdmans, 2001), 65–74, 98ff. and 118–19.

119 Jüngel, *God as the Mystery of the World*, 316–17.

120 Jüngel, *God as the Mystery of the World*, 317.

121 Jüngel, *God as the Mystery of the World*, 317. While Barth does say 'love is God' (*CD* IV/2, 756) this is no authorization for moving from the general to the particular. In fact he states that love and God may be equated 'presupposing that the content of the terms remains the same' (756) and insists, in a way that

our preunderstanding of what love is; it is presumed that we know the truth and that revelation completes that knowledge.[122] This leads to the mutual conditioning which Barth rejected:

> Our consideration of the essence of love brings us back to our insight that God is love. On the basis of this consideration, we have gained a pre-understanding of the identification of God and love ... *Now it is our task to think through this identification of God and love in such a way that the subject and predicate in the statement 'God is love' interpret each other.*[123]

Consequently, while Jüngel can perceive a 'dialectic of being and non-being ... which belongs to the essence of love',[124] Barth emphatically rejects any idea that nonbeing belongs to the essence of God[125] and

Jüngel does not, that God would still be perfect love without loving us (755) and that his love is grounded only in God and 'not at all in man' (771). This is a point that also has been noticed by George Hunsinger who asserts that: 'The main difference [between Jüngel and Barth] ... was that Jüngel surrendered the Trinity's eternal antecedence as something pure, self-subsisting and absolute. Pure antecedence was replaced by the idea of dialectical identity. For Jüngel, one could not think of God as God without referring at the same time to the human Jesus ... God's eternal being (*ousia*) was determined by his relation to the Crucified' ('Karl Barth and Some Protestant Theologians', 321). Hunsinger astutely concludes that for Jüngel 'The immanent Trinity is not a doctrine of pure antecedence, but a "summarizing concept" for the economic Trinity' (313, citing Jüngel, *God as Mystery of the Word*, 346). In any case, Barth still insisted on giving precedence to divine over human love by not moving from the general to the particular, cf. 755, 777–8. By love, Barth means the inconceivable action ad extra of God in the Son and Spirit which can only be acknowledged, 760. 'Only His act can be the basis of ours ... We have thus to gain a full and clear picture of the act of His love before we can speak meaningfully of the act of ours' (760). See also *CD* I/2, 136, 162, *CD* II/1, 275, 308–9 and *CD* IV/2, 64 and 68. Christopher R. J. Holmes, *Revisiting the Divine Attributes*, notes that 'Jüngel is less careful than Barth in affirming the *asymmetrical* order that exists between the immanent and economic Trinity: God's immanent essence always *precedes* his covenantal working' (124).

122 Jüngel, *God as the Mystery of the World*, 317.
123 Jüngel, *God as the Mystery of the World*, 326, emphasis mine.
124 Jüngel, *God as the Mystery of the World*, 325.
125 Cf. esp. Karl Barth, *CD* IV/4, 146–7.

refuses to ascribe darkness and nothingness any existence in light of Christ.

While Jüngel, like Alan Torrance is closer to Barth's method in intention than Moltmann, Pannenberg or Peters, he gives a status to experience which is clearly at variance with Barth's method.[126] As he makes experience co-extensive with God himself (God's love cannot contradict our experiences of love) he is led to give a reality to 'nothingness' which it does not actually have.[127] Instead of beginning his theology exclusively from the certainty that the reality of Jesus himself, true God and true man, is the norm for truth he begins as follows:

> From the material and dogmatic perspective, talk about God which is oriented to the crucified man Jesus must understand God's deity *on the basis of his humanity revealed in Jesus.* Thus, we must deal with problems which emerge in the *context* of the questions of God's thinkability, God's speakability, and God's humanity.[128]

Why doesn't he say that talk about God must understand the truth of his deity from the deity revealed in the history of the cross? Certainly the truth about humanity is revealed in Jesus, but Jüngel implies that humanity itself is part of God in such a way that it, in itself has the power of the Godhead. Thus, in spite of his valid criticisms of Pannenberg[129] and Rahner,[130] Jüngel's own criterion leaves him with difficulties similar to Rahner's.[131]

In contrast to Barth's *analogia fidei*, Jüngel believes that the danger of drawing 'God, world, and man, or creator, creation, and creature … together into a structure of being which then makes it possible to understand God on the basis of the ordering of the created world under him',[132]

126 Indeed, according to Jüngel's own presentation of Barth's theology in *The Doctrine of the Trinity*, esp. 25ff., this very compromise is excluded. See also Jüngel, *God's Being is in Becoming*, 37ff.

127 Jüngel, *God as the Mystery of the World*, 216–25.

128 Jüngel, *God as the Mystery of the World*, 14, emphasis mine. God's humanity is now the context for understanding God, revelation, Christ and love.

129 Jüngel, *God as the Mystery of the World*, 17, n. 6.

130 Jüngel, *God as the Mystery of the World*, for example, 222, n. 67, 251, n. 11 and 262, n. 1.

131 Jüngel, *God as the Mystery of the World*, 220ff. 'Thus, "in the beginning the 'word' is with God, belongs to God as the word of love in that he expresses himself in order to address others"' (222).

132 Jüngel, *God as the Mystery of the World*, 282.

is polemically overstressed. Thus, Jüngel partially adopts Przywara's doctrine of analogy seeking to clarify it in light of the gospel.[133] Believing that Przywara *intended* the same thing as Protestant critics of the *analogia entis*,[134] that is, to maintain that God is wholly other and yet factually involved in creaturely being,[135] Jüngel holds, with Balthasar that 'there is no trace of the phantom of the analogia entis, which Karl Barth makes it out to be, to be found in him (Przywara)'.[136] For Jüngel, Przywara 'protects the holy grail of mystery', that is, God's transcendence, even though he falsely concludes that God will always remain 'something unknown';[137] and instead of drawing God into the world (as Protestant polemics would have it) Przywara's doctrine leaves God free (transcendent). Jüngel believes the 'later' Barth recognized that the *analogia entis* was not really a 'grasping after God';[138] but doesn't Przywara's doctrine

133 Jüngel, *God as the Mystery of the World*, 261, that is, 'as an "introduction to mystery" (*introductio in mysterium*)'. Also 262, n. 1. Jüngel is aware of Rahner's position on the analogy of being as an ' "analogy of having being" ' which suggests that 'man is necessarily a hearer of the word, namely, of the possible word of God' (262, n.1). Such an anthropology 'understands itself as "the metaphysics of a *potentia oboedientialis* for the revelation of the supernatural God" ' [Jüngel citing Rahner's *Hearers of the Word*, trans. M. Richards, 162]. Jüngel observes that 'a debate with Przywara and Rahner would require another book' but interestingly notes that his dialogue will be implicit; nonetheless he states that he is aware of the ultimate promise of Rahner's religious philosophy: 'the person who must attend to the possible word of God as an anthropological necessity will, once he has grasped this necessity, not find it difficult "to recognize the holy Roman Catholic Church as the seat of the genuine revelation of the living God" ' (*HW*, 177 cited in *God as the Mystery of the Word*, 262 n.1). Here Jüngel opts for a more evangelical view of analogy that might lead to a more ecumenical view of ecclesiology.

134 Jüngel, *God as the Mystery of the World*, 283ff.

135 Jüngel, *God as the Mystery of the World*, 284ff.

136 Jüngel, *God as the Mystery of the World*, 282.

137 Jüngel, *God as the Mystery of the World*, 284–5. Thus, there is never a conclusion. The Augustinian 'unrest for God' arrives at no end. There is always that greater dissimilarity even in the midst of the similarity.

138 Jüngel, *God as the Mystery of the World*, 282. Cf. Grover Foley, 'The Catholic Critics of Karl Barth In Outline and Analysis', *SJT*, vol. 14, no. 2 (1961), 136–55, 149 where he notes that Barth, in reply to Brunner and to Balthasar 'cautions against all speculations on a "new Barth." ' Could this be why

draw God, world and humanity together into a concept of similarity and difference precisely by introducing us to God's mystery through a general concept of mystery? While the later Barth may have been concerned that the *analogia entis* would overlook God's nearness more than his otherness,[139] he still held that we could not know it as God's nearness unless we *first* perceived his otherness. Thus, Barth's objection was primarily to the *method* of the *analogia entis* (including the method of Przywara, Balthasar and Rahner), that is, to the idea that theology could proceed from a general understanding of love or mystery toward an accurate understanding God's particular love and God's being as mystery.[140]

As Jüngel's doctrine of analogy compromises this method, it is inconsistent. On the one hand he maintains, with Barth, that:

> God by no means first becomes his goal when he aims toward man. He is adequate to himself ... A strict distinction must be maintained between the eternal derivation of God from God and the temporal derivation of man from God in order to recognize the factual relationship which obtains between the two, the factual grace relation between God's eternal becoming and our temporal becoming in faith.[141]

On the other hand, he asserts that:

> God *aims* in himself at what is other. God aims in his divine eternal becoming toward the incarnation of man, toward the becoming of the world. God aims in his eternal begetting toward creation ... In this creative being of God the Son as the aim of God the Father, God

Jüngel thinks that Barth discovered the 'analogy of faith as the precondition for ... proper talk about God'? *God as the Mystery of the World*, 282. For Barth even the analogy of faith could not be a precondition for grasping the meaning of revelation.

139 Jüngel, *God as the Mystery of the World*, 282.

140 This is the case for Barth of course because faith never means standing on ourselves but only on Christ and this faith comes from the Holy Spirit as a miraculous act of God; thus 'we must look at Christ Himself and not our experiences of him, because the love of God is shed abroad in our hearts by the Holy Spirit' (*CD* I/2, 248–9, and Rom. 5:5). For a detailed discussion of this and a clear contrast between Rahner and Barth on how their anthropologies differ, see Molnar, *Faith, Freedom and the Spirit*, 100ff.

141 Jüngel, *God as the Mystery of the World*, 384.

is aiming at man. In that God the Father loves the Son, in the event of this divine self-love, God is aiming selflessly at his creation.[142]

The absence of a distinction here between God eternally begetting the Son and *freely* deciding to create through the Son leads Jüngel to conclude that:

> In the event of love, man corresponds to the God who has come to the world in both the most intensive and most extensive ways. For this God is love. In the event of love man is at his most mysterious, not because he is most ununderstandable when he loves and is loved (that is always true, in a certain sense), but because he, as lover and beloved, corresponds to the God who reveals himself as love and who as love works invisibly. *In the event of love, God and man share the same mystery.*[143]

142 Jüngel, *God as the Mystery of the World*, 384.

143 Jüngel, *God as the Mystery of the World*, 392, emphasis mine. The same point is repeated on 395 in connection with faith, love and hope as described in 1 Cor. 13:13. Compare the 'later' Barth, 'the divine love and the human are always two different things and cannot be confused' (*CD* IV/2, 778). The difference between Barth and Jüngel here is traceable to their very different conceptualization of God's freedom at this point. For Barth (the later Barth) God 'reveals Himself as the One who, even though he did not love us and were not revealed to us, even though we did not exist at all, still loves in and for Himself as surely as He is and is God; who loves us by reason and in consequence of the fact that He is the One who loves in his freedom in and for Himself, and is God as such' (*CD* IV/2, 755). For this reason Barth can ask: 'What is it that God wills when He loves us? He certainly does not will anything for Himself – for what have we to give Him? But He does not will Himself without us. In all the fullness of His Godhead, in which He might well have been satisfied with Himself, He wills Himself together with us. He wills Himself in fellowship with us ... He wills Himself ... as His gift freely imparted to us ... It is in this way that He loves us – man. And in this sense His love is creative love; love which does not ask or seek or demand or awaken and set in motion our love as though it were already present in us, but which creates it as something completely new, making us free for love as for an action which differs wholly and utterly from all that we have done hitherto' (*CD* IV/2, 777). Here it is worth mentioning that, according to one contemporary interpretation, Jüngel holds that the resurrection discloses the fact that God identified himself with this dead man (Jesus) and the life that was lived by this dead man. Thus, 'the concept of "identification" is being asked

Our *human* acts of love may correspond with God's free love revealed in Christ but they do not share the *same mystery*.[144] The mystery of God

to do all the work which the traditional language of incarnation, hypostatic union, and so on, was asked to perform' (McCormack, *Orthodox and Modern*, 255). Consequently, 'The unity of God with Jesus takes place in the event of identification, which Jüngel locates at the end of Jesus' life rather than at its beginning' (255). But, if Jesus *is* God acting *as* man only at the end and not at the beginning of his life, then the whole meaning of the hypostatic union has been undermined by a Nestorian separation running through Jesus's human life until his death. This may well be the case because Jüngel has allowed a general definition of love to shape his Christology at that point. While McCormack thinks that Jüngel is not completely clear about the kind of unity he has offered here, McCormack theorizes that because love means giving oneself so unreservedly 'that one's being is determined from without' suggests that ' "the being of this dead man determines God's being in such a way that one must speak of a differentiation of God and God" ' (255). However, it is not the man Jesus who determines God's eternal being in differentiation; it is the preexistent eternal Father, Son and Spirit who acts as one in the incarnation, life, death and resurrection of the man Jesus who was and is the eternal Son become flesh for us from the moment of his conception by the Holy Spirit in the womb of the virgin Mary. Therefore, it is precisely the idea that God is, in the words of McCormack, 'determined in this way by Jesus' (255), that undermines a proper doctrine of the immanent Trinity. It cannot and does not allow the antecedent love of the Father, Son and Spirit to determine the relevance of Jesus's human life and death for us, but mistakenly reverses these, with problematic results.

144 This conclusion illustrates the problem inherent in the way LaCugna exploited Jüngel's unfortunate characterization of the doctrine of the immanent Trinity as a summary concept for our experience of God within the economy. As seen earlier, LaCugna concludes that trinitarian life is our life and that we become by grace what God is by nature. Such thinking confuses human and divine being and action and in the long run undermines a proper understanding of theological anthropology and love. For Barth, of course, God alone frees us to love – that is our new creation as children of God – but a human person 'is not God, of course, but only a child of God – and this by grace and not by nature. When [a human person] loves, therefore, he cannot give what God gives. Even that which he can give he gives only on the basis and according to the model of the divine self-giving' (*CD* IV/2, 778). The corrective here would be a doctrine of the immanent Trinity that would point to the constant need to distinguish God's free love from our experiences of love which are marked by sin and limited in their dependence on God. Such a doctrine of the immanent

precedes and the human mystery may follow but they do not arise out of some mysteriousness which they have in common. As Jüngel thinks that it is no longer a problem to classify God and the world together, he is led to a Docetic view which he clearly did not intend: 'In the event of love, the believer has the decisive criterion to judge whether humanity's ways to itself are humane ways ... What serves love is human ... But what hinders love is inhuman.'[145] However, if the essence of love is selflessness[146] and if God's love cannot contradict a human experience of selflessness, then one could argue, against Barth's view,[147] that as long as we are selfless, love cannot mean obedience to Christ alone with a specific form of moral behavior corresponding to the divine

Trinity, when properly conceived, would point us to the God who loves in and for himself even in loving us and is thus able to enable our free love as something entirely new which is not native to us in our experiences of love in ourselves since as sinners we are not really free for God and thus for others. This is a point that is missed by Werner G. Jeanrond, 'Love and Death: Christian Eschatology in an Interreligious Context', 131–41, in *Indicative of Grace-Imperative of Freedom: Essays in Honour of Eberhard Jüngel in His 80th Year*, (ed.) R. David Nelson (London: Bloomsbury T & T Clark, 2014), when he argues that 'The gospels do not introduce a different or new kind of love ... in the way Jesus related to his fellow humans, friends and foes alike, he powerfully explored the depth of love and its transformative potential for humankind ... It must be one of the most tragic misunderstandings of Christian theology ever to reduce this God-given virtue of love to an inner Christian doctrine' (135). When that happens, Jeanrond believes, Christians are 'reducing the power of love to a merely Christian horizon instead of appreciating the capacity of all genuine love to enlarge any human horizon' (135). Here Jeanrond is critical of Barth, Jüngel, Luther and others, but he has missed a crucial point, namely, that the love revealed in Jesus Christ simply cannot be understood by confusing it with a general understanding of human love so that one might suppose, as Jeanrond does, that 'Criteria of truth within and between traditions must, of course, be developed, however not without reference to human communication and love, *but on the basis of both*' (136, emphasis mine). Of course, Jeanrond is right to maintain that in interreligious dialogue Christians must interact with others with love; but that hardly means that Christians should then assume that it is our experiences of love that will transform us as only God can, did and does in his Word and Spirit.

145 Jüngel, *God as the Mystery of the World*, 392.

146 Jüngel, *God as the Mystery of the World*, 298.

147 For example, *CD* IV/2, 776ff.

command.[148] This is no small issue today, since a number of theologians now attempt to justify behavior that is clearly excluded on the basis of the biblical revelation by abstractly arguing that as long as people are selfless and faithful, then that makes what had been previously regarded as immoral behavior acceptable. Apparently the problem of the creature grasping and controlling revelation in a general definition of love and freedom persists today and cannot be solved by choosing the language of parables[149] over the language of scholastic theology.

How does Rahner's axiom affect Jüngel's Christology? While Jüngel perceives the affirmation of certain 'vestiges of the Trinity' as 'a dogmatic problem of the first rank',[150] his solution exhibits the same ambivalence which led Rahner to redefine the immanent trinitarian relations in light of history. Jüngel correctly stresses that 'Revelation cannot first gain worldly speech through interpretation'; yet he also believes an 'objection to Barth's thesis is unavoidable' because 'Revelation has as such world speech as part of itself – else it could not reveal. The world must be conceived within the concept of revelation'.[151] However, everything depends on how this secularity is perceived. What exactly is the

---

148 On this point see esp. *CD* IV/2, 768–81. Hence, Barth can say 'Only from the deep quiet of the knowledge that grace is given does there follow the genuine disquiet of the knowledge that we need it, and not *vice versa*. It is the Gospel, and not a Law abstracted from the Gospel, that compels us to recognise our transgression ... To believe is to admit that we are at the end of ourselves because God wills to make a new beginning with us and has actually done so' (*CD* IV/2, 769). This has happened in the love of God expressed in the fact that Jesus Christ is the one in whom and by whom we are forgiven sinners since in him we have been converted to God who is love. Thus, 'To believe is to consider the assault that God Himself will immediately and necessarily mount against us if even for a moment or by a hair's breadth we seek our security in ourselves' (770). That security is ours only in and from Christ and only in the power of his Holy Spirit. This is all lost if it is thought that we can transform ourselves and others by love; such an idea misses the fact that we have in reality already been transformed in Christ in God's judgment which he suffered for us and by God's grace as his free act of forgiveness.

149 Jüngel, *God as the Mystery of the World*, 282ff. It would appear at times that Jüngel ascribes to parables a power which Barth held came only from Holy Spirit!

150 Jüngel, *God as the Mystery of the World*, 348.

151 Jüngel, *God as the Mystery of the World*, 348–9.

basis for this inclusion of the world in the concept of revelation? Where is the distinction between God's Word and the humanity of Jesus to be drawn? Jüngel answers:

> The concept of revelation is a *special* human history ... but not in and of itself. It is so by the power of a process of becoming which is not founded in its own historicity. *Such* a history speaks then, by virtue of the revelation taking place within it, of the God who reveals himself. And then it is necessary to say of that history that it is the trace of the triune God, the 'vestige of the Trinity'.[152]

However, it is at this very point that a kind of mutual conditioning that compromises the freedom of revelation enters. The immanent Trinity does not refer to a being existing independently of history even while in closest union with it in Christ. Indeed, 'If God were only the one who loves himself eternally, then the differentiation between God and God would be pointless, and God would actually not love at all in his absolute identity'.[153] Thus, for Jüngel the only permissible

152 Jüngel, *God as the Mystery of the World*, 349. Moltmann's view is quite similar (*Trinity and Kingdom*, 161).

153 Jüngel, *God as the Mystery of the World*, 329. We are a long way from Barth's constant insistence in *CD* Volumes 1 through 4, that as Father, Son and Spirit, God does not need anyone or anything in order to be fully one who loves. He could have remained God without us and would have suffered no lack. Barth avoided this difficulty by insisting that 'It is not ... to satisfy a law of love, nor because love is a reality even God must obey, that He must be the Father of the Son ... Love is God, the supreme law and ultimate reality, because God is love and not *vice versa*' (*CD* I/1, 483). Thus, Barth argued that: 'The eternal generation of the Son by the Father tells us first and supremely that God is not at all lonely even without the world and us. His love has its object in Himself. And so one cannot say that our existence as that of the recipients of God's Word is constitutive for the concept of the Word' (*CD* I/1, 139–40). See also n. 143 for Barth's assertion of this very point in *CD* IV/2, 755. This perception of God's freedom is enabled by a clear doctrine of the immanent Trinity and as seen throughout this book, even those who claim to follow Barth most closely, tend to blur this particular but crucial point. This is an issue also noticed by Ivor J. Davidson, 'The Crucified One', 29–49, *Indicative of Grace-Imperative of Freedom* (ed.) Nelson, 46 when he asks: 'In working back to the immanent Trinity from the economic, does Jüngel risk compromising something which others have traditionally been highly keen to maintain: the primacy of God's triunity and plenitude in himself regardless of

distinction between the immanent and economic Trinity occurs 'when the economic doctrine of the Trinity deals with God's history with man, and the immanent doctrine of the Trinity is *its* summarizing concept'.[154] However, as long as this is the case, the immanent Trinity cannot possibly be the indispensable premise of the economic Trinity (Barth's view) in an *irreversible* sequence that invariably dictates a certain form of knowledge and practice in dogmatics and ethics, that is, one that moves from above to below.[155] Rather, the immanent Trinity

any world?'. Davidson also says that Jüngel's view of the cross does not provide 'any serious account of sin and judgment' and so undercuts the meaning of 'Christian obedience' (47). As also noted above, Hunsinger gets this just right when he says that: 'Not even the human Jesus was necessary to God's eternal self-existence as the Holy Trinity' ('Karl Barth and Some Protestant Theologians', 312). By contrast Jüngel says: 'We have seen that God is love precisely in that he loves his Son in his identity with man, that is, with the scandalously murdered man Jesus' (*God as the Mystery of the World*, 329). This confirms Hunsinger's judgment that for Jüngel, 'The death of Jesus belonged to the concept of God's deity' ('Karl Barth and Some Protestant Theologians', 312). Of course God does love his Son in his identity with the man Jesus, but at this point Jüngel fails to distinguish the eternal love of the Father and Son in the Spirit from the love that freely and by grace chooses to love us in his Son. He fails to allow Barth's statement of the freedom of God's love to shape his thought here as when Barth insisted that: 'We cannot over-emphasise God's freedom and sovereignty in this act [of election]. We cannot assert too strongly that in the election of grace it is a matter of the decision and initiative of the divine good-pleasure, that as the One who elects God has absolute precedence over the One who is elected, more particularly when we remember that the theme of the divine election is primarily the relationship between God and man in the person of Jesus Christ. Who has the initiative in this relationship? Who has precedence? Who decides? Who rules? God, always God' (*CD* II/2, 177).

154 Jüngel, *God as the Mystery of the World*, 346.

155 *CD* I/1, 242. Among the innumerable references to this both early and later in the *CD*, I cite these three here: 'We have to think of man in the event of real faith as, so to speak, opened up from above. From above, not from below!' Also, 'We had Pentecost in view when we called revelation an event that from man's standpoint has dropped down vertically from heaven' (*CD* I/1, 331). Much later Barth argued that 'the movement from below to above which takes place originally in this man [Jesus] does not compete with the movement of

can only have as much independence as we are willing to give it on the basis of our experiences of faith in the crucified Jesus.[156] Thus, for Jüngel, the *man* Jesus is a 'vestige of the Trinity'.[157] From here Jüngel presents a type of Christology from below which culminates in Pannenberg's most dubious assertion noted in Chapter 6: 'What is true in God's eternity is decided with retroactive validity only from the perspective of what occurs temporally with the importance of the ultimate ... thus the truth of the incarnation – is also decided only retroactively from the perspective of Jesus' resurrection for the whole of Jesus' human existence on the one hand ... and thus also for God's eternity, on the other.'[158] We have seen the inadequacy of this view earlier.

Jüngel concludes that: 'It would appear then, based on the theology of the Crucified One, that God who is love is better understood as the absolutely selfless essence.'[159] Thus,

> A 'still greater selflessness in the midst of a very great, and justifiably great self-relatedness' is nothing other than a self-relationship which in freedom goes beyond itself, overflows itself, and gives itself away. It is pure overflow, overflowing being for the sake of another and only then for the *sake of itself*. That is love. And that is the God who is love: the one who always heightens and expands his own being in such great self-relatedness still more selfless and *thus* overflowing. Based on that insight, Karl Rahner's thesis should be given unqualified agreement: '*The economic Trinity is the immanent Trinity and the immanent Trinity is the economic Trinity*' ... The thesis that the 'economic' Trinity is the 'immanent' Trinity, and vice versa opens up the possibility of a new foundation for the doctrine of the Trinity, in that it makes the express constitution of

God from above to below. It takes place because and as the latter takes place' (*CD* IV/2, 47).

156 Jüngel, *God as the Mystery of the World*, 376–7. While Jüngel correctly rejects the ideas that God is unknown in principle or a being who can be understood as possessing being (Rahner), he gives to experience a place Barth did not give it and this I believe opens the door to the problems we have been considering.

157 Jüngel, *God as the Mystery of the World*, 349.

158 Jüngel, *God as the Mystery of the World*, 363, n. 39.

159 Jüngel, *God as the Mystery of the World*, 369.

the trinitarian concept of God possible through a theology of the Crucified One.[160]

160 Jüngel, *God as the Mystery of the World*, 369–70. Some emphases mine. Of course, as seen earlier, one of the more perplexing features of Rahner's theology is that he claims to be basing it on the economic trinitarian actions within history and so he does believe that some type of theology of the cross is necessary. However, all too frequently his starting point is human self-transcending experience and not Jesus Christ himself as attested in the New Testament. This problem is especially clear in the way he approaches his understanding of the resurrection as we saw in Chapter 7. And Jüngel's thinking, as already discussed, begins with a prior understanding of love and uses that to express his trinitarian theology of the cross. We have already noted that the chief problem with that approach is that it led to the idea that the 'death of Jesus belonged to the concept of God's deity' and that he was finally led to surrender 'the Trinity's eternal antecedence as something pure, self-subsisting and absolute' by instead embracing a notion of 'dialectical identity' (Hunsinger, 'Karl Barth and Some Protestant Theologians', 312). In other words, even though Jüngel knew and maintained the importance of the immanent Trinity for understanding God's freedom and love, here he undermined the actual meaning of the doctrine as it functioned in Barth's theology to express God's *free* love in se and ad extra. From another perspective, it is interesting to note that John Webster thinks that Jüngel's theology of the word 'tends to attribute to language the regenerative power more normally reserved for Christ and Spirit'. Webster believes that this may result from 'Jüngel's reticence in developing an operative account of Christ's risen presence or of the Spirit's agency; he shares this feature with much theology in the tradition of Bultmann' ('Systematic Theology after Barth: Jüngel, Jenson, and Gunton', *The Modern Theologians: An Introduction to Christian Theology Since 1918* (ed.) David F. Ford with Rachel Muers, Third Edition, [Oxford: Blackwell, 2005], 249–63, 253). Webster discusses these issues in his introduction to the new edition of *God's Being is in Becoming*, xx–xxii. It seems clear that he thinks that Barth's view of the resurrection, the Holy Spirit and Christian existence offers the account that he finds less than fully operative in Jüngel. Webster wonders whether Jüngel's handling of the relation between Barth and Bultmann 'can be supported, not simply by Barth's earlier doctrine of the Trinity but also by the theology of Christian existence in *Church Dogmatics IV*' (John Webster, Translator's Introduction to *God's Being is in Becoming*, xxi). In Colin Gunton's estimation Jüngel's 'attention to the part played by the immanent Trinity in maintaining a non-necessary relation between God and the world has saved him from submission to the shibboleths

Have we not here explained the *how* of the trinitarian relations and of Christology? Are we not now standing within the mystery rather than recognizing it in faith? Are we not back to Barth's original question of whether there can be any foundation for the doctrine of the Trinity other than the scriptural revelation itself? The foundation here obviously can be derived from and corroborated by *experience* within history. While Barth certainly would say that the immanent trinitarian actions ad extra include us with all our experiences in a real relationship with God through faith, grace and revelation, he would never introduce the notion of mutual conditioning into the Godhead precisely because it is a relation with God and not an apotheosis. As we have seen throughout this book, he would never accept the *vice versa* of Rahner's axiom without the careful qualifications that are required by an actual perception of God's internal and external freedom. That is why I have consistently argued that it is not advisable to give Rahner's axiom unqualified agreement.[161]

of modern immanentism' ('The Being and Attributes of God. Eberhard Jüngel's Dispute with the Classical Philosophical Tradition', 7–22, in *The Possibilities of Theology: Studies in the Theology of Eberhard Jüngel* in his Sixtieth Year, (ed.) John Webster [Edinburgh: T & T Clark, 1994]), 22. In light of this discussion, we might simply say that while Jüngel did not embrace the overt immanentism found, for example, in the thinking of Ted Peters and Catherine LaCugna, his way of stating the function of the doctrine of the immanent Trinity together with his unequivocal acceptance of Rahner's axiom of identity caused some inconsistency in his thinking on this matter.

161 This is where it is important to mention Alan E. Lewis's misguided claim, discussed earlier in Chapter 4, that Barth 'illogically' drove a wedge between the economic and immanent Trinity when he maintained that God could have remained satisfied with his own eternal glory, but chose not to (*Between Cross and Resurrection*, 208ff.). We have repeatedly seen that no such wedge is introduced with this important acknowledgment by Barth of God's eternal freedom and love as the basis for his gracious acts ad extra as creator, reconciler and redeemer. Barth rightly would not allow God's eternal triune being and act to be defined by his relations ad extra. Lewis was also puzzled by my criticism of Jüngel for attempting to understand God's love by first seeking a general definition of love (253). Yet that very criticism follows from Barth's important insight that the relation between God and us is an irreversible one that can only be explained from the love of God actualized and revealed in the history of Jesus himself (Jn. 3: 16). As mentioned earlier, Lewis compromises

The most important lessons to be learned from Jüngel's analysis are that: (1) contemporary theology must continue to stress, with Barth, that the inclusion of history in revelation is and always remains the result of God's free grace – it is a miracle whose *how* cannot ultimately be explained, but one that must be accepted in faith; (2) contemporary theology cannot ignore the problem of sin when it comes to constructing theological analogies; (3) contemporary theology must stick rigorously to its proper starting point which is the love of God revealed in Jesus Christ and therefore it must not allow retrospective views of history or experience to determine the free love of the immanent Trinity – when this happens then God's free love, which is the basis of human freedom itself, is compromised by the fact that it becomes indistinguishable from our human love, which is unfortunately marred by sin and in need of reconciliation; (4) finally, contemporary theology must be clear that the immanent Trinity is and remains the indispensable presupposition for the economic trinitarian actions within history. Such an acknowledgment of God's freedom will lead theologians specifically and conceptually to distinguish their trinitarian thinking from the actions of God within the economy with the result that it will be seen with clarity that when we truly know God it is an event that takes place within the mystery of the divine Trinity.

the freedom of grace envisioned by Barth by contending that God needs the world (210), that God's nature needs perfecting (212–14 and 218ff. where Lewis follows Moltmann with some reservations), and that God could not have done other than he did in Christ (209ff.). Moreover, Lewis makes love the subject and God the predicate saying 'The ineffable love which takes God down that path is free and sovereign, even if there is no possibility for God to be or act otherwise' (211). However, love does not take God down the path of creation, reconciliation and redemption. The triune God who loves chooses to go down that path in full loving freedom in his grace, mercy and righteousness. While Lewis rightly stresses that Jüngel has done much to establish God's priority, we have shown in this chapter that when Jüngel argues that (1) a preunderstanding of love is necessary to grasp God's love for us in Christ, (2) what serves love is human, (3) God and humanity share the same mystery and (4) nothingness is part of God's eternal being, he is clearly inconsistent with his own belief in God's freedom by introducing the mutual conditioning associated with the vice versa of Rahner's axiom which he unfortunately adopted without hesitation. Both Jüngel and Lewis allow selflessness, abstractly considered, to define God's free selfless love for us exercised in Christ and the Spirit.

In the next chapter it will be helpful to analyze the thought of one more important contemporary theologian who is more sympathetic to Barth than Moltmann and Pannenberg, but who nevertheless is also critical of Barth in ways somewhat similar to Alan Torrance. This will not be an exhaustive discussion of Colin Gunton's important trinitarian theology; rather it will be a discussion that focuses on a number of key issues that relate to the need for a contemporary doctrine of the immanent Trinity, that is, one that recognizes that human freedom is supported by divine freedom and that Christ is and must remain the starting point and conclusion of Christian theological reflection. Important among our considerations will be the connection between Atonement and the Trinity.

Chapter 10

THE PROMISE OF TRINITARIAN THEOLOGY: COLIN GUNTON, KARL BARTH AND THE DOCTRINE OF THE IMMANENT TRINITY

Among contemporary theologians, Colin Gunton sees the positive meaning of a proper doctrine of the immanent Trinity with clarity and consistency.[1] After noting the importance of the revival of trinitarian theology in recent years, Gunton observes that with this revival certain dangers have also arisen. 'The first set of dangers derives from a mistaken attempt to remain concretely relevant by casting doubt on the necessity of an immanent, or, better, ontological Trinity.'[2] According to Gunton, Robert Jenson's tendency to focus exclusively on the economic Trinity has been reinforced by the work of Ted Peters and Catherine LaCugna, both of whom explicitly contest the importance of a doctrine of the immanent Trinity. Gunton rightly notes that Peters makes God's internal constitution dependent on his relations with creation, while LaCugna follows Harnack's view that when the early church went

---

1 He is certainly not alone. Aside from the clarity on the subject provided by Karl Barth and Thomas F. Torrance, we saw earlier that George Hunsinger offers an impeccable understanding of a properly functioning doctrine of the immanent Trinity as does John Webster. Among others, Christopher R. J. Holmes, '"A Specific Form of Relationship": On the Dogmatic Implications of Barth's Account of Election and Commandment for his Theological Ethics', 182–200 in (ed.) Dempsey, *Trinity and Election*; Philip G. Ziegler, 'Some Remarks on Christian Freedom' in (ed.) Nelson, *Indicative of Grace – Imperative of Freedom*, 255–66; Fred Sanders, *The Image of the Immanent Trinity: Rahner's Rule and the Theological Interpretation of Scripture* (New York: Peter Lang, 2004); Kevin J. Vanhoozer, *Remythologizing Theology: Divine Action, Passion, and Authorship* and Scott Swain, *The God of the Gospel*, should also be included in this list.

2 Gunton, *The Promise of Trinitarian Theology*, second edn, xvii.

beyond a simple description of God's action within history, to reflect on an ontology of the divine being, it made a mistake.

> It follows that any doctrine of an immanent Trinity, even one derived from an understanding of the economy, is to be rejected ... From the outset it is made clear that we must not 'reify the idea of communion by positing an intradivine "community" or society of persons that exists alongside, or above, the human community.'³

As seen in Chapters 1 and 6, LaCugna's idea that a doctrine of the immanent Trinity reflects our reifying certain thinking is deeply indebted to the thought of Gordon Kaufman, who is quite unable to allow any ontological otherness to God's existence. This is important, because it opens the door to the kind of agnosticism that places the lever in our hands for defining God, grace, revelation, faith and salvation. We have also seen the problems associated with Ted Peters's attempt to understand the Trinity as a description of our experience of the beyond and intimate; the chief problem of course was his inability to recognize and maintain either divine or human freedom.⁴

In response to both these misguided views, Gunton correctly insists that it is precisely the doctrine of the immanent Trinity that is necessary 'as a foundation for the relative independence and so integrity of worldly reality ... and thus for human freedom.'⁵ As seen earlier, Gunton rightly asserts that the problem with these views is that they do not in fact escape the pantheist position that effectively undermines both

---

3 Gunton, *The Promise of Trinitarian Theology*, second edn, xviii.

4 Gunton directly opposes the pantheistic tendencies in the thinking of Catherine LaCugna and Ted Peters saying: 'If God is truly revealed in Jesus Christ, then that is what he is like eternally' and 'a distinction between God's reality and that of the world serves the world's interest. The doctrine of the eternal Trinity serves as a foundation for the relative independence and so integrity of worldly reality also, and thus for human freedom,' *Father, Son and Holy Spirit: Toward a Fully Trinitarian Theology* (London: T & T Clark, 2003), 23–4. For my review of this book, see *Pro Ecclesia* (Fall 2005), XIV, 4, 494–6.

5 Gunton, *The Promise of Trinitarian Theology*, second edn, xviii. For a recent discussion of these issues, see Uche Anizor, *Trinity and Humanity: An Introduction to the Theology of Colin Gunton* (Carlisle, UK: Paternoster Press, 2016). See also *The Theology of Colin Gunton* (ed.) Lincoln Harvey (London: T & T Clark International, 2010).

divine and human freedom. Gunton notes that it is neither just a matter of an abstract assertion of the divine freedom nor is it a matter of asserting any sort of arbitrary deistic view of divine freedom. Rather, it is a matter of seeing and acknowledging God's actual freedom for us that is grounded in his freedom in se. Like Barth, however, Gunton urges that God's freedom is self-grounded and not at all dependent on history for its reality. Consequently, God really can have an intimate involvement in and with his creation in what Gunton, following Irenaeus, calls the two hands of God, that is, his Word and Spirit.

However, there is another set of dangers that Gunton perceives and seeks to avoid, namely, any attempt to use the doctrine of the immanent Trinity as a weapon in a battle for certain social or ethical causes espoused by particular theologians. While the promise of trinitarian theology certainly consists in the fact that 'everything looks – and, indeed, is – different in the light of the Trinity',[6] Gunton quite rightly wishes to avoid the idea that this doctrine or any other can be wielded as a principle used by us in idealist or projectionist ways.[7] The primary defect in this second set of dangers is 'that they turn Christ into a world principle at the expense of Jesus of Nazareth, and treat his cross as a focus for the suffering of God rather than as the centre of that history in which God overcomes sin and evil'.[8] In other words, Gunton appropriately wishes to stress that if the doctrine of the Trinity is detached from the doctrine of the atonement it ceases to be a description of the Christian God but instead becomes 'an uncritical validation of modern culture – or whatever – and so effectively Christianity's opposite'.[9] Interestingly, Gunton opposes any idea that trinitarian theology is only edifying to those within the Christian community and instead insists that the theology of the Trinity 'could be the centre of Christianity's appeal to the unbeliever, as the good news of a God who enters into free relations of creation and redemption with his world. In the light of the theology of the Trinity, everything looks different'.[10] What he specifically and rightly opposes is any attempt to employ 'some non-trinitarian apologetic, some essentially monotheistic "natural theology"' in this

6 Gunton, *The Promise of Trinitarian Theology*, second edn, 4–5.

7 This same argument is made in *Father, Son and Holy Spirit*, 24–5.

8 Gunton, *The Promise of Trinitarian Theology*, second edn, xx. See also Chapter 10.

9 Gunton, *The Promise of Trinitarian Theology*, second edn, xx.

10 Gunton, *The Promise of Trinitarian Theology*, second edn, 7.

context.[11] This would have disastrous consequences for Christian theology not only because it would lead to a failure to respect the particularities of Christian revelation but because it would, in effect, allow a human conception of unity to define God's unity with the result that the *homoousion* of the Father, Son and Spirit would be denied or compromised as well. With Barth, Gunton appropriately believes that there is 'an asymmetrical relationship between knowing and being, and we are not obliged to accept the apparent view of Rahner that the thesis "the Economic Trinity is the Immanent Trinity" is also true "reciprocally (*umgekehrt*)"'.[12] Gunton thinks that Barth's view of the relationship between the immanent and economic Trinity is similar to John Zizioulas's view, that is, 'the distinction is "nothing else essentially but a device created by the Greek Fathers to safeguard the absolute transcendence of God without alienating him from the world"'.[13]

What then is the importance of the doctrine of the immanent Trinity for Colin Gunton? The doctrine asserts that because God is already a being-in-relation, before the creation of the world, he does not need the world. Those who believe that God must be either an 'unfeeling monarch' or one who needs the world, therefore, confuse two points: (1) the proper objection to a God who is immutable, unfeeling and distant does not necessarily imply that 'for God to enter into relation with the world he must need it in some way';[14] (2) trinitarian theology does not teach that God is unrelated to the world but that he is indeed involved 'in creation, reconciliation and redemption. However, what it also enables us to say is that far from being dependent upon the world God is free to create a world which can be itself, that is to say, free according to its own order of being.'[15] Any sort of pantheism compromises both God's freedom to create, reconcile and redeem the world and the very existence and independence of the world. A doctrine of the immanent Trinity that is formulated from the economic trinitarian actions ad extra will see and maintain with clarity that God's involvement with the world is free and thus can indeed enable the world to be truly itself in relation to God in his otherness. This would be the kind of contemporary doctrine

11 Gunton, *The Promise of Trinitarian Theology*, second edn, 7.

12 Colin E. Gunton, *Theology through the Theologians: Selected Essays 1972–1995* (Edinburgh: T&T Clark, 1996), 123.

13 Gunton, *Theology through the Theologians*, 123.

14 Gunton, *The Promise of Trinitarian Theology*, second edn, 142.

15 Gunton, *The Promise of Trinitarian Theology*, second edn, 142–3.

of the immanent Trinity that we are in search of because it formulates its view of the immanent Trinity only from God's economic trinitarian actions within history and not from some other existential or idealistic source.

Interestingly, Gunton prefers to speak of otherness and relation instead of transcendence and immanence because he believes that transcendence can easily be understood quantitatively or as the opposite of immanence with the false idea that transcendence and immanence are opposites. This is one of the reasons that he argues for 'a stronger distinction between economic and immanent Trinity, between God in eternity and God in time … the distinction between economic and immanent Trinity achieves more than a concept of God's freedom. It is, as we have seen, a matter of human freedom as well.'[16] Gunton thus prefers the terms 'otherness' and 'relation'. These latter terms are better alternatives because they are not 'contraries … but correlatives which require and interpret each other. Only that which is other than something else can be related to it. Otherness and relation can therefore be conceived as correlatives rather than rivals.'[17] Gunton's positive point is to stress, against monism and pantheism, that 'because God has otherness – personal freedom and "space" – within the dynamics of his being, he is able to grant to the world space to be itself'.[18]

Otherness and relation are not only important terms for a proper understanding of God's relation with the world but they shed light on relations within creation. Hence, our relation to the non-human world becomes confused if the otherness between the two is not recognized and respected. That is, if the world is personalized or if it is made the object of worship (as in some forms of creation spirituality), its very nature is misunderstood and so also is our true responsibility for the world. Also, in terms of interpersonal relations, Gunton correctly insists that monistic or totalitarian societies actually violate both the unique and distinctive being of each person and the privacy of each person. 'To relate rightly to other people is to intend them in their otherness and particularity, to allow them room to be themselves.'[19] Importantly, this view of the immanent Trinity does not lead Gunton to separate God from the world. Rather, 'the doctrine of creation, trinitarianly

---

16 Gunton, *The Promise of Trinitarian Theology*, second edn, 134–5.

17 Gunton, *The Promise of Trinitarian Theology*, second edn, 202.

18 Gunton, *The Promise of Trinitarian Theology*, second edn, 202.

19 Gunton, *The Promise of Trinitarian Theology*, second edn, 203.

conceived, enables us to understand the world as other than God, but as the product of a free act of creation and of a continuing free related-ness'.[20] In other words when God's otherness is properly acknowledged it will be seen that God's otherness includes his own internal relations as well as his free external relations with us.

Gunton and Barth

While Gunton agrees with Barth that because of human finitude and sin we need God's revelation in order to know him in truth and that 'such knowledge cannot be merely a human achievement, but rather must, as a human achievement, also be the gift of the Holy Spirit',[21] he also believes that we should go further than Barth and make links between the theo-logical implications of revelation and other intellectual, moral and aes-thetic concerns: 'Revelation speaks to and constitutes human reason, but in such a way as to liberate the energies that are inherent in created rationality'.[22] Here we have what appears to be only a minor linguistic distinction between Barth and Gunton that has major theological impli-cations. Would Barth agree that revelation liberates energies inherent in created rationality or might he not insist that created rationality needs to be placed on an entirely new footing in order to operate properly?[23] In other words, from Barth's point of view, Gunton's analysis in this context, underplays the seriousness of sin and the fact that revelation is offensive to us – it does not just release something inherent in created being – but rather completely transforms human reason in a way that goes against what we would consider reasonable apart from grace, faith and revela-tion. This is why, as seen in Chapter 2, Barth insisted that revelation causes offense.[24] It is hidden apart from faith and goes against what we would consider reasonable. Perhaps it is not an accident that the word 'faith' rarely appears in Gunton's theology of the Trinity.

20 Gunton, *The Promise of Trinitarian Theology*, second edn, 203.

21 Colin E. Gunton, *The One, The Three and the Many: God, Creation and the Culture of Modernity* (hereafter: *The One, the Three and the Many*) (Cambridge: Cambridge University Press, 1993), 211.

22 Gunton, *The One, the Three and the Many*, 212.

23 See, for example, *CD* II/1, § 26. The Knowability of God, 63–178.

24 For more on this idea of revelation causing offense, see Molnar, *Faith, Freedom and the Spirit*, 97, 391f. and 400.

This difference between Barth and Gunton is important. For Barth, 'The form of God's Word ... is in fact the form of the cosmos which stands in contradiction [*Widerspruch*] to God. It has as little ability to reveal God to us as we have to recognize [*zu erkennen*] God in it.'[25] For Gunton, 'As finite and temporal, yet created in the image of God, human beings *have* spirit because they are open to God, each other and the world in the peculiar although limited way that characterizes personal beings.'[26] Barth is quite consistent in taking sin seriously as understood in light of God's revelation in Christ: for him we are not in fact open to God but can only become open through the mystery and miracle of faith given by the Holy Spirit and determined by its object, that is, Christ himself the incarnate Word. Barth will not equate the Holy Spirit with the human spirit of personal beings. Curiously, Gunton argues that the 'main difference between the human and the divine is expressed in the claim that God *is* spirit, while finite persons *have* spirit ... God *is* spirit by virtue of the unqualified openness of the triune persons to each other and his free and unnecessitated movement outwards.'[27] By contrast T. F. Torrance understands the Spirit absolutely and relatively:

> Absolutely considered the Spirit is God of God, and like the Son whole God of whole God, so that the Being of the Spirit is the Being ... of the Godhead. 'God is Spirit', as Jesus said to the woman of Samaria. In this absolute sense 'Spirit' refers to the Deity, without distinction of Persons, and is equally applicable to the Father, the Son and the Holy Spirit. Considered relatively, however, the Spirit is Person ... who in distinction from and together with the Persons of the Father and the Son belongs with them to the one Being of God. The Holy Spirit is, then, like the Father and the Son, both *ousia* and *hypostasis*, and with the Persons of the Father and the Son is eternally in God and inseparable from him who is *one Being, three Persons*.[28]

Torrance does not try to explain *how* God is Spirit by saying it is by virtue of the openness of the persons to each other and by virtue of an unnecessitated movement outward. These inward and outward actions

---

25 *CD* I/1, 166. *KD* I/1, 172–3 translation slightly revised.

26 Gunton, *The One, the Three and the Many*, 188.

27 Gunton, *The One, the Three and the Many*, 188.

28 T. F. Torrance, *The Christian Doctrine of God*, 147–8. This issue will be discussed further in the Appendix.

disclose the fact that God is Spirit in his unique way but it is not by virtue of these actions that he *is* Spirit – he *is* Spirit simply because he is. Torrance thus simply states the objective fact that God is Spirit because he is – and he is Spirit as the eternal Father, Son and Holy Spirit who objectively indwells us.

> Our receiving of the Spirit is objectively grounded in and derives from Christ who as the incarnate Son was anointed by the Spirit in his humanity and endowed with the Spirit without measure, not for his own sake (for he was eternally one in being with the Spirit in God) but for our sakes, and who then mediates the Spirit to us through himself ... Our receiving of the Spirit, therefore, is not independent of or different from the vicarious receiving of the Spirit by Christ himself but is a sharing in it.[29]

Here Torrance makes an important distinction between Christ receiving the Spirit while yet eternally being one in being with the Spirit. This is a distinction that hardly figures in Gunton's analysis.

This apparently minor linguistic difference between Barth and Gunton can be seen in their different emphasis on Christ's humanity. It is precisely because Barth insisted that Christ's humanity *as such* could not be the starting point for Christology that he also insisted that there is *no* analogy which is true in itself.[30] By contrast, Gunton's search for transcendentals appears to operate at least in part on the assumption that there are certain concepts (analogies) that are inherently true.[31] It is because Barth acknowledged the continuing priority of the Word in

---

29 Torrance, *The Christian Doctrine of God*, 148.

30 Cf. Barth, *CD* II/1, 194, 226 and 358. See *CD* IV/3.2, 509 for how Barth carries through this insight in connection with his understanding of vocation by defining illumination as 'a seeing of which man was previously incapable but of which he is now capable. It is thus his advancement to knowledge ... not with new and special organs ... not in virtue of his own capacity to use them, but in virtue of the missing capacity which he is now given by God's revelation. "Jesus, give me sound and serviceable eyes; touch Thou mine eyes." It is as He does this that they become serviceable ... It is all a process which like others really implies knowledge in man. But it is all an original creation of the One who enables him to know.'

31 See, for example, *The One, the Three and the Many*, 141ff. Unlike Robert Jenson, Gunton does not want to jettison the concept of analogy altogether, but

the incarnation, reconciliation and redemption, that he also insisted on the priority of faith by stressing that there could be no exclusive interest in Christ's humanity and that his humanity should not become the determinative element in Christology or Dogmatics. Thus, for Barth, faith recognizes that the Word is indeed the determinative element in the incarnation since the Word alone gives Jesus's humanity its true meaning. As the priority of the creator over creature is not blurred but clarified in Christ, Barth insists on the positive and negative aspects of the divine freedom by emphasizing the irreversibility of analogous concepts in his doctrine of God.[32] In connection with Christology, Barth stressed both the *enhypostasis* (God actually became flesh for us) and the *anhypostasis* (Christ's humanity draws its meaning from the immanent Trinity and not from history). Barth preferred the ancient to the modern Christologies because they grappled with the problem of Christology, namely, Jesus Christ as *vere Deus vere homo* in his unique

one of the marks of Gunton's view is that he believes that there are concepts 'that enable us to *think* our world ... inherent within certain words there lies the possibility of *conceiving* things as they are' (*The Promise of Trinitarian Theology*, second edn, 138). For Barth, of course, this possibility of conceiving things as they are must continually come from God himself through the Holy Spirit and so is not a possibility inherent in certain concepts. See, for example, *CD* II/1, 194 and 226. As the object of faith determines our knowledge of God, so too the object of faith determines our knowledge of the world for Barth. That is why he argued that the covenant was the internal basis of creation. The ultimate problem here is that Gunton conceives creation as open to God and Barth correctly insists that creation is not open to God but continually must become open through God.

32 See *CD* II/1, 301ff. See Barth's illuminating discussion of this issue in *The Göttingen Dogmatics*, 156ff. Barth insisted that, while our knowledge of the Son takes place through the incarnate, in Jesus, 'he is also the Logos of God beyond his union with humanity, just as the Trinity is more than the incarnation. As the Father is not just the Creator, so the Logos is what he is even apart from Jesus Christ' (156). Since for Barth the man Jesus never existed apart from the Logos, he rejected any notion that the Logos was 'enclosed in the human nature' (158). While he believed that the Logos indwells Christ's human nature, he rejected the idea that the divine freedom from limitation applied to the flesh just as it did to the Logos because 'we may not say that the Logos subsists only in the human nature of Christ' (158). He thus rejected the idea the Jesus was revealer in his humanity as such.

self-sufficient existence,[33] and not an apotheosis;[34] meaning was found *only* in him.

As seen previously, Barth understood revelation as the unveiling of what is veiled because he took seriously the miraculous nature of human knowledge of God.[35] That God unveils himself implies a real knowledge of the immanent Trinity and of his will for us, but because Christ alone is the norm, human interpretation and the fact of Christ can never be reversed.[36] This then is the thinking that eventually led Barth to argue that any view of Christ that saw God's revealing activity wholly as a property of the man Jesus has allowed 'man to set himself on the same platform as God, to grasp Him there and thus to become His master'.[37] The error of mysticism,[38] of Schleiermacher,[39] of Hegel[40] and in general of nineteenth century theology consists in their uncritical presumption of *identity* here.[41] They failed to note God's holiness, that is, his right to make himself known as he chooses by 'entering the sphere of our existence', while at the same time 'He still inhabits and asserts the sphere which is proper to Him and to Him alone ... the Godhead is not so immanent in Christ's humanity that it does not also remain transcendent to it, that its immanence ceases to be an event in the Old Testament sense, always a new thing, something that God brings into being in specific circumstances'.[42] This is why Barth insists that God cannot be classified with other 'supreme ideas' such as freedom and immortality

33 Cf. *CD* I/2, 23 and *CD* IV/1, 179ff.

34 *CD* I/2, 129.

35 See *CD* I/1, 168. While human freedom is not set aside or weakened by an encounter with God (*CD* I/1, 246ff.), 'it cannot in any sense be regarded as its [human freedom] product, as the result of an intuition' *CD* I/1, 247.

36 See *CD* I/ 2, 6ff.

37 *CD* I/1, 323. In *CD* IV/3.2, 504 Barth insisted that vocation could not be controlled by us for the same reason, that is, because the emphasis even here must be on 'the concrete person of Jesus Christ who as the Son of God calls him by the Holy Spirit'.

38 *CD* II/1, 409 and Karl Barth, *Protestant Theology in the Nineteenth Century: Its Background & History* (hereafter: *Protestant Theology in the Nineteenth Century*) (Valley Forge, PA: Judson Press, 1973), 468 and 471fff.

39 Barth, *Protestant Theology in the Nineteenth Century*, 468 and 471ff.

40 Barth, *Protestant Theology in the Nineteenth Century*, 412ff., esp. 418–20.

41 *CD* II/1, 291ff.

42 *CD* I/1, 322–3. This is why Barth rejects any sort of divinization of Christ's human nature, (*CD* IV/1, 132) and why he insists that in becoming a

and then known; this, because his *esse* really is his *act*. Therefore, 'no self-determination of the second partner [the creature] can influence the first, whereas the self-determination of the first, *while not cancelling the self-determination* of the second, is the sovereign predetermination which precedes it absolutely'.[43] The very being of the Christian God revealed not only excludes *any* pantheistic or panentheistic attempt to define his relation with creatures, but it excludes any attempt to ascribe meaning directly to human concepts or experiences; it excludes the attempt to correlate otherness and transcendence following such a procedure.

By contrast, Colin Gunton, in partial reliance on John Zizioulas and in connection with ecclesiology, criticizes Barth's doctrine of election because it has been taken to imply universal salvation. 'The moment of truth in the contention is that if election is ordered christologically, and with greater emphasis on the divine Christ than on the human Jesus of Nazareth, the fate of us all appears to have been pre-determined in eternity'.[44] Gunton notes that an ecclesiology that is then ordered to a 'monophysite or docetically tending christology has even more disastrous effects'[45] which he detects in the documents of Vatican II. What is Gunton's remedy? He suggests

a greater stress on the fact that the ecclesiological significance of Jesus derives equally from the humanity of the incarnate ... that Jesus is

man Christ did not change himself into a man so that his divinity in some sense ceased, *CD* IV/2, 401ff. See also *CD* II/1, 360ff. Considering that God was in Christ reconciling the world to himself (2 Cor. 5:19) Barth maintains that: 'This reconciling action of God is the *being* of God in Christ, but it is this reconciling *action* that is the being. The Son "glorifies" the Father, yet not without the Father glorifying the Son (Jn. 17:1). It is not any son that speaks here, but the Son of this Father, who even as the Father of this Son remains the Father in heaven, the Father who sends the Son' (*CD* I/1, 323–4). The key here is that in revealing and reconciling there is no loss of mystery so that 'He assumes a form, yet not in such a way that any form will compass Him. Even as He gives Himself He remains free to give Himself afresh or to refuse Himself' (*CD* I/1, 324).

43 *CD* II/1, 312, emphasis mine.

44 Gunton, *The Promise of Trinitarian Theology*, 1991, 67. Additional criticisms along these lines may be seen in C. E. Gunton, *Christ and Creation* (Grand Rapids, MI: Eerdmans, 1992), 94ff.

45 Gunton, *The Promise of Trinitarian Theology*, 1991, 67.

without sin does not imply that he is omniscient, or even infallible ... It is part of the being of a human person to be contingent and fallible (though not, of course, to be sinful) ... In view of the temptations and the trial in Gethsemane, may we claim even indefectibility of Jesus? He did, indeed, escape defection. But how? Not through some inbuilt divine programming, though that is the way it is has often been made to appear, but by virtue of his free acceptance of the Spirit's guidance.[46]

Some crucial difficulties arise in connection with this analysis. Unlike Barth, Gunton does not consistently maintain the dialectical unity and distinction within the priority of the action of the Word in what George Hunsinger has called the Chalcedonian pattern.[47] Instead, he emphasizes the Holy Spirit in such a way that it becomes virtually impossible to maintain two insights that are crucial to Barth's theology and are important in preserving both divine and human freedom: (1) he argues that Jesus's significance derives equally from his humanity; and (2) he argues that the Spirit rather than the Word is the source of Jesus's authentic humanity. While Jesus's humanity is crucial because what is not assumed is not saved, and while it is important to stress, as both Gunton and Barth do indeed stress, that the Word assumed our sinful humanity and not some idealized humanity, Gunton's emphasis on Jesus's humanity sometimes appears to eliminate the significance of his being the Word incarnate and at times actually tends to separate the actions of the Word and Spirit instead of seeing these actions in their *perichoretic* unity.

Thus, for instance, in the passage just cited, he argues that Jesus is not omniscient or infallible and that his indefectibility is traceable to his free acceptance of the Spirit's guidance; but why is Jesus's indefectibility traceable *only* to the Spirit's guidance and Jesus's free human acceptance of that guidance? Is it not the case that the incarnation refers to a mystery and miracle involving the Word who, in Barth's theology, never ceases to be the subject of the events of incarnation, reconciliation and redemption? Isn't the mystery of Jesus Christ identical with the fact that while not ceasing to be divine and thus omniscient, he became a man who did indeed share our ignorance and limitations in order to overcome them on our behalf? When Barth speaks of the Spirit's activity

46 Gunton, *The Promise of Trinitarian Theology*, 1991, 67–8.
47 For a discussion of this 'Chalcedonian pattern', see Chapter 3, n. 74.

within history, he always links that activity to the activity of the Word with the result that he never plays off the Word and Spirit against each other. By contrast, Gunton, who follows the thought of Edward Irving argues that 'the Spirit … is the source of Jesus' authentic humanity'.[48] Accordingly, Gunton intends to correct what he sees as Barth's tendency to universalize election for christological reasons with Irving's approach which limits that universality to redemption for pneumatological reasons. Thus, 'election has to do … with the mysterious activity of the Spirit, communicating the benefits of redemption to particular people at particular times';[49] but what are those benefits and how can they be discerned without faith in Christ himself as the giver of those benefits? Here it seems Gunton leaves out the action of the Word which takes place in and through the action of the Holy Spirit.

A closer look at some of Gunton's criticisms of Barth in relation to Barth's own position might help bring to light a point that I would like to emphasize here, namely, the continuing need to acknowledge the importance of Barth's insight that the Word is and remains the subject of the event of the incarnation and the one who even now speaks his Word to us through the words of scripture in the power of the Holy Spirit. While Gunton is quite right to stress, in line with the Eastern tradition, the fact that when the Holy Spirit is properly acknowledged and emphasized, then Jesus's full humanity and ours, together with the eschatological nature of our redemption, will come more clearly into view, it is equally important that we not fail to acknowledge and emphasize the inseparability of the Spirit and the Word. It is also important to make room for the fact that in the Holy Spirit, God continues to speak his Word to us here and now in and through the historical witness of scripture. One of the ways that Barth stresses the historicity of revelation is by showing how scripture, as a human document, is also God's Word.

In this connection we will compare Barth and Gunton on five episodes in Jesus's life: (1) the relation of the virgin birth to the beginning of Jesus's life, (2) Jesus's baptism and the temptations, (3) Jesus's death on the cross, (4) Jesus's resurrection and (5) Jesus's ascension. Gunton contends that the Western tradition, beginning with Augustine and 'culminating in Barth'[50] failed to do justice to Jesus's humanity because of its failure to give proper emphasis to the Holy Spirit.

---

48 Sykes, *Karl Barth*, 63.
49 Sykes, *Karl Barth*, 64.
50 Gunton, *Christ and Creation*, 50.

The Virgin Birth

Gunton contends that the virgin birth has been used to screen Jesus from the pressures of human existence or to express his total involvement in our humanity. He notes that the doctrine of the Immaculate Conception completely shields Jesus from participating in our sinful flesh while Barth's understanding of the virgin birth has a similar outcome with the opposite intent. Since Barth's concern is to say that at the beginning and end of Jesus's earthly life there was a miracle, 'a new divine initiative, a mystery of revelation,'[51] he pays less attention to the divine action *within* creation and instead focuses on God's action *toward* creation. Thus when Barth speaks of God acting solely through God and that ' "God can be known solely through God" ' this indicates that he is unable 'to specify an action of the Spirit except in terms of "God Himself in His freedom exercised in revelation to be present to His creature" '.[52] The problem with Barth, accordingly, is not with what he says but with what he does not say. Barth misses the point that the Holy Spirit is 'the one enabling the creation truly to be itself'.[53]

Gunton wishes to avoid tritheism while relying on Edward Irving to offset this apparent one-sidedness in Barth's thought and so he stresses that when the function of the Holy Spirit is properly emphasized, then it is seen that Jesus

> is indeed part of the network of creation, in all its fallenness. By forming a body for the Word in the womb of Mary, the Spirit shows that the being of the human Jesus is not merely the passive object of the eternal Son's determination: it is also flesh of our flesh ... That is the point of denying that Jesus bore the flesh of unfallen Adam. If he did, what is his *saving* relation to us in our lostness?[54]

In this context then the virgin birth should be seen as a statement about Christ's humanity, which is that of fallen creatures, but is led to perfection by the Holy Spirit. Hence 'the doctrine of the virgin birth is not to "prove" the divinity of Christ, but to link together divine initiative and true humanity. Jesus is within the world as human, and yet as new

---

51 Gunton, *Christ and Creation*, 51.
52 Gunton, *Christ and Creation*, 51.
53 Gunton, *Christ and Creation*, 50.
54 Gunton, *Christ and Creation*, 52.

act of creation by God.'[55] While it must be admitted that Barth does not say that the Holy Spirit is the 'perfecting cause of creation' in the sense described by Gunton, though he is aware of this, he does say a number of things that are underplayed or missing from Gunton's account.

First, Barth insists that the incarnation is an action of the Word, that is, the Word or Son of God is and remains the subject of the event of incarnation. Thus,

> As the Son of God made His own this one specific possibility of human essence and existence and made it a reality, this Man came into being, and He, the Son of God, became this Man ... Thus the reality of Jesus Christ is that God Himself in person is actively present in the flesh. God Himself in person is the Subject of a real human being and acting. And just because God is the Subject of it, this being and acting are real. They are genuinely and truly human being and acting. Jesus Christ is not a demigod. He is not an angel. Nor is He an ideal man. He is a man as we are, equal to us as a creature ... equal to us in the state and condition into which our disobedience has brought us.[56]

Barth therefore insists that in the incarnation

> the Word is the Subject. Nothing befalls him; but in the becoming asserted of Him He acts. The becoming asserted of Him is not, therefore, to be regarded as an element in the world process as such ... It cannot be regarded as one of its evolutionary possibilities ... God's Word becoming a creature must be regarded as a new creation ... it is a sovereign divine act, and it is an act of lordship different from creation.[57]

This is why Barth regards the equation 'very God very man' as irreversible. If Jesus is to be seen not only as God who is man but as man who is God then 'it is so because it has pleased very God to be very man'.[58] Jesus is indeed the incarnate Word but it is the Word who speaks, acts, reveals and reconciles us. It is 'the Word and not the flesh. The Word is what

55 Gunton, *Christ and Creation*, 53.
56 Barth, *CD* I/2, 150–1.
57 *CD* I/2, 134.
58 *CD* I/2, 136.

He is even before and apart from His being flesh. Even as incarnate He derives His being to all eternity from the Father and from Himself, and not from the flesh.'[59] While it is important to stress the action of the Holy Spirit as Gunton does, it is also important to see that the Word and Spirit are both active in the incarnation and therefore emphasis on the Spirit does not have to imply, as it seems to imply for Gunton, that the Word's activity must be restricted. Nor should it imply that Jesus's human actions are pre-programmed. Gunton wants to say that Jesus's free human actions are enabled by the Spirit *rather than* determined by the Word;[60] but why can we not say that Jesus's free human actions, as the actions of the Word are indeed enabled by the Spirit in such a way that we cannot ultimately explain *how* this can be so? Rather we must simply confess the fact that it is so. In one sense, as T. F. Torrance says, the Word restricts his activity so as to submit obediently to the Father's will on the cross out of love for us.[61] Still, he does not cease being divine in the incarnation, but acts as God become man.[62]

---

59 *CD* I/2, 136.

60 There are also some problematic assertions that Gunton makes regarding the Spirit within the immanent Trinity as when he claims that 'the Spirit perfects the divine communion by being the dynamic of the Father's and the Son's being who they distinctly are', *Father, Son and Holy Spirit*, 86. In addition, he claims that the Spirit is the 'perfecter both of the eternal divine communion … and of God's love for the *other* in creation and redemption' (86). However, does this idea of the Spirit 'perfecting' what is supposed to be the self-sufficient and perfect life of the immanent Trinity as the one who loves in freedom, not undermine the sovereignty of God in himself and of his grace when he acts effectively for us as reconciler and redeemer?

61 Thus, Torrance believes that 'Jesus Christ came among us sharing to the full the poverty of our ignorance, without ceasing to embody in himself all the riches of the wisdom of God, in order that we might be redeemed from our ignorance through sharing in his wisdom' (*The Trinitarian Faith*, 187). Christ's ignorance however was 'an economic and vicarious ignorance … by way of a deliberate restraint on his divine knowledge throughout a life of continuous *kenosis* in which he refused to transgress the limits of the creaturely and earthly conditions of human nature' (187). For more on this, see Molnar, *Torrance: Theologian of the Trinity*, 155ff.

62 Thus, Torrance also insists that: 'The self-humiliation of God in Jesus Christ, his *kenosis* or *tapeinosis*, does not mean the self-limitation of God or the curtailment of his power, but the staggering exercise of his power within

Gunton, who follows John Owen, makes an unfortunate separation of God's Word and Spirit acting ad extra. Thus, 'Owen *limits* the direct operation of the Word ... Owen holds that "The only singular immediate act of the person of the Son on the human nature was the *assumption* of it into subsistence with himself" ... the humanity [of Jesus] is not subverted by the immanently operating Word.'[63] Where then does the human Jesus receive the capacity to do God's work? For Owen, '"The Holy Ghost ... is the *immediate, peculiar, efficient* cause of all external divine operations: for God worketh by his Spirit, or in him immediately applies the power and efficacy of the divine excellencies unto their operation ..."'[64] However, as we have just seen, for Barth and T. F. Torrance, the direct operation of the Word is not limited to only one aspect of the incarnation and is not simply equated with the action of the Son 'on the human nature'. For Barth it is the action of the Son as man within human history that counts. Still, as we have just seen, he does not cease being divine in the incarnation but acts as God become man. Owen's view would be tantamount to saying that in the incarnation God ceased to be divine when he became man. However, Barth also did not envision Jesus's activity as 'determined' by the Word as subject in the sense that his actions were less than free human actions of obedience on Jesus's part under the guidance of the Holy Spirit; nor did Torrance.[65]

Second, contrary to Gunton's assertion, Barth indeed insists on the fact that Jesus's humanity is the humanity of sinful creatures: 'The Word is not only the eternal Word of God but 'flesh' as well, i.e., all that we are and exactly like us even in our opposition to Him. It is because of this that He makes contact with us and is accessible for us.'[66] Barth notes

the limitations of our contingent existence in space and time ... God is revealed to have the inconceivable power of becoming little and contingent, while remaining what he eternally and almightily is' (*The Christian Doctrine of God*, 214–15).

63 Gunton, *The Promise of Trinitarian Theology*, 70. For a discussion of how thinking such as this relates to Torrance's understanding, see Molnar, *Faith, Freedom and the Spirit*, 252ff.

64 Gunton, *The Promise of Trinitarian Theology*, 70.

65 See Molnar, *Torrance: Theologian of the Trinity*, 158–9 and *The Trinitarian Faith*, 188–9. For Torrance's helpful and important discussion of the virgin birth, see Torrance, *Incarnation* (ed.) Walker, 88–104.

66 *CD* I/2, 151.

that while Jesus himself did not commit sin, he nonetheless shared our sinful flesh and thus experienced God's judgment in our stead. 'He bore innocently what Adam and all of us in Adam have been guilty of. Freely He entered into solidarity and necessary association with our lost existence. Only in this way "could" God's revelation to us, our reconciliation with Him, manifestly become an event in Him and by Him.'[67]

Third, in speaking of the *Natus ex Maria virgine* Barth stresses that we are dealing with a mystery and miracle. However, Barth does not think of the miracle at the beginning of Jesus's human life and the miracle at the end of his life (the resurrection) as indications that he is not fully human, as Gunton seems to suggest. Rather, Barth insists that Jesus was born as no one else was born and that we must acknowledge the unique object in question. Still, according to Barth, Jesus was not born because of 'male generation' but because of 'female conception'.[68] The *conceptus de Spiritu sancto*, which according to Barth is the more important creedal clause, positively states the 'coming of His Word into human existence' and asserts that this is not just any mystery but that here

> God's reality becomes one with human reality. By its *natus ex Maria* it states that the person of Jesus Christ is the real son of a real mother, the son born of the body, flesh and blood of his mother, both of them as real as all the other sons of other mothers. It is thus that Jesus Christ is born and not otherwise. In this complete sense, He, too, is a man ... He is man in a different way from the other sons of other mothers. But the difference ... is so great, so fundamental and comprehensive, that it does not impair the completeness and genuineness of His humanity.[69]

For all its mystery and miraculous nature, Christmas is an event that concerns creatures – not in any monistic sense but in the sense that the Lord makes it so: 'It is not an event in the loneliness of God, but an event between God and man. Man is not there only

---

67 *CD* I/2, 152.

68 *CD* I/2, 185.

69 *CD* I/2, 185. Importantly Barth notes that this miracle had already acquired the practical importance of 'a protection against gnostic and docetic ideas like those of Valentinus, according to whom Christ had received nothing from His human mother, but had assumed a heavenly body newly created for this purpose' (185).

in a supplementary capacity ... he participates in the event as one of the principals ... as the real man he is. The Word became flesh.'[70] However, the fact of this participation is the result and embodiment of God's grace and judgment:

> In that grace is imparted to him he is given not simply to be the spectator of an unusual event, but to participate in an event which contradicts and withstands him. Something decisive befalls him ... something ... which he can affirm and appreciate only in faith and not otherwise. Of course, in the judgment in which he is placed grace is concealed.[71]

Judgment here is signified by the fact that: (1) 'human nature possesses no capacity for becoming the human nature of Jesus Christ ... It cannot be the work-mate of God'. It becomes this 'by the divine Word'. Mary's virginity is not the denial of humanity in God's presence but 'of any power, attribute or capacity in [us] for God'. This power comes to Mary from God and in that sense it cannot be explained, but can only be acknowledged. It is clear then that Barth does not ignore the humanity of Christ but stresses that humanity in such a way that he respects the fact that the *how* of this event cannot be explained but can only be accepted. (2) Barth insists that the creature whose flesh the Word assumes has lost 'his pure creatureliness' because 'he became disobedient to his Creator'.[72] This nature, which is marked by sin, must be judged (opposed and negated) so that we can humanly act as God's fellow-workers. For flesh to be united with God is a mystery that must be wrought, and that is what is signified by the *natus ex virgine*. Barth insists that it was not the miracle that made possible God's becoming man in Christ and the new beginning that took place there. Barth insists that

> we can as little say that as we can say on Mk. 2: 1–12 that the truth and reality of the fact that the Son of man has power on earth to forgive sins was made possible and effected by the healing of the paralytic. The forgiveness of sins is manifestly the thing signified, while the healing is the sign, quite inseparable from, but very significantly

70 *CD* I/2, 186.
71 *CD* I/2, 187–8.
72 *CD* I/2, 188.

related to, this thing signified, yet neither identical with it nor a condition of it . . .[73]

This is why Barth insists that knowledge of what is here revealed is knowledge of faith.

How then does Barth understand the action of the Holy Spirit in all of this? When Barth speaks of the Holy Spirit he says that when the Church depicts the Holy Spirit it refers to God in the strictest and fullest sense, the Lord (i.e., what Gunton portrays as God's transcendence). This means that humanity relies on God 'upon whose grace he is utterly thrown, and in whose promise alone his future consists'.[74] Jesus's human nature is conceived by the Holy Spirit. If we are clear about this then we will realize that there is no parallel between God the Holy Spirit and other deities which are the product of human mythology. The 'mythical miracles' associated with the gods invented by us are not real miracles, that is, 'signs of God, the Lord of the world'.[75] If God himself, God the Holy Spirit is the author of this sign (the virgin birth), as he indeed is, then it cannot be understood as a natural possibility. It must be acknowledged as 'a pure divine beginning' and thus we cannot inquire 'as to whether or how this reality can be anything else but a pure divine beginning'.[76] It is the divinity of the Holy Spirit as the author of Christ's human nature together with the miraculous nature of the virgin birth that makes the virgin birth 'a sign of the mystery of Christmas';[77] but why, Barth asks, is the Holy Spirit in particular named here? As Gunton remarks in a somewhat disparaging way, Barth says (with nuances left out of Gunton's reference): 'The Holy Spirit is God Himself in His freedom exercised in revelation to be present to His creature, even to dwell in him personally, and thereby to achieve his meeting with Himself in His Word and by this achievement to make it possible'.[78] The Holy Spirit enables us to believe, to be free for God and his work and to be an object of God's reconciliation. The Holy Spirit guarantees that human beings can participate in revelation and reconciliation.

73 *CD* I/2, 189.
74 *CD* I/2, 197.
75 *CD* I/2, 197.
76 *CD* I/2, 198.
77 *CD* I/2, 198.
78 *CD* I/2, 198.

It must be remembered that by revelation Barth aims to describe all that God does as Emmanuel or God with us. It is not noetic in place of emphasizing Jesus's saving significance as Gunton says.[79] However, as we have seen, for Barth, that which is noetic includes all aspects of human freedom.[80] Hence, God acts for us as our creator, reconciler and redeemer and thus includes us in Christ in a genuine participation in his own inner knowledge, love and freedom. Barth, however, insists on the fact that the virgin birth indicates to us that since God the Holy Spirit creates for us the possibility of being his free children in the church, the whence and whither of the Christian life remain a mystery grounded in an act that can be effected only by God in the unity of his Spirit and Word. Hence, Barth also insists that the virgin birth 'eliminates the last surviving possibility of understanding the *vere Deus vere homo* intellectually, as an idea or an arbitrary interpretation in the sense of docetic or ebionite Christology. It leaves only the spiritual understanding ... in which God's own work is seen in God's own light.'[81]

Several other important points are made by Barth which show that he is much more aware than Gunton allows of the function of the Holy Spirit in relation to Christ's humanity and ours. Indeed, I would say that Barth's trinitarian understanding of the matter is clearer than Gunton's in the sense that he does not relegate the action of the Word into a corner and leave the rest to the Spirit. Rather, he sees the Spirit acting together with the Word: 'The very possibility of human nature's being adopted into unity with the Son of God is the Holy Ghost. Here, then at this fontal point in revelation, the Word of God is not without the Spirit of God ... there is the togetherness of Spirit and Word.'[82] Further, Barth insists that human freedom takes place in and through the Holy Spirit; that God claims us for himself in the Spirit; that in virtue of the Holy Spirit there is 'a Church in which God's Word can be ministered, because it has the language for it ... The freedom which the Holy Spirit gives us in this understanding and in this sphere ... so

---

79 Gunton, *The Promise of Trinitarian Theology*, 20.

80 See John Webster, *Barth's Moral Theology: Human Action in Barth's Thought*, (Edinburgh: T & T Clark and Grand Rapids, MI: Eerdmans, 1998), 108, for his response to Gunton's criticism of Barth for underplaying the role of the Holy Spirit. It is precisely Barth's view of the Holy Spirit that enables him to give proper weight to human self-determination (freedom).

81 *CD* I/2, 177.

82 *CD* I/2, 199.

far as it is His own freedom and so far as he gives us nothing else and no less than Himself – is the freedom of the Church, the children of God.'[83] This freedom is involved in the assumption of human nature by the Son of God: 'Through the Spirit flesh, human nature, is assumed into unity with the Son of God ... this Man can be God's Son and at the same time the Second Adam and as such ... the prototype of all who are set free for His sake and through faith in Him.'[84] Barth even insists that: 'The sign of the baptism in Jordan, like the sign of the Virgin birth, points back to the mystery of this Man's being which was real in itself apart from this sign ... [it] means that the Holy Spirit is the mystery of this being.'[85] The mystery to which Barth refers is the fact that when the Spirit descended on Jesus (cf. Jn. 1:32f.) he descended on Jesus who 'actually is the beloved Son of God' and this could not mean that Jesus became the Son of God because of the Spirit's descent. In sum, for Barth the Spirit is important because first, 'it refers back the mystery of the human existence of Jesus Christ to the mystery of God Himself ... that God Himself creates a possibility, a power, a capacity, and assigns it to man, where otherwise there would be sheer impossibility'.[86] Second, it refers back to the 'connexion which exists between our reconciliation and the existence of the Reconciler, to the primary realisation of the work of the Spirit'.[87]

One final point, while we saw earlier that adoptionist thinking threatens much contemporary Christology, with trinitarian implications,[88] Barth is straightforward about the matter precisely because of his view of the Holy Spirit: 'The man Jesus of Nazareth is not the true Son of God because He was conceived by the Holy Spirit and born of the Virgin Mary ... He is the true Son of God and because this is an inconceivable mystery intended to be acknowledged as such, therefore He is conceived by the Holy Spirit and born of the Virgin Mary.'[89] For this reason, he must be acknowledged as the one he is: 'The mystery does not rest upon the miracle. The miracle rests upon the mystery.'[90]

---

83 *CD* I/2, 198.

84 *CD* I/2, 199.

85 *CD* I/2, 199.

86 *CD* I/2, 199.

87 *CD* I/2, 200.

88 See also Molnar, *Incarnation and Resurrection* for more such examples.

89 *CD* I/2, 202. See also *CD* IV/1, 207.

90 *CD* I/2, 202.

Jesus's Baptism and the Temptations

Since the tradition has neglected the importance of these two events, Gunton believes that the charges of Docetism leveled at orthodox Christology are justified. Indeed he links Barth with this tradition since he argues that there is 'a fundamental flaw in his [Barth's] doctrine of God ... because he is weaker in handling the detail of that [Christ's] humanity, his theology can take on a docetic air.'[91] For the tradition, the baptism has been taken to reveal the Trinity: 'The Father acknowledges the Son and sends the Spirit.'[92] However, Gunton wants to consider 'those relationships that concern him [Jesus] as a human being, abstracting them, so far as is possible without distortion, from the ways in which, as the eternal Son, he is related to the Father and to the world.'[93] It will be remembered that for Barth we can never for a moment consider Jesus's humanity or his human relationships in abstraction from faith in the mystery of his being as the Word or Son incarnate – the very idea that this is possible consists in a separation of that which cannot be separated, that is, Jesus's divinity and humanity. That is why Barth rejected abstract Jesus worship. As we shall see shortly, Barth was adamant about this point in his Christology and Gunton's unwillingness to accept the limitation which Barth held was imposed by revelation itself is the key to their different epistemologies.

In any case, Gunton argues that in order to focus on the *human* savior we must see that the Spirit directs Jesus's human life as the prophet, priest and king of Israel. In this context the general human relevance of the temptation stories becomes clear: 'If Jesus did not share our human trials, he is as irrelevant to our needs as if he had not borne the same flesh.'[94] Gunton rightly opposes any docetic account of the temptations which might suggest that Jesus did not experience conflict here. In this regard he cites Edward Irving against Schleiermacher to say: 'Jesus was enabled to resist temptation not by some immanent conditioning, but by virtue of his obedience to the guidance of the Spirit.'[95] Barth is here criticized once again for not incorporating Jesus's free obedience into his theology at this point: 'His freedom is that he accepts it as a gift from the Father's sending of the Spirit. Freedom is ...

---

91 Sykes, *Karl Barth*, 60.
92 Gunton, *Christ and Creation*, 53.
93 Gunton, *Christ and Creation*, 47.
94 Gunton, *Christ and Creation*, 53.
95 Gunton, *Christ and Creation*, 54.

something exercised in relation to other persons ... it is the gift of the Spirit who is God *over against us*, God in personal otherness enabling us to be free.'[96] Thus, for Gunton, in remaining true to his call to be the Messiah of Israel Jesus 'establishes his freedom'.[97] Gunton wants to stress, with Irving, that Jesus's relation to the Spirit changes because of his glorification: only after his resurrection could Jesus pour out the Spirit that led him during his life. Jesus's human actions as priest, prophet and king illustrate that (1) Jesus's humanity is 'perfected by the Spirit'; (2) 'In the perfect offering of himself to the Father through the eternal Spirit we witness one sample – and Irving can even speak of this as a *random* sample – of the creation in its integrity.'[98] As creation has fallen into sin and disruption it has therefore lost its directedness to God. This is what is restored in Jesus's free obedience in a way that respects his and our freedom.

Interestingly, Karl Barth insisted that: 'The Son of God exists with man and as man in this fallen and perishing state. We should be explaining the incarnation docetically and therefore explaining it away if we did not put it like this, if we tried to limit in any way the solidarity with the cosmos which God accepted in Jesus Christ.'[99] Hence, Barth insisted that God did not evade our fallen state but 'exposed Himself to and withstood the temptation which man suffers and in which he becomes a sinner and the enemy of God'.[100] Jesus's sinlessness consists in the fact that he 'was obedient in that He willed to take our place as sinners and did, in fact, take our place. [His sinlessness] did not consist in an abstract and absolute purity, goodness and virtue. It consisted in His actual freedom from sin itself, from the basis of all sins.'[101] However, this freedom is not pre-programmed for Barth any more than it was in the gospels. This freedom consists in the fact that, unlike Adam, Jesus did not try to become his own judge but acknowledged that God was the only righteous judge. Jesus

> was a man as we are. His condition was no different from ours. He
> took our flesh, the nature of man as he comes from the fall. In this

---

96 Gunton, *Christ and Creation*, 55.
97 Gunton, *Christ and Creation*, 55.
98 Gunton, *Christ and Creation*, 57.
99 *CD* IV/1, 215.
100 *CD* IV/1, 215.
101 *CD* IV/1, 258.

nature He is exposed every moment to the temptation to a renewal of sin – the temptation of impenitent being and thinking and speaking and action. His sinlessness was not therefore His condition. It was the act of His being in which He defeated temptation in His condition which is ours, in the flesh.[102]

At his baptism in the Jordan, Jesus entered his way as the Judge who was then judged in our place on the cross. This has significance precisely because this man was and is the Son of God incarnate. This is the mystery of Jesus Christ and his sinlessness manifests the miracle of the grace of reconciliation. Barth analyzes the temptation stories indicating that Jesus was led by the same Spirit that the Baptist had seen descending on him in the Jordan into the wilderness in order to be tempted. Barth insists that while others should refrain from temptation, Jesus was willing to expose himself to it; and what was Jesus's temptation? It consisted in the fact that Jesus might not have been true to his calling by choosing to avoid the cross. This would have meant, however, that without his obedience, the enmity of the world against God would have continued. Barth does a masterful job analyzing the temptation stories in the gospels and he shows clearly an awareness of Jesus's human experience and even identification with our fallen condition. However, he does so in full awareness that the mystery of Jesus's existence is that as man he was also the eternal Son who could forgive sins and judge us as well as experience judgment in our place and on our behalf. Barth's analysis of Jesus in Gethsemane takes full account of Jesus's human struggle and of his prayer that if it was in accordance with God's will his suffering might not have to be experienced. Nevertheless he was obedient. Yet it was not his obedience that caused our freedom from sin. His obedience was a sign of the fact that he could and did overcome sin: 'In the power of this prayer [in Gethsemane] Jesus received, i.e., He renewed, confirmed and put into effect, His freedom to finish His work, to execute the divine judgment by undergoing it Himself.'[103] Experiencing this burden on behalf of all others Jesus once for all liberated the human race from sin. In his prayer 'there took place quite simply the completion of the penitence and obedience which He had begun to render at Jordan and which He had maintained in the wilderness'.[104]

---

102 *CD* IV/1, 258–9.
103 *CD* IV/1, 271.
104 *CD* IV/1, 272.

Unlike Gunton, Barth is able to do justice to the fact that what took place in the human life of Jesus was in fact the act of God the Son in the unity of his divine and human natures and under the direction of the Spirit. The mystery of Jesus's suffering and death cannot for a moment be separated from his being as the eternal Son of the eternal Father and assigned in that way to his free obedience. His free obedience was every bit a human action, but it was at the same time the action of the Son of God. This did not make it any less free. Rather, this mystery gives it its true meaning. It is important to acknowledge the working of the Spirit as Gunton insists; but Barth's theology offers an important additional feature without which the action of the Spirit is in danger of being separated from the Word once again. Barth insists that Jesus's human actions are never merely the actions of a human being who was not also the eternal Son of God. In that regard, Jesus himself is the reconciler and the subject of the events of incarnation and reconciliation. That is the mystery of the Christian faith.

In spite of the important contributions Gunton has made to our understanding of the proper relation between the immanent and economic Trinity, there remains a problem with his theological epistemology. Instead of arguing with Barth that our knowledge of God is an event enclosed in the mystery of the Trinity, Gunton at times appears to imply that relationality is the subject while God's act becomes the predicate. Thus, he argues 'to a theology of being from structures of relations. Who we are is made known to us through the relations in which we stand ... Those relations reveal different ranges of mutuality and reciprocity, but they all ... provide us with mirrors in which we may see ourselves as we are'.[105] Gunton rejects Barth's view of God as one in three modes of being, not because it is modalist (though Gunton suspects that Barth's thinking tends toward modalism), but because 'it fails to reclaim the relational view of the person from the ravages of modern individualism. To be personal ... is not to be an individual centre of consciousness or something like that ... but to be one whose being consists in relations of mutual constitution with other persons'.[106] Hence, for Gunton: 'That is one of the glories of trinitarian thinking, for it enables unique and fruitful insight into the nature of being – all being – in relation.'[107] Here, once again, however, we must ask whether it

105 Gunton, *Christ and Creation*, 72.
106 Gunton, *The Promise of Trinitarian Theology, second edn*, 195.
107 Gunton, *The Promise of Trinitarian Theology, second edn*, 195–6.

is trinitarian thinking grounded in our experience of relations that can accomplish all this; is it not the case that even our trinitarian thinking cannot displace God's own act of unveiling which is here necessary for a proper understanding of divine and human relations? Do the relations in which we stand make known who we are or is it God himself in his Word and Spirit who does this in and through our faith as we read scripture and live the Christian life? This important difference, in my view, stems from a failure to distinguish the immanent and economic Trinity precisely by separating God's Word and Spirit at the point where Barth refused to do so.[108]

Jesus's Death

In connection with Jesus's death, Gunton stresses the action of the Spirit in order to illuminate two features of Jesus's humanity: (1) the involvement of the incarnate Son in the network of the fallen creation and (2) his obedience to the Father's will that took place in the temptations and ministry.

> The relation of the human Jesus to the creation is therefore describable as a saving one. What he achieves, freely because through the enabling of the Spirit, is a matter of redemption because he offers

108 In his appreciative yet critical response to Colin Gunton, John Webster 'Gunton and Barth' in *The Theology of Colin Gunton* (ed.) Lincoln Harvey, 17–31, concludes his discussion of Gunton's various criticisms of Barth's theology including the fact that 'he associated Barth rather too quickly with what he took to be the features of Augustine's theology' by noting that Gunton did not do justice to Barth's interest in Reformed theology. From the Reformed tradition Barth learned and emphasized 'the strictly non-reversible yet utterly real relation of God and God's active human creatures'. In Webster's judgment 'he learned the perils' of associating God's freedom 'with pure transcendence' without attending to Christology and the Christian life from early on by reading Calvin and the Christology of the Reformed confessions (28). In response to Gunton's dislike of Barth's Reformed Christology, which Gunton thought displayed 'docetic tendencies' along with Barth's 'prioritising of the divine nature of the incarnate one, and the absence of an operative pneumatology', Webster quite rightly judges 'that his [Gunton's] criticisms of Barth in this matter are in large part misplaced, and rest on a separation of Word and Spirit which gives little room to the Word's continuing activity in the history of the incarnate one' (28).

to God the Father, through the Spirit, a renewed and cleansed sample of the life in the flesh in which human being consists.[109]

Therefore, contrary to Barth's view, Gunton insists that Jesus's miraculous birth 'belongs dogmatically more with the temptation and cross than with the resurrection'.[110] This, because it indicates the beginning of Jesus's human story that moves toward the cross. As the Father's new creation was initiated through Jesus's birth, so the cross is where Jesus, through the Spirit 'perfected the obedience that he had learned through his temptation and ministry'.[111] Hence, 'his obedience is salvific because here we have a representative sample of fallen flesh purified and presented to God the Father'.[112]

The question that must be asked of this analysis from the perspective of Barth's theology, however, is what happened to the particularity of the Son as an actor in all of this? Is it because of Jesus's free obedience, even as enabled by the Spirit, that redemption is achieved? Or is it because the offering he made to the Father was an offering made by the Son of God himself in the flesh? As T. F. Torrance has put it:

> After all, it was not the *death* of Jesus that constituted atonement, but Jesus Christ the Son of God offering Himself in sacrifice for us. Everything depends on *who* He was, for the significance of His acts in life and death depends on the nature of His Person ... we must allow the Person of Christ to determine for us the nature of His saving work, rather than the other way round.[113]

Gunton's stress on the Spirit and on the humanity of Jesus is important. However, by transferring the emphasis away from the person and work of Christ himself as the savior, his thinking underplays the mysterious and miraculous nature of Jesus's entire earthly life, including his death and resurrection. This man Jesus was God acting among us forgiving sins, healing and restoring us from death (sin) to new life. For Barth, 'the man Jesus – not although but because He is the Son of God – is

---

109 Gunton, *Christ and Creation*, 58–9.

110 Gunton, *Christ and Creation*, 59.

111 Gunton, *Christ and Creation*, 59.

112 Gunton, *Christ and Creation*, 59.

113 T. F. Torrance, *God and Rationality*, 64. For further discussion of this point, see Molnar, *Torrance: Theologian of the Trinity*, 146ff.

the creature of God which, by fulfilling the will and doing the work of the Creator, and being one with Him, does not lose its existence as a creature'. As Barth rightly insisted: 'This Son [of John's Gospel] is in no sense a being devoid of will ... there are texts which imply the exercise of a very energetic will on the part of Jesus ... there can be no question of supposing that Jesus is a sort of vacuum, the mere place where God lives and does His work as another and a stranger'.[114]

Barth also takes the problem of sin far more seriously than Gunton in that he believes that our old sinful lives are doomed to death – they are not merely perfected, but brought from death to new life. These are problems that Barth consistently attempted to counter by his insistence that there never was a time when Jesus's humanity could or should be considered in itself apart from the fact that it is the humanity of the eternal Son or Word of God. If Jesus's human life is solely the work of the Spirit, then does that not raise the question of whether or not the significance of the Word is left out of both the immanent and the economic Trinity? There is in fact, as Barth stressed, no way to God the Father, except through the Son. Barth astutely saw the problem here when he wrote:

> Jesus does ... the work of the Saviour. But He really does it. It is not merely His fate to execute it. It does not simply happen in Him. 'No one taketh my life from me, but I lay it down of myself ... and I have power to take it again.' And this laying down of His life is the fulfillment of the commandments which He has received [Jn] (10:18).[115]

This is what Barth meant when he wrote that 'God acts as Jesus acts'.[116] He had in mind Jn. 9:33 where the man born blind observed: 'If this man were not of God he could do nothing.' Importantly, 'He acts in the name of God, and therefore in His own name ... In what spirit but the Holy Spirit could the will to do so be born?'[117] Consequently, for Barth 'it is not merely the eternal but the incarnate Logos and therefore the man Jesus who is included in this circle [of the inner life of the Godhead]. He did not give up His eternal divinity when He concealed

114 *CD* III/2, 64.
115 *CD* III/2, 64–5.
116 *CD* III/2, 62.
117 *CD* III/2, 62.

it to become man. He is still in the bosom of the Father ... even in His coming to this world. Only on this assumption does Johannine Christology make sense.'[118] It is precisely at this point in his theological anthropology that Barth appeals to the doctrine of perichoresis to insist that the doctrine of the Trinity helps us understand the unity and trinity of God disclosed by Jesus in his relation with the Father. Indeed, Barth insists that it is precisely the inner life of the Trinity that is the very foundation of Jesus's human life among us. 'The Johannine Jesus, too, proclaims Himself unequivocally to be man. His history, too, is plainly a human history ... the particular concern of the Fourth Gospel [in opposition to Docetism] ... was a desire to show that the eternal divine Logos was this man Jesus.'[119]

Unlike Gunton, however, Barth insists that Jesus's laying down his life for his friends is the same thing as God's so loving the world that he gave his only begotten Son.

> The giving of the Son by the Father indicates a mystery, a hidden movement in the inner life of the Godhead. But in the self-sacrifice of the man Jesus for His friends this intra-divine movement is no longer hidden but revealed. For what the man Jesus does by this action is to lay bare this mystery, to actualise the human and therefore the visible ... aspect of this portion of the divine history of this primal moment of divine volition and execution.[120]

In his haste to emphasize the human story of Jesus in abstraction from his action as the Word or Son, Gunton has, to a certain extent, made Jesus a passive object who does little more than illustrate for us certain human features that are attributed to the action of the Spirit rather than the Word. For Barth, in virtue of the eternal perichoresis of the Father, Son and Spirit, we have an active disclosure of the love of God in Jesus's human action because he is included in and expressive of the eternal love of the immanent Trinity.

Gunton believes that in Barth election is conceived binitarianly with the result that the kenotic dimensions of Christ's life are underplayed and Barth loses a sense of eschatology; in addition, it is said that Barth's focus on our human relations with God leads him to neglect creation

118 *CD* III/2, 65.
119 *CD* III/2, 66.
120 *CD* III/2, 66.

itself.[121] In response to this, one might ask whether Matt. 11:27 is also too binitarian? Further, while Gunton wishes to see Jesus's human actions as enabled by the Spirit so as to avoid any idea that they are programmed or '*determined* by the (immanent) Word',[122] Barth actually insisted that election should be understood as the continual choice of a living subject, that is, Christ himself as electing God and elected man. If election is seen this way then the Word would also be seen as active in a non-determinative way in the history of Jesus and precisely by his positing a truly limited humanity in that Jesus was a man of his time.[123] Rather than making Jesus a timeless metaphysical idea, Barth insisted that all theological reflection had to begin and end with him as he was and is, namely, as electing God who was elected man. Gunton believes that Barth 'centered his development [of his treatise on the Trinity] on a conception of Jesus Christ as revelation'.[124] Alan Torrance makes a similar criticism by arguing that the root of the doctrine of the Trinity for Barth was 'the biblical concept of revelation'.[125] This thinking, which is of course indebted to Wolfhart Pannenberg, is not exactly accurate.

While Barth does say that his concept of revelation is decisive, he also makes it very clear that it is revelation itself, namely, Jesus himself who is the root of the doctrine. Hence, Barth writes:

> What we do in fact gather from the doctrine of the Trinity is who the God is who reveals Himself, and this is why we present the doctrine here as an interpretation of revelation. We are not saying, then, that revelation is the basis of the Trinity, as though God were the triune God only in His revelation and only for the sake of His revelation. What we are saying is that revelation is the basis of the doctrine of the Trinity ... We arrive at the doctrine of the Trinity by no other way than that of an analysis of the concept of revelation.[126]

121 Gunton, *Christ and Creation*, 95.

122 Gunton, *The Promise of Trinitarian Theology*, 70.

123 In this regard, John Webster rightly speaks of a 'non-oppositional account of God's transcendence of creaturely time' in (ed.) Harvey, *The Theology of Colin Gunton*, 27.

124 Gunton, *The Promise of Trinitarian Theology*, 20.

125 Torrance, *Persons in Communion*, 239.

126 Barth, *CD* I/1, 312. See also *CD* I/1, 346 where Barth insists that 'the root of the doctrine of the Trinity lies in revelation, and that it can lie only in this if it is not to become at once the doctrine of another and alien God'. Importantly, in the original version of *KD* I/1, 366, the text reads: '*daß die*

It is obvious from the context here that Barth's concept of revelation is determined by revelation itself, which he cites three times as the basis for the doctrine. This is extremely important, because if Jesus Christ is the starting point, then Barth's concepts of revelation and of the Trinity stand or fall by the extent to which they faithfully describe the reality of God present and active in the history of Jesus himself.[127]

Jesus's Resurrection

According to Colin Gunton, the resurrection of Jesus extends his 'relations with the chosen people of God ... universally'.[128] Here, Gunton is willing to speak of a retroactive force in that the resurrection 'brings it about that this man is not just for and against Israel, the mediator of her salvation and judgement, but that his eschatological rule is universal'.[129]

Wurzel der Trinitätslehre in der Offenbarung liegt und nur in der Offenbarung liegen kann, wenn sie nicht sofort die Lehr von einem anderen, fremden Gott'. Notice that Barth does not locate the root of the doctrine in the *idea* or *concept* of revelation but in revelation itself and he repeats this twice to make sure there is no misunderstanding. It will of course be remembered that for Barth, 'revelation denotes the Word of God itself in the act of its being spoken in time ... It is the condition which conditions all things without itself being conditioned ... [It] means the unveiling of what is veiled ... Revelation as such is not relative. Revelation in fact does not differ from the person of Jesus Christ nor from the reconciliation accomplished in him. To say revelation is to say "The Word became flesh"' (*CD* I/I, 118–19). This, of course, is what is revealed in the resurrection and ascension of Jesus Christ, the incarnate Word (*CD* IV/2, 149). Barth earlier in *CD* I/1 claimed that 'the basis or root of the doctrine of the Trinity, if it has one and is thus legitimate dogma – and it does have one and is thus legitimate dogma – lies in revelation' (*CD* I/1, 311). Therefore, when Barth speaks of arriving at the doctrine by an analysis of the concept of revelation, he clearly means that the anchor for the veracity of that concept is revelation itself in its identity with the Word made flesh.

127 This position stands opposed to those who argue that Barth had a second doctrine of the Trinity that was based on Christology later in the *Church Dogmatics* and that this was different from his earlier view based on the concept of revelation.

128 Gunton, *Christ and Creation*, 61.

129 Gunton, *Christ and Creation*, 61. Astutely aware of the problems with theories such as Rahner's anonymous Christianity, Gunton insists: 'To proclaim the universality of Jesus is not to condemn to hell all those who do not respond

Gunton rejects all subjectivist and Bultmannian views of the resurrection because he believes that creation's promised perfection is here realized by the Spirit. Like Robert Jenson before him, Gunton asks 'who it was [who] raised Jesus from the dead'.[130] In one sense, Gunton notes that it is indeed an action of the triune God, but in virtue of the fact that scripture appropriates certain actions to certain persons of the Trinity, Gunton also stresses that 'Incarnation and salvation must be understood as peculiarly the work of the Son' and argues that Jesus's resurrection should also be interpreted 'trinitarianly'. Here he objects to T. F. Torrance's understanding of Jesus's resurrection as the completion of his active obedience as the incarnate Son, asserting that unless 'this is balanced by a firm assertion of the passivity of the Son, the link, made so firmly in Paul between Jesus' resurrection, as the first fruits, and ours is likely to be difficult to maintain'.[131]

Here again Gunton wishes to emphasize pneumatology. The Spirit should here be seen as the one who perfects creation and who is the agent of the eschatological act of resurrection. It is therefore as the first fruits of the transformation of the whole of creation that Jesus is the future for the world. 'If the resurrection is to be more than a revelation of the meaning of Christ and the will of the Father; if, that is to say, it is to *do* as well as simply *show* something ... then it is as the beginnings of an eschatological redemption that we must see it ... The resurrection brings it about that the particular humanity of Jesus becomes the basis of universal redemption.'[132]

Gunton thus stresses two key points. First,

the resurrection establishes the representative status of Christ, because, as 'the first-born among many ...', Rom. 8:29, he becomes the means whereby, through the Spirit, other created reality becomes

to him. It is to leave to the mercy of God the means of the final realisation of the kingdom' (61).

130 Gunton, *Christ and Creation*, 62.

131 Gunton, *Christ and Creation*, 62-3. For Torrance's view of this matter and some of the implications involved, see Molnar, *Incarnation and Resurrection*, 142-3, 256, 378, n. 15 and *Faith, Freedom and the Spirit*, 253 and 323. Torrance, of course, affirms that both the Father and the Spirit raised Jesus from the dead, but that did not mean that he did not also raise himself in perfect Amen to the Father completing his life of obedience for us in that event.

132 Gunton, *Christ and Creation*, 63-4.

perfected. It is … a matter of relationality: of how the relations to God of this human life become through the agency of the Spirit, the means of restoring to right relation those who had sought their own way and thus gone astray.[133]

Second, 'the churchly dimension of the matter is shown by the fact that the Spirit, by relating his people to the Father through the crucified and risen Jesus, moves towards perfection those first created in the image and likeness of their maker'.[134]

Again, what is completely missing from this analysis is any recognition of the active mediation of Jesus, recognized in faith, as the Word or Son of God not only revealing himself, but revealing the work of salvation that he himself had accomplished on our behalf. This does not take place without the Spirit but in the Spirit. However, when Gunton observes that the Holy Spirit brings it about 'that the particular humanity of Jesus becomes the basis of universal redemption' this implies a practical separation of Jesus's humanity and divinity and indeed suggests that it is Jesus's humanity as such that is a kind of passive focal point for the redemption of humanity. This needs to be balanced by the fact that Jesus's resurrection was only seen and understood by those with faith in him – faith given and received by the Holy Spirit. As T. F. Torrance notes: 'The Spirit is said to speak … what he has received from the Son'.[135] Hence, the mystery and miracle of this event must be respected. It must be acknowledged that the power of the resurrection is the very power of God creating new life out of death, a power that was not absent from Jesus's person and work even before the resurrection. The resurrection is not merely the perfecting of human life – it is the restoration of human life from the brink of extinction. This is why Barth insisted that the resurrection could not be described as 'an operation proper to the *humanitas Christi* but rather as something done to it, as a being raised from the dead by God … the Godhead is not so immanent in Christ's humanity that it does not also remain transcendent to it'.[136] Hence, for Barth,

133 Gunton, *Christ and Creation*, 64.
134 Gunton, *Christ and Creation*, 64–5.
135 Torrance, *The Trinitarian Faith*, 248.
136 *CD* I/1, 323.

the power and continuity in which the man Jesus of Nazareth was in fact the revealed Word ... consisted here too in the power and continuity of the divine action in this form [the man Jesus] and not in the continuity of this form as such ... Revealing could obviously not be ascribed to His existence as such. His existence as such is indeed given up to death, and it is in this way, from death, from this frontier, since the Crucified was raised again, that He is manifested as the Son of God.[137]

Barth could speak powerfully about the resurrection in a way that Gunton does not:

The Church exists among Jews and Gentiles because Jesus in His resurrection does not shatter the power of death in vain but with immediate effect; because as the witness to eternal life He cannot remain alone but at once awakens, gathers and sends forth recipients, partners and co-witnesses of this life ... Man elected by God is man made participant by God in eternal salvation. It is this man whom God's community in its perfect, its Church form can reveal. It reveals that even death is surrounded by life, even hell (in all its terrible reality) by the kingdom of the beloved Son of God.[138]

Here a proper understanding of the power of the resurrection is tied to a proper understanding of predestination. For Barth, as is well known, predestination or election is unequivocally linked with Jesus Christ himself as electing God and elected man. However, for Barth, election which is indeed the sum of the gospel, is a living action on the part of the living God. It is not, as Gunton and Jenson assume, identical with a timeless and static past action of God: 'It is not the case, then that God did will but that now He no longer wills, or wills only the effects of His willing ... God is never an echo. He is and continues to be and always will be an independent note or sound. The predestination of God is unchanged and unchangeably God's activity.'[139] Here Barth strongly

137 *CD* I/1, 323.

138 *CD* II/2, 264–5.

139 *CD* II/2, 183. Barth continues by saying that: 'The point we have to make against the older doctrine is this, that while in other respects it laid too great stress upon God's freedom, in this context it came very near to thinking of this freedom in such a way that in predestination God became His own prisoner' (184).

opposes the idea that God could in any sense become 'His own prisoner'. Barth thus insisted that:

> Only as concrete decree, only as an act of divine life in the Spirit, is it the law which precedes all creaturely life. In virtue of its character and content this decree can never be rigid and fixed. It can never belong only to the past ... since it is an act of divine life in the spirit ... it is the presupposition of all the movement of creaturely life ... [it is] an act which occurs in the very midst of time no less than in that far distant pre-temporal eternity. It is the present secret, and in the history of salvation the revealed secret, of the whole history, encounter and decision between God and man ... If it is true that the predestinating God not only is free but remains free, that He does not cease to make use of His freedom but continues to decide, then in the course of God's eternal deciding we have constantly to reckon with new decisions in time ... developments and alterations ... are always possible and do in fact take place.[140]

For Barth, then, 'The Word of the divine steadfastness is the resurrection of Jesus from the dead, His exaltation, His session at the right hand of the Father. By these events God confirms the fact that the Elect is the only-begotten Son of God who can suffer death but cannot be holden of death, who by His death must destroy death.'[141] That is why Barth insists that: 'To believe in Jesus means to have His resurrection and prayer both in the mind and in the heart. And this means to be elected. For it is the man that does this who "in Him" is the object of the divine election.'[142] In Barth's theology then, the mystery of faith consists in the fact that the man Jesus, as Son of God, not only died for our sins out of love for us, but rose again from the dead and in this very power of the resurrection he continues to interact with us now in the power of his Holy Spirit. He speaks his Word which can be heard and obeyed in faith. The Spirit unites us to him and thus enables

---

140 *CD* II/2, 184–7.

141 *CD* II/2, 125.

142 *CD* II/2, 127. It is worth contrasting this specific factor, that is, Jesus's own resurrection and prayer, which is the basis of hope for Christians, with Karl Rahner's belief in an 'anonymous' experience of the resurrection in our existential hope for something definitive at the end of life. See Chapter 7 and Molnar, *Incarnation and Resurrection*, 62f. et al.

the transformation of our humanity. It goes without saying that like Gunton, Barth's theology of the resurrection, with special clarity in *CD* III/2, stresses its objective facticity against any subjectivist or Bultmannian interpretation.[143]

Jesus's Ascension

For Gunton the ascension is a historical event in the sense that it happened within history. It is 'the final closure of Jesus' earthly career' and involves 'the taking up of his humanity into God'.[144] Gunton correctly rejects the idea that there has always been a humanity of God and insists, against Barth, that the ascension is not merely revelation but event, that is, 'something which brings about a new state of affairs. History is decisive'.[145] Here, Gunton makes a clear distinction between the immanent and economic Trinity to argue that Jesus is humanly taken into the eternity of God and lives as the mediator. This does not, he says, imply a change in the inner being of God.

Gunton does not wish to see the resurrection as a retroactive force in Pannenberg's sense which implies that Jesus's oneness with God was realized in the resurrection, and thus that 'he was not uniquely one with the Father [before the resurrection], but that after it he is made to have been one with him all along'.[146] In Gunton's view, Pannenberg's thinking also underplays the fact that the Holy Spirit is 'the one by whom we understand Jesus to have been from the beginning one with the Father'.[147] Gunton wants to give the Spirit structural significance in Jesus's human life which he finds missing from both Pannenberg and Barth. Gunton is therefore critical of the fact that the ascension has often been treated as an appendix to the resurrection 'as for example in Barth's treatment of the virgin birth and resurrection as miracles to mark the beginning and end of Jesus' earthly life'.[148] By contrast, Gunton argues that it is the ascension 'that establishes Jesus as the eternal mediator between heaven and earth, by virtue of that which he did and suffered as man'.

---

143 See, for example, Molnar, *Incarnation and Resurrection*, chapters one and four.

144 Gunton, *Christ and Creation*, 65.

145 Gunton, *Christ and Creation*, 65–6.

146 Gunton, *Christ and Creation*, 66.

147 Gunton, *Christ and Creation*, 66.

148 Gunton, *Christ and Creation*, 66–7.

Ascension thus completes 'the earthwards movement of the Son, the opening of heaven to earth'.[149]

Interestingly, many of Gunton's criticisms of Barth are echoed by Douglas Farrow in his important book on the Ascension. Farrow also accuses Barth of a kind of Christomonism and Docetism. He also believes that a residue of natural theology caused Barth to define eternity by time and that Barth's doctrine of election 'seals the historical Jesus in eternity'.[150] However, like Gunton, Farrow tends to separate God's actions in his Word and Spirit, as for example, when he criticizes T. F. Torrance saying: 'To look beyond Jesus' humanity to the operation of his divinity in order to explain his "towering authority" over the world is a move that runs counter to everything we have been saying. We must look instead to the Spirit …'.[151] Why should we look to the Spirit *instead* of the Word? Should we not instead look to the Spirit to be enlightened by the Word through sharing in his new humanity, as T. F. Torrance rightly held?[152] In Farrow's view 'it is only by means of the Spirit … that this human work of filling and fulfilling, satisfying and perfecting, is achieved'.[153] Why *only* by the Spirit? Can we separate the Spirit from the Word at this important point without falling into some form of Docetism or adoptionism? It is no accident that Farrow totally rejects any idea of a *Logos asarkos* while, as we have seen earlier, Barth insisted that such an idea was essential to enable us to see the free basis that God's actions ad extra have in the inner being of God.

149 Gunton, *Christ and Creation*, 67.

150 In light of the lengthy statement from Barth just cited (in text at n. 140) indicating that election (predestination) must never be understood as 'rigid and fixed' and thus cannot be regarded as simply belonging to the past since it is 'an act of divine life in the Spirit', this is a strange statement by Farrow.

151 Farrow, *Ascension and Ecclesia*, 266.

152 See, for example, *The Trinitarian Faith*, 248ff. Following Athanasius, Torrance writes: 'It is because the Word and the Spirit mutually inhere in one another that the Holy Spirit is not dumb but eloquent of Christ the incarnate Word' (249, see also 267ff.). For Torrance, Jesus 'makes our humanity in him partake of the Holy Spirit with which he has been anointed and sanctified *as man* for our sakes, and thereby unites it through himself with the Godhead. It is that perfected or consecrated humanity in Jesus Christ which constitutes the life-giving substance of the Church and the perpetual source of its renewal' (267).

153 Farrow, *Ascension and Ecclesia*, 267.

This thinking leads to the odd conclusion that Jesus's *human* pre-existence is what is being referred to in the gospel of John, a view that Gunton himself rightly criticizes. Even more puzzlingly, as seen in Chapter 3, Farrow contends: 'That he [Jesus] goes [ascends] makes him the way [to the Father].'[154] This is reminiscent of Gunton's observation that the ascension 'establishes Jesus as the eternal mediator … by virtue of that which he did and suffered as man'. However, is it really by virtue of his human actions that Jesus *becomes* the mediator and the way to the Father? Or is it not the case that mysteriously and miraculously from the very beginning of his earthly way, Jesus was the way to the Father and the eternal mediator, just because he was the Word incarnate? Farrow insists that 'Jesus-history' rather than Jesus the incarnate Word as the living subject of these events, is his theological criterion. However, in my view it is precisely his understanding of Jesus-history, which as we have already seen, is defined as 'the sanctification of our humanity through the life and passion and heavenly intercession of Jesus',[155] that leaves out the most important ingredient in Christology that Barth's theology supplies – namely the fact that it is precisely because this man was God himself active among us that leads to the sanctification of our humanity in his, through the activity of the Holy Spirit. Importantly, Farrow believes that people today stumble more over Jesus's humanity than his divinity. Yet his very analysis shows that the greatest problem today is the same as it always has been: the attempt to construct a Christology that bypasses Jesus's actual uniqueness as truly divine and human without separation or confusion.

In fact, Barth's theology never loses its emphasis on the unity of the Word and Spirit acting ad extra because Barth insisted that Father, Son and Spirit were also one ad intra and indeed he insists that our sanctification is traceable to the action of God incarnate and not to Jesus's human action as such. This is why Barth continually stresses that true theological knowledge takes place in faith as a work of God in and through our human activity without mixture and confusion of divine and human action.[156] As noted earlier, Farrow's thinking leads him to search for a 'eucharistic world-view'[157] while Barth clearly and correctly recognized that *all* world-views represent human attempts to avoid the

---

154 Farrow, *Ascension and Ecclesia*, 36.
155 Farrow, *Ascension and Ecclesia*, 6.
156 See, for example, *CD* II/1, 55f.
157 Farrow, *Ascension and Ecclesia*, 73, 78.

Lordship of Jesus Christ.[158] In Barth's thinking any such search betrays its docetic tendency at the outset by allowing a world view rather than the living Christ to be its criterion of theological truth. Beyond that, the very idea that Jesus humanly preexisted his birth on earth[159] – even if it is understood retroactively in Farrow's sense – suggests a docetic understanding of humanity just because it cannot admit that Jesus's humanity is just as fully limited as ours, in the sense that it came into being at a particular point in time. It is just here that a proper understanding of the *Logos asarkos* would have allowed Farrow to make a distinction made by Barth. He could have said that, while God's eternal decree is to be God for us, and that while this decree indicates God's eternal attitude toward the world (with Jesus Christ as the beginning of all God's ways and works ad extra), still God is and remains the free Lord of both his inner life and his works ad extra. Therefore one cannot collapse God's pretemporal, supratemporal and posttemporal existence manifested in the history of Jesus into 'Jesus-history' without calling into question God's freedom in se which is the basis, meaning and goal of all created freedom. In my opinion this is indeed what finally happens to Farrow when he concludes: 'here, in this man, we encounter an expression of the love of God that has eternal validity'.[160] Why does he not say that here, in this man we encounter God himself – not just *an* expression of God's love – but God himself in the flesh as the subject of this event in his unity with the Holy Spirit loving us in the sending of his only begotten Son into the world for our salvation (Jn. 3: 16)?

With respect to Barth's view of Christ's ascension, he argues that the resurrection and ascension add 'only the new fact that in this event He was to be seen and was actually seen as the One He was and is. He did not become different in this event'.[161] What did Barth mean by this? He meant that the significance of Jesus's resurrection and ascension 'is not to be found in a continuation of His being in a changed form which is its fulfilment. The being of Jesus Christ was and is perfect and complete in itself in His history as the true Son of God and Son of Man. It does not need to be transcended or augmented by new qualities or further developments'.[162] Rather, the covenant was indeed fulfilled in him with the reconciliation of the world.

158 See, for example, *CD* IV/3.1, 254ff. and Chapter 3.
159 Farrow, *Ascension and Ecclesia*, 297.
160 Farrow, *Ascension and Ecclesia*, 293.
161 *CD* IV/2, 133.
162 *CD* IV/2, 132.

His being as such (if we may be permitted this abstraction for a moment) was and is the end of the old and the beginning of the new form of this world even without His resurrection and ascension. He did not and does not lack anything in Himself. What was lacking was only the men to see and hear it as the work and Word of God – the praise and thanksgiving and obedience of their thoughts and words and works.[163]

Does this mean that the historical events of resurrection and ascension then were unnecessary or meaningless? No. What Barth intends to say is that the power of the resurrection was not absent from the life of Jesus even before the actual occurrences and that the actual occurrences mean the disclosure of his glory and the exaltation of humanity in him.

In fact, Barth's understanding of this matter is anti-docetic: 'Like all men, the man Jesus has His lifetime … a fixed span with a particular duration … The eternal content of his life must not cause us to miss or to forget or to depreciate this form … as though we could see and have the content without it … It is as a man of His time, and not otherwise that He is the Lord of time.'[164] For Barth, 'At bottom Docetism is "the failure to respect the historically unique character of the redemptive deed of Christ".'[165] In this context Barth insists on the historical nature of the resurrection because as a man of his time Jesus appeared among the apostles as 'the Resurrected'.[166] It was by their specific historical memory of the 40 days and not by some timeless idea that the apostles and churches they founded lived in relation to Jesus.

In his physical resurrection from the dead Jesus is the 'Revealer of His hidden glory as God's eternal Word incarnate'.[167] However, this has significance for us because, as Jn. 20:30 says: 'These [signs] are recorded so that you may believe that Jesus is the Christ, the Son of God, and that believing this you may have life through his name.' Barth also insists that the ascension, together with the empty tomb, are indispensable for understanding the Easter message. They 'mark the limits of the Easter period'.[168] Both are indicated rather than described because for Barth

---

163 *CD* IV/2 132–3.
164 *CD* III/2, 440.
165 *CD* III/2, 441.
166 *CD* III/2, 442.
167 *CD* III/2, 451.
168 *CD* III/2, 452.

the content of the New Testament witness was neither the empty tomb nor the fact that the disciples saw Jesus 'go up to heaven',[169] but 'that when they had lost Him through death they were sought and found by Him as the Resurrected'.[170] The empty tomb and ascension therefore are signs of Easter as the virgin birth is the sign of the nativity.

For Barth the ascension serves a positive function by pointing forward and upward. As the empty tomb marks the beginning of Easter history, so the ascension marks its end. Still, for Barth 'the ascension – Jesus's disappearance into heaven – is the sign of the Resurrected, not the Resurrected Himself'.[171] For Barth the point of the ascension then is that when Jesus left the disciples, 'He entered the side of the created world [heaven] which was provisionally inaccessible and incomprehensible ... This does not mean ... that he ceased to be a creature'.[172] He was a creature who lived and acted as God incarnate and now had been taken up into heaven and would come again. He would be with them always even to the end of the world (Matt. 28:20). This is an important text that Barth often repeats in order to stress that it is the living Jesus Christ who is risen and ascended and that it is indeed this same glorified Jesus Christ who is the object of faith and hope and who will come again to complete for the rest of history what was a completed event for us in his history. For Barth, 'The ascension is the proleptic sign of the *parousia*, pointing to the Son of Man who will finally and visibly emerge from the concealment of His heavenly existence and come on the clouds of heaven (Mt. 24:30)'.[173] The ascension is thus indispensable as a sign of the fact that at the conclusion of the Easter history Jesus is not to be sought in any kind of hiddenness but in the hiddenness of God, a hiddenness that 'burgeons with the conclusive revelation still awaited in the future'.[174]

While Barth might agree with Gunton that Jesus's ascension completes the earthward movement of the Son, his thinking certainly calls into question Gunton's belief that Jesus is established as the mediator by virtue of that which he did and suffered as man. For Barth the mystery and miracle that Jesus Christ was and is means that what he

---

169 *CD* III/2, 453.
170 *CD* III/2, 453.
171 *CD* III/2, 453.
172 *CD* III/2, 454.
173 *CD* III/2, 454.
174 *CD* III/2, 454.

did and suffered as man disclosed who he was and what he actually accomplished by virtue of who he was. From the beginning, that is, from his conception, Jesus was already the mediator in a mysterious and miraculous way because he was the Word incarnate. This activity obviously did not take place without the action of the Holy Spirit. This was indeed the power of the resurrection that was hidden from the disciples and revealed in the Easter history. Jesus himself was and is actively the mediator as the only man who was God. Thus when T. F. Torrance finds Jesus's 'towering authority' in his divinity, this insight is not opposed to the fact that the Spirit enables Jesus's free human activity; rather this insight complements the fact that Jesus could reconcile the world and could forgive sins because he was uniquely the Son of God in the flesh. That is why theological knowledge is the knowledge of faith – it begins by, in and through the Holy Spirit who unites us to Christ as the one who speaks his Word as a revelation of the Father. According to Barth, Jesus's resurrection revealed that he was and is 'the bearer of all power in heaven and earth'.[175] In this sense, the ascension is the concluding form of the Risen Christ's appearances by which he created faith and created the Church. Barth also stresses Calvin's view that the ascension is

> the *end* of these appearances of the Risen One … God's revelation having taken place once and for all in Christ, the Ascension makes a separation, a distance between Him and His disciples, between Him and the world generally. Ended is the time of His direct, His 'worldly' presence in the world, to which the forty days unmistakably belonged. There dawns – one could also say, there returns, the time of the *Church*.[176]

In the time between the resurrection and ascension and his second coming Jesus is present indirectly and in faith as God and man and through the Holy Spirit so that reconciliation may be acknowledged and lived as free grace: 'It is no longer and not yet the time for the "beholding of His glory" (Jn. i. 14; cf. 2 Cor. v. 7)'.[177]

175 Barth, *Credo*, 113.
176 Barth, *Credo*, 113–14.
177 Barth, *Credo*, 114. For an important and helpful discussion of Christ's 'threefold' *Parousia* in Barth, see Drury, *The Resurrected God*, 131ff., the first referring to Christ's resurrection (the Easter history), the second to Christ's intermediate form of presence in the outpouring of the Holy Spirit as the

The difference between Barth and Farrow and Gunton then concerns the fact that for Barth the ascension shows the kind of power Jesus exercised in his earthly life and in his risen and ascended life. Farrow and Gunton insist that something new happened in history to Jesus and that history is determinative here. Barth insists that something new happened to Jesus in history too, but that it is the power of the Word incarnate that is determinative here. Thus, for Barth we must acknowledge that Christ's history was a completed event while at the same time we must acknowledge that he is coming again to complete the redemption which is a reality in his risen and ascended existence, as the hope of our future. Here once again a clear distinction between the immanent and economic Trinity allows Barth to steer clear of any suggestion that history rather than God acting within history determines past, present and future meaning.

Conclusion

More than any other modern theologian, besides Thomas F. Torrance, Colin E. Gunton sees the importance of a contemporary doctrine of the immanent Trinity. Gunton clearly wishes to avoid any sort of illegitimate agnosticism and the pantheism and dualism that follow. He vigorously opposes any sort of projectionism. Further, he certainly avoids grounding theology in transcendental experience and sees that everything looks different in the light of the Trinity. He wishes to maintain Christ's uniqueness and particularity and makes every effort to avoid any sort of modalism or idealism.

But in recent years especially, Gunton has become more and more critical of Barth's theology because he believes that Barth paid less attention to Jesus's humanity and to ours. This critique is based on Gunton's belief that Barth's doctrine of the Spirit is inadequate. I have contrasted

---

presence of Christ between his resurrection and ascension and his second and final return at the end as the goal of history (the third form). While some of Drury's analysis is indeed problematic, as when he claims that 'God is the source, event, and result of Christ's resurrection' (178), there is a great deal of helpful information showing the connection between Barth's trinitarian theology and his view of the resurrection. See my review of this book in the *Journal of Theological Studies*, vol. 67, no. 1 (2016), 380–3.

Gunton and Barth on key theological issues that Gunton himself suggests might allow for greater emphasis on history and humanity to show that Barth's doctrine of the Spirit requires, in a way that Gunton's does not, that there can be no separation of the Spirit and Word without falling into the dangers of Ebionite and Docetic Christology. Ultimately, the difficulty here concerns the fact that Gunton is willing to abstract from Jesus's being as the Word in areas of his reflection and then search for transcendentals or analogies grounded in a concept of relationality that is not always dictated by the immanent Trinity.

Chapter 11

CONCLUSION

There is a thread that runs through this book. That thread suggests that there is a tendency today among theologians to allow experience, history or some principle of relationality rather than the Word of God revealed to dictate the meaning of theological categories. A contemporary doctrine of the immanent Trinity should recognize that while the formulation of the doctrine of the Trinity begins with an experience of God in the economy, it nonetheless directs us away from our experiences and ideas and toward God's Word and Spirit as the source of theological knowledge. To be sure, God meets us in our experiences of faith and hope and enables us to know and love him and thus also to love others; but the object of trinitarian reflection is and remains God and never becomes our experiences of faith, hope or love. In this sense, the doctrine of the immanent Trinity is a description of who God is who meets us in and through our experiences and not simply a description of salvation history or of our experiences of faith, hope and love. We have seen repeatedly that whenever and wherever theologians think the doctrine is simply a way of describing the Christian experiences of faith, hope, love or salvation, such thinking invariably substitutes some form of trinitarian thinking for the trinitarian God acting ad extra. We have also seen that while the triune God eternally elects us in his Son Jesus Christ and thus acts freely as our creator, reconciler and redeemer, it would be a mistake to logically reverse the doctrines of election and the Trinity; such a reversal inevitably leads to thinking that advances the idea that history in some sense constitutes God's triunity. That manner of thinking always ends by reducing the immanent to the economic Trinity with problematic results.

It has been my contention that there are at least four indicators that suggest that much trinitarian theology today has failed to recognize the need for a suitable doctrine of the immanent Trinity. As we have seen, these indicators are: (1) the trend toward making God, in some sense, dependent on and indistinguishable from history; (2) the lack of precision in Christology which leads to the idea that Jesus, in his humanity as such is the revealer; (3) the failure to distinguish the Holy Spirit from the human spirit; (4) a trend to begin theology with experiences of self-transcendence, thus allowing experience rather than the object of faith to determine the truth of theology.

I have argued that a proper doctrine of the immanent Trinity is one that recognizes, respects and upholds God's freedom in se and ad extra; a doctrine that realizes that human freedom is grounded in God's freedom for us exercised in his Word and Spirit. I have stressed that such a doctrine will not become embroiled in what Rahner called wild conceptual acrobatics by speculating about God's inner nature in abstraction from God's own self-communication in the economic Trinity. I have argued that a proper doctrine of the immanent Trinity will acknowledge that our relations with God are irreversible so that while we can and must say that we meet the immanent Trinity in our encounter with the economic Trinity, still we cannot simply assert that the economic Trinity *is* the immanent Trinity and vice versa. Instead, as Barth insisted, a 'deliberate and sharp distinction' must be drawn; one that allows for the fact of God's free grace.

I have stressed therefore that theologians should neither separate nor confuse the immanent and economic Trinity and that because theology really is faith (in the triune God), as enabled by the Holy Spirit uniting us to Christ and through him to the Father, seeking understanding and not understanding seeking faith, we must adhere to the economic Trinity for our information about the immanent Trinity. This is crucial, because even some theologians who, as we have seen, do not deny the relevance of the immanent Trinity altogether, tend to allow some principle of relationality, history, temporality or transcendence and immanence to be defined first from a general ontology based on some form of transcendental experience. Only then do they turn to the economy to see how the doctrine of the Trinity may enrich that ontology. We have even seen how some theologians virtually substitute election for the immanent Trinity with the result that even the eternal triune God's very existence as Father, Son and Holy Spirit is conceived to be constituted by election. Thus, the very idea that God exists only for his revelation or for the sake of his revelation is embraced; such thinking, I have argued, is at variance with Karl Barth's most important insights regarding the doctrine of the immanent Trinity. I have tried to show that a contemporary doctrine of the immanent Trinity would prevent any such thinking simply because it would lead to the positive recognition that God has in fact exercised his transcendent freedom to be for us specifically in Christ and the Spirit. These are not just concepts describing Christian experience however; they are not concepts that we invest with meaning according to our own social, psychological, historical, political or even theological goals and ideals. Jesus Christ and the Holy Spirit cannot be ignored or bypassed even for a moment because in fact there is no other way to God the Father than through the Son. This is not an imperialistic projection of Christian self-consciousness, nor is it in any sense an attempt to open up a gap between the immanent and the economic Trinity since, as I have argued, there is only one eternal Trinity who acts for us in his Word and Spirit, such that the immanent Trinity cannot be separated from the economic Trinity any more than, in virtue of election and of the incarnation, Christ's humanity can be separated from his divinity. However, of course, they cannot be confused or blended together either. We are bound by the grace and thus also by the judgment of God to Jesus Christ, the incarnate Son, to know God and to live in freedom. So finding our way to God the Father through Christ and in his Holy Spirit can be nothing but a humble acceptance of God's actual judgment and grace which, because God is truly free in himself, God can and does exercise effectively for us throughout history, including now and in the future.

I have agreed with Karl Barth, who believed that the content of the doctrine of the Trinity is that God is the eternal Father, Son and Holy Spirit and that God's internal relations could not be reduced to God's relations with us as creator, mediator and redeemer. This fact itself, which is in accord with T. F. Torrance's view that what God is toward us, he is eternally in himself, is indeed the surest of facts, beyond which there can be no other which can serve as the root of the doctrine of the Trinity today. There is no escaping Athanasius's observation that: 'It is more pious and more accurate to signify God from the Son and call him Father, than to name him from his works and call him Unoriginate.' The central difficulty surrounding contemporary trinitarian theology is precisely the failure to stick to this particular approach to God. From this Athanasian insight it follows that God can only be known with certainty and clarity from God himself as he includes us in his own eternal knowing and loving through faith and by grace and thus by revelation. Every attempt to understand the Christian God that bypasses the Son of God incarnate amounts to a human attempt to construct the image of God without God himself and even against God himself, even if that attempt may claim to be eminently theological and its claims construct an ontology based on Christian doctrines such as election, salvation or grace.

This very limitation then is what is still disregarded most in contemporary trinitarian theology. Karl Rahner, who is considered one of the preeminent theologians of the twentieth century, and who, with Karl Barth, was famous for having restored the doctrine to the center of Christian faith and practice, did not allow Jesus Christ to be his exclusive starting point as Barth surely did. Therefore, in that very way, he bypassed the sure foundation for trinitarian theology and, as we have seen, he allowed his thinking about the Trinity to be shaped not only by his analysis of transcendental experience, but also by his philosophy and theology of the symbol. The result was a kind of universalism that claimed that we can experience Christ and Christ's resurrection without knowing about him specifically, and by simply thematizing our own transcendental experiences. I have addressed his work extensively because his methodology has affected so many other modern theologians, whose work is a logical outworking of his faulty premises.

This is a form of self-justifying theology that I have shown to be excluded from a trinitarian theology that begins and ends its reflections with Jesus Christ himself who is the Son of God incarnate simply because he is – without any need for proof or verification from Christian experience or ideology. His existence in history for us simply calls for acknowledgment, not verification – only he can verify who he is in and through the power of his Holy Spirit. One of the key functions of a proper doctrine of the immanent Trinity is to allow for the fact that God sets the terms for theological insight; not the church and certainly not humanity with its questions and insights, however important they may be, humanly speaking.

I have discussed Karl Barth's deliberate and consistent rejection of Ebionite and Docetic Christology because it reflected his constant attempt to begin his trinitarian theology with Jesus Christ himself and not with some idea of divinity or some experience of Jesus's importance for the community. This led him to a clear distinction (but not a separation) of the immanent and economic Trinity. We have seen that this is still not the dominant view today. We have also seen that much modern theology of the Trinity tends to assume that Jesus is in some sense the revealer in his humanity as such. This lack of precision in Christology leads to an emphasis on Jesus's humanity that tends to ignore the all-important fact that this man was and is God and it thus also underplays the consequent need for faith in him as he truly is before understanding who we are and what we are liberated to be in him. Even the most sophisticated contemporary trinitarian theologies seem to allow an emphasis on the Holy Spirit to displace the action of the Word in union with the Holy Spirit. For some, there is a tendency to confuse the Holy Spirit with the human spirit. For others, there is the tendency toward adoptionism and thus toward the separation of the Word and Spirit. Yet if T. F. Torrance and Karl Barth are right in stressing that the very center of Christian theology concerns the fact that Jesus really was God, then any adoptionist overtones simply reflect the fact that contemporary theology finds it difficult, perhaps even a little embarrassing, that it must begin at this particular place and this place alone, namely, with Jesus who is the eternally begotten Son of the Father who came down from heaven for us and for our salvation.

A proper doctrine of the immanent Trinity that made a 'deliberate and sharp' distinction between the immanent and economic Trinity would continually return to Jesus Christ himself, prompted by his Holy Spirit to understand divine and human freedom. Since such a doctrine speaks of the eternal Father, Son and Spirit as the foundation for human freedom and for the relative independence of the created world in general, proper theological thinking can never be agnostic. Agnostic thinking, as we have seen, speaks of a divine incomprehensibility as of a void left for us to fill with as many images of transcendence (and/or immanence) as we can muster. However, we have seen that a proper doctrine of the immanent Trinity indicates at once the danger and irrelevance of such thinking. God's being and act are God's very definite acts as creator, lord, reconciler and redeemer; they are the acts of God who is eternally the Father, Son and Holy Spirit. These are not just freely chosen symbols drawn from human experience but, as Barth boldly maintained, statements of who God, the immanent Trinity eternally is and would have been even if he never decided to create and relate with us; there is, as Barth powerfully maintained, nothing higher or better to God than that God is the eternal Father, Son and Holy Spirit. He is in eternity as he has revealed himself to be and this must be seen and stated without introducing gender or other limited human experiences into the divine being, as we have seen. While God is and remains incomprehensible even in his revelation, he nevertheless is known and knowable as a very definite object in faith and by grace; that is why Barth helpfully distinguished between God's primary and secondary objectivity. Here is the true mystery of the triune God that is at once both veiled and unveiled by God's own act. God is not an object we can control existentially either in thought or in prayer; but the Christian God is still Emmanuel – God with us. Yet this God is and remains the only divine subject in the encounter and the roles may never be reversed. A sound doctrine of the immanent Trinity recognizes this freedom of God in his grace, mercy and love as the basis of our own human freedom and our own ability to love God and love our neighbor; it recognizes what Barth referred to as the antecedent existence of the Father, Son and Spirit. Every theology that fails to allow this antecedent existence to shape what is said about the immanent and economic Trinity also fails to respect God's judgment and grace and thus fails to explicate truly who God is and who we are in relation to God.

It is unfortunate but true that wherever this false kind of agnosticism is allowed to function, namely, in theologies that do not keep to God's economic trinitarian self-revelation, God becomes dependent on creation, history and humanity in some way, shape or form. This dependence, we have seen, dominates the thinking of those who explicitly reject, ignore or merely pay lip service to a doctrine of the immanent Trinity. It also affects the thinking of those who accept the doctrine but see it mainly as a description of the events of salvation or the experience of salvation. It especially affects the thinking of those who believe that election and the Trinity should be logically reversed, as well as those who, while recognizing the problem in this reversal, embrace the thinking that underlies such a misguided proposal. Any such dependence, however, whether it is blatantly untheological or apparently profoundly theological, represents a failure to respect the fact that God alone reveals God. God alone establishes and maintains fellowship (communion) between himself and creatures. Consequently, pantheism is one of the chief threats to contemporary trinitarian theology. If God cannot in fact be distinguished from our own experiences and thoughts about ourselves and the world we live in, as he certainly cannot in a pantheistic or panentheistic view, then trinitarian theology, for all its attempts to reinvigorate the Christian life, actually makes Christianity more irrelevant than ever. What could be more irrelevant than a theology that really believes trinitarian life is our life or that we become by grace what God is by nature? Our life is doomed to death and in need of a reconciler and redeemer. Our new life is hidden with Christ in God. Pantheism, which makes the truth dependent on one's point of view, never even sees the need for another outside itself, because from the very outset, pantheism identifies God with creation and sees them as in some sense mutually dependent. It is precisely such thinking that places the key to salvation in the hands of Christians as they attempt to live the Christian life. However, it is just such a form of self-reliance that has been rendered illusory by what has happened on our behalf in the history of Jesus Christ himself and his ongoing history, through the Spirit and in the Church and world today. A proper doctrine of the immanent Trinity would recognize God's freedom in such a way that our constant need for Jesus's active Lordship would lead us away from any sort of self-reliance or self-justification and toward Jesus Christ coming again. He is the only one who is and remains the way, the truth and the life – neither an idea of him nor an experience of him and not a doctrine about him – but Jesus the risen, ascended and advent Lord himself, who guides us now in truth through his Holy Spirit.

We therefore end where we began, that is, with a recognition of God's freedom to be and to have been the eternal Father, Son and Spirit who existed prior to and apart from creation; we also recognize that God is not limited by his freedom *in se* so that he is also free to be for us in a way that surpasses all forms of created communion. This freedom for us which includes both judgment and grace, is the surest of facts on which a theology of the Trinity can indeed build. However, it is a fact that will only be clearly seen and understood where and when a clear doctrine of the immanent Trinity is expressed. Such a doctrine, as we have seen, necessarily maintains a 'deliberate and sharp' distinction between the immanent and the economic Trinity in each of its theological reflections.

APPENDIX

Since I have relied on the thinking of Thomas F. Torrance throughout this book, I think it would be instructive to explore Colin Gunton's criticisms of Torrance's trinitarian theology which appear in a volume on the theology of T. F. Torrance titled *The Promise of Trinitarian Theology: Theologians in Dialogue with T. F. Torrance*. My goal here is to clarify a number of important issues that have emerged in our attempt to construct a proper doctrine of the immanent Trinity. In addition, I would like to explore however briefly, the problem of the *filioque* which has not yet been discussed.

We begin with four critical issues which Gunton considers in relation to the doctrine of the immanent Trinity. The first concerns the justification for a theological move from the economic to the immanent Trinity and in this regard Gunton believes Torrance's method is generally the same as Barth's, that is, God is toward us what he is in himself. The second question concerns the function of the doctrine. Here Gunton insists that Torrance properly opted for a distinction between the immanent and economic Trinity in order to reject any idealist attempt to confuse the two by confusing the order of knowing with the order of being, as Rahner apparently had done. Again, Torrance is perceived to be similar to Barth here. It is in connection with the third and fourth points that Gunton's criticisms of T. F. Torrance emerge.

Let us consider these briefly as they relate especially to a doctrine of the immanent Trinity. How should we understand the terms 'being' and 'person'? Gunton rightly notes that for Torrance we do not begin thinking about the triune God either with God's oneness or his threeness but rather with the fact that God is simultaneously one being, three persons. Still, Gunton finds fault with Torrance's use of the term *perichoresis*. Accordingly, he believes that for Torrance *perichoresis* 'serves to hold powerfully together ... the identity of the divine Being and the intrinsic unity of the three divine Persons'.[1] This, Gunton believes, is not the usual function of the term; its usual function, he thinks, is to show 'how three distinct persons can yet constitute one God'. Thus, according to Gunton, Torrance believes that *perichoresis* led to a new concept of persons in which 'the relations between persons belongs to what they are'. He, therefore, says that its meaning, for Torrance, is derived mainly from the economy 'rather than in reflection on the relation of the eternal persons'.[2]

Is this really what Torrance believes? A close reading of Torrance on his understanding of *perichoresis* shows that his use of the term is intimately connected with the term *homoousion* and that its meaning is strictly governed 'by the mutual indwelling of the Father and the Son and the Spirit'.[3] Torrance notes that Gregory Nazianzen originally used the term to speak of Christ's divine and human natures, but that it was then changed to refer to 'the complete mutual containing or interpenetration of the three divine Persons, Father, Son and Holy Spirit, in one God'.[4] Further, Torrance insists that while it is through revelation that we know of the 'coinherent relations within the one being of God',[5] still the meaning of this concept was grounded on the relations within God's being made known in revelation. This is why Torrance insists that:

> Just as we take our knowledge of the Father from our knowledge of the Son, so we must take our knowledge of the Spirit from our knowledge of the Son, and in him from our knowledge of the Father: that is, from the inner relations which the Father, Son and Holy Spirit have with one another in the one indivisible being of the Holy Trinity.[6]

Indeed, Torrance argues that: 'It is on that inner divine basis, and not on any creaturely basis outside of God, that the life and work of Christ the incarnate Son of God are to be understood as that of the one Mediator between God and men, who is himself God and man'.[7] Therefore, it is

---

1 Colin Gunton, 'Being and Person: T. F. Torrance's Doctrine of God', in *The Promise of Trinitarian Theology: Theologians in Dialogue with T. F. Torrance* (hereafter: 'Being and Person') ed. Elmer M. Colyer (Lanham, MD: Rowman & Littlefield, 2001), 124–5.

2 Gunton, 'Being and Person', 125.

3 Torrance, *The Christian Doctrine of God*, 102.

4 Torrance, *The Christian Doctrine of God*, 102.

5 Torrance, *The Trinitarian Faith*, 305.

6 Torrance, *The Trinitarian Faith*, 306.

7 Torrance, *The Trinitarian Faith*, 308.

incorrect to suggest that *perichoresis* is understood by Torrance mainly from the economy and not from the relations of the eternal persons. Indeed it is not *perichoresis*, thus understood, that is Torrance's theological criterion, but by his own reckoning, that criterion is the inner trinitarian relations of the Father, Son and Spirit.

How does all of this relate to the understanding of being and person? Torrance follows Gregory Nazianzen in order to avoid any hint of subordinationism and to affirm a view of person that is not to be equated with 'mode of being' as Basil understood this. Of course, Gunton opposes Barth's appeal to 'mode of being' rather than person and follows Alan Torrance's view in this matter; a view that we have already discussed in Chapter 9. Gunton argues for the retrieval of the concept of the person in order to overcome problems in the Church and in the world. Such a concept, he believes, enables theology to emphasize 'the ontological compatibility of the one and the many'.[8] In relation to God, the concept enables recognition 'of divine oneness in which the individuality of the particular persons is also stressed, because Father, Son and Spirit in their interrelatedness make God to be the God that he is'.[9] Here Gunton comes dangerously near to allowing relationality, personally understood, to define who God is as Father, Son and Spirit. Can the term 'person' really do all of this? Or is it not the case that even the term 'person' must receive its meaning from the eternal Trinity? If it does, then the onto-relations of the Father, Son and Spirit would define for us the word 'person' instead of allowing the word 'person' to define both the problem of the one and the many and the inner constitution of God. For Torrance, of course, an onto-relational understanding of the trinitarian persons means 'an understanding of the three divine Persons in the one God in which the ontic relations between them belong to what they essentially are in themselves in their distinctive *hypostases*'.[10] The question that must be asked of Colin Gunton is: do the Father, Son and Spirit *make* God to be the God he is, or do they reveal the God he is from eternity to eternity in the freedom of his transcendence?

Here, Gunton once more attributes to Barth the suspicion of modalism and attempts to connect this supposed weakness in Barth with T. F. Torrance's analysis by suggesting that, because Torrance sees the trinitarian Persons as relations and because he believes that the term 'Father' is not a name for being (*ousia*), that he too is guilty of a kind of modalistic

---

8 Gunton, 'Being and Person', 126.
9 Gunton, 'Being and Person', 126.
10 Torrance, *The Christian Doctrine of God*, 102.

tendency. However, this charge neglects Torrance's important distinction between knowing God absolutely and relatively. Speaking of the Father, Son and Holy Spirit relatively refers to them as Persons in relation to each other, while speaking of Father, Son and Holy Spirit absolutely refers to their divine Being.[11] Torrance's view stems from Athanasius and Gregory Nazianzen and asserts that *ousia* refers to 'being in its internal relations and *hypostasis* as being in its objective relations'.[12] For this reason, the Persons must be seen as 'more than distinctive relations, for they really subsist, and coexist hypostatically, in the one Being of God without being confused with one another, for they are *other* than one another'.[13] Gunton also misses the fact that, for Torrance, the concept of *perichoresis* does not just indicate the oneness of the Persons but it also

> deepens and strengthens our understanding of the hypostatic distinctions within the Trinity ... it does not dissolve the distinctions between the three divine Persons unipersonally into the one Being of God ... it establishes those distinctions by showing that it is precisely through their reciprocal relations with one another, and in virtue of their incommunicable characteristics as Father, Son and Holy Spirit, that the three divine Persons constitute the very Communion which the one God eternally is, or which they eternally are.[14]

It is here that Gunton asks about the nature of that subsistence. As what, he asks, do they really subsist? He rejects Torrance's assertion that Basil identified person with modes of being and he rejects the idea that relation can describe person. However, here, he was not paying attention to Torrance, because while Torrance did say that the persons are relations relatively, he insisted that 'the *Being* of the Godhead is to be understood as fully and intrinsically *personal* as the Father of the Lord Jesus Christ'.[15] Here Gunton wishes to follow Basil and assert that persons are

11 Torrance, *The Christian Doctrine of God*, 131 and Torrance, *Trinitarian Perspectives*, 28. For more on this, see Molnar, *Torrance: Theologian of the Trinity*, 56, 65f., 209 and 344f.

12 Torrance, *Trinitarian Perspectives*, 28.

13 Torrance, *Trinitarian Perspectives*, 28.

14 Torrance, *The Christian Doctrine of God*, 175. Cf. also Molnar, 'Introduction to the Second Edition of Thomas F. Torrance's *The Christian Doctrine of God*', xxx–xxxi.

15 Torrance, *Trinitarian Perspectives*, 27.

not relations but rather 'are constituted by their relations to one another'.[16] Do we really want to say that persons are *constituted* by their relations? Do they *need* to be constituted this way? Or should we rather not say that the persons subsisting in God are who they are by virtue of their relations? The difference here concerns the implication that we can know *how* God is constituted when, in fact, we only know that he is constituted as Father, Son and Spirit from revelation. This is where Barth insisted that the *how* of the trinitarian self-revelation could not be explained but could only be accepted and then understood because such knowledge is a miracle that is begun, upheld and completed by God himself in the power of his Spirit.[17]

This is an extremely important insight recognized by Augustine, emphasized by Athanasius and repeated by Thomas F. Torrance: 'We can no more offer an account of the "how" of these divine relations and actions [than] we can define the Father, the Son and the Holy Spirit and delimit them from one another';[18] indeed Torrance cites Athanasius to stress this point: 'Thus far human knowledge goes. Here the cherubim spread the covering of their wings.'[19] For Torrance, 'just as we cannot comprehend *how* God created the world out of nothing, or *how* he brought Jesus Christ forth from the grave, so we are unable to grasp *how* his redemptive and providential activity makes all things, material as well as spiritual, to serve his eternal purpose of love'.[20] This is not an argument for agnosticism, which both Barth and Torrance reject. Rather it is a recognition that we do not know God as God knows himself and so we cannot intrude into the divine mystery with an explanation and delimitation of the persons of the Trinity.

Furthermore, the difference between Torrance and Gunton here concerns the implication that in Gunton's thought there is implied an element of causality with respect to the fact that it is suggested that their relations cause the divine unity, when in truth the divine unity exists and is manifest in and through the relations. Here, Gunton accuses Torrance of showing little interest in the way in which the persons are distinctly themselves. Yet, as we have just noted, Torrance insists that because we are not God we can only begin to think from a center in God and not from a center in ourselves. We must recognize that this center can be provided only by God in Christ and through the Holy Spirit. However,

---

16 Gunton, 'Being and Person', 128.

17 See especially *CD* I/1, 475ff.

18 Torrance, *The Christian Doctrine of God*, 193 and Barth, *CD* I/1, 475f.

19 Torrance, *The Christian Doctrine of God*, 193.

20 Torrance, *The Christian Doctrine of God*, 226. Cf. also 233.

since this is so, we cannot define and delimit the Father, Son and Holy Spirit without trying to redefine God in our own image. Torrance follows Athanasius and speaks in quite distinct ways of the Father as Creator, of the Son as Reconciler and of the Holy Spirit as the Redeemer. However, his thinking allows itself to be shaped by revelation rather than a pre-supposed notion of person. It appears that Gunton's primary concern with Torrance here is to question the traditional Western notion that the works of God ad extra are undivided. Yet the twin dangers evident in his objection to Torrance are those of tritheism and adoptionism.

How then are being and person related within the immanent Trinity? Here, Gunton cites Torrance's view that is indebted to G. L. Prestige: 'In precise theological usage *ousia* now refers to "being" not simply as that which is but to what it is in respect of its internal reality, while *hypostasis* refers to "being" not just in its independent subsistence but in its objective otherness.'[21] Gunton professes not to know what to make of these formulations and suggests that they tend toward modalism since they imply that God exists one way inwardly and another outwardly. Yet that is exactly opposed to what Torrance intended, namely, that

> while both *ousia* and *hypostasis* describe 'being' as such, in the trinitarian formulation 'one Being, three Persons', Being or οὐσία is being considered in its internal relations, and Person or ὑπόστασις is being considered in its otherness, i.e. in the objective relations between the Persons. In the case of the Father, this would amount to a distinction between the Father considered absolutely, as he is in himself, and the Father considered relatively to the Son, although of course it is one and the same Fatherly Being that is being considered . . .[22]

Hence, by making a distinction between God's absolute and relative being within the immanent Trinity, Torrance could show that God's oneness is the oneness of being of the God who is three persons, one being. For Torrance, there is no oneness of God that is not the one-ness of the being of the Father in the Son and the Spirit who, in virtue of *perichoresis*, mutually interpenetrate each other without dissolution or separation of their distinct onto-relations. Consequently, Torrance did not refer to God's inward and outward relations in this context as Gunton assumes and so he did not present any modalistically tinged

21 See Torrance, *The Christian Doctrine of God*, 130 and Gunton, 'Being and Person', 129.

22 Torrance, *The Christian Doctrine of God*, 131.

notion that God exists in one way immanently and another way economically. Such a conclusion is at variance with Torrance's most basic theological insights. In fact Torrance insists that what God is toward us he is in himself, and that precisely is one God who is equally divine as Father, Son and Spirit ad intra and ad extra. On this fact rests the validity of the incarnation, reconciliation and redemption.

Gunton believes that Torrance's emphasis on the *homoousion* leads him to stress God's being 'at the expense of the divine *persons*'.[23] Gunton attributes this to his belief that Torrance reads Eastern Orthodox theologians too much through Western eyes, especially through Augustinian eyes. As in other writings, Gunton appears to place these issues in the context of the problem of the one and the many. That at least raises the question of whether or not we are dealing primarily with God's being and act or with the philosophical problem of the one and the many.

While it must be admitted that the Eastern Fathers are often read through Western eyes, I do not believe this charge is a proper one to level at Torrance. Gunton argues that Torrance's vision is more patristic than biblical; there is little exegesis of scripture in his trinitarian texts. Indeed, according to Gunton, Torrance's main effort is to choose texts that allow him to unify the immanent and economic Trinity as much as possible. Here Gunton wishes that Torrance would have paid more attention to the 'apparently subordinationist texts of 1 Corinthians 15 and some of those in the Fourth Gospel'.[24] But what is the point here? Torrance is very clear, for instance, that Jesus freely shared our ignorance. He very clearly rejects Docetism and adoptionism as dualistic attempts to read the New Testament without accepting the 'non-dualist frame of reference deriving from Israel'.[25] However, he also insists that while the incarnate Son is subordinate to the Father, such subordinationism cannot be read back into the immanent Trinity.[26] Further,

23 Gunton, 'Being and Person', 129.

24 Gunton, 'Being and Person', 129.

25 See Torrance, *Space, Time and Resurrection*, 42. See also *The Christian Doctrine of God*, chapter 3, 'The Biblical Frame' and his books *Incarnation* (ed.) Walker and *The Atonement: The Person and Work of Christ*, ed. Robert T. Walker (Downers Grove, IL: InterVarsity Press, 2009) for fairly extensive biblical references.

26 Here Torrance differs from Barth, who believes that there was 'a superiority and a subordination' (*CD* IV/1, 201ff.) within God on the basis of which he could say that in the incarnation, it is God's own obedience that we meet in Jesus's human obedience. Barth's thinking here is indeed intriguing,

Footnote 26 (*cont.*)

and he makes every effort to distinguish the immanent and economic Trinity, while avoiding heretical notions of subordinationism and modalism. Still, an ambiguity in his own thought remains as when he describes the incarnation: 'He does not do it [become incarnate] without any correspondence to, but as the strangely logical final continuation of, the history in which He is God' (203). If the obedience of the Son of God incarnate is the continuation of the history of his obedience in the immanent Trinity, where is the distinction between God's free existence as Father, Son and Spirit who did not need to become incarnate (which Barth also insists upon even in this context) and his free new action ad extra? There is an ambiguity here and it may be due to the fact that the element of subordinationism that Barth thinks that he can maintain without compromising the equality of the persons in the immanent Trinity is the result of thinking that the Son and Spirit were 'caused' by the Father in the Basilian sense rejected by Torrance. Or it may be due to the fact that Barth has unwittingly read back the Son's incarnate action on our behalf into the immanent Trinity instead of seeing it consistently as a condescension grounded in God's eternal love and freedom. Even if one translates the original *wunderbar konsequenter letzter Fortsetzung* (*KD* IV/1, 223) saying 'wonderfully consistent final continuation', or perhaps even 'miraculously final continuation', instead of 'logical final continuation', and even if one stresses, as Barth does, that this is in 'correspondence' with God's eternal history, there still remains the difficulty attached to the word *Fortsetzung* (continuation), which seems to suggest a blurring of the distinction between God's internal and external actions. For discussion of some additional difficulties and for a full discussion of the differences between Torrance and Barth on these issues, see Molnar, 'The obedience of the Son in the theology of Karl Barth and of Thomas F. Torrance', *SJT* (2014) and *Faith, Freedom, and the Spirit*, chapter seven. See also Molnar, 'The Importance of the Doctrine of Justification in the Theology of Thomas F. Torrance and of Karl Barth' *SJT*, vol. 70, no. 1 (2017). For George Hunsinger's insightful view of these matters, see *Reading Barth with Charity*, 115–27. Importantly, Hunsinger suggests that it might have been better if Barth stuck to his earlier view regarding super and subordination within the immanent Trinity expressed in *CD* III/2, 371: 'For all the rich differentiation of God, there is no higher and lower in his unity, no prior and posterior in his individual perfections. There is order in God, but no subordination or superordination'. Hunsinger concludes by saying that he 'cannot see that Barth's doctrine of antecedence would have required anything more' (117). This conclusion is right on target and if Barth had stuck to this position then Barth would not have opened himself to the charge by T. F. Torrance that there was a residual element of subordinationism in his doctrine of the Trinity. As I have argued, Torrance was more consistent in not confusing the order of the persons

Torrance is crystal clear about the fact that the human Jesus never exists except as the Word incarnate. Is Gunton in search of a human Jesus here who can be understood without regard for the fact that this man was and is the eternally begotten Son of the Father? Torrance's scriptural exegesis actually makes much of Matt. 11:27 and of Jesus's bodily resurrection not only to stress that what God is toward us he is in himself, but that if we are to know God in accordance with God's own nature, our knowledge must be grounded in a center in God himself. This is how Torrance could maintain 'the integrity and wholeness of the humanity of the Incarnate Son.'[27] This commits him to a reading of scripture as a whole in such a way that Jesus, the incarnate Word is the one who unifies his reading of it. It is for this reason that there is, for Torrance, no way that scripture can be read to imply subordinationism within the immanent Trinity. This is not just a patristic insight but a biblically based patristic insight.

Gunton wonders whether Torrance reads the *homoousion* back into Athanasius himself in such a way as to compromise the 'particular being of the three persons'[28] as when he writes that 'the fullness of the Father's Being is the Being of the Son and of the Spirit.'[29] Is this statement a valid reading of Athanasius' belief in 'the all-holy Father of Christ beyond all created being'?[30] The first question to be asked of Gunton is whether we want to speak of the 'particular being' of the persons of the Trinity at all. Does this not tend toward tritheism? Torrance insists that the particularity of the Father, Son and Spirit is not the particularity of particular beings but of three uniquely divine persons in the one being of God. This is indeed the gist of his books on Trinity. Hence Torrance's emphasis in this context is that Father, Son and Spirit are always both together and individually fully God. What is more, if the statement quoted by Gunton is read in context, it is very clear that Torrance does not blur the particularities of the Father, Son and Spirit and does not distort Athanasius. When Torrance said that 'the Father's Being is the Being of the Son and Spirit' he wanted to stress that his understanding of being was not taken from Aristotle, but was instead shaped under the influence of God's self-revelation in Christ, in a manner similar to the way Athanasius thought

within the Trinity with their being. See Molnar, 'Theological Issues Involved in the *Filioque*', *Ecumenical Perspectives on the Filioque for the 21st Century*, ed. Myk Habets, 24–34.

27 Torrance, *Space, Time and Resurrection*, 42.

28 Gunton, 'Person and Being', 131.

29 See, for example, Torrance, *The Christian Doctrine of God*, 116.

30 Gunton, 'Person and Being', 130.

about God's being. Hence, Torrance was strictly interpreting the being of God following Athanasius's statement that: ' "It would be more godly and true to signify God from the Son and call him Father, than to name God from his works alone and call him Unoriginate." '[31]

Gunton is also unhappy with the fact that Torrance did not engage more with the work of John Zizioulas so that persons might be seen as beings *in relation to* others rather than simply as relations. This, Gunton believes, would enable theologians to give equal weight to the one and the many; but is that really the goal of trinitarian theology? While it is certainly true that all good dogmatics is also ethics and while it is also true that individualism and collectivism are unacceptable, the question remains as to whether a new understanding of the term 'person' in relation will solve all of this. Do we not need to look exclusively to the person and work of Christ at precisely this point? Can we allow persons in relation to become the subject here with Christ and the Holy Spirit perhaps becoming the predicate? This is certainly a danger at this point.

The final issue to be addressed here concerns Torrance's understanding of the *filioque*. Gunton sees at least two areas of concern in relation to the Western view. First, if we think the Spirit proceeds from the Son as well as from the Father, then the Spirit is seen to be subordinate to the Son and 'is reduced to the margins … to do little more than apply Christ's work in the Church or to the individual believer'.[32] This leads to 'a failure to do justice to the full humanity of the incarnate Son of God'.[33]

Here, Gunton cites Torrance's important paper on 'The Mind of Christ in Worship: The Problem of Apollinarianism in the Liturgy', to show that Torrance had a healthy concern to stress the fact that Christ's priestly ministry as man offering himself is the focus of our worship. Still, Torrance is criticized for not paying much attention to the detailed gospel presentations of Jesus's life, death, resurrection and ascension. This is a surprising assertion especially in light of Torrance's biblical analysis in *Space, Time and Resurrection*.[34] However, it is also surprising in light of the fact that what Torrance in fact has to say is grounded in

31 Torrance, *The Christian Doctrine of God*, 117.

32 Gunton, 'Person and Being', 132.

33 Gunton, 'Person and Being', 132.

34 Torrance's important books on the Incarnation and Atonement which represented edited versions of his Edinburgh lectures were not available to Gunton, at least in the published form that we now have them. However, Torrance does offer a full discussion of Christ's resurrection and ascension along with their implications in *Space, Time and Resurrection*.

and controlled by the biblical revelation itself. Nonetheless, we are told that another problem of the *filioque* is the Western tendency toward modalism, that is, in the Western search for the One, the question arises as to who or what ultimately unifies our experience; the temptation of the West is to find the unity of all things 'in some deity or divine principle over and above the Triune revelation'.[35]

Here is where the disagreement between Torrance and Zizioulas emerges. Should we follow Zizioulas and say that the Father is the cause of everything, including the triune communion? Or should we say, with T. F. Torrance, that 'we must understand the Triune communion as a whole to be the metaphysical source of unity'?[36] Gunton sees this as a question of whether the double procession encourages modalism. Does it?

Gunton wonders that if the Spirit comes from the Father *and* the Son, will we not then wonder what it is that gives the Father and Son *their* underlying unity? In Gunton's view, double procession invites us to seek a deeper cause than the Trinity and thus opens the door to modalism. Western minds, he believes, inevitably tend that way. Gunton stresses that neither Torrance nor Barth are actually modalists, but that today we need to stress the persons more in order to overcome any underlying tendency to modalism.

This requires several comments. First, Barth did support the *filioque*, but not because of a modalist tendency and certainly not by thinking beyond and apart from revelation. In fact, his main argument in favor of this was to insist that just as the Spirit proceeds from the Father and Son, so we have no direct mystical access to God that would bypass the Son's incarnate mediation.[37] Indeed, his intention was to safeguard the

35 Gunton, 'Person and Being', 133.

36 Gunton, 'Person and Being', 133.

37 Thus, 'if our thinking is not to leave the soil of revelation, a distinction must be acknowledged in the reality of what the Son and the Spirit are antecedently in Themselves' *CD* I/1, 474. This will lead to a recognition that the Holy Spirit is different from the Son and the Father as well, without being separated from the Father and Son. For a discussion of Barth's understanding of the *filioque*, see David Guretzki, *Karl Barth on the Filioque* (Farnham: Ashgate, 2009). In his discussion of Barth and Torrance, Guretzki indicates their similarities in that they appeal to Athanasius to extend the *homoousion* 'fully to the Holy Spirit' using the concept of *perichoresis*. However, he misstates Torrance's position when he says that 'Torrance is ready to speak of a procession of the Spirit from "the whole Being of God to whom the Father and the Son with the Spirit belong"' (129). Torrance actually was arguing that the homoousial

Footnote 37 (*cont.*)

relation of the Spirit with the Father and the Son means not only that the Spirit is coequal with the Father and the Son, but that since the Spirit too is 'God of God' therefore 'we have to do not just with a two-way relationship between the Father and the Son in which the Spirit is some kind of connecting link, but with an active three-way or perichoretic relationship between the Father, the Son and the Holy Spirit' (*The Christian Doctrine of God*, 191). Then, to make his point clearer he says that this approach 'is reinforced by consideration of the truth that *God is Spirit*, "Spirit" cannot be restricted to the Person of the Holy Spirit, but must apply to the whole Being of God to whom the Father and the Son with the Spirit belong' (191). Notice that Torrance does not here say the Spirit proceeds from the 'whole Being of God' – he was making a completely different point, namely, that God is Spirit and that that applies not just to the person of the Spirit but to the Father and Son as well. Then he concludes by saying that a proper view 'of the procession of the Spirit must be of procession from the whole spiritual Being of God the Father which the Holy Spirit has entirely in common with the Father and the Son' (191). Guretzki's misstatement was to leave out Torrance's affirmation that the Spirit proceeds from 'the whole spiritual Being of God the Father'. This is extremely important because Torrance wants to affirm that the Spirit can be said to proceed from the Father *and* the Son as long as this does not imply two ultimate principles of origin and he thinks we can also say that the Spirit proceeds from the Father *through* the Son as long as this is not taken to mean that the monarchy resides solely in the person of the Father. That would lead to the idea of a derived deity which Torrance rightly rejects. Since God is Spirit, Torrance thus wants to affirm, with Epiphanius that: ' "The Holy Spirit ever is from the same Being of the Father and the Son, for God is Spirit" ' (191). Hence, for Torrance, 'The Holy Spirit is the Spirit of the Son by Nature as well as the Spirit of the Father by Nature' so that 'the Spirit proceeds from the Father and is given by the Son, as from the one Being which they both equally share, but share also with the Holy Spirit himself, for the Father is not Father and the Son is not Son apart from the Holy Spirit' (191). Had Guretzki paid attention to these developments in Torrance's argument he never would have concluded that Barth was 'concerned, in a way that Torrance was not, to safeguard the unique relational dialectic that exists between the Father and the Son in the Holy Spirit' (130). Yet that is exactly what Torrance ended up arguing, without using the word dialectic of course. Since Guretzki misstated Torrance's idea of the procession of the Spirit from the Being of the Father rather than just from the person of the Father, he claims that while 'Torrance's view of the Spirit's procession from the monarchy of the Trinity' may be 'dogmatically deduced', nonetheless 'it is not clear that it is intelligible

inseparable relation between the Spirit and the Son in both the economic and immanent Trinity. Barth was sensitive to the fact that the *filioque* was uncharitably added to the creed, yet Barth believed that from the very beginning both East and West did not disagree materially about the procession of the Spirit even when this expression was used. Barth also insisted that passages such as Jn. 15:26, which speak of the Spirit proceeding from the Father, could not be isolated from other texts which clearly call him the Spirit of the Son. Hence, he explicitly affirmed the *filioque* because for Barth

or coherent' (134). Thus, he asks 'what might it possibly mean for one divine hypostasis to proceed from all three hypostases, including itself?' (134). This very question manifests a striking misunderstanding of Torrance's position. He never says that one divine hypostasis (presumably the Spirit) proceeds from all three hypostases. Nor does he ever say or imply that the Spirit proceeds from itself. Those would indeed be absurd statements. What he does say is that since each of the persons of the Trinity are perichoretically related, therefore the procession of the Spirit is from the being of the Father and that as such, since God is Spirit, the perichoretic unity of the persons (which he always clearly maintains in their distinctive relations) is such that one could never claim that the Spirit proceeds only from the person of the Father, as that would lead to ideas of a derived deity or subordinationism or both. Within this view one could never advance the false idea that there are two ultimate sources of the Spirit within the Godhead; therefore this would eliminate the perceived need for the *filioque*. So when Torrance speaks of the 'Triune Monarchy' (192) all that he wants to affirm is that all three persons of the Trinity are God from God such that there is an eternal Trinity in Unity and Unity in Trinity. Torrance certainly is willing to speak of the Monarchy of the Father in the sense that he is first in order within the Trinity but this order cannot be confused with the being of the persons without doing damage to the Unity in Trinity and Trinity in Unity of God (*The Christian Doctrine of God*, 176). However, for Torrance the Spirit does not proceed from the being of God in some general sense, but from the being of the Father through the Son 'perichoretically understood' (191). This thinking ingeniously 'does not allow of any procession of the Spirit from the Father and the Son alone, as if the Spirit himself did not belong to the Father-Son relation in the Holy Trinity equally with the Father and the Son' (191). As just stated, it disallows any idea that the Spirit proceeds from 'two ultimate Principles or Origins' (191). For more on the views of Torrance and Barth regarding these matters, see Molnar 'Theological Issues Involved in the *Filioque*' (ed.) Habets.

statements about the divine modes of being antecedently in themselves cannot be different in content from those that are to be made about their reality in revelation. All our statements concerning what is called the immanent Trinity have been reached simply as confirmations or underlinings or, materially, as *the indispensable premises of the economic Trinity*.[38]

As Torrance notes, this was the original intention of the *filioque* clause,[39] even though it had damaging effect because it was unecumenically introduced by the West into the creed. Torrance himself partially agrees with Barth's view. While he rejects 'the element of "subordinationism" in his doctrine of the Holy Trinity ... as a hang-over from Latin theology but also from St Basil's doctrine of the Trinity', he also agreed with Barth that the Nicene *homoousion* should apply to the doctrine of the Holy Spirit. Thus, 'we cannot but trace back the historical mission of the Spirit from the incarnate Son to the eternal mission of the Spirit from the Father. But I would argue that the problem of the *filioque* was created by an incipient subordinationism in the Cappadocian doctrine of the Trinity.'[40] Whatever one's final judgment may be with respect to Barth's view of the *filioque*, Torrance's analysis on this issue deserves careful attention. If Torrance is right, and I think he is, then his suggestion could be the basis of far-reaching ecumenical agreement.

Briefly, Torrance believes that if the *filioque* is set back again on the Athanasian (and 'Cyrilian') basis[41] then the problems associated with it fall away. Torrance believes that if we accept Athanasius's notion of coinherence, this would lead us to admit that in the Trinity 'no Person is before or after Another, no Person is greater or less, but all three Persons are coeternal and coequal in their substantive relations with one another'.[42] If this is taken seriously then the mission of the Holy Spirit from the Father and the gift of the Spirit by the Son will be governed by the fact that each person is wholly God and that therefore the Holy Spirit 'proceeds from the Father through the Son'. This eliminates both the idea that there is more than one source of deity and the idea that the Son is less than the Father. What Torrance wants to say is that if we consider the procession of the Holy Spirit from the Father in light

38 *CD* I/1, 479, emphasis mine.
39 Torrance, *Theology in Reconstruction*, 218–19.
40 Torrance, *Karl Barth*, 131–2.
41 Cf. Torrance, *Trinitarian Perspectives*, 20.
42 Torrance, *Trinitarian Perspectives*, 20.

of the fact that each Person of the Godhead 'is perfectly and wholly God'[43] then we can say 'that the Holy Spirit proceeds ultimately from the Triune Being of the Godhead.'[44] This must mean that the Spirit 'proceeds from out of the mutual relations within the One Being of the Holy Trinity in which the Father indwells the Spirit and is himself indwelt by the Spirit'. Further, 'since God *is* Spirit, "Spirit" cannot be restricted to the Person of the Holy Spirit',[45] but must also be applied to the eternal communion of the Father, Son and Holy Spirit. Hence the Spirit proceeds from the Being of the Father. This eliminates any false notion of causality that would suggest that the Son proceeds from the Person of the Father and this transcends the rift between East and West. This also eliminates any idea of two ultimate principles in God (Father and Son) and is seen as a procession from mutual relations within the being of God 'who is Trinity in Unity and Unity in Trinity'.[46]

What Torrance opposes here is the Cappadocian conception of God's unity 'as deriving "from the Person of the Father" … thereby replacing the Nicene formula "from the Being of the Father …"'[47] This thinking does not sufficiently affirm the *homoousion* of the Spirit. Still, the Cappadocians did not think of the Holy Spirit as created. Nonetheless, Torrance believes that it was the Cappadocian thinking that actually led Western church leaders to insert the *ex Patre filioque* clause unecumenically into the Creed, thus creating the impasse between East and West.[48]

The West assumed that if the Spirit proceeds from the Father and is sent by the Son, then such thinking would suggest that 'the Son would be regarded as subordinate to the Father, as an adopted creature of God, and not really as God of God'.[49] The East believed that the *filioque* suggested two ultimate principles in the Godhead and thus opted to speak of the Spirit as proceeding from the Father alone. This was defended on the basis of John's gospel, which implied a distinction between

43 Torrance, *Trinitarian Perspectives*, 112.

44 Torrance, *Trinitarian Perspectives*, 112–13. The key here, however, as indicated in n. 37 is that one must not understand this statement to refer to some generic or general notion of the deity but to the perichoretically related persons of the Trinity in their full and equal deity.

45 Torrance, *Trinitarian Perspectives*, 113.

46 Torrance, *Trinitarian Perspectives*, 113.

47 Torrance, *The Christian Doctrine of God*, 186.

48 In Barth's view this impasse was created more by this action than by any material disagreement.

49 Torrance, *The Christian Doctrine of God*, 186.

procession and mission, that is, 'between the *eternal* procession of the Spirit from the Father, and the *historical* mission of the Spirit from the Son'.[50] However, this raises the question of whether the sending of the Spirit by the Son has only to do with revelation and faith instead of being 'grounded immanently in the eternal being of God'.[51] If this is the case then that would undercut the *homoousial* relation of the Holy Spirit to God the Father. This thinking, exacerbated by the Basilian and Palamite distinction between the divine being and energies, led both toward agnosticism and dualism, and undermined the Nicene emphasis on the identity of God's being and act; it separated the immanent and economic Trinity.

Hence, Torrance prefers to say that 'the Spirit is from the Father but from the Father in the Son. Since the Holy Spirit like the Son is of the Being of God, and belongs to the Son … he could not but proceed from or out of the Being of God inseparably from and through the Son'.[52] For Athanasius the problem of the double procession of the Spirit did not arise, because he believed that it would be irreverent 'to ask *how* the Spirit proceeds from God' since that would have suggested 'an ungodly attempt to intrude into the holy mystery of God's being'.[53] For Athanasius then, the procession of the Spirit is bound up with the Son's generation and these divine actions exceed and transcend all human thoughts. Therefore, since the Son and Spirit 'are both *of the Being* of the Father … the idea that the Spirit derives from the *Being* of the Son just did not arise and could not have arisen for Athanasius'.[54] This then is T. F. Torrance's solution to the problem of the *filioque*. Thus for Torrance, we can say both that the Holy Spirit proceeds from the Father and the Son and from the Father through the Son as long as monarchy is not limited to the Father; as long as there is no distinction drawn between the underived Deity of the Father and the derived Deity of the Son and as long as the Holy Spirit is seen to belong 'homoousially with the Father and the Son in their two-way relation with one another in the divine Triunity'.[55] What is so astonishing and helpful about Torrance's proposal is that he simultaneously avoids any hint of modalism or subordinationism.

50 Torrance, *The Christian Doctrine of God*, 186.

51 Torrance, *The Christian Doctrine of God*, 187.

52 Torrance, *The Christian Doctrine of God*, 188.

53 Torrance, *The Christian Doctrine of God*, 188

54 Torrance, *The Christian Doctrine of God*, 188.

55 Torrance, *The Christian Doctrine of God*, 190.

Hence, the question to be raised to Gunton is what exactly is it in the notion of person that he adopts from John Zizioulas that leads him to criticize Torrance for modalist leanings? The answer, I suggest, is to be found in the belief that person is more basic than substance or being. If person is believed to be more basic than being, then it strikes me that one will be tempted to explain the *how* of God's triune being when in fact we can only reason in faith from the fact of it which remains a mystery. Further, if person is believed to be more basic than being, then some form of adoptionism in Christology and some separation of the Spirit from the Word will inevitably threaten. It is no accident that, as we have seen throughout this book, adoptionism threatens to weaken much contemporary Christology and thereby lead to some form of self-justification. Nor is it an accident that even in the most sophisticated Christologies, whenever the Spirit is separated from the Word, then Jesus's activity as the subject of the events of reconciliation and revelation is also called into question; but then the unity of the Father, Son and Spirit is also called into question. Torrance's thinking therefore not only has the advantage of healing the wounds that exist between East and West, but it helps theologians realize that the strength of trinitarian theology rests, as it always has, on the fact that Jesus Christ is the eternally begotten Son of the Father and that this takes place in the unity of the Holy Spirit. It is not then to be found in his human activity within history except as that human activity is the activity of the Word of God incarnate.

SELECTED BIBLIOGRAPHY

Ables, Travis. 'The Grammar of Pneumatology in Barth and Rahner: A Reconsideration'. *International Journal of Systematic Theology* 11 (2) (April 2009), 208–24.

Achtemeier, Elizabeth. 'Exchanging God for "No Gods"'. *Speaking the Christian God: The Holy Trinity and the Challenge of Feminism*. Edited by Alvin F. Kimel, Jr., 1–16. Grand Rapids, MI: Eerdmans, 1992.

Anizor, Uche. *Trinity and Humanity: An Introduction to the Theology of Colin Gunton*. Carlisle, UK: Paternoster Press, 2016.

Aquinas, St Thomas. *Summa Theologica: Complete English Edition in Five Volumes*. Translated by Fathers of the English Dominican Province. Westminster, MD: Christian Classics, 1948.

Athanasius. *Athanasius, Select Works and Letters in A Select Library of Nicene and Post-Nicene Fathers*. Translated and edited by Philip Schaff and Henry Wace, Vol. 4. New York: Charles Scribner's Sons, 1903. *Epistle of Athanasius Concerning the Arian Bipartite Council Held at Ariminum and Seleucia*.

Athanasius. *Four Discourses against the Arians 1.34. A Select Library of Nicene and Post-Nicene Fathers of the Christian Church Second Series*. Translated and edited by Philip Schaff and Henry Wace. Edinburgh: T&T Clark, 1987.

Athanasius. *Letters of Saint Athanasius Concerning the Holy Spirit*. Translated by C.R.B. Shapland. London: Epworth Press, 1951.

Augustine. *The Trinity*. Translated by Edmund Hill, O.P. Edited by John E. Rotelle O.S.A. Brooklyn, New York: New City Press, 1991.

Ayres, Lewis. *Nicaea and Its Legacy: An Approach to Fourth-Century Trinitarian Theology*. New York: Oxford University Press, 2004.

Balthasar, Hans Urs von. *The Theology of Karl Barth: Exposition and Interpretation*. Translated by Edward T. Oakes, S.J. San Francisco: Ignatius Press, 1992.

Barth, Karl. *Ad limina apostolorum: An Appraisal of Vatican II*. Translated by Keith R. Crim. Richmond, VA: John Knox Press, 1968.

Barth, Karl. *Anselm: Fides quaerens intellectum. Anselm's Proof of the Existence of God in the Context of his Theological Scheme*. Richmond, VA: John Knox Press, 1960.

Barth, Karl. *Church Dogmatics*. 4 vols. in 13 pts.

Barth, Karl. Vol. 1, pt 1: *The Doctrine of the Word of God*. Edited by G. W. Bromiley and T. F. Torrance. Translated by G. W. Bromiley. Edinburgh: T&T Clark, 1975.

Barth, Karl. Vol. 1, pt 2: *The Doctrine of the Word of God*. Edited by G. W. Bromiley and T. F. Torrance. Translated by G. T. Thomson and H. Knight. Edinburgh: T&T Clark, 1970.

Barth, Karl. Vol. 2, pt 1: *The Doctrine of God*. Edited by G. W. Bromiley and T .F. Torrance. Translated by T. H. L. Parker, W. B. Johnston, H. Knight and J. L. M. Haire. Edinburgh: T&T Clark, 1964.

Barth, Karl. Vol. 2, pt 2: *The Doctrine of God*. Edited by G. W. Bromiley and T. F. Torrance. Translated by G. W. Bromiley, J. C. Campbell, I. Wilson, J. Strathearn McNab, H. Knight and R. A. Stewart. Edinburgh: T&T Clark, 1967.

Barth, Karl. Vol. 3, pt 1: *The Doctrine of Creation*. Edited by G. W. Bromiley and T. F. Torrance. Translated by J. W. Edwards, O. Bussey and H. Knight. Edinburgh: T&T Clark, 1970.

Barth, Karl. Vol. 3, pt 2: *The Doctrine of Creation*. Edited by G. W. Bromiley and T. F. Torrance. Translated by H. Knight, G. W. Bromiley, J. K. S. Reid and R. H. Fuller. Edinburgh: T&T Clark, 1968.

Barth, Karl. Vol. 3, pt 3: *The Doctrine of Creation*. Edited by G. W. Bromiley and T. F. Torrance. Translated by G. W. Bromiley and R. J. Ehrlich. Edinburgh: T&T Clark, 1976.

Barth, Karl. Vol. 3, pt 4: *The Doctrine of Creation*. Edited by G. W. Bromiley and T. F. Torrance. Translated by A. T. MacKay, T. H. L. Parker, H. Knight, H. A. Kennedy and J. Marks. Edinburgh: T&T Clark, 1969.

Barth, Karl. Vol. 4, pt 1: *The Doctrine of Reconciliation*. Edited by G. W. Bromiley and T. F. Torrance. Translated by by G. W. Bromiley. Edinburgh: T&T Clark, 1974.

Barth, Karl. Vol. 4, pt 2: *The Doctrine of Reconciliation*. Edited by G. W. Bromiley and T. F. Torrance. Translated by by G. W. Bromiley. Edinburgh: T&T Clark, 1967.

Barth, Karl. Vol. 4, pt 3: *The Doctrine of Reconciliation*. First Half. Edited by G. W. Bromiley and T. F. Torrance. Translated by G. W. Bromiley. Edinburgh: T&T Clark, 1976.

Barth, Karl. Vol. 4, pt 3: *The Doctrine of Reconciliation*. Second Half. Edited by G. W. Bromiley and T. F. Torrance. Translated by by G. W. Bromiley. Edinburgh: T&T Clark, 1969.

Barth, Karl. Vol. 4, pt 4: *The Doctrine of Reconciliation*. Fragment. *Baptism as the Foundation of the Christian Life*. Edited by G. W. Bromiley and T. F. Torrance. Translated by by G. W. Bromiley. Edinburgh: T&T Clark, 1969.

Barth, Karl. Vol. 4, pt 4: *The Christian Life*. Lecture Fragments. Translated by Geoffrey W. Bromiley. Grand Rapids, MI: William B. Eerdmans Publishing Company, 1981.

Barth, Karl. *Credo*. Translated by Robert McAfee Brown. New York: Charles Scribner's Sons, 1962.

Barth, Karl. *Deliverance to the Captives*. Translated by Marguerite Wieser. New York: Harper & Row, 1959.

Barth, Karl. *Die Kirchliche Dogmatik*. 4 vols. in 13 pts.

Barth, Karl. Vol. 1, pt 1: *Die Lehre Von Wort Gottes: Prolegmona Zur Kirchlichen Dogmatik*. Evangelischer Verlag AG Zollikon-Zürich, 1955.

Barth, Karl. Vol. 2, pt 1: *Die Lehre Von Gott (Dritte Auflage)*. Evangelischer Verlag AG Zollikon- Zürich, 1948.

Barth, Karl. Vol. 4, p. 1: *Die Lehre Von Der Versöhnung*. Evangelischer Verlag AG Zollikon-Zürich, 1955.

Barth, Karl. *Ethics*. Edited by Dietrich Braun. Translated by Geoffrey W. Bromiley. New York: Seabury Press, 1981.

Barth, Karl. *Evangelical Theology: An Introduction*. Translated by Grover Foley. Grand Rapids, MI: Eerdmans, 1963.

Barth, Karl. *Letters 1961–1968*. Edited by Jürgen Fangemeier and Hinrich Stoevesandt. Translated and Edited by Geoffrey W. Bromiley. Grand Rapids, MI: Eerdmans, 1981.

Barth, Karl. *Protestant Theology in the Nineteenth Century: Its Background and History*. Translated by Brian Cozens and John Bowden. Valley Forge, PA: Judson Press, 1973.

Barth, Karl. *The Göttingen Dogmatics: Instruction in the Christian Religion Volume One*. Translated by Geoffrey W. Bromiley. Grand Rapids, MI: Eerdmans, 1991.

Barth, Karl. *The Holy Spirit and the Christian Life*. Foreword by Robin W. Lovin. Translated by R. Birch Hoyle. Louisville, KY: Westminster/John Knox Press, 1993.

Barth, Karl. *The Humanity of God*. Translated by Thomas Wieser and John Newton Thomas. Richmond, VA: John Knox Press, 1968.

Barth, Karl. *Theology and Church (Shorter Writings 1920–1928)*. Translated by Louise Pettibone Smith. With an Introduction (1962) by T. F. Torrance. London: SCM Press Ltd., 1962.

Bauckham, Richard J. 'Moltmann's Messianic Christology'. *Scottish Journal of Theology* 44 (1991), 519–31.

Bauckham, Richard J. *The Theology of Jürgen Moltmann*. Edinburgh: T&T Clark, 1995.

Bender, Kimlyn J. *Karl Barth's Christological Ecclesiology*. Eugene, OR: Cascade Books, 2013.

Biggar, Nigel (ed.). *Reckoning with Barth: Essays in Commemoration of the Centenary of Karl Barth's Birth*. London: Mowbray, 1988.

Boff, Leonardo. *Trinity and Society*. Translated by Paul Burns. Maryknoll, NY: Orbis, 1988.

Bonzo, J. Matthew. *Indwelling the Forsaken Other: The Trinitarian Ethics of Jürgen Moltmann*. Eugene, OR: Pickwick, 2009.

Bromiley, Geoffrey W. *Introduction to the Theology of Karl Barth*. Edinburgh: T&T Clark, 1995.

Bultmann, Rudolf. *Jesus Christ and Mythology*. New York: Charles Scribner's Sons, 1958.

Bultmann, Rudolf. 'New Testament and Mythology'. *Kerygma and Myth: A Theological Debate*. Edited by Hans Werner Bartsch, 1–44. New York: Harper Torchbooks, 1961.

Burghardt, Walter J., S.J. *Long Have I Loved You: A Theologian Reflects on his Church*. New York: Orbis Books, 2000.

Burke, Patrick. *Reinterpreting Rahner: A Critical Study of His Major Themes.* New York: Fordham University Press, 2002.

Busch, Eberhard. *Karl Barth: His Life from Letters and Autobiographical Facts.* Translated by John Bowden. Philadelphia: Fortress Press, 1976.

Busch, Eberhard. *The Great Passion: An Introduction to Karl Barth's Theology.* Edited by Darrell L. Guder and Judith J. Guder. Translated by Geoffrey W. Bromiley. Grand Rapids, MI: Eerdmans, 2004.

Carr, Anne. 'Theology and Experience in the Thought of Karl Rahner'. *Journal of Religion* 53 (1973), 359–76.

Carr, Anne. *Transforming Grace: Christian Tradition and Women's Experience.* San Francisco: Harper & Row, 1988.

Castelo, Daniel. 'Moltmann's Dismissal of Divine Impassibility: Warranted?' *Scottish Journal of Theology* 61 (4) (2008), 396–407.

Chadwick, Henry. *The Early Church.* New York: Penguin, 1967.

Clarkson, John F., S.J., et al. (trans. and eds) *The Church Teaches: Documents of the Church in English Translation.* London: Herder, 1955.

Coffey, David. *Deus Trinitas: The Doctrine of the Triune God.* New York: Oxford University Press, 1999.

Coffey, David. 'In Response to Paul Molnar'. *Irish Theological Quarterly* 67 (2002), 375–8.

Coffey, David. 'The "Incarnation" of the Holy Spirit in Christ'. *Theological Studies* 45.3 (September 1984), 466–80.

Coffey, David. 'The Theandric Nature of Christ'. *Theological Studies* 60 (3) (September 1999), 405–31.

Congar, Yves. *I Believe in the Holy Spirit,* vol. III, *The River of the Water of Life (Rev 22:1) Flows in the East and in the West.* Translated by David Smith. New York: Crossroad, 1997.

Cunningham, David S. *These Three Are One: The Practice of Trinitarian Theology.* Oxford: Blackwell, 1998.

Daly, Mary. *Beyond God the Father: Toward a Philosophy of Women's Liberation.* Boston, MA: Beacon Press, 1985.

Davidson, Ivor J. 'The Crucified One'. *Indicative of Grace-Imperative of Freedom: Essays in Honour of Eberhard Jüngel in His 80th Year.* Edited by R. David Nelson, 29–49. London: Bloomsbury T&T Clark, 2014.

Davidson, Ivor J. 'Salvation's Destiny: Heirs of God'. *God of Salvation: Soteriology in Theological Perspective.* Edited by Ivor J. Davidson and Murray A. Rae, 155–75. Farnham, UK: Ashgate, 2011.

Davis, Stephen T., Daniel Kendall, S.J. and Gerald O'Collins, S.J. (eds). *The Trinity: An Interdisciplinary Symposium on the Trinity.* Oxford: Oxford University Press, 1999.

Dawson, R. Dale. *The Resurrection in Karl Barth.* Aldershot: Ashgate, 2007.

Del Colle, Ralph. *Christ and the Spirit: Spirit-Christology in Trinitarian Perspective.* New York: Oxford University Press, 1994.

Dempsey, Michael T. (ed.). *Trinity and Election in Contemporary Theology*. Grand Rapids, MI: Eerdmans, 2011.

Diller, Kevin. 'Is God *Necessarily* Who God Is? Alternatives for the Trinity and Election Debate'. *Scottish Journal of Theology* 66 (2) (2013), 209–20.

DiNoia, J. A., O.P. 'Karl Rahner'. *The Modern Theologians*, Vol. 1. Edited by David F. Ford. Oxford: Blackwell, 1989.

Donovan, Daniel. 'Revelation and Faith'. *Cambridge Companion to Karl Rahner*. Edited by Declan Marmion and Mary E. Hines, 83–97. Cambridge: Cambridge University Press, 2007.

Drury, John. *The Resurrected God: Karl Barth's Trinitarian Theology of Easter*. Minneapolis, MN: Fortress, 2014.

Duffy, Stephen J. 'Experience of Grace'. *The Cambridge Companion to Karl Rahner*. Edited by Declan Marmion and Mary E. Hines, 43–62. Cambridge: Cambridge University Press, 2007.

Dych, William V., S.J. *Karl Rahner*. Collegeville, MN: The Liturgical Press, 1992.

Dych, William V., S.J. 'Theology in a New Key'. *A World of Grace: An Introduction to the Themes and Foundations of Karl Rahner's Theology*. Edited by Leo J. O'Donovan, S.J. New York: Crossroad, 1981.

Eilers, Kent. *Faithful to Save: Pannenberg on God's Reconciling Action*. London/New York: Bloomsbury, T&T Clark, 2011.

Farrow, Douglas. *Ascension and Ecclesia: On the Significance of the Doctrine of the Ascension for Ecclesiology and Christian Cosmology*. Grand Rapids, MI: Eerdmans, 1999.

Fergusson, David A.S. 'Interpreting the Resurrection'. *Scottish Journal of Theology* 38 (1985), 287–305.

Feuerbach, Ludwig. *The Essence of Christianity*. Translated by George Eliot. Introduction by Karl Barth. Foreword by H. Richard Niebuhr. New York: Harper Torchbooks, 1957.

Fiddes, Paul S. *Participating in God: A Pastoral Doctrine of the Trinity*. Louisville, KY: Westminster John Knox Press, 2000.

Fiddes, Paul S. 'Relational Trinity: Radical Perspective'. *Two Views on the Doctrine of the Trinity*. Edited by Jason S. Sexton and Stanley N. Gundry, 159–85. Grand Rapids, MI: Zondervan, 2014.

Fiddes, Paul S. *The Creative Suffering of God*. Oxford: Clarendon Press, 1988.

Fletcher, Jeannine Hill. 'Rahner and Religious Diversity'. *The Cambridge Companion to Karl Rahner*. Edited by Declan Marmion and Mary E. Hines, 235–48. Cambridge: Cambridge University Press, 2007.

Foley, Grover. 'The Catholic Critics of Karl Barth in Outline and Analysis'. *Scottish Journal of Theology* 14 (1961), 136–51.

Ford, David F. and Muers, Rachel (eds). *The Modern Theologians: An Introduction to Christian Theology Since 1918*. Third Edition. Oxford: Blackwell, 2005.

Fortmann, Edmund J. *The Triune God: An Historical Study of the Doctrine of the Trinity*. Philadelphia: Westminster Press, 1972.

Frye, Roland M. 'Language for God and Feminist Language: Problems and Principles'. *Scottish Journal of Theology* 41 (4) (1988), 441–69.

Frye, Roland M. 'Language for God and Feminist Language: Problems and Principles'. *Speaking the Christian God: The Holy Trinity and the Challenge of Feminism*. Edited by Alvin F. Kimel, Jr. Grand Rapids, MI: Eerdmans, 1992, 17–43.

Galvin, John P. 'The Invitation of Grace'. *A World of Grace: An Introduction to the Themes and Foundations of Karl Rahner's Theology*. Edited by Leo J. O'Donovan, S.J., 64–75. New York: Crossroad, 1981.

Gathercole, Simon. 'Pre-existence, and the Freedom of the Son in Creation and Redemption: An Exposition in Dialogue with Robert Jenson'. *International Journal of Systematic Theology* 7 (1) (January 2005), 38–51.

Giles, Kevin. *The Eternal Generation of the Son: Maintaining Orthodoxy in Trinitarian Theology*. Downers Grove, IL: InterVarsity Press, 2012.

Giles, Kevin. 'Barth and Subordinationism'. *Scottish Journal of Theology* 64 (3) (2011), 327–46.

Gilson, Etienne. *God and Philosophy*. New Haven: Yale University Press, 1979.

Gockel, Matthias. 'How to Read Karl Barth with Charity: A Critical Reply to George Hunsinger'. *Modern Theology* 32 (2) (April 2016), 259–67.

Godsey, John. *Karl Barth's Table Talk*. Richmond, VA: John Knox, 1962.

Gregory of Nyssa. *Against Eunomius Book I, § 42. Select Writings and Letters of Gregory, Bishop of Nyssa*. Translated by William Moore and Henry Wilson. *Nicene and Post-Nicene Fathers of the Christian Church*. Grand Rapids, MI: Eerdmans, 1988.

Grenz, Stanley J. *Rediscovering the Triune God: The Trinity in Contemporary Theology*. Minneapolis, MN: Fortress, 2004.

Grenz, Stanley J. and Roger E. Olson. *20th Century Theology: God and the World in a Transitional Age*. Carlisle: Paternoster Press, 1992.

Groppe, Elizabeth T. 'Catherine Mowry LaCugna's Contribution To Trinitarian Theology'. *Theological Studies* 63 (2002), 730–63.

Gunton, Colin. *A Brief Theology of Revelation*. Edinburgh: T&T Clark, 1995.

Gunton, Colin. *Becoming and Being: The Doctrine of God in Charles Hartshorne and Karl Barth*. London: Oxford University Press, 1978.

Gunton, Colin. 'Being and Person: T.F. Torrance's Doctrine of God'. *The Promise of Trinitarian Theology: Theologians in Dialogue with T.F. Torrance*. Edited by Elmer M. Colyer. Lanham, MD: Rowman & Littlefield, 2001.

Gunton, Colin. *Christ and Creation*. Grand Rapids, MI: Eerdmans, 1992.

Gunton, Colin. 'Review of Ted Peters, *GOD as Trinity*'. *Theology Today* 51 (1) (1994), 174–6.

Gunton, Colin. *The Actuality of Atonement*. Edinburgh: T&T Clark, 1994.

Gunton, Colin. 'The Being and Attributes of God. Eberhard Jüngel's Dispute with the Classical Philosophical Tradition'. *The Possibilities of*

Theology: Studies in the Theology of Eberhard Jüngel in his Sixtieth Year. Edited by John Webster, 7–22. Edinburgh: T&T Clark, 1994.

Gunton, Colin. *The One, the Three and the Many*. Cambridge: Cambridge University Press, 1993.

Gunton, Colin. *Theology through the Theologians: Selected Essays 1972–1995*. Edinburgh: T&T Clark, 1996.

Gunton, Colin. *The Promise of Trinitarian Theology*. Edinburgh: T&T Clark, 1991.

Gunton, Colin. *The Promise of Trinitarian Theology*. Second Edition. Edinburgh: T&T Clark, 1997.

Gunton, Colin. *The Triune Creator: A Historical and Systematic Study*. Edinburgh Studies in Constructive Theology. Grand Rapids, MI: Eerdmans, 1998.

Gunton, Colin. 'Two Dogmas Revisited: Edward Irving's Christology'. *Scottish Journal of Theology* 41 (1988), 359–76.

Gunton, Colin. *Yesterday and Today: A Study of Continuities in Christology*. Grand Rapids, MI: Eerdmans, 1983.

Gunton, Colin (ed.). *God and Freedom: Essays in Historical and Systematic Theology*. Edinburgh: T&T Clark, 1995.

Gunton, Colin (ed.). *The Cambridge Companion to Christian Doctrine*. Cambridge: Cambridge University Press, 1997.

Gunton, Colin (ed.). *The Doctrine of Creation: Essays in Dogmatics, History and Philosophy*. Edinburgh: T&T Clark, 1997.

Guretzki, David. *Karl Barth on the Filioque*. Farnham: Ashgate, 2009.

Habets, Myk. *Theology in Transposition: A Constructive Appraisal of T.F. Torrance*. Minneapolis, MN: Fortress, 2013.

Habets, Myk and Tolliday, Phillip (eds). *Trinitarian Theology After Barth*. Eugene, OR: Pickwick, 2011.

Haight, Roger. *Jesus: Symbol of God*. Maryknoll, NY: Orbis, 1999.

Hanson, R. P. C. *The Search for the Christian Doctrine of God*. Edinburgh: T&T Clark, 1988.

Harnack, Adolf von. *History of Dogma*. Vols I, III and VI. Translated by Neil Buchanan. New York: Dover, 1961.

Harvey, Lincoln (ed.). *The Theology of Colin Gunton*. London: T&T Clark International, 2010.

Hector, Kevin W. 'God's Trinity and Self-Determination: A Conversation with Karl Barth, Bruce McCormack, and Paul Molnar'. *International Journal of Systematic Theology* 7 (3) (2005): 246–61.

Hector, Kevin W. 'God's Trinity and Self-Determination: A Conversation with Karl Barth, Bruce McCormack, and Paul Molnar'. *Trinity and Election in Contemporary Theology*. Edited by Michael T. Dempsey, 29–46. Grand Rapids, MI: Eerdmans, 2011.

Hector, Kevin W. 'Immutability, Necessity and Triunity: Towards a Resolution of the Trinity and Election Controversy'. *Scottish Journal of Theology* 65 (1) (2012), 64–81.

Heltzel, Peter Goodwin and Collins Winn, Christian T. 'Karl Barth, Reconciliation, and the Triune God'. *Cambridge Companion to the Trinity.* Edited by Peter C. Phan, 171–91. Cambridge: Cambridge University Press, 2011.

Hensley, Jeffrey. 'Trinity and Freedom: A Response to Molnar'. *Scottish Journal of Theology* 61 (1) 83–95.

Heron, Alasdair I. C. *A Century of Protestant Theology.* Philadelphia: Westminster Press, 1980.

Heron, Alasdair I. C. *The Holy Spirit in the Bible, the History of Christian Thought, and Recent Theology.* Philadelphia: Westminster Press, 1983.

Hick, John. *The Metaphor of God Incarnate: Christology in a Pluralistic Age.* Louisville, KY: Westminster/John Knox Press, 1993.

Hilary of Poitiers. *On the Trinity. A Select Library of Nicene and Post-Nicene Fathers of the Christian Church Second Series*, Vol. IX. Translated by Philip Schaff and Henry Wace. Grand Rapids, MI: Eerdmans, 1997.

Hill, William J. *The Three-Personed God: The Trinity as a Mystery of Salvation.* Washington, DC: The Catholic University of America Press, 1982.

Holmes, Christopher R. J. '"A Specific Form of Relationship": On the Dogmatic Implications of Barth's Account of Election and Commandment for His Theological Ethics'. *Trinity and Election in Contemporary Theology.* Edited by Michael T. Dempsey, 182–200. Grand Rapids, MI: Eerdmans, 2011.

Holmes, Christopher R. J. *Revisiting the Doctrine of the Divine Attributes: In Dialogue with Karl Barth, Eberhard Jüngel, and Wolf Krötke.* New York: Peter Lang, 2007.

Holmes, Christopher R. J. 'The Person and Work of Christ Revisited: In Conversation with Karl Barth'. *Anglican Theological Review*, 95 (1) (2013), 37–55.

Hunsinger, George. *Disruptive Grace: Studies in the Theology of Karl Barth.* Grand Rapids, MI: Eerdmans, 2000.

Hunsinger, George. 'Election and the Trinity: Twenty-Five Theses on the Theology of Karl Barth'. *Modern Theology* 24 (2) (April 2008), 179–98.

Hunsinger, George. 'Election and the Trinity: Twenty-Five Theses on the Theology of Karl Barth'. *Trinity and Election in Contemporary Theology.* Edited by Michael T. Dempsey, 91–114. Grand Rapids, MI: Eerdmans, 2011.

Hunsinger, George. *Evangelical, Catholic and Reformed: Doctrinal Essays on Barth and Related Themes.* Grand Rapids, MI: Eerdmans, 2015.

Hunsinger, George. *How to Read Karl Barth: The Shape of his Theology.* New York: Oxford University Press, 1991.

Hunsinger, George. 'Karl Barth's Doctrine of the Trinity, and Some Protestant Doctrines After Barth'. *The Oxford Handbook of the Trinity.* Edited by Gilles Emery, O.P. and Matthew Levering, 294–313. New York: Oxford University Press, 2011.

Hunsinger, George. *Reading Barth with Charity: A Hermeneutical Proposal.* Grand Rapids, MI: Baker Academic, 2015.

Hunsinger, George. Review of Jürgen Moltmann, *The Trinity and the Kingdom*. *The Thomist* 47 (1983), 124–39.

Hunsinger, George. 'Robert Jenson's *Systematic Theology*: A Review Essay'. *Scottish Journal of Theology* 55 (2) (2002), 161–200.

Hunsinger, George. 'Schleiermacher and Barth: Two Divergent Views of Christ and Salvation', *Evangelical, Catholic and Reformed: Doctrinal Essays on Barth and Related Themes*, 146–68. Grand Rapids, MI: Eerdmans, 2015.

Hunsinger, George. 'The Daybreak of the New Creation: Christ's Resurrection in Recent Theology' *Scottish Journal of Theology* 57 (2) (2004), 163–81.

Hunsinger, George. *The Eucharist and Ecumenism: Let us Keep the Feast*. Cambridge: Cambridge University Press, 2008.

Hunsinger, George. 'The Mediator of Communion: Karl Barth's Doctrine of the Holy Spirit'. *Cambridge Companion to Karl Barth*. Edited by John Webster, 177–94. Cambridge: Cambridge University Press, 2000.

Imhof, Paul and Biallowons, Hubert (eds). *Karl Rahner in Dialogue: Conversations and Interviews 1965–1982*. Translated by Harvey D. Egan. New York: Crossroad, 1986.

Jeanrond, Werner G. 'Love and Death: Christian Eschatology in an Interreligious Context'. *Indicative of Grace-Imperative of Freedom: Essays in Honour of Eberhard Jüngel in His 80th Year*. Edited by R. David Nelson, 131–41. London: Bloomsbury T&T Clark, 2014.

Jenson, Robert W. *God According to the Gospel: The Triune Identity*. Philadelphia: Fortress Press, 1982.

Jenson, Robert W. *God after God*. New York: The Bobbs-Merrill Company, 1969.

Jenson, Robert W. 'Once More the *Logos Asarkos*'. *International Journal of Systematic Theology* 13 (2) (April 2011), 130–3.

Jenson, Robert W. *Systematic Theology Volume 1: The Triune God*. New York: Oxford University Press, 1997.

Jenson, Robert W. *Systematic Theology. Volume II: The Works of God*. New York: Oxford University Press, 1999.

Johnson, Adam J. *God's Being in Reconciliation: The Theological Basis of the Unity and Diversity of the Atonement in the Theology of Karl Barth*. New York and London: T&T Clark International, 2012.

Johnson, Elizabeth A. *Quest for the Living God: Mapping Frontiers in the Theology of God*. New York: Continuum, 2008.

Johnson, Elizabeth A. 'Redeeming the Name of Christ'. *Freeing Theology: The Essentials of Theology in Feminist Perspective*. Edited by Catherine Mowry LaCugna, 115–37. HarperSanFrancisco: Harper Collins, 1993.

Johnson, Elizabeth A. *She Who Is: The Mystery of God in Feminist Theological Discourse*. New York: Crossroad, 1992.

Johnson, William Stacy. *The Mystery of God: Karl Barth and the Postmodern Foundations of Theology*. Columbia Series in Reformed Theology. Louisville, KY: Westminster/John Knox Press, 1997.

Jones, Paul Dafydd. 'Obedience, Trinity, and Election: Thinking with and Beyond the *Church Dogmatics*'. *Trinity and Election in Contemporary Theology*. Edited by Michael T. Dempsey, 138–61. Grand Rapids, MI: Eerdmans, 2011.

Jones, Paul Dafydd. *The Humanity of Christ: Christology in Karl Barth's Church Dogmatics*. London: T&T Clark, 2008.

Jüngel, Eberhard. *God as the Mystery of the World: On the Foundation of the Theology of the Crucified One in the Dispute between Theism and Atheism*. Translated by Darrell L. Guder. Grand Rapids, MI: Eerdmans, 1983.

Jüngel, Eberhard. *God's Being Is in Becoming: The Trinitarian Being of God in the Theology of Karl Barth, A Paraphrase*. Translated and Introduction by John Webster. Grand Rapids, MI: Eerdmans, 2001.

Jüngel, Eberhard. *The Doctrine of the Trinity: God's Being Is in Becoming*. Translated by Horton Harris. London: Scottish Academic Press, 1976.

Jüngel, Eberhard. *Theological Essays*. Translated and edited by J. B. Webster. Edinburgh: T&T Clark, 1989.

Kang, Phee Seng. ' The Epistemological Significance of Ὁμοούσιον in the Theology of Thomas F. Torrance'. *Scottish Journal of Theology* 45 (1992), 341–66.

Kantzer Komline, Han-Luen. 'Friendship and Being: Election and Trinitarian Freedom in Moltmann and Barth'. *Modern Theology* 29 (1) (January 2013), 1–17.

Kärkkäinen, Veli-Matti. *The Trinity: Global Perspectives*. Louisville, KY: Westminster John Knox Press, 2007.

Kasper, Walter. *The God of Jesus Christ*. Translated by Matthew J. O'Connell. New York: Crossroad, 1986.

Kaufman, Gordon D. *An Essay on Theological Method*. Atlanta: Scholars Press, 1990.

Kaufman, Gordon D. *God – Mystery – Diversity: Christian Theology in a Pluralistic World*. Minneapolis, MN: Fortress Press, 1996.

Kaufman, Gordon D. *God The Problem*. Cambridge, MA: Harvard University Press, 1972.

Kaufman, Gordon D. *In Face of Mystery: A Constructive Theology*. Cambridge, MA: Harvard University Press, 1993.

Kaufman, Gordon D. *Systematic Theology: A Historicist Perspective*. New York: Charles Scribner's Sons, 1968.

Kaufman, Gordon D. *The Theological Imagination: Constructing the Concept of God*. Philadelphia: Westminster Press, 1981.

Kaufman, Gordon D. *Theology for a Nuclear Age*. Philadelphia: Westminster Press, 1985.

Kelly, J.N.D. *Early Christian Doctrines*. New York: Harper & Row, 1978.

Kilby, Karen. *Karl Rahner*. Fount Christian Thinkers, Series Edited by Peter Vardy. London: Fount Paperbacks an Imprint of HarperCollins, 1997.

Kilby, Karen. 'Karl Rahner'. *The Modern Theologians: An Introduction to Christian Theology Since 1918*. Edited by David F. Ford and Rachel Muers, Third Edition, 92-104. Oxford: Blackwell, 2005.

Kilby, Karen. *Karl Rahner: Theology and Philosophy*. London and New York: Routledge, 2004.

Kilby, Karen. 'Philosophy, Theology and Foundationalism in the Thought of Karl Rahner'. *Scottish Journal of Theology* 55 (2) (2002), 127-40.

Kimel, Alvin F., Jr (ed.). *Speaking the Christian God: The Holy Trinity and the Challenge of Feminism*. Grand Rapids, MI: Eerdmans, 1992.

Knitter, Paul F. *No Other Name? A Critical Survey of Christian Attitudes toward the World Religions*. New York: Orbis, 1985.

Knox, John. *The Humanity and Divinity of Christ: A Study of Pattern in Christology*. New York: Cambridge University Press, 1967.

LaCugna, Catherine Mowry. *God for Us: The Trinity and Christian Life*. San Francisco, CA: HarperSanFrancisco, 1991.

LaCugna, Catherine Mowry. Review Symposium on Catherine Mowry LaCugna's *God for Us: The Trinity and Christian Life*. *Horizons* 20 (1) (1993), 127-42.

LaCugna, Catherine Mowry. 'The Trinitarian Mystery of God'. *Systematic Theology: Roman Catholic Perspectives*. Edited by Francis Schüssler Fiorenza and John P. Galvin, 151-92. Minneapolis, MN: Fortress Press, 1991.

LaCugna, Catherine Mowry (ed.). *Freeing Theology: The Essentials of Theology in Feminist Perspective*. San Francisco: HarperSanFrancisco, 1993.

Lane, Dermot A. *The Reality of Jesus*. New York: Paulist Press, 1975.

Lauber, David. *Barth on the Descent into Hell: God, Atonement and the Christian Life*. Aldershot: Ashgate, 2004.

Leonard, Ellen. 'Experience as a Source for Theology'. *Proceedings of the Forty-Third Annual Convention of the Catholic Theological Society of America*. Edited by George Kilcourse. Toronto, 43 (1988), 44-61.

Lewis, Alan E. *Between Cross and Resurrection: A Theology of Holy Saturday*. Grand Rapids, MI: Eerdmans, 2001.

Long, D. Stephen. *Saving Karl Barth: Hans Urs Von Balthasar's Preoccupation*. Minneapolis, MN: Fortress Press, 2014.

Macquarrie, John. *Jesus Christ in Modern Thought*. Philadelphia: Trinity Press International, 1990.

Marshall, Bruce D. 'The Absolute and the Trinity'. *Pro Ecclesia* 23 (2) (Spring 2014), 147-64.

Marshall, Bruce D. *Trinity and Truth*. Cambridge: Cambridge University Press, 2000.

Martin, Francis. *The Feminist Question: Feminist Theology in the Light of Christian Tradition*. Grand Rapids, MI: Eerdmans, 1994.

McBrien, Richard P. *Catholicism Completely Revised and Updated*. San Francisco: HarperSanFrancisco, 1994.

McCormack, Bruce L. 'Barth's Critique of Schleiermacher Reconsidered'. *Theological Theology: Essays in Honour of John Webster*. Edited by R.

David Nelson, Darren Sarisky and Justin Stratis, 167–79. London/
New York: Bloomsbury, T&T Clark, 2015.

McCormack, Bruce L. 'Divine Impassibility or Simply Divine Constancy?
Implications of Karl Barth's Later Christology for Debates over
Impassibility'. *Divine Impassibility and the Mystery of Human Suffering.*
Edited by James F. Keating and Thomas Joseph White, O.P., 150–86. Grand
Rapids, MI: Eerdmans, 2009.

McCormack, Bruce L. 'Divine Revelation and Human Imagination: Must
We Choose Between the Two?' *Scottish Journal of Theology* 37 (4) (1984),
431–55.

McCormack, Bruce L. 'Election and the Trinity: Theses in Response to George
Hunsinger'. *Scottish Journal of Theology* 63 (2) (2010), 203–24.

McCormack, Bruce L. 'Election and the Trinity: Theses in Response to George
Hunsinger'. *Trinity and Election in Contemporary Theology.* Edited by
Michael T. Dempsey, 115–37. Grand Rapids, MI: Eerdmans, 2011.

McCormack, Bruce L. 'God *Is* His Decision: The Jüngel-Gollwitzer "Debate"
Revisited'. *Theology as Conversation: The Significance of Dialogue in
Historical and Contemporary Theology, A Festschrift for Daniel L. Migliore.*
Edited by Bruce L. McCormack and Kimlyn J. Bender, 48–66. Grand
Rapids, MI: Eerdmans, 2009.

McCormack, Bruce L. 'Grace and Being: The Role of God's Gracious Election
in Karl Barth's Theological Ontology'. *The Cambridge Companion to Karl
Barth.* Edited by John Webster, 92–110. Cambridge: Cambridge University
Press, 2000.

McCormack, Bruce L. 'Grace and Being: The Role of God's Gracious Election
in Karl Barth's Theological Ontology'. *Orthodox and Modern: Studies
in the Theology of Karl Barth*, 183–200. Grand Rapids, MI: Baker
Academic, 2008.

McCormack, Bruce L. *Karl Barth's Critically Realistic Dialectical
Theology: Its Genesis and Development 1909–1936.* Oxford: Clarendon
Press, 1995.

McCormack, Bruce L. 'Karl Barth's Historicized Christology: Just How
"Chalcedonian" Is It?'. *Orthodox and Modern: Studies in the Theology of
Karl Barth*, 201–34. Grand Rapids, MI: Baker Academic, 2008.

McCormack, Bruce L. *Mapping Modern Theology: A Thematic and Historical
Introduction.* Edited by Kelly M. Kapic and Bruce L. McCormack. Grand
Rapids, MI: Baker Academic, 2012.

McCormack, Bruce L. *Orthodox and Modern: Studies in the Theology of Karl
Barth.* Grand Rapids, MI: Baker Academic, 2008.

McCormack, Bruce L. 'Processions and Missions: A Point of Convergence
between Thomas Aquinas and Karl Barth'. *Thomas Aquinas and Karl
Barth: An Unofficial Catholic-Protestant Dialogue.* Edited by Bruce L.
McCormack and Thomas Joseph White, O.P., 99–126. Grand Rapids,
MI: Eerdmans, 2013.

McCormack, Bruce L. 'Seek God Where He May Be Found: A Response to Edwin Chr. Van Driel'. *Orthodox and Modern: Studies in the Theology of Karl Barth*, 261–77. Grand Rapids, MI: Baker Academic, 2008.

McCormack, Bruce L. 'Seek God Where He May Be Found: A Response to Edwin Chr. Van Driel'. *Scottish Journal of Theology* 60 (1) (2007): 62–79.

McCormack, Bruce L. 'The Actuality of God: Karl Barth in Conversation with Open Theism'. *Engaging the Doctrine of God: Contemporary Protestant Perspectives*. Edited by Bruce L. McCormack, 185–244. Grand Rapids, MI: Eerdmans, 2008.

McCormack, Bruce L. 'The Doctrine of the Trinity after Barth: An Attempt to Reconstruct Barth's Doctrine in the Light of His Later Christology'. *Trinitarian Theology After Barth*. Edited by Myk Habets and Phillip Tolliday, 87–120. Eugene, OR: Pickwick, 2011.

McCormack, Bruce L. 'The Lord and Giver of Life: A "Barthian" Defense of the *Filioque*'. *Rethinking Trinitarian Theology: Disputed Questions and Contemporary Issues in Trinitarian Theology*. Edited by Robert J. Woźniak and Giulio Maspero, 230–53. New York: T&T Clark, 2012.

McCormack, Bruce L. (ed.). *Engaging the Doctrine of God: Contemporary Protestant Perspectives*. Grand Rapids, MI: Baker Academic, 2008.

McFague, Sallie. *Models of God: Theology for an Ecological Nuclear Age*. Philadelphia: Fortress Press, 1987.

McFague, Sallie. *The Body of God: An Ecological Theology*. Minneapolis, MN: Fortress Press, 1993.

McGrath, Alister E. *A Scientific Theology: Volume I Nature*. Grand Rapids, MI: Eerdmans, 2001.

McGrath, Alister E. *Thomas F. Torrance: An Intellectual Biography*. Edinburgh: T&T Clark, 1999.

McKenny, Gerald. *The Analogy of Grace: Karl Barth's Moral Theology*. Oxford: Oxford University Press, 2010.

Molnar, Paul D. 'A Response: Beyond Hegel with Karl Barth and T.F. Torrance'. *Pro Ecclesia* 23 (2) (Spring 2014), 165–73.

Molnar, Paul D. 'Barth and Contemporary Roman Catholic Theology'. *The Oxford Handbook of Karl Barth*, Edited by Paul Dafydd Jones and Paul T. Nimmo, forthcoming.

Molnar, Paul D. 'Can the Electing God Be God Without Us? Some Implications of Bruce McCormack's Understanding of the Doctrine of Election for the Doctrine of the Trinity'. *Neue Zeitschrift für Systematische Theologie und Religionsphilosophie* 49 (2) (2007), 199–222.

Molnar, Paul D. 'Can the Electing God Be God Without Us? Some Implications of Bruce McCormack's Understanding of the Doctrine of Election for the Doctrine of the Trinity'. *Trinity and Election in Contemporary Theology*. Edited by Michael T. Dempsey, 63–90. Grand Rapids, MI: Eerdmans, 2011.

Molnar, Paul D. 'Can We Know God Directly? Rahner's Solution from Experience'. *Theological Studies* 46 (1985), 228–61.

Molnar, Paul D. 'Classical Trinity: Catholic Perspective'. *Two Views on The Doctrine of the Trinity.* Edited by Jason S. Sexton and Stanley N. Gundry, 69–95. Grand Rapids, MI: Zondervan, 2014.

Molnar, Paul D. '*Deus Trinitas*: Exploring Some Dogmatic Implications of David Coffey's Biblical Approach to the Trinity'. *Irish Theological Quarterly* 67 (1) (Spring 2002), 33–54.

Molnar, Paul D. 'Experience and Knowledge of the Trinity in the Theology of Ted Peters: Occasion for Clarity or Confusion?' *Irish Theological Quarterly* 64 (1999), 219–43.

Molnar, Paul D. *Faith, Freedom and the Spirit: The Economic Trinity in Barth, Torrance and Contemporary Theology.* Downers Grove, IL: InterVarsity Press (Academic), 2015.

Molnar, Paul D. *Incarnation and Resurrection: Toward a Contemporary Understanding.* Grand Rapids, MI: Eerdmans, 2007.

Molnar, Paul D. 'Incarnation, Resurrection and the Doctrine of the Trinity: A Comparison of Thomas F. Torrance and Roger Haight'. *International Journal of Systematic Theology* 5 (2) (July, 2003), 147–67.

Molnar, Paul D. 'Introduction to the Second Edition of Thomas F. Torrance's *The Christian Doctrine of God, One Being Three Persons*'. London: Bloomsbury T&T Clark, 2016. Cornerstones Series ix–xxxi.

Molnar, Paul D. 'Is God Essentially Different from His Creatures? Rahner's Explanation from Revelation'. *The Thomist* 51 (1987), 575–631.

Molnar, Paul D. *Karl Barth and the Theology of the Lord's Supper. A Systematic Investigation.* New York: Peter Lang, 1996.

Molnar, Paul D. 'Karl Barth and the Importance of Thinking Theologically within the Nicene Faith'. *Ecclesiology* 11 (2015), 153–76.

Molnar, Paul D. 'Love of God and Love of Neighbor in the Theology of Karl Rahner and Karl Barth'. *Modern Theology* 20 (4) (October 2004), 567–99.

Molnar, Paul D. 'Moltmann's Post-Modern Messianic Christology: A Review Discussion'. *The Thomist* 56 (1992), 669–93.

Molnar, Paul D. 'Myth and Reality: Analysis and Critique of Gordon Kaufman and Sallie McFague on God, Christ, and Salvation'. *Cultural Encounters: A Journal for the Theology of Culture* 1 (2) (Summer 2005), 23–48.

Molnar, Paul D. 'Natural Theology Revisited: A Comparison of T.F. Torrance and Karl Barth'. *Zeitschrift Für Dialektische Theologie* 20 (1) (December 2005), 53–83.

Molnar, Paul D. 'Orthodox and Modern: Just How Modern Was Barth's Later Theology?' *Theology Today* 67 (2010): 51–6.

Molnar, Paul D. 'Reflections on Pannenberg's Systematic Theology'. *The Thomist* 58 (1994), 501–12.

Molnar, Paul D. 'Response to David Coffey'. *Irish Theological Quarterly* 68 (2003), 51–65.

Molnar, Paul D. Review of *Father, Son & Holy Spirit: Toward a Fully Trinitarian Theology*. London: T&T Clark, 2003. *Pro Ecclesia* XIV (4) (Fall 2005), 494–96.

Molnar, Paul D. Review of John Drury, *The Resurrected God: Karl Barth's Trinitarian Theology of Easter*. Minneapolis, MN: Fortress, 2014. *Journal of Theological Studies*, vol. 67, no. 1 (2016), 380–3.

Molnar, Paul D. Review of Kapic, Kelly M. and McCormack, Bruce L. (eds). *Mapping Modern Theology: A Thematic and Historical Introduction*. Grand Rapids, MI: Baker Academic, 2012, *Scottish Journal of Theology* 69 (2) (2016), 252–45.

Molnar, Paul D. Review of Stanley J. Grenz, *Rediscovering the Triune God: The Trinity in Contemporary Theology*. Minneapolis, MN: Fortress Press, 2004. *Scottish Journal of Theology* 60 (4) (2007), 492–95.

Molnar, Paul D. 'Some Dogmatic Consequences of Paul F. Knitter's Unitarian Theocentrism'. *The Thomist* 55 (1991), 449–95.

Molnar, Paul D. 'Some Problems with Pannenberg's Solution to Barth's "Faith Subjectivism"'. *Scottish Journal of Theology* 48 (1995), 315–39.

Molnar, Paul D. 'The Function of the Immanent Trinity in the Theology of Karl Barth: Implications for Today'. *Scottish Journal of Theology* 42 (1989), 367–99.

Molnar, Paul D. 'The Function of the Trinity in Moltmann's Ecological Doctrine of Creation'. *Theological Studies* 51 (1990), 673–97.

Molnar, Paul D. 'The Importance of the Doctrine of Justification in the Theology of Thomas F. Torrance and of Karl Barth'. *Scottish Journal of Theology* 70 (1) (2017), forthcoming.

Molnar, Paul D. 'The obedience of the Son in the Theology of Karl Barth and of Thomas F. Torrance' *Scottish Journal of Theology* 67 (1) (2014): 50–69.

Molnar, Paul D. 'The Perils of Embracing a "Historicized Christology."' *Modern Theology* 30 (4) (2014): 454–80.

Molnar, Paul D. 'The Trinity, Election and God's Ontological Freedom: A Response to Kevin W. Hector'. *International Journal of Systematic Theology* 8 (3) (2006): 294–306.

Molnar, Paul D. 'The Trinity, Election and God's Ontological Freedom: A Response to Kevin W. Hector'. *Trinity and Election in Contemporary Theology*. Edited by Michael T. Dempsey, 47–62. Grand Rapids, MI: Eerdmans, 2011.

Molnar, Paul D. 'Theological Issues Involved in the *Filioque*'. *Ecumenical Perspectives on the Filioque for the 21st Century*. Edited by Myk Habets, 20–39. London: T&T Clark, 2014.

Molnar, Paul D. 'Thomas F. Torrance and the problem of universalism'. *Scottish Journal of Theology* 68 (2) (2015): 164–86.

Molnar, Paul D. *Thomas F. Torrance: Theologian of the Trinity*. Aldershot: Ashgate, 2009.

Molnar, Paul D. '"Thy Word is Truth": *Barth on Scripture*'. Edited by George Hunsinger, 151–72. Grand Rapids, MI: Eerdmans, 2012.

Molnar, Paul D. '"Thy Word Is Truth": The Role of Faith in Reading Scripture Theologically with Karl Barth'. *Scottish Journal of Theology* 63 (1) (2010): 70–92.

Molnar, Paul D. 'Was Barth a Pro-Nicene Theologian? Reflections on *Nicaea and Its Legacy*'. *Scottish Journal of Theology* 64 (2011), 347–59.

Molnar, Paul D. 'What Does It Mean to Say That Jesus Christ Is Indispensable to a Properly Conceived Doctrine of the Immanent Trinity?' in response to Jeffrey Hensley, *Scottish Journal Theology* 61 (1) (2008): 96–106.

Moltmann, Jürgen. *God in Creation: A New Theology of Creation and the Spirit of God*. Translated by Margaret Kohl. New York: Harper & Row, 1985.

Moltmann, Jürgen. *History and the Triune God: Contributions to Trinitarian Theology*. Translated by John Bowden. New York: Crossroad, 1992.

Moltmann, Jürgen. *The Spirit of Life: A Universal Affirmation*. Translated by Margaret Kohl. Minneapolis, MN: Fortress Press, 1993.

Moltmann, Jürgen. *The Trinity and the Kingdom: The Doctrine of God*. Translated by Margaret Kohl. New York: Harper & Row, 1981.

Moltmann, Jürgen. *The Way of Jesus Christ: Christology in Messianic Dimensions*. Translated by Margaret Kohl. San Francisco: HarperCollins, 1989.

Murphy, Francesca Aran. *God is Not a Story: Realism Revisited*. Oxford: Oxford University Press, 2007.

Myers, Benjamin. 'Election, Trinity, and the History of Jesus: Reading Barth with Rowan Williams'. *Trinitarian Theology After Barth*. Edited by Myk Habets and Phillip Tolliday. Eugene, OR: Pickwick Publications, 2011, 121–37.

Myers, Benjamin. 'Faith as Self-Understanding: Towards a Post-Barthian Appreciation of Rudolf Bultmann'. *International Journal of Systematic Theology* 10 (1) (January 2008), 21–35.

Nelson, R. David. (ed.). *Indicative of Grace-Imperative of Freedom: Essays in Honour of Eberhard Jüngel in His 80th Year*. London: Bloomsbury T&T Clark, 2014.

Neuner, Joseph, S.J., Roos, Heinrich, S.J. and Rahner, Karl, S.J. (eds). *The Teaching of the Catholic Church*. Cork: The Mercier Press, 1966.

Nimmo, Paul T. 'Barth and the Election-Trinity Debate: A Pneumatological View'. *The Trinity and Election in Contemporary Theology*. Edited by Michael T. Dempsey, 162–81. Grand Rapids, MI: Eerdmans, 2011.

Nimmo, Paul T. *Being in Action: The Theological Shape of Barth's Ethical Vision*. New York: T&T Clark, 2007.

Nimmo, Paul T. 'Karl Barth and the *concursus Dei*: A Chalcedonianism Too Far?' *International Journal of Systematic Theology* 9 (1) (2007), 58–72.

Nordling, Cherith Fee. *Knowing God by Name: A Conversation between Elizabeth A. Johnson and Karl Barth*. New York: Peter Lang, 2010.

O'Donovan, Leo J., S.J. 'A Journey into Time: The Legacy of Karl Rahner's Last Years'. *Theological Studies* 46 (1985), 621–46.

O'Donovan, Leo J., S.J. (ed.) *A World of Grace: An Introduction to the Themes and Foundations of Karl Rahner's Theology*. New York: Crossroad, 1981.

Olson, Roger. 'Wolfhart Pannenberg's Doctrine of the Trinity'. *Scottish Journal of Theology* 43 (1990), 175–206.

Otto, Randall E. 'The Use and Abuse of Perichoresis in Recent Theology' *Scottish Journal of Theology* 54 (3) (August 2001), 366–84.

Pagels, Elaine. *The Gnostic Gospels*. New York: Random House, 1979.

Pagels, Elaine. 'The Gnostic Jesus and Early Christian Politics'. University Lecture in Religion at Arizona State University, 28 January 1982.

Pannenberg, Wolfhart. *An Introduction to Systematic Theology*. Grand Rapids, MI: Eerdmans, 1991.

Pannenberg, Wolfhart. *Faith and Reality*. Translated by John Maxwell. Philadelphia: Westminster Press, 1977.

Pannenberg, Wolfhart. 'Eternity, Time and the Trinitarian God'. *Trinity, Time, and Church: A Response to the Theology of Robert W. Jenson*. Edited by Colin E. Gunton, 62–70. Grand Rapids, MI: Eerdmans, 2000.

Pannenberg, Wolfhart. *Jesus – God and Man*. Second Edition. Translated by Lewis L. Wilkins and Duane A. Priebe. Philadelphia: Westminster Press, 1977.

Pannenberg, Wolfhart. *Systematic Theology, Volume 1*. Translated by Geoffrey W. Bromiley. Grand Rapids, MI: Eerdmans, 1991.

Pannenberg, Wolfhart. *Systematic Theology, Volume 2*. Translated by Geoffrey W. Bromiley. Grand Rapids, MI: Eerdmans, 1994.

Peters, Ted. *GOD as Trinity: Relationality and Temporality in Divine Life*. Louisville, KY: Westminster/John Knox Press, 1993.

Price, Robert B. *Letters of the Divine Word: The Perfections of God in Karl Barth's Church Dogmatics*. London: Bloomsbury T&T Clark, 2011.

Powell, Samuel M. *The Trinity in German Thought*. Cambridge: Cambridge University Press, 2001.

Rahner, Karl, S.J. (ed.) *Encyclopedia of Theology. The Concise Sacramentum Mundi*. New York: Seabury, 1975.

Rahner, Karl, S.J. *Foundations of Christian Faith: An Introduction to the Idea of Christianity*. Translated by William V. Dych. New York: A Crossroad Book, Seabury Press, 1978.

Rahner, Karl, S.J. *Hearer of the Word: Laying the Foundation for a Philosophy of Religion*. Translated by Joseph Donceel. Edited and Introduction by Andrew Tallon. New York: Continuum, 1994.

Rahner, Karl, S.J. *Hearers of the Word*. Translated by Michael Richards. New York: Herder & Herder, 1969.

Rahner, Karl, S.J. *Spirit in the World*. Translated by William Dych, S.J. New York: Herder & Herder, 1968.

Rahner, Karl, S.J. *The Church and the Sacraments*, Quaestiones disputatae, 9. Translated by W. J. O'Hara. New York: Herder & Herder, 1968.

Rahner, Karl, S.J. *The Trinity*. Translated by Joseph Donceel. New York: Herder & Herder, 1970.

Rahner, Karl, S.J. *Theological Investigations.* 23 vols.

Rahner, Karl, S.J. Vol. 1: *God, Christ, Mary and Grace.* Translated by Cornelius Ernst, O.P. Baltimore: Helicon Press, 1961.

Rahner, Karl, S.J. Vol. 2: *Man in the Church.* Translated by Karl-H. Kruger. Baltimore: Helicon Press, 1966.

Rahner, Karl, S.J. Vol. 3: *Theology of the Spiritual Life.* Translated by Karl-H. Kruger and Boniface Kruger. Baltimore: Helicon Press, 1967.

Rahner, Karl, S.J. Vol. 4: *More Recent Writings.* Translated by Kevin Smyth. Baltimore: Helicon Press, 1966.

Rahner, Karl, S.J. Vol. 5: *Later Writings.* Translated by Karl-H. Kruger. Baltimore: Helicon Press, 1966.

Rahner, Karl, S.J. Vol. 6: *Concerning Vatican Council II.* Translated by Karl-H. Kruger and Boniface Kruger. Baltimore: Helicon Press, 1969.

Rahner, Karl, S.J. Vol. 7: *Further Theology of the Spiritual Life 1.* Translated by David Bourke. New York: Herder & Herder, 1971.

Rahner, Karl, S.J. Vol. 8: *Further Theology of the Spiritual Life 2.* Translated by David Bourke. New York: Herder & Herder, 1971.

Rahner, Karl, S.J. Vol. 9: *Writings of 1965–1967, 1.* Translated by Graham Harrison. New York: Herder & Herder, 1972.

Rahner, Karl, S.J. Vol. 10: *Writings of 1965–1967, 2.* Translated by David Bourke. New York: Herder & Herder, 1973.

Rahner, Karl, S.J. Vol. 11: *Confrontations 1.* Translated by David Bourke. New York: Seabury Press, 1974.

Rahner, Karl, S.J. Vol. 12: *Confrontations 2.* Translated by David Bourke. New York: Seabury Press, 1974.

Rahner, Karl, S.J. Vol. 13: *Theology, Anthropology, Christology.* Translated by David Bourke. London: Darton, Longman & Todd, 1975.

Rahner, Karl, S.J. Vol. 14: *Ecclesiology, Questions of the Church, the Church in the World.* Translated by David Bourke. New York: Seabury Press, 1976.

Rahner, Karl, S.J. Vol. 15: *Penance in the Early Church.* Translated by David Bourke. New York: Seabury Press, 1976.

Rahner, Karl, S.J. Vol. 16: *Experience of the Spirit: Source of Theology.* Translated by David Morland. New York: Seabury Press, 1976.

Rahner, Karl, S.J. Vol. 17: *Jesus, Man, and the Church.* Translated by Margaret Kohl. New York: Crossroad, 1981.

Rahner, Karl, S.J. Vol. 18: *God and Revelation.* Translated by Edward Quinn. New York: Crossroad, 1983.

Rahner, Karl, S.J. Vol. 19: *Faith and Ministry.* Translated by Edward Quinn. New York: Crossroad, 1983.

Rahner, Karl, S.J. Vol. 20: *Concern for the Church.* Translated by Edward Quinn. New York: Crossroad, 1986.

Rahner, Karl, S.J. Vol. 21: *Science and Christian Faith.* Translated by Hugh M. Riley. New York: Crossroad, 1988.

Rahner, Karl, S.J. Vol. 22: *Humane Society and the Church of Tomorrow.* Translated by Joseph Donceel, S.J. New York: Crossroad, 1991.

Rahner, Karl, S.J. Vol. 23: *Final Writings*. Translated by Joseph Donceel, S.J. and Hugh M. Riley. New York: Crossroad, 1992.

Rahner, Karl, S.J. and Joseph Ratzinger. *Revelation and Tradition*. Quaestiones disputatae, 17. Translated by W. J. O'Hara. New York: Herder & Herder, 1966.

Rahner, Karl, S.J. and Herbert Vorgrimler. *Theological Dictionary*. Edited by Cornelius Ernst, O.P. Translated by Richard Strachan. New York: Herder & Herder, 1965.

Rahner, Karl, S.J. and Karl-Heinz Weger, S.J. *Our Christian Faith Answers for the Future*. Translated by Francis McDonagh. New York: Crossroad, 1981.

Ratzinger, Joseph Cardinal. *Principles of Catholic Theology: Building Stones for a Fundamental Theology*. Translated by Sister Mary Frances McCarthy, SND. San Francisco: Ignatius Press, 1987.

Rusch, William G. (ed. and trans.). 'Athanasius's Orations against the Arians', *The Trinitarian Controversy, Sources of Early Christian Thought*. Philadelphia: Fortress Press, 1980.

Sanders, Fred. *The Image of the Immanent Trinity: Rahner's Rule and the Theological Interpretation of Scripture*. New York: Peter Lang, 2004.

Schweizer, Eduard. *Jesus*. Translated by David E. Green. Atlanta: John Knox Press, 1971.

Schwöbel, Christoph (ed.). *Trinitarian Theology Today: Essays on Divine Being and Act*. Edinburgh: T&T Clark, 1995.

Schoonenberg, Piet, S.J. *The Christ: A Study of the God-Man Relationship in the Whole of Creation and in Jesus Christ*. New York: Herder & Herder, 1971.

Shults, F. LeRon. *The Postfoundationalist Task of Theology: Wolfhart Pannenberg and the New Theological Rationality*. Grand Rapids, MI: Eerdmans, 1999.

Soulen, R. Kendall. *The Divine Name(s) and the Holy Trinity: Distinguishing the Voices Volume One*. Louisville, KY: Westminster John Knox Press, 2011.

Sumner, Darren O. *Karl Barth and the Incarnation: Christology and the Humility of God*. London: Bloomsbury T&T Clark, 2014.

Swain, Scott R. *The God of the Gospel: Robert Jenson's Trinitarian Theology*. Downers Grove, IL: InterVarsity Press, 2013.

Swain, Scott R. and Allen, Michael. 'The Obedience of the Eternal Son'. *International Journal of Systematic Theology* 15 (2) (April 2013): 114–34.

Sykes, S. W. (ed.). *Karl Barth: Centenary Essays*. New York: Cambridge University Press, 1989.

Taylor, Iain. *Pannenberg on the Triune God*. London: T&T Clark, 2007.

The New Testament of the New Jerusalem Bible with Complete Introductions and Notes. Garden City, NY: Image Books, 1986.

Thompson, John. *Modern Trinitarian Perspectives*. New York: Oxford University Press, 1994.

Thompson, John. *The Holy Spirit in the Theology of Karl Barth*. Allison Park, PA: Pickwick Publications, 1991.

Thompson, Thomas R. 'Interpretatio in bonem partem: Jürgen Moltmann on the Immanent Trinity'. In *Theology as Conversation: the Significance of Dialogue in Historical and Contemporary Theology*. Edited by Bruce L. McCormack and Kimlyn J. Bender, 159–78. Grand Rapids, MI: Eerdmans, 2009.

Tillich, Paul. *The Shaking of the Foundations*. New York: Charles Scribner's Sons, 1948.

Torrance, Alan J. *Persons in Communion: Trinitarian Description and Human Participation*. Edinburgh: T&T Clark, 1996.

Torrance, Alan J. 'The Trinity'. In *The Cambridge Companion to Karl Barth*. Edited by John Webster, 72–91. Cambridge: Cambridge University Press, 2000.

Torrance, James B. *Worship, Community and the Triune God of Grace*. Downers Grove, IL: InterVarsity Press, 1996.

Torrance, Thomas F. *Atonement: The Person and Work of Christ*. Edited by Robert T. Walker. Downers Grove, IL: IVP Academic, 2009.

Torrance, Thomas F. *Christian Theology and Scientific Culture*. New York: Oxford University Press, 1981.

Torrance, Thomas F. *Divine and Contingent Order*. Edinburgh: T&T Clark, 1998.

Torrance, Thomas F. 'Ecumenism and Rome'. *Scottish Journal of Theology* 37 (1984), 59–64.

Torrance, Thomas F. *God and Rationality*. London: Oxford University Press, 1971; reissued Edinburgh: T&T Clark, 1997.

Torrance, Thomas F. *Incarnation: The Person and Life of Christ*. Edited by Robert T. Walker. Downers Grove, IL: IVP Academic, 2008.

Torrance, Thomas F. 'Karl Barth and the Latin Heresy'. *Scottish Journal of Theology* 39 (1986), 461–82.

Torrance, Thomas F. *Karl Barth, Biblical and Evangelical Theologian*. Edinburgh: T&T Clark, 1990.

Torrance, Thomas F. *Preaching Christ Today: The Gospel and Scientific Thinking*. Grand Rapids, MI: Eerdmans, 1994.

Torrance, Thomas F. *Reality and Evangelical Theology*. Philadelphia: Westminster Press, 1982.

Torrance, Thomas F. *Space, Time and Incarnation*. London: Oxford University Press, 1969; reissued Edinburgh: T&T Clark, 1997.

Torrance, Thomas F. *Space, Time and Resurrection*. Grand Rapids, MI: Eerdmans, 1976; reissued Edinburgh: T&T Clark, 1998.

Torrance, Thomas F. *The Christian Doctrine of God, One Being Three Persons*. Edinburgh: T&T Clark, 1996.

Torrance, Thomas F. 'The Deposit of Faith'. *Scottish Journal of Theology* 36 (1983), 1–28.

Torrance, Thomas F. *The Doctrine of Jesus Christ*. Eugene, OR: Wipf and Stock, 2002.

Torrance, Thomas F. *The Ground and Grammar of Theology*.
Charlottesville: University Press of Virginia, 1980; reissued
Edinburgh: T&T Clark, 2001.

Torrance, Thomas F. *The Trinitarian Faith: The Evangelical Theology of the
Ancient Catholic Church*. Edinburgh: T&T Clark, 1988.

Torrance, Thomas F. *Theological Science*. New York: Oxford University
Press, 1978.

Torrance, Thomas F. *Theology in Reconciliation*. London: Geoffrey
Chapman, 1975.

Torrance, Thomas F. *Theology in Reconstruction*. London: SCM Press, 1965.

Torrance, Thomas F. 'Toward an Ecumenical Consensus on the Trinity'.
Theologische Zeitschrift 31 (1975), 337–50.

Torrance, Thomas F. 'Toward an Ecumenical Consensus on the Trinity'.
Trinitarian Perspectives: Toward Doctrinal Agreement. Edinburgh: T&T
Clark, 1994, 77–102.

Torrance, Thomas F. *Trinitarian Perspectives: Toward Doctrinal Agreement*.
Edinburgh: T&T Clark, 1994.

Tracy, David. 'Approaching the Christian Understanding of God'. *Systematic
Theology: Roman Catholic Perspectives*. Edited by Francis Schüssler Fiorenza
and John P. Galvin, 133–48. Minneapolis, MN: Fortress Press, 1991.

Tracy, David. 'Trinitarian Speculation and the Forms of Divine Disclosure'.
The Trinity: An Interdisciplinary Symposium on the Trinity. Edited by
Stephen T. Davis, Daniel Kendall, S.J. and Gerald O'Collins, S.J., 273–93.
Oxford: Oxford University Press, 1999.

Tseng, Shao Kai. *Karl Barth's Infralapsarian Theology: Origins and Development
1920–1953*. Downers Grove, IL: InterVarsity Press, 2016.

Van Beeck, Frans Josef, S.J. 'Trinitarian Theology as Participation'. *The
Trinity: An Interdisciplinary Symposium on the Trinity*. Edited by Stephen
T. Davis, Daniel Kendall, S.J. and Gerald O'Collins, S.J., 295–325.
Oxford: Oxford University Press, 1999.

Van Den Brink, Gijsbert. 'Social Trinitarianism: A Discussion of Some Recent
Theological Criticisms'. *International Journal of Systematic Theology* 16 (3)
(July 2014), 331–50.

Vanhoozer, Kevin J. *Remythologizing Theology: Divine Action, Passion, and
Authorship*. Cambridge: Cambridge University Press, 2010.

Vorgrimler, Herbert. *Understanding Karl Rahner: An Introduction to his Life
and Thought*. New York: Crossroad, 1986.

Wainwright, Arthur. *The Trinity in the New Testament*. London: SPCK, 1980.

Webster, John. *Barth's Ethics of Reconciliation*. Cambridge: Cambridge
University Press, 1995.

Webster, John. *Barth's Moral Theology: Human Action in Barth's Thought*.
Edinburgh: T&T Clark; Grand Rapids, MI: Eerdmans, 1998.

Webster, John. 'Gunton and Barth'. *The Theology of Colin Gunton*. Edited by
Lincoln Harvey, 17–31. London: T&T Clark International, 2010.

Webster, John. Review of *Divine Freedom and the Doctrine of the Immanent Trinity: In Dialogue with Karl Barth and Contemporary Theology*. The *Journal of Theological Studies* 56 (part 1) (April 2005), 289–90.

Webster, John. 'Systematic Theology after Barth: Jüngel, Jenson, and Gunton'. *The Modern Theologians: An Introduction to Christian Theology Since 1918*. Edited by David F. Ford and Rachel Muers, Third Edition, 249–63. Oxford: Blackwell, 2005.

Webster, John. 'Trinity and Creation'. *International Journal of Systematic Theology* 12 (1) (January 2010): 4–19.

Webster, John. (ed.). *The Cambridge Companion to Karl Barth*. Cambridge: Cambridge University Press, 2000.

Williams, Rowan. 'Barth on the Triune God'. *Karl Barth: Studies of His Theological Method*. Edited by S.W. Sykes, 147–93. Oxford: Clarendon, 1979.

Wiseman, James A., O.S.B. ' "I Have Experienced God": Religious Experience in the Theology of Karl Rahner'. *American Benedictine Review*. March (1993), 22–57.

Wong, Joseph H. P. *Logos-Symbol in the Christology of Karl Rahner*. Rome: Las-Roma, 1984.

Wong, Kam Ming. *Wolfhart Pannenberg on Human Destiny*. Aldershot: Ashgate, 2008.

Ziegler, Philip G. 'Some Remarks on Christian Freedom'. *Indicative of Grace-Imperative of Freedom: Essays in Honour of Eberhard Jüngel in His 80th Year*. Edited by R. David Nelson, 255–66. London: Bloomsbury T&T Clark, 2014.

Zizioulas, John D. *Being as Communion: Studies in Personhood and the Church*. Foreword by John Meyendorff. Contemporary Greek Theologians, 4. Crestwood, New York: St Vladimir's Seminary Press, 1993.

INDEX OF NAMES

INDEX OF SUBJECTS